GENERAL MOTORS | FULL-SIZE TRUCKS 1988-98 REPAIR MANUAL

CHILTON'S

President — Dean F. Morgantini, S.A.E.
Vice President–Finance — Barry L. Beck
Vice President–Sales — Glenn D. Potere

Executive Editor — Kevin M. G. Maher, A.S.E.

Manager–Consumer Automotive — Richard Schwartz, A.S.E.
Manager–Marine/Recreation — James R. Marotta, A.S.E.

Production Specialists — Brian Hollingsworth, Melinda Possinger
Project Managers — Will Kessler, A.S.E., S.A.E., Thomas A. Mellon, A.S.E., S.A.E., Richard Rivele, Todd W. Stidham, A.S.E., Ron Webb

Editor — Thomas A. Mellon, A.S.E., S.A.E.

CHILTON ™ *Automotive Books*

PUBLISHED BY **W. G. NICHOLS, INC.**

Manufactu...
© 1996 C...
1020 And...
West Che...
ISBN 0-8...
Library of Congress Catalog...
3456789012 8765432109

™ Chilton is a registered trademark of Cahners Business Information, a division of Reed Elsevier, Inc., and has been licensed to W. G. Nichols, Inc.

www.chiltononline.com

Contents

Contents

SAFETY NOTICE

Proper service and repair procedures are vital to the safe, reliable operation of all motor vehicles, as well as the personal safety of those performing repairs. This manual outlines procedures for servicing and repairing vehicles using safe, effective methods. The procedures contain many NOTES, CAUTIONS and WARNINGS which should be followed, along with standard procedures to eliminate the possibility of personal injury or improper service which could damage the vehicle or compromise its safety.

It is important to note that repair procedures and techniques, tools and parts for servicing motor vehicles, as well as the skill and experience of the individual performing the work vary widely. It is not possible to anticipate all of the conceivable ways or conditions under which vehicles may be serviced, or to provide cautions as to all possible hazards that may result. Standard and accepted safety precautions and equipment should be used when handling toxic or flammable fluids, and safety goggles or other protection should be used during cutting, grinding, chiseling, prying, or any other process that can cause material removal or projectiles.

Some procedures require the use of tools specially designed for a specific purpose. Before substituting another tool or procedure, you must be completely satisfied that neither your personal safety, nor the performance of the vehicle will be endangered.

Although information in this manual is based on industry sources and is complete as possible at the time of publication, the possibility exists that some car manufacturers made later changes which could not be included here. While striving for total accuracy, NP/Chilton cannot assume responsibility for any errors, changes or omissions that may occur in the compilation of this data.

PART NUMBERS

Part numbers listed in this reference are not recommendations by Chilton for any product brand name. They are references that can be used with interchange manuals and aftermarket supplier catalogs to locate each brand supplier's discrete part number.

SPECIAL TOOLS

Special tools are recommended by the vehicle manufacturer to perform their specific job. Use has been kept to a minimum, but where absolutely necessary, they are referred to in the text by the part number of the tool manufacturer. These tools can be purchased, under the appropriate part number, from your local dealer or regional distributor, or an equivalent tool can be purchased locally from a tool supplier or parts outlet. Before substituting any tool for the one recommended, read the SAFETY NOTICE at the top of this page.

ACKNOWLEDGMENTS

Portions of this manual have been reprinted with permission of the General Motors Corporation, Service Technology Group.

1

GENERAL INFORMATION AND MAINTENANCE

HOW TO USE THIS BOOK

This Chilton's Total Car Care manual for 1988–98 ½, ¾ and 1 ton Chevrolet and GMC Pick-ups, Blazers, Jimmys, Tahoes, Yukons and Suburbans is intended to help you learn more about the inner workings of your vehicle, while saving you money on its upkeep and operation.

The beginning of the book will likely be referred to the most, since that is where you will find information for maintenance and tune-up. The other sections deal with the more complex systems of your vehicle. Systems (from engine through brakes) are covered to the extent that the average do-it-yourselfer can attempt. This book will not explain such things as rebuilding a differential because the expertise required and the special tools necessary make this uneconomical. It will, however, give you detailed instructions to help you change your own brake pads and shoes, replace spark plugs, and perform many more jobs that can save you money and help avoid expensive problems.

A secondary purpose of this book is a reference for owners who want to understand their vehicle and/or their mechanics better.

Where to Begin

Before removing any bolts, read through the entire procedure. This will give you the overall view of what tools and supplies will be required. So read ahead and plan ahead. Each operation should be approached logically and all procedures thoroughly understood before attempting any work.

If repair of a component is not considered practical, we tell you how to remove the part and then how to install the new or rebuilt replacement. In this way, you at least save labor costs.

Avoiding Trouble

Many procedures in this book require you to "label and disconnect . . ." a group of lines, hoses or wires. Don't be think you can remember where everything goes—you won't. If you hook up vacuum or fuel lines incorrectly, the vehicle may run poorly, if at all. If you hook up electrical wiring incorrectly, you may instantly learn a very expensive lesson.

You don't need to know the proper name for each hose or line. A piece of masking tape on the hose and a piece on its fitting will allow you to assign your own label. As long as you remember your own code, the lines can be reconnected by matching your tags. Remember that tape will dissolve in gasoline or solvents; if a part is to be washed or cleaned, use another method of identification. A permanent felt-tipped marker or a metal scribe can be very handy for marking metal parts. Remove any tape or paper labels after assembly.

Maintenance or Repair?

Maintenance includes routine inspections, adjustments, and replacement of parts which show signs of normal wear. Maintenance compensates for wear or deterioration. Repair implies that something has broken or is not working. A need for a repair is often caused by lack of maintenance. for example: draining and refilling automatic transmission fluid is maintenance recommended at specific intervals. Failure to do this can shorten the life of the transmission/transaxle, requiring very expensive repairs. While no maintenance program can prevent items from eventually breaking or wearing out, a general rule is true: MAINTENANCE IS CHEAPER THAN REPAIR.

Two basic mechanic's rules should be mentioned here. First, whenever the left side of the vehicle or engine is referred to, it means the driver's side. Conversely, the right side of the vehicle means the passenger's side. Second, screws and bolts are removed by turning counterclockwise, and tightened by turning clockwise unless specifically noted.

Safety is always the most important rule. Constantly be aware of the dangers involved in working on an automobile and take the proper precautions. Please refer to the information in this section regarding SERVICING YOUR VEHICLE SAFELY and the SAFETY NOTICE on the acknowledgment page.

Avoiding the Most Common Mistakes

Pay attention to the instructions provided. There are 3 common mistakes in mechanical work:

1. Incorrect order of assembly, disassembly or adjustment. When taking something apart or putting it together, performing steps in the wrong order usually just costs you extra time; however, it CAN break something. Read the entire procedure before beginning. Perform everything in the order in which the instructions say you should, even if you can't see a reason for it. When you're taking apart something that is very intricate, you might want to draw a picture of how it looks when assembled in order to make sure you get everything back in its proper position. When making adjustments, perform them in the proper order. One adjustment possibly will affect another.

2. Overtorquing (or undertorquing). While it is more common for overtorquing to cause damage, undertorquing may allow a fastener to vibrate loose causing serious damage. Especially when dealing with aluminum parts, pay attention to torque specifications and utilize a torque wrench in assembly. If a torque figure is not available, remember that if you are using the right tool to perform the job, you will probably not have to strain yourself to get a fastener tight enough. The pitch of most threads is so slight that the tension you put on the wrench will be multiplied many times in actual force on what you are tightening.

There are many commercial products available for ensuring that fasteners won't come loose, even if they are not torqued just right (a very common brand is Loctite®). If you're worried about getting something together tight enough to hold, but loose enough to avoid mechanical damage during assembly, one of these products might offer substantial insurance. Before choosing a threadlocking compound, read the label on the package and make sure the product is compatible with the materials, fluids, etc. involved.

3. Crossthreading. This occurs when a part such as a bolt is screwed into a nut or casting at the wrong angle and forced. Crossthreading is more likely to occur if access is difficult. It helps to clean and lubricate fasteners, then to start threading the bolt, spark plug, etc. with your fingers. If you encounter resistance, unscrew the part and start over again at a different angle until it can be inserted and turned several times without much effort. Keep in mind that many parts have tapered threads, so that gentle turning will automatically bring the part you're threading to the proper angle. Don't put a wrench on the part until it's been tightened a couple of turns by hand. If you suddenly encounter resistance, and the part has not seated fully, don't force it. Pull it back out to make sure it's clean and threading properly.

Be sure to take your time and be patient, and always plan ahead. Allow yourself ample time to perform repairs and maintenance.

TOOLS AND EQUIPMENT

▶ **See Figures 1 thru 15**

Without the proper tools and equipment it is impossible to properly service your vehicle. It would be virtually impossible to catalog every tool that you would need to perform all of the operations in this book. It would be unwise for the amateur to rush out and buy an expensive set of tools on the theory that he/she may need one or more of them at some time.

The best approach is to proceed slowly, gathering a good quality set of those tools that are used most frequently. Don't be misled by the low cost of bargain tools. It is far better to spend a little more for better quality. Forged wrenches, 6 or 12-point sockets and fine tooth ratchets are by far preferable to their less expensive counterparts. As any good mechanic can tell you, there are few worse experiences than trying to work on a vehicle with bad tools.

Your monetary savings will be far outweighed by frustration and mangled knuckles.

Begin accumulating those tools that are used most frequently: those associated with routine maintenance and tune-up. In addition to the normal assortment of screwdrivers and pliers, you should have the following tools:

• Wrenches/sockets and combination open end/box end wrenches in sizes ⅛–¾ in. and/or 3mm–19mm ¹³⁄₁₆ in. or ⅝ in. spark plug socket (depending on plug type).

➡**If possible, buy various length socket drive extensions. Universal-joint and wobble extensions can be extremely useful, but be careful when using them, as they can change the amount of torque applied to the socket.**

- Jackstands for support.
- Oil filter wrench.
- Spout or funnel for pouring fluids.
- Grease gun for chassis lubrication (unless your vehicle is not equipped with any grease fittings)
- Hydrometer for checking the battery (unless equipped with a sealed, maintenance-free battery).
- A container for draining oil and other fluids.
- Rags for wiping up the inevitable mess.

In addition to the above items there are several others that are not absolutely necessary, but handy to have around. These include an equivalent oil absorbent gravel, like cat litter, and the usual supply of lubricants, antifreeze and fluids. This is a basic list for routine maintenance, but only your personal needs and desire can accurately determine your list of tools.

After performing a few projects on the vehicle, you'll be amazed at the other tools and non-tools on your workbench. Some useful household items are: a large turkey baster or siphon, empty coffee cans and ice trays (to store parts), a

ball of twine, electrical tape for wiring, small rolls of colored tape for tagging lines or hoses, markers and pens, a note pad, golf tees (for plugging vacuum lines), metal coat hangers or a roll of mechanic's wire (to hold things out of the way), dental pick or similar long, pointed probe, a strong magnet, and a small mirror (to see into recesses and under manifolds).

A more advanced set of tools, suitable for tune-up work, can be drawn up easily. While the tools are slightly more sophisticated, they need not be outrageously expensive. There are several inexpensive tach/dwell meters on the market that are every bit as good for the average mechanic as a professional model. Just be sure that it goes to a least 1200–1500 rpm on the tach scale and that it works on 4, 6 and 8-cylinder engines. The key to these purchases is to make them with an eye towards adaptability and wide range. A basic list of tune-up tools could include:

- Tach/dwell meter.
- Spark plug wrench and gapping tool.
- Feeler gauges for valve adjustment.
- Timing light.

Fig. 1 All but the most basic procedures will require an assortment of ratchets and sockets

TCCS1200

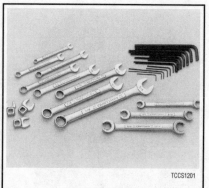

Fig. 2 In addition to ratchets, a good set of wrenches and hex keys will be necessary

TCCS1201

Fig. 3 A hydraulic floor jack and a set of jackstands are essential for lifting and supporting the vehicle

TCCS1202

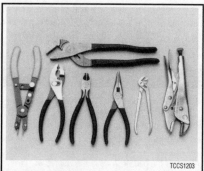

Fig. 4 An assortment of pliers, grippers and cutters will be handy for old rusted parts and stripped bolt heads

TCCS1203

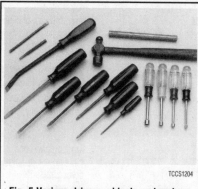

Fig. 5 Various drivers, chisels and prybars are great tools to have in your toolbox

TCCS1204

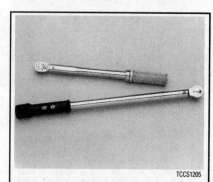

Fig. 6 Many repairs will require the use of a torque wrench to assure the components are properly fastened

TCCS1205

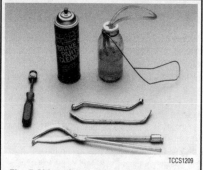

Fig. 7 Although not always necessary, using specialized brake tools will save time

TCCS1209

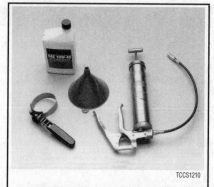

Fig. 8 A few inexpensive lubrication tools will make maintenance easier

TCCS1210

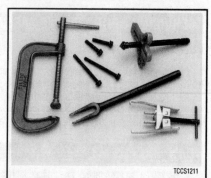

Fig. 9 Various pullers, clamps and separator tools are needed for many larger, more complicated repairs

TCCS1211

Fig. 10 A variety of tools and gauges should be used for spark plug gapping and installation

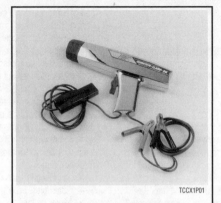

Fig. 11 Inductive type timing light

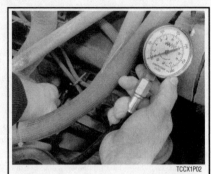

Fig. 12 A screw-in type compression gauge is recommended for compression testing

Fig. 13 A vacuum/pressure tester is necessary for many testing procedures

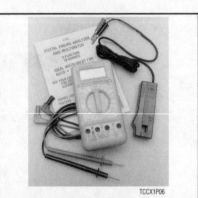

Fig. 14 Most modern automotive multimeters incorporate many helpful features

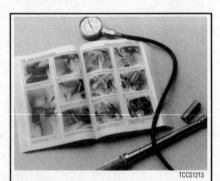

Fig. 15 Proper information is vital, so always have a Chilton Total Car Care manual handy

The choice of a timing light should be made carefully. A light which works on the DC current supplied by the vehicle's battery is the best choice; it should have a xenon tube for brightness. On any vehicle with an electronic ignition system, a timing light with an inductive pickup that clamps around the No. 1 spark plug cable is preferred.

In addition to these basic tools, there are several other tools and gauges you may find useful. These include:
- Compression gauge. The screw-in type is slower to use, but eliminates the possibility of a faulty reading due to escaping pressure.
- Manifold vacuum gauge.
- 12V test light.
- A combination volt/ohmmeter
- Induction Ammeter. This is used for determining whether or not there is current in a wire. These are handy for use if a wire is broken somewhere in a wiring harness.

As a final note, you will probably find a torque wrench necessary for all but the most basic work. The beam type models are perfectly adequate, although the newer click types (breakaway) are easier to use. The click type torque wrenches tend to be more expensive. Also keep in mind that all types of torque wrenches should be periodically checked and/or recalibrated. You will have to decide for yourself which better fits your pocketbook, and purpose.

Special Tools

Normally, the use of special factory tools is avoided for repair procedures, since these are not readily available for the do-it-yourself mechanic. When it is possible to perform the job with more commonly available tools, it will be pointed out, but occasionally, a special tool was designed to perform a specific function and should be used. Before substituting another tool, you should be convinced that neither your safety nor the performance of the vehicle will be compromised.

Special tools can usually be purchased from an automotive parts store or from your dealer. In some cases special tools may be available directly from the tool manufacturer.

SERVICING YOUR VEHICLE SAFELY

♦ See Figures 16, 17 and 18

It is virtually impossible to anticipate all of the hazards involved with automotive maintenance and service, but care and common sense will prevent most accidents.

The rules of safety for mechanics range from "don't smoke around gasoline," to "use the proper tool(s) for the job." The trick to avoiding injuries is to develop safe work habits and to take every possible precaution.

Do's

- Do keep a fire extinguisher and first aid kit handy.
- Do wear safety glasses or goggles when cutting, drilling, grinding or prying, even if you have 20–20 vision. If you wear glasses for the sake of vision, wear safety goggles over your regular glasses.
- Do shield your eyes whenever you work around the battery. Batteries contain sulfuric acid. In case of contact with, flush the area with water or a mixture of water and baking soda, then seek immediate medical attention.
- Do use safety stands (jackstands) for any undervehicle service. Jacks are for raising vehicles; jackstands are for making sure the vehicle stays raised until you want it to come down.
- Do use adequate ventilation when working with any chemicals or hazardous materials. Like carbon monoxide, the asbestos dust resulting from some brake lining wear can be hazardous in sufficient quantities.
- Do disconnect the negative battery cable when working on the electrical system. The secondary ignition system contains EXTREMELY HIGH VOLTAGE. In some cases it can even exceed 50,000 volts.
- Do follow manufacturer's directions whenever working with potentially hazardous materials. Most chemicals and fluids are poisonous.

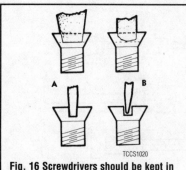

Fig. 16 Screwdrivers should be kept in good condition to prevent injury or damage which could result if the blade slips from the screw

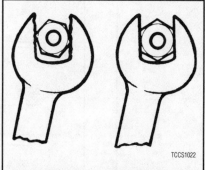

Fig. 17 Using the correct size wrench will help prevent the possibility of rounding off a nut

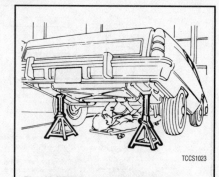

Fig. 18 NEVER work under a vehicle unless it is supported using safety stands (jackstands)

• Do properly maintain your tools. Loose hammerheads, mushroomed punches and chisels, frayed or poorly grounded electrical cords, excessively worn screwdrivers, spread wrenches (open end), cracked sockets, slipping ratchets, or faulty droplight sockets can cause accidents.

• Likewise, keep your tools clean; a greasy wrench can slip off a bolt head, ruining the bolt and often harming your knuckles in the process.

• Do use the proper size and type of tool for the job at hand. Do select a wrench or socket that fits the nut or bolt. The wrench or socket should sit straight, not cocked.

• Do, when possible, pull on a wrench handle rather than push on it, and adjust your stance to prevent a fall.

• Do be sure that adjustable wrenches are tightly closed on the nut or bolt and pulled so that the force is on the side of the fixed jaw.

• Do strike squarely with a hammer; avoid glancing blows.

• Do set the parking brake and block the drive wheels if the work requires a running engine.

Don'ts

• Don't run the engine in a garage or anywhere else without proper ventilation—EVER! Carbon monoxide is poisonous; it takes a long time to leave the human body and you can build up a deadly supply of it in your system by simply breathing in a little at a time. You may not realize you are slowly poisoning yourself. Always use power vents, windows, fans and/or open the garage door.

• Don't work around moving parts while wearing loose clothing. Short sleeves are much safer than long, loose sleeves. Hard-toed shoes with neoprene soles protect your toes and give a better grip on slippery surfaces. Watches and jewelry is not safe working around a vehicle. Long hair should be tied back under a hat or cap.

• Don't use pockets for toolboxes. A fall or bump can drive a screwdriver deep into your body. Even a rag hanging from your back pocket can wrap around a spinning shaft or fan.

• Don't smoke when working around gasoline, cleaning solvent or other flammable material.

• Don't smoke when working around the battery. When the battery is being charged, it gives off explosive hydrogen gas.

• Don't use gasoline to wash your hands; there are excellent soaps available. Gasoline contains dangerous additives which can enter the body through a cut or through your pores. Gasoline also removes all the natural oils from the skin so that bone dry hands will suck up oil and grease.

• Don't service the air conditioning system unless you are equipped with the necessary tools and training. When liquid or compressed gas refrigerant is released to atmospheric pressure it will absorb heat from whatever it contacts. This will chill or freeze anything it touches.

• Don't use screwdrivers for anything other than driving screws! A screwdriver used as a prying tool can snap when you least expect it, causing injuries. At the very least, you'll ruin a good screwdriver.

• Don't use an emergency jack (that little ratchet, scissors, or pantograph jack supplied with the vehicle) for anything other than changing a flat! These jacks are only intended for emergency use out on the road; they are NOT designed as a maintenance tool. If you are serious about maintaining your vehicle yourself, invest in a hydraulic floor jack of at least a 1½ ton capacity, and at least two sturdy jackstands.

FASTENERS, MEASUREMENTS AND CONVERSIONS

Bolts, Nuts and Other Threaded Retainers

▶ See Figures 19 and 20

Although there are a great variety of fasteners found in the modern car or truck, the most commonly used retainer is the threaded fastener (nuts, bolts, screws, studs, etc.). Most threaded retainers may be reused, provided that they are not damaged in use or during the repair. Some retainers (such as stretch bolts or torque prevailing nuts) are designed to deform when tightened or in use and should not be reinstalled.

Whenever possible, we will note any special retainers which should be replaced during a procedure. But you should always inspect the condition of a retainer when it is removed and replace any that show signs of damage. Check all threads for rust or corrosion which can increase the torque necessary to achieve the desired clamp load for which that fastener was originally selected. Additionally, be sure that the driver surface of the fastener has not been compromised by rounding or other damage. In some cases a driver surface may become only partially rounded, allowing the driver to catch in only one direction. In many of these occurrences, a fastener may be installed and tightened, but the driver would not be able to grip and loosen the fastener again.

If you must replace a fastener, whether due to design or damage, you must ALWAYS be sure to use the proper replacement. In all cases, a retainer of the

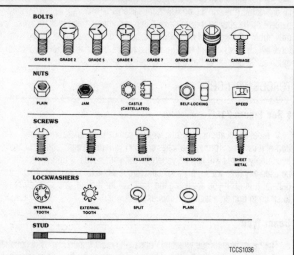

Fig. 19 There are many different types of threaded retainers found on vehicles

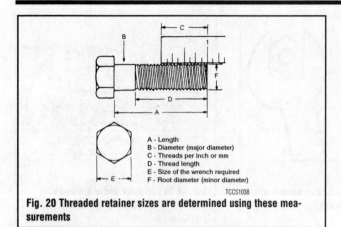

A - Length
B - Diameter (major diameter)
C - Threads per inch or mm
D - Thread length
E - Size of the wrench required
F - Root diameter (minor diameter)

TCCS1038

Fig. 20 Threaded retainer sizes are determined using these measurements

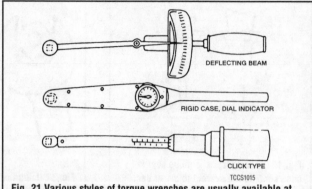

DEFLECTING BEAM

RIGID CASE, DIAL INDICATOR

CLICK TYPE

TCCS1015

Fig. 21 Various styles of torque wrenches are usually available at your local automotive supply store

same design, material and strength should be used. Markings on the heads of most bolts will help determine the proper strength of the fastener. The same material, thread and pitch must be selected to assure proper installation and safe operation of the vehicle afterwards.

Thread gauges are available to help measure a bolt or stud's thread. Most automotive and hardware stores keep gauges available to help you select the proper size. In a pinch, you can use another nut or bolt for a thread gauge. If the bolt you are replacing is not too badly damaged, you can select a match by finding another bolt which will thread in its place. If you find a nut which threads properly onto the damaged bolt, then use that nut to help select the replacement bolt.

※※ WARNING

Be aware that when you find a bolt with damaged threads, you may also find the nut or drilled hole it was threaded into has also been damaged. If this is the case, you may have to drill and tap the hole, replace the nut or otherwise repair the threads. NEVER try to force a replacement bolt to fit into the damaged threads.

Torque

Torque is defined as the measurement of resistance to turning or rotating. It tends to twist a body about an axis of rotation. A common example of this would be tightening a threaded retainer such as a nut, bolt or screw. Measuring torque is one of the most common ways to help assure that a threaded retainer has been properly fastened.

When tightening a threaded fastener, torque is applied in three distinct areas, the head, the bearing surface and the clamp load. About 50 percent of the measured torque is used in overcoming bearing friction. This is the friction between the bearing surface of the bolt head, screw head or nut face and the base material or washer (the surface on which the fastener is rotating). Approximately 40 percent of the applied torque is used in overcoming thread friction. This leaves only about 10 percent of the applied torque to develop a useful clamp load (the force which holds a joint together). This means that friction can account for as much as 90 percent of the applied torque on a fastener.

TORQUE WRENCHES

♦ See Figure 21

In most applications, a torque wrench can be used to assure proper installation of a fastener. Torque wrenches come in various designs and most automotive supply stores will carry a variety to suit your needs. A torque wrench should be used any time we supply a specific torque value for a fastener. Again, the general rule of "if you are using the right tool for the job, you should not have to strain to tighten a fastener" applies here.

Beam Type

The beam type torque wrench is one of the most popular types. It consists of a pointer attached to the head that runs the length of the flexible beam (shaft) to a scale located near the handle. As the wrench is pulled, the beam bends and the pointer indicates the torque using the scale.

Click (Breakaway) Type

Another popular design of torque wrench is the click type. To use the click type wrench you pre-adjust it to a torque setting. Once the torque is reached, the wrench has a reflex signaling feature that causes a momentary breakaway of the torque wrench body, sending an impulse to the operator's hand.

Pivot Head Type

♦ See Figure 22

Some torque wrenches (usually of the click type) may be equipped with a pivot head which can allow it to be used in areas of limited access. BUT, it must be used properly. To hold a pivot head wrench, grasp the handle lightly, and as you pull on the handle, it should be floated on the pivot point. If the handle comes in contact with the yoke extension during the process of pulling, there is a very good chance the torque readings will be inaccurate because this could alter the wrench loading point. The design of the handle is usually such as to make it inconvenient to deliberately misuse the wrench.

→It should be mentioned that the use of any U-joint, wobble or extension will have an effect on the torque readings, no matter what type of wrench you are using. For the most accurate readings, install the socket directly on the wrench driver. If necessary, straight extensions (which hold a socket directly under the wrench driver) will have the least effect on the torque reading. Avoid any extension that alters the length of the wrench from the handle to the head/driving point (such as a crow's foot). U-joint or wobble extensions can greatly affect the readings; avoid their use at all times.

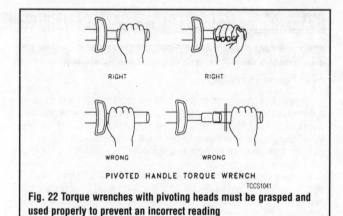

RIGHT

RIGHT

WRONG

WRONG

PIVOTED HANDLE TORQUE WRENCH

TCCS1041

Fig. 22 Torque wrenches with pivoting heads must be grasped and used properly to prevent an incorrect reading

Rigid Case (Direct Reading)

A rigid case or direct reading torque wrench is equipped with a dial indicator to show torque values. One advantage of these wrenches is that they can be held at any position on the wrench without affecting accuracy. These wrenches are often preferred because they tend to be compact, easy to read and have a great degree of accuracy.

TORQUE ANGLE METERS

Because the frictional characteristics of each fastener or threaded hole will vary, clamp loads which are based strictly on torque will vary as well. In most applications, this variance is not significant enough to cause worry. But, in certain applications, a manufacturer's engineers may determine that more precise clamp loads are necessary (such is the case with many aluminum cylinder heads). In these cases, a torque angle method of installation would be specified. When installing fasteners which are torque angle tightened, a predetermined seating torque and standard torque wrench are usually used first to remove any compliance from the joint. The fastener is then tightened the specified additional portion of a turn measured in degrees. A torque angle gauge (mechanical protractor) is used for these applications.

Standard and Metric Measurements

▶ See Figure 23

Throughout this manual, specifications are given to help you determine the condition of various components on your vehicle, or to assist you in their installation. Some of the most common measurements include length (in. or cm/mm), torque (ft. lbs., inch lbs. or Nm) and pressure (psi, in. Hg, kPa or mm Hg). In most cases, we strive to provide the proper measurement as determined by the manufacturer's engineers.

Though, in some cases, that value may not be conveniently measured with what is available in your toolbox. Luckily, many of the measuring devices which are available today will have two scales so the Standard or Metric measurements may easily be taken. If any of the various measuring tools which are available to you do not contain the same scale as listed in the specifications, use the accompanying conversion factors to determine the proper value.

The conversion factor chart is used by taking the given specification and multiplying it by the necessary conversion factor. For instance, looking at the first line, if you have a measurement in inches such as "free-play should be 2 in." but your ruler reads only in millimeters, multiply 2 in. by the conversion factor of 25.4 to get the metric equivalent of 50.8mm. Likewise, if the specification was given only in a Metric measurement, for example in Newton Meters (Nm), then look at the center column first. If the measurement is 100 Nm, multiply it by the conversion factor of 0.738 to get 73.8 ft. lbs.

CONVERSION FACTORS

LENGTH–DISTANCE

Inches (in.)	x 25.4	= Millimeters (mm)	x .0394	= Inches
Feet (ft.)	x .305	= Meters (m)	x 3.281	= Feet
Miles	x 1.609	= Kilometers (km)	x .0621	= Miles

VOLUME

Cubic Inches (in3)	x 16.387	= Cubic Centimeters	x .061	= in3
IMP Pints (IMP pt.)	x .568	= Liters (L)	x 1.76	= IMP pt.
IMP Quarts (IMP qt.)	x 1.137	= Liters (L)	x .88	= IMP qt.
IMP Gallons (IMP gal.)	x 4.546	= Liters (L)	x .22	= IMP gal.
IMP Quarts (IMP qt.)	x 1.201	= US Quarts (US qt.)	x .833	= IMP qt.
IMP Gallons (IMP gal.)	x 1.201	= US Gallons (US gal.)	x .833	= IMP gal.
Fl. Ounces	x 29.573	= Milliliters	x .034	= Ounces
US Pints (US pt.)	x .473	= Liters (L)	x 2.113	= Pints
US Quarts (US qt.)	x .946	= Liters (L)	x 1.057	= Quarts
US Gallons (US gal.)	x 3.785	= Liters (L)	x .264	= Gallons

MASS–WEIGHT

Ounces (oz.)	x 28.35	= Grams (g)	x .035	= Ounces
Pounds (lb.)	x .454	= Kilograms (kg)	x 2.205	= Pounds

PRESSURE

Pounds Per Sq. In. (psi)	x 6.895	= Kilopascals (kPa)	x .145	= psi
Inches of Mercury (Hg)	x .4912	= psi	x 2.036	= Hg
Inches of Mercury (Hg)	x 3.377	= Kilopascals (kPa)	x .2961	= Hg
Inches of Water (H₂O)	x .07355	= Inches of Mercury	x 13.783	= H₂O
Inches of Water (H₂O)	x .03613	= psi	x 27.684	= H₂O
Inches of Water (H₂O)	x .248	= Kilopascals (kPa)	x 4.026	= H₂O

TORQUE

Pounds–Force Inches (in-lb)	x .113	= Newton Meters (N·m)	x 8.85	= in-lb
Pounds–Force Feet (ft-lb)	x 1.356	= Newton Meters (N·m)	x .738	= ft-lb

VELOCITY

Miles Per Hour (MPH)	x 1.609	= Kilometers Per Hour (KPH)	x .621	= MPH

POWER

Horsepower (Hp)	x .745	= Kilowatts	x 1.34	= Horsepower

FUEL CONSUMPTION*

Miles Per Gallon IMP (MPG)	x .354	= Kilometers Per Liter (Km/L)	
Kilometers Per Liter (Km/L)	x 2.352	= IMP MPG	
Miles Per Gallon US (MPG)	x .425	= Kilometers Per Liter (Km/L)	
Kilometers Per Liter (Km/L)	x 2.352	= US MPG	

*It is common to covert from miles per gallon (mpg) to liters/100 kilometers (1/100 km), where mpg (IMP) x 1/100 km = 282 and mpg (US) x 1/100 km = 235.

TEMPERATURE

Degree Fahrenheit (°F) = (°C x 1.8) + 32
Degree Celsius (°C) = (°F − 32) x .56

TCCS1044

Fig. 23 Standard and metric conversion factors chart

SERIAL NUMBER IDENTIFICATION

Vehicle

▶ See Figures 24 and 25

The Vehicle Identification Number (VIN) plate is mounted on the driver's side of the instrument panel, and is visible through the windshield.

The models covered in this book are full size C/K trucks including the Tahoe, Blazer, Jimmy, Yukon and Suburban. Starting in 1992 the Blazer was renamed the Blazer/Tahoe and Jimmy the Jimmy/Yukon.

The 5th digit on the vehicle identification number is the vehicle line and chassis type:

- C and R are 2-wheel drive conventional cabs
- V and K are 4-wheel drive conventional cabs

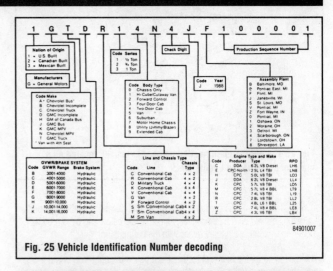

Fig. 25 Vehicle Identification Number decoding

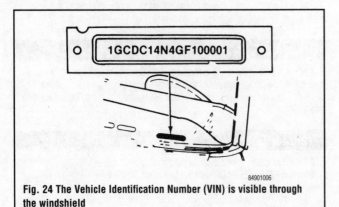

Fig. 24 The Vehicle Identification Number (VIN) is visible through the windshield

Engine

▶ See Figure 26

On the 4.8L, inline 6-cylinder engine, the engine identification number is found on a machined pad on the left side of the block, just rear of center, below the engine side cover.

On the 1988–92 4.3L V6 engine, the engine identification number is found on a machined pad on the block, at the front just below the right side cylinder head.

VEHICLE IDENTIFICATION CHART

Engine Code							Model Year	
Engine Series (ID/VIN)	Engine Displacement Liters	Cubic Inches	No. of Cylinders	Fuel System	Eng. Mfg.		Code	Year
Z	4.3	263 (4293)	6	TBI	CPC		J	1988
W	4.3	263 (4293)	6	CSFI	CPC		K	1989
T	4.8	292 (4785)	6	1BC	CPC		L	1990
H	5.0	305 (4999)	8	①	CPC		M	1991
M	5.0	305 (4999)	8	CSFI	CPC		N	1992
K	5.7	350 (5735)	8	TBI	CPC		P	1993
R	5.7	350 (5735)	8	CSFI	CPC		R	1994
C	6.2	379 (6210)	8	D	DDA		S	1995
J	6.2	379 (6210)	8	D	DDA		T	1996
F	6.5	395 (6473)	8	②	CPC		V	1997
P	6.5	395 (6473)	8	D	CPC		W	1998
S	6.5	395 (6473)	8	TD	CPC			
N	7.4	454 (7440)	8	TBI	CPC			
W	7.4	454 (7440)	8	4BC	CPC			
J	7.4	454 (7440)	8	MFI	CPC			

The 10th digit of the Vehicle Identification Number (VIN) is the year code and the 8th digit is the engine code.

① 4BC or TBI	D-Diesel	
② D or TD/HO	DDA-Detroit Diesel Allison	
1BC-1 Barrel Carburetor	HO-High Output	
4BC-4 Barrel Carburetor	MFI-Multi-port Fuel Injection	
CPC-Chevrolet/Pontiac of Canada	TBI-Throttle Body Injection	
CSFI-Central Sequential Fuel Injection	TD-Turbo Diesel	

91021C01

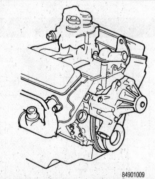

Fig. 26 The engine identification number is usually located on a machined pad on the engine block

On the 1993–98 4.3L V6 engine, the engine identification number is found on a machined pad on the rear of the cylinder block, below and behind the left cylinder head where the engine mates with the bellhousing.

On V8 gasoline engines, the engine identification number is usually found on a machined pad on the block, at the front just below the right side cylinder head. The engine identification number is sometimes also found on a machined pad on the left, rear upper side of the block, where the engine mates with the bellhousing.

On V8 diesel engines, the engine identification number is found on a machined pad on the front of the block, between the left cylinder head and the thermostat housing, and/or on a machined pad on the left rear of the block, just behind the left cylinder head. In the following example, engine number F1210TFA is broken down as follows:

- F—Manufacturing Plant. F-Flint and T-Tonawanda

- 12—Month of Manufacture (December)
- 10—Day of Manufacturer (Tenth)
- T—Truck engine
- FA—Transmission and Engine Combination

Transmission

The Muncie 117mm 4-speed transmission is numbered on the rear of the case, above the output shaft.

The 4-Speed 85mm and 5-Speed 85mm transmissions are numbered on the right rear of the case.

The NVG 3500 5-speed transmissions are numbered on the top, left side of the case, near the bellhousing.

The NVG 4500 5-speed transmissions are numbered on the top, left side of the case, near the bellhousing.

The NVG 5LM60 5-speed transmissions are numbered on the lower left side, about halfway back on the case.

The automatic transmissions are identified by a plate attached to the right side, which is stamped with the serial number.

Drive Axle

The drive axle serial number is stamped on the axle shaft housing, where it connects to the differential housing.

Front axles on four wheel drive models are marked on the front of the left axle tube.

Transfer Case

All transfer cases have a build tag attached to the case.

On the NP205, it is attached to the bolt retaining the Power Take Off (PTO) cover.

GENERAL ENGINE SPECIFICATIONS

Year	Engine ID/VIN	Engine Displacement Liters (cc)	No. of Cyl.	Fuel System Type	Net Horsepower @ rpm	Net Torque @ rpm (ft. lbs.)	Compression Ratio	Oil Pressure (lbs. @ rpm)
1994	S	6.5 (6473)	8	D	190@3400 [1]	380@1700	21.5:1	40-45@2000
	N	7.4 (7440)	8	TBI	230@3600 [2]	385@1600 [3]	8.0:1	40@2000
1995	Z	4.3 (4293)	6	TBI	160@4000	235@2400	9.1:1	18@2000 [4]
	H	5.0 (4999)	8	TBI	175@4200	265@2800	9.0:1	18@2000 [4]
	K	5.7 (5735)	8	TBI	200@4000	310@2400	9.1:1	18@2000 [4]
	F	6.5 (6473)	8	D	140@3600	255@1900	21.5:1	40-45@2000
	P	6.5 (6473)	8	D	150@3600	280@2000	21.5:1	40-45@2000
	S	6.5 (6473)	8	D	190@3400	380@1700	21.5:1	40-45@2000
	N	7.4 (7440)	8	TBI	230@3600 [5]	385@1600 [6]	8.0:1	40@2000
1996	W	4.3 (4293)	6	CSFI	200@4400	255@2800	9.2:1	18@2000 [4]
	M	5.0 (4999)	8	CSFI	220@4600	285@2800	9.4:1	18@2000 [4]
	R	5.7 (5735)	8	CSFI	255@4600	330@2800	9.4:1	18@2000 [4]
	F	6.5 (6473)	8	D	180@3400 [9]	360@1800 [9]	21.5:1	40-45@2000
	P	6.5 (6473)	8	D	180@3400 [9]	360@1800 [9]	21.5:1	40-45@2000
	S	6.5 (6473)	8	D	180@3400 [9]	360@1800 [9]	21.5:1	40-45@2000
	J	7.4 (7440)	8	MFI	290@4000 [9]	410@3200 [9]	9.0:1	26@2000
1997	W	4.3 (4293)	6	CSFI	200@4400	255@2800	9.2:1	18@2000 [4]
	M	5.0 (4999)	8	CSFI	230@4600	285@2800	9.4:1	18@2000 [4]
	R	5.7 (5735)	8	CSFI	255@4600	330@2800	9.4:1	18@2000 [4]
	F	6.5 (6473)	8	D	180@3400 [9]	360@1800 [9]	21.5:1	40-45@2000
	P	6.5 (6473)	8	D	180@3400 [9]	360@1800 [9]	21.5:1	40-45@2000
	S	6.5 (6473)	8	D	180@3400 [9]	360@1800 [9]	21.5:1	40-45@2000
	J	7.4 (7440)	8	MFI	290@4000 [9]	410@3200 [9]	9.0:1	26@2000
1998	W	4.3 (4293)	6	CSFI	200@4400	255@2800	9.2:1	18@2000 [4]
	M	5.0 (4999)	8	CSFI	230@4600	285@2800	9.4:1	18@2000 [4]
	R	5.7 (5735)	8	CSFI	255@4600	330@2800	9.4:1	18@2000 [4]
	F	6.5 (6473)	8	D	180@3400 [9]	360@1800 [9]	21.5:1	40-45@2000
	P	6.5 (6473)	8	D	180@3400 [9]	360@1800 [9]	21.5:1	40-45@2000
	S	6.5 (6473)	8	D	180@3400 [9]	360@1800 [9]	21.5:1	40-45@2000
	J	7.4 (7440)	8	MFI	290@4000 [9]	410@3200 [9]	9.0:1	26@2000

1BC—1 Barrel Carburetor
4BC—4 Barrel Carburetor
CSFI—Central Sequential Fuel Injection
D—Diesel
MFI—Multi-port Fuel Injection
TBI—Throttle Body Injection
TD/HO—Turbo Diesel/High Output

[1] C/K pick-up—160@4000
[2] C/K heavy duty pick-up—155@4000
[3] C/K pick-up—230@2400
C/K heavy duty pick-up—230@2400

[1] Below 850 GVWR—211@4000
C/K pick-up—155@4000
[2] Below 850 GVWR—300@2800
Above 8500 GVWR—30@2400
[3] 454 SS—255@4000
[4] 454 SS—405@2400
[5] Heavy duty—8.6:1
[6] Heavy duty—8.3:1
[7] Minimum PSI
[8] Heavy duty—290@3400
[9] Heavy duty—385@1800

GENERAL ENGINE SPECIFICATIONS

Year	Engine ID/VIN	Engine Displacement Liters (cc)	No. of Cyl.	Fuel System Type	Net Horsepower @ rpm	Net Torque @ rpm (ft. lbs.)	Compression Ratio	Oil Pressure (lbs. @ rpm)
1988	Z	4.3 (4293)	6	TBI	145@4000	230@2400	9.3:1	30@2000
	T	4.8 (4785)	6	1BC	115@3400	215@1600	8.0:1	50@2000
	H	5.0 (4999)	8	4BC	165@4400	240@2000	9.0:1	18@2000
	K	5.7 (5735)	8	TBI	[1]	[2]	8.5:1	18@2000
	C	6.2 (6210)	8	D	130@3600	240@2000	21.0:1	35@2000
	J	6.2 (6210)	8	D	135@3600	240@2000	21.0:1	35@2000
	N	7.4 (7440)	8	TBI	230@3600	385@1600	8.0:1	40@2000
	W	7.4 (7440)	8	4BC	240@3800	375@3200	8.0:1	40@2000
1989	Z	4.3 (4293)	6	TBI	145@4000	230@2400	9.3:1	30@2000
	T	4.8 (4785)	6	1BC	115@3400	215@1600	8.0:1	50@2000
	H	5.0 (4999)	8	TBI	170@4400	270@2400	9.0:1	18@2000
	K	5.7 (5735)	8	TBI	[3]		8.5:1	18@2000
	C	6.2 (6210)	8	D	145@3600	255@1900	21.0:1	35@2000
	J	6.2 (6210)	8	D	155@3500	257@2000	21.0:1	35@2000
	N	7.4 (7440)	8	TBI	230@3600	385@1600	8.0:1	40@2000
	W	7.4 (7440)	8	4BC	230@3800	375@3200	8.0:1	40@2000
1990	Z	4.3 (4293)	6	TBI	170@4000	270@2400	9.3:1 [7]	18@2000
	H	5.0 (4999)	8	TBI	170@4000	270@2400	9.0:1 [7]	18@2000
	K	5.7 (5735)	8	TBI	145@3600	255@1900	8.5:1 [7]	35@2000
	C	6.2 (6210)	8	D	155@3500	257@2000	21.0:1	40@2000
	J	6.2 (6210)	8	D	230@3600	385@1600	21.0:1	18@2000
	N	7.4 (7440)	8	TBI	230@3600	385@1600	8.0:1	18@2000
1991	Z	4.3 (4293)	6	TBI	170@4000	270@2400	9.3:1 [7]	18@2000 [4]
	H	5.0 (4999)	8	TBI	145@3600	255@1900	9.0:1 [7]	18@2000 [4]
	C	6.2 (6210)	8	D	155@3500	257@2000	21.0:1	35@2000
	J	6.2 (6210)	8	D	230@3500	385@1600	21.0:1	40@2000
	N	7.4 (7440)	8	TBI	160@4000	235@2400	9.3:1	18@2000 [4]
1992	Z	4.3 (4293)	6	TBI	160@4000	235@2400	9.3:1	18@2000 [4]
	H	5.0 (4999)	8	TBI	175@4400	270@2400	9.0:1	18@2000 [4]
	K	5.7 (5735)	8	TBI	140@3600	255@1900	8.5:1 [8]	18@2000 [4]
	C	6.2 (6210)	8	D	150@3600	280@1700	21.3:1	35@2000
	J	6.2 (6210)	8	D	190@3400	380@1700	21.0:1	40@2000
	F	6.5 (6473)	8	TD	230@3600 [8]	385@1600 [8]	8.0:1	40-45@2000
	N	7.4 (7440)	8	TBI	230@3600	385@1600	8.0:1	40-45@2000
1993	Z	4.3 (4293)	6	TBI	160@4000	235@2400	9.3:1	18@2000 [4]
	H	5.0 (4999)	8	TBI	175@4400	270@2400	9.0:1	18@2000 [4]
	K	5.7 (5735)	8	TBI	140@3600	255@1900	8.5:1 [8]	18@2000 [4]
	C	6.2 (6210)	8	D	150@3600	280@1700	21.3:1	35@2000
	J	6.2 (6210)	8	D	190@3400	380@1700	21.0:1	40@2000
	F	6.5 (6473)	8	TD	230@3600 [8]	385@1600 [8]	8.0:1	40-45@2000
	N	7.4 (7440)	8	TBI	160@4000	235@2400	9.1:1	18@2000 [4]
1994	Z	4.3 (4293)	6	TBI	200@4000	265@2800	9.0:1	18@2000 [4]
	H	5.0 (4999)	8	TBI	200@4000	310@2400	9.1:1	18@2000 [4]
	K	5.7 (5735)	8	TBI	140@3600	255@1900	21.5:1	40-45@2000
	F	6.5 (6473)	8	D	150@3600	280@2000	21.5:1	40-45@2000
	P	6.5 (6473)	8	D	150@3600	280@2000	21.5:1	40-45@2000

On the NP231, NP233 and NP241, it is attached to the rear case half.

On the NV241 and NV243, it is attached to the rear case half.

On the Borg Warner 4401/4470, it is attached to an extension housing bolt.

Service Parts Identification Label

♦ See Figure 27

The service parts identification label, commonly known as the option list, is usually located on the inside of the glove compartment door. On some trucks, you may have to look for it on an inner fender panel. The label lists the vehicle serial number, wheelbase, all Regular Production Options (RPOs) and all special equipment. Probably, the most valuable piece of information on this label is the paint code, a useful item when you have occasion to need paint.

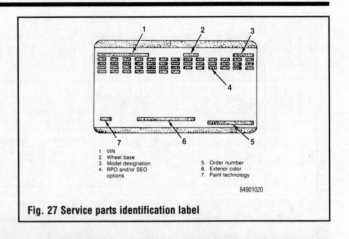

1. VIN
2. Wheel base
3. Model designation
4. RPO and/or SEO options
5. Order number
6. Exterior color
7. Paint technology

84901020

Fig. 27 Service parts identification label

ROUTINE MAINTENANCE AND TUNE-UP

Proper maintenance and tune-up is the key to long and trouble-free vehicle life. Studies have shown that a properly tuned and maintained vehicle can achieve better gas mileage than an out-of-tune vehicle. As a conscientious owner and driver, set aside a Saturday morning, say once a month, to check or replace items which could cause major problems later. Keep your own personal log to jot down which services you performed, how much the parts cost you, the date, and the exact odometer reading at the time. Keep all receipts for such items as engine oil and filters, so that they may be referred to in case of related problems or to determine operating expenses. As a do-it-yourselfer, these receipts are the only proof you have that the required maintenance was performed. In the event of a warranty problem, these receipts will be invaluable.

The literature provided with your vehicle when it was originally delivered includes the factory recommended maintenance schedule. If you no longer have this literature, replacement copies are usually available from the dealer.

Air Cleaner

♦ See Figures 28, 29 and 30

The element should be replaced at the recommended intervals shown in the Maintenance Intervals chart later in this section. If your truck is operated under severely dusty conditions or severe operating conditions, more frequent changes will certainly be necessary. Inspect the element at least twice a year. Early spring and early fall are always good times for inspection. Remove the element and check for any perforations or tears in the filter. Check the cleaner housing for signs of dirt or dust that may have leaked through the filter element or in through the snorkel tube. Position a droplight on one side of the element and look through the filter at the light. If no glow of light can be seen through the element material, replace the filter. If holes in the filter element are apparent or signs of dirt seepage through the filter are evident, replace the filter.

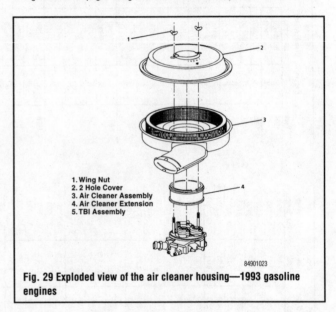

1. Wing Nut
2. 2 Hole Cover
3. Air Cleaner Assembly
4. Air Cleaner Extension
5. TBI Assembly

84901023

Fig. 29 Exploded view of the air cleaner housing—1993 gasoline engines

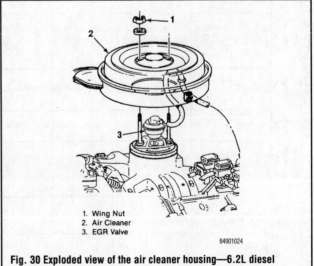

1. Air cleaner
2. Seal
3. Extension
4. Stud
5. Nut - 18 inch lbs.

FRT

84901021

Fig. 28 Typical air cleaner housing assembly components—1988–92 gasoline engines

1. Wing Nut
2. Air Cleaner
3. EGR Valve

84901024

Fig. 30 Exploded view of the air cleaner housing—6.2L diesel engines

UNDERHOOD MAINTENANCE COMPONENT LOCATIONS—R/V-SERIES

1. Coolant recovery reservoir
2. Battery
3. Radiator cap
4. Engine oil dipstick
5. Radiator hose (upper)
6. Air filter element (under housing)
7. Brake master cylinder
8. Windshield washer fluid reservoir
9. Automatic transmission dipstick (behind air cleaner housing)
10. Oil filler cap
11. Distributor (behind air cleaner housing)

91021P01

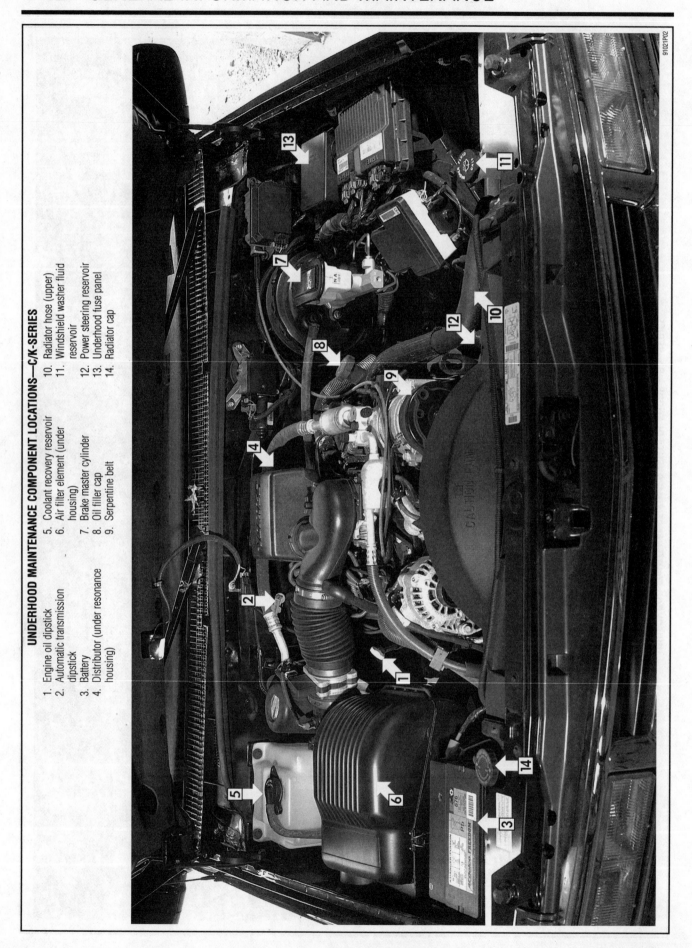

UNDERHOOD MAINTENANCE COMPONENT LOCATIONS—C/K-SERIES

1. Engine oil dipstick
2. Automatic transmission dipstick
3. Battery
4. Distributor (under resonance housing)
5. Coolant recovery reservoir
6. Air filter element (under housing)
7. Brake master cylinder
8. Oil filler cap
9. Serpentine belt
10. Radiator hose (upper)
11. Windshield washer fluid reservoir
12. Power steering reservoir
13. Underhood fuse panel
14. Radiator cap

REMOVAL & INSTALLATION

▶ **See Figures 31, 32, 33, 34 and 35**

1. On older model vehicles, loosen the wingnut(s) and lift off the housing cover. On newer model vehicles, unfasten the retaining clips and separate the two case halves.

2. On the 6.5L diesel, position the cover with the air cleaner flexible hose off to the side.

3. Withdraw the element from the housing and discard it.

4. With a clean rag, remove any dirt or dust from the front cover and also from the element seating surface.

To install:

5. Position and install the new filter element so that it seats properly in the housing.

6. On the 6.5L diesel, position the cover with the attached hose over the element and snap the retaining clips into place.

7. On early model vehicles, install the housing lid and tighten the wingnut(s) to about 18 inch lbs. (2 Nm).

8. On late model vehicles, place the housing cover into position and engage the retaining clip.

❉❉ WARNING

Do not drive the vehicle with air cleaner removed. Doing so will allow dirt and a variety of other foreign particles to enter the engine and cause damage and wear. Also, backfiring could cause a fire in the engine compartment.

Fuel Filter

REMOVAL & INSTALLATION

Carbureted Gasoline Engines

FILTER IN CARBURETOR

▶ **See Figure 36**

The fuel filter should be serviced at the interval given on the Maintenance Interval chart. Two types of fuel filters are used, a bronze type and a paper element type. Filter replacement should be attempted only when the engine is cold. Additionally, it is a good idea to place some absorbent rags under the fuel fittings to catch the gasoline which will spill out when the lines are loosened.

1. Disengage the fuel line connection at the intake fuel filter nut. Plug the opening to prevent loss of fuel.

2. Remove the intake fuel filter nut from the carburetor with a 1 in. open end wrench (or adjustable wrench).

3. Remove the filter element and spring.

4. Check the element for restrictions by blowing on the cone end. Air should pass freely.

5. Clean or replace the element, as necessary.

To install:

6. Install the element spring, then the filter element in the carburetor. Bronze filters should have the small section of the cone facing out.

87981P01

Fig. 31 Loosen the wingnut and remove it from the air cleaner cover

87981P02

Fig. 32 Removing the air cleaner cover

87981P03

Fig. 33 Remove the old air cleaner element

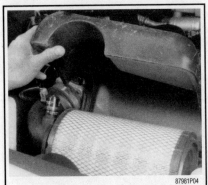

87981P04

Fig. 34 On newer vehicles, lift up the air cleaner cover—1996 truck shown

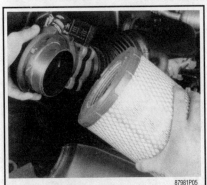

87981P05

Fig. 35 Remove the filter element—1996 truck shown

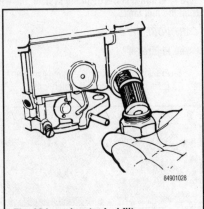

84901028

Fig. 36 In-carburetor fuel filter

7. Install a new gasket on the intake fuel nut. Install the nut in the carburetor body and tighten securely.

8. Install the fuel line and tighten the connector.

INLINE FILTER

Some trucks may have an inline filter. This is a can-shaped device located in the fuel line between the pump and the carburetor. It may be made of either plastic or metal. To replace the filter:

1. Place some absorbent rags under the filter. Remember, it will be full of gasoline when removed.

2. Use a pair of pliers to expand the clamp on one end of the filter, then slide the clamp down past the point to which the filter pipe extends in the rubber hose. Do the same with the other clamp.

3. Gently twist and pull the hoses free of the filter pipes. Remove and discard the old filter.

➡**Most replacement filters come with new hoses that should be installed with a new filter.**

4. Install the new filter into the hoses, slide the clamps back into place, and check for leaks with the engine idling.

Fuel Injected Gasoline Engines

EXCEPT CARTRIDGE TYPE

▶ **See Figures 37 and 38**

The inline filter on the fuel injected models is found along the frame rail.
1. Properly relieve the fuel system pressure.

❋❋ CAUTION

The 220 TBI unit used on the V6 and V8 engines contains a constant bleed feature in the pressure regulator that relieves pressure any time the engine is turned off. Therefore, no special relief procedure is required, however, a small amount of fuel may be released when the fuel line is disconnected. To reduce the chance of personal injury, cover the fuel line with cloth to collect the fuel and then place the cloth in an approved container.

2. Disconnect the fuel lines.
3. Remove the fuel filter from the retainer or mounting bolt.
To install:
4. Install the filter and tighten the bolt to 12 ft. lbs. (16 Nm). Connect the fuel lines and tighten the nuts to 20 ft. lbs. (26 Nm).
5. Road test the truck and check for any leaks.

➡**The filter has an arrow (fuel flow direction) on the side of the case, be sure to install it correctly in the system, the with arrow facing away from the fuel tank.**

CARTRIDGE TYPE

▶ **See Figure 39**

1. Properly relieve the fuel system pressure.
2. Disconnect the negative battery cable.

3. Turn the filter housing counterclockwise and allow the fuel to drain into a suitable container.
4. Remove the filter housing and gasket from the base.
5. Remove the fuel filter cartridge.
6. Inspect the filter housing for signs of corrosion or damage, replace as necessary.
To install:
7. Appalt a few drops of clean engine oil to the new housing gasket and install the gasket.
8. Install a new filter cartridge and the place the filter housing into position.
9. Tighten the housing by turning it clockwise until the gasket seats, then tighten the housing an additional ¾ turn.
10. Connect the negative battery cable.
11. Start the engine and check for fuel leaks.
12. Repair as necessary.

Diesel Engines

6.2L ENGINE

▶ **See Figures 40 and 41**

The fuel/water separator is usually located on the header assembly.
1. Drain the fuel from the fuel filter by opening both the air bleed and the water drain valve allowing the fuel to drain out into an appropriate container.
2. Remove the fuel tank cap to release any pressure or vacuum in the tank.
3. Unstrap both bail wires with a screwdriver and remove the filter.
To install:
4. Before installing the new filter, insure that both filter mounting plate fittings are clear of dirt.
5. Install the new filter, snap into place with the bail wires.
6. Close the water drain valve and open the air bleed valve. Connect a ⅛ in. (3mm) I.D. hose to the air bleed port and place the other end into a suitable container.
7. Disconnect the fuel injection pump shut off solenoid wire.
8. Crank the engine for 10–15 seconds, then wait one minute for the starter motor to cool. Repeat until clear fuel is observed coming from the air bleed.

➡**If the engine is to be cranked, or starting attempted with the air cleaner removed, care must be taken to prevent dirt from being pulled into the air inlet manifold which could result in engine damage.**

9. Close the air bleed valve, reconnect the injection pump solenoid wire and replace the fuel tank cap.
10. Start the engine, allow it to idle for 5 minutes and check the fuel filter for leaks.

6.5L ENGINE

▶ **See Figure 42**

1. Remove the fuel tank cap to release any pressure or vacuum in the tank.
2. If equipped, remove the upper intake manifold cover.
3. Open the air bleed valve on top of the filter assembly.
4. Spin off the element nut at the top of the filter—it looks like a large knurled knob.
5. Lift the filter element out of the header assembly.

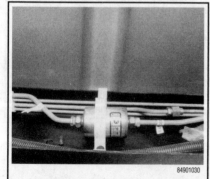
Fig. 37 The fuel filter is found along the frame rail

Fig. 38 Using two flare nut wrenches, disconnect the fuel lines

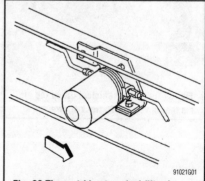
Fig. 39 The cartridge type fuel filter is located along the frame rail

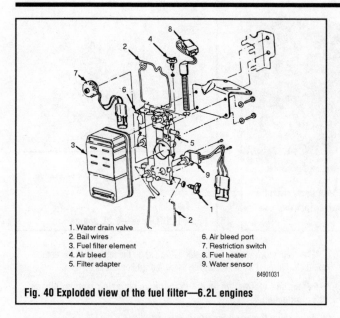

1. Water drain valve
2. Bail wires
3. Fuel filter element
4. Air bleed
5. Filter adapter
6. Air bleed port
7. Restriction switch
8. Fuel heater
9. Water sensor

84901031

Fig. 40 Exploded view of the fuel filter—6.2L engines

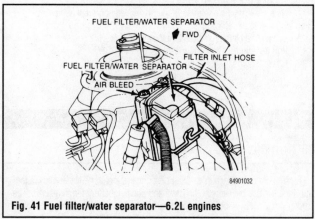

84901032

Fig. 41 Fuel filter/water separator—6.2L engines

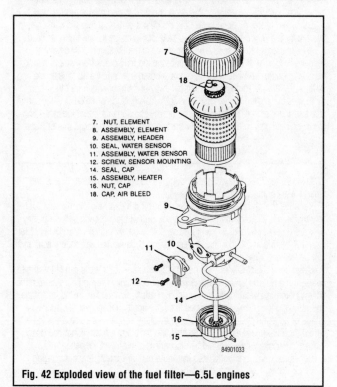

7. NUT, ELEMENT
8. ASSEMBLY, ELEMENT
9. ASSEMBLY, HEADER
10. SEAL, WATER SENSOR
11. ASSEMBLY, WATER SENSOR
12. SCREW, SENSOR MOUNTING
14. SEAL, CAP
15. ASSEMBLY, HEATER
16. NUT, CAP
18. CAP, AIR BLEED

84901033

Fig. 42 Exploded view of the fuel filter—6.5L engines

To install:

6. Clean the mating surfaces on the header assembly and the filter. Align the widest key slot in the element cap with that in the header assembly, push the element down until the two surfaces make contact, then tighten the nut by hand.

7. Open the air bleed valve on top of the filter assembly. Connect a hose to the bleeder valve and insert the other end into a suitable glass container.

8. Disconnect the fuel injection pump shut-down solenoid wire or the FUEL SOL relay center fuse (whichever applies to your vehicle, then crank the engine in 10–15 second intervals until clear, clean fuel is coming out of the hose.

➥**Wait about one minute between cranking intervals!**

9. Remove the hose and close the bleeder valve.

10. Connect the shut-down solenoid wire or fuse and install the fuel cap. Start the engine and allow it to idle for a few minutes. Check for leaks.

PCV Valve

▶ **See Figure 43**

➥**Diesel engines do not utilize a PCV system.**

The PCV valve, which is the heart of the positive crankcase ventilation system, should be changed as noted in the Maintenance Intervals chart at the end of this section. The main thing to keep in mind is that the valve should be free of dirt and residue and should be in working order. As long as the valve is not showing signs of becoming damaged or gummed up, it should perform its function properly. When the valve becomes sticky and will not operate freely, it should be replaced.

The PCV valve is used to control the rate at which crankcase vapors are returned to the intake manifold. The action of the valve plunger is controlled by intake manifold vacuum and the spring. During deceleration and idle, when manifold vacuum is high, it overcomes the tension of the valve spring and the plunger bottoms in the manifold end of the valve housing. Because of the valve construction, it reduces, but does not stop, the passage of vapors to the intake manifold. When the engine is lightly accelerated or operated at constant speed, spring tension matches intake manifold vacuum pull and the plunger takes a mid-position in the valve body, allowing more vapors to flow into the manifold.

The valve is either mounted on the valve cover or in the line which runs from the intake manifold to the crankcase. Do not attempt to adjust or repair the valve. If the valve is faulty, replace it.

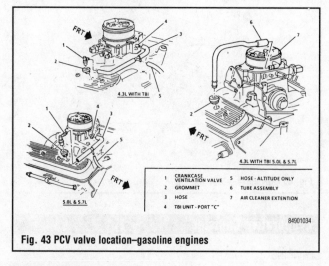

1	CRANKCASE VENTILATION VALVE
2	GROMMET
3	HOSE
4	TBI UNIT - PORT "C"
5	HOSE - ALTITUDE ONLY
6	TUBE ASSEMBLY
7	AIR CLEANER EXTENTION

84901034

Fig. 43 PCV valve location–gasoline engines

REMOVAL & INSTALLATION

▶ **See Figures 44 and 45**

1. Remove the PCV valve from the cylinder head cover or from the manifold-to-crankcase hose.

2. Visually inspect all hose connections and hoses for cracks, clogs or deterioration and replace as necessary.

Fig. 44 Pull the PCV valve out of the cylinder head

87981P07

Fig. 45 Disconnect the PCV valve from the hose and remove the valve from the vehicle

87981P08

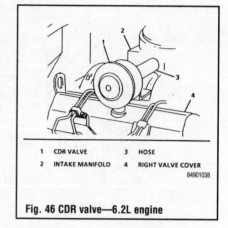

| 1 | CDR VALVE | 3 | HOSE |
| 2 | INTAKE MANIFOLD | 4 | RIGHT VALVE COVER |

84901038

Fig. 46 CDR valve—6.2L engine

Crankcase Depression Regulator and Flow Control Valve

SERVICING

◆ See Figures 46 and 47

➥This system is found only on diesel engines.

The Crankcase Depression Regulator (CDR) is designed to scavenge crankcase vapors in basically the same manner as the PCV valve on gasoline engines. The valve is located by the right cylinder head cover. On this system, the valve and filter are replaced as an assembly.

The ventilation pipes and tubes should also be cleaned and replaced as wear and tear dictates.

➥Do not attempt to test the crankcase controls on these diesels. Instead, clean the valve cover filter assembly and vent pipes and check the vent pipes. Replace the breather cap assembly every 30,000 miles (48,000 km). Replace all rubber fittings as required every 15,000 miles (24,000 km).

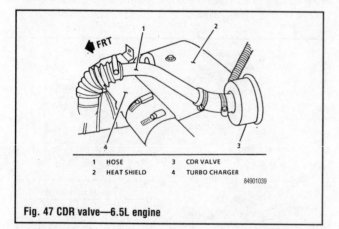

| 1 | HOSE | 3 | CDR VALVE |
| 2 | HEAT SHIELD | 4 | TURBO CHARGER |

84901039

Fig. 47 CDR valve—6.5L engine

Evaporative Canister

SERVICING

The only regular maintenance that need be performed on the evaporative emission canister is to regularly change the filter (on those 1988–90 models which utilize one; 1991–98 trucks do not have a canister filter) and check the condition of the hoses. If any hoses need replacement, use only hoses which are marked EVAP. No other type should be used. Whenever the vapor vent hose is replaced, the restrictor adjacent to the canister should also be replaced.

The evaporative emission canister is located on the left side of the engine compartment, with a filter located in its bottom (if applicable).

➥For further information on the evaporative emission system, please refer to Section 4.

To service the canister filter:

1. Note the installed positions of the hoses, tagging them as necessary, in case any have to be removed.
2. Loosen the clamps and remove the canister.
3. Pull the filter out and throw it away.
4. Install a new canister filter.
5. Install the canister and tighten the clamps.
6. Check the hoses.

Battery

PRECAUTIONS

Always use caution when working on or near the battery. Never allow a tool to bridge the gap between the negative and positive battery terminals. Also, be careful not to allow a tool to provide a ground between the positive cable/terminal and any metal component on the vehicle. Either of these conditions will cause a short circuit, leading to sparks and possible personal injury.

Do not smoke or all open flames/sparks near a battery; the gases contained in the battery are very explosive and, if ignited, could cause severe injury or death.

All batteries, regardless of type, should be carefully secured by a battery hold-down device. If not, the terminals or casing may crack from stress during vehicle operation. A battery which is not secured may allow acid to leak, making it discharge faster. The acid can also eat away at components under the hood.

Always inspect the battery case for cracks, leakage and corrosion. A white corrosive substance on the battery case or on nearby components would indicate a leaking or cracked battery. If the battery is cracked, it should be replaced immediately.

GENERAL MAINTENANCE

Always keep the battery cables and terminals free of corrosion. Check and clean these components about once a year.

Keep the top of the battery clean, as a film of dirt can help discharge a battery that is not used for long periods. A solution of baking soda and water may be used for cleaning, but be careful to flush this off with clear water. DO NOT let any of the solution into the filler holes. Baking soda neutralizes battery acid and will de-activate a battery cell.

Batteries in vehicles which are not operated on a regular basis can fall victim to parasitic loads (small current drains which are constantly drawing current from the battery). Normal parasitic loads may drain a battery on a vehicle that is in storage and not used for 6–8 weeks. Vehicles that have additional accessories such as a phone or an alarm system may discharge a battery sooner. If the vehicle is to be stored for longer periods in a secure area and the alarm system is not necessary, the negative battery cable should be disconnected to protect the battery.

Remember that constantly deep cycling a battery (completely discharging and recharging it) will shorten battery life.

BATTERY FLUID

▶ See Figure 48

Check the battery electrolyte level at least once a month, or more often in hot weather or during periods of extended vehicle operation. On non-sealed batteries, the level can be checked either through the case (if translucent) or by removing the cell caps. The electrolyte level in each cell should be kept filled to the split ring inside each cell, or the line marked on the outside of the case.

If the level is low, add only distilled water through the opening until the level is correct. Each cell must be checked and filled individually. Distilled water should be used, because the chemicals and minerals found in most drinking water are harmful to the battery and could significantly shorten its life.

If water is added in freezing weather, the vehicle should be driven several miles to allow the water to mix with the electrolyte. Otherwise, the battery could freeze.

Although some maintenance-free batteries have removable cell caps, the electrolyte condition and level on all sealed maintenance-free batteries must be checked using the built-in hydrometer "eye." The exact type of eye will vary. But, most battery manufacturers, apply a sticker to the battery itself explaining the readings.

➡ Although the readings from built-in hydrometers will vary, a green eye usually indicates a properly charged battery with sufficient fluid level. A dark eye is normally an indicator of a battery with sufficient fluid, but which is low in charge. A light or yellow eye usually indicates that electrolyte has dropped below the necessary level. In this last case, sealed batteries with an insufficient electrolyte must usually be discarded.

Checking the Specific Gravity

▶ See Figures 49, 50 and 51

A hydrometer is required to check the specific gravity on all batteries that are not maintenance-free. On batteries that are maintenance-free, the specific gravity is checked by observing the built-in hydrometer "eye" on the top of the battery case.

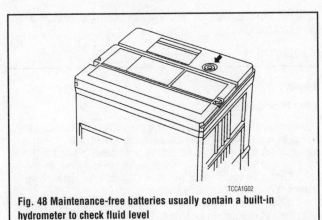

Fig. 48 Maintenance-free batteries usually contain a built-in hydrometer to check fluid level

TCCA1G02

✳✳ CAUTION

Battery electrolyte contains sulfuric acid. If you should splash any on your skin or in your eyes, flush the affected area with plenty of clear water. If it lands in your eyes, get medical help immediately.

The fluid (sulfuric acid solution) contained in the battery cells will tell you many things about the condition of the battery. Because the cell plates must be kept submerged below the fluid level in order to operate, the fluid level is extremely important. And, because the specific gravity of the acid is an indication of electrical charge, testing the fluid can be an aid in determining if the battery must be replaced. A battery in a vehicle with a properly operating charging system should require little maintenance, but careful, periodic inspection should reveal problems before they leave you stranded.

At least once a year, check the specific gravity of the battery. It should be between 1.20 and 1.26 on the gravity scale. Most auto stores carry a variety of inexpensive battery hydrometers. These can be used on any non-sealed battery to test the specific gravity in each cell.

The battery testing hydrometer has a squeeze bulb at one end and a nozzle at the other. Battery electrolyte is sucked into the hydrometer until the float is lifted from its seat. The specific gravity is then read by noting the position of the float. If gravity is low in one or more cells, the battery should be slowly charged and checked again to see if the gravity has come up. Generally, if after charging, the specific gravity between any two cells varies more than 50 points (0.50), the battery should be replaced, as it can no longer produce sufficient voltage to guarantee proper operation.

CABLES

▶ See Figures 52 thru 57

Once a year (or as necessary), the battery terminals and the cable clamps should be cleaned. Loosen the clamps and remove the cables, negative cable first. On top post batteries, the use of a puller specially made for this purpose is recommended. These are inexpensive and available in most parts stores. Side terminal battery cables are secured with a small bolt.

Clean the cable clamps and the battery terminal with a wire brush, until all corrosion, grease, etc., is removed and the metal is shiny. It is especially important to clean the inside of the clamp thoroughly (an old knife is useful here), since a small deposit of oxidation there will prevent a sound connection and inhibit starting or charging. Special tools are available for cleaning these parts, one type for conventional top post batteries and another type for side terminal batteries. It is also a good idea to apply some dielectric grease to the terminal, as this will aid in the prevention of corrosion.

After the clamps and terminals are clean, reinstall the cables, negative cable last; DO NOT hammer the clamps onto battery posts. Tighten the clamps securely, but do not distort them. Give the clamps and terminals a thin external coating of grease after installation, to retard corrosion.

Check the cables at the same time that the terminals are cleaned. If the cable insulation is cracked or broken, or if the ends are frayed, the cable should be replaced with a new cable of the same length and gauge.

Fig. 49 On non-sealed batteries, the fluid level can be checked by removing the cell caps

TCCA1P07

Fig. 50 If the fluid level is low, add only distilled water until the level is correct

TCCA1P08

Fig. 51 Check the specific gravity of the battery's electrolyte with a hydrometer

TCCA1P09

Fig. 52 Loosen the battery cable retaining nut . . .

Fig. 53 . . . then disconnect the cable from the battery

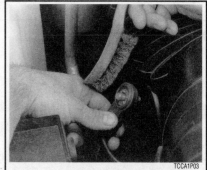

Fig. 54 A wire brush may be used to clean any corrosion or foreign material from the cable

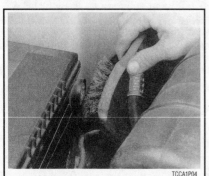

Fig. 55 The wire brush can also be used to remove any corrosion or dirt from the battery terminal

Fig. 56 The battery terminal can also be cleaned using a solution of baking soda and water

Fig. 57 Before connecting the cables, it's a good idea to coat the terminals with a small amount of dielectric grease

CHARGING

> ✳✳ **CAUTION**
>
> **The chemical reaction which takes place in all batteries generates explosive hydrogen gas. A spark can cause the battery to explode and splash acid. To avoid personal injury, be sure there is proper ventilation and take appropriate fire safety precautions when working with or near a battery.**

A battery should be charged at a slow rate to keep the plates inside from getting too hot. However, if some maintenance-free batteries are allowed to discharge until they are almost "dead," they may have to be charged at a high rate to bring them back to "life." Always follow the charger manufacturer's instructions on charging the battery.

REPLACEMENT

When it becomes necessary to replace the battery, select one with an amperage rating equal to or greater than the battery originally installed. Deterioration and just plain aging of the battery cables, starter motor, and associated wires makes the battery's job harder in successive years. This makes it prudent to install a new battery with a greater capacity than the old.

Belts

INSPECTION

▶ See Figures 58, 59, 60, 61 and 62

Inspect the belts for signs of glazing or cracking. A glazed belt will be perfectly smooth from slippage, while a good belt will have a slight texture of fabric visible. Cracks will usually start at the inner edge of the belt and run outward. All worn or damaged drive belts should be replaced immediately. It is best to replace all drive belts at one time, as a preventive maintenance measure, during this service operation.

ADJUSTMENT

V-Belts

▶ See Figures 63 and 64

Belt tension should be checked with a gauge made for the purpose. If a tension gauge is not available, tension can be checked with moderate thumb pressure applied to the belt at its longest span midway between pulleys. If the belt has a free span less than 12 in. (305mm), it should deflect approximately ⅛–¼ in. (3–6mm). If the span is longer than 12 in. (305mm), deflection can range between ⅛ in. (3mm) and ⅜ in. (9.5mm).

If a tension gauge is available use the following procedure:

1. Place a belt tension gauge at the center of the greatest span of a warm, not hot, drive belt and measure the tension.
2. If the belt is not within the specification, loosen the component mounting bracket and adjust to specification.
3. Run the engine at idle for 15 minutes to allow the belt to reseat itself in the pulleys.
4. Allow the drive belt to cool and re-measure the tension. Adjust as necessary to meet the following specifications:
   - V6, V8 gasoline engines: used—90 ft. lbs. (122Nm); new—135 ft. lbs. (183 Nm).
   - 6—4.8L: used—90 ft. lbs. (122 Nm); new—169 ft. lbs. (229 Nm).
   - V8—6.2L/6.5L diesel: used—67 ft. lbs. (90 Nm); new—146 ft. lbs. (197 Nm).

➡A belt is considered "used" after 15 minutes of operation.

Serpentine Belts

The serpentine belt tension can be checked by simply observing the belt acceptable belt wear range indicator located on the tensioner spindle. If the belt does not meet the specified range, it must be replaced.

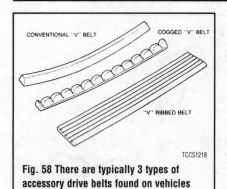

Fig. 58 There are typically 3 types of accessory drive belts found on vehicles today

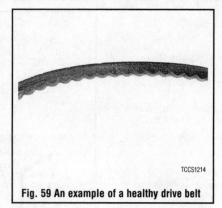

Fig. 59 An example of a healthy drive belt

Fig. 60 Deep cracks in this belt will cause flex, building up heat that will eventually lead to belt failure

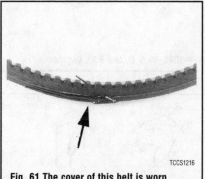

Fig. 61 The cover of this belt is worn, exposing the critical reinforcing cords to excessive wear

Fig. 62 Installing too wide a belt can result in serious belt wear and/or breakage

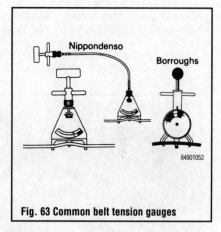

Fig. 63 Common belt tension gauges

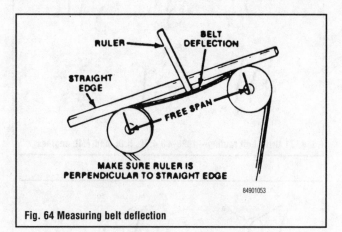

Fig. 64 Measuring belt deflection

REMOVAL & INSTALLATION

V-Belts

▶ See Figures 65, 66 and 67

1. Loosen the driven accessory's pivot and mounting bolts. Remove the belt.
2. Install the belt. Move the accessory toward or away from the engine until the tension is correct. You can use a wooden hammer handle, or broomstick, as a lever, but do not use anything metallic, such as a prybar. Certain models may utilize an adjusting bolt to do this work for you. Simply loosen the mounting bolt and turn the adjuster.
3. Tighten the bolts and recheck the tension. If new belts have been installed, run the engine for a few minutes, then recheck and readjust as necessary.

It is better to have belts too loose than too tight, because overtight belts will lead to bearing failure, particularly in the water pump and alternator. However, loose belts place an extremely high impact load on the driven component due to the whipping action of the belt.

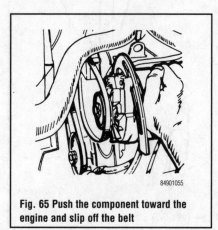

Fig. 65 Push the component toward the engine and slip off the belt

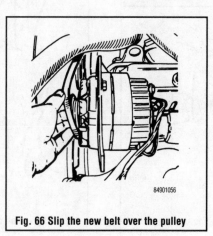

Fig. 66 Slip the new belt over the pulley

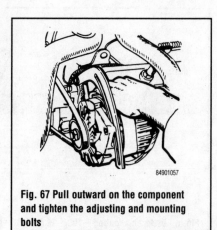

Fig. 67 Pull outward on the component and tighten the adjusting and mounting bolts

Serpentine Belts

◆ **See Figure 68**

1. On all models except the 7.4L engine with an Air Injector Reactor (AIR) pump (California emissions only), use a ½ in. breaker bar with a socket placed on the tensioner pulley bolt, rotate the tensioner to relieve belt tension.

2. On all 7.4L engines with an AIR pump (California emissions only), use a suitable wrench on the pulley axis bolt to rotate the tensioner clockwise to relieve belt tension.

3. Remove the serpentine belt.

To install:

4. Route the belt over all the pulleys except the tensioner.

5. On all models except the 7.4L engine with an AIR pump (California emissions only), place the breaker bar and socket on the tensioner pulley bolt and rotate the tensioner to the released position.

6. Install the belt and return the pulley to its original position.

7. On all 7.4L engines with an AIR pump (California emissions only), use a suitable wrench on the pulley axis bolt to rotate the tensioner clockwise to relieve belt tension.

8. Install the belt and return the pulley to its original position.

9. Check that the belt is properly seated in each pulley.

Fig. 68 Rotate the tensioner with a breaker bar to relieve belt tension

BELT ROUTING

◆ **See Figures 69 thru 88**

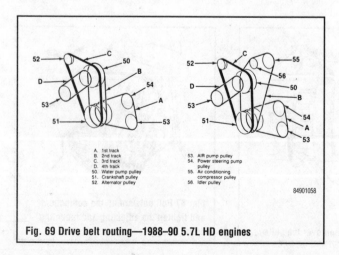

Fig. 69 Drive belt routing—1988–90 5.7L HD engines

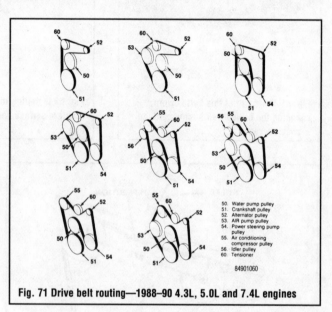

Fig. 70 Drive belt routing—1988–90 5.7L and 6.2L engines

Fig. 71 Drive belt routing—1988–90 4.3L, 5.0L and 7.4L engines

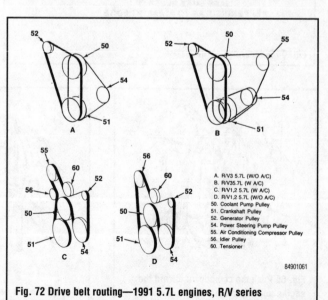

Fig. 72 Drive belt routing—1991 5.7L engines, R/V series

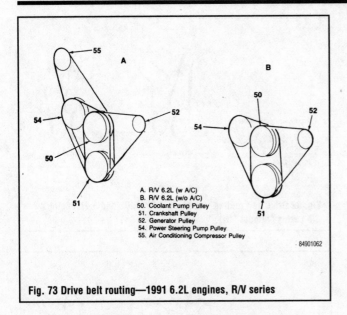

Fig. 73 Drive belt routing—1991 6.2L engines, R/V series

A. R/V 6.2L (w A/C)
B. R/V 6.2L (w/o A/C)
50. Coolant Pump Pulley
51. Crankshaft Pulley
52. Generator Pulley
54. Power Steering Pump Pulley
55. Air Conditioning Compressor Pulley

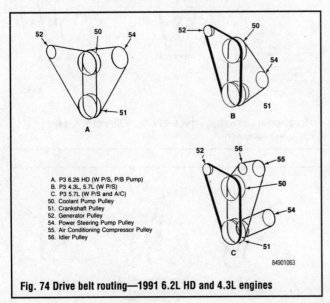

A. P3 6.26 HD (W P/S, P/B Pump)
B. P3 4.3L, 5.7L (W P/S)
C. P3 5.7L (W P/S and A/C)
50. Coolant Pump Pulley
51. Crankshaft Pulley
52. Generator Pulley
54. Power Steering Pump Pulley
55. Air Conditioning Compressor Pulley
56. Idler Pulley

Fig. 74 Drive belt routing—1991 6.2L HD and 4.3L engines

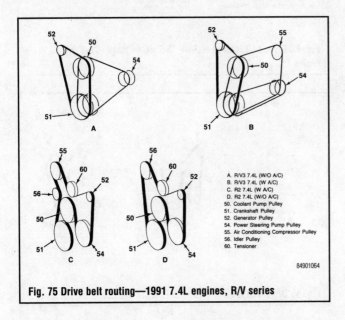

A. R/V3 7.4L (W/O A/C)
B. R/V3 7.4L (W A/C)
C. R2 7.4L (W A/C)
D. R2 7.4L (W/O A/C)
50. Coolant Pump Pulley
51. Crankshaft Pulley
52. Generator Pulley
54. Power Steering Pump Pulley
55. Air Conditioning Compressor Pulley
56. Idler Pulley
60. Tensioner

Fig. 75 Drive belt routing—1991 7.4L engines, R/V series

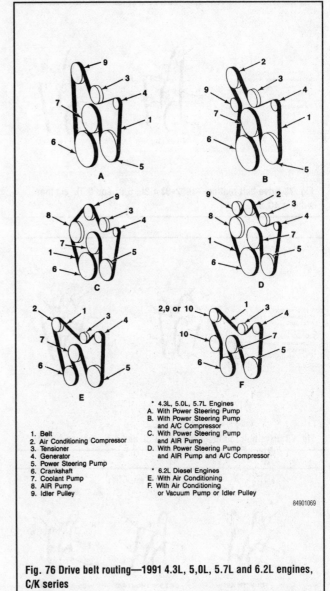

* 4.3L, 5.0L, 5.7L Engines
A. With Power Steering Pump
B. With Power Steering Pump and A/C Compressor
C. With Power Steering Pump and AIR Pump
D. With Power Steering Pump and AIR Pump and A/C Compressor

* 6.2L Diesel Engines
E. With Air Conditioning
F. With Air Conditioning or Vacuum Pump or Idler Pulley

1. Belt
2. Air Conditioning Compressor
3. Tensioner
4. Generator
5. Power Steering Pump
6. Crankshaft
7. Coolant Pump
8. AIR Pump
9. Idler Pulley

Fig. 76 Drive belt routing—1991 4.3L, 5,0L, 5.7L and 6.2L engines, C/K series

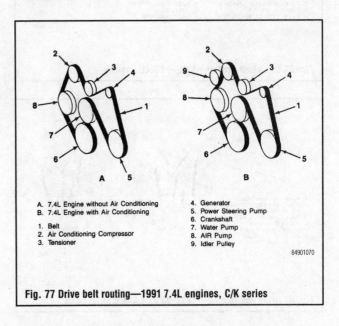

A. 7.4L Engine without Air Conditioning
B. 7.4L Engine with Air Conditioning

1. Belt
2. Air Conditioning Compressor
3. Tensioner
4. Generator
5. Power Steering Pump
6. Crankshaft
7. Water Pump
8. AIR Pump
9. Idler Pulley

Fig. 77 Drive belt routing—1991 7.4L engines, C/K series

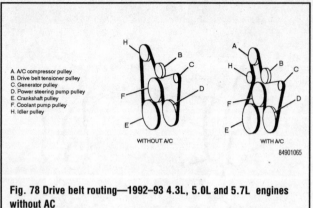

A. A/C compressor pulley
B. Drive belt tensioner pulley
C. Generator pulley
D. Power steering pump pulley
E. Crankshaft pulley
F. Coolant pump pulley
H. Idler pulley

WITHOUT A/C

WITH A/C

84901065

Fig. 78 Drive belt routing—1992–93 4.3L, 5.0L and 5.7L engines without AC

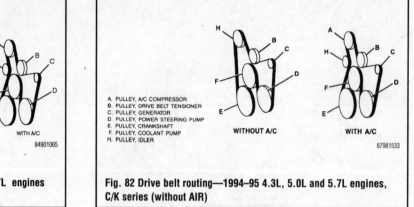

A. PULLEY, A/C COMPRESSOR
B. PULLEY, DRIVE BELT TENSIONER
C. PULLEY, GENERATOR
D. PULLEY, POWER STEERING PUMP
E. PULLEY, CRANKSHAFT
F. PULLEY, COOLANT PUMP
H. PULLEY, IDLER

WITHOUT A/C

WITH A/C

87981533

Fig. 82 Drive belt routing—1994–95 4.3L, 5.0L and 5.7L engines, C/K series (without AIR)

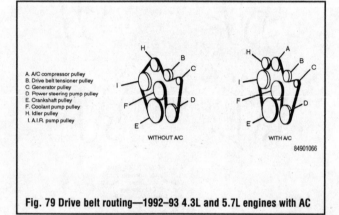

A. A/C compressor pulley
B. Drive belt tensioner pulley
C. Generator pulley
D. Power steering pump pulley
E. Crankshaft pulley
F. Coolant pump pulley
H. Idler pulley
I. A.I.R. pump pulley

WITHOUT A/C

WITH A/C

84901066

Fig. 79 Drive belt routing—1992–93 4.3L and 5.7L engines with AC

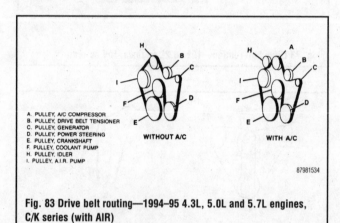

A. PULLEY, A/C COMPRESSOR
B. PULLEY, DRIVE BELT TENSIONER
C. PULLEY, GENERATOR
D. PULLEY, POWER STEERING
E. PULLEY, CRANKSHAFT
F. PULLEY, COOLANT PUMP
H. PULLEY, IDLER
I. PULLEY, A.I.R. PUMP

WITHOUT A/C

WITH A/C

87981534

Fig. 83 Drive belt routing—1994–95 4.3L, 5.0L and 5.7L engines, C/K series (with AIR)

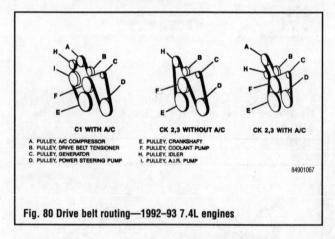

C1 WITH A/C

CK 2,3 WITHOUT A/C

CK 2,3 WITH A/C

A. PULLEY, A/C COMPRESSOR
B. PULLEY, DRIVE BELT TENSIONER
C. PULLEY, GENERATOR
D. PULLEY, POWER STEERING PUMP
E. PULLEY, CRANKSHAFT
F. PULLEY, COOLANT PUMP
H. PULLEY, IDLER
I. PULLEY, A.I.R. PUMP

84901067

Fig. 80 Drive belt routing—1992–93 7.4L engines

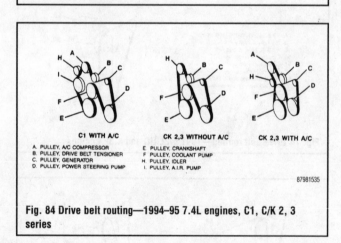

C1 WITH A/C

CK 2,3 WITHOUT A/C

CK 2,3 WITH A/C

A. PULLEY, A/C COMPRESSOR
B. PULLEY, DRIVE BELT TENSIONER
C. PULLEY, GENERATOR
D. PULLEY, POWER STEERING PUMP
E. PULLEY, CRANKSHAFT
F. PULLEY, COOLANT PUMP
H. PULLEY, IDLER
I. PULLEY, A.I.R. PUMP

87981535

Fig. 84 Drive belt routing—1994–95 7.4L engines, C1, C/K 2, 3 series

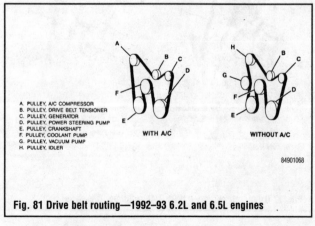

A. PULLEY, A/C COMPRESSOR
B. PULLEY, DRIVE BELT TENSIONER
C. PULLEY, GENERATOR
D. PULLEY, POWER STEERING PUMP
E. PULLEY, CRANKSHAFT
F. PULLEY, COOLANT PUMP
G. PULLEY, VACUUM PUMP
H. PULLEY, IDLER

WITH A/C

WITHOUT A/C

84901068

Fig. 81 Drive belt routing—1992–93 6.2L and 6.5L engines

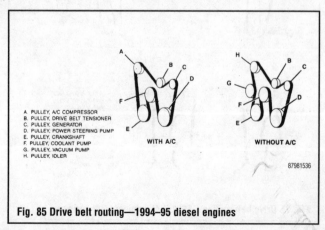

A. PULLEY, A/C COMPRESSOR
B. PULLEY, DRIVE BELT TENSIONER
C. PULLEY, GENERATOR
D. PULLEY, POWER STEERING PUMP
E. PULLEY, CRANKSHAFT
F. PULLEY, COOLANT PUMP
G. PULLEY, VACUUM PUMP
H. PULLEY, IDLER

WITH A/C

WITHOUT A/C

87981536

Fig. 85 Drive belt routing—1994–95 diesel engines

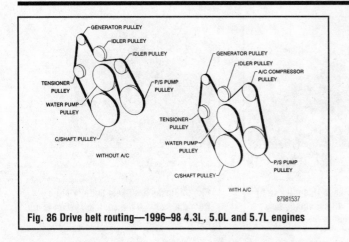

Fig. 86 Drive belt routing—1996–98 4.3L, 5.0L and 5.7L engines

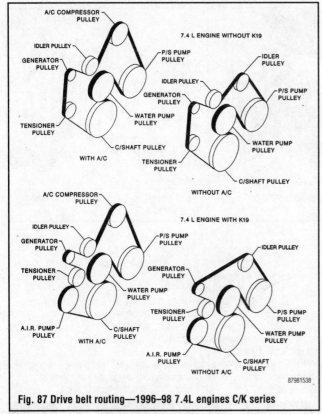

Fig. 87 Drive belt routing—1996–98 7.4L engines C/K series

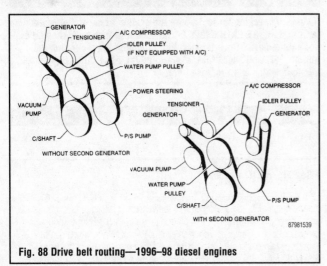

Fig. 88 Drive belt routing—1996–98 diesel engines

Hoses

INSPECTION

♦ See Figures 89, 90, 91 and 92

Upper and lower radiator hoses along with the heater hoses should be checked for deterioration, leaks and loose hose clamps at least every 15,000 miles (24,000 km). It is also wise to check the hoses periodically in early spring and at the beginning of the fall or winter when you are performing other maintenance. A quick visual inspection could discover a weakened hose which might have left you stranded if it had remained unrepaired.

Whenever you are checking the hoses, make sure the engine and cooling system are cold. Visually inspect for cracking, rotting or collapsed hoses, and replace as necessary. Run your hand along the length of the hose. If a weak or swollen spot is noted when squeezing the hose wall, the hose should be replaced.

Fig. 89 The cracks developing along this hose are a result of age-related hardening

REMOVAL & INSTALLATION

♦ See Figures 93, 94, 95 and 96

1. Remove the radiator pressure cap.

❋❋ CAUTION

Never remove the pressure cap while the engine is running, or personal injury from scalding hot coolant or steam may result. If possible, wait until the engine has cooled to remove the pressure cap. If this is not possible, wrap a thick cloth around the pressure cap and turn it slowly to the stop. Step back while the pressure is released from the cooling system. When you are sure all the pressure has been released, use the cloth to turn and remove the cap.

2. Position a clean container under the radiator and/or engine draincock or plug, then open the drain and allow the cooling system to drain to an appropriate level. For some upper hoses, only a little coolant must be drained. To remove hoses positioned lower on the engine, such as a lower radiator hose, the entire cooling system must be emptied.

❋❋ CAUTION

When draining coolant, keep in mind that cats and dogs are attracted by ethylene glycol antifreeze, and are quite likely to drink any that is left in an uncovered container or in puddles on the ground. This will prove fatal in sufficient quantity. Always drain coolant into a sealable container. Coolant may be reused unless it is contaminated or several years old.

3. Loosen the hose clamps at each end of the hose requiring replacement. Clamps are usually either of the spring tension type (which require pliers to squeeze the tabs and loosen) or of the screw tension type (which require screw or hex drivers to loosen). Pull the clamps back on the hose away from the connection.

Fig. 90 A hose clamp that is too tight can cause older hoses to separate and tear on either side of the clamp

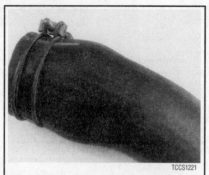

Fig. 91 A soft spongy hose (identifiable by the swollen section) will eventually burst and should be replaced

Fig. 92 Hoses are likely to deteriorate from the inside if the cooling system is not periodically flushed

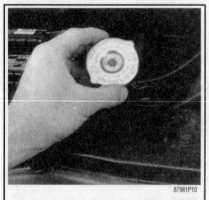

Fig. 93 Remove the radiator cap

Fig. 94 Loosen the hose clamps at each end of the hose requiring replacement and remove the hose

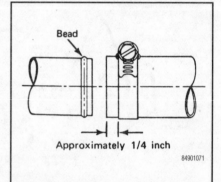

Fig. 95 Position the hose clamp so that it is about ¼ in. from the end of the hose

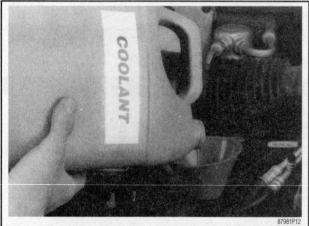

Fig. 96 Properly refill the cooling system with a suitable mixture of ethylene glycol coolant and water

4. Twist, pull and slide the hose off the fitting, taking care not to damage the neck of the component from which the hose is being removed.

➡ If the hose is stuck at the connection, do not try to insert a screwdriver or other sharp tool under the hose end in an effort to free it, as the connection and/or hose may become damaged. Heater connections especially may be easily damaged by such a procedure. If the hose is to be replaced, use a single-edged razor blade to make a slice along the portion of the hose which is stuck on the connection, perpendicular to the end of the hose. Do not cut deep so as to prevent damaging the connection. The hose can then be peeled from the connection and discarded.

5. Clean both hose mounting connections. Inspect the condition of the hose clamps and replace them, if necessary.

To install:

6. Dip the ends of the new hose into clean engine coolant to ease installation.

7. Slide the clamps over the replacement hose, then slide the hose ends over the connections into position.

8. Position and secure the clamps at least ¼ in. (6.35mm) from the ends of the hose. Make sure they are located beyond the raised bead of the connector.

9. Close the radiator or engine drains and properly refill the cooling system with the clean drained engine coolant or a suitable mixture of ethylene glycol coolant and water.

10. If available, install a pressure tester and check for leaks. If a pressure tester is not available, run the engine until normal operating temperature is reached (allowing the system to naturally pressurize), then check for leaks.

✳✳ CAUTION

If you are checking for leaks with the system at normal operating temperature, BE EXTREMELY CAREFUL not to touch any moving or hot engine parts. Once temperature has been reached, shut the engine OFF, and check for leaks around the hose fittings and connections which were removed earlier.

CV-Boots

INSPECTION

▶ See Figures 97 and 98

The CV (Constant Velocity) boots should be checked for damage each time the oil is changed and any other time the vehicle is raised for service. These boots keep water, grime, dirt and other damaging matter from entering the CV-joints. Any of these could cause early CV-joint failure which can be expensive to repair. Heavy grease thrown around the inside of the front wheel(s) and on the brake caliper/drum can be an indication of a torn boot.

Thoroughly check the boots for missing clamps and tears. If the boot is damaged, it should be replaced immediately. Please refer to Section 7 for procedures.

Spark Plugs

♦ See Figure 99

A typical spark plug consists of a metal shell surrounding a ceramic insulator. A metal electrode extends downward through the center of the insulator and protrudes a small distance. Located at the end of the plug and attached to the side of the outer metal shell is the side electrode. The side electrode bends in at a 90° angle so that its tip is just past and parallel to the tip of the center electrode. The distance between these two electrodes (measured in thousandths of an inch or hundredths of a millimeter) is called the spark plug gap.

The spark plug does not produce a spark but instead provides a gap across which the current can arc. The coil produces anywhere from 20,000 to 50,000 volts (depending on the type and application) which travels through the wires to the spark plugs. The current passes along the center electrode and jumps the gap to the side electrode, and in doing so, ignites the air/fuel mixture in the combustion chamber.

SPARK PLUG HEAT RANGE

♦ See Figure 100

Spark plug heat range is the ability of the plug to dissipate heat. The longer the insulator (or the farther it extends into the engine), the hotter the plug will operate; the shorter the insulator (the closer the electrode is to the block's cooling passages) the cooler it will operate. A plug that absorbs little heat and remains too cool will quickly accumulate deposits of oil and carbon since it is not hot enough to burn them off. This leads to plug fouling and consequently to misfiring. A plug that absorbs too much heat will have no deposits but, due to the excessive heat, the electrodes will burn away quickly and might possibly

km). As the gap increases, the plug's voltage requirement also increases. It requires a greater voltage to jump the wider gap and about two to three times as much voltage to fire the plug at high speeds than at idle. The improved air/fuel ratio control of modern fuel injection combined with the higher voltage output of modern ignition systems will often allow an engine to run significantly longer on a set of standard spark plugs, but keep in mind that efficiency will drop as the gap widens (along with fuel economy and power).

When you're removing spark plugs, work on one at a time. Don't start by removing the plug wires all at once, because, unless you number them, they may become mixed up. Take a minute before you begin and number the wires with tape.

1. Disconnect the negative battery cable, and if the vehicle has been run recently, allow the engine to thoroughly cool.

2. Carefully twist the spark plug wire boot to loosen it, then pull upward and remove the boot from the plug. Be sure to pull on the boot and not on the wire, otherwise the connector located inside the boot may become separated.

3. Using compressed air, blow any water or debris from the spark plug well to assure that no harmful contaminants are allowed to enter the combustion chamber when the spark plug is removed. If compressed air is not available, use a rag or a brush to clean the area.

→Remove the spark plugs when the engine is cold, if possible, to prevent damage to the threads. If removal of the plugs is difficult, apply a few drops of penetrating oil or silicone spray to the area around the base of the plug, and allow it a few minutes to work.

4. Using a spark plug socket that is equipped with a rubber insert to properly hold the plug, turn the spark plug counterclockwise to loosen and remove the spark plug from the bore.

✳✳ WARNING

Be sure not to use a flexible extension on the socket. Use of a flexible extension may allow a shear force to be applied to the plug. A shear force could break the plug off in the cylinder head, leading to costly and frustrating repairs.

Fig. 97 CV-boots must be inspected periodically for damage

Fig. 98 A torn boot should be replaced immediately

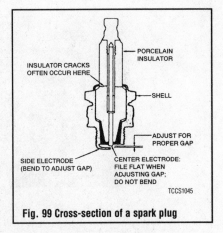

Fig. 99 Cross-section of a spark plug

lead to preignition or other ignition problems. Preignition takes place when plug tips get so hot that they glow sufficiently to ignite the air/fuel mixture before the actual spark occurs. This early ignition will usually cause a pinging during low speeds and heavy loads.

The general rule of thumb for choosing the correct heat range when picking a spark plug is: if most of your driving is long distance, high speed travel, use a colder plug; if most of your driving is stop and go, use a hotter plug. Original equipment plugs are generally a good compromise between the 2 styles and most people never have the need to change their plugs from the factory-recommended heat range.

REMOVAL & INSTALLATION

A set of spark plugs usually requires replacement after about 20,000–30,000 miles (32,000–48,000 km), depending on your style of driving. In normal operation plug gap increases about 0.001 in. (0.025mm) for every 2500 miles (4000

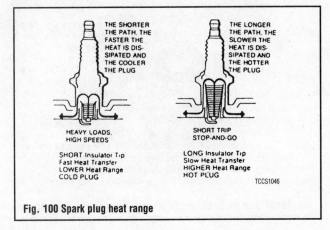

Fig. 100 Spark plug heat range

To install:

5. Inspect the spark plug boot for tears or damage. If a damaged boot is found, the spark plug wire must be replaced.

6. Using a wire feeler gauge, check and adjust the spark plug gap. When using a gauge, the proper size should pass between the electrodes with a slight drag. The next larger size should not be able to pass while the next smaller size should pass freely.

7. Carefully thread the plug into the bore by hand. If resistance is felt before the plug is almost completely threaded, back the plug out and begin threading again. In small, hard to reach areas, an old spark plug wire and boot could be used as a threading tool. The boot will hold the plug while you twist the end of the wire and the wire is supple enough to twist before it would allow the plug to crossthread.

⁎⁎ WARNING

Do not use the spark plug socket to thread the plugs. Always carefully thread the plug by hand or using an old plug wire to prevent the possibility of crossthreading and damaging the cylinder head bore.

8. Carefully tighten the spark plug. If the plug you are installing is equipped with a crush washer, seat the plug, then tighten about ¼ turn to crush the washer. If you are installing a tapered seat plug, tighten the plug to specifications provided by the vehicle or plug manufacturer.

9. Apply a small amount of silicone dielectric compound to the end of the spark plug lead or inside the spark plug boot to prevent sticking, then install the boot to the spark plug and push until it clicks into place. The click may be felt or heard, then gently pull back on the boot to assure proper contact.

INSPECTION & GAPPING

▶ **See Figures 101, 102, 103, 104 and 105**

Check the plugs for deposits and wear. If they are not going to be replaced, clean the plugs thoroughly. Remember that any kind of deposit will decrease the efficiency of the plug. Plugs can be cleaned on a spark plug cleaning machine, which can sometimes be found in service stations, or you can do an acceptable

A normally worn spark plug should have light tan or gray deposits on the firing tip.

A carbon fouled plug, identified by soft, sooty, black deposits, may indicate an improperly tuned vehicle. Check the air cleaner, ignition components and engine control system.

This spark plug has been left in the engine too long, as evidenced by the extreme gap- Plugs with such an extreme gap can cause misfiring and stumbling accompanied by a noticeable lack of power.

An oil fouled spark plug indicates an engine with worn poston rings and/or bad valve seals allowing excessive oil to enter the chamber.

A physically damaged spark plug may be evidence of severe detonation in that cylinder. Watch that cylinder carefully between services, as a continued detonation will not only damage the plug, but could also damage the engine.

A bridged or almost bridged spark plug, identified by a build-up between the electrodes caused by excessive carbon or oil build-up on the plug.

Fig. 101 Inspect the spark plug to determine engine running conditions

TCCA1P40

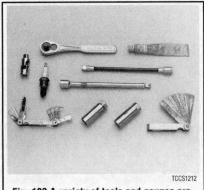

Fig. 102 A variety of tools and gauges are needed for spark plug service

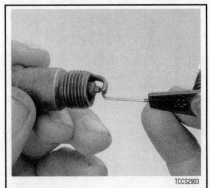

Fig. 103 Checking the spark plug gap with a feeler gauge

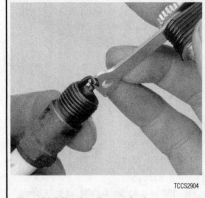

Fig. 104 Adjusting the spark plug gap

job of cleaning with a stiff brush. If the plugs are cleaned, the electrodes must be filed flat. Use an ignition points file, not an emery board or the like, which will leave deposits. The electrodes must be filed perfectly flat with sharp edges; rounded edges reduce the spark plug voltage by as much as 50%.

Check spark plug gap before installation. The ground electrode (the L-shaped one connected to the body of the plug) must be parallel to the center electrode and the specified size wire gauge (please refer to the Tune-Up Specifications chart for details) must pass between the electrodes with a slight drag.

➡ NEVER adjust the gap on a used platinum type spark plug.

Always check the gap on new plugs as they are not always set correctly at the factory. Do not use a flat feeler gauge when measuring the gap on a used plug, because the reading may be inaccurate. A round-wire type gapping tool is the best way to check the gap. The correct gauge should pass through the electrode gap with a slight drag. If you're in doubt, try one size smaller and one larger. The smaller gauge should go through easily, while the larger one shouldn't go through at all. Wire gapping tools usually have a bending tool attached. Use that to adjust the side electrode until the proper distance is obtained. Absolutely never attempt to bend the center electrode. Also, be careful not to bend the side electrode too far or too often as it may weaken and break off within the engine, requiring removal of the cylinder head to retrieve it.

Spark Plug Wires

TESTING

♦ See Figures 106 and 107

At every tune-up/inspection, visually check the spark plug cables for burns cuts, or breaks in the insulation. Check the boots and the nipples on the distributor cap and/or coil. Replace any damaged wiring.

Every 50,000 miles (80,000 Km) or 60 months, the resistance of the wires should be checked with an ohmmeter. Wires with excessive resistance will cause misfiring, and may make the engine difficult to start in damp weather.

To check resistance:
1. Remove the distributor cap, leaving the wires in place.
2. Connect one lead of an ohmmeter to an electrode within the cap.
3. Connect the other lead to the corresponding spark plug terminal (remove it from the spark plug for this test).
4. Replace any wire which shows a resistance over 30,000 ohms. Generally speaking, however, resistance should not be over 25,000 ohms, and 30,000 ohms must be considered the outer limit of acceptability.

It should be remembered that resistance is also a function of length. The longer the wire, the greater the resistance. Thus, if the wires on your truck are longer than the factory originals, the resistance will be higher, possibly outside these limits.

REMOVAL & INSTALLATION

When installing new wires, replace them one at a time to avoid mixups. Start by replacing the longest one first.
1. Remove the spark plug wire by gripping the boot firmly and disengaging the wire from the spark plug and the distributor.
2. Install the boot of the new wire firmly over the spark plug. Route the wire over the same path as the original.

Distributor Cap and Rotor

REMOVAL & INSTALLATION

Carbureted Engines

♦ See Figures 108, 109, 110 and 111

1. Remove the feed and module wire terminal connectors from the distributor cap.
2. Remove the retainer and spark plug wires from the cap.
3. Depress and release the 4 distributor cap-to-housing retainers and lift off the cap assembly.

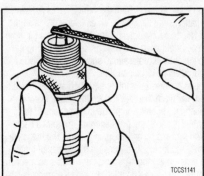

Fig. 105 If the standard plug is in good condition, the electrode may be filed flat—WARNING: do not file platinum plugs

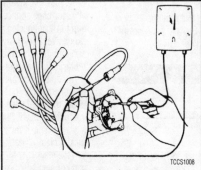

Fig. 106 Checking plug wire resistance through the distributor cap with an ohm-meter

Fig. 107 Checking individual plug wire resistance with a digital ohmmeter

Fig. 108 Loosen the distributor hold-down fasteners

Fig. 109 If necessary, label and remove the spark plug wires from the distributor cap

Fig. 110 Remove the distributor cap . . .

Fig. 111 . . . then the rotor from the distributor

4. Remove the 4 coil cover screws and cover.
5. Using a finger or a blunt drift, push the spade terminals up out of the distributor cap.
6. Remove all 4 coil screws and lift the coil, coil spring and rubber seal washer out of the cap coil cavity.
7. Remove the two rotor attaching screws (if equipped) and rotor.
8. Using a new distributor cap and rotor, reverse the above procedures to assemble, being sure to clean and lubricate the rubber seal washer with dielectric lubricant.

Fuel Injected Engines

1. Tag and remove the spark plug wires.
2. Loosen the cap retaining fasteners and remove the cap.
3. Remove the rotor from the distributor shaft.
4. Installation is the reverse of removal.

INSPECTION

1. Remove the distributor cap and rotor as described in this section.
2. Check the cap for wear, electrode cracks or damage. Replace if defective.
3. Check the rotor for cracks and wear. Replace if defective.

Ignition Timing

GENERAL INFORMATION

➡This procedure does not apply to diesel engines.

Ignition timing is the measurement, in degrees of crankshaft rotation, of the point at which the spark plugs fire in each of the cylinders. It is measured in degrees before or after Top Dead Center (TDC) of the compression stroke. Ignition timing is controlled by turning the distributor in the engine.

Ideally, the air/fuel mixture in the cylinder will be ignited by the spark plug just as the piston passes TDC of the compression stroke. If this happens, this piston will be beginning the power stroke just as the compressed and ignited air/fuel mixture starts to expand. The expansion of the air/fuel mixture then forces the piston down on the power stroke and turns the crankshaft.

Because it takes a fraction of a second for the spark plug to ignite the gases in the cylinder, the spark plug must fire a little before the piston reaches TDC. Otherwise, the mixture will not be completely ignited as the piston passes TDC and the full benefit of the explosion will not be used by the engine. The timing measurement is given in degrees of crankshaft rotation before the piston reaches TDC (BTDC). If the setting for the ignition timing is 5 degrees BTDC, the spark plug must fire 5 degrees before that piston reaches TDC. This only holds true, however, when the engine is at idle speed.

As the engine speed increases, the pistons go faster. The spark plugs have to ignite the fuel even sooner if it is to be completely ignited when the piston reaches TDC. To do this, the distributor has a means to advance the timing of the spark as the engine speed increases.

If the ignition is set too far advanced (BTDC), the ignition and expansion of the fuel in the cylinder will occur too soon and tend to force the piston down while it is still traveling up. This causes engine ping. If the engine is too far retarded after TDC (ATDC), the piston will have already passed TDC and started on its way down when the fuel is ignited. This will cause the piston to be forced down for only a portion of its travel. This will result in poor engine performance and lack of power.

Timing should be checked at each tune-up and any time the points are adjusted or replaced. It isn't likely to change much with HEI. The timing marks consist of a notch on the rim of the crankshaft pulley or vibration damper and a graduated scale attached to the engine front (timing) cover. A stroboscopic flash (dynamic) timing light must be used, as a static light is too inaccurate for emission controlled engines.

There are three basic types of timing lights available. The first is a simple neon bulb with two wire connections. One wire connects to the spark plug terminal and the other plugs into the end of the spark plug wire for the No. 1 cylinder, thus connecting the light in series with the spark plug. This type of light is pretty dim and must be held very closely to the timing marks to be seen. Sometimes a dark corner has to be sought out to see the flash at all. This type of light is very inexpensive. The second type operates from the vehicle battery—two alligator clips connect to the battery terminals, while an adapter enables a third clip to be connected between No. 1 spark plug and wire. This type is a bit more expensive, but it provides a nice bright flash that you can see even in bright sunlight. It is the type most often seen in professional shops. The third type replaces the battery power source with 115 volt current.

Some timing lights have other features built into them, such as dwell meters, or tachometers. These are convenient, in that they reduce the tangle of wires under the hood when you're working, but may duplicate the functions of tools you already have. One worthwhile feature, which is becoming more of a necessity with higher voltage ignition systems, is an inductive pickup. The inductive pickup clamps around the No. 1 spark plug wire, sensing the surges of high voltage electricity as they are sent to the plug. The advantage is that no mechanical connection is inserted between the wire and the plug, which eliminates false signals to the timing light. A timing light with an inductive pickup should be used on HEI systems.

CHECKING & ADJUSTMENT

HEI Systems

1. Start the engine and allow it to reach operating temperature. Stop the engine and connect the timing light to the No. 1 (left front) spark plug wire, at the plug or at the distributor cap. You can also use the No. 6 wire, if it is more convenient. Numbering is illustrated in this section.

➥Do not pierce the plug wire insulation with HEI; it will cause a miss. The best method is an inductive pickup timing light.

2. Clean off the timing marks and mark the pulley or damper notch and timing scale with white chalk.
3. Disconnect and plug the vacuum line at the distributor on models with a carburetor. This is done to prevent any distributor vacuum advance. On fuel injected models, disengage the timing connector which comes out of the harness conduit next to the distributor, this will put the system in the bypass mode. Check the underhood emission sticker for any other hoses or wires which may need to be disconnected.
4. Start the engine and adjust the idle speed to that specified on the Underhood Emissions label. With automatic transmission, set the specified idle speed in Park. It will be too high, since it is normally (in most cases) adjusted in Drive. You can disconnect the idle solenoid, if any, to get the speed down. Otherwise, adjust the idle speed screw.

The tachometer connects to the **TACH** terminal on the distributor and to a ground on models with a carburetor. On models with fuel injection, the tachometer connects to the **TACH** terminal on the ignition coil. Some tachometers must connect to the **TACH** terminal and to the positive battery terminal. Some tachometers won't work with HEI.

❊❊ WARNING

Never ground the HEI TACH terminal; serious system damage will result.

5. Aim the timing light at the pointer marks. Be careful not to touch the fan, because it may appear to be standing still. If the pulley or damper notch isn't aligned with the proper timing mark (see the Underhood Emissions label), the timing will have to be adjusted.

➥TDC or Top Dead Center corresponds to 0B, or BTDC, or Before Top Dead Center may be shown as BEFORE. A, or ATDC, or After Top Dead Center may be shown as AFTER.

6. Loosen the distributor base clamp locknut. You can buy trick wrenches which make this task a lot easier.
7. Turn the distributor slowly to adjust the timing, holding it by the body and not the cap. Turn the distributor in the direction of rotor rotation to retard, and against the direction of rotation to advance.
8. Tighten the locknut. Check the timing again, in case the distributor moved slightly as you tightened it.
9. Reinstall the distributor vacuum line or the timing connector. Correct the idle speed.
10. Stop the engine and disconnect the timing light.

Distributor Ignition (DI) Systems

1995 MODELS

➥Refer to the underhood label for the proper timing setting.

1. Engage the parking brake, block the wheels and set the transmission in P.
2. Disconnect the Ignition Control (IC) system by disengaging the "set timing connector". This is a single wire sealed connector that has a tan with black stripe lead. This wire comes out of the wiring harness below the heater case.
3. With the ignition switch **OFF**, connect the timing light pickup lead to the No. 1 spark plug wire.
4. Start the engine and point the timing light at the timing mark on the balancer or pulley and check the timing.
5. If the timing is not within specifications refer to the underhood emission sticker, loosen the distributor hold-down bolt. Slowly rotate the distributor until the proper timing setting is achieved.
6. Tighten the hold-down bolt and recheck the timing.

7. Turn the ignition **OFF**, remove the timing light and engage the "set timing" connector.

1996–98 MODELS

➥The distributor on the 4.3L engine is non-adjustable and any attempt to adjust the distributor could cause cross firing. This procedure applies to the 5.0L, 5.7L and 7.4L engines.

The ignition timing is preset and cannot be adjusted. If the distributor position is moved, crossfiring may be induced. To check distributor position the following:

➥An OBD-II compliant scan tool is required for this procedure

1. With the ignition **OFF** install scan tool to the Data Link Connector (DLC).
2. Start the engine and bring the vehicle to operating temperature.
3. Monitor cam retard on the scan tool.
4. If cam retard is between –2 and +2, the distributor is properly adjusted.
5. If cam retard is not between –2 and +2, the distributor must adjusted.
6. With the engine **OFF** loosen the distributor hold-down bolt.
7. Start the engine and check the cam retard reading. Rotate the distributor counterclockwise to compensate for a negative reading and clockwise to compensate for a positive reading.
8. Momentarily raise the engine speed to over 1000 RPM and check the cam retard reading.
9. If the proper reading is not achieved repeat Steps 7 and 8.
10. When the proper reading has been achieved, tighten the distributor hold-down bolt and disconnect the scan tool.

Valve Lash

All engines described in this book use hydraulic lifters, which require no periodic adjustment. In the event of cylinder head removal or any operation that requires disturbing the rocker arms, the rocker arms will have to be adjusted.

ADJUSTMENT

4.8L Engines

1. Remove the rocker arm cover.
2. Mark the distributor housing at the No. 1 and No. 6 wire positions and remove the cap.
3. Turn the crankshaft until the rotor points to the No. 1 position. The following valves can be adjusted:
   - No. 1 exhaust and intake
   - No. 2 intake
   - No. 3 exhaust
   - No. 4 intake
   - No. 5 exhaust

To adjust a valve, back off the adjusting nut until lash (play) is felt at the pushrod. Tighten the nut just until all lash is removed. This can be determined by rotating the pushrod with your fingers. When all lash is removed, the pushrod will stop rotating. When all play is removed, tighten the nut 1 full turn (360°).

4. Rotate the crankshaft until the rotor points to the No. 6 position. The following valves can be adjusted:
   - No. 2 exhaust
   - No. 3 intake
   - No. 4 exhaust
   - No. 5 intake
   - No. 6 intake and exhaust
5. Install the distributor cap.
6. Install the rocker cover.

V6 and V8 Engines

♦ See Figure 112

Valve adjustment on 1991–98 7.4L engines and 1995–98 models equipped with V6 engines is not required. These models use a positive stop shoulder. On models with a positive stop shoulder, simply tighten the rocker arm retainers to the torque listed in the torque specifications chart in this section.

On models not equipped with positive stop shoulders, perform the steps outlined in this procedure.

1. Remove the rocker covers and gaskets.
2. Crank the engine until the mark on the damper aligns with the **TDC** or **0** mark on the timing tab and the engine is in No. 1 firing position. This can be determined by placing your finger on the No. 1 cylinder valves as the marks align. If the valves do not move, it is in No. 1 firing position. If the valves move, it is in No. 6 firing position (No. 4 on the V6) and the crankshaft should be rotated 1 more revolution to the No. 1 firing position. To adjust a valve, back off the adjusting nut until lash (play) is felt at the pushrod. Tighten the nut just until all lash is removed. This can be determined by rotating the pushrod with your fingers. When all lash is removed, the pushrod will stop rotating. When all play is removed, tighten the nut 1 full turn (360°).
3. With the engine in No. 1 firing position, the following valves can be adjusted:

V6 Engines
- Exhaust—1, 5, 6
- Intake—1, 2, 3

V8 Engines
- Exhaust—1, 3, 4, 8
- Intake—1, 2, 5, 7

4. Crank the engine 1 full revolution until the marks are again in alignment. This is No. 6 firing position (No. 4 on the V6). The following valves can now be adjusted:

V6 Engines
- Exhaust—2, 3, 4
- Intake—4, 5, 6

V8 Engines
- Exhaust—2, 5, 6, 7
- Intake—3, 4, 6, 8

5. Reinstall the rocker arm covers using new gaskets.
6. Install the distributor cap and wire assembly.

Idle Speed and Mixture Adjustments

CARBURETED ENGINES

Mixture screws are concealed under staked-in plugs. Idle mixture is adjustable only during carburetor overhaul, and requires the addition of propane as an artificial mixture enricher. For these reasons, mixture adjustments are not considered part of routine maintenance. Refer to Section 5 for these procedures.

4.8L Engines

CURB IDLE SPEED

▶ See Figure 113

With the idle speed solenoid energized, turn the solenoid body to establish the curb idle speed shown on your underhood sticker.

BASE IDLE SPEED

With the solenoid wire disconnected, turn the ⅛ in. hex head solenoid plunger adjusting screw to establish the base idle speed shown on your underhood sticker.

5.7L Engines

▶ See Figures 114 and 115

1. All adjustments should be made with the engine at normal operating temperature, air cleaner on, choke open, and air conditioning off, unless otherwise noted. Set the parking brake and block the rear wheels. Automatic transmissions should be set in Drive, manuals in Neutral, unless otherwise noted in the procedures or on the emission control label.

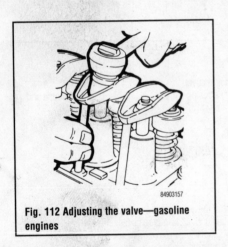

Fig. 112 Adjusting the valve—gasoline engines

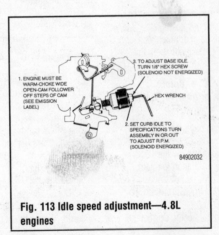

Fig. 113 Idle speed adjustment—4.8L engines

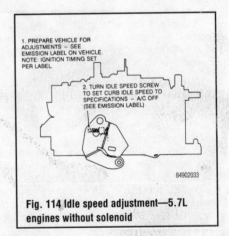

Fig. 114 Idle speed adjustment—5.7L engines without solenoid

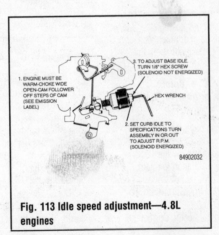

Fig. 115 Idle speed adjustment—5.7L engines with solenoid

2. Refer to the underhood emission sticker and prepare the vehicle for adjustment as specified on the sticker. On models without a solenoid, turn the idle speed screw to obtain the idle speed listed in the underhood emission control label. On models with a solenoid, turn the solenoid screw to obtain the idle speed listed in the underhood emission control label. Disconnect the wire at the air conditioning compressor and turn the air conditioning on. Rev the engine momentarily to fully extend the solenoid plunger. Turn the solenoid screw to obtain the solenoid idle speed listed on the underhood emission sticker. Reconnect the air conditioning wire at the compressor.

GASOLINE FUEL INJECTED ENGINES

The fuel injected vehicles are controlled by a computer which supplies the correct amount of fuel during all engine operating conditions and controls idle speed; no adjustment is necessary or possible.

DIESEL ENGINES

Idle Speed

▶ See Figure 116

➡A special tachometer suitable for diesel engines must be used. A gasoline engine type tach will not work with the diesel engine.

1. Set the parking brake and block the drive wheels.
2. Run the engine up to normal operating temperature. The air cleaner must be mounted and all accessories turned off.
3. Install the diesel tachometer as per the manufacturer's instructions.
4. Adjust the low idle speed screw on the fuel injection pump to the specification listed on the underhood label in Neutral or P for both manual and automatic transmissions.

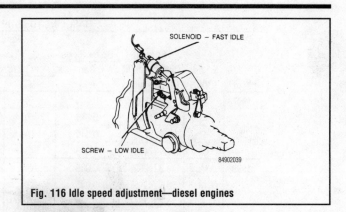

Fig. 116 Idle speed adjustment—diesel engines

GASOLINE TUNE-UP SPECIFICATIONS

Year	Engine ID/VIN	Engine Displacement Liters (cc)	Spark Plugs Gap (in.)	Ignition Timing (deg.) MT	Ignition Timing (deg.) AT	Fuel Pump (psi)	Idle Speed (rpm) MT	Idle Speed (rpm) AT	Valve Clearance In.	Valve Clearance Ex.
1988	Z	4.3 (4293)	0.040	①	①	9-13	700	700	HYD	HYD
	T	4.8 (4785)	0.035	8B	8B	5.0	700	700	HYD	HYD
	H	5.0 (4999)	0.045	4B	4B	4.0-6.5	700	700	HYD	HYD
	K	5.7 (5735)	0.045	4B	4B	4.0-6.5	700	700	HYD	HYD
	N	7.4 (7440)	0.045	4B	4B	9-13	700	700	HYD	HYD
	W	7.4 (7440)	0.045	4B	4B	4.0-6.5	700	700	HYD	HYD
1989	Z	4.3 (4293)	0.040	①	①	9-13	700	700	HYD	HYD
	T	4.8 (4785)	0.035	8B	8B	5.0	700	700	HYD	HYD
	H	5.0 (4999)	0.045	4B	4B	4.0-6.5	700	700	HYD	HYD
	K	5.7 (5735)	0.045	4B	4B	4.0-6.5	700	700	HYD	HYD
	N	7.4 (7440)	0.045	4B	4B	9-13	700	700	HYD	HYD
	W	7.4 (7440)	0.045	4B	4B	4.0-6.5	700	700	HYD	HYD
1990	Z	4.3 (4293)	0.040	①	①	9-13	①	①	HYD	HYD
	T	4.8 (4785)	0.035	①	①	9-13	①	①	HYD	HYD
	H	5.0 (4999)	0.045	①	①	9-13	①	①	HYD	HYD
	K	5.7 (5735)	0.045	①	①	9-13	①	①	HYD	HYD
	N	7.4 (7440)	0.045	①	①	9-13	①	①	HYD	HYD
	W	7.4 (7440)	0.045	①	①	5.0	①	①	HYD	HYD
1991	Z	4.3 (4293)	0.040	①	①	9-13	①	①	HYD	HYD
	H	5.0 (4999)	0.045	①	①	9-13	①	①	HYD	HYD
	K	5.7 (5735)	0.045	①	①	9-13	①	①	HYD	HYD
	N	7.4 (7440)	0.045	①	①	9-13	①	①	HYD	HYD
1992	Z	4.3 (4293)	0.035	①	①	9-13	①	①	HYD	HYD
	H	5.0 (4999)	0.045	①	①	9-13	①	①	HYD	HYD
	K	5.7 (5735)	0.045	①	①	9-13	①	①	HYD	HYD
	N	7.4 (7440)	0.045	①	①	9-13	①	①	HYD	HYD
1993	Z	4.3 (4293)	0.035	①	①	9-13	①	①	HYD	HYD
	H	5.0 (4999)	0.045	①	①	9-13	①	①	HYD	HYD
	K	5.7 (5735)	0.045	①	①	9-13	①	①	HYD	HYD
	N	7.4 (7440)	0.045	①	①	9-13	①	①	HYD	HYD
1994	Z	4.3 (4293)	0.035	①	①	9-13	①	①	HYD	HYD
	H	5.0 (4999)	0.045	①	①	9-13	①	①	HYD	HYD
	K	5.7 (5735)	0.045	①	①	9-13	①	①	HYD	HYD
	N	7.4 (7440)	0.045	①	①	9-13	①	①	HYD	HYD
1995	Z	4.3 (4293)	0.035	①	①	9-13	①	①	HYD	HYD
	H	5.0 (4999)	0.045	①	①	9-13	①	①	HYD	HYD
	K	5.7 (5735)	0.045	①	①	9-13	①	①	HYD	HYD
	N	7.4 (7440)	0.045	①	①	9-13	①	①	HYD	HYD
1996	W	4.3 (4293)	0.035	①	①	60-66	①	①	HYD	HYD
	M	5.0 (4999)	0.045	①	①	60-66	①	①	HYD	HYD
	R	5.7 (5735)	0.045	①	①	60-66	①	①	HYD	HYD
	J	7.4 (7440)	0.045	①	①	60-66	①	①	HYD	HYD

91021C04

GASOLINE TUNE-UP SPECIFICATIONS

Year	Engine ID/VIN	Engine Displacement Liters (cc)	Spark Plugs Gap (in.)	Ignition Timing (deg.) MT	Ignition Timing (deg.) AT	Fuel Pump (psi)	Idle Speed (rpm) MT	Idle Speed (rpm) AT	Valve Clearance In.	Valve Clearance Ex.
1997	W	4.3 (4293)	0.035	①	①	60-66	①	①	HYD	HYD
	M	5.0 (4999)	0.045	①	①	60-66	①	①	HYD	HYD
	R	5.7 (5735)	0.045	①	①	60-66	①	①	HYD	HYD
	J	7.4 (7440)	0.045	①	①	60-66	①	①	HYD	HYD
1998	W	4.3 (4293)	0.035	①	①	60-66	①	①	HYD	HYD
	M	5.0 (4999)	0.045	①	①	60-66	①	①	HYD	HYD
	R	5.7 (5735)	0.045	①	①	60-66	①	①	HYD	HYD
	J	7.4 (7440)	0.045	①	①	60-66	①	①	HYD	HYD

NOTE: The Vehicle Emission Control Information label often reflects specification changes made during production.

The label figures must be used if they differ from those in this chart

HYD—Hydraulic

NA—Not Available

① Refer to the underhood label

91021C05

➡**All idle speeds are to be set within 25 rpm of the specified values.**

5. Adjust the fast idle speed as follows:
   a. Remove the connector from the fast idle solenoid. Use an insulated jumper wire from the battery positive terminal to the solenoid terminal to energize the solenoid.
   b. Open the throttle momentarily to ensure that the fast idle solenoid plunger is energized and fully extended.
   c. Adjust the extended plunger by turning the hex-head screw to an engine speed of 800 rpm (check the underhood label) in Neutral.
   d. Remove the jumper wire and reinstall the connector to the fast idle solenoid.
6. Disconnect and remove the tachometer.

Air Conditioning System

SYSTEM SERVICE & REPAIR

➡**It is recommended that the A/C system be serviced by an EPA Section 609 certified automotive technician utilizing a refrigerant recovery/recycling machine.**

The do-it-yourselfer should not service his/her own vehicle's A/C system for many reasons, including legal concerns, personal injury, environmental damage and cost.

According to the U.S. Clean Air Act, it is a federal crime to service or repair (involving the refrigerant) a Motor Vehicle Air Conditioning (MVAC) system for money without being EPA certified. It is also illegal to vent R-12 and R-134a refrigerants into the atmosphere. State and/or local laws may be more strict than the federal regulations, so be sure to check with your state and/or local authorities for further information.

➡**Federal law dictates that a fine of up to $25,000 may be levied on people convicted of venting refrigerant into the atmosphere.**

When servicing an A/C system you run the risk of handling or coming in contact with refrigerant, which may result in skin or eye irritation.or frostbite. Although low in toxicity (due to chemical stability), inhalation of concentrated refrigerant fumes is dangerous and can result in death; cases of fatal cardiac arrhythmia have been reported in people accidentally subjected to high levels of refrigerant. Some early symptoms include loss of concentration and drowsiness.

➡**Generally, the limit for exposure is lower for R-134a than it is for R-12. Exceptional care must be practiced when handling R-134a.**

Also, some refrigerants can decompose at high temperatures (near gas heaters or open flame), which may result in hydrofluoric acid, hydrochloric acid and phosgene (a fatal nerve gas).

It is usually more economically feasible to have a certified MVAC automotive technician perform A/C system service on your vehicle.

R-12 Refrigerant Conversion

If your vehicle still uses R-12 refrigerant, one way to save A/C system costs down the road is to investigate the possibility of having your system converted to R-134a. The older R-12 systems can be easily converted to R-134a refrigerant by a certified automotive technician by installing a few new components and changing the system oil.

The cost of R-12 is steadily rising and will continue to increase, because it is no longer imported or manufactured in the United States. Therefore, it is often possible to have an R-12 system converted to R-134a and recharged for less than it would cost to just charge the system with R-12.

If you are interested in having your system converted, contact local automotive service stations for more details and information.

PREVENTIVE MAINTENANCE

Although the A/C system should not be serviced by the do-it-yourselfer, preventive maintenance should be practiced to help maintain the efficiency of the vehicle's A/C system. Be sure to perform the following:

• The easiest and most important preventive maintenance for your A/C system is to be sure that it is used on a regular basis. Running the system for five minutes each month (no matter what the season) will help ensure that the seals and all internal components remain lubricated.

➡**Some vehicles automatically operate the A/C system compressor whenever the windshield defroster is activated. Therefore, the A/C system would not need to be operated each month if the defroster was used.**

• In order to prevent heater core freeze-up during A/C operation, it is necessary to maintain proper antifreeze protection. Be sure to properly maintain the engine cooling system.

• Any obstruction of or damage to the condenser configuration will restrict air flow which is essential to its efficient operation. Keep this unit clean and in proper physical shape.

➡**Bug screens which are mounted in front of the condenser (unless they are original equipment) are regarded as obstructions.**

• The condensation drain tube expels any water which accumulates on the bottom of the evaporator housing into the engine compartment. If this tube is obstructed, the air conditioning performance can be restricted and condensation buildup can spill over onto the vehicle's floor.

SYSTEM INSPECTION

Although the A/C system should not be serviced by the do-it-yourselfer, system inspections should be performed to help maintain the efficiency of the vehicle's A/C system. Be sure to perform the following:

The easiest and often most important check for the air conditioning system consists of a visual inspection of the system components. Visually inspect the system for refrigerant leaks, damaged compressor clutch, abnormal compressor drive belt tension and/or condition, plugged evaporator drain tube, blocked condenser fins, disconnected or broken wires, blown fuses, corroded connections and poor insulation.

A refrigerant leak will usually appear as an oily residue at the leakage point in the system. The oily residue soon picks up dust or dirt particles from the surrounding air and appears greasy. Through time, this will build up and appear to be a heavy dirt impregnated grease.

For a thorough visual and operational inspection, check the following:
• Check the surface of the radiator and condenser for dirt, leaves or other material which might block air flow.
• Check for kinks in hoses and lines. Check the system for leaks.
• Make sure the drive belt is properly tensioned. During operation, make sure the belt is free of noise or slippage.
• Make sure the blower motor operates at all appropriate positions, then check for distribution of the air from all outlets.

➡ **Remember that in high humidity, air discharged from the vents may not feel as cold as expected, even if the system is working properly. This is because moisture in humid air retains heat more effectively than dry air, thereby making humid air more difficult to cool.**

Windshield Wipers

ELEMENT (REFILL) CARE & REPLACEMENT

♦ **See Figures 117, 118 and 119**

For maximum effectiveness and longest element life, the windshield and wiper blades should be kept clean. Dirt, tree sap, road tar and so on will cause

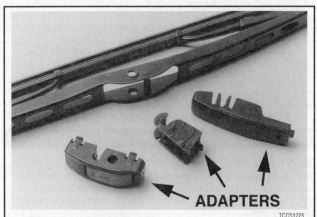

Fig. 117 Most aftermarket blades are available with multiple adapters to fit different vehicles

streaking, smearing and blade deterioration if left on the glass. It is advisable to wash the windshield carefully with a commercial glass cleaner at least once a month. Wipe off the rubber blades with the wet rag afterwards. Do not attempt to move wipers across the windshield by hand; damage to the motor and drive mechanism will result.

To inspect and/or replace the wiper blade elements, place the wiper switch in the **LOW** speed position and the ignition switch in the **ACC** position. When the wiper blades are approximately vertical on the windshield, turn the ignition switch to **OFF**.

Examine the wiper blade elements. If they are found to be cracked, broken or torn, they should be replaced immediately. Replacement intervals will vary with usage, although ozone deterioration usually limits element life to about one year. If the wiper pattern is smeared or streaked, or if the blade chatters across the glass, the elements should be replaced. It is easiest and most sensible to replace the elements in pairs.

If your vehicle is equipped with aftermarket blades, there are several different types of refills and your vehicle might have any kind. Aftermarket blades and arms rarely use the exact same type blade or refill as the original equipment.

Regardless of the type of refill used, be sure to follow the part manufacturer's instructions closely. Make sure that all of the frame jaws are engaged as the refill is pushed into place and locked. If the metal blade holder and frame are allowed to touch the glass during wiper operation, the glass will be scratched.

Tires and Wheels

Common sense and good driving habits will afford maximum tire life. Make sure that you don't overload the vehicle or run with incorrect pressure in the tires. Either of these will increase tread wear. Fast starts, sudden stops and sharp cornering are hard on tires and will shorten their useful life span.

➡ **For optimum tire life, keep the tires properly inflated, rotate them often and have the wheel alignment checked periodically.**

Inspect your tires frequently. Be especially careful to watch for bubbles in the tread or sidewall, deep cuts or underinflation. Replace any tires with bubbles in the sidewall. If cuts are so deep that they penetrate to the cords, discard the tire. Any cut in the sidewall of a radial tire renders it unsafe. Also look for uneven tread wear patterns that may indicate the front end is out of alignment or that the tires are out of balance.

TIRE ROTATION

♦ **See Figure 120**

Tires must be rotated periodically to equalize wear patterns that vary with a tire's position on the vehicle. Tires will also wear in an uneven way as the front steering/suspension system wears to the point where the alignment should be reset.

Rotating the tires will ensure maximum life for the tires as a set, so you will not have to discard a tire early due to wear on only part of the tread. Regular rotation is required to equalize wear.

When rotating "unidirectional tires," make sure that they always roll in the same direction. This means that a tire used on the left side of the vehicle must not be switched to the right side and vice-versa. Such tires should only be

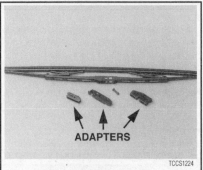

Fig. 118 Choose a blade which will fit your vehicle, and that will be readily available next time you need blades

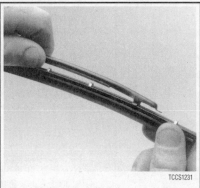

Fig. 119 When installed, be certain the blade is fully inserted into the backing

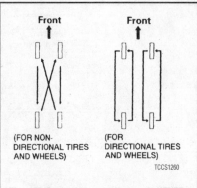

Fig. 120 Compact spare tires must NEVER be used in the rotation pattern

rotated front-to-rear or rear-to-front, while always remaining on the same side of the vehicle. These tires are marked on the sidewall as to the direction of rotation; observe the marks when reinstalling the tire(s).

Some styled or "mag" wheels may have different offsets front to rear. In these cases, the rear wheels must not be used up front and vice-versa. Furthermore, if these wheels are equipped with unidirectional tires, they cannot be rotated unless the tire is remounted for the proper direction of rotation.

➡The compact or space-saver spare is strictly for emergency use. It must never be included in the tire rotation or placed on the vehicle for everyday use.

TIRE DESIGN

♦ See Figure 121

For maximum satisfaction, tires should be used in sets of four. Mixing of different brands or types (radial, bias-belted, fiberglass belted) should be avoided. In most cases, the vehicle manufacturer has designated a type of tire on which the vehicle will perform best. Your first choice when replacing tires should be to use the same type of tire that the manufacturer recommends.

When radial tires are used, tire sizes and wheel diameters should be selected to maintain ground clearance and tire load capacity equivalent to the original specified tire. Radial tires should always be used in sets of four.

✳✳ CAUTION

Radial tires should never be used on only the front axle.

When selecting tires, pay attention to the original size as marked on the tire. Most tires are described using an industry size code sometimes referred to as P-Metric. This allows the exact identification of the tire specifications, regardless of the manufacturer. If selecting a different tire size or brand, remember to check the installed tire for any sign of interference with the body or suspension while the vehicle is stopping, turning sharply or heavily loaded.

Snow Tires

Good radial tires can produce a big advantage in slippery weather, but in snow, a street radial tire does not have sufficient tread to provide traction and control. The small grooves of a street tire quickly pack with snow and the tire behaves like a billiard ball on a marble floor. The more open, chunky tread of a snow tire will self-clean as the tire turns, providing much better grip on snowy surfaces.

To satisfy municipalities requiring snow tires during weather emergencies, most snow tires carry either an M + S designation after the tire size stamped on the sidewall, or the designation "all-season." In general, no change in tire size is necessary when buying snow tires.

Most manufacturers strongly recommend the use of 4 snow tires on their vehicles for reasons of stability. If snow tires are fitted only to the drive wheels, the opposite end of the vehicle may become very unstable when braking or turning on slippery surfaces. This instability can lead to unpleasant endings if the driver can't counteract the slide in time.

Note that snow tires, whether 2 or 4, will affect vehicle handling in all non-snow situations. The stiffer, heavier snow tires will noticeably change the turn-

ing and braking characteristics of the vehicle. Once the snow tires are installed, you must re-learn the behavior of the vehicle and drive accordingly.

➡**Consider buying extra wheels on which to mount the snow tires. Once done, the "snow wheels" can be installed and removed as needed. This eliminates the potential damage to tires or wheels from seasonal removal and installation. Even if your vehicle has styled wheels, see if inexpensive steel wheels are available. Although the look of the vehicle will change, the expensive wheels will be protected from salt, curb hits and pothole damage.**

TIRE STORAGE

If they are mounted on wheels, store the tires at proper inflation pressure. All tires should be kept in a cool, dry place. If they are stored in the garage or basement, do not let them stand on a concrete floor; set them on strips of wood, a mat or a large stack of newspaper. Keeping them away from direct moisture is of paramount importance. Tires should not be stored upright, but in a flat position.

INFLATION & INSPECTION

♦ See Figures 122 thru 127

The importance of proper tire inflation cannot be overemphasized. A tire employs air as part of its structure. It is designed around the supporting strength of the air at a specified pressure. For this reason, improper inflation drastically reduces the tire's ability to perform as intended. A tire will lose some air in day-to-day use; having to add a few pounds of air periodically is not necessarily a sign of a leaking tire.

Two items should be a permanent fixture in every glove compartment: an accurate tire pressure gauge and a tread depth gauge. Check the tire pressure (including the spare) regularly with a pocket type gauge. Too often, the gauge on the end of the air hose at your corner garage is not accurate because it suffers too much abuse. Always check tire pressure when the tires are cold, as pressure increases with temperature. If you must move the vehicle to check the tire inflation, do not drive more than a mile before checking. A cold tire is generally one that has not been driven for more than three hours.

A plate or sticker is normally provided somewhere in the vehicle (door post, hood, tailgate or trunk lid) which shows the proper pressure for the tires. Never counteract excessive pressure build-up by bleeding off air pressure (letting some air out). This will cause the tire to run hotter and wear quicker.

✳✳ CAUTION

Never exceed the maximum tire pressure embossed on the tire! This is the pressure to be used when the tire is at maximum loading, but it is rarely the correct pressure for everyday driving. Consult the owner's manual or the tire pressure sticker for the correct tire pressure.

Once you've maintained the correct tire pressures for several weeks, you'll be familiar with the vehicle's braking and handling personality. Slight adjustments in tire pressures can fine-tune these characteristics, but never change the cold pressure specification by more than 2 psi. A slightly softer tire pressure will give a softer ride but also yield lower fuel mileage. A slightly harder tire will give crisper dry road handling but can cause skidding on wet surfaces. Unless you're fully attuned to the vehicle, stick to the recommended inflation pressures.

All automotive tires have built-in tread wear indicator bars that show up as ½ in. (13mm) wide smooth bands across the tire when ¹⁄₁₆ in. (1.5mm) of tread remains. The appearance of tread wear indicators means that the tires should be replaced. In fact, many states have laws prohibiting the use of tires with less than this amount of tread.

You can check your own tread depth with an inexpensive gauge or by using a Lincoln head penny. Slip the Lincoln penny (with Lincoln's head upside-down) into several tread grooves. If you can see the top of Lincoln's head in 2 adjacent grooves, the tire has less than ¹⁄₁₆ in. (1.5mm) tread left and should be replaced. You can measure snow tires in the same manner by using the "tails" side of the Lincoln penny. If you can see the top of the Lincoln memorial, it's time to replace the snow tire(s).

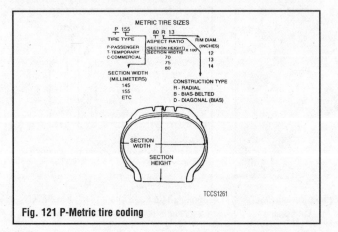

Fig. 121 P-Metric tire coding

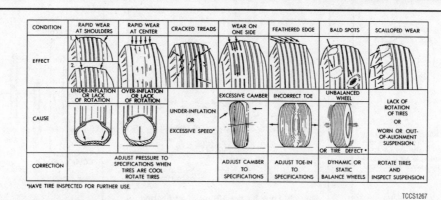

CONDITION	RAPID WEAR AT SHOULDERS	RAPID WEAR AT CENTER	CRACKED TREADS	WEAR ON ONE SIDE	FEATHERED EDGE	BALD SPOTS	SCALLOPED WEAR
EFFECT							
CAUSE	UNDER-INFLATION OR LACK OF ROTATION	OVER-INFLATION OR LACK OF ROTATION	UNDER-INFLATION OR EXCESSIVE SPEED*	EXCESSIVE CAMBER	INCORRECT TOE	UNBALANCED WHEEL OR TIRE DEFECT *	LACK OF ROTATION OF TIRES OR WORN OR OUT-OF-ALIGNMENT SUSPENSION.
CORRECTION	ADJUST PRESSURE TO SPECIFICATIONS WHEN TIRES ARE COOL ROTATE TIRES			ADJUST CAMBER TO SPECIFICATIONS	ADJUST TOE-IN TO SPECIFICATIONS	DYNAMIC OR STATIC BALANCE WHEELS	ROTATE TIRES AND INSPECT SUSPENSION

*HAVE TIRE INSPECTED FOR FURTHER USE.

TCCS1267

Fig. 122 Common tire wear patterns and causes

Fig. 123 Tires with deep cuts, or cuts which bulge, should be replaced immediately

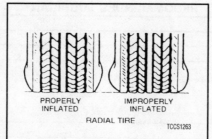

PROPERLY INFLATED   IMPROPERLY INFLATED

RADIAL TIRE

TCCS1263

Fig. 124 Radial tires have a characteristic sidewall bulge; don't try to measure pressure by looking at the tire. Use a quality air pressure gauge

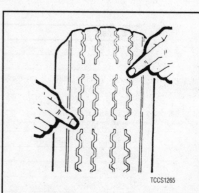

TCCS1265

Fig. 125 Tread wear indicators will appear when the tire is worn

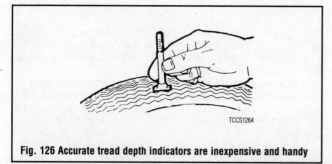

TCCS1264

Fig. 126 Accurate tread depth indicators are inexpensive and handy

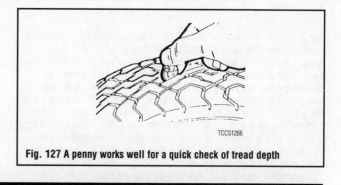

TCCS1266

Fig. 127 A penny works well for a quick check of tread depth

FLUIDS AND LUBRICANTS

Fluid Disposal

Used fluids such as engine oil, transmission fluid, antifreeze and brake fluid are hazardous wastes and must be disposed of properly. Before draining any fluids, consult with your local authorities; in many areas, waste oil, antifreeze, etc. is being accepted as a part of recycling programs. A number of service stations and auto parts stores are also accepting waste fluids for recycling.

Be sure of the recycling center's policies before draining any fluids, as many will not accept different fluids that have been mixed together.

Fuel and Oil Recommendations

OIL

▶ See Figures 128, 129 and 130

The Society of Automotive Engineers (SAE) grade number indicates the viscosity of the engine oil; its resistance to flow at a given temperature. The lower the SAE grade number, the lighter the oil. For example, the mono-grade oils begin with SAE 5 weight, which is a thin light oil, and continue in viscosity up to SAE 80 or 90 weight, which are heavy gear lubricants. These oils are also known as "straight weight", meaning they are of a single viscosity, and do not vary with engine temperature.

Multi-viscosity oils offer the important advantage of being adaptable to temperature extremes. These oils have designations such as 10W-40, 20W-50, etc. The 10W-40 means that in winter (the "W" in the designation) the oil acts like a thin 10 weight oil, allowing the engine to spin easily when cold and offering rapid lubrication. Once the engine has warmed up, however, the oil acts like a straight 40 weight, maintaining good lubrication and protection for the engine's internal components. A 20W-50 oil would therefore be slightly heavier than and not as ideal in cold weather as the 10W-40, but would offer better protection at higher rpm and temperatures because when warm it acts like a 50 weight oil. Whichever oil viscosity you choose when changing the oil, make sure you are anticipating the temperatures your engine will be operating in until the oil is changed again. Refer to the oil viscosity chart for oil recommendations according to temperature.

The American Petroleum Institute (API) designation indicates the classification of engine oil used under certain given operating conditions. Only oils designated for

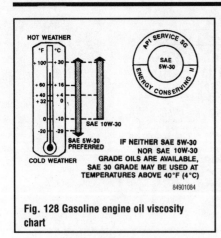

Fig. 128 Gasoline engine oil viscosity chart

Fig. 129 Look for the API oil identification label when choosing your engine oil

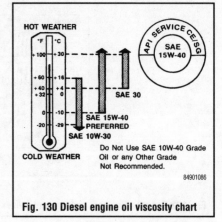

Fig. 130 Diesel engine oil viscosity chart

RECOMMENDED LUBRICANTS

Component	Lubricant
Engine Oil	API SG/CE
Coolant	Ethylene Glycol Anti-Freeze
Manual Transmission	
Muncie 117mm	API GL5, SAE 80W-90
Getrag 85mm	Synchromesh Transmission Fluid
NVG 4500	Castrol Syntorq GL-4
NVG 5LM60	Synchromesh Transmission Fluid
Automatic Transmission	AFT Dexron® II
Transfer Case	
Differential	API GL-5, SAE 80W-90
Master Cylinder	DOT 3 Brake Fluid
Power Steering	GM Power Steering Fluid
Manual Steering Gear	GM Lubricant
Multi-Purpose Grease	NLGI #2

84901151

use "Service SG, SH" or greater should be used. Oils of the SG, SH or its superseding oil type perform a variety of functions inside the engine in addition to the basic function as a lubricant. Through a balanced system of metallic detergents and polymeric dispersants, the oil prevents the formation of high and low temperature deposits and also keeps sludge and particles of dirt in suspension. Acids, particularly sulfuric acid, as well as other by-products of combustion, are neutralized. Both the SAE grade number and the APE designation can be found on top of the oil can.

Diesel engines also require SG, SH or greater engine oil. In addition, the oil must qualify for a CC or greater rating. The API has a number of different diesel engine ratings, including CB, CC, and CD. Any of these other oils are fine as long as the designation CC appears on the container label along with them. Do not use oil labeled only SG, SH or only CC. Both designations must always appear together.

For recommended oil viscosities, refer to the chart. Note that 10W-30 and 10W-40 grade oils are not recommended for sustained high speed driving when the temperature rises above the indicated limit.

Synthetic Oil

There are many excellent synthetic and fuel-efficient oils currently available that can provide better gas mileage, longer service life, and in some cases better engine protection. These benefits do not come without a few hitches, however; the main one being the price of synthetic oils, which in most cases is more expensive per quart of conventional oil.

Synthetic oil is not for every truck and every type of driving, so you should consider your engine's condition and your type of driving. Also, check your truck's warranty conditions regarding the use of synthetic oils.

FUEL

Gasoline Engines

It is important to use fuel of the proper octane rating in your truck. Octane rating is based on the quantity of anti-knock compounds added to the fuel and it determines the speed at which the gas will burn. The lower the octane rating, the faster it burns. The higher the octane, the slower the fuel will burn and a greater percentage of compounds in the fuel prevent spark ping (knock), detonation and preignition (dieseling).

As the temperature of the engine increases, the air/fuel mixture exhibits a tendency to ignite before the spark plug is fired. If fuel of an octane rating too low for the engine is used, this will allow combustion to occur before the piston has completed its compression stroke, thereby creating a very high pressure very rapidly.

Fuel of the proper octane rating, for the compression ratio and ignition timing of your truck, will slow the combustion process sufficiently to allow the spark plug enough time to ignite the mixture completely and smoothly. Many non-catalyst models are designed to run on regular fuel. The use of some super-premium fuel is no substitution for a properly tuned and maintained engine. Chances are that if your engine exhibits any signs of spark ping, detonation or pre-ignition when using regular fuel, the ignition timing should be checked against specifications or the cylinder head should be removed for decarbonizing.

Vehicles equipped with catalytic converters must use UNLEADED GASOLINE ONLY. Use of unleaded fuel shortened the life of spark plugs, exhaust systems and EGR valves and can damage the catalytic converter. Most converter equipped models are designed to operate using unleaded gasoline with a minimum rating of 87 octane. Use of unleaded gas with octane ratings lower than 87 can cause persistent spark knock which could lead to engine damage.

Light spark knock may be noticed when accelerating or driving up hills. The slight knocking may be considered normal (with 87 octane) because the maximum fuel economy is obtained under condition of occasional light spark knock. Gasoline with an octane rating higher than 87 may be used, but it is not necessary (in most cases) for proper operation.

If spark knock is constant, when using 87 octane, at cruising speeds on level ground, ignition timing adjustment may be required.

➡**Your engine's fuel requirement can change with time, mainly due to carbon buildup, which changes the compression ratio. If your engine** pings, knocks or runs on, switch to a higher grade of fuel. Sometimes just changing brands will cure the problem. If it becomes necessary to retard the timing from specifications, don't change it more than a few degrees. Retarded timing will reduce power output and fuel mileage and will increase the engine temperature.

Diesel Engines

Diesel engines require the use of diesel fuel. At no time should gasoline be substituted. Two grades of diesel fuel are manufactured, No. 1 and No. 2, although No. 2 grade is generally more available. Better fuel economy results from the use of No. 2 grade fuel. In some northern parts of the U.S. and in most parts of Canada, No. 1 grade fuel is available in the winter or a winterized blend of No. 2 grade is supplied in winter months. When the temperature falls below 20F (-7C), No. 1 grade or winterized No. 2 grade fuel are the only fuels that can be used. Cold temperatures cause unwinterized No. 2 to thicken (it actually gels), blocking the fuel lines and preventing the engine from running.
- Do not use home heating oil in your truck.
- Do not use ether or starting assist fluids in your truck.
- Do not use any fuel additives recommended for use in gasoline engines.

It is normal that the engine noise level is louder during the warm-up period in winter. It is also normal that whitish/blue smoke may be emitted from the exhaust after starting and during warm-up. The amount of smoke depends upon the outside temperature.

Engine

✳✳ CAUTION

Prolonged and repeated skin contact with used engine oil, with no effort to remove the oil, may be harmful. Always follow these simple precautions when handling used motor oil:

- Avoid prolonged skin contact with used motor oil.

- Remove oil from skin by washing thoroughly with soap and water or waterless hand cleaner. Do not use gasoline, thinners or other solvents.
- Avoid prolonged skin contact with oil-soaked clothing.

OIL LEVEL CHECK

▶ See Figures 131, 132 and 133

Every time you stop for fuel, check the engine oil as follows:
1. Park the truck on level ground.
2. When checking the oil level it is best for the engine to be at operating temperature, although checking the oil immediately after a stopping will lead to a false reading. Wait a few minutes after turning off the engine to allow the oil to drain back into the crankcase.
3. Open the hood and locate the dipstick which is on the left side of the engine. Pull the dipstick from its tube, wipe it clean and reinsert it.
4. Pull the dipstick out again and, holding it horizontally, read the oil level. The oil should be between the **FULL** or **OPERATING RANGE** and **ADD** or **ADD OIL** marks on the dipstick.
5. If the oil is below the **ADD** mark, add oil of the proper viscosity through the capped opening on the top of the cylinder head cover. See the "Oil and Fuel Recommendations" chart in this section for the proper viscosity and rating of acceptable oils.
6. Reinsert the dipstick and check the oil level again after adding any oil. Be careful not to overfill the crankcase. Approximately one quart of oil will raise the level from the **ADD** to the **FULL**. Excess oil will generally be consumed at an accelerated rate.

OIL & FILTER CHANGE

▶ See Figures 134, 135, 136 and 137

The oil should be changed every 7500 miles (12,000 km). General Motors recommends changing the oil filter with every other oil change; we suggest that the filter be changed with every oil change. There is approximately 1 quart of

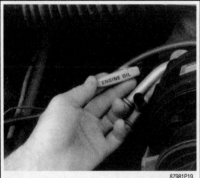

Fig. 131 Remove the oil dipstick and check the oil level

Fig. 132 Remove the oil filler cap

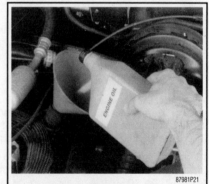

Fig. 133 Using a funnel, add the proper grade and viscosity of oil

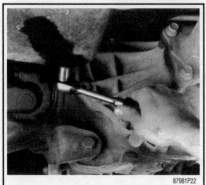

Fig. 134 With the proper size socket, loosen the drain plug

Fig. 135 Remove the drain plug while maintaining a slight upward force, to keep the oil from running out prematurely

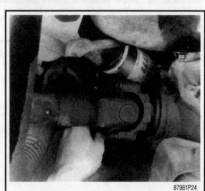

Fig. 136 With a filter wrench, loosen the oil filter counterclockwise

Fig. 137 Before installing a new oil filter, coat the rubber gasket with clean oil

dirty oil left remaining in the old oil filter if it is not changed! A few dollars more every year seems a small price to pay for extended engine life—so change the filter every time you change the oil!

The oil drain plug is located on the bottom, rear of the oil pan (bottom of the engine, underneath the truck).

The mileage figures given are the recommended intervals assuming normal driving and conditions. If your truck is being used under dusty, polluted or off-road conditions, change the oil and filter more frequently than specified. The same goes for trucks driven in stop-and-go traffic or only for short distances. Always drain the oil after the engine has been running long enough to bring it to normal operating temperature. Hot oil will flow easier and more contaminants will be removed along with the oil than if it were drained cold. To change the oil and filter:

➡ **If the engine is equipped with an oil cooler, this will also have to be drained, using the drain plug. Be sure to add enough oil to fill the cooler in addition to the engine.**

1. Warm the oil by running the engine for a short period of time or at least until the needle on the temperature gauge rises above the **C** mark. This will make the oil flow more freely from the oil pan.

2. Park on a level surface, apply the parking brake and block the wheels.

3. Stop the engine. Raise the hood and remove the oil filler cap from the top of the valve cover. This allows the air to enter the engine as the oil drains. Remove the dipstick, wipe it off and set it aside.

4. Position a suitable oil drain pan under the drain plug.

➡ **All diesel and gasoline engines hold approximately 5–8 quarts of oil (give or take), so choose a drain pan that exceeds this amount to allow for movement of the oil when the pan is pulled from under the vehicle. This will prevent time lost to the cleaning up of messy oil spills.**

5. With the proper size socket or wrench (DO NOT use pliers or vise grips), loosen the drain plug. Back out the drain plug while maintaining a slight upward force on it to keep the oil from running out around it (and your hand). Allow the oil to drain into the drain pan.

✳✳ **CAUTION**

The engine oil will be hot. Keep your arms, face and hands away from the oil as it is draining.

6. Remove the drain pan and wipe any excess oil from the area around the hole using a clean rag.

7. Clean the threads of the drain plug and the drain plug gasket to remove any sludge deposits that may have accumulated.

8. Place the drain pan under the oil filter location to prevent spilling any oil from the filter on to the ground.

9. With a filter wrench, loosen the oil filter counterclockwise and back the filter off the filter post the rest of the way by hand. Keep the filter end up so that the oil does not spill out. Tilt the filter into the drain pan to drain the oil.

10. Remove the drain pan from under the vehicle and position it off to the side.

11. With a clean rag, wipe off the filter seating surface to ensure a proper seal. Make sure that the old gasket is not stuck to the seating surface. If it is, remove it and thoroughly clean the seating surface of the old gasket material.

12. Open a container of new oil and smear some of this oil onto the rubber gasket of the new oil filter. Get a feel for where the filter post is and start the filter by hand until the gasket contacts the seat. Turn the filter an additional ¾ turn with your hand.

13. Install the drain plug and metal gasket. Be sure that the plug is tight enough that the oil does not leak out, but not tight enough to strip the threads. Over time you will develop a sense of what the proper tightness of the drain plug is. If a torque wrench is available, tighten the plug to 18 ft. lbs. (25 Nm).

➡ **Replace the drain plug gasket at every third or fourth oil change.**

14. Through a suitable plastic or metal funnel, add clean new oil of the proper grade and viscosity through the oil filler on the top of the valve cover. Be sure that the oil level registers near the (full) mark on the dipstick.

15. Install and tighten the oil filler cap.

16. Start the engine and allow it to run for several minutes. Check for leaks at the filter and drain plug. Sometimes leaks will not be revealed until the engine reaches normal operating temperature.

17. Stop the engine and recheck the oil level. Add oil as necessary.

When you have finished this job, you will notice that you now possess several quarts of dirty oil. The best thing to do with it is to pour it into plastic jugs, such as milk or anti-freeze containers. Then, find a gas station or service garage which accepts waste oil for recycling and dispose of it there.

Manual Transmission

FLUID RECOMMENDATION

- Muncie 117mm: API GL-5, SAE 80W-90
- Getrag 85mm: Syncromesh Transmission Fluid
- NVG 4500: Castrol Syntorq GL-4
- NVG 5LM60: Syncromesh Transmission Fluid
- NVG 3500: Syncromesh Transmission Fluid

LEVEL CHECK

◗ **See Figure 138**

Check the lubricant level at least twice a year, even more frequently if driven in deep water.

1. With the truck parked on a level surface, remove the filler plug from the side of the transmission case. Be careful not to take out the drain plug at the bottom.

2. If lubricant begins to trickle out of the hole, there is enough. If not, carefully insert a finger (watch out for sharp threads) and check that the level is up to the edge of the hole.

3. If not, add sufficient lubricant with a funnel and tube, or a squeeze bulb to bring it to the proper level. You can also use a common kitchen baster.

4. Install the plug and tighten to 17 ft. lbs. (23 Nm) on the Muncie and Getrag; 30 ft. lbs. (40 Nm) on NVG 4500; and 44 ft. lbs. (60 Nm) on the NVG 5LM60. Road test the truck and check for any leaks.

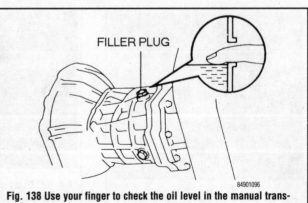

Fig. 138 Use your finger to check the oil level in the manual transmission

DRAIN & REFILL

No intervals are specified for changing the transmission lubricant, but it is a good idea on a used vehicle, one that has been worked hard, or one driven in deep water. The vehicle should be on a level surface and the lubricant should be at operating temperature.

1. Position the truck on a level surface.
2. Place a pan of sufficient capacity under the transmission drain plug.
3. Remove the upper (fill) plug to provide a vent opening.
4. Remove the lower (drain) plug and let the lubricant drain out.

❋ CAUTION

The oil will be hot! Be careful when you remove the plug or you'll be taking a bath in hot gear oil.

5. Install the drain plug and tighten to 17 ft. lbs. (23 Nm) on the Muncie and Getrag; 30 ft. lbs. (40 Nm) on NVG 4500; and 44 ft. lbs. (60 Nm) on the NVG 5LM60.
6. Add lubricant with a suction gun or squeeze bulb.
7. Reinstall the filler plug. Run the engine and check for leaks.

Automatic Transmission

FLUID RECOMMENDATIONS

Use Dexron III® or its superseding fluid type.

LEVEL CHECK

▶ **See Figures 139, 140 and 141**

Check the level of the fluid at least once a month. The fluid level should be checked with the engine at normal operating temperature and running. If the truck

has been running at high speed for a long period, in city traffic on a hot day, or pulling a trailer, let it cool down for about thirty minutes before checking the level.

1. Park the truck on a level surface with the engine idling. Shift the transmission into **P** and set the parking brake.
2. Remove the dipstick (on newer models, you may have to flip up the handle first), wipe it clean and reinsert if firmly. Be sure that it has been pushed all the way in.
3. Remove the dipstick and check the fluid level while holding it horizontally. All models have a HOT and a COLD side to the dipstick.
   - **COLD**: the fluid level should fall in this range when the engine has been running for only a short time.
   - **HOT**: the fluid level should fall in this range when the engine has reached normal running temperatures.
4. Early models have two dimples below the ADD mark, the level should be between these when the engine is cold.
5. If the fluid level is not within the proper area on either side of the dipstick, pour ATF into the dipstick tube. This is easily done with the aid of a funnel. Check the level often as you are filling the transmission. Be extremely careful not to overfill it. Overfilling will cause slippage, seal damage and overheating. Approximately one pint of ATF will raise the level from one notch to the other.

❋ WARNING

The fluid on the dipstick should always be a bright red color. It if is discolored (brown or black), or smells burnt, serious transmission troubles, probably due to overheating, should be suspected. The transmission should be inspected by a qualified service technician to locate the cause of the burnt fluid.

DRAIN & REFILL

▶ **See Figures 142, 143, 144 and 145**

1. The fluid should be drained with the transmission warm. It is easier to change the fluid if the truck is raised somewhat from the ground, but this is not always easy without a lift. The transmission must be level for it to drain properly.

87981P25

Fig. 139 Remove the dipstick to check the transmission fluid level

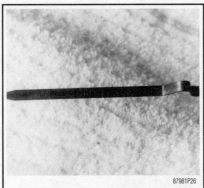

87981P26

Fig. 140 Hold the dipstick horizontally and check the fluid level

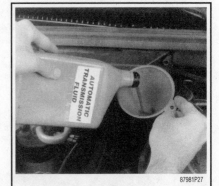

87981P27

Fig. 141 Use a funnel to add transmission fluid

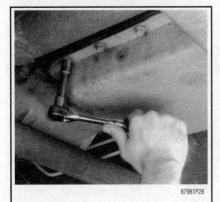

87981P28

Fig. 142 Loosen all the pan bolts

87981P29

Fig. 143 Pull one corner of the pan down to drain most of the fluid and remove the pan

87981P30

Fig. 144 Remove the old pan gasket and clean both gasket mating surfaces

Fig. 145 Remove the filter from the transmission

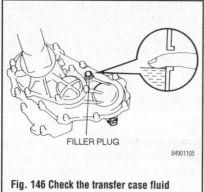

Fig. 146 Check the transfer case fluid level with your finger

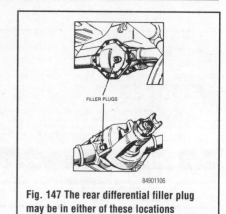

Fig. 147 The rear differential filler plug may be in either of these locations

2. Place a shallow pan underneath to catch the transmission fluid (about 5 pints). Loosen all the pan bolts, then pull one corner down to drain most of the fluid. If it sticks, VERY CAREFULLY pry the pan loose. You can buy aftermarket drain plug kits that makes this operation a bit less messy, once installed.

➡**If the fluid removed smells burnt, serious transmission troubles, probably due to overheating, should be suspected.**

3. Remove the pan bolts and empty out the pan. On some models, there may not be much room to get at the screws at the front of the pan.

4. Clean the pan with solvent and allow it to air dry. If you use a rag to wipe it out, you risk leaving bits of lint and threads in the transmission.

5. Remove the filter or strainer retaining bolts. On the Turbo Hydra-Matic 400, there are two screws securing the filter or screen to the valve body. A reusable strainer may be found on some models. The strainer may be cleaned in solvent and air dried thoroughly. The filter and gasket must be replaced.

To install:

6. Install a new gasket and filter.

7. Install a new gasket on the pan, and tighten the bolts evenly to 18 ft. lbs. (25 Nm) in a crisscross pattern.

8. Add DEXRON®III or its superseding type of transmission fluid through the dipstick tube. The correct amount is in the Capacities Chart. Do not overfill.

9. With the gearshift lever in **Park**, start the engine and let it idle. Do not race the engine.

10. Move the gearshift lever through each position, holding the brakes. Return the lever to **Park**, and check the fluid level with the engine idling. The level should be between the two dimples on the dipstick, about ¼ in. (6mm) below the ADD mark. Add fluid, if necessary.

11. Check the fluid level after the truck has been driven enough to thoroughly warm up the transmission. If the transmission is overfilled, the excess must be drained off. Overfilling causes aerated fluid, resulting in transmission slippage and probable damage.

Transfer Case

FLUID RECOMMENDATIONS

Use Dexron II® or its superseding fluid type on models through 1994. On 1995–98 models, use Dexron III® or its superseding fluid.

LEVEL CHECK

▶ **See Figure 146**

Check the four wheel drive transfer case lubricant at least twice a year.

1. With the truck parked on a level surface, remove the filler plug from the rear of the transfer case (behind the transmission). Be careful not to take out the drain plug at the bottom.

2. If lubricant trickles out, there is enough. If not, carefully insert a finger and check that the level is up to the edge of the hole, EXCEPT in full time four wheel drive cases which should be ½ in. (13mm) below the hole.

3. Lubricant may be added, if necessary, with a funnel and tube, or a squeeze bulb.

4. Tighten the plug to 18 ft. lbs. (25 Nm).

DRAIN & REFILL

1. With the transfer case warmed up, park on a level surface.

2. Slide a pan of a least 6 pts. capacity under the case drain plug.

3. Remove the filler plug from the rear of the transfer case (behind the transmission). Remove the drain plug from the bottom.

4. Wipe the area clean and install the drain plug.

5. Add lubricant with a suction gun or squeeze bulb.

6. When the lubricant level is up to the bottom of the filler hole, install the plug and tighten it to specifications.

- 4401 and 4470 models: 18 ft. lbs. (25 Nm).
- NV241 and NV243 models: 35 ft. lbs. (47 Nm).

Front and Rear Drive Axles

FLUID RECOMMENDATIONS

Front axles use SAE 80W-90, GL-5 Gear Lubricant. Rear axles use SAE 80W-90 gear oil. Posi-traction axles must use special lubricant available from dealers and most auto parts stores. If the special fluid is not used, noise, uneven operation, and damage will result. There is also a Posi-traction additive used to cure noise and slippage. Posi-traction axles have an identifying tag, as well as a warning sticker near the jack or on the rear wheel well.

LEVEL CHECK

▶ **See Figures 147 and 148**

The oil level in the front and/or rear differentials should be checked at least twice a year. If driven in deep water it should be checked immediately afterward. The fluid level in the front axle should be ½ in. (13mm) below the filler plug opening. The fluid level in the rear axle should be up to the bottom of the filler plug opening. Lubricant may be added with a suction gun or squeeze bulb.

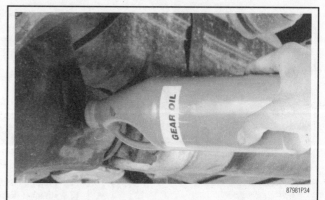

Fig. 148 If necessary, fill with the proper fluid

1. Park on level ground.
2. Remove the filler plug from the differential housing cover.
3. If lubricant trickles out there is enough. If not, carefully insert a finger and check that the level is up to the bottom of the hole. Locking front hubs should be run in the LOCK position for at least 10 miles (6 km) each month to assure proper lubrication to the front axle.
4. Fill with the proper fluid, install the plug and tighten to:

REAR:
- 8½ in.—25 ft. lbs. (34 Nm)
- 9½ and 10½ in.—19 ft. lbs. (24 Nm)
- 9¾–10½ in.—10 ft. lbs. (14 Nm)
- 12 in.—35 ft. lbs. (47 Nm)

FRONT:
- All—80 ft. lbs. (110 Nm)

DRAIN & REFILL

▶ See Figures 149, 150 and 151

No intervals are specified for changing axle lubricant, but it is a good idea every year or so. If you have driven in water over the axle vents, change the fluid immediately.
1. Park the vehicle on the level with the axles at normal operating temperature.
2. Place a pan of at least 6 pints capacity under the differential housing.
3. Remove the filler plug.
4. If you have a drain plug, remove it. If not, unbolt and remove the differential cover.
5. Install the drain plug, or differential cover. Use a new gasket if the differential cover has been removed.
6. Install the drain plug and tighten it so it will not leak. Do not overtighten.

➡ It is usually a good idea to replace the gasket at this time.

7. Refill the differential with the proper lubricant—do not overfill!
8. Install the filler plug and tighten both plugs to:

REAR:
- 8½ in.—25 ft. lbs. (34 Nm)
- 9½ and 10½ in.—19 ft. lbs. (24 Nm)
- 9¾–10½ in.—10 ft. lbs. (14 Nm)
- 12 in.—35 ft. lbs. (47 Nm)

FRONT:
- All: 80 ft. lbs. (110 Nm)
9. Road test the truck and check for any leaks.

Cooling System

▶ See Figures 152, 153, 154, 155 and 156

The cooling system was filled at the factory with a high quality coolant solution that is good for year around operation and protects the system from freezing down to -20F (-29C) (-32F/36C in Canada). It is good for two full calendar years or 24,000 miles (38,500 km), whichever occurs first, provided that the proper concentration of coolant is maintained.

The hot coolant level should be at the FULL HOT mark on the expansion tank and the cold coolant level should be at the FULL COLD mark on the tank. Do not remove the radiator cap to check the coolant level.

FLUID RECOMMENDATIONS

On 1988–95 models, the coolant mixture in Chevy/GMC trucks is 50/50 ethylene glycol and water for year round use. Use a good quality anti-freeze with water pump lubricants, rust inhibitors and other corrosion inhibitors along with acid neutralizers.

On 1996–98 models, Use a 50/50 mixture of DEX-COOL® coolant and water. Do not mix any other type of coolant with the DEX-COOL® as they are incompatible and may cause damage to the cooling system.

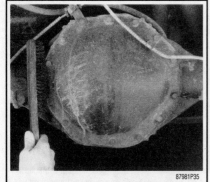

Fig. 149 Using a wire brush, clean the bolts and edges of the differential cover

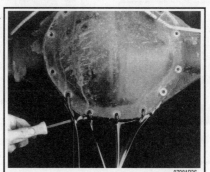

Fig. 150 After removing the bolts, carefully pry the bottom of the cover off and drain the fluid

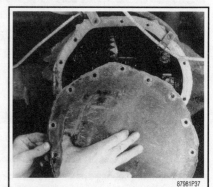

Fig. 151 After the oil has drained, remove the differential cover

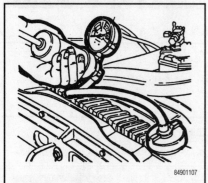

Fig. 152 The system should be pressure-tested once a year

Fig. 153 Remove any debris from the radiator's cooling fins

Fig. 154 Coolant condition can be checked with an inexpensive tester

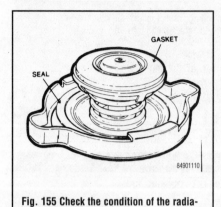

Fig. 155 Check the condition of the radiator cap gasket and seal

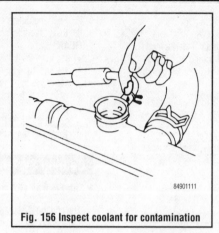

Fig. 156 Inspect coolant for contamination

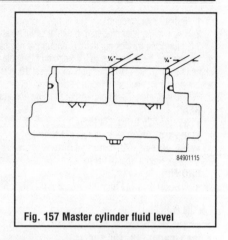

Fig. 157 Master cylinder fluid level

LEVEL CHECK

1. Check the level on the see-through expansion tank.

✳✳ CAUTION

The radiator coolant is under pressure when hot. To avoid the danger of physical harm, coolant level should be checked or replenished only when the engine is cold. To remove the radiator cap when the engine is hot, first cover the cap with a thick rag, or wear a heavy glove for protection. Press down on the cap slightly and slowly turn it counterclockwise until it reaches the first stop. Allow all the pressure to vent (indicated when the hissing sound stops). When the pressure is released, press down on the cap and continue to rotate it counterclockwise. Some radiator caps have a lever for venting the pressure, but you should still exercise extreme caution when removing the cap.

2. Check the level and, if necessary, add coolant through the expansion tank to the proper level. Use a 50/50 mix of ethylene glycol anti-freeze and water. Alcohol or methanol base coolants are not recommended. Anti-freeze solutions should be used, even in summer, to prevent rust and to take advantage of the solution's higher boiling point compared to plain water. This is imperative on air conditioned trucks; the heater core can freeze if it isn't protected. Coolant should be added through the coolant recovery tank, not the radiator filler neck.

✳✳ WARNING

Never add large quantities of cold coolant to a hot engine! A cracked engine block may result!

Each year the cooling system should be serviced as follows:
- Wash the radiator cap and filler neck with clean water.
- Check the coolant for proper level and freeze protection.
- Have the system pressure tested 15 psi. (103 kPa), If a replacement cap is installed, be sure that it conforms to the original specifications.
- Tighten the hose clamps and inspect all hoses. Replace hoses that are swollen, cracked or otherwise deteriorated.
- Clean the frontal area of the radiator core and the air conditioning condenser, if so equipped.

DRAINING & FLUSHING

The cooling system in you truck accumulates some internal rust and corrosion in its normal operation. A simple method of keeping the system clean is known as flushing the system. It is performed by circulating a can of radiator flush through the system, and then draining and refilling the system with the normal coolant. Radiator flush is marketed by several different manufacturers, and is available in cans at auto departments, parts stores, and many hardware stores. This operation should be performed every 30,000 miles (48,000 km) or once a year.

✳✳ CAUTION

When draining the coolant, keep in mind that cats and dogs are attracted by ethylene glycol anti-freeze, and are quite likely to drink any that is left in an uncovered container or in puddles on the ground. This will prove fatal in sufficient quantity. Always drain the coolant into a sealable container. Coolant should be reused unless it is contaminated or several years old.

1. Drain the existing anti-freeze and coolant. Open the radiator and engine drain petcocks (located near the bottom of the radiator and engine block, respectively), or disconnect the bottom radiator hose at the radiator outlet.
2. Close the petcock or reconnect the lower hose and fill the system with water—hot water if the system has just been run.
3. Add a can of quality radiator flush to the radiator or recovery tank, following any special instructions on the can.
4. Idle the engine as long as specified on the can of flush, or until the upper radiator hose gets hot.
5. Drain the system again. There should be quite a bit of scale and rust in the drained water.
6. Repeat this process until the drained water is mostly clear.
7. Close all petcocks and connect all hoses.
8. Flush the coolant recovery reservoir with water and leave empty.
9. Determine the capacity of your truck's cooling system (see Capacities specifications in this guide). Add a 50/50 mix of ethylene glycol anti-freeze and water to provide the desired protection.
10. Run the engine to operating temperature, then stop the engine and check for leaks. Check the coolant level and top up if necessary.
11. Check the protection level of your anti-freeze mix with an anti-freeze tester (a small, inexpensive syringe type device available at any auto parts store). The tester has five or six small colored balls inside, each of which signify a certain temperature rating. Insert the tester in the recovery tank and suck just enough coolant into the syringe to float as many individual balls as you can (without sucking in too much coolant and floating all the balls at once). A table supplied with the tester will explain how many floating balls equal protection down to a certain temperature (three floating balls might mean the coolant will protect your engine down to +5F (-15C), for example).

Brake Master Cylinder

FLUID RECOMMENDATIONS

▶ **See Figure 157**

Use only Heavy Duty Brake fluid meeting or exceeding DOT 3 standards.

LEVEL CHECK

▶ **See Figures 158 and 159**

Chevrolet and GMC trucks are equipped with a dual braking system, allowing a vehicle to be brought to a safe stop in the event of failure in either front or rear brakes. The dual master cylinder has 2 entirely separate reservoirs, one connected to the front brakes and the other connected to the rear brakes. In the event of failure in either portion, the remaining part is not affected. Fluid level in the master cylinder should be checked on a regular basis.

The master cylinder is mounted to the left side of the firewall.

1. Clean all of the dirt from around the cover of the master cylinder.
2. Be sure that the vehicle is resting on a level surface.
3. Carefully pry the clip from the top of the master cylinder to release the cover. On some later models, just pull up on the tabs.
4. The fluid level should be approximately ¼ in. (6mm) from the top of the master cylinder or at least above the **MIN** mark. If not, add fluid until the level is correct. Replacement fluid should be Delco Supreme No. 11, DOT 3, or its equivalent. It is normal for the fluid level to fall as the disc brake pads wear. If the fluid level in the master cylinder is excessively low, check the brake system for leaks and wear.

❋❋ WARNING

Brake fluid dissolves paint! It also absorbs moisture from the air. Never leave a container or the master cylinder uncovered any longer than necessary!

5. Install the cover of the master cylinder. On most models there is a rubber gasket under the cover, which fits into two slots on the cover. Be sure that this is seated properly.
6. Push the clip back into place and be sure that it seats in the groove on the top of the cover.

Clutch Master Cylinder

FLUID RECOMMENDATIONS

Use hydraulic clutch fluid or heavy duty brake fluid meeting DOT 3 standards.

LEVEL CHECK

The clutch master cylinder is located on the firewall in the engine compartment.

1. Clean all of the dirt from around the cover of the master cylinder.
2. Be sure that the vehicle is resting on a level surface.
3. Carefully remove the cover from the master cylinder.
4. The fluid level should be approximately ¼ in. (6mm) from the top of the master cylinder or at least above the **MIN** mark. If not, add fluid until the level is correct. Replacement fluid should be Delco Supreme No. 11, DOT 3, or its equivalent.
5. Install the cover of the master cylinder.

Power Steering Pump

FLUID RECOMMENDATION

Use GM Power Steering fluid, or its equivalent.

LEVEL CHECK

▶ See Figures 160, 161 and 162

Check the dipstick in the pump reservoir when the fluid is at operating temperature. The fluid should be between the **HOT** and **COLD** marks. If the fluid is at room temperature, the fluid should be between the **ADD** and **COLD** marks. The fluid does not require periodic changing.

On systems with a remote reservoir, the level should be maintained approximately ½–1 in. (13–25mm) from the top with the wheels in the full left turn position.

Steering Gear

FLUID RECOMMENDATIONS

Use GM Lubricant (part No. 1051052).

Fig. 158 Remove the master cylinder cover

Fig. 159 Add brake fluid until the level is correct

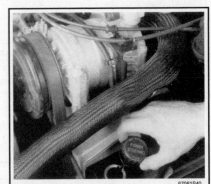

Fig. 160 Remove the power steering pump dipstick

Fig. 161 Hold the dipstick horizontally and check the power steering fluid level

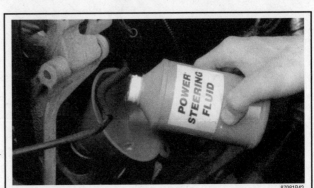

Fig. 162 Add power steering fluid to the pump and fill it to the proper level

LEVEL CHECK

No lubrication is needed for the life of the gear, except in the event of seal replacement or overhaul, when the gear should be refilled with a 13 oz. container of Steering Gear Lubricant (Part No. 1051052) which meets GM Specification GM 4673M, or its equivalent.

Chassis Greasing

◆ See Figures 163, 164, 165, 166 and 167

Refer to the diagrams for chassis points to be lubricated. Not all vehicles have all the fittings illustrated. Water resistant EP chassis lubricant (grease) conforming to GM specification 6031–M should be used for all chassis grease points.

Every year or 7500 miles (12,067 km) the front suspension ball joints, both upper and lower on each side of the truck, must be greased. Most trucks covered in this guide should be equipped with grease nipples on the ball joints, although some may have plugs which must be removed and nipples fitted.

✳✳ WARNING

Do not pump so much grease into the ball joint that excess grease squeezes out of the rubber boot. This destroys the watertight seal.

1. Raise up the front end of the truck and safely support it with jackstands. Block the rear wheels and firmly apply the parking brake.

2. If the truck has been parked in temperatures below 20F (-7C) for any length of time, park it in a heated garage for an hour or so until the ball joints loosen up enough to accept the grease.

3. Depending on which front wheel you work on first, turn the wheel and tire outward, either full-lock right or full-lock left. You now have the ends of the upper and lower suspension control arms in front of you; the grease nipples are visible pointing up (top ball joint) and down (lower ball joint) through the end of each control arm.

4. If the nipples are not accessible enough, remove the wheel and tire.

5. Wipe all dirt and crud from the nipples or from around the plugs (if installed). If plugs are on the truck, remove them and install grease nipples in the holes (nipples are available in various thread sizes at most auto parts stores).

6. Using a hand operated, low pressure grease gun loaded with a quality chassis grease, grease the ball joint only until the rubber joint boot begins to swell out.

The steering linkage should be greased at the same interval as the ball joints. Grease nipples are installed on the steering tie rod ends on most models.

7. Wipe all dirt and crud from around the nipples at each tie rod end.

8. Using a hand operated, low pressure grease gun loaded with a suitable chassis grease, grease the linkage until the old grease begins to squeeze out around the tie rod ends.

9. Wipe off the nipples and any excess grease. Also grease the nipples on the steering idler arms.

Use chassis grease on the parking brake cable where it contacts the cable guides, levers and linkage.

Apply a small amount of clean engine oil to the kickdown and shift linkage points at 7500 mile (12,000 km) intervals.

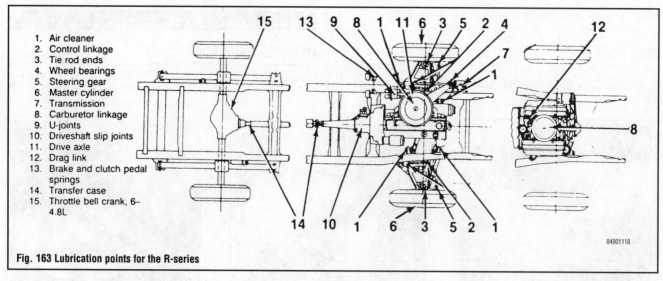

1. Air cleaner
2. Control linkage
3. Tie rod ends
4. Wheel bearings
5. Steering gear
6. Master cylinder
7. Transmission
8. Carburetor linkage
9. U-joints
10. Driveshaft slip joints
11. Drive axle
12. Drag link
13. Brake and clutch pedal springs
14. Transfer case
15. Throttle bell crank, 6–4.8L

84901118

Fig. 163 Lubrication points for the R-series

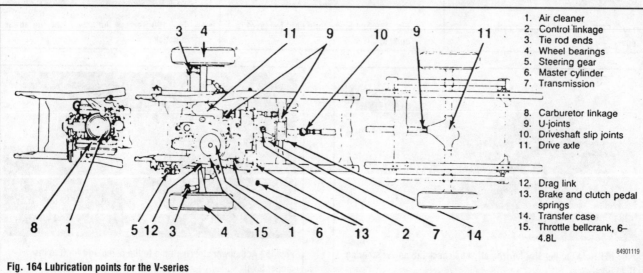

1. Air cleaner
2. Control linkage
3. Tie rod ends
4. Wheel bearings
5. Steering gear
6. Master cylinder
7. Transmission
8. Carburetor linkage
9. U-joints
10. Driveshaft slip joints
11. Drive axle
12. Drag link
13. Brake and clutch pedal springs
14. Transfer case
15. Throttle bellcrank, 6–4.8L

84901119

Fig. 164 Lubrication points for the V-series

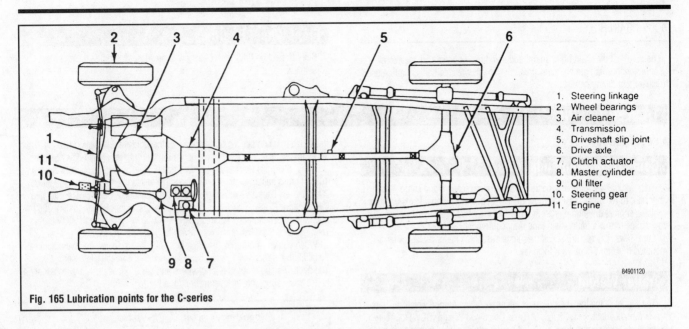

1. Steering linkage
2. Wheel bearings
3. Air cleaner
4. Transmission
5. Driveshaft slip joint
6. Drive axle
7. Clutch actuator
8. Master cylinder
9. Oil filter
10. Steering gear
11. Engine

84901120

Fig. 165 Lubrication points for the C-series

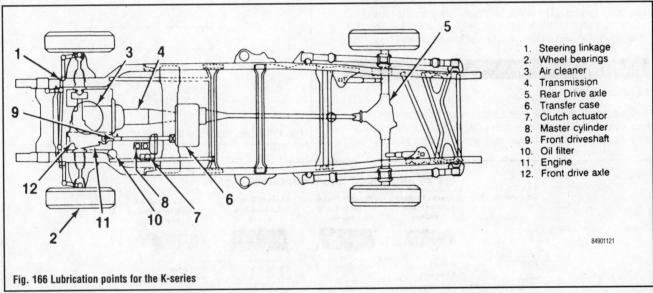

1. Steering linkage
2. Wheel bearings
3. Air cleaner
4. Transmission
5. Rear Drive axle
6. Transfer case
7. Clutch actuator
8. Master cylinder
9. Front driveshaft
10. Oil filter
11. Engine
12. Front drive axle

84901121

Fig. 166 Lubrication points for the K-series

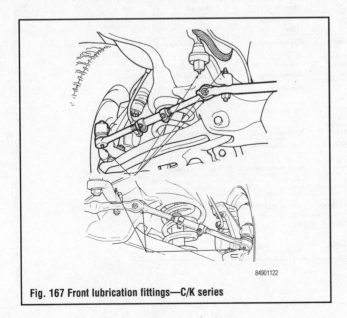

84901122

Fig. 167 Front lubrication fittings—C/K series

Body Lubrication and Maintenance

LOCK CYLINDERS

Apply graphite lubricant sparingly through the key slot. Insert the key and operate the lock several times to be sure that the lubricant is worked into the lock cylinder.

HOOD LATCH & HINGES

Clean the latch surfaces and apply clean engine oil to the latch pilot bolts and the spring anchor. Also lubricate the hood hinges with engine oil. Use a chassis grease to lubricate all the pivot points in the latch release mechanism.

DOOR HINGES

The gas tank filler door and truck doors should be wiped clean and lubricated with clean engine oil once a year. The door lock cylinders and latch mechanisms should be lubricated periodically with a few drops of graphite lock lubricant or a few shots of silicone spray.

BODY DRAIN HOLES

Be sure that the drain holes in the doors and rocker panels are cleared of obstruction. A small punch, screwdriver or unbent wire coat hanger can be used to clear them of any debris.

TRAILER TOWING

▶ See Figure 168

General Recommendations

Your vehicle was primarily designed to carry passengers and cargo. It is important to remember that towing a trailer will place additional loads on your vehicles engine, drive train, steering, braking and other systems. However, if you decide to tow a trailer, using the prior equipment is a must.

Local laws may require specific equipment such as trailer brakes or fender mounted mirrors. Check your local laws.

Trailer Weight

The weight of the trailer is the most important factor. A good weight-to-horse-power ratio is about 35:1, 35 lbs. of Gross Combined Weight (GCW) for every horsepower your engine develops. Multiply the engine's rated horsepower by 35 and subtract the weight of the vehicle passengers and luggage. The number remaining is the approximate ideal maximum weight you should tow, although a numerically higher axle ratio can help compensate for heavier weight.

Hitch (Tongue) Weight

▶ See Figure 169

Calculate the hitch weight in order to select a proper hitch. The weight of the hitch is usually 9–11% of the trailer gross weight and should be measured with the trailer loaded. Hitches fall into various categories: those that mount on the

Front Wheel Bearings

Refer to Section 8 for wheel bearing removal, repacking, installation and adjustment.

frame and rear bumper, the bolt-on type, or the weld-on distribution type used for larger trailers. Axle mounted or clamp-on bumper hitches should never be used.

Check the gross weight rating of your trailer. Tongue weight is usually figured as 10% of gross trailer weight. Therefore, a trailer with a maximum gross weight of 2000 lbs. will have a maximum tongue weight of 200 lbs. Class I trailers fall into this category. Class II trailers are those with a gross weight rating of 2000–3000 lbs., while Class III trailers fall into the 3500–6000 lbs. category. Class IV trailers are those over 6000 lbs. and are for use with fifth wheel trucks, only.

When you've determined the hitch that you'll need, follow the manufacturer's installation instructions, exactly, especially when it comes to fastener torques. The hitch will subjected to a lot of stress and good hitches come with hardened bolts. Never substitute an inferior bolt for a hardened bolt.

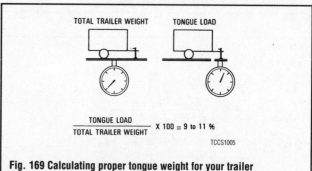

$$\frac{\text{TONGUE LOAD}}{\text{TOTAL TRAILER WEIGHT}} \times 100 = 9 \text{ to } 11 \text{ \%}$$

TCCS1005

Fig. 169 Calculating proper tongue weight for your trailer

Recommended Equipment Checklist

Equipment	Class I Trailers Under 2,000 pounds	Class II Trailers 2,000-3,500 pounds	Class III Trailers 3,500-6,000 pounds	Class IV Trailers 6,000 pounds and up
Hitch	Frame or Equalizing	Equalizing	Equalizing	Fifth wheel Pick-up truck only
Tongue Load Limit**	Up to 200 pounds	200-350 pounds	350-600 pounds	600 pounds and up
Trailer Brakes	Not Required	Required	Required	Required
Safety Chain	3/16" diameter links	1/4" diameter links	5/16" diameter links	—
Fender Mounted Mirrors	Useful, but not necessary	Recommended	Recommended	Recommended
Turn Signal Flasher	Standard	Constant Rate or heavy duty	Constant Rate or heavy duty	Constant Rate or heavy duty
Coolant Recovery System	Recommended	Required	Required	Required
Transmission Oil Cooler	Recommended	Recommended	Recommended	Recommended
Engine Oil Cooler	Recommended	Recommended	Recommended	Recommended
Air Adjustable Shock Absorbers	Recommended	Recommended	Recommended	Recommended
Flex or Clutch Fan	Recommended	Recommended	Recommended	Recommended
Tires	•••	•••	•••	•••

NOTE The information in this chart is a guide. Check the manufacturer's recommendations for your car if in doubt
  *Local laws may require specific equipment such as trailer brakes or fender mounted mirrors. Check your local laws
    Hitch weight is usually 10-15% of trailer gross weight and should be measured with trailer loaded
  **Most manufacturer's do not recommend towing trailers of over 1,000 pounds with compacts. Some intermediates
    cannot tow Class III trailers
  ***Check manufacturer's recommendations for your specific car trailer combination
    —Does not apply

84901131

Fig. 168 Recommended trailer towing equipment

Engine

One of the most common, if not THE most common, problems associated with trailer towing is engine overheating. If you have a cooling system without an expansion tank, you'll definitely need to get an aftermarket expansion tank kit, preferably one with at least a 2 quart capacity. These kits are easily installed on the radiator's overflow hose, and come with a pressure cap designed for expansion tanks.

Aftermarket engine oil coolers are helpful for prolonging engine oil life and reducing overall engine temperatures. Both of these factors increase engine life. While not absolutely necessary in towing Class I and some Class II trailers, they are recommended for heavier Class II and all Class III towing. Engine oil cooler systems usually consist of an adapter, screwed on in place of the oil filter, a remote filter mounting and a multi-tube, finned heat exchanger, which is mounted in front of the radiator or air conditioning condenser.

Transmission

An automatic transmission is usually recommended for trailer towing. Modern automatics have proven reliable and, of course, easy to operate, in trailer towing. The increased load of a trailer, however, causes an increase in the temperature of the automatic transmission fluid. Heat is the worst enemy of an automatic transmission. As the temperature of the fluid increases, the life of the fluid decreases.

It is essential, therefore, that you install an automatic transmission cooler. The cooler, which consists of a multi-tube, finned heat exchanger, is usually installed in front of the radiator or air conditioning compressor, and hooked in-line with the transmission cooler tank inlet line. Follow the cooler manufacturer's installation instructions.

Select a cooler of at least adequate capacity, based upon the combined gross weights of the vehicle and trailer.

Cooler manufacturers recommend that you use an aftermarket cooler in addition to, and not instead of, the present cooling tank in your radiator. If you do want to use it in place of the radiator cooling tank, get a cooler at least two sizes larger than normally necessary.

➡**A transmission cooler can, sometimes, cause slow or harsh shifting in the transmission during cold weather, until the fluid has a chance to come up to normal operating temperature. Some coolers can be purchased with or retrofitted with a temperature bypass valve which will allow fluid flow through the cooler only when the fluid has reached above a certain operating temperature.**

Handling a Trailer

Towing a trailer with ease and safety requires a certain amount of experience. It's a good idea to learn the feel of a trailer by practicing turning, stopping and backing in an open area such as an empty parking lot.

JUMP STARTING A DEAD BATTERY

▶ **See Figure 170**

Whenever a vehicle is jump started, precautions must be followed in order to prevent the possibility of personal injury. Remember that batteries contain a small amount of explosive hydrogen gas which is a by-product of battery charging. Sparks should always be avoided when working around batteries, especially when attaching jumper cables. To minimize the possibility of accidental sparks, follow the procedure carefully.

✷ CAUTION

NEVER hook the batteries up in a series circuit or the entire electrical system will go up in smoke, including the starter!

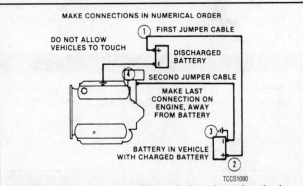

Fig. 170 Connect the jumper cables to the batteries and engine in the order shown

Jump Starting Precautions

- Be sure that both batteries are of the same polarity (have the same terminal, in most cases NEGATIVE grounded).
- Be sure that the vehicles are not touching or a short could occur.
- On non-sealed batteries, be sure the vent cap holes are not obstructed.
- Do not smoke or allow sparks anywhere near the battery.
- In cold weather, make sure the battery electrolyte is not frozen. This can occur more readily in a battery that has been in a state of discharge.
- Do not allow electrolyte to contact your skin or clothing.

Jump Starting Procedure

SINGLE BATTERY GASOLINE AND DIESEL ENGINE MODELS

1. Make sure that the voltages of the 2 batteries are the same. Most batteries and charging systems are of the 12 volt variety.
2. Pull the jumping vehicle (with the good battery) into a position so the jumper cables can reach the dead battery and that vehicle's engine. Make sure that the vehicles do NOT touch.
3. Place the transmissions of both vehicles in **Neutral** (MT) or **P** (AT), as applicable, then firmly set their parking brakes.

➡**If necessary for safety reasons, the hazard lights on both vehicles may be operated throughout the entire procedure without significantly increasing the difficulty of jumping the dead battery.**

4. Turn all lights and accessories OFF on both vehicles. Make sure the ignition switches on both vehicles are turned to the **OFF** position.
5. Cover the battery cell caps with a rag, but do not cover the terminals.
6. Make sure the terminals on both batteries are clean and free of corrosion for good electrical contact.
7. Identify the positive (+) and negative (-) terminals on both batteries.
8. Connect the first jumper cable to the positive (+) terminal of the dead battery, then connect the other end of that cable to the positive (+) terminal of the booster (good) battery.
9. Connect one end of the other jumper cable to the negative (-) terminal on the booster battery and the final cable clamp to an engine bolt head, alternator bracket or other solid, metallic point on the engine with the dead battery. Try to pick a ground on the engine that is positioned away from the battery in order to minimize the possibility of the 2 clamps touching should one loosen during the procedure. DO NOT connect this clamp to the negative (-) terminal of the bad battery.

✷ CAUTION

Be very careful to keep the jumper cables away from moving parts (cooling fan, belts, etc.) on both engines.

10. Check to make sure that the cables are routed away from any moving parts, then start the donor vehicle's engine. Run the engine at moderate speed for several minutes to allow the dead battery a chance to receive some initial charge.
11. With the donor vehicle's engine still running slightly above idle, try to start the vehicle with the dead battery. Crank the engine for no more than 10

seconds at a time and let the starter cool for at least 20 seconds between tries. If the vehicle does not start in 3 tries, it is likely that something else is also wrong or that the battery needs additional time to charge.

12. Once the vehicle is started, allow it to run at idle for a few seconds to make sure that it is operating properly.

13. Turn ON the headlights, heater blower and, if equipped, the rear defroster of both vehicles in order to reduce the severity of voltage spikes and subsequent risk of damage to the vehicles' electrical systems when the cables are disconnected. This step is especially important to any vehicle equipped with computer control modules.

14. Carefully disconnect the cables in the reverse order of connection. Start with the negative cable that is attached to the engine ground, then the negative cable on the donor battery. Disconnect the positive cable from the donor battery and finally, disconnect the positive cable from the formerly dead battery. Be careful when disconnecting the cables from the positive terminals not to allow the alligator clips to touch any metal on either vehicle or a short and sparks will occur.

DUAL BATTERY DIESEL MODELS

▶ See Figure 171

Some diesel model vehicles utilize two 12 volt batteries, one on either side of the engine compartment. The batteries are connected in a parallel circuit (positive terminal to positive terminal and negative terminal to negative terminal). Hooking the batteries up in a parallel circuit increases battery cranking power without increasing total battery voltage output. The output will remain at 12 volts. On the other hand, hooking two 12 volt batteries in a series circuit (positive terminal to negative terminal and negative terminal to positive terminal) increases the total battery output to 24 volts (12 volts plus 12 volts).

✴✴ WARNING

Never hook the batteries up in a series circuit or the entire electrical system will be damaged, including the starter motor.

In the event that a dual battery vehicle needs to be jump started, use the following procedure:

1. Turn the heater blower motor **ON** to help protect the electrical system from voltage surges when the jumper cables are connected and disconnected.
2. Turn all lights and other switches **OFF**.

➡**The battery cables connected to one of the diesel vehicle's batteries may be thicker than those connected to its other battery. (The passenger side battery often has thicker cables.) This set-up allows relatively high jump starting current to pass without damage. If so, be sure to connect**

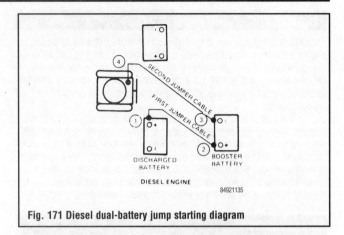

Fig. 171 Diesel dual-battery jump starting diagram

the positive jumper cable to the appropriate battery in the disabled vehicle. If there is no difference in cable thickness, connect the jumper cable to either battery's positive terminal. Similarly, if the donor vehicle also utilizes two batteries, the jumper cable connections should be made to the battery with the thicker cables; if there is no difference in thickness, the connections can be made to either donor battery.

3. Connect the end of a jumper cable to one of the disabled diesel's positive (+) battery terminals, then connect the clamp at the other end of the same cable to the positive terminal (+) on the jumper battery.
4. Connect one end of the other jumper cable to the negative battery terminal (-) on the jumper battery, then connect the other cable clamp to an engine bolt head, alternator bracket or other solid, metallic point on the disabled vehicle's engine. DO NOT connect this clamp to the negative terminal (-) of the disabled vehicle's battery.

✴✴ CAUTION

Be careful to keep the jumper cables away from moving parts (cooling fan, belts, etc.) on both engines.

5. Start the engine on the vehicle with the good battery and run it at a moderate speed.
6. Start the engine of the vehicle with the discharged battery.
7. When the engine starts on the vehicle with the discharged battery, remove the cable from the engine block before disconnecting the cable from the positive terminal.

JACKING

▶ See Figures 172 thru 179

Your vehicle was supplied with a jack for emergency road repairs. This jack is fine for changing a flat tire or other short term procedures not requiring you to go beneath the vehicle. If it is used in an emergency situation, carefully follow the instructions provided either with the jack or in your owner's manual. Do

not attempt to use the jack on any portions of the vehicle other than specified by the vehicle manufacturer. Always block the diagonally opposite wheel when using a jack.

A more convenient way of jacking is the use of a garage or floor jack. You may use the floor jack to raise the truck in the positions indicated in the accompanying illustration and photographs.

Fig. 172 Raising the front of the vehicle using a hydraulic jack

Fig. 173 Place the jackstand under the lower control arm

Fig. 174 Raising the rear of the vehicle using a hydraulic jack placed under the rear axle differential

Never place the jack under the radiator, engine or transmission components. Severe and expensive damage will result when the jack is raised. Additionally, never jack under the floorpan or bodywork; the metal will deform.

Whenever you plan to work under the vehicle, you must support it on jackstands or ramps. Never use cinder blocks or stacks of wood to support the vehicle, even if you're only going to be under it for a few minutes. Never crawl under the vehicle when it is supported only by the tire-changing jack or other floor jack.

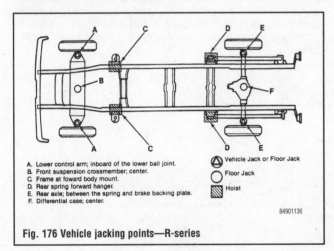

Fig. 175 Place the jackstand under the rear axle, near the wheel assembly

A. Lower control arm; inboard of the lower ball joint.
B. Front suspension crossmember; center.
C. Frame at forward body mount.
D. Rear spring forward hanger.
E. Rear axle; between the spring and brake backing plate.
F. Differential case; center.

△ Vehicle Jack or Floor Jack
○ Floor Jack
▨ Hoist

84901136

Fig. 176 Vehicle jacking points—R-series

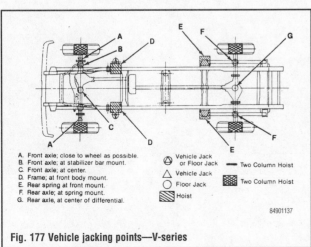

A. Front axle; close to wheel as possible.
B. Front axle; at stabilizer bar mount.
C. Front axle; at center.
D. Frame; at front body mount.
E. Rear spring at front mount.
F. Rear axle; at spring mount.
G. Rear axle, at center of differential.

△ Vehicle Jack or Floor Jack
△ Vehicle Jack
○ Floor Jack
▨ Hoist

▬ Two Column Hoist
▨ Two Column Hoist

84901137

Fig. 177 Vehicle jacking points—V-series

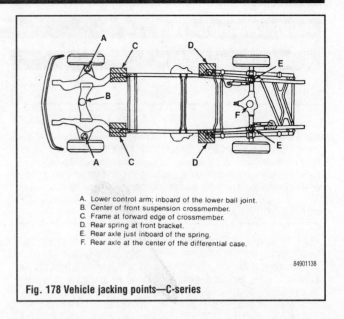

A. Lower control arm; inboard of the lower ball joint.
B. Center of front suspension crossmember.
C. Frame at forward edge of crossmember.
D. Rear spring at front bracket.
E. Rear axle just inboard of the spring.
F. Rear axle at the center of the differential case.

84901138

Fig. 178 Vehicle jacking points—C-series

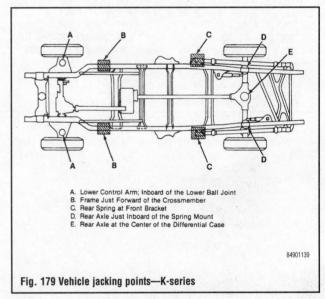

A. Lower Control Arm; Inboard of the Lower Ball Joint
B. Frame Just Forward of the Crossmember
C. Rear Spring at Front Bracket
D. Rear Axle Just Inboard of the Spring Mount
E. Rear Axle at the Center of the Differential Case

84901139

Fig. 179 Vehicle jacking points—K-series

➡Always position a block of wood or small rubber pad on top of the jack or jackstand to protect the lifting point's finish when lifting or supporting the vehicle.

Small hydraulic, screw, or scissors jacks are satisfactory for raising the vehicle. Drive-on trestles or ramps are also a handy and safe way to both raise and support the vehicle. Be careful though, some ramps may be too steep to drive your vehicle onto without scraping the front bottom panels. Never support the vehicle on any suspension member (unless specifically instructed to do so by a repair manual) or by an underbody panel.

Jacking Precautions

The following safety points cannot be overemphasized:
• Always block the opposite wheel or wheels to keep the vehicle from rolling off the jack.
• When raising the front of the vehicle, firmly apply the parking brake.
• When the drive wheels are to remain on the ground, leave the vehicle in gear to help prevent it from rolling.
• Always use jackstands to support the vehicle when you are working underneath. Place the stands beneath the vehicle's jacking brackets. Before climbing underneath, rock the vehicle a bit to make sure it is firmly supported.

MAINTENANCE INTERVALS

General Recommendations

BUT THE OWNER'S MANUAL IS DIFFERENT?

We have provided a maintenance interval chart which is based on both the manufacturer's specific information and general industry standards. The time and mileage given should be sufficient to meet or beat the manufacturer's warranty requirements. If, for some reason, your owner's manual differs from this schedule, we would recommend that you follow the more conservative of the two in order to be sure that all maintenance occurs in a timely manner.

BUT THE REPLACEMENT PART IS DIFFERENT?

Another thing to remember is that maintenance intervals may vary with the type of replacement parts which are used. Spark plugs and synthetic oils are two good examples of this. Although we have suggested changing your oil and filter every 3,000 miles, use of a synthetic oil may allow you to lengthen or even double this mileage, IF your usage fits the proper patterns (highway miles, above freezing, with little stop-and-go and no excessive speeds . . .). The recommendation we give for spark plugs is based on conventional plugs with an electronic ignition system, which probably covers most vehicles on the road. But, if you use special plugs, like the increasingly popular long-life Platinum plugs, you may easily be able to double the recommended replacement interval. The key here is to pay attention to the directions supplied with your replacement parts (and if you have never replaced an item before, check with the manufacturer for suggestions about original equipment).

IS MY DRIVING "NORMAL" OR "SEVERE"?

Sometimes we are puzzled at how manufacturer's chose the term "Normal" for the style of driving which most refer to in their maintenance charts as the opposite of "Severe." Check your owner's manual and you will likely see that you are NOT normal. Sorry to be the one to tell you, but it's probably true.

You see, to be "Normal" according to most manufacturer's driving and maintenance recommendations you would have to: Drive the car for more than 10 miles or so (to make sure it properly warms up) almost every time you start it (never under freezing conditions, but not in excessive heat, dry or dusty conditions either). Most miles would have to be on the highway, NOT stop-and-go (few red lights or stop signs), with no excessive idling (in traffic or curbside), but NOT at excessive speeds. Well, some of you reading this will find that this applies . . . but most wont.

If ALL of these conditions apply, then most manufacturers call your driving style "Severe" and lump it in with trailer towing, racing, cab or delivery driving or even police or fire vehicle usage. The truth is that most usage probably falls somewhere in between. Actual severe usage, such as those that we have just listed, should require a LOT of attention to all of the various systems of a car (including early replacement of all fluids). But, the average person, who does not race or tow, will be fine with the 3,000 mile/3 month engine oil change and most of the other recommendations we have given. If you compare those recommendations with your manufacturer, you will probably find that they have listed those intervals for "SEVERE" usage and not "NORMAL." Maybe it is just a play on words. Just remember that it is your money (that you are driving around every day) and possibly even your life (kept safe by tires and brakes . . .) so remember the general rule, maintenance is cheaper than repair. Don't be afraid of not being "Normal." Go ahead and admit that your driving is "Severe" and maintain your vehicle to match.

The charts we have included fall into two categories, Maintenance Schedule I (or what most manufacturers would call "SEVERE") and Maintenance Schedule II (what most manufacturers would call "NORMAL"). Schedule I should be followed if that vast majority of your usage is not comprised of highway miles in mild temperatures. Schedule I should also be followed if your truck is used in heavy traffic, frequent stop and go driving, carrying loads or towing, is exposed to excessive dusty or dirty conditions, or is operated in extreme low or high temperatures. As we explained earlier, we suspect most people should follow Schedule I.

GASOLINE ENGINES WITH LIGHT DUTY EMISSIONS— MAINTENANCE SCHEDULE I

Item No.	Service	Miles (000) / Kilometers (000)	3/5	6/10	7.5/12.5	9/15	12/20	15/25	18/30	21/35	22.5/37.5	24/40	27/45	30/50	33/55	36/60	37.5/62.5	39/65	42/70	45/75	48/80	51/85	52.5/87.5	54/90	57/95	60/100
1	Engine Oil Change*—Every 3 Months, or		+	+		+	+	+	+	+		+	+	+	+	+		+	+	+	+	+		+	+	+
	Oil Filter Change*—Every 3 Months, or		+	+		+	+	+	+	+		+	+	+	+	+		+	+	+	+	+		+	+	+
2	Chassis Lubrication—Every 12 Months, or		+	+		+	+	+	+	+		+	+	+	+	+		+	+	+	+	+		+	+	+
3	Clutch Fork Ball Stud Lubrication													+												+
5	Cooling System Service*—Every 24 Months or													+												+
6	Air Cleaner Filter Replacement*													+												+
7	Front Wheel Bearing Repack							+												+						+
8	Transmission Service																									
10	Fuel Filter Replacement*													+												+
11	Spark Plugs Replacement*													+												+
12	Spark Plug Wire Inspection*																									+
14	Electronic Vacuum Regulator Valve (EVRV) Inspection*																									+
15	Engine Timing Check*																									+
16	Fuel Tank, Cap and Lines Inspection*																									+
18	Engine Accessory Drive Belt(s) Inspection*																									+
24	Tire and Wheel Rotation																									
25	Drive Axle Service																									
26	Brake Systems Inspection																									

FOOTNOTES.
*An Emission Control Service

THE SERVICES SHOWN ON THIS CHART UP TO 60,000 MILES (100 000 km) ARE TO BE DONE AFTER 60,000 MILES AT THE SAME INTERVALS.

91021C07

GASOLINE ENGINES WITH LIGHT DUTY EMISSIONS— MAINTENANCE SCHEDULE II

Item No.	Service	Miles (000) / Kilometers (000)	3/5	6/10	7.5/12.5	9/15	12/20	15/25	18/30	21/35	22.5/37.5	24/40	27/45	30/50	33/55	36/60	37.5/62.5	39/65	42/70	45/75	48/80	51/85	52.5/87.5	54/90	57/95	60/100
1	Engine Oil Change*—Every 12 Months, or				•			•			•			•			•			•			•			•
	Oil Filter Change*—Every 12 Months, or				•						•						•						•			
2	Chassis Lubrication—Every 12 Months, or				•			•			•			•			•			•			•			•
3	Clutch Fork Ball Stud Lubrication																									•
5	Cooling System Service*—Every 24 Months or													•												•
6	Air Cleaner Filter Replacement*																									•
7	Front Wheel Bearing Repack																									
8	Transmission Service																									•
10	Fuel Filter Replacement*																									•
11	Spark Plugs Replacement*													•												•
12	Spark Plug Wire Inspection*																									•
14	Electronic Vacuum Regulator Valve (EVRV) Inspection*																									•
15	Engine Timing Check*																									•
16	Fuel Tank, Cap and Lines Inspection*																									•
18	Engine Accessory Drive Belt(s) Inspection*																									•
24	Tire and Wheel Rotation																									
25	Drive Axle Service																									
26	Brake Systems Inspection																									

FOOTNOTES:
*An Emission Control Service

THE SERVICES SHOWN ON THIS CHART UP TO 60,000 MILES (100 000 km) ARE TO BE DONE AFTER 60,000 MILES AT THE SAME INTERVALS.

91021C08

GASOLINE ENGINES WITH HEAVY DUTY EMISSIONS—　　　　MAINTENANCE SCHEDULE I

Item No.	Service	Miles (000) → 3	6	9	12	15	18	21	24	27	30	33	36	39	42	45	48	51	54	57	60
	Kilometers (000) →	5	10	15	20	25	30	35	40	45	50	55	60	65	70	75	80	85	90	95	100
1	Engine Oil Change*—Every 3 Months, or	+	+	+	+	+	+	+	+	+	+	+	+	+	+	+	+	+	+	+	+
	Oil Filter Change*—Every 3 Months, or	+	+	+	+	+	+	+	+	+	+	+	+	+	+	+	+	+	+	+	+
2	Chassis Lubrication—Every 12 Months, or	+	+	+	+	+	+	+	+	+	+	+	+	+	+	+	+	+	+	+	+
3	Clutch Fork Ball Stud Lubrication												+								+
5	Cooling System Service*—Every 24 Months or								+								+				
6	Air Cleaner Filter Replacement▲*								+								+				
7	Front Wheel Bearing Repack				+				+				+				+				
8	Transmission Service																				
10	Fuel Filter Replacement*				+				+				+				+				+
11	Spark Plugs Replacement*										+								+		
12	Spark Plug Wire Inspection*																				+
13	EGR System Inspection*																				+
14	Electronic Vacuum Regulator Valve (EVRV) Inspection*												+								
15	Engine Timing Check▲*								+							+					
16	Fuel Tank, Cap and Lines Inspection*																				+
17	Thermostatically Controlled Air Cleaner Inspection▲*								+							+					
18	Engine Accessory Drive Belt(s) Inspection*				+				+				+			+					+
19	Evaporative Control System Inspection*																				+
20	Shields and Underhood Insulation Inspection▲■				+				+				+			+					+
21	Air Intake System Inspection▲■								+							+					
22	Thermostatically Controlled Engine Cooling Fan Check ▲■— Every 12 Months or				+				+							+					
24	Tire and Wheel Rotation																				
25	Drive Axle Service																				
26	Brake Systems Inspection																				

FOOTNOTES:
*　An Emission Control Service
▲　Also a Noise Emission Control Service
■　Applicable only to vehicles sold in the United States

THE SERVICES SHOWN ON THIS CHART UP TO 60,000 MILES (100 000 km) ARE TO BE DONE AFTER 60,000 MILES AT THE SAME INTERVALS.

91201C09

GASOLINE ENGINES WITH HEAVY DUTY EMISSIONS—　　　　MAINTENANCE SCHEDULE II

Item No.	Service	Miles (000) → 3	6	9	12	15	18	21	24	27	30	33	36	39	42	45	48	51	54	57	60
	Kilometers (000) →	5	10	15	20	25	30	35	40	45	50	55	60	65	70	75	80	85	90	95	100
1	Engine Oil Change*—Every 12 Months, or		•		•		•		•		•		•		•		•		•		•
	Oil Filter Change*—Every 12 Months, or		•				•				•				•				•		
2	Chassis Lubrication—Every 12 Months, or		•		•		•		•		•		•		•		•		•		•
3	Clutch Fork Ball Stud Lubrication										•										
5	Cooling System Service*—Every 24 Months or								•								•				
6	Air Cleaner Filter Replacement▲*								•								•				
7	Front Wheel Bearing Repack								•								•				
8	Transmission Service																				
10	Fuel Filter Replacement*								•								•				
11	Spark Plugs Replacement*									•									•		
12	Spark Plug Wire Inspection*																				•
13	EGR System Inspection*																				•
14	Electronic Vacuum Regulator Valve (EVRV) Inspection*																				•
15	Engine Timing Check▲*								•												
16	Fuel Tank, Cap and Lines Inspection*																				
17	Thermostatically Controlled Air Cleaner Inspection▲*										•										
18	Engine Accessory Drive Belt(s) Inspection*				•				•				•				•				•
19	Evaporative Control System Inspection*				•																
20	Shields and Underhood Insulation Inspection▲■				•				•				•				•				•
21	Air Intake System Inspection▲■								•												
22	Thermostatically Controlled Engine Cooling Fan Check ▲■— Every 12 Months or				•				•								•				•
24	Tire and Wheel Rotation																				
25	Drive Axle Service																				
26	Brake Systems Inspection																				

FOOTNOTES:
*　An Emission Control Service
▲　Also a Noise Emission Control Service
■　Applicable only to vehicles sold in the United States

THE SERVICES SHOWN ON THIS CHART UP TO 60,000 MILES (100 000 km) ARE TO BE DONE AFTER 60,000 MILES AT THE SAME INTERVALS.

91021C10

6.2L AND 6.5L DIESEL ENGINES— MAINTENANCE SCHEDULE I†

Item No.	Service — Miles (000)	2.5	5	7.5	10	12.5	15	17.5	20	22.5	25	27.5	30	32.5	35	37.5	40	42.5	45	47.5	50	52.5	55	57.5	60
	Kilometers (000)	4	8	12	16	20	24	28	32	36	40	44	48	52	56	60	64	68	72	76	80	84	88	92	96
1	Engine Oil Change*—Every 3 Months, or	+	+	+	+	+	+	+	+	+	+	+	+	+	+	+	+	+	+	+	+	+	+	+	+
	Oil Filter Change*—Every 3 Months, or	+	+	+	+	+	+	+	+	+	+	+	+	+	+	+	+	+	+	+	+	+	+	+	+
2	Chassis Lubrication—Every 12 Months, or	+	+	+	+	+	+	+	+	+	+	+	+	+	+	+	+	+	+	+	+	+	+	+	+
3	Clutch Fork Ball Stud Lubrication												+												+
4	Engine Idle Speed Adjustment*		+										+												+
5	Cooling System Service*—Every 24 Months or												+												+
6	Air Cleaner Filter Replacement*★																								
7	Front Wheel Bearing Repack						+												+						
8	Transmission Service																								
9	CDRV System Inspection*																								+
10	Fuel Filter Replacement*												+												+
13	EGR System Inspection*																								+
18	Drive Belt(s) Inspection																								+
20	Shields and Underhood Insulation Inspection■▲				+					+			+				+				+				+
21	Air Intake System Inspection■▲				+					+			+				+				+				+
22	Thermostatically Controlled Engine Cooling Fan Check■▲—Every 12 Months or				+					+			+				+				+				+
23	Exhaust Pressure Regulator Valve Inspection*																								+
24	Tire and Wheel Rotation																								
25	Drive Axle Service																								
26	Brake Systems Inspection																								

FOOTNOTES:
★ Change filter every 15,000 miles (24 000 km), except when operating in dusty conditions. Dusty conditions may require more frequent filter replacement. Extreme dust and dirt operating conditions (off-road), may require the air filter to be checked as often as every 300 miles (483 km) and replaced as necessary.
* An Emission Control Service
■ Applicable only to trucks sold in the United States.
▲ Also, a Noise Control Service (applicable to vehicles with engine VIN Code J).
† This maintenance schedule applies to all diesel engines available.

THE SERVICES SHOWN ON THIS CHART UP TO 60,000 MILES (100 000 km) ARE TO BE DONE AFTER 60,000 MILES AT THE SAME INTERVALS.

91021C11

6.2L AND 6.5L DIESEL ENGINES— MAINTENANCE SCHEDULE II†

Item No.	Service — Miles (000)	2.5	5	7.5	10	12.5	15	17.5	20	22.5	25	27.5	30	32.5	35	37.5	40	42.5	45	47.5	50	52.5	55	57.5	60
	Kilometers (000)	4	8	12	16	20	24	28	32	36	40	44	48	52	56	60	64	68	72	76	80	84	88	92	96
1	Engine Oil Change*—Every 12 Months, or			•			•			•			•			•			•			•			•
	Oil Filter Change*—Every 12 Months, or			•			•			•			•			•			•			•			•
2	Chassis Lubrication—Every 12 Months, or			•			•			•			•			•			•			•			•
3	Clutch Fork Ball Stud Lubrication												•												•
4	Engine Idle Speed Adjustment*		•										•												•
5	Cooling System Service*—Every 24 Months or												•												•
6	Air Cleaner Filter Replacement*												•												•
7	Front Wheel Bearing Repack												•												•
8	Transmission Service																								
9	CDRV System Inspection*												•												•
10	Fuel Filter Replacement*												•												•
13	EGR System Inspection*												•												•
18	Drive Belt(s) Inspection												•												•
20	Shields and Underhood Insulation Inspection■▲				•					•			•				•				•				
21	Air Intake System Inspection■▲				•					•			•				•				•				
22	Thermostatically Controlled Engine Cooling Fan Check■▲—Every 12 Months or				•					•			•				•				•				
23	Exhaust Pressure Regulator Valve Inspection*												•												•
24	Tire and Wheel Rotation																								
25	Drive Axle Service																								
26	Brake Systems Inspection																								

FOOTNOTES:
* An Emission Control Service
■ Applicable only to trucks sold in the United States.
▲ Also, a Noise Control Service (applicable to vehicles with engine VIN Code J).
† This maintenance schedule applies to all diesel engines available.

THE SERVICES SHOWN ON THIS CHART UP TO 60,000 MILES (100 000 km) ARE TO BE DONE AFTER 60,000 MILES AT THE SAME INTERVALS.

91021C12

CAPACITIES

91021C14

Year	Engine ID/VIN	Engine Displacement Liters (cc)	Engine Oil with Filter	Transmission (pts.) 4-Spd	5-Spd	Auto.	Transfer Case (pts.)	Drive Axle Front (pts.)	Drive Axle Rear (pts.)	Fuel Tank (gal.)	Cooling System (qts.) W/AC	Wo/AC
1996	W	4.3 (4293)	4.5	-	⑪	⑫	-	-	③	⑧	13.0	13.0
	M	5.0 (4999)	5.0	-	⑪	⑫	⑬	④	③	⑧	18.0	17.5
	R	5.7 (5735)	5.0⑩	-	⑪	⑫	⑬	④	③	⑧	20.0⑱	17.5⑱
	F/P/S	6.5 (6489)	7.0	-	-	⑫	⑬	④	③	⑧	27.5	27.5
	J	7.4 (7440)	7.0⑨	-	⑪	⑫	⑬	④	③	⑧	27.5⑱	27.5⑱
1997	W	4.3 (4293)	4.5	-	⑪	⑫	-	-	③	⑧	13.0	13.0
	M	5.0 (4999)	5.0	-	⑪	⑫	⑬	④	③	⑧	18.0	17.5
	R	5.7 (5735)	5.0⑩	-	⑪	⑫	⑬	④	③	⑧	20.0⑱	17.5⑱
	F/P/S	6.5 (6489)	7.0	-	-	⑫	⑬	④	③	⑧	27.5	27.5
	J	7.4 (7440)	7.0⑨	-	⑪	⑫	⑬	④	③	⑧	27.5⑱	27.5⑱
1998	W	4.3 (4293)	4.5	-	⑪	⑫	-	-	③	⑧	13.0	13.0
	M	5.0 (4999)	5.0	-	⑪	⑫	⑬	④	③	⑧	18.0	17.5
	R	5.7 (5735)	5.0⑩	-	⑪	⑫	⑬	④	③	⑧	20.0⑱	17.5⑱
	F/P/S	6.5 (6489)	7.0	-	-	⑫	⑬	④	③	⑧	27.5	27.5
	J	7.4 (7440)	7.0⑨	-	⑪	⑫	⑬	④	③	⑧	27.5⑱	27.5⑱

Footnotes:

① 117mm: 8.4 pts.
  85mm: 3.6 pts.
② THM400/4B0LE: 8.4 pts.
  THM700-R4/4L60: 10.00 pts.
③ 8 1/4 in.: 4.2 pts.
  9 1/2 in. 5.5 pts.
  10 1/2 in.: 5.5 pts.
④ 15/25 Series: 3.5 pts.
  35 series: 4.4 pts.
⑤ Standard: 26 gal.
  Optional: 34 gal.
⑥ 15/25 Series: 1.4 pts.
  35 Series: 2.75 pts.
⑦ 15/25 Series: 2.3 pts.
  35 Series: 2.75 pts.
⑧ Pick-up: Short-26; Long-34
  Chassis cab: Side-22; Rear-31
⑨ C3500 HD: 6.0 qts.
⑩ 85mm: 3.6 qts.
  NVG 4500: 9.5 pts.

⑪ K1/K2: 2.8 pts.
  K3: 5.5 pts.
⑫ NVG 3500: 4.4 pts.
  NVG 4500: 8.0 pts.
⑬ C3500 HD: w/AC-25; w/o AC-26.5
⑭ C3500 HD: w/AC-28.5; w/o AC-26.5
⑮ C3500 HD: 8 pts.
⑯ C3500 HD: w/AC-27; w/o AC-26.5
⑰ 4L60: 10.00 pts.
  4L80E: 15.4 pts.
⑱ T-5: 5.92 pts.
  3500: 4.4 pts.
  4500: 8.0 pts.
⑲ 241/243: 4.5 pts.
  233/231: 2.5 pts.
  440/4470: 6.6 pts. 233/231: 2.5 pts.
  4472: 2.6 pts.

CAPACITIES

91021C13

Year	Engine ID/VIN	Engine Displacement Liters (cc)	Engine Oil with Filter	Transmission (pts.) 4-Spd	5-Spd	Auto.	Transfer Case (pts.)	Drive Axle Front (pts.)	Drive Axle Rear (pts.)	Fuel Tank (gal.)	Cooling System (qts.) W/AC	Wo/AC
1988	Z	4.3 (4293)	5.0	①	-	②	⑥	-	③	⑧	10.9	10.9
	T	4.8 (4785)	5.0	①	-	②	⑥	-	③	⑧	13.8	13.8
	H	5.0 (4999)	5.0	①	3.6	②	1.4	1.75	③	⑧	18.0	17.5
	K	5.7 (5735)	5.0	①	3.6	②	⑥	④	③	⑧	18.0	17.5
	C/J	6.2 (6210)	7.0		3.6	②	⑥	④	③	⑧	25.0	25.0
	N/W	7.4 (7440)	6.0			②	⑥	④	③	⑧	25.0	25.0
1989	Z	4.3 (4293)	5.0	①	3.6	②	⑥	-	③	⑧	10.9	10.9
	T	4.8 (4785)	5.0	①	-	②	⑥	-	③	⑧	13.8	13.8
	H	5.0 (4999)	5.0	①	3.6	②	1.4	1.75	③	⑧	18.0	17.5
	K	5.7 (5735)	5.0	①	3.6	②	⑥	④	③	⑧	18.0	17.5
	C/J	6.2 (6210)	7.0		3.6	②	⑥	④	③	⑧	25.0	25.0
	N/W	7.4 (7440)	6.0			②	⑥	④	③	⑧	25.0	25.0
1990	Z	4.3 (4293)	5.0	①	3.6	②	⑥	-	③	⑧	10.9	10.9
	H	5.0 (4999)	5.0	①	3.6	②	1.4	1.75	③	⑧	18.0	17.5
	K	5.7 (5735)	5.0	①	3.6	②	⑥	④	③	⑧	18.0	17.5
	C/J	6.2 (6210)	7.0		3.6	②	⑥	④	③	⑧	25.0	25.0
	N	7.4 (7440)	6.0			②	⑥	④	③	⑧	25.0	25.0
1991	Z	4.3 (4293)	5.0	①	-	10.0	-	-	③	⑧	10.9	10.9
	H	5.0 (4999)	5.0	①	⑳	10.0	⑥	④	③	⑧	18.0	17.5
	K	5.7 (5735)	5.0	①	⑳	10.0	⑥	④	③	⑧	18.0	18.0
	C/J	6.2 (6210)	7.0		⑳	10.0	⑥	④	③	⑧	25.0	25.0
	N	7.4 (7440)	7.0		⑳	10.0	⑥	④	③	⑧	25.0	25.0
1992	Z	4.3 (4293)	4.5		-	10.0	-	-	③	⑧	11.0	10.9
	H	5.0 (4999)	5.0		⑳	10.0	⑥	④	③	⑧	18.0	17.5
	K	5.7 (5735)	5.0⑩		⑳	10.0	⑥	④	③	⑧	18.0⑬	17.5⑬
	F	6.5 (6489)	7.0		-	10.0	⑥	④	③	⑧	25.0	25.0
	N	7.4 (7440)	7.0		⑳	10.0	⑥	④	③	⑧	26.5	26.5
1993	Z	4.3 (4293)	4.5		-	10.0	-	-	③	⑧	11.0	11.0
	H	5.0 (4999)	5.0		⑳	10.0	⑥	④	③	⑧	18.0	17.5
	K	5.7 (5735)	5.0⑩		⑳	10.0	⑥	④	③	⑧	18.0⑬	17.5⑬
	C/J	6.2 (6210)	7.0		-	10.0	⑥	④	③	⑧	25.0	25.0
	F	6.5 (6489)	7.0		-	10.0	⑥	④	③	⑧	26.5	26.5
	N	7.4 (7440)	7.0⑨		⑳	10.0	⑥	④	③	⑧	25.0⑬	23.0⑬
1994	Z	4.3 (4293)	5.0		-	10.0	-	-	③	⑧	11.0	11.0
	H	5.0 (4999)	5.0		⑳	10.0	⑥	④	③	⑧	11.0	11.0
	K	5.7 (5735)	5.0⑩		⑳	10.0	⑥	④	③	⑧	18.0⑬	17.5⑬
	F/P/S	6.5 (6489)	7.0		-	10.0	⑥	④	③	⑧	18.0	18.0
	N	7.4 (7440)	7.0⑨		⑳	10.0	⑥	④	③	⑧	25.0⑬	23.0⑬
1995	Z	4.3 (4293)	5.0		-	10.0	-	-	③	⑧	11.0	11.0
	H	5.0 (4999)	5.0		⑳	10.0	⑥	④	③	⑧	18.0	17.5
	K	5.7 (5735)	5.0⑩		⑳	10.0	⑥	④	③	⑧	18.5	18.0
	F/P/S	6.5 (6489)	7.0		-	10.0	⑥	④	③	⑧	26.5	26.5
	N	7.4 (7440)	7.0⑩		⑳	10.0	⑥	④	③	⑧	25.0	25.0

2

ENGINE
ELECTRICAL

HIGH ENERGY IGNITION (HEI) SYSTEM

Description and Operation

▶ **See Figures 1 and 2**

The General Motors HEI system is a pulse-triggered, transistorized controlled, inductive discharge ignition system. The entire HEI system (except for the ignition coil) is contained within the distributor cap.

The distributor, in addition to housing the mechanical and vacuum advance mechanisms, contains the electronic control module, and the magnetic triggering device. The magnetic pick-up assembly contains a permanent magnet, a pole piece with internal teeth, and a pick-up coil (not to be confused with the ignition coil).

In the HEI system, as in other electronic ignition systems, the breaker points have been replaced with an electronic switch—a transistor—which is located

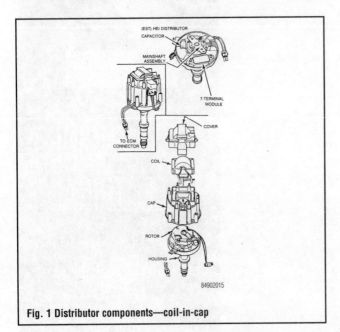

Fig. 1 Distributor components—coil-in-cap

84902015

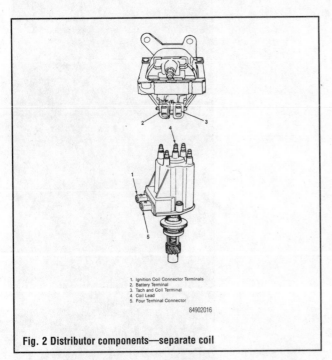

1. Ignition Coil Connector Terminals
2. Battery Terminal
3. Tach and Coil Terminal
4. Coil Lead
5. Four Terminal Connector

84902016

Fig. 2 Distributor components—separate coil

within the control module. This switching transistor performs the same function the points did in an conventional ignition system. It simply turns coil primary current on and off at the correct time. Essentially then, electronic and conventional ignition systems operate on the same principle.

The module which houses the switching transistor is controlled (turned on and off) by a magnetically generated impulse induced in the pick-up coil. When the teeth of the rotating timer align with the teeth of the pole piece, the induced voltage in the pick-up coil signals the electronic module to open the coil primary circuit. The primary current then decreases, and a high voltage is induced in the ignition coil secondary windings which is then directed through the rotor and high voltage leads (spark plug wires) to fire the spark plugs.

In essence then, the pick-up coil module system simply replaces the conventional breaker points and condenser. The condenser found within the distributor is for radio suppression purposes only and has nothing to do with the ignition process. The module automatically controls the dwell period, increasing it with increasing engine speed. Since dwell is automatically controlled, it cannot be adjusted. The module itself is non-adjustable and non-repairable and must be replaced if found defective.

HEI SYSTEM PRECAUTIONS

Before going on to troubleshooting, it might be a good idea to take note of the following precautions:

Timing Light Use

Inductive pick-up timing lights are the best kind to use if your truck is equipped with HEI. Timing lights which connect between the spark plug and the spark plug wire occasionally (not always) give false readings.

Spark Plug Wires

The plug wires used with HEI systems are of a different construction than conventional wires. When replacing them, make sure you get the correct wires, since conventional wires won't carry the voltage. Also, handle them carefully to avoid cracking or splitting them and never pierce them.

Tachometer Use

Not all tachometers will operate or indicate correctly when used on a HEI system. While some tachometers may give a reading, this does not necessarily mean the reading is correct. In addition, some tachometers hook up differently from others. If you can't figure out whether or not your tachometer will work on your truck, check with the tachometer manufacturer.

HEI Systems Testers

Instruments designed specifically for testing HEI systems are available from several tool manufacturers. Some of these will even test the module itself. However, the tests given in the following section will require only an ohmmeter and a voltmeter.

Diagnosis and Testing

The symptoms of a defective component within the HEI system are exactly the same as those you would encounter in a conventional system. Some of these symptoms are:
- Hard or no Starting
- Rough Idle
- Fuel Poor Economy
- Engine misses under load or while accelerating

If you suspect a problem in the ignition system, there are certain preliminary checks which you should carry out before you begin to check the electronic portions of the system. First, it is extremely important to make sure the vehicle battery is in a good state of charge. A defective or poorly charged battery will cause the various components of the ignition system to read incorrectly when they are being tested. Second, make sure all wiring connections are clean and tight, not only at the battery, but also at the distributor cap, ignition coil, and at the electronic control module.

SECONDARY SPARK TEST

Since the only change between electronic and conventional ignition systems is in the distributor component area, it is imperative to check the secondary ignition circuit first. If the secondary circuit checks out properly, then the engine condition is probably not the fault of the ignition system. To check the secondary ignition system, perform a simple spark test.

1. Remove one of the plug wires and insert some sort of extension in the plug socket. An old spark plug with the ground electrode removed makes a good extension.

2. Hold the wire and extension about ¼ in. (.009mm) away from the block and crank the engine. If a normal spark occurs, then the problem is most likely not in the ignition system.

3. Check for fuel system problems, or fouled spark plugs.

4. If, however, there is no spark or a weak spark, then further ignition system testing will have to be done. Troubleshooting techniques fall into two categories, depending on the nature of the problem. The categories are (1) Engine cranks, but won't start or (2) Engine runs, but runs rough or cuts out.

Engine Fails to Start

1. If the engine won't start, perform a spark test as described earlier. If no spark occurs, check for the presence of normal battery voltage at the battery (**BAT**) terminal in the distributor cap. The ignition switch must be in the **ON** position for this test.

2. If battery voltage is not present, this indicates an open circuit in the ignition primary wiring leading to the distributor. In this case, you will have to check wiring continuity back to the ignition switch using a test light.

3. If there is battery voltage at the **BAT** terminal, but no spark at the plugs, then the problem lies within the distributor assembly. Go on to test the ignition coil.

Engine Runs, But Runs Roughly or Cuts Out

1. Make sure the plug wires are in good shape first. There should be no obvious cracks or breaks. You can check the plug wires with an ohmmeter, but do not pierce the wires with a probe.

2. If the plug wires are OK, remove the cap assembly, and check for moisture, cracks, chips, or carbon tracks, or any other high voltage leaks or failures.

3. Replace the cap if you find any defects. Make sure the timer wheel rotates when the engine is cranked. If everything is all right so far, go on to test the ignition coil.

IGNITION COIL

Carbureted Engines

1. Connect an ohmmeter between the **TACH** and **BAT** terminals in the distributor cap. The primary coil resistance should be less than one ohm (zero or nearly zero).

2. To check the coil secondary resistance, connect an ohmmeter between the rotor button and the **BAT** terminal. Then connect the ohmmeter between the

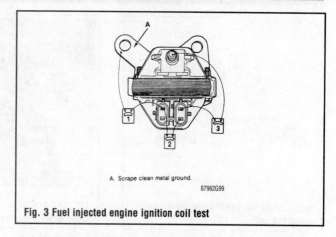

A. Scrape clean metal ground.

87982G99

Fig. 3 Fuel injected engine ignition coil test

ground terminal and the rotor button. The resistance in both cases should be between 6000 and 30,000 ohms.

3. Replace the coil only if the readings in Step 1 and 2 are infinite.

➡ **These resistance checks will not disclose shorted coil windings. This condition can be detected only with scope analysis or a suitably designed coil tester. If these instruments are unavailable, replace the coil with a known good coil as a final coil test.**

Fuel Injected Engines

♦ See Figure 3

1. Tag and disconnect the distributor lead and wiring from the coil.

2. Connect an ohmmeter as shown in Step 1 of the accompanying illustration. Place the ohmmeter on the high scale. The reading should be infinite.

3. Connect an ohmmeter as shown in Step 2 of the same illustration. Place the ohmmeter on the low scale. The reading should be very low or zero. If not replace the coil.

4. Connect an ohmmeter as shown in Step 3 of the same illustration. Place the ohmmeter on the high scale. The meter should not read infinite. If it does replace the coil.

5. Connect the distributor lead and wiring.

PICK-UP COIL

♦ See Figures 4, 5 and 6

1. To test the pick-up coil, first disconnect the white and green module leads. Set the ohmmeter on the high scale and connect it between a ground and either the white or green lead. Any resistance measurement less than infinity requires replacement of the pick-up coil.

2. Pick-up coil continuity is tested by connecting the ohmmeter (on low range) between the white and green leads. Normal resistance is between 500 and 1500 ohms. Move the vacuum advance arm while performing this test. This will detect any break in coil continuity. Such a condition can cause intermittent misfiring. Replace the pick-up coil if the reading is outside the specified limits.

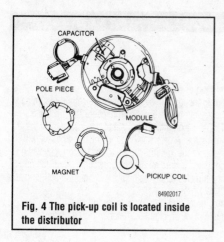

84902017

Fig. 4 The pick-up coil is located inside the distributor

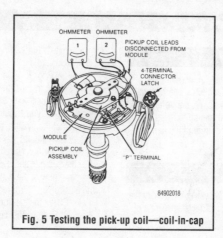

84902018

Fig. 5 Testing the pick-up coil—coil-in-cap

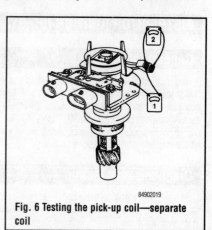

84902019

Fig. 6 Testing the pick-up coil—separate coil

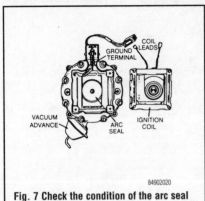

Fig. 7 Check the condition of the arc seal under the coil

Fig. 8 Be careful not to break the locktabs when unplugging the connectors

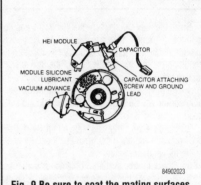

Fig. 9 Be sure to coat the mating surfaces with silicone lubricant

3. If no defects have been found at this time, and you still have a problem, then the module will have to be checked. If you do not have access to a module tester, the only possible alternative is a substitution test. If the module fails the substitution test, replace it.

Ignition Coil

REMOVAL & INSTALLATION

Carbureted Engines

♦ See Figure 7

1. Disconnect the feed and module wire terminal connectors from the distributor cap.
2. Remove the ignition set retainer.
3. Remove the 4 coil cover-to-distributor cap screws and coil cover.
4. Remove the 4 coil-to-distributor cap screws.
5. Using a blunt drift, press the coil wire spade terminals up out of distributor cap.
6. Lift the coil up out of the distributor cap.
7. Remove and clean the coil spring, rubber seal washer and coil cavity of the distributor cap.
8. Coat the rubber seal with a dielectric lubricant furnished in the replacement ignition coil package.
9. Reverse the above procedures to install.

Fuel Injected Engines

♦ See Figure 8

1. Make sure that the ignition switch is in the **OFF** position.
2. Tag and disconnect the coil wire and the connector on the side of the coil.

3. Remove the nuts holding the coil and bracket assembly to the engine and lift out the coil. The coil is riveted to the bracket, to remove it will require drilling the rivets and punching them out.
4. Position the coil on the engine and tighten the nuts.
5. Connect the coil wire and electrical connectors.

Vacuum Advance Unit

REMOVAL & INSTALLATION

1. Remove the distributor cap and rotor as previously described.
2. Disconnect the vacuum hose from the vacuum advance unit.
3. Remove the two vacuum advance retaining screws, pull the advance unit outward, rotate and disengage the operating rod from its tang.
4. Reverse the above procedure to install.

Ignition Module

REMOVAL & INSTALLATION

♦ See Figure 9

1. Remove the distributor cap and rotor as previously described.
2. Disconnect the harness connector and pickup coil spade connectors from the module. Be careful not to damage the wires when removing the connector.
3. Remove the two screws and module from the distributor housing.
4. Coat the bottom of the new module with dielectric silicone lubricant. This is usually supplied with the new module. Reverse the above procedure to install.

DISTRIBUTOR IGNITION (DI) SYSTEM

General Information

The Distributor Ignition (DI) system consists of the distributor, Hall effect switch (camshaft position sensor), ignition coil, secondary wires, spark plugs, knock sensor and the crankshaft position sensor. The system is controlled by the Vehicle Control Module (VCM). The VCM using information from various engine sensors, controls the spark timing, dwell, and the firing of the ignition coil. It is used on the 1993–98 models.

Diagnosis and Testing

The symptoms of a defective component within the DI system are exactly the same as those you would encounter in a conventional or HEI system. Some of these symptoms are:

- Hard or no Starting
- Rough Idle
- Fuel Poor Economy
- Engine misses under load or while accelerating

If you suspect a problem in the ignition system, there are certain preliminary checks which you should carry out before you begin to check the electronic portions of the system. First, it is extremely important to make sure the vehicle battery is in a good state of charge. A defective or poorly charged battery will cause the various components of the ignition system to read incorrectly when they are being tested. Second, make sure all wiring connections are clean and tight, not only at the battery, but also at the distributor cap, ignition coil, and at the electronic control module.

1. Check the cap for tiny holes and carbon tracks as follows.
   a. Remove the cap and place an ohmmeter lead on the cap terminal.

b. Use the other lead to probe all the other terminals and the center carbon ball.

2. If the readings are not infinite, the cap must be replaced.

SECONDARY SPARK TEST

It is imperative to check the secondary ignition circuit first. If the secondary circuit checks out properly, then the engine condition is probably not the fault of the ignition system. To check the secondary ignition system, perform a simple spark test.

1. Remove one of the plug wires and insert some sort of extension in the plug socket. An old spark plug with the ground electrode removed makes a good extension.

2. Hold the wire and extension about ¼ in. (0.25mm) away from the block and crank the engine.

3. If a normal spark occurs, then the problem is most likely not in the ignition system. Check for fuel system problems, or fouled spark plugs.

4. If, however, there is no spark or a weak spark, then test the ignition coil and the camshaft and crankshaft position sensors. For testing the camshaft and crankshaft position sensors, refer to Section 4.

IGNITION COIL

▶ **See Figure 10**

➡**Make sure the ignition switch is OFF.**

1. Tag and disconnect the wires from the ignition coil.

2. Using a digital ohmmeter set on the high scale, probe the ignition coil as shown in Step 1 of the accompanying illustration.

3. The reading should be infinite. If not replace the coil.

4. Using the low scale of the ohmmeter, probe the ignition coil as shown in Step 2 of the accompanying illustration. The reading should be 0.1 ohms, if not replace the coil.

5. Using the high scale of the ohmmeter, probe the ignition coil as shown in

Step 3 of the accompanying illustration. The reading should be 5k–25k ohms, if not replace the coil.

6. Reconnect the wires to the ignition coil.

Ignition Coil

REMOVAL & INSTALLATION

▶ **See Figures 11, 12 and 13**

1. Tag and unplug the wiring connectors from the coil and the coil wire.

2. Unfasten the retainers securing the coil bracket and coil to the manifold.

3. Remove the coil and bracket and drill out the two rivets securing the coil to the bracket.

4. Remove the coil from the bracket.

To install:

➡**The replacement coil kit may come with the two screws to attach the coil to the bracket. If not, you must supply your own screws.**

5. Fasten the coil to the bracket using two screws.

6. Fasten the coil and bracket to the manifold. Tighten the retainers until they are snug.

7. Engage the coil wire and the wiring connectors to the coil.

Distributor

REMOVAL

▶ **See Figures 14, 15, 16 and 17**

1. Disconnect the negative battery cable.

2. Tag and remove the spark plug wires and the coil leads from the distributor.

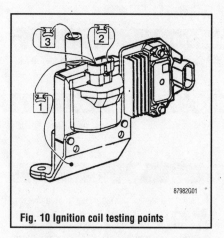

Fig. 10 Ignition coil testing points

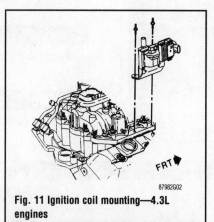

Fig. 11 Ignition coil mounting—4.3L engines

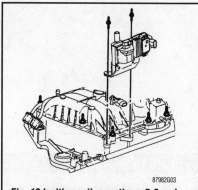

Fig. 12 Ignition coil mounting—5.0 and 5.7L engines

Fig. 13 Ignition coil mounting—7.4L engines

Fig. 14 Mark the distributor and tag the spark plug wires

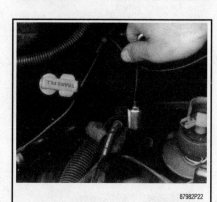

Fig. 15 A distributor wrench can be used to loosen the hold-down bolt

3. Unplug the electrical connector at the base of the distributor.
4. Loosen the distributor cap fasteners and remove the cap.
5. Using a marker, matchmark the rotor-to-housing and housing-to-engine block positions so that they can be matched during installation.
6. Loosen and remove the distributor hold-down bolt and clamp.
7. Remove the distributor from the engine.

INSTALLATION

Engine Not Disturbed

1. Install the distributor in the engine making sure that the matchmarks are properly aligned.
2. If the rotor-to-housing and housing-to-engine marks are not aligned, the distributor gear may be off a tooth or more. If this is the case repeat the installation process until the marks are perfectly aligned.
3. Install the hold-down clamp and bolt, then tighten the bolt to 20 ft. lbs. (27 Nm).
4. Install the distributor cap and attach the electrical connector at the base of the distributor.
5. Attach the spark plug wires and coil leads.
6. Connect the negative battery cable.

Engine Disturbed

1. Remove the No. 1 cylinder spark plug.
2. Turn the engine using a socket wrench on the large bolt on the front of the crankshaft pulley. Place a finger near the No. 1 spark plug hole and turn the

Fig. 16 Remove the distributor hold-down bolt and clamp

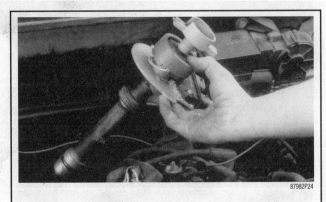

Fig. 17 Be sure to mark the distributor position before removing it

crankshaft until the piston reaches Top Dead Center (TDC). As the engine approaches TDC, you will feel air being expelled by the No. 1 cylinder. If the position is not being met, turn the engine another full turn (360 degree). Once the engine's position is correct, install the spark plug.
3. Align the pre-drilled indent hole in the distributor driven gear with the white painted alignment line on the lower portion of the shaft housing.
4. Using a long screwdriver, align the oil pump drive shaft in the engine in the mating drive tab in the distributor.
5. Install the distributor in the engine.
6. When the distributor is fully seated, the rotor segment should be aligned with the pointer cast in the distributor base. The pointer will have a "6" or "8" cast into it indicating a 6 or 8-cylinder engine. If the rotor segment is not within a few degrees of the pointer, the distributor gear may be off a tooth or more. If this is the case repeat the process until the rotor aligns with the pointer.
7. Install the cap and fasten the mounting screws.
8. Install the hold-down clamp and bolt, then tighten the bolt to 20 ft. lbs. (27 Nm).
9. Engage the electrical connections and the spark plug wires.

Crankshaft Position Sensor

For information on the Crankshaft Position (CKP) sensor, please refer to Section 4.

Camshaft Position Sensor

For information on the Camshaft Position (CMP) sensor, please refer to Section 4.

FIRING ORDERS

♦ **See Figures 18, 19, 20 and 21**

➡ **To avoid confusion, remove and tag the spark plug wires one at a time, for replacement.**

If a distributor is not keyed for installation with only one orientation, it could have been removed previously and rewired. The resultant wiring would hold the correct firing order, but could change the relative placement of the plug towers in relation to the engine. For this reason it is imperative that you label all wires before disconnecting any of them. Also, before removal, compare the current wiring with the accompanying illustrations. If the current wiring does not match, make notes in your book to reflect how your engine is wired.

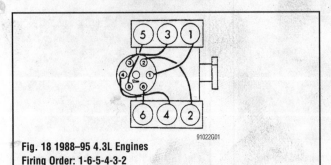

Fig. 18 1988–95 4.3L Engines
Firing Order: 1-6-5-4-3-2
Distributor Rotation: Clockwise

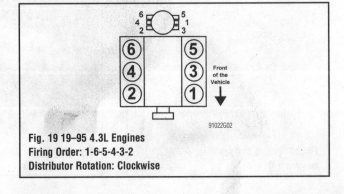

Fig. 19 19–95 4.3L Engines
Firing Order: 1-6-5-4-3-2
Distributor Rotation: Clockwise

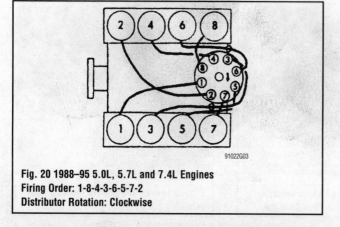

Fig. 20 1988–95 5.0L, 5.7L and 7.4L Engines
Firing Order: 1-8-4-3-6-5-7-2
Distributor Rotation: Clockwise

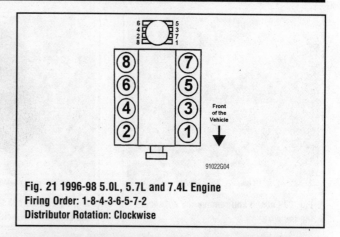

Fig. 21 1996-98 5.0L, 5.7L and 7.4L Engine
Firing Order: 1-8-4-3-6-5-7-2
Distributor Rotation: Clockwise

CHARGING SYSTEM

Alternator Precautions

To prevent damage to the alternator and regulator, the following precautionary measures must be taken when working with the electrical system.
• Never reverse the battery connections. Always check the battery polarity visually. This is to be done before any connections are made to ensure that all of the connections correspond to the battery ground polarity of the car.
• Booster batteries must be connected properly. Make sure the positive cable of the booster battery is connected to the positive terminal of the battery which is getting the boost.
• Disconnect the battery cables before using a fast charger; the charger has a tendency to force current through the diodes in the opposite direction for which they were designed.
• Never use a fast charger as a booster for starting the vehicle.
• Never disconnect the voltage regulator while the engine is running, unless as noted for testing purposes.
• Do not ground the alternator output terminal.
• Do not operate the alternator on an open circuit with the field energized.
• Do not attempt to polarize the alternator.
• Disconnect the battery cables and remove the alternator before using an electric arc welder on the vehicle.
• Protect the alternator from excessive moisture. If the engine is to be steam cleaned, cover or remove the alternator.

Alternator

TESTING

▶ **See Figure 22**

If you suspect a defect in your charging system, first perform these general checks before going on to more specific tests.
1. Check the condition of the alternator belt and tighten it if necessary.
2. Clean the battery cable connections at the battery. Make sure the connections between the battery wires and the battery clamps are good. Reconnect the negative terminal only and proceed to the next step.
3. With the key **OFF**, insert a test light between the positive terminal on the battery and the disconnected positive battery terminal clamp. If the test light comes on, there is a short in the electrical system of the truck. The short must be repaired before proceeding. If the light does not come on, proceed to the next step.

➡ **If the truck is equipped with an electric clock, the clock must be disconnected.**

4. Check the charging system wiring for any obvious breaks or shorts.
5. Check the battery to make sure it is fully charged and in good condition.
There are many possible ways in which the charging system can malfunction. Often the source of a problem is difficult to diagnose, requiring special equipment and a good deal of experience. This is usually not the case, however, where the charging system fails completely and causes the dashboard warning

light to come on or the battery to become dead. To troubleshoot a complete system failure only two pieces of equipment are needed: a test light, to determine that current is reaching a certain point; and a current indicator (ammeter), to determine the direction of the current flow and its measurement in amps.
This test works under three assumptions:
• The battery is known to be good and fully charged.
• The alternator belt is in good condition and adjusted to the proper tension.
• All connections in the system are clean and tight.

➡ **In order for the current indicator to give a valid reading, the truck must be equipped with battery cables which are of the same gauge size and quality as original equipment battery cables.**

6. With the ignition switch **ON**, engine not running, the charge indicator light should be on. If not disengage the wiring harness at the alternator and use a fused jumper wire with a 5-amp fuse, ground the "L" terminal in the wiring harness.
   a. If the lamp lights, replace the alternator.
   b. If the lamp does not light, check for an open circuit between the grounding lead and the ignition switch.
7. With the ignition switch **ON** and the engine running, the lamp should be off. If not, stop the engine, turn the ignition switch **ON**, and disconnect the wiring harness.
   a. If the lamp goes out, replace the alternator.
   b. If the lamp stays on, check for a grounded "L" terminal wire.
8. If the vehicle voltmeter shows high or low voltage readings with the engine running:
   a. Disengage the wiring harness from the alternator.
   b. With the engine off and ignition switch **ON**, connect a digital multimeter set on the DC scale, from ground to the "L" terminal in the wiring harness. The reading should be battery voltage, if not there is an open, grounded or high resistance circuit between the terminal and the battery. Repair this circuit before performing any more tests.

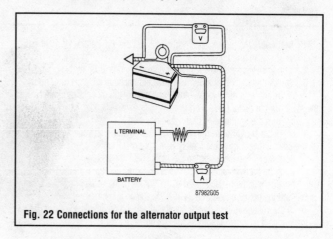

Fig. 22 Connections for the alternator output test

Fig. 23 Loosen and remove the nut securing the wire

Fig. 24 Don't break the locktab securing the harness connector in the alternator

Fig. 25 Loosen and remove the alternator retaining bolts . . .

9. Engage the harness connect to the alternator and run the engine at 2500 RPM with the accessories off.

10. Measure the voltage at the battery. If it is above 16 volts, replace the alternator.

11. With the engine off, connect an ammeter at the alternator output terminal. The ammeter must have the capability to measure 115 amps of current.

12. Connect a digital multimeter set on the DC scale across the alternator and a carbon pile across the battery.

    a. Run the engine at 2500 RPM, turn on all the accessories and load the battery with a carbon pile to obtain maximum amperage. Maintain voltage at 13 volts or more.

    b. If the output is within 15 amps of the rated output, the alternator is OK. Refer to the alternator specifications in this section.

    c. If the output is not within 15 amps, the alternator must be replaced.

REMOVAL & INSTALLATION

▶ **See Figures 23, 24, 25 and 26**

1. Disconnect the negative battery cable.
2. Disconnect and tag all wiring to the alternator.
3. If equipped, remove the alternator brace bolt.
4. Remove the drive belt.
5. Support the alternator and remove the mounting bolts. Remove the alternator.

To install:

6. Install the unit and tighten the bolts to the following torques:

On 4.3L, 4.8L, 5.0L and 5.7L engines:
- Top (right) mount bolt: 18 ft. lbs. (25 Nm)
- Lower (left) mount bolt: 37 ft. lbs. (50 Nm)
- Bracket bolt: 18 ft. lbs. (25 Nm)

Fig. 26 . . . then remove the alternator from the vehicle

On 7.4L engines:
- Lower mount bolt: 18 ft. lbs. (25 Nm)
- Upper mount bolt: 37 ft. lbs. (50 Nm)
- Upper bracket bolt: 18 ft. lbs. (25 Nm)
- Lower bracket bolt: 24 ft. lbs. (33 Nm)

On 6.2L and 6.5L diesel engines:
- Top mount bolt: 18 ft. lbs. (25 Nm)
- Lower mount nut: 17 ft. lbs. (23 Nm)
- Bracket bolt: 18 ft. lbs. (25 Nm)

7. Reconnect the wire at the alternator.
8. Reconnect the negative battery cable.
9. Adjust the belt to have ½ in. (13mm) depression under thumb pressure on its longest run.

STARTING SYSTEM

Starter

TESTING

1. Make sure the battery is fully charged and that the battery terminal connections are clean and tight.

2. Check the starter motor wiring for damage and/or open and shorted wires.

3. Check that all starter motor electrical connections are clean and tight.

4. If the starter motor cranks slowly and the solenoid clicks or chatters, test the starter motor as follows:

    a. Turn the ignition key to the start position.

    b. Use a Digital Volt Ohm Meter (DVOM) set to read voltage. Measure the cranking voltage at the battery terminal posts.

    c. If the voltage is less than 9.6 volts check the battery.

    d. If the battery voltage is 9.6 volts or more continue with the test.

    e. Connect the negative lead of the DVOM to the battery negative terminal and the positive lead of the DVOM to the engine block.

5. If the voltage is less than 0.5 volts, attach the positive lead of the DVOM to the starter **B** terminal and crank the engine.

6. If the voltage reading is less than 9.0 volts, replace the starter motor.

7. If the starter motor does not crank and there is no sound from the solenoid, test the starter motor as follows:

    a. Turn the headlights and the dome light on.

    b. Turn the ignition key to the **START** position.

    c. If the lights stay bright, turn the radio, heater and turn signals on.

    d. If the accessories you have turned on do not operate properly, check the bulkhead connector fusible link and the ignition switch connections.

    e. If the accessories operate properly, continue with the test.

    f. Make sure the ignition key is still in the **START** position.

    g. If your vehicle is equipped with a automatic transmission, using a Digital Volt Ohm Meter (DVOM) set to read voltage, connect the negative lead of the DVOM to the battery negative terminal and the positive lead of the DVOM to the starter **S** terminal.

    h. If the voltage is 9.6 volts or more, replace the starter motor.

    i. If the voltage is 9.6 volts or less, attach the positive lead of the DVOM to the ignition switch solenoid terminal.

    j. If the voltage is 9.6 volts or more, repair the purple wire from the ignition switch to the starter.

    k. If the voltage is less than 9.6 volts, replace the ignition switch.

l. If your vehicle is equipped with a manual transmission, using a Digital Volt Ohm Meter (DVOM) set to read voltage, connect the negative lead of the DVOM to a good known ground and the positive lead of the DVOM to the neutral/start switch. Turn the ignition key to the **START** position and depress the clutch.

m. If there is more than 9.6 volts present at one terminal, test the switch connector and adjustment. If the adjustment and connector are functioning properly, replace the switch.

n. If there is less than 9.6 volts present at both terminals, make sure the ignition key is still in the **START** position.

o. Test the voltage at the ignition switch solenoid terminal.

p. If the voltage is 9.6 volts or more, repair the yellow feed wire from the ignition switch.

q. If the voltage is less than 9.6 volts, replace the ignition switch.

REMOVAL & INSTALLATION

▶ **See Figures 27, 28, 29 and 30**

The following is a general procedure for all trucks covered in this manual, and may vary slightly depending on model and series.
1. Disconnect the negative battery cable at the battery.
2. Raise and support the vehicle.
3. Disconnect and tag all wires at the solenoid terminal.

➡**Reinstall all nuts as soon as they are removed, since the thread sizes are different.**

4. Remove the front bracket from the starter and the mounting bolts. On engines with a solenoid heat shield, remove the front bracket upper bolt and detach the bracket from the starter.
5. Remove the front bracket bolt or nut. Lower the starter, front end first, then remove the unit from the truck.
To install:
6. Position the starter and tighten all bolts as follows:
R/V Series:
- Thru-bolts: 40 ft. lbs. (54 Nm)
- Bracket bolt: 30 ft. lbs. (41 Nm)

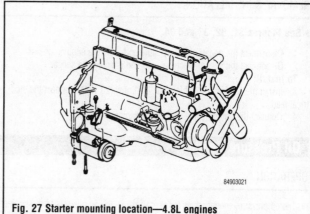
Fig. 27 Starter mounting location—4.8L engines

- Nut (gas): 11 ft. lbs. (15 Nm)
- Nut (diesel): 90 inch lbs. (10 Nm)
C/K Series:
- Thru-bolts: 35 ft. lbs. (45 Nm)
- Bracket bolt (diesel): 24 ft. lbs. (33 Nm)
- Nut (diesel): 75 inch lbs. (8.5 Nm)
7. Reconnect all wires.

SOLENOID REPLACEMENT

1. Disconnect the negative battery cable.
2. Remove the screw and washer from the field strap terminal.
3. Remove the two solenoid-to-housing retaining screws and the motor terminal bolt.
4. Remove the solenoid by twisting the unit 90 degrees.
5. To replace the solenoid, reverse the above procedure. Make sure the return spring is on the plunger, and rotate the solenoid unit into place on the starter.

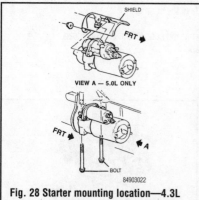
Fig. 28 Starter mounting location—4.3L and 5.0L engines; 5.7L and 7.4L similar

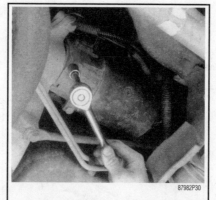
Fig. 29 Remove the starter retaining bolts

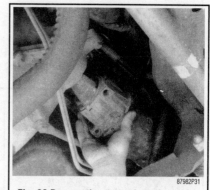
Fig. 30 Remove the starter from the vehicle

SENDING UNITS AND SENSORS

The sensors covered in this section are not related to engine control. They are for gauges and warning lights only. For sensors related to engine control refer to Electronic Engine Controls in Section 4.

Coolant Temperature Sender

OPERATION

The coolant temperature sender changes resistance as the coolant temperature increases and decreases.

TESTING

1. Check the instrument cluster fuse condition and replace as necessary.
2. Check the sender wire for damage and repair as necessary.
3. Unplug the sender electrical connection.
4. Attach one end of a jumper wire to the sender electrical connector and the other end of the jumper wire to ground.
5. If the gauge functions properly, replace the sender.

REMOVAL & INSTALLATION

♦ See Figures 31, 32, 33 and 34

1. Disconnect the negative battery cable and drain the engine coolant.
2. Disconnect the sensor electrical lead and unscrew the sensor.
To install:
3. Install the sensor and tighten it to 17 ft. lbs. (23 Nm). Connect the electrical lead.
4. Connect the battery cable and fill the engine with coolant.

Oil Pressure Sender

OPERATION

The oil pressure sender relays to the dash gauge the oil pressure in the engine.

TESTING

1. Check the instrument cluster fuse condition and replace as necessary.
2. Check the sender wire for damage and repair as necessary.
3. Unplug the sender electrical connection.
4. Attach one end of a jumper wire to the sender electrical connector and the other end of the jumper wire to ground.
5. If the gauge reads functions properly, replace the sender.

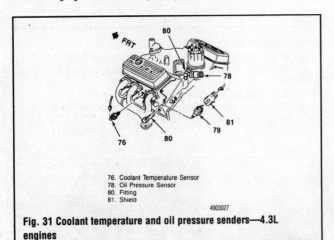

76. Coolant Temperature Sensor
78. Oil Pressure Sensor
80. Fitting
81. Shield

4903027

Fig. 31 Coolant temperature and oil pressure senders—4.3L engines

REMOVAL & INSTALLATION

1. Disconnect the negative battery cable and drain the engine oil.
2. Disconnect the sensor electrical lead and unscrew the sensor. The sensor can be found on the top side of the engine, near the distributor.
To install:
3. Coat the first two or three threads with sealer. Install the sensor and tighten until snug. Engage the electrical lead.
4. Connect the battery cable and fill the engine with oil.

Auxiliary Fan Switch

OPERATION

The auxiliary fan circuit contains the auxiliary fan, coolant temperature sensor and a relay. When the sensor reaches a predetermined temperature, it closes the circuit to the relay. This energizes the relay sending 12 volts to the auxiliary fan. When the temperature decreases below the set point of the sensor, the circuit opens and the voltage is no longer applied to the auxiliary fan.

TESTING

1. Check the condition of the fan switch and wiring. Repair as necessary.
2. Attach one end of a jumper wire to a good 12 volt power source and the other end of the jumper wire to the orange wire at the cooling fan relay.
3. The fan should operate. If the fan does operate the switch is probably defective.
4. If the fan does not operate, unplug the fan electrical harness and apply 12 volts directly to the fan. If the fan does not operate, the fan motor is probably defective. If the fan does operate, the relay could be defective.

REMOVAL & INSTALLATION

1. Disconnect the negative battery cable.
2. Disconnect the sensor electrical lead and unscrew the sensor. The sensor can be found on the right side of the engine.
To install:
3. Install the sensor or relay and connect the electrical lead.
4. Connect the battery cable.

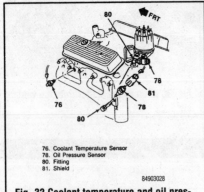

76. Coolant Temperature Sensor
78. Oil Pressure Sensor
80. Fitting
81. Shield

84903028

Fig. 32 Coolant temperature and oil pressure senders—5.0L and 5.7L engines

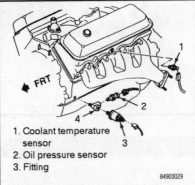

1. Coolant temperature sensor
2. Oil pressure sensor
3. Fitting

84903029

Fig. 33 Coolant temperature and oil pressure senders—7.4L engines

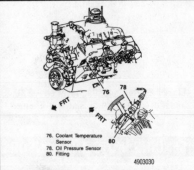

76. Coolant Temperature Sensor
78. Oil Pressure Sensor
80. Fitting

4903030

Fig. 34 Coolant temperature and oil pressure senders—6.2L and 6.5L diesel engines

3

ENGINE AND ENGINE OVERHAUL

4.3L VIN Z ENGINE MECHANICAL SPECIFICATIONS

Description	English Specifications	Metric Specifications
General Information		
Engine type	V6	
Displacement	4.3L	262
Bore	4.00 in.	101.64mm
Stroke	3.480 in.	88.88mm
Firing order	1-6-5-4-3-2	
Oil pressure	①	①
Cylinder Bore		
Diameter	4.0007-4.0017 in.	101.618-101.643mm
Out-of-round (max.)	0.001 in.	0.02mm
Taper		
Thrust side (max.)	0.0005 in.	0.012mm
Relief side (max.)	0.001 in.	0.02mm
Piston		
Clearance	0.0007-0.0017 in.	0.0177-0.0431mm
Piston Ring		
Compression rings		
Groove clearance		
Top	0.0012-0.0032 in.	0.0304-0.0812mm
Second	0.0012-0.0032 in.	0.0304-0.0812mm
Gap		
Top	0.010-0.020 in.	0.254-0.508mm
Second	0.010-0.025 in.	0.2540-0.635mm
Oil rings		
Groove clearance	0.002-0.007 in.	0.050-0.177mm
Gap	0.015-0.055 in.	0.381-1.397mm
Piston Pin		
Diameter	0.9270-0.9273 in.	23.545-23.548mm
Clearance in piston	0.0002-0.0007 in.	0.0050-0.0177mm
Fit in rod (interference)	0.0008-0.0016 in.	0.0203-0.0406mm
Crankshaft		
Main journal		
Diameter		
No.1	2.4484-2.4493 in.	62.189-62.212mm
Nos. 2, 3 and 4	2.4481-2.4490 in.	62.18162.204mm
No.4	2.4479-2.4488 in.	62.176-62.199mm
Taper		
Production (max.)	0.0002 in.	0.0050mm
Service limit (max.)	0.001 in.	0.0254mm
Out-of-round		
Production (max.)	0.0002 in.	0.0050mm
Service limit (max.)	0.001 in.	0.0254mm
Main bearing clearance		
Production		
No.1	0.0008-0.0020 in.	0.0203-0.0508mm
Nos. 2, 3 and 4	0.0011-0.0023 in.	0.0279-0.05842mm
No.4	0.0017-0.0032 in.	0.04318-0.08128mm

91023C01

4.3L VIN Z ENGINE MECHANICAL SPECIFICATIONS

Description	English Specifications	Metric Specifications
Crankshaft (cont.)		
Main bearing clearance (cont.)		
Service limit		
No.1	0.0010-0.0015 in.	0.0254-0.0381mm
Nos. 2 and 3	0.0010-0.0025 in.	0.0254-0.0635mm
No. 4	0.0025-0.0035 in.	0.0635-0.0889mm
Crankshaft end-play	0.005-0.018 in.	0.127-0.4572mm
Crankshaft run-out (max.)	0.001 in.	0.0254mm
Crankpin		
Taper		
Production	0.0005 in.	0.0127mm
Service limit (max.)	0.001 in.	0.0254mm
Out-of-round		
Production	0.0005 in.	0.0127mm
Service limit (max.)	0.001 in.	0.0254mm
Rod bearing clearance		
Production	0.0013-0.0035 in.	0.03302-0.0889mm
Service limit	0.0030 in.	0.0762mm
Rod side clearance	0.015-0.046 in.	0.381-1.1684mm
Camshaft		
Lobe lift		
Intake	0.232-0.236 in.	5.892-5.994mm
Exhaust	0.255-0.259 in.	6.477-6.578mm
Journal diameter	1.8682-1.8692 in.	47.452-47.477mm
Camshaft end-play	0.004-0.012 in.	0.101-0.304mm
Valve System		
Lifter	Hydraulic	
Rocker arm ratio	1.50:1	
Valve lash		
Intake/Exhaust	②	②
Face angle		
Intake/Exhaust	45°	
Seat angle		
Intake/Exhaust	46°	
Seat run-out (max.)		
Intake/Exhaust	0.002 in.	0.0508mm
Seat width		
Intake	0.035-0.060 in.	0.889-1.524mm
Exhaust	0.062-0.093 in.	1.5748-2.3622mm
Stem clearance		
Production		
Intake	0.0010-0.0027 in.	0.0254-0.0685mm
Exhaust	0.0010-0.0027 in.	0.0254-0.0685mm
Service (high limit production)		
Intake	+ 0.001 in.	+ 0.0254mm
Exhaust	+ 0.002 in.	+ 0.0508mm

91023C02

4.3L VIN Z ENGINE MECHANICAL SPECIFICATIONS

Description	English Specifications	Metric Specifications
Valve System (cont.)		
Valve spring (outer)		
Free length	2.03 in.	51.562mm
Pressure		
Closed	76-84 lbs. @ 1.70 in.	338-374 N @ 43mm
Open	194-206 lbs. @ 1.25 in.	863-916.7 N @ 31.75mm
Installed height	1.690-1.710 in.	42.926-43.434mm
Valve spring damper		
Free length	1.86 in.	47.244mm
Approximate number of coils	4	

① 6 psi @ 1000 rpm, 18 psi @ 2000 rpm and 24 psi @ 4000 rpm
② Tighten the rocker arm nut to 20 ft. lbs. (27 Nm)

91023C03

4.3L VIN W ENGINE MECHANICAL SPECIFICATIONS

Description	English Specifications	Metric Specifications
Piston Pin		
Diameter Nos. 2 and 3	0.9267-0.9271 in.	23.545-23.548mm
Clearance in piston		
Production	0.0002-0.0007 in.	0.009-0.024mm
Service limit (max.)	0.001 in.	0.0025mm
Fit in rod (interference)	0.0008-0.0016 in.	0.021-0.040mm
Crankshaft		
Main journal		
Diameter		
No.1	2.4488-2.4495 in.	62.199-62.217mm
Nos. 2 and 3	2.4485-2.4494 in.	62.191-62.215mm
No. 4	2.4480-2.4489 in.	62.179-62.203mm
Taper		
Production (max.)	0.0003-0.001 in.	0.007-0.025mm
Out-of-round		
Production (max.)	0.0002 in.	0.0050mm
Service limit (max.)	0.001 in.	0.025mm
Main bearing clearance		
Production		
No.1	0.0008-0.0020 in.	0.0043-0.0508mm
Service limit		
No.1	0.0010-0.0020 in.	0.0254-0.05mm
Nos. 2, 3 and 4	0.0010-0.0020 in.	0.025-0.064mm
Crankshaft end-play	0.002-0.008 in.	0.050-0.20mm
Crankshaft run-out (max.)	0.001 in.	0.025mm
Connecting Rod		
Connecting rod journal		
Diameter	2.2487-2.2497 in.	57.117-57.142mm
Taper		
Production (max.)	0.0002 in.	0.007mm
Service limit (max.)	0.001 in.	0.025mm
Out-of-round		
Production (max.)	0.0002 in.	0.007mm
Service limit (max.)	0.001 in.	0.025mm
Rod bearing clearance		
Production	0.0013-0.0035 in.	0.033-0.088mm
Service limit	0.0010-0.0030 in.	0.025-0.076mm
Rod side clearance		
Camshaft		
Lobe lift		
Intake	0.286-0.290 in.	0.0726-0.0736mm
Exhaust	0.292-0.296 in.	0.0741-0.0751mm
Journal diameter	1.8682-1.8692 in.	47.452-47.478mm
Camshaft end-play	0.001-0.009 in.	0.0254-0.228mm
Balance Shaft		
Front bearing journal		
Diameter	2.1648-2.1654 in.	55.985-55.001mm
		863-916.7 N @ 31.75mm
Rear bearing journal		
Diameter	1.4994-1.5000 in.	38.084-38.100mm
Clearance	0.001-0.0036 in.	0.0254-0.09144mm

91023C05

4.3L VIN W ENGINE MECHANICAL SPECIFICATIONS

Description	English Specifications	Metric Specifications
General Information		
Engine type	90 degree V6	
Displacement	4.3L, 262	
Bore	4.00 in.	101.60mm
Stroke	3.480 in.	88.38mm
Compression ratio	9.2:1	
Firing order	1-6-5-4-3-2	
Oil pressure	①	①
Lubrication System		
Oil capacity without filter change	4 quarts	3.75 liters
Oil capacity with filter change add	0.42 quarts	0.398 liters
Oil Pan		
Engine block clearance tolerance (max.)	0.010 in.	0.254mm
Cylinder Head		
Surface flatness (max.)	0.004 in.	0.102mm
Exhaust manifold		
Surface flatness (max.)	0.010 in.	0.254mm
Intake Manifold		
Surface flatness (max.)	0.010 in.	0.254mm
Cylinder Bore		
Diameter	4.0007-4.0017 in.	101.618-101.643mm
Out-of-round (max.)		
Production	0.001 in.	0.02mm
Service limit	0.002 in.	0.05mm
Taper		
Production thrust side (max.)	0.0005 in.	0.012mm
Production relief side (max.)	0.001 in.	0.02mm
Service limit (max.)	0.001 in.	0.02mm
Piston		
Clearance		
Production	0.0007-0.002 in.	0.0001-0.005mm
Service limit (max.)	0.070 in.	0.0024mm
Piston Rings (end gap measured in the cylinder bore)		
Compression rings		
Groove clearance		
Top	0.02-0.06 in.	0.050-0.15mm
Second	0.0012-0.0032 in.	0.10-0.20mm
Gap	0.0042 in.	0.107mm
Production		
Top	0.010-0.016 in.	0.25-0.40mm
Second	0.40-0.66 in.	0.018-0.026mm
Service limit (max.)	0.06-0.035 in.	0.25-0.88mm
Gap		
Production (max.)	0.002-0.007 in.	0.051-0.20mm
Service limit (max.)	0.002-0.008 in.	0.051-0.20mm
Oil rings		
Groove clearance		
Production	0.015-0.050 in.	0.003-0.0127mm
Gap		
Production	0.0094-0.065 in.	0.25-1.65mm
Service limit (max.)		

91023C04

4.3L VIN W ENGINE MECHANICAL SPECIFICATIONS

Description	English Specifications	Metric Specifications
Valve System		
Lifter	Hydraulic roller type	
Rocker arm ratio	1.50:1	
Valve lash		
Intake/Exhaust	No adjustment	
Face angle		
Intake/Exhaust	45°	
Seat angle		
Intake/Exhaust	46°	
Seat run-out (max.)		
Intake/Exhaust	0.002 in.	0.0508mm
Seat width		
Intake	0.035-0.060 in.	0.889-1.524mm
Exhaust	0.062-0.093 in.	1.5748-2.3622mm
Stem clearance		
Production		
Intake	0.0011-0.0027 in.	0.025-0.069mm
Exhaust	0.0011-0.0027 in.	0.025-0.069mm
Service limit		
Intake	+ 0.001 in.	+ 0.0254mm
Exhaust	+ 0.002 in.	+ 0.0508mm
Valve spring		
Free length	2.03 in.	52mm
Pressure		
Closed	76-84 lbs. @ 1.70 in.	338-374 N @ 43mm
Open	187-203 lbs. @ 1.27 in.	832-903 N @ 32mm
Installed height	1.690-1.710 in.	42.926-43.434mm
Valve lift		
Intake	0.414 in.	10.51mm
Exhaust	0.428 in.	10.87mm

① 6 psi @ 1000 rpm, 18 psi @ 2000 rpm and 24 psi @ 4000 rpm

91023C08

4.8L ENGINE MECHANICAL SPECIFICATIONS

Description	English Specifications	Metric Specifications
General Information		
Engine type	Inline 6 cylinder	
Displacement	4.8L	292 (CID)
Bore	3.88 in.	98.55mm
Stroke	4.12 in.	104.64mm
Compression ratio	8.0:1	
Firing order	1-5-3-6-2-4	
Oil pressure	30 psi @ 2000 rpm	
Piston		
Clearance	0.0026-0.0036 in.	0.0660-0.0914mm
Piston Rings		
Gap		
Top	0.010-0.020 in.	0.254-0.508mm
Second	0.010-0.020 in.	0.254-0.508mm
Oil	0.015-0.055 in.	0.381-1.397mm
Side clearance		
Top	0.0020-0.0040 in.	0.0508-0.1016mm
Second	0.0020-0.0040 in.	0.0508-0.1016mm
Oil	0.0050-0.0055 in.	0.127-0.139mm
Crankshaft		
Main journal		
Diameter	2.2979-2.2994 in.	58.366-58.404mm
Main bearing oil clearance	①	①
Crankshaft end-play	0.0020-0.0060 in.	0.050-0.152mm
Connecting Rod		
Connecting rod journal		
Diameter	2.0990-2.1000 in.	53.314-53.340mm
Oil clearance	0.0010-0.0026 in.	0.0254-0.0660mm
Side clearance	0.0060-0.0170 in.	0.1524-0.4318mm
Camshaft		
Elevation		
Intake	0.2313-0.2317 in.	5.875-5.885mm
Exhaust	0.2313-0.2317 in.	5.875-5.885mm
Journal diameter	1.8677-1.8697 in.	47.4395-47.4903mm
Camshaft end-play	0.0039-0.0080 in.	0.0762-0.2032mm
Valve System		
Lifter	Hydraulic	
Face angle		
Intake/Exhaust	45°	
Seat angle		
Intake/Exhaust	46°	
Spring test	175 lbs. @ 1.26 in.	778.75 N @ 32.004mm
Spring installed height	1.66 in.	42.164mm
Stem-to-guide clearance		
Intake	0.0010-0.0027 in.	0.0254-0.0685mm
Exhaust	0.0015-0.0032 in.	0.0381-0.0812mm
Stem diameter		
Intake/exhaust	0.3410-0.3417 in.	8.6614-8.67918 in.
Intake/exhaust	0.3410-0.3417 in.	8.6614-8.67918 in.

① Nos. 1-6: 0.0010-0.0024 in. (0.0254-0.0609mm)
No. 7: 0.0016-0.0035 in. (0.0406-0.0889mm)

91023C07

5.0L VIN H ENGINE MECHANICAL SPECIFICATIONS

Description	English Specifications	Metric Specifications
General Information		
Engine type	V8	
Displacement	5.0L	305 (CID)
Bore	3.736 in.	94.894mm
Stroke	3.480 in.	88.392mm
Compression ratio	9.1:1	
Firing order	1-8-4-3-6-5-7-2	
Oil pressure	①	①
Cylinder Bore		
Diameter	3.7350-3.7385 in.	94.869-94.957mm
Out-of-round (max.)		
Production	0.001 in.	0.0254mm
Service limit	0.002 in.	0.0508mm
Taper		
Production thrust side (max.)	0.0005 in.	0.0127mm
Production relief side (max.)	0.001 in.	0.0254mm
Service limit (max.)	0.001 in.	0.0254mm
Piston		
Clearance		
Production	0.0007-0.0021 in.	0.0177-0.0533mm
Service limit (max.)	0.0027 in.	0.0685mm
Piston Rings		
Compression rings		
Groove clearance		
Production		
Top	0.0012-0.0032 in.	0.3048-0.0812mm
Second	0.0012-0.0032 in.	0.3048-0.0812mm
Service limit (max.)	plus or minus 0.001 in.	
Gap		
Production		
Top	0.010-0.020 in.	0.254-0.508mm
Second (max.)	0.018-0.026 in.	0.4572-0.6604mm
Service limit (max.)	plus or minus 0.001 in.	
Oil rings		
Groove clearance		
Production	0.002-0.007 in.	0.050-0.177mm
Service limit (max.)	plus or minus 0.001 in.	
Gap		
Production	0.010-0.030 in.	0.254-0.762mm
Service limit (max.)	plus or minus 0.001 in.	
Piston Pin		
Diameter	0.9270-0.9271 in.	23.545-23.548mm
Clearance in piston		
Production	0.0004-0.0008 in.	0.010-0.020mm
Service limit (max.)	plus or minus 0.001 in.	
Fit in rod (interference)	0.0008-0.0016 in.	0.020-0.040mm

91023C08

5.0L VIN H ENGINE MECHANICAL SPECIFICATIONS

Description	English Specifications	Metric Specifications
Crankshaft		
Main journal		
Diameter		
No. 1	2.4484-2.4493 in.	62.189-62.212mm
No. 2, 3 and 4	2.4481-2.4490 in.	62.181-62.204mm
No. 5	2.4479-2.4488 in.	62.176-62.199mm
Taper		
Production (max.)	0.0002 in.	0.0050mm
Service limit (max.)	0.001 in.	0.025mm
Out-of-round (max.)		
Production (max.)	0.0002 in.	0.0050mm
Service limit (max.)	0.001 in.	0.025mm
Main bearing clearance		
Production		
No.1	0.0008-0.0020 in.	0.0203-0.0508mm
Nos. 2 and 3	0.0011-0.0023 in.	0.0279-0.0584mm
No. 5	0.0017-0.0032 in.	0.0431-0.0812mm
Service limit		
No.1	0.0010-0.0015 in.	0.0254-0.0381mm
Nos. 2, 3 and 4	0.0010-0.0025 in.	0.0254-0.0635mm
No. 5	0.0025-0.0035 in.	0.0635-0.0889mm
Crankshaft end-play	0.002-0.006 in.	0.0508-0.1524mm
Crankpin		
Diameter	2.0988-2.0998 in.	53.3095-53.3349mm
Taper		
Production (max.)	0.0005 in.	0.0127mm
Service limit (max.)	0.001 in.	0.025mm
Out-of-round		
Production (max.)	0.0005 in.	0.0127mm
Service limit (max.)	0.001 in.	0.025mm
Rod bearing clearance		
Production	0.0013-0.0035 in.	0.0330-0.0889mm
Service limit (max.)	0.003 in.	0.0762mm
Rod side clearance	0.006-0.014 in.	0.1524-0.3556mm
Camshaft		
Lobe lift		
Intake	0.2316-0.2356 in.	5.8826-5.9842mm
Exhaust	0.2545-0.2585 in.	6.4943-6.5659mm
Journal diameter	1.8692-1.8692 in.	47.4522-47.4776mm
Valve System		
Lifter	Hydraulic	
Rocker arm ratio	1.50:1	
Valve lash		
Intake/Exhaust	②	②
Face angle		
Intake/Exhaust	45°	
Seat angle		
Intake/Exhaust	46°	
Seat run-out (max.)		
Intake/Exhaust	0.002 in.	0.0508mm

91023C09

5.0L VIN H ENGINE MECHANICAL SPECIFICATIONS

Description	English Specifications	Metric Specifications
Valve System (cont.)		
Seat width		
Intake	1/32-1/16 in.	863-916.7 N @ 31.75mm
Exhaust	1/16-3/32 in.	0.0625-0.0937mm
Stem clearance		
Production		
Intake	0.0010-0.0027 in.	0.0254-0.06858mm
Exhaust	0.0010-0.0027 in.	0.0254-0.06858mm
Service limit		
Intake	High limit + 0.001 in.	High limit + 0.001 in.
Exhaust	High limit + 0.002 in.	High limit + 0.002 in.
Valve spring		
Free length	2.03 in.	51.562mm
Pressure		
Closed	76-84 lbs. @ 1.70 in.	338-373 N @ 43.18mm
Open	194-206 lbs. @ 1.25 in.	863-916 N @ 31.75mm
Installed height	1.2932 in.	1.72mm
Valve lift		
Intake	1.86 in.	47.24mm
Exhaust	4	

① 6 psi @ 1000 rpm, 18 psi @ 2000 rpm and 24 psi @ 4000 rpm
② One turn down from zero lash

91023C10

5.7L VIN K ENGINE MECHANICAL SPECIFICATIONS

Description	English Specifications	Metric Specifications
General Information		
Engine type	V8	
Displacement	5.7L	350 (CID)
Bore	4.00 in.	101.6mm
Stroke	3.480 in.	88.392mm
Compression ratio		9.4:1
Firing order		1-8-4-3-6-5-7-2
Oil pressure	①	①
Oil filter torque	15 ft. lbs.	20 Nm
Cylinder Bore		
Diameter	3.735-3.7384 in.	94.881-94.958mm
Out-of-round (max.)		
Production	0.001 in.	0.0254mm
Service limit	0.002 in.	0.0508mm
Taper		
Production thrust side (max.)	0.0005 in.	0.0127mm
Production relief side (max.)	0.001 in.	0.0254mm
Service limit (max.)	0.001 in.	0.0254mm
Piston		
Clearance		
Production	0.0007-0.0001 in.	0.018-0.053mm
Service limit (max.)	0.0007-0.0026 in.	0.018-0.068mm
Piston Rings (end gaps measured in cylinder bore)		
Compression rings		
Groove clearance		
Production		
Top	0.0012-0.0027 in.	0.030-0.070mm
Second	0.0012-0.0032 in.	0.040-0.080mm
Service limit (max.)		
Top	0.0012-0.0035 in.	0.030-0.090mm
Second	0.0015-0.004 in.	0.040-0.100mm
Gap		
Production		
Top	0.010-0.020 in.	0.25-0.51mm
Second	0.018-0.026 in.	0.46-0.66mm
Service limit (max.)		
Top	0.010-0.025 in.	0.25-0.65mm
Second	0.018-0.035 in.	0.46-0.90mm
Oil rings		
Groove clearance		
Production	0.002-0.006 in.	0.051-0.177mm
Service limit (max.)	0.002-0.009 in.	0.051-0.22mm
Gap		
Production	0.010-0.030 in.	0.25-0.76mm
Service limit (max.)	0.010-0.035 in.	0.25-0.89mm
Piston Pin		
Diameter	0.9270-0.9271 in.	23.545-23.548mm
Clearance in piston		
Production	0.0005-0.0009 in.	0.010-0.020mm
Service limit (max.)	0.0005-0.0010 in.	0.013-0.025mm
Fit in rod (interference)	0.0008-0.0016 in.	0.021-0.040mm

91023C11

5.7L VIN K ENGINE MECHANICAL SPECIFICATIONS

Description	English Specifications	Metric Specifications
Crankshaft		
Main journal		
Diameter		
No. 1	2.4484-2.4493 in.	62.189-62.212mm
No. 2, 3 and 4	2.4484-2.4491 in.	62.189-62.207mm
No. 5	2.4484-2.4491 in.	62.189-62.207mm
Taper		
Production (max.)	0.0002 in.	0.0050mm
Out-of-round		
Production (max.)	0.002 in.	0.005 in.
Production (max.)	0.001 in.	0.025mm
Main bearing clearance		
Production		
No. 1	0.0007-0.0021 in.	0.018-0.053mm
No. 2, 3 and 4	0.0009-0.0024 in.	0.022-0.061mm
No. 5	0.0010-0.0027 in.	0.025-0.069mm
Service limit		
No. 1	0.0010-0.0020 in.	0.025-0.051mm
No. 2, 3 and 4	0.0010-0.0025 in.	0.025-0.064mm
No. 5	0.0015-0.0030 in.	0.038-0.076mm
Crankshaft end-play	0.002-0.008 in.	0.05-0.20mm
Crankshaft run-out at rear flange	0.0015 in.	0.038mm
Connecting Rod		
Rod journal diameter	2.0978-2.0998 in.	53.284-53.334mm
Rod journal taper		
Production (max.)	0.0003 in.	0.007mm
Service limit (max.)	0.0010 in.	0.025mm
Rod out-of-round		
Production (max.)	0.0003 in.	0.007mm
Service limit (max.)	0.0010 in.	0.025mm
Rod bearing clearance		
Production	0.0013-0.0035 in.	0.033-0.088mm
Service limit	0.0010-0.0030 in.	0.025-0.076mm
Rod side clearance	0.006-0.014 in.	0.16-0.35mm
Camshaft		
Lobe lift		
Intake	0.274-0.278 in.	6.97-7.07mm
Exhaust	0.283-0.287 in.	7.20-7.30mm
Journal diameter	1.8677-1.8697 in.	47.4522-47.4776mm
End play	0.004-0.012 in.	0.11-0.30mm
Valve System		
Lifter	Hydraulic	
Rocker arm ratio	1.50:1	
Valve lash		
Intake/Exhaust	②	②
Face angle		
Intake/Exhaust	45°	
Seat angle		863-916.7 N @ 31.75mm
Intake/Exhaust	46°	
Seat run-out (max.)		
Intake/Exhaust	0.002 in.	0.0508mm

91023C12

5.7L VIN K ENGINE MECHANICAL SPECIFICATIONS

Description	English Specifications	Metric Specifications
Valve System (cont.)		
Seat width		
Intake	0.045-0.070 in.	1.14-1.78mm
Exhaust	0.065-0.098 in.	1.65-2.49mm
Stem clearance		
Production		
Intake	0.0010-0.0027 in.	0.025-0.069mm
Exhaust	0.0010-0.0027 in.	0.025-0.068mm
Service limit		
Intake	0.0010-0.0037 in.	0.025-0.094mm
Exhaust	0.0010-0.0027 in.	0.025-0.094mm
Valve spring		
Free length	2.02 in.	51.3mm
Pressure		
Closed	76-84 lbs. @ 1.70 in.	338-374 N @ 43.2mm
Open	187-203 lbs. @ 1.27 in.	832-903 N @ 32.3mm
Installed height	1.67-1.70 in.	42.92-43.43mm
Cylinder Head		
Surface flatness		
At the exhaust manifold deck	0.002 in.	0.05mm
At the engine block deck	0.004 in.	0.10mm
At the intake manifold deck	0.004 in.	0.10mm

① 6 psi @ 1000 rpm, 18 psi @ 2000 rpm and 24 psi @ 4000 rpm
② One turn down from zero lash

91023C13

5.0L VIN M ENGINE MECHANICAL SPECIFICATIONS

Description	English Specifications	Metric Specifications
General Information		
Engine type	V8	
Displacement	5.0L	305 (CID)
Bore	3.736 in.	94.894mm
Stroke	3.480 in.	88.392mm
Compression ratio	9.4:1	
Firing order	1-8-4-3-6-5-7-2	
Oil pressure	①	①
Cylinder Bore		
Diameter	3.7350-3.7385 in.	94.869-94.957mm
Out-of-round (max.)		
Production	0.001 in.	0.0254mm
Service limit	0.002 in.	0.0508mm
Taper		
Production thrust side (max.)	0.0005 in.	0.0127mm
Production relief side (max.)	0.001 in.	0.0254mm
Service limit (max.)	0.001 in.	0.0254mm
Piston		
Clearance		
Production	0.0007-0.0021 in.	0.0177-0.0533mm
Service limit (max.)	0.0027 in.	0.0686mm
Piston Rings		
Compression rings		
Groove clearance		
Production		
Top	0.0012-0.0032 in.	0.3048-0.0812mm
Second	0.0012-0.0032 in.	0.3048-0.0812mm
Service limit (max.)	plus or minus 0.001 in.	
Gap		
Production		
Top	0.010-0.020 in.	0.254-0.508mm
Second	0.018-0.026 in.	0.4572-0.660mm
Service limit (max.)	plus or minus 0.001 in.	
Oil rings		
Groove clearance		
Production	0.002-0.007 in.	0.050-0.177mm
Service limit (max.)	plus or minus 0.001 in.	
Gap		
Production	0.010-0.030 in.	0.254-0.762mm
Service limit (max.)	plus or minus 0.001 in.	
Piston Pin		
Diameter	0.9270-0.9271 in.	23.545-23.548mm
Clearance in piston		
Production	0.0004-0.0006 in.	0.010-0.020mm
Service limit (max.)	plus or minus 0.001 in.	
Fit in rod (interference)	0.0008-0.0016 in.	0.020-0.040mm

91023C14

5.0L VIN M ENGINE MECHANICAL SPECIFICATIONS

Description	English Specifications	Metric Specifications
Crankshaft		
Main journal		
Diameter		
No. 1	2.4484-2.4493 in.	62.189-62.212mm
Nos. 2, 3 and 4	2.4481-2.4490 in.	62.181-62.204mm
No. 5	2.4479-2.4488 in.	62.176-62.199mm
Taper		
Production (max.)	0.0002 in.	0.0050mm
Service limit (max.)	0.001 in.	0.025mm
Out-of-round		
Production (max.)	0.0002 in.	0.0050mm
Service limit (max.)	0.001 in.	0.025mm
Main bearing clearance		
Production		
No. 1	0.0008-0.0020 in.	0.0203-0.0508mm
Nos. 2, 3 and 4	0.0011-0.0023 in.	0.0279-0.0584mm
No. 5	0.0017-0.0032 in.	0.0431-0.0812mm
Service limit		
No. 1	0.0010-0.0015 in.	0.0254-0.0381mm
Nos. 2, 3 and 4	0.0010-0.0025 in.	0.0254-0.0635mm
No. 5	0.0025-0.0035 in.	0.0635-0.0889mm
Crankshaft end-play	0.002-0.006 in.	0.0508-0.1524mm
Crankpin		
Diameter	2.0988-2.0998 in.	53.3095-53.3349mm
Taper		
Production (max.)	0.0005 in.	0.0127mm
Service limit (max.)	0.001 in.	0.025mm
Out-of-round		
Production (max.)	0.0005 in.	0.0127mm
Service limit (max.)	0.001 in.	0.025mm
Rod bearing clearance		
Production	0.0013-0.0035 in.	0.0330-0.0889mm
Service limit (max.)	0.003 in.	0.0762mm
Rod side clearance	0.006-0.014 in.	0.1524-0.3556mm
Camshaft		
Lobe lift		
Intake	0.2316-0.2356 in.	5.8826-5.9842mm
Exhaust	0.2545-0.2585 in.	6.4943-6.5659mm
Journal diameter	1.8682-1.8692 in.	47.4522-47.4776mm
Valve System		
Lifter	Hydraulic	
Rocker arm ratio	1.50:1	
Valve lash	②	②
Face angle		
Intake/Exhaust	45°	
Seat angle		
Intake/Exhaust	46°	
Seat run-out (max.)		
Intake/Exhaust	0.002 in.	0.0508mm

91023C15

5.0L VIN M ENGINE MECHANICAL SPECIFICATIONS

Description	English Specifications	Metric Specifications
Valve System (cont.)		
Seat width		
Intake	1/32-1/16 in.	
Exhaust	1/16-3/32 in.	
Stem clearance		
Production		
Intake	0.0010-0.0027 in.	0.0254-0.06858mm
Exhaust	0.0010-0.0027 in.	0.0254-0.06858mm
Service limit		
Intake	High limit + 0.001 in.	
Exhaust	High limit + 0.002 in.	
Valve spring		
Free length	2.03 in.	51.562mm
Pressure		
Closed	76-84 lbs. @ 1.70 in.	338-373 N @ 43.18mm
Open	194-206 lbs. @ 1.25 in.	863-916 N @ 31.75mm
Installed height	1 23/32 in.	1.72mm
Valve lift		
Intake	1.86 in.	47.24mm
Exhaust	4	

① 6 psi @ 1000 rpm, 18 psi @ 2000 rpm and 24 psi @ 4000 rpm
② One turn down from zero lash

91023C16

5.7L VIN R ENGINE MECHANICAL SPECIFICATIONS

Description	English Specifications	Metric Specifications
General Information		
Engine type		V8
Displacement	5.7L	350 (CID)
Bore	4.00 in.	101.6mm
Stroke	3.480 in.	88.392mm
Compression ratio	9.4:1	
Firing order	1-8-4-3-6-5-7-2	
Oil pressure	①	①
Oil filter torque	15 ft. lbs.	20 Nm
Cylinder Bore		
Diameter	4.0007-4.0017 in.	101.618-101.643mm
Out-of-round (max.)		
Production	0.001 in.	0.0254mm
Service limit	0.002 in.	0.0508mm
Taper		
Production thrust side (max.)	0.0005 in.	0.0127mm
Production relief side (max.)	0.001 in.	0.0254mm
Service limit (max.)	0.001 in.	0.0254mm
Piston		
Clearance		
Production	0.0007-0.0021 in.	0.0177-0.0533mm
Service limit (max.)	0.0007-0.0026 in.	0.018-0.066mm
Piston Rings (end gaps measured in cylinder bore)		
Compression rings		
Groove clearance		
Production		
Top	0.0012-0.0027 in.	0.030-0.070mm
Second	0.0012-0.0032 in.	0.040-0.080mm
Service limit (max.)		
Top	0.0012-0.0035 in.	0.030-0.090mm
Second	0.0015-0.004 in.	0.040-0.100mm
Gap		
Production		
Top	0.012-0.022 in.	0.30-0.58mm
Second	0.020-0.028 in.	0.51-0.71mm
Service limit (max.)		
Top	0.012-0.025 in.	0.30-0.85mm
Second	0.016-0.035 in.	0.46-0.90mm
Oil rings		
Groove clearance		
Production	0.002-0.006 in.	0.051-0.177mm
Service limit (max.)	0.002-0.0078 in.	0.051-0.195mm
Gap		
Production	0.010-0.030 in.	0.25-0.76mm
Service limit (max.)	0.010-0.030 in.	0.25-0.785mm
Piston Pin		
Diameter	0.9270-0.9271 in.	23.545-23.548mm
Clearance in piston		
Production	0.0005-0.0009 in.	0.010-0.020mm
Service limit (max.)	0.0005-0.0010 in.	0.013-0.025mm
Fit in rod (interference)	0.0008-0.0016 in.	0.021-0.040mm

91023C17

5.7L VIN R ENGINE MECHANICAL SPECIFICATIONS

Description	English Specifications	Metric Specifications
Crankshaft		
Main journal		
Diameter		
No. 1	2.4484-2.4493 in.	62.189-62.212mm
No. 2, 3 and 4	2.4484-2.4491 in.	62.189-62.207mm
No. 5	2.4484-2.4491 in.	62.189-62.207mm
Taper		
Production (max.)	0.0002 in.	0.0050mm
Out-of-round		
Production (max.)	0.002 in.	0.005 in.
Service limit (max.)	0.002 in.	0.005 in.
Main bearing clearance		
Production		
No. 1	0.0007-0.0021 in.	0.018-0.053mm
No. 2, 3 and 4	0.0009-0.0024 in.	0.022-0.061mm
No. 5	0.0010-0.0027 in.	0.025-0.069mm
Service limit		
No. 1	0.0010-0.0020 in.	0.025-0.051mm
No. 2, 3 and 4	0.0010-0.0025 in.	0.025-0.064mm
No. 5	0.0015-0.0030 in.	0.038-0.076mm
Crankshaft end-play	0.002-0.008 in.	0.05-0.20mm
Crankshaft run-out at rear flange	0.0015 in.	0.038mm
Connecting Rod		
Rod journal diameter	2.0978-2.0998 in.	53.284-53.334mm
Rod journal taper		
Production (max.)	0.0003 in.	0.007mm
Service limit (max.)	0.0010 in.	0.025mm
Rod out-of-round		
Production (max.)	0.0003 in.	0.007mm
Service limit (max.)	0.0010 in.	0.025mm
Rod bearing clearance		
Production	0.0013-0.0035 in.	0.033-0.088mm
Service limit	0.0010-0.0030 in.	0.025-0.076mm
Rod side clearance	0.006-0.014 in.	0.16-0.35mm
Camshaft		
Lobe lift		
Intake	0.274-0.278 in.	6.97-7.07mm
Exhaust	0.283-0.287 in.	7.20-7.30mm
Journal diameter	1.8677-1.8697 in.	47.4522-47.4776mm
End play	0.004-0.012 in.	0.11-0.30mm
Valve System		
Lifter	Hydraulic roller	
Rocker arm ratio	1.50:1	
Valve lash		
Intake/Exhaust	②	②
Face angle		
Intake/Exhaust	45°	
Seat angle		
Intake/Exhaust	46°	
Seat run-out (max.)		
Intake/Exhaust	0.002 in.	0.0508mm

91023C18

5.7L VIN R ENGINE MECHANICAL SPECIFICATIONS

Description	English Specifications	Metric Specifications
Valve System (cont.)		
Seat width		
Intake	0.040-0.065 in.	1.02-1.65mm
Exhaust		
Light duty	0.065-0.098 in.	1.65-2.49mm
Heavy duty	0.059-0.101 in.	1.50-2.56mm
Stem clearance		
Production		
Intake	0.0010-0.0027 in.	0.025-0.069mm
Exhaust	0.0010-0.0027 in.	0.025-0.069mm
Service limit		
Intake	0.0010-0.0037 in.	0.025-0.094mm
Exhaust	0.0010-0.0027 in.	0.025-0.094mm
Valve spring		
Free length	2.02 in.	51.3mm
Pressure		
Closed	76-84 lbs. @ 1.70 in.	338-374 N @ 43.2mm
Open	187-203 lbs. @ 1.27 in.	832-903 N @ 32.3mm
Installed height	1.67-1.70 in.	42.92-43.43mm
Cylinder Head		
Surface flatness		
At the exhaust manifold deck	0.002 in.	0.05mm
At the engine block deck	0.004 in.	0.10mm
At the intake manifold deck	0.004 in.	0.10mm

① 6 psi @ 1000 rpm, 18 psi @ 2000 rpm and 24 psi @ 4000 rpm
② One turn down from zero lash

91023C19

7.4L VIN N/W ENGINE MECHANICAL SPECIFICATIONS

Description	English Specifications	Metric Specifications
General Information		
Engine type		V8
Displacement	7.4L	454 (CID)
Bore	4.25 in.	107.95mm
Stroke	4.00 in.	101.6mm
Compression ratio	7.9:1	
Firing order	1-8-4-3-6-5-7-2	
Oil pressure	①	①
Cylinder Bore		
Diameter	4.2500-4.2504 in.	107.65-107.96mm
Out-of-round (max.)		
Production	0.001 in.	0.0254mm
Service limit	0.002 in.	0.0508mm
Taper		
Production thrust side (max.)	0.0005 in.	0.0127mm
Production relief side (max.)	0.001 in.	0.0254mm
Service limit (max.)	0.001 in.	0.254mm
Piston		
Clearance		
Production	0.0018-0.0030 in.	0.0457-0.0762mm
Service limit (max.)	0.036 in.	0.9144mm
Piston Rings (end gaps measured in cylinder bore)		
Compression rings		
Groove clearance		
Production		
Top	0.0012-0.0029 in.	0.0304-0.0736mm
Second	0.0012-0.0029 in.	0.0304-0.0736mm
Service limit (max.)		
Top	Hi limit production + 0.010 in. (0.254mm)	
Second	Hi limit production + 0.010 in. (0.254mm)	
Gap		
Production		
Top	0.010-0.018 in.	0.254-0.711mm
Second (max.)	0.016-0.024 in.	0.406mm-0.609
Service limit (max.)		
Top	Hi limit production + 0.010 in. (0.254mm)	
Second		
Oil rings		
Groove clearance		
Production	0.0050-0.0065 in.	0.127-0.165mm
Service limit (max.)	Hi limit production + 0.001 in. (0.0254mm)	
Gap		
Production	0.010-0.030 in.	0.254-0.762mm
Service limit (max.)	Hi limit production + 0.010 in. (0.254mm)	
Piston Pin		
Diameter	0.98945-0.98965 in.	25.132-25.137mm
Clearance in piston		
Production	0.0002-0.0007 in.	0.0050-0.0177mm
Service limit (max.)	0.001 in.	0.0254mm
Fit in rod (interference)	0.0031-0.0021 in.	0.0787-0.0533mm

91023C20

7.4L VIN N/W ENGINE MECHANICAL SPECIFICATIONS

Description	English Specifications	Metric Specifications
Crankshaft		
Main journal		
Diameter		
Nos. 1-5	2.7482-2.7489 in.	69.804-69.822mm
Taper		
Production (max.)	0.0004 in.	0.0101mm
Service limit (max.)	0.001 in.	0.0254mm
Out-of-round		
Production (max.)	0.0004 in.	0.0101mm
Service limit (max.)	0.001 in.	0.0254mm
Main bearing clearance		
Production		
Nos. 1, 2, 3 and 4	0.0017-0.0030 in.	0.04318-0.0762mm
No. 5	0.0025-0.0038 in.	0.0635-0.09652mm
Service limit		
Nos. 1, 2, 3 and 4	0.0010-0.0030 in.	0.0254-0.0762mm
No. 5	0.0025-0.0040 in.	0.0635-0.1016mm
Crankshaft end-play	0.005-0.011 in.	0.127-0.2794mm
Crankpin		
Taper		
Production (max.)	0.0005 in.	0.0127mm
Service limit (max.)	0.001 in.	0.0254mm
Out-of-round		
Production (max.)	0.0005 in.	0.0127mm
Service limit (max.)	0.001 in.	0.0254mm
Rod bearing clearance		
Production	0.0011-0.0029 in.	0.0279-0.0736mm
Service limit (max.)	0.003 in.	0.076mm
Camshaft		
Lobe lift		
Intake	0.2467-0.2507 in.	6.2661-6.3677mm
Exhaust	0.2717-0.2517 in.	6.9011-6.3931mm
Journal diameter	1.9477-1.9497 in.	49.471-49.522mm
Valve System		
Lifter	Hydraulic	
Rocker arm ratio	1.70:1	
Valve lash	Net lash	
Face angle		
Intake/Exhaust	45°	
Seat angle		
Intake/Exhaust	46°	
Seat run-out (max.)		
Intake/Exhaust	0.002 in.	0.0508mm

91023C21

7.4L VIN J ENGINE MECHANICAL SPECIFICATIONS

Description	English Specifications	Metric Specifications
General Information		
Engine type	V8	
Displacement	7.4L	454 (CID)
Bore	4.25 in.	107.95mm
Stroke	4.00 in.	101.6mm
Compression ratio	9.0:1	
Firing order	1-8-4-3-6-5-7-2	
Oil pressure	①	①
Cylinder Bore		
Diameter	4.2500-4.2507 in.	107.950-107.968mm
Out-of-round (max.)		
Production	0.001 in.	0.0254mm
Service limit	0.002 in.	0.0508mm
Taper		
Production thrust side (max.)	0.0005 in.	0.0127mm
Production relief side (max.)	0.001 in.	0.0254mm
Service limit (max.)	0.001 in.	0.254mm
Piston		
Clearance		
Production	0.0018-0.0030 in.	0.0457-0.0762mm
Service limit (max.)	0.0018-0.0048 in.	0.0457-0.219mm
Piston Rings		
Compression rings		
Groove clearance		
Production		
Top	0.0012-0.0029 in.	0.0304-0.0736mm
Second	0.0012-0.0029 in.	0.0304-0.0736mm
Service limit (max.)	0.0012-0.0039 in.	0.305-0.991mm
Gap		
Production		
Top	0.010-0.018 in.	0.254-0.711mm
Second	0.016-0.024 in.	0.406-0.609mm
Service limit (max.)	0.016-0.034 in.	0.406-0.863mm
Oil rings		
Groove clearance		
Production	0.0050-0.0065 in.	0.127-0.165mm
Service limit (max.)	0.0050-0.0075 in.	0.127-0.191mm
Gap		
Production	0.010-0.030 in.	0.254-0.762mm
Service limit (max.)	0.010-0.040 in.	0.254-1.016mm
Piston Pin		
Diameter	0.9895-0.9897 in.	25.132-25.137mm
Clearance in piston		
Production	0.0002-0.0007 in.	0.0050-0.0177mm
Service limit (max.)	0.0002-0.0010 in.	0.005-0.025mm
Fit in rod (interference)	0.0031-0.0021 in.	0.0787-0.0533mm

91023C23

7.4L VIN N/W ENGINE MECHANICAL SPECIFICATIONS

Description	English Specifications	Metric Specifications
Valve System (cont.)		
Seat width		
Intake	1/32-1/16 in.	0.0312-0.0625mm
Exhaust	1/16-3/32 in.	0.0625-0.0937mm
Stem clearance	863-916.7 N @ 31.75mm	
Production		
Intake	0.0010-0.0027 in.	0.0254-0.0685mm
Exhaust	0.0012-0.0029 in.	0.0304-0.0736mm
Service limit		
Intake	High limit + 0.001 in. (0.0254mm)	
Exhaust	High limit + 0.002 in. (0.050mm)	
Valve spring		
Free length	2.15 in.	54.61mm
Pressure		
Closed	76-84 lbs. @ 1.838 in.	338-373 N @ 46.682mm
Open	205-225 lbs. @ 1.408 in.	912-1001 N @ 35.763mm
Installed height	1.838 in.	46.685mm

① 10 psi @ 600 rpm (minimum), 25 psi @ 2000 rpm with engine at operating temperature

91023C22

7.4L VIN J ENGINE MECHANICAL SPECIFICATIONS

Description	English Specifications	Metric Specifications
Crankshaft		
Run-out (max.)	0.002 in.	0.0508mm
Main journal		
Diameter		
Nos. 1-5	2.7482-2.7489 in.	69.804-69.822mm
Taper		
Production (max.)	0.0004 in.	0.0101mm
Service limit (max.)	0.001 in.	0.0254mm
Out-of-round		
Production (max.)	0.0004 in.	0.0101mm
Service limit (max.)	0.001 in.	0.0254mm
Main bearing clearance		
Production		
No. 1	0.0017-0.0030 in.	0.043-0.076mm
Nos. 2, 3 and 4	0.0011-0.0024 in.	0.028-0.061mm
No. 5	0.0025-0.0038 in.	0.063-0.0965mm
Service limit		
Nos. 1, 2, 3 and 4	0.0010-0.0030 in.	0.0254-0.0762mm
No. 5	0.0025-0.0040 in.	0.0635-0.1016mm
Crankshaft end-play	0.005-0.011 in.	0.127-0.2794mm
Crankpin		
Diameter	2.1990-2.1996 in.	55.854-55.869mm
Taper		
Production (max.)	0.0005 in.	0.0127mm
Service limit (max.)	0.001 in.	0.0254mm
Out-of-round		
Production (max.)	0.0005 in.	0.0127mm
Service limit (max.)	0.001 in.	0.0254mm
Rod bearing clearance		
Production	0.0011-0.0029 in.	0.0279-0.0736mm
Service limit (max.)	0.0011-0.0039 in.	0.028-0.099mm
Rod side clearance	0.0013-0.0230 in.	0.033-0.584mm
Camshaft		
Run-out	0.002 in.	0.0508mm
Lobe lift		
Intake	0.2821-0.2841 in.	7.165-7.216mm
Exhaust	0.2823-0.2863 in.	7.170-7.272mm
Journal diameter	1.9477-1.9497 in.	49.471-49.522mm
Valve System		
Lifter	Hydraulic, roller followers	
Rocker arm ratio	1.70:1	
Valve lash		
Intake/Exhaust	Net lash	
Face angle		
Intake/Exhaust	45°	
Seat angle		
Intake/Exhaust	46°	
Seat run-out (max.)		
Intake/Exhaust	0.002 in.	0.0508mm

91023C24

7.4L VIN J ENGINE MECHANICAL SPECIFICATIONS

Description	English Specifications	Metric Specifications
Valve System (cont.)		
Seat width		
Intake	0.030-0.060 in.	0.762-1.524mm
Exhaust	0.060-0.095 in.	863-916.7 N @ 31.75mm
Stem clearance		
Production		
Intake	0.0010-0.0029 in.	0.0254-0.0737mm
Exhaust	0.0012-0.0031 in.	0.030-0.077mm
Service limit		
Intake	0.0010-0.0037 in.	0.025-0.094mm
Exhaust	0.0012-0.0049 in.	0.030-0.124mm
Valve spring		
Pressure		
Closed	71-79 lbs. @ 1.838 in.	316-351 N @ 46.685mm
Open	238-262 lbs. @ 1.347 in.	1059-1165 N @ 34.213mm
Installed height	1.838 in.	46.685mm

① 10 psi @ 600 rpm (minimum), 25 psi @ 2000 rpm with engine at operating temperature

91023C25

6.2 DIESEL ENGINE MECHANICAL SPECIFICATIONS

Description	English Specifications	Metric Specifications
General Information		
Engine type	V8	
Displacement	6.2L	379 (CID)
Bore	3.976 in.	101mm
Stroke	3.818 in.	97mm
Compression ratio	21.3:1	
Firing order	1-8-7-2-6-5-4-3	①
Oil pressure	①	
Cylinder Bore		
Diameter	3.9758-3.9789 in.	100.987-101.065mm
Out-of-round (max.)	0.0007 in.	0.02mm
Taper Thrust side (max.)	0.0007 in.	0.02mm
Piston		
Clearance		
Bohn pistons		
Bores 1-6	0.0035-0.0045 in.	0.089-0.115mm
Bores 7 and 8	0.0044-0.0050 in.	0.102-0.128mm
Zollner pistons ②		
Bores 1-6	0.0044-0.0054 in.	0.112-0.138mm
Bores 7 and 8	0.0049-0.0059 in.	0.125-0.151mm
Piston Rings		
Compression rings		
Groove clearance		
Top	0.0029-0.0070 in.	0.076-0.178mm
Second	0.0029-0.039 in.	0.75-1.00mm
Gap		
Top	0.011-0.021 in.	0.30-0.55mm
Second	0.0029-0.039 in.	0.75-1.00mm
Oil rings		
Groove clearance	0.00155-0.0037 in.	0.040-0.096mm
Gap	0.010-0.020 in.	0.25-0.51mm
Piston Rings (end gap measured in the cylinder bore)		
Diameter	1.2203-1.2206 in.	30.9961-31.0039mm
Clearance	0.0003-0.0012 in.	0.0081-0.0309mm
Fit in rod	0.0003-0.0012 in.	0.0081-0.0309mm
Crankshaft		
Main journal		
Diameter		
Nos. 1-4	2.9494-2.9504 in.	74.917-74.941mm
No. 5	2.9492-2.9502 in.	74.912-74.936mm
Taper (max.)	0.0001 in.	0.005mm
Out-of-round (max.)	0.0001 in.	0.005mm
Main bearing clearance		
Production		
Nos. 1-4	0.0017-0.0032 in.	0.045-0.083mm
No. 5	0.002-0.003 in.	0.055-0.083mm

91023C26

6.2 DIESEL ENGINE MECHANICAL SPECIFICATIONS

Description	English Specifications	Metric Specifications
Crankshaft (cont.)		
Crankshaft end-play	0.003-0.0098 in.	0.10-0.25mm
Crankpin		
Diameter	2.398-2.399 in.	60.913-60.939mm
Taper (max.)	0.0001 in.	0.005mm
Out-of-round (max.)	0.0001 in.	0.005mm
Rod bearing clearance	0.0017-0.0039 in.	0.045-0.100mm
Rod side clearance	0.0066-0.0240 in.	0.17-0.63mm
Camshaft		
Lobe lift		
Intake	0.278-0.282 in.	7.083-7.183mm
Exhaust	0.278-0.282 in.	7.083-7.183mm
Journal diameter		
Nos. 1-4	2.164-2.166 in.	54.975-55.025mm
No. 5	2.006-2.008 in.	50.975-51.025mm
Journal clearance	0.001-0.003 in.	0.026-0.101mm
End-play	0.002-0.012 in.	0.051-0.305mm
Valve System		
Lifter	Hydraulic roller	
Rocker arm ratio	1.50:1	
Valve lash		
Intake/Exhaust	Non-adjustable	
Face angle		
Intake/Exhaust	45°	
Seat angle		
Intake/Exhaust	46°	
Seat run-out (max.)		
Intake/Exhaust	0.00196 in.	0.05mm
Seat width		
Intake	0.029-0.060 in.	0.89-1.53mm
Exhaust	0.061-0.092 in.	1.57-2.36mm
Stem clearance		
Intake	0.001-0.002 in.	0.026-0.069mm
Exhaust	0.001-0.002 in.	0.026-0.069mm
Valve spring		
Pressure		
Closed	80 lbs. @ 1.81 in.	356 N @ 46.0mm
Open	230 lbs. @ 1.40 in.	1025 N @ 35.3mm
Installed height	1.81 in.	46mm
Timing chain free-play		
New chain	0.500 in.	12.7mm
Used chain	0.800 in.	20.3mm

① 10 psi @ idle, 40-45 psi @ 2000 rpm with engine at operating temperature

② Not used in production

91023C27

6.5 DIESEL ENGINE MECHANICAL SPECIFICATIONS

Description	English Specifications	Metric Specifications
General Information		
Engine type	V8	
Displacement	6.5L	396 (CID)
Bore	4.06 in.	103mm
Stroke	3.82 in.	97mm
Compression ratio	21.3:1	
Firing order	1-8-7-2-6-5-4-3	
Oil pressure	①	①
Cylinder Bore		
Diameter	②	②
Out-of-round (max.)	0.0008 in.	0.002mm
Taper (max.)	0.0008 in.	0.002mm
Piston		
Diameter	③	③
Bore clearance		
Nos 1-6	0.0037-0.0047 in.	0.094-0.120mm
Nos. 7 and 8	0.0042-0.0052 in.	0.107-0.133mm
Piston Rings		
Compression rings	Keystone type ring	
Groove clearance		
Top	0.0015-0.0052 in.	0.039-0.079mm
Second		
Gap		
Top	0.010-0.020 in.	0.26-0.51mm
Second	0.029-0.039 in.	0.75-1.00mm
Oil rings		
Groove clearance	0.0016-0.0035 in.	0.040-0.090mm
Gap	0.010-0.020 in.	0.25-0.51mm
Piston Pin		
Diameter	1.2212-1.2216 in.	30.9961-31.0039mm
Pin-to-piston bore	0.0004-0.0006 in.	0.0101-0.153mm
Pin-to-connecting rod bushing	0.0003-0.0012 in.	0.0081-0.0909mm
Piston Rings (end gap measured in the cylinder bore)		
Main journal		
Diameter	④	
Taper (max.)	0.0018-0.0033 in.	0.005-0.083mm
Out-of-round (max.)	0.005-0.083 in.	0.0018-0.0033mm
Main bearing clearance		
Nos. 1-4	0.0018-0.0033 in.	0.045-0.083mm
No. 5	0.0022-0.0037 in.	0.055-0.092mm
Crankshaft end-play	0.0039-0.0010 in.	0.10-0.25mm
Rod bearing clearance	0.0018-0.0039 in.	0.045-0.100mm
Rod side clearance	0.0020-0.0120 in.	0.17-0.0395mm
Camshaft		
Lobe lift		
Intake	0.278-0.282 in.	7.083-7.183mm
Exhaust	0.278-0.282 in.	7.083-7.183mm
Journal diameter		
Nos. 1-4	2.1658-2.1680 in.	54.970-55.025mm
No. 5	2.0082-2.0104 in.	50.970-51.025mm

91023C28

6.5 DIESEL ENGINE MECHANICAL SPECIFICATIONS

Description	English Specifications	Metric Specifications
Camshaft (cont.)		
Journal clearance		
Nos. 1-4	0.0010-0.0046 in.	0.025-0.118mm
No. 5	0.0008-0.0044 in.	0.020-0.113mm
End-play	0.002-0.012 in.	0.051-0.305mm
Valve System		
Lifter	Hydraulic roller	
Rocker arm ratio	1.50:1	
Valve lash		
Intake/Exhaust	Non-adjustable	
Face angle		
Intake/Exhaust	45°	
Seat angle		
Intake/Exhaust	46°	
Seat run-out (max.)		
Intake/Exhaust	0.002 in.	0.5mm
Seat width		
Intake	0.0351-0.0603 in.	0.89-1.53mm
Exhaust	0.0618-0.0930 in.	1.57-2.36mm
Stem clearance		
Intake	0.001-0.002 in.	0.026-0.069mm
Exhaust	0.001-0.002 in.	0.026-0.069mm
Valve spring		
Pressure		
Closed	80 lbs. @ 1.81 in.	356 N @ 46.0mm
Open	230 lbs. @ 1.40 in.	1025 N @ 35.3mm
Installed height	1.81 in.	46mm
Timing chain free-play		
New chain	0.500 in.	12.7mm
Used chain	0.800 in.	20.3mm

91023C29

① 10 psi @ idle, 40-45 psi @ 2000 rpm with engine at operating temperature

② Note: cylinder No. 7 and No. 8 require a 0.0005 in. (0.013mm) additional piston-to-bore clearance

③ Production standard: -JT or JT:
Bore diameter 1-6: 4.0571-4.0578 in. (102.972-102.990mm)
Bore diameter 7-8: 4.0576-4.0583 in. (102.985-103.003mm)
Production standard: -S or ST
Bore diameter 1-6: 4.0628-4.0633 in. (103.117-103.130mm)
Bore diameter 7-8: 4.0633-4.0638 in. (103.130-103.143mm)
Service standard: -JT:
Bore diameter 1-6: 4.0570-4.0578 in. (102.972-102.990mm)
Bore diameter 7-8: 4.0576-4.0583 in. (102.985-103.003mm)
Service Hi limit-GT
Bore diameter 1-6: 4.0587-4.0592 in. (103.013-103.026mm)
Bore diameter 7-8: 4.0592-4.0597 in. (103.026-103.039mm)
Service 0.50mm OS, -0.50mm OST
Bore diameter 1-6: 4.0782-4.0784 in. (103.508-103.512mm)
Bore diameter 7-8: 4.0787-4.0789 in. (103.521-103.525mm)

④ Production standard: -JT or JT.
Skirt diameter: 4.0529-4.0536 in. (102.865-102.883mm)
Production standard: -S or ST
Skirt diameter: 4.0585-4.0592 in. (103.008-103.026mm)
Service standard: JT
Skirt diameter: 4.0529-4.0536 in. (102.865-102.883mm)
Service Hi limit-GT
Skirt diameter: 4.0544-4.0551 in. (102.904-102.922mm)
Service 0.50mm OS, -0.50 OST
Skirt diameter: 4.0789-4.0746 in. (103.399-103.417mm)

④ Nos. 1-4:
Blue: 2.9517-2.9520 in. (74.917-74.925mm)
Orange or red: 2.9520-2.9524 in. (74.925-74.933mm)
White: 2.9524-2.9527 in. (74.933-74.942mm)
No. 5:
Blue: 2.9515-2.9518 in. (74.912-74.920mm)
Orange or red: 2.9518-2.9522 in. (74.920-74.928mm)
White: 2.9522-2.9525 in. (74.928-74.936mm)

Engine

REMOVAL & INSTALLATION

※※ CAUTION

When draining the coolant, keep in mind that cats and dogs are attracted by ethylene glycol antifreeze, and are quite likely to drink any that is left in an uncovered container or in puddles on the ground. This will prove fatal in sufficient quantity. Always drain the coolant into a sealable container. Coolant should be reused unless it is contaminated or several years old.

4.8L Engines

1. Matchmark and remove the hood.
2. Disconnect the negative battery cable.
3. Remove the battery.
4. Drain the cooling system.
5. Drain the engine oil.
6. Disconnect the accelerator cable from the carburetor throttle lever.
7. On trucks with automatic transmission, remove the detent cable from the throttle lever.
8. Remove the air cleaner assembly.
9. Mark and disconnect all necessary electrical wiring from the engine.
10. Mark and disconnect all necessary vacuum hoses from the engine.
11. Disconnect the radiator hoses at the radiator.
12. Disconnect the heater hoses at the engine.
13. Remove the radiator.

※※ CAUTION

Please refer to Section 1 before discharging the compressor or disconnecting air conditioning lines. Damage to the air conditioning system or personal injury could result. Consult your local laws concerning refrigerant discharge and recycling. In many areas it may be illegal for anyone but a certified technician to service the A/C system. Always use an approved recovery station when discharging the air conditioning.

14. On trucks with air conditioning, discharge the system using an approved recovery/recycling machine.
15. Remove the air conditioning condenser.
16. Remove the fan assembly and water pump pulley.
17. Disconnect and plug the fuel line at the fuel pump.
18. Raise and support the truck on jackstands.
19. Remove the starter.
20. Remove the flywheel cover.
21. Disconnect the exhaust pipe from the exhaust manifold.
22. Support the weight of the engine with a shop crane and remove the engine mount through-bolts.
23. If equipped with an automatic transmission, remove the torque converter-to-flexplate bolts.
24. If equipped with 4WD, unbolt the strut rods at the engine mounts.
25. Remove the bell housing-to-engine retaining bolts.
26. Support the transmission with a floor jack.
27. Using the shop crane, carefully remove the engine from the vehicle.

To install:
Installation is the reverse of removal but please perform the following important steps.
28. Tighten the bell housing-to-engine retaining bolts to 30 ft. lbs. (40 Nm).
29. If equipped with 4WD, bolt the strut rods to the engine mounts. Tighten the bolts to 45 ft. lbs. (61 Nm).
30. If equipped with an automatic transmission, install the torque converter-to-flexplate bolts. Tighten the bolts to 40 ft. lbs. (54 Nm).
31. Install the engine mount through-bolts. Tighten them to 60 ft. lbs. (81 Nm). Remove the shop crane.
32. Connect the exhaust pipe at the exhaust manifold. Tighten the nuts to 20 ft. lbs. (27 Nm).

4.3L, 5.0L and 5.7L Engines

1. Disconnect the negative battery cable.
2. Remove the hood.
3. Drain the cooling system.
4. Remove the air cleaner assembly.
5. Remove the accessory drive belt, fan and water pump pulley.
6. Remove the radiator and shroud.

※※ CAUTION

Please refer to Section 1 before discharging the compressor or disconnecting air conditioning lines. Damage to the air conditioning system or personal injury could result. Consult your local laws concerning refrigerant discharge and recycling. In many areas it may be illegal for anyone but a certified technician to service the A/C system. Always use an approved recovery station when discharging the air conditioning.

7. On vehicles with air conditioning, discharge the system using an approved recovery/recycling machine.
8. Remove the air conditioning condenser.
9. Disconnect the heater hoses at the engine.
10. Disconnect the accelerator, cruise control and detent linkage (if equipped).
11. Disconnect the air conditioning compressor, (if equipped), and lay aside.
12. Remove the power steering pump and lay aside.
13. Disconnect the engine wiring harness from the engine.
14. Disconnect and tag the fuel line(s) from the intake manifold to the rear of the block.
15. Disconnect and tag the vacuum lines from the intake manifold.
16. Remove the distributor.
17. Raise the vehicle and support it safely.
18. Drain the engine oil.
19. Disconnect the exhaust pipes from the manifold.
20. Disconnect the strut rods at the engine mountings, (if equipped).
21. Remove the flywheel or torque converter cover.
22. Disconnect the wiring along the oil pan rail.
23. Remove the starter.
24. Disconnect the wire for the fuel gauge.
25. On vehicles equipped with automatic transmission, remove the converter-to-flexplate bolts.
26. Lower the vehicle and suitably support the transmission. Attach a suitable lifting fixture to the engine.
27. Remove the bell housing-to-engine bolts.
28. Remove the rear engine mounting-to-frame bolts and the front through-bolts and remove the engine.

※※ CAUTION

The EPA warns that prolonged contact with used engine oil may cause a number of skin disorders, including cancer! You should make every effort to minimize you exposure to used engine oil. Protective gloves should be worn when changing the oil. Wash your hands and any other exposed skin areas as soon as possible after exposure to used engine oil. Soap and water, or waterless hand cleaner should be used.

To install:
Installation is the reverse of removal but please perform the following important steps.
29. Raise the vehicle and support it safely.
30. Tighten the engine mounting bolts and nuts to the specifications listed in the torque specification chart at the end of this section.
31. Tighten the bell housing-to-engine bolts 35 ft. lbs. (47 Nm).
32. Install the converter-to-flex bolts and torque to 46 ft. lbs. (63 Nm).

7.4L Engines

1. Remove the hood.
2. Disconnect the negative battery cable.

3. Drain the cooling system.

4. Remove the air cleaner assembly.

5. Remove the radiator and fan shroud.

6. Disconnect and tag all necessary engine wiring.

7. Disconnect the accelerator, cruise control and TVS linkage.

8. Disconnect the fuel supply lines.

9. Disconnect all necessary vacuum wires.

10. Disconnect the air conditioning compressor and lay aside. Do not disconnect the lines.

11. Dismount the power steering pump and position it out of the way. It's not necessary to disconnect the fluid lines.

12. Raise the vehicle and support it on jackstands.

13. Disconnect the exhaust pipes from the manifold.

14. Remove the starter.

15. Remove the torque converter cover.

16. Remove the converter-to-flexplate bolts.

17. Lower the vehicle and suitably support the transmission. Attach a suitable lifting fixture to the engine.

18. Remove the bell housing-to-engine bolts.

19. Remove the rear engine mounting-to-frame bolts and the front through-bolts and remove the engine.

To install:

Installation is the reverse of removal but please pay attention to the following important steps.

20. Tighten the engine mounting bolts and nuts to the specifications listed in the torque specification chart at the end of this section.

21. Tighten the bell housing-to-engine bolts to 35 ft. lbs. (47 Nm).

22. Tighten the converter-to-flexplate bolts to 46 ft. lbs. (63 Nm).

6.2L and 6.5L Diesel Engines

✳✳ CAUTION

When draining the coolant, keep in mind that cats and dogs are attracted by ethylene glycol antifreeze, and are quite likely to drink any that is left in an uncovered container or in puddles on the ground. This will prove fatal in sufficient quantity. Always drain the coolant into a sealable container. Coolant should be reused unless it is contaminated or several years old.

1. Disconnect the negative battery cable.

2. Raise the vehicle and support it safely.

3. Remove the flywheel or torque converter cover.

4. On vehicles equipped with automatic transmission, remove the converter-to-flexplate bolts.

5. Disconnect the exhaust pipes from the manifold.

6. Remove the starter.

7. Remove the bell housing bolts.

8. Remove the engine mounting through-bolts.

9. Disconnect the block heater wiring.

10. Disconnect the wiring harness, transmission cooler lines, and a battery cable clamp at the oil pan.

11. Disconnect the fuel return lines at the engine.

12. Disconnect the oil cooler lines at the engine.

13. Lower the vehicle.

14. Remove the hood.

15. Drain the cooling system.

16. Remove the air cleaner and cover the mouth of the intake manifold.

17. Remove the alternator wires and clips.

18. Disconnect the wiring at the injector pump.

19. Disconnect the wiring from the rocker cover including the glow plug wires.

20. Disconnect the EGR/EPR solenoids, glow plug controller and temperature solenoid and move the harness aside.

21. Disconnect the left or right ground strap.

22. Remove the upper fan shroud and fan.

23. Disconnect the power steering pump and reservoir and lay to one side.

24. Disconnect the accelerator, cruise control and detent cables at the injection pump.

25. Disconnect the heater hose at the engine.

26. Remove the radiator.

27. Support the transmission with a suitable jack.

28. Remove the engine.

To install:

Installation is the reverse of removal but please perform the following important steps.

29. Tighten the engine mounting bolts and nuts to the specifications listed in the torque specification chart at the end of this section.

30. Tighten the bell housing-to-engine bolts to 30 ft. lbs. (40 Nm).

31. Tighten the converter-to-flexplate bolts to 46 ft. lbs. (63 Nm).

Valve/Cylinder Head Cover

REMOVAL & INSTALLATION

Gasoline Engines

EXCEPT 1997–98 7.4L ENGINES

▶ See Figures 1, 2, 3 and 4

1. Disconnect the negative battery cable. Remove the air cleaner.

2. Tag, disconnect and reposition as necessary any vacuum or PCV hoses that obstruct the cylinder head covers.

3. If necessary, remove the air cleaner box and the intake duct.

4. Disconnect electrical wire(s) (spark plug, etc.) from the cylinder head cover clips. You may also have to remove or move the alternator brace and PCV pipe.

5. Unbolt and remove the cover(s).

➡ **Do not pry the covers off if they seem stuck. Instead, gently tap around each cover with a rubber mallet until the old gasket or sealer breaks loose.**

To install:

6. Install a new gasket or apply RTV (or any equivalent) sealer to the cover prior to installation. If using sealer, follow directions on the tube.

7. Install the cover and mounting bolts. Tighten the bolts to the specifications listed in the torque specification chart at the end of this section.

8. Installation of the remaining components is the reverse of removal.

1997–98 7.4L ENGINES

1. Disconnect the negative battery cable.

2. If removing the right side cover, perform the following steps:

a. Remove the air cleaner assembly.

b. Tag and disconnect the spark plug wires from the spark plugs and move the wires aside so that they will not interfere with the valve cover removal.

c. Remove the vent tube from the valve cover.

d. Remove the throttle body unit and the throttle body studs.

e. Unfasten the valve cover retainers and remove the cover.

f. Remove the old valve cover gasket, then clean any gasket residue from the gasket mating surfaces.

g. Inspect the valve cover and its sealing surfaces for distortion. Replace as necessary.

3. If removing the left side cover, perform the following steps:

a. Remove the PCV valve, tube and the EGR inlet tube.

b. Tag and disconnect the spark plug wires from the spark plugs and move the wires aside so that they will not interfere with the valve cover removal.

c. Unfasten the valve cover retainers and remove the cover.

d. Remove the old valve cover gasket, then clean any gasket residue from the gasket mating surfaces.

e. Inspect the valve cover and its sealing surfaces for distortion. Replace as necessary.

To install:

4. If installing the right side cover, perform the following steps:

a. Install a new valve cover gasket.

b. Install the valve cover and its retainers. Tighten the retainers to 72 inch lbs. (8 Nm).

c. Install the throttle body studs in the upper intake manifold. Tighten the studs to 108 inch lbs. (12Nm).

5. Install all of the remaining components is the reverse of removal. Tighten the valve cover retainers to 72 inch lbs. (8 Nm).

Fig. 1 Unfasten and remove the cover bolts

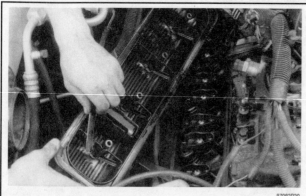

Fig. 2 Remove the old gasket material

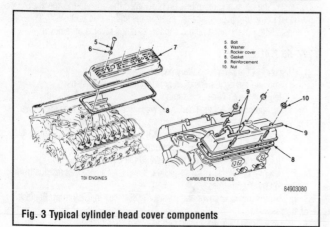

5. Bolt
6. Washer
7. Rocker cover
8. Gasket
9. Reinforcement
10. Nut

Fig. 3 Typical cylinder head cover components

APPLY A 3/32 INCH BEAD OF R.T.V. (ROOM TEMPERATURE VULCANIZING) SEALER ON THE VALVE COVER AS SHOWN

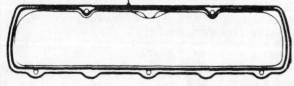

Fig. 4 Correct RTV application on the cylinder head cover

Diesel Engines

EXCEPT 1996–98 MODELS

1. If removing/installing the right side cover, perform the following steps:

  a. Remove the intake manifold.

  b. Remove the fuel injection lines for all except the No. 5 and No. 7 injectors.

  c. Disconnect the glow plug wires.

  d. Remove the wiring harness from the clip.

  e. Remove the CDR valve.

  f. Remove the cover bolts.

  g. Remove the cover. If the cover sticks, jar it loose with a plastic or rubber mallet. NEVER pry it loose!

  h. Installation is the reverse of removal. Clean all old RTV gasket material from the mating surfaces. Apply a 5/16 in. (8mm) bead of sealer to the head mating surfaces. Tighten the cover bolts to 16 ft. lbs. (22 Nm).

2. If removing/installing the left side cover, perform the following steps:

  a. Remove the intake manifold.

  b. Remove the fuel injection lines.

  c. On trucks with air conditioning, remove the upper fan shroud.

  d. On trucks with air conditioning, remove the compressor drive belt.

  e. On trucks with air conditioning, remove the left exhaust manifold.

  f. Remove the dipstick tube

  g. On trucks with air conditioning, dismount the compressor and move it out of the way. It may be possible to avoid disconnecting the refrigerant lines. If not, Discharge the system and disconnect the lines. Cap all openings at once. See Section 1 for discharging procedures.

  h. Remove the dipstick tube front bracket from the stud.

  i. Remove the wiring harness brackets.

  j. Remove the rocker arm cover bolts and fuel return bracket.

  k. Remove the cover. If the cover sticks, jar it loose with a plastic or rubber mallet. NEVER pry it loose!

  l. Installation is the reverse of removal. Clean all old RTV gasket material from the mating surfaces. Apply a 5/16 in. (8 mm) bead of sealer to the head mating surfaces. Tighten the cover bolts to 16 ft. lbs. (22 Nm).

1996–98 MODELS

♦ See Figure 5

1. Remove the intake manifold cover.

➥Do not bend the fuel lines to facilitate valve cover removal as this may damage the lines.

2. Mark the fuel line clips an brackets to ensure proper installation.

3. Remove the fuel injection lines and clips.

4. If removing the right side cover, remove the CDR valve, CDR hose and the long pencil brace to the turbocharger.

5. Remove the ground strap.

6. If removing the right side valve cover, remove the heater hose.

7. If removing the left side valve cover, remove the oil level indicator tube and bracket.

8. Remove the fuel return line clip from the valve cover stud.

9. Remove the wiring harness at the rear of the valve cover from the clips and set the harness aside.

10. If removing the right side cover, remove the turbocharger heat shield.

11. Unfasten the valve cover retainers.

  a. Unfasten the valve cover retainers and remove the cover.

  b. Remove the RTV sealer from the valve, then clean any RTV sealer residue from the valve cover mating surfaces.

  c. Inspect the valve cover and its sealing surfaces for distortion. Replace as necessary.

To install:

12. Installation is the reverse of removal, but please pay careful attention to the following important steps.

➥Do not allow and RTV sealant to enter the valve cover bolt holes. This will cause a condition referred to as valve lock, and when the bolts are tightened the cylinder head casing could be damaged.

13. Apply a 3/16 inch (5mm) bead of RTV sealant to the valve covers,

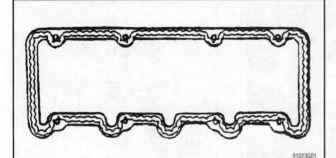

Fig. 5 Apply a bead of RTV sealant to the valve covers, inboard of the bolt holes—1996–98 6.5L diesel engine

inboard of the bolt holes. The sealer must be wet to the touch when the cover bolts are tightened.

14. Install the valve cover and the bolts. Tighten the bolts to 16 ft. lbs. (22 Nm).

Pushrod (Engine Side) Cover

REMOVAL & INSTALLATION

➡This applies to 4.8L engines only.

1. Disconnect the negative battery cable.
2. Remove the oil dipstick tube.
3. Remove the distributor.
4. Remove the side cover bolts.
5. Carefully pry off the side cover.
6. Remove all traces of the old gasket.
7. Installation is the reverse of removal. Use sealer on both sides of the gasket. Tighten the bolts to 80 inch lbs. (9 Nm).

Rocker Arms

REMOVAL & INSTALLATION

4.8L Engines

♦ See Figure 6

1. Remove the rocker arm cover.
2. Remove the rocker arm nut.
3. Remove the rocker arm and ball.
To install:
4. Coat the replacement rocker arm with Molykote, or its equivalent, and the rocker arm and pivot with SAE 90 gear oil, and install the pivots.

5. Install the nut. See the valve lash adjustment procedure later in this section.
6. Install the cover.

4.3L, 5.0L, 5.7L and 7.4L Engines

♦ See Figures 7, 8, 9 and 10

1. Remove the cylinder head cover.
2. Remove the rocker arm nut. If you are only replacing the pushrod, back the nut off until you can swing the rocker out of the way.
3. Remove the rocker arms and balls as a unit.

➡Always remove each set of rocker arms (one set per cylinder) as a unit.

4. Lift out the pushrods and pushrod guides.
To install:
5. Install the pushrods and their guides. Make sure that they seat properly in each lifter.
6. Position a set of rocker arms (for one cylinder) in the proper location.

➡Install the rocker arms for each cylinder only when the lifters are off the cam lobe and both valves are closed.

7. Coat the replacement rocker arm with Molykote, or its equivalent, and the rocker arm and pivot with SAE 90 gear oil, and install the pivots.
8. Install the nuts and tighten alternately as detailed in the valve lash adjustment procedure later in this section.

6.2L and 6.5L Diesel Engines

♦ See Figures 11 and 12

➡Rotate the engine until the mark on the crankshaft balancer is at the 2 o'clock position. Rotate the crankshaft counterclockwise 3½ in. (88mm) aligning the crankshaft balancer mark with the first lower water pump bolt, about the 12:30 position. This will ensure that no valves are close to a piston crown

1. Remove the cylinder head cover.
2. The rocker assemblies are mounted on two short rocker shafts per cylinder head, with each shaft operating four rockers. Remove the two bolts which secure each rocker shaft assembly, and remove the shaft. Mark the shafts so they can be installed in their original locations.
3. Remove the pushrods. The pushrods MUST be installed in the original direction! A paint stripe usually identifies the upper end of each rod, but if you can't see it, make sure to mark each rod yourself.
4. Insert a small prybar into the end of the rocker shaft bore and break off the end of the nylon retainers. Pull off the retainers with pliers and then slide off the rockers.
To install:
5. Make sure first that the rocker arms and springs go back on the shafts in the exact order in which they were removed. Its a good idea to coat them with engine oil.
6. Center the rockers on the corresponding holes in the shaft and install new plastic retainers using a ½ in. (13mm) drift.

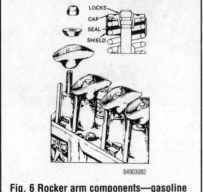

Fig. 6 Rocker arm components—gasoline engines

Fig. 7 Remove the rocker arm nut

Fig. 8 Remove the rocker arms

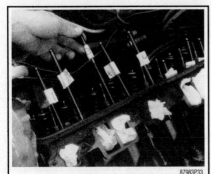

Fig. 9 Tag the pushrods before removal, as they must be installed in the same order

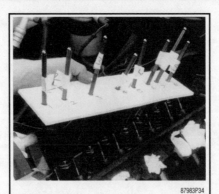

Fig. 10 A piece of cardboard may be used to hold the pushrods in order

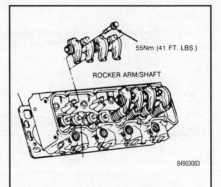

Fig. 11 Rocker shaft assembly—diesel engines

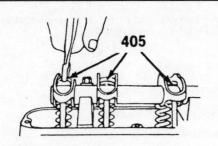

405. Rocker Arm Retainers

Fig. 12 Removing the rocker arm retainers

7. Install the pushrods with their marked ends up.

8. Install the rocker shaft assemblies and make sure that the ball ends of the pushrods seat themselves in the rockers.

9. Rotate the engine clockwise until the mark on the torsional damper aligns with the **0** on the timing tab. Rotate the engine counterclockwise 3½ in. (88mm) measured at the damper. You can estimate this by checking that the mark on the damper is now aligned with the FIRST lower water pump bolt. BE CAREFUL! This ensures that the piston is away from the valves.

10. Install the rocker shaft bolts and tighten them to 40 ft. lbs. (55 Nm).

11. Install the cylinder head cover.

Thermostat

REMOVAL & INSTALLATION

Gasoline Engines

▶ See Figures 13, 14, 15 and 16

✳ CAUTION

Never open, service or drain the radiator or cooling system when hot; serious burns can occur from the steam and hot coolant. Also, when draining engine coolant, keep in mind that cats and dogs are attracted to ethylene glycol antifreeze and could drink any that is left in an uncovered container or in puddles on the ground. This will prove fatal in sufficient quantities. Always drain coolant into a sealable container. Coolant should be reused unless it is contaminated or is several years old.

1. Drain the radiator until the coolant is below the thermostat level (below the level of the intake manifold).

2. Remove the water outlet elbow assembly from the engine. Remove the thermostat from the engine, or, on the 4.8L, from inside the adapter elbow.

To install:

3. Clean the gasket surfaces on the water outlet elbow and the intake manifold. Use a new gasket when installing the elbow to the manifold.

4. Install the new thermostat making sure the spring side is inserted into the engine, or, on the 4.8L, downward into the thermostat housing. Tighten the ther-

Fig. 13 Remove the thermostat housing bolts

Fig. 14 Remove the thermostat housing from the engine

Fig. 15 Remove the thermostat from the housing

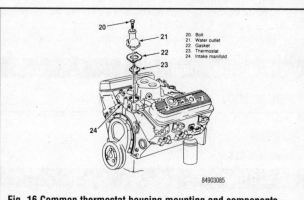

Fig. 16 Common thermostat housing mounting and components—gasoline engines

mostat housing bolts to 20 ft. lbs. (28 Nm). On the 4.3L, 5.0L, 5.7L tighten the studs to 21 ft. lbs. (28 Nm). On the 7.4L tighten the bolts to 27 ft. lbs. (37 Nm).
5. Refill the cooling system. Start the engine and check for leaks.

Diesel Engines

1988–95 MODELS

♦ See Figures 17 and 18

1. Remove the upper fan shroud.
2. Drain the cooling system to a point below the thermostat.
3. Remove the engine oil dipstick tube brace and the oil fill brace.
4. Remove the upper radiator hose.
5. Remove the water outlet.
6. Remove the thermostat and gasket.

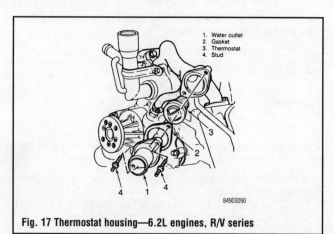

1. Water outlet
2. Gasket
3. Thermostat
4. Stud

Fig. 17 Thermostat housing—6.2L engines, R/V series

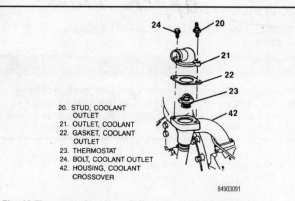

20. STUD, COOLANT OUTLET
21. OUTLET, COOLANT
22. GASKET, COOLANT OUTLET
23. THERMOSTAT
24. BOLT, COOLANT OUTLET
42. HOUSING, COOLANT CROSSOVER

Fig. 18 Thermostat housing—6.2L and 6.5L diesel engines—1988–95 C/K series

7. Installation is the reverse of removal.
8. Use a new gasket coated with sealer, Make sure that the spring end of the thermostat is in the engine. Tighten the bolts to 35 ft. lbs. (47 Nm) on 1988–91 models and 31 ft. lbs. (42 Nm) on 1992–95 models.

1996–98 MODELS

♦ See Figure 19

1. Drain the cooling system to a point below the thermostat.
2. Disconnect the upper radiator (inlet) hose from the thermostat outlet.
3. Unfasten the thermostat housing bolt and stud, then remove the housing.
4. Remove the gasket and the thermostat.
5. Clean any remaining gasket from the thermostat hosing mating surfaces.
To install:
6. Place the thermostat into position in the housing, then install the gasket.
7. Install the thermostat housing, the bolt and the stud. Tighten the bolt and stud to 31 ft. lbs. (42 Nm).
8. Install the remaining components in the reverse order of removal.

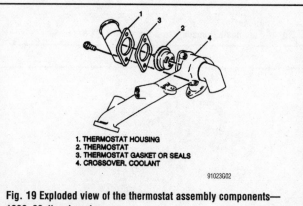

1. THERMOSTAT HOUSING
2. THERMOSTAT
3. THERMOSTAT GASKET OR SEALS
4. CROSSOVER, COOLANT

Fig. 19 Exploded view of the thermostat assembly components—1996–98 diesel engines

Thermostat Housing Crossover

REMOVAL & INSTALLATION

♦ See Figures 20, 21 and 22

➡ This is found on the 6.2 and 6.5L diesel engines only.

✳ CAUTION

Never open, service or drain the radiator or cooling system when hot; serious burns can occur from the steam and hot coolant. Also, when draining engine coolant, keep in mind that cats and dogs are attracted to ethylene glycol antifreeze and could drink any that is left in an uncovered container or in puddles on the ground. This will prove fatal in sufficient quantities. Always drain coolant into a sealable container. Coolant should be reused unless it is contaminated or is several years old.

1. Drain the cooling system.
2. Remove the engine cover.
3. Remove the air cleaner and CDR valve.
4. Remove the air cleaner resonator and bracket.
5. Remove the upper fan shroud.
6. Remove the upper alternator bracket.
7. Remove the bypass hose.
8. Remove the upper radiator hose.
9. Disconnect the heater hose.
10. Remove the attaching bolts and lift out the crossover.
To install:
11. Thoroughly clean the mating surfaces.
12. Position the crossover, using new gaskets coated with sealer.

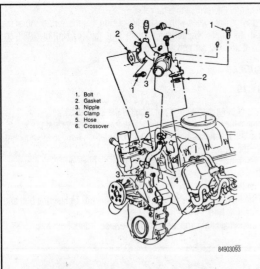

1. Bolt
2. Gasket
3. Nipple
4. Clamp
5. Hose
6. Crossover

84903093

Fig. 20 Thermostat housing crossover—1988–91 R/V series

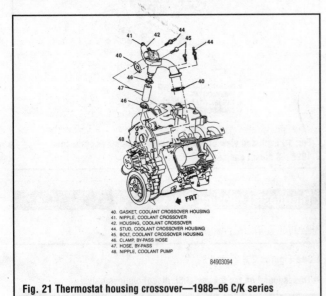

40. GASKET, COOLANT CROSSOVER HOUSING
41. NIPPLE, COOLANT CROSSOVER
42. HOUSING, COOLANT CROSSOVER
44. STUD, COOLANT CROSSOVER HOUSING
45. BOLT, COOLANT CROSSOVER HOUSING
46. CLAMP, BY-PASS HOSE
47. HOSE, BY-PASS
48. NIPPLE, COOLANT PUMP

84903094

Fig. 21 Thermostat housing crossover—1988–96 C/K series

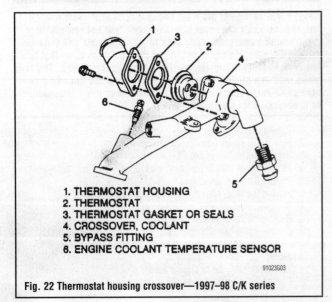

1. THERMOSTAT HOUSING
2. THERMOSTAT
3. THERMOSTAT GASKET OR SEALS
4. CROSSOVER, COOLANT
5. BYPASS FITTING
6. ENGINE COOLANT TEMPERATURE SENSOR

91023G03

Fig. 22 Thermostat housing crossover—1997–98 C/K series

13. Install the attaching bolts and tighten them to 35 ft. lbs. (47 Nm) on 1988–91 engines, or 31 ft. lbs. (42 Nm) on 1992–98 engines.
14. Installation of the remaining components is the reverse of removal.

Upper Intake Manifold

REMOVAL & INSTALLATION

4.3L Engines

1996–98 MODELS

✳✳ CAUTION

Fuel injection systems remain under pressure, even after the engine has been turned OFF. The fuel system pressure must be relieved before disconnecting any fuel lines. Failure to do so may result in fire and/or personal injury.

1. Disconnect the negative battery cable.
2. Drain and recycle the engine coolant.
3. Remove the air cleaner box and intake duct.
4. Remove the wiring harness connectors and brackets and move them aside.
5. Disconnect the throttle linkage and bracket from the upper intake manifold.
6. Remove the cruise control cable (if equipped).
7. Remove the fuel lines and bracket at the rear of the lower intake manifold.
8. Remove the brake booster vacuum hose at the upper intake manifold.
9. Remove the PCV hose from the upper intake manifold.
10. Remove the ignition coil and bracket.
11. Remove the purge solenoid and bracket.

➥**Note the location of the manifold bolts and studs before removal for reassembly in their original positions.**

12. Remove the intake manifold bolts and studs.

➥**Do not disassemble the CSFI unit.**

13. Remove the upper intake manifold.
To install:
14. Install the upper intake manifold gasket.
15. Install the upper intake manifold.

➥**When installing the upper intake manifold be careful not to pinch the injector wires between the upper and lower intake manifolds.**

16. Install the upper intake manifold mounting bolts and studs in the same locations as prior to removal.
17. Tighten the bolts and studs in a crisscross pattern to 88 inch lbs. (10 Nm).
18. Install the remaining components in the reverse of removal.

5.0 and 5.7L Engines   *Upper Intake*

1996–98 MODELS

➥**The lower intake manifold gaskets are NOT reusable on the 5.0L and 5.7L engines.**

✳✳ CAUTION

Fuel injection systems remain under pressure, even after the engine has been turned OFF. The fuel system pressure must be relieved before disconnecting any fuel lines. Failure to do so may result in fire and/or personal injury.

1. Disconnect the negative battery cable.
2. Remove the air cleaner intake duct.
3. Remove the wiring harness connectors and brackets and move them aside.
4. Disconnect the throttle linkage and bracket from the upper intake manifold.

5. Remove the cruise control cable (if equipped).
6. Remove the PCV valve and hose.
7. Remove the fuel lines and bracket from the intake to the rear of the block.
8. Remove the ignition coil and bracket.
9. Remove the purge solenoid and bracket.

➡**Note the location of the manifold bolts and studs before removal for reassembly in their original positions.**

10. Remove the intake manifold bolts and studs.

➡**Do not disassemble the CSFI unit.**

11. Remove the upper intake manifold.
To install:
12. Install the upper intake manifold gasket.
13. Install the upper intake manifold.

➡**When installing the upper intake manifold, be careful not to pinch the injector wires between the upper and lower intake manifolds.**

14. Install the upper intake manifold mounting bolts and studs in the same locations as prior to removal.
15. Tighten the bolts and studs in a crisscross pattern in 2 steps first to 45 inch lbs. (5 Nm) then to 83 inch lbs. (10 Nm).
16. Installation of the remaining components is the reverse of removal.

7.4L Engines

1996–98 MODELS

▶ **See Figures 23 and 24**

1. Disconnect the negative battery cable.
2. Remove the air cleaner intake duct.
3. Remove the wiring harness connectors and brackets and move them aside.
4. Remove the throttle and cruise control linkage (if equipped).
5. Remove the throttle body electrical connectors.
6. Remove the PCV valve and hose.
7. Remove the EGR inlet tube.
8. Remove the purge solenoid and connectors.
9. Remove the ignition coil and bracket.
10. Remove the No. 8 spark plug wire from the distributor.
11. Unfasten the upper intake manifold bolts and remove the upper intake manifold.
To install:
12. Clean all parts well. Clean all traces of gasket from the sealing surfaces.
13. Install a new upper intake manifold gasket.

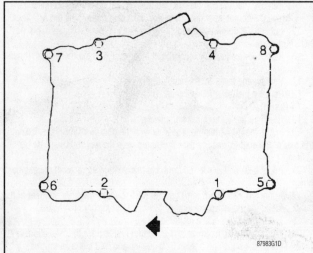

Fig. 23 Upper intake manifold bolt tightening sequence—1996 7.4L engines

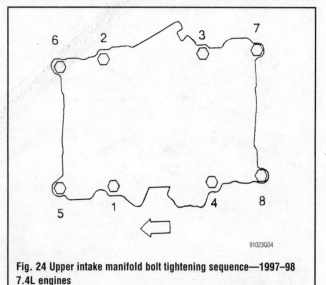

Fig. 24 Upper intake manifold bolt tightening sequence—1997–98 7.4L engines

14. Carefully place the upper intake manifold into position.
15. Install the upper intake manifold bolts and tighten them in sequence to 17 ft. lbs. (22 Nm) on 1996 models. On 1997–98 models tighten the bolts in two steps. On the first pass, tighten the bolts in sequence to 72 inch lbs. (8 Nm). On the second and final pass, tighten the bolts in sequence to 10 ft. lbs. (14 Nm).
16. Install the remaining components in the reverse of removal.

Lower Intake Manifold

➡**For the 4.8L engine, please refer to the Combination Manifold procedure.**

REMOVAL & INSTALLATION

4.3L Engines

1988–95 MODELS

▶ **See Figures 25, 26 and 27**

1. Disconnect the negative battery cable. Drain the cooling system.
2. Remove the air cleaner assembly.

➡**Mark the relationship of the distributor and rotor for proper reassembly.**

3. Remove the distributor.
4. Disconnect the accelerator and cruise control cables with their brackets.
5. Remove the rear air conditioner compressor bracket, the alternator bracket and the idler pulley bracket at the manifold.
6. Unplug all electrical connections and vacuum lines from the manifold. Remove the EGR valve if necessary.
7. Disconnect the fuel line at the intake manifold.
8. Remove the heater pipe.
9. Disconnect the upper radiator hose and pull it off.
10. Tag and disconnect the power brake vacuum pipe and the EGR vacuum line.
11. Tag and disconnect the coil wires and if necessary remove the coil.
12. Remove the sensors and bracket on the right side. Disconnect the wiring harness on the right side and position it out of the way.

➡**Mark the location of the intake manifold studs for proper reassembly**

13. Remove the intake manifold bolts. Remove the manifold and the gaskets. Remember to reinstall the O-ring between the intake manifold and timing chain cover during assembly, if so equipped.
To install:

➡**Before installing the intake manifold, be sure that the gasket surfaces are thoroughly clean.**

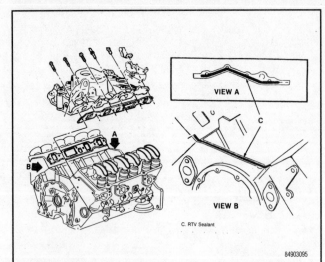

Fig. 25 Intake manifold installation—4.3L engine shown, 5.0L and 5.7L engines similar

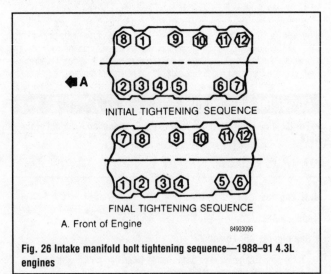

Fig. 26 Intake manifold bolt tightening sequence—1988–91 4.3L engines

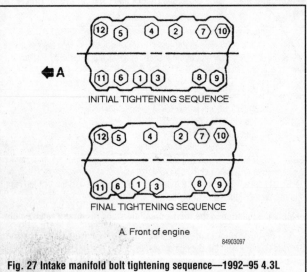

Fig. 27 Intake manifold bolt tightening sequence—1992–95 4.3L engines

14. Use plastic gasket retainers to prevent the manifold gasket from slipping out of place, if so equipped. Coat the front and rear sealing surfaces with a 0.19 in. (5mm) bead of RTV sealant. Extend the bead approximately ½ in. (13mm) down each head to help retain the gaskets.

15. Install the manifold and the gaskets. Remember to reinstall the O-ring between the intake manifold and timing chain cover, if so equipped.

16. Install the intake manifold bolts and tighten them to 35 ft. lbs. (48 Nm) in the sequence shown.

17. Install the remaining components in the reverse of removal.

1996–98 MODELS

♦ See Figure 28

1. Drain and recycle the engine coolant.
2. Remove the upper intake manifold using the recommended procedure outlined in this section.
3. Remove the distributor.
4. Disconnect the upper radiator hose from the thermostat housing.
5. Disconnect the heater hose from the lower intake manifold.
6. Remove the coolant by-pass hose.

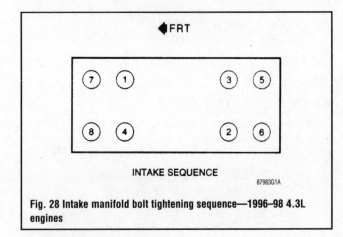

Fig. 28 Intake manifold bolt tightening sequence—1996–98 4.3L engines

7. Remove the EGR valve.
8. Disconnect the fuel pressure and return lines from the lower intake manifold.
9. Disconnect the wiring harnesses and brackets from the lower manifold.
10. Disconnect the throttle cable, the cruise control cable (if equipped) and the bracket from the manifold.
11. Remove the transmission oil level indicator and tube, if equipped.
12. Remove the EGR tube, clamp and bolt.
13. Remove the PCV valve and vacuum hoses.
14. Remove the A/C compressor and bracket, but do NOT disconnect the lines. Move the compressor out of the way. Take care not to kink the A/C lines.
15. Loosen the compressor mounting bracket and slide it forward, but do NOT remove it.
16. Remove the alternator bracket bolt located next to the thermostat, if necessary.
17. Remove the lower intake manifold bolts.
18. Remove the lower intake manifold.

To install:

19. Clean all gasket surfaces completely.
20. Install the intake manifold gaskets with the port blocking plates facing the rear of the engine. Factory gaskets should have the words "This Side Up" visible.
21. Apply gasket sealer to the front and rear sealing surfaces of the engine block.
22. Apply a 0.197 inch (5mm) bead of RTV sealer to the front and rear of the block. Extend the sealer approximately ½-inch (13mm) onto the heads.
23. Install the lower intake manifold.
24. Apply sealer to the lower intake manifold bolts prior to installation.
25. Install the bolts and tighten in sequence and in 3 steps as follows:

a. First step to 26 inch lbs. (3 Nm).
b. Second step to 106 inch lbs. (12 Nm).
c. Final step to 11 ft. lbs. (15 Nm).
26. Installation of the remaining components is the reverse of removal.

5.0L and 5.7L Engines

1988–95 MODELS

♦ **See Figures 25, 29, 30, 31 and 32**

1. Disconnect the negative battery cable. Drain the cooling system.
2. Remove the air cleaner assembly.
3. Remove the upper radiator hose from the thermostat housing.
4. Disconnect the heater pipe at the rear of the manifold.
5. Disconnect the rear alternator brace at the manifold.
6. Disengage all electrical connections and vacuum lines from the manifold. Remove the EGR valve if necessary.

➡ **Mark the relationship of the distributor and rotor for proper reassembly**

7. Remove the distributor.
8. Disconnect the fuel line at the intake manifold.
9. Remove the accelerator and cruise control linkage.
10. Remove the air conditioner compressor rear bracket.
11. Remove the brake booster vacuum pipe and then disconnect the coil wires.
12. Remove the emission control sensors and their bracket from the right side.
13. Remove the fuel line bracket at the rear of the manifold and position the fuel lines out of the way.
14. Remove the bracket behind the idler pulley.
15. Remove the carburetor or TBI unit if necessary. Refer to Section 5 for this procedure.

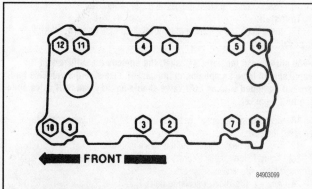

Fig. 29 Intake manifold bolt tightening sequence—1988–95 5.0L and 5.7L engines

➡ **Mark the location of the intake manifold studs for proper reassembly**

16. Remove the intake manifold bolts. Remove the manifold and the gaskets. Remember to reinstall the O-ring between the intake manifold and timing chain cover during assembly, if so equipped.

To install:

➡ **Before installing the intake manifold, be sure that the gasket surfaces are thoroughly clean.**

17. Use plastic gasket retainers to prevent the manifold gasket from slipping out of place, if so equipped. Place a ³⁄₁₆ in. (5mm) bead of RTV type silicone sealer on the front and rear ridges of the cylinder block-to-manifold mating surfaces. Extend the bead ½ in. (13mm) up each cylinder head to seal and retain the manifold side gaskets.
18. Install the manifold and the gaskets. Remember to reinstall the O-ring between the intake manifold and timing chain cover, if so equipped.
19. Install the intake manifold bolts and tighten in the proper sequence. Tighten to 35 ft. lbs. (48Nm).
20. Install the remaining components in the reverse of removal.

1996–98 MODELS Lower Intake

♦ **See Figure 33**

1. Remove the upper intake manifold using the recommended procedure outlined in this section.
2. Remove the distributor.
3. Disconnect the upper radiator hose from the thermostat housing.
4. Disconnect the heater hose from the lower intake manifold.
5. Remove the coolant by-pass hose.
6. Remove the EGR valve.
7. Disconnect the fuel pressure and return lines from the lower intake manifold.
8. Disconnect the wiring harnesses and brackets from the lower manifold.
9. Disconnect the throttle cable, the cruise control cable (if equipped) and the bracket from the manifold.
10. If necessary, remove the left side valve cover.
11. Remove the transmission oil level indicator and tube, if equipped.
12. Remove the EGR tube, clamp and bolt.
13. Remove the PCV valve and vacuum hoses.
14. Remove the A/C compressor and bracket, but do NOT disconnect the lines. Move the compressor out of the way. Take care not to kink the A/C lines.
15. Loosen the compressor mounting bracket and slide it forward, but do NOT remove it.
16. Remove the power brake vacuum tube.
17. If necessary, remove the alternator rear bracket bolt.
18. Remove the lower intake manifold bolts.
19. Remove the lower intake manifold.

To install:
20. Clean all gasket surfaces completely.
21. Install the intake manifold gaskets with the port blocking plates facing the rear. Factory gaskets should have the words "This Side Up" visible.
22. Apply gasket sealer to the front and rear sealing surfaces of the engine block.

Fig. 30 Remove the intake manifold retaining bolts

Fig. 31 Remove the intake manifold

Fig. 32 Using a scraper, clean the intake manifold gasket mating surfaces

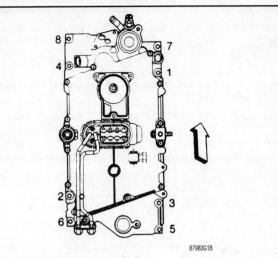

Fig. 33 Intake manifold bolt tightening sequence—1996–98 5.0L and 5.7L engines

23. Apply a 0.197 inch (5mm) bead of RTV sealer to the front and rear of the block. Extend the sealer approximately ½-inch (13mm) onto the heads.
24. Install the lower intake manifold.
25. Apply sealer to the lower intake manifold bolts prior to installation.
26. Install the bolts and tighten in sequence and in 3 steps as follows:
    a. First step to 71 inch lbs. (8 Nm).
    b. Second step to 106 inch lbs. (12 Nm).
    c. Final step to 11 ft. lbs. (15 Nm).
27. Install the remaining components in the reverse of removal.

Diesel Engines

1988–95 MODELS

▶ See Figure 34

1. Disconnect both batteries.
2. Remove the air cleaner assembly.
3. Remove the alternator rear bracket.
4. Remove the EPR/EGR boost solenoids and bracket.
5. Tag and disconnect the Crankcase Depression Regulator (CDR) hose.
6. Tag and disconnect the EGR and crankcase vent hoses.
7. Remove the intake manifold bolts. The injection line clips are retained by these bolts.
8. Remove the intake manifold.

➡If the engine is to be further serviced with the manifold removed, install protective covers over the intake ports.

To install:
9. Clean the manifold gasket surfaces on the cylinder heads and install new gaskets before installing the manifold.

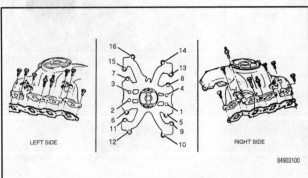

LEFT SIDE   RIGHT SIDE

Fig. 34 Intake manifold bolt tightening sequence—1988–95 diesel engines

➡The gaskets have an opening for the EGR valve on light duty installations. An insert covers this opening on heavy duty installations.

10. Install the manifold. Tighten the bolts in the sequence illustrated to 32 ft. lbs. (42 Nm).
11. Installation of the remaining components is the reverse of removal.

1996–98 MODELS

▶ See Figure 35

1. Disconnect the negative battery cable.
2. Remove the fuel filter.
3. Drain the cooling system.
4. Remove the thermostat bolts.
5. Remove the fuel line return hose and its retaining clips.

➡Mark the location of the EGR/boost or boost (whichever your vehicle is equipped with) solenoid studs so that they can be installed in their original positions.

6. Remove the EGR/boost or boost (whichever your vehicle is equipped with) solenoids with the bracket from the intake manifold studs.
7. Remove the heater hose bracket and the vacuum hoses from the EGR valve.
8. Remove the long pencil brace that attaches to the turbocharger.
9. Remove the upper radiator hose.
10. Remove the fuel filter assembly and the POE wiring harness bracket to the rear of the lower intake manifold.
11. Remove the intake manifold that runs from the turbocharger to the upper intake manifold.
12. Mark the location of the fuel line clips and brackets so that they can be installed in their original positions.
13. Remove the intake manifold studs and the fuel line clips.
14. Remove the intake manifold and the gasket.
15. If any further work is to performed around the intake manifold area, cover the intake ports to prevent any dirt entering the ports.
16. Use a scraper to clean the gasket mating surfaces.
To install:
17. Installation is the reverse of removal but please note the following important steps.

➡Be sure to use the correct gasket, the engines that utilize an EGR valve should have an opening in the gasket. Likewise the vehicles that are not equipped with an EGR valve should not have an EGR valve opening in the gasket.

18. Remove any covers placed over the intake ports to prevent dirt from entering the ports.
19. Install the new gaskets and the intake manifold.
20. Apply Teflon® sealer to bolts 9, 11, 13 and 15, as these bolts are exposed to the crankcase.
21. Apply a threadlocker sealer to bolts 1, 2, 3 , 4, 5, 6 , 7, 8, 10, 12, 14 and 16.
22. Install the intake manifold studs and the fuel line clips. Tighten the studs to 31 ft. lbs. (42 Nm) in the sequence illustrated.

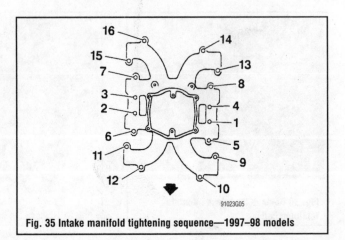

Fig. 35 Intake manifold tightening sequence—1997–98 models

23. Tighten the clamps for the turbocharger connector hose 50 inch lbs. (6 Nm).

➡ **When installing the upper intake manifold, if equipped with an O-ring between the upper and lower manifolds, always replace this O-ring as failure to do so could cause a derivability problem.**

24. Install the fuel return line hose and the fuel filter. Tighten the fuel filter bolts to 31 ft. lbs. (42 Nm).

7.4L Engines

1988-95 MODELS

▶ **See Figures 36, 37 and 38**

1. Disconnect the battery.
2. Drain the cooling system.
3. Remove the air cleaner assembly.
4. Remove the upper radiator hose, thermostat housing and the bypass hose, if necessary.
5. Disconnect the heater hose and pipe.
6. Tag and disconnect all electrical connections and vacuum lines from the manifold and move them to the side.
7. Disconnect the accelerator linkage and if equipped, the cruise control cable.
8. Disconnect the TVS cable.
9. Remove the fuel line at the manifold.
10. Remove the TBI unit, if necessary.

➡ **Mark the relationship of the distributor and rotor for proper reassembly**

11. Remove the distributor, if necessary.
12. Remove the cruise control transducer, if equipped.
13. Disconnect the ignition coil wires and remove the coil if necessary.
14. Remove the EGR solenoid and bracket and the MAP sensor and bracket.
15. Remove the air conditioning compressor rear bracket.
16. Remove the front alternator/AIR pump bracket, if necessary.
17. Remove the intake manifold bolts.

2. Remove the upper intake manifold using the recommended procedure outlined in this section.
3. Remove the A/C lines at the compressor.
4. Remove the distributor using the recommended procedure. Mark the relationship of the distributor housing and rotor for proper reassembly.

❊❊ CAUTION

Never open, service or drain the radiator or cooling system when hot; serious burns can occur from the steam and hot coolant. Also, when draining engine coolant, keep in mind that cats and dogs are attracted to ethylene glycol antifreeze and could drink any that is left in an uncovered container or in puddles on the ground. This will prove fatal in sufficient quantities. Always drain coolant into a sealable container. Coolant should be reused unless it is contaminated or is several years old.

5. Drain the engine coolant. Remove the upper radiator hose at the thermostat housing.
6. Disconnect the heater hose from the manifold.
7. Disconnect the fuel line brackets and rail.
8. Disconnect the water pump by-pass hose.
9. Unfasten the lower intake manifold bolts and remove the lower intake manifold and gaskets.

To install:
10. Clean all parts well:
   a. Clean all traces of gasket from the sealing surfaces.
   b. Inspect for cracks, broken flanges and gasket surface damage.
   c. Clean excessive carbon buildup in the exhaust passages.
   d. Clean scale and deposits from the coolant passages.
   e. Clean the EGR passage of carbon deposits.
11. Install the gaskets to the cylinder head in their proper position. Factory-type gaskets should be stamped "This Side Up".
12. Install the front and rear intake manifold seals to the block.
13. Apply a ¾₁₆-inch (5mm) bead of RTV GM #1052289, or equivalent, to the four seal corners of the block. Extend the bead approximately ½-inch (13mm) up the cylinder head to seal and retain the gaskets.
14. Carefully place the lower intake manifold into position on the engine.

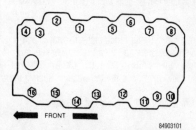

Fig. 36 Intake manifold bolt tightening sequence—1988-90 7.4L engines

84903101

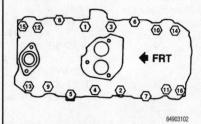

Fig. 37 Intake manifold bolt tightening sequence—1991-94 7.4L engines

84903102

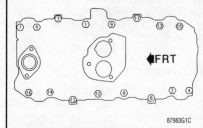

Fig. 38 Intake manifold bolt tightening sequence—1995 7.4L engines

87983G1C

18. Remove the manifold and the gaskets and seals.

➡ **Remember to reinstall the O-ring between the intake manifold and timing chain cover during assembly, if so equipped.**

To install:
➡ **Before installing the intake manifold, be sure that the gasket surfaces are thoroughly clean.**

19. Install the manifold and the gaskets and seals.
20. Install the intake manifold bolts. Tighten the bolts to 30 ft. lbs. (40 Nm) in the proper sequence.
21. Installation of the remaining components is the reverse of removal.

1996-98 MODELS

▶ **See Figure 39**

1. Have the A/C system discharged. Recover the refrigerant using the appropriate recycling equipment.

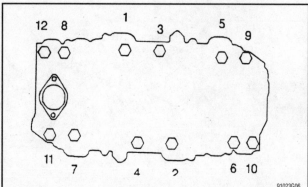

Fig. 39 Lower intake manifold bolt tightening sequence—1996-98 models

91023G06

15. Apply sealer, GM #1052080, or equivalent, to the lower intake manifold bolts. Install the lower manifold bolts and tighten them in sequence to 30 ft. lbs. (40 Nm).

16. Install the remaining components in the reverse of removal.

17. Have the A/C system recharged.

Exhaust Manifold

→For the 4.8L engine, please refer to the Combination Manifold procedure.

REMOVAL & INSTALLATION

4.3L Engines

▶ See Figure 40

On some engines, tab locks are used on the front and rear pairs of bolts on each exhaust manifold. When removing the bolts, straighten the tabs from beneath the truck using a suitable tool. When installing the tab locks, bend the tabs against the sides of the bolt, not over the top of the bolt.

1988–94 MODELS

1. Disconnect the negative battery cable. Remove the air cleaner assembly.

2. Raise the vehicle and support it with jackstands.

3. Remove the hot air shroud, (if so equipped). Disconnect the exhaust pipe at the manifold.

4. Lower the truck.

5. Disconnect the oxygen sensor wire on the left side manifold. Do not remove the sensor unless you intend to replace it.

6. Disconnect the rear power steering pump bracket at the left manifold.

7. Remove the heat stove pipe on the right side manifold.

8. Remove the AIR hose at the check valve.

9. Remove the manifold bolts and remove the manifold(s). Some models have lock tabs on the front and rear manifold bolts which must be removed before removing the bolts. These tabs can be bent with a drift pin.

To install:

10. Clean both the manifold and cylinder block mating surfaces and install the manifold. Install the flat washers and then the tab washers and insert the bolts. Tighten the two center bolts to 26 ft. lbs. (36 Nm); the outside bolts to 20 ft. lbs. (28 Nm) and then bend the tab washers against the bolt heads.

11. Installation of the remaining components is the reverse of removal.

1995–98 MODELS

1. Disconnect the negative battery cable.

2. Raise the vehicle and support it with jackstands.

3. Remove the hot air shroud, (if so equipped). Disconnect the exhaust pipe at the manifold.

4. Lower the truck.

5. If removing the left side manifold, remove the EGR inlet pipe.

6. Unfasten the manifold retainers and remove the manifold.

To install:

7. Clean the exhaust manifold mating surfaces to remove any gasket residue.

8. Install the manifold and tighten the retainers in the following sequence:

- Bolts on the center exhaust tube: 26 ft. lbs. (36 Nm)
- Bolts on the front and rear exhaust tubes: 20 ft. lbs. (28 Nm)

9. Bend the tab washers over the bolts.

10. Install the remaining components in the reverse of removal.

5.0L and 5.7L Engines

1988–95 MODELS

▶ See Figures 41, 42, 43, 44 and 45

On some engines, tab locks are used on the front and rear pairs of bolts on each exhaust manifold. When removing the bolts, straighten the tabs from beneath the truck using a suitable tool. When installing the tab locks, bend the tabs against the sides of the bolt, not over the top of the bolt.

1. Disconnect the negative battery cable. Remove the air cleaner.

2. Raise the truck and support it with jackstands.

3. Remove the hot air shroud, (if so equipped). Disconnect the exhaust pipe at the manifold.

4. Lower the truck.

5. Disconnect the oxygen sensor wire on the left side manifold. Do not remove the sensor unless you intend to replace it.

6. Remove the AIR hose at the check valve.

7. Remove the heat stove pipe on the right side manifold.

8. Disconnect the rear power steering pump bracket at the left manifold.

9. Remove the dipstick tube bracket on the right manifold.

10. Remove the manifold bolts and remove the manifold(s). Some models have locktabs on the front and rear manifold bolts which must be removed before removing the bolts. These tabs can be bent with a drift pin or needle-nose pliers.

To install:

11. Clean both the manifold and cylinder block mating surfaces and install the manifold. Install the flat washers and then the tab washers and insert the bolts. Tighten the two center bolts to 26 ft. lbs. (36 Nm); the outside bolts to 20 ft. lbs. (28 Nm) and then bend the tab washers against the bolt heads.

12. Install the remaining components in the reverse of removal.

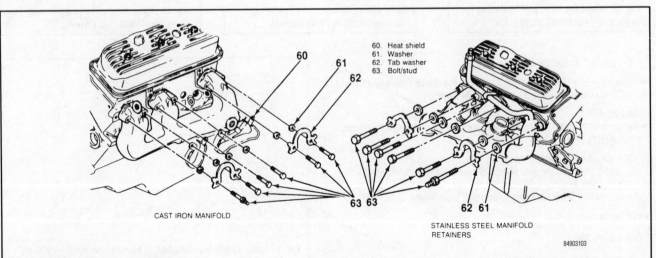

60. Heat shield
61. Washer
62. Tab washer
63. Bolt/stud

CAST IRON MANIFOLD

STAINLESS STEEL MANIFOLD RETAINERS

84903103

Fig. 40 Exhaust manifold—4.3L engines

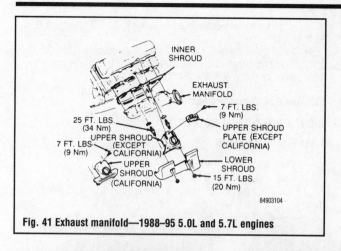

Fig. 41 Exhaust manifold—1988–95 5.0L and 5.7L engines

Fig. 42 Remove the exhaust pipe from the manifold

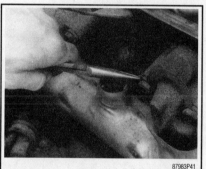

Fig. 43 Use a pair of needlenose pliers to bend back the locktabs on the exhaust manifold

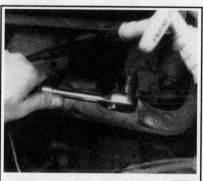

Fig. 44 Loosen and remove the exhaust manifold bolts

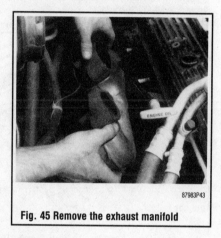

Fig. 45 Remove the exhaust manifold

1996–98 MODELS

▶ See Figure 46

1. Disconnect the negative battery cable.
2. Raise the vehicle and support it with jackstands.
3. Disconnect the exhaust pipe at the manifold.
4. Lower the truck.
5. If removing the left side manifold, remove the EGR inlet pipe.
6. Remove the engine oil level indicator bracket from the right side manifold.
7. Unfasten the manifold retainers and remove the manifold.

To install:

8. Clean the exhaust manifold mating surfaces to remove any gasket residue.
9. Install the manifold and tighten the retainers in the following sequence:

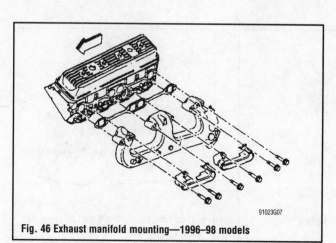

Fig. 46 Exhaust manifold mounting—1996–98 models

- First pass: 15 ft. lbs. (20 Nm)
- Final pass: 22 ft. lbs. (30 Nm)

10. Bend the tab washers over the bolts.
11. Installation of the remaining components is the reverse of removal.

7.4L Engines

RIGHT SIDE—1988–95 MODELS

1. Disconnect the negative battery cable.
2. Remove the heat stove pipe.
3. Remove the dipstick tube.
4. Disconnect the AIR hose at the check valve.
5. Remove the spark plugs.
6. Disconnect the exhaust pipe at the manifold.
7. Remove the manifold bolts and spark plug heat shields.
8. Remove the manifold.

To install:

9. Clean the mating surfaces.
10. Clean the stud threads.
11. Install the manifold and bolts. Tighten the bolts to 40 ft. lbs. (54 Nm) starting from the center bolts and working towards the outside.
12. Install the remaining components.

LEFT SIDE—1988–95 MODELS

1. Disconnect the negative battery cable.
2. Disconnect the oxygen sensor wire.
3. Disconnect the AIR hose at the check valve.
4. Remove the spark plugs.
5. Disconnect the exhaust pipe at the manifold.
6. Remove the manifold bolts and spark plug heat shields.
7. Remove the manifold.

To install:

8. Clean the mating surfaces.
9. Clean the stud threads.

10. Install the manifold and bolts. Tighten the bolts to 40 ft. lbs. (54 Nm) starting from the center bolts and working towards the outside.

11. Installation of the remaining components is the reverse of removal.

1996–98 MODELS

▶ See Figure 47

1. Disconnect the negative battery cable.
2. If removing the right side manifold, remove the oil level indicator tube.
3. If removing the left side manifold, remove the EGR inlet pipe.
4. Remove the spark plugs.
5. Remove the exhaust pipe from the manifold.
6. Unfasten the heat shield nuts and remove the heat shield.
7. Unfasten the exhaust manifold retainers, then remove the manifold.
8. Clean any gasket material from the manifold mating surfaces, also clean the manifold mounting studs.

To install:

9. Install the remaining components in the reverse order of removal but please note the following steps.

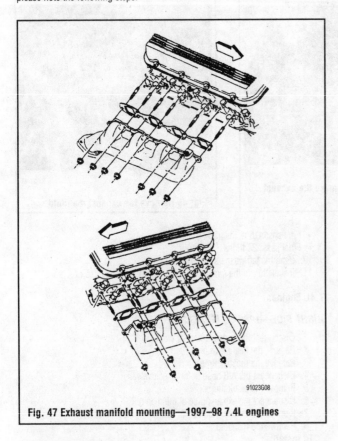

Fig. 47 Exhaust manifold mounting—1997–98 7.4L engines

10. Install the exhaust manifold and the manifold nuts. Tighten the nuts to 22 ft. lbs. (30 Nm).

11. Install the heat shields and nuts. Tighten the nuts to 15 ft. lbs. (20 Nm).

12. If removed from the right side manifold, install the oil level indicator tube. Tighten the bolt to 40 ft. lbs. (54 Nm).

6.2L and 6.5L Diesel Engines

RIGHT SIDE—1988–95 MODELS

▶ See Figures 48 and 49

1. Disconnect the batteries.
2. Jack up the vehicle and safely support it with jackstands.
3. Disconnect the exhaust pipe from the manifold flange and lower the truck.
4. Disconnect the glow plug wires.
5. Remove the air cleaner duct, box and if necessary the duct bracket.
6. Remove the glow plug wires.
7. Remove the turbocharger on the 6.5L, if equipped.
8. Remove the manifold bolts and remove the manifold.

To install:

9. Clean all mating surfaces and install the manifold. Tighten the bolts to 26 ft. lbs. (35 Nm).

10. Install the remaining components.

LEFT SIDE—1988–95 MODELS

▶ See Figure 50

1. Disconnect the batteries, negative cable first.
2. Remove the dipstick tube nut, and remove the dipstick tube.
3. Disconnect the glow plug wires.
4. Raise the vehicle and safely support it with jackstands.
5. Disconnect the exhaust pipe at the manifold flange.
6. Remove the manifold bolts. Remove the manifold from underneath the truck.

To install:

7. Install the manifold and tighten the bolts to 25 ft. lbs. (35 Nm).
8. Installation of the remaining components is the reverse of removal.

RIGHT SIDE—1996–98 MODELS

1. Disconnect the batteries.
2. Remove the air cleaner duct and box.
3. Jack up the vehicle and safely support it with jackstands.
4. Disconnect the exhaust pipe from the manifold flange.
5. Disconnect the glow plug wires.
6. Remove the glow plug wires.
7. Lower the truck.
8. Remove the turbocharger.
9. Remove the glow plugs and their shields.
10. Unfasten the manifold bolts and remove the manifold.

To install:

11. Clean all mating surfaces and install the manifold. Tighten the bolts to 26 ft. lbs. (35 Nm).

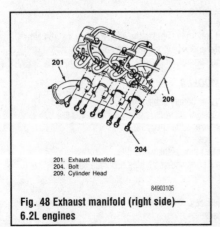

201. Exhaust Manifold
204. Bolt
209. Cylinder Head

84903105

Fig. 48 Exhaust manifold (right side)—6.2L engines

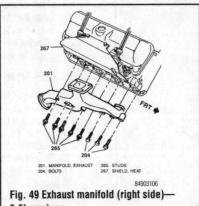

201. MANIFOLD, EXHAUST   265. STUDS
204. BOLTS   267. SHIELD, HEAT

84903106

Fig. 49 Exhaust manifold (right side)—6.5L engines

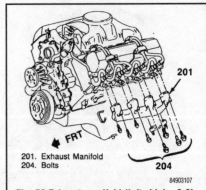

201. Exhaust Manifold
204. Bolts

84903107

Fig. 50 Exhaust manifold (left side)—6.2L and 6.5L engines

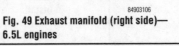

12. Install the remaining components in the reverse of removal.

LEFT SIDE—1996–98 MODELS

▶ See Figure 51

1. Disconnect the batteries, negative cable first.
2. Raise the vehicle and safely support it with jackstands.
3. Remove the glow plugs.
4. Disconnect the exhaust pipe at the manifold flange.
5. Unfasten the manifold bolts. Remove the manifold from underneath the truck.
6. Clean the manifold mating surfaces.

To install:

7. Install the manifold and tighten the bolts to 25 ft. lbs. (35 Nm).
8. Install the remaining components.

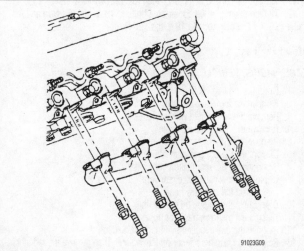

Fig. 51 Typical exhaust manifold mounting—1996–98 6.5L diesel engine

Combination Manifold

REMOVAL & INSTALLATION

4.8L Engines

▶ See Figure 52

1. Disconnect the negative battery cable.
2. Remove the air cleaner.
3. Disconnect the throttle controls at the bellcrank.
4. Remove the carburetor.
5. Disconnect and label the fuel and vacuum lines from the manifold.
6. Remove the AIR pump and bracket.
7. Disconnect the PCV hose.
8. Disconnect the exhaust pipe.
9. Remove the manifold heat stove.
10. Remove the clamps, bolts and washers and remove the combination manifold.
11. Separate the manifolds by removing the bolts and nuts.

To install:

12. Clean the mating surfaces.
13. Clean the stud threads.
14. Assemble the manifolds with a new gasket and leave the nuts finger-tight.
15. Install a new gasket over the manifold studs on the cylinder head and install the manifold assembly.
16. Install the bolts, clamps and nuts.

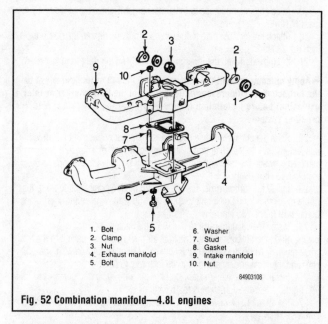

1. Bolt
2. Clamp
3. Nut
4. Exhaust manifold
5. Bolt
6. Washer
7. Stud
8. Gasket
9. Intake manifold
10. Nut

84903108

Fig. 52 Combination manifold—4.8L engines

➡ Always tighten the manifold-to-cylinder head bolts and nuts to 38 ft. lbs. (52 Nm) before tightening the manifold center bolts and nuts to 44 ft. lbs. (60 Nm).

17. Installation of the remaining components is the reverse of removal.

Turbocharger

REMOVAL & INSTALLATION

▶ See Figure 53

➡ This applies to 6.5L diesel engines only.

1. Disconnect the negative battery cables.
2. Remove the upper intake manifold cover.
3. Remove the self-tapping screw that holds the CDR valve vent tube bracket to the top of the turbocharger and then remove the valve and tube.
4. Remove the air cleaner extension from the air cleaner and compressor inlet.
5. Remove the fasteners securing the air cleaner housing where it attaches to the wheel arch and lift it off the duct.
6. If necessary, remove the right front wheel and the inner splash shield to access the turbocharger back flange nut.
7. Tag and remove the vacuum hose to the waste gate actuator.
8. Remove the turbocharger braces.
9. Loosen the hose clamps at the upper intake manifold to the turbocharger.
10. If necessary, use a prytool to break the seal between the connector hose, turbocharger, the compressor outlet, and the intake extension. Slide the connector hose over the intake extension.
11. Disconnect the exhaust clamp at the turbocharger
12. Disconnect the oil feed hose and the oil return pipe.
13. Loosen the turbocharger mounting bolts, then remove the turbocharger and exhaust manifold.

To install:

14. Clean all mating surfaces and coat any turbocharger fasteners with anti-seize compound.
15. Position the unit on the exhaust manifold and tighten the bolts to 43 ft. lbs. (58 Nm).
16. Install the turbocharger and the exhaust manifold assembly. Tighten the manifold bolts and studs to 43 ft. lbs. (58 Nm).
17. Connect the oil return pipe with a new gasket and tighten the bolt to 19 ft. lbs. (26 Nm).
18. Lubricate the oil feed hole at the top of the turbocharger with a small amount (1–2cc) of engine oil and rotate the compressor wheel by hand. This will lubricate the turbocharger shaft bearings.

19. Attach the oil feed hose to the turbocharger. Tighten the fitting to 13 ft. lbs. (17 Nm).

20. Attach the exhaust pipe to the turbocharger and tighten the clamp to 71 inch lbs. (8 Nm).

21. If removed, install the inner splash shield and the right front wheel.

➡**Apply silicone sealant GM part number 9985943 or its equivalent to the turbocharger compressor outlet hose (not the turbocharger or inlet extension) before installation to prevent oil leakage from the closed breather system.**

22. Slide the connector hose over the compressor outlet and then slide the inlet extension into the other end of the connector hose making sure the hose is centered between the inlet and outlet and the inlet. Tighten the clamps to 50 inch lbs. (6 Nm).

23. Install the turbocharger braces. Tighten the long brace nut to 26 ft. lbs. (34 Nm) and the long brace bolt to 37 ft. lbs. (50 Nm). Tighten the short brace bolts to 19 ft. lbs. (25 Nm).

24. Install the vacuum hose to the waste gate actuator.

25. Slide the air cleaner onto the front air inlet duct and attach it to the wheelhousing using the bolts. Tighten the large diameter bolt to 22 ft. lbs. (30 Nm) and the smaller diameter bolt to 45 inch lbs. (5 Nm).

26. Install the air cleaner extension onto the air cleaner and compressor outlet. Tighten the extension clamps to 15 inch lbs. (1.7 Nm).

27. Install the CDR valve and tube, making sure to tighten the self-tapping screw securely.

28. Install the intake manifold cover bolts and tighten to 90 inch lbs. (11Nm).

29. Connect the negative battery cables.

30. Run the engine for at least two minutes after installing the turbocharger. While the engine is running, check for oil leaks at the supply and return hoses.

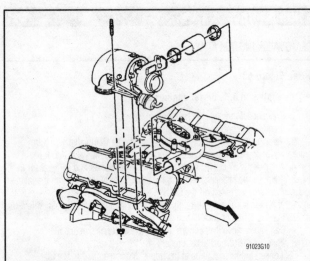

91023G10

Fig. 53 Exploded view of the turbocharger mounting—diesel engines

Radiator

REMOVAL & INSTALLATION

> **❋❋ CAUTION**
>
> Never open, service or drain the radiator or cooling system when hot; serious burns can occur from the steam and hot coolant. Also, when draining engine coolant, keep in mind that cats and dogs are attracted to ethylene glycol antifreeze and could drink any that is left in an uncovered container or in puddles on the ground. This will prove fatal in sufficient quantities. Always drain coolant into a sealable container. Coolant should be reused unless it is contaminated or is several years old.

Gasoline Engines

➡ **See Figures 54, 55, 56 and 57**

1. Drain the cooling system.
2. Unfasten the upper fan shroud bolts and remove the upper fan shroud.
3. If equipped, remove the upper panel fasteners and the panel.
4. If equipped, remove the upper insulators and brackets.
5. Disconnect the radiator upper and lower hoses and, if applicable, the transmission coolant lines.
6. Remove the coolant recovery system line, if so equipped.
7. Remove the oil coolant lines, if equipped.
8. Remove the lower fan shroud bolts and the lower fan shroud.
9. Remove radiator from the lower brackets and insulators.

To install:

10. Install the remaining components in the reverse order of removal but please note the following steps.
11. Tighten the shroud bolts to 71 inch lbs. (9 Nm).
12. Tighten the engine oil cooler pipe bolts to 18 ft. lbs. (24 Nm) and the transmission oil cooler bolts to 19 ft. lbs. (26 Nm).

Diesel Engines

EARLY MODEL VEHICLES

1. Drain the cooling system.
2. Remove the air intake snorkel.
3. Remove the windshield washer bottle.
4. Remove the hood release cable.
5. Remove the upper fan shroud.
6. Disconnect the upper radiator hose.
7. Disconnect the transmission cooler lines.
8. Unplug the low coolant sensor wire.
9. Disconnect the overflow hose.
10. Disconnect the engine oil cooler lines.
11. Disconnect the lower radiator hose.
12. Remove the brake master cylinder. See Section 9.
13. Remove the fasteners securing the radiator, then remove the radiator from the vehicle.

To install:

14. Position the radiator at its mounting points and install its retainers. Tighten to 71 inch lbs. (9 Nm).
15. Install the remaining components.

LATE MODEL VEHICLES

> **❋❋ CAUTION**
>
> Never open, service or drain the radiator or cooling system when hot; serious burns can occur from the steam and hot coolant. Also,

87983P44

Fig. 54 Remove the radiator upper panel fasteners

Fig. 55 Remove the radiator upper panel

87983P45

Fig. 56 Disconnect the transmission cooler lines

87983P46

Fig. 57 After the fasteners are removed, lift the radiator from the vehicle

87983P23

when draining engine coolant, keep in mind that cats and dogs are attracted to ethylene glycol antifreeze and could drink any that is left in an uncovered container or in puddles on the ground. This will prove fatal in sufficient quantities. Always drain coolant into a sealable container. Coolant should be reused unless it is contaminated or is several years old.

1. Drain the cooling system.
2. Unfasten the upper fan shroud bolts and remove the upper fan shroud.
3. If equipped, remove the upper panel fasteners and the panel.
4. If equipped, remove the upper insulators and brackets.
5. Disconnect the radiator upper and lower hoses and, if applicable, the transmission coolant lines.
6. Remove the coolant recovery system line, if so equipped.
7. Remove the oil coolant lines, if equipped.
8. Remove the lower fan shroud bolts and the lower fan shroud.
9. Remove radiator from the lower brackets and insulators.

To install:

10. Install the remaining components in the reverse order of removal but please note the following steps.
11. Tighten the shroud bolts to 71 inch lbs. (9 Nm).
12. Tighten the engine oil cooler pipe bolts to 18 ft. lbs. (24 Nm) and the transmission oil cooler bolts to 19 ft. lbs. (26 Nm).

Engine Fan

REMOVAL & INSTALLATION

4.3L, 5.0L and 5.7L Engines

♦ See Figures 58 and 59

1. Disconnect the negative battery cable.
2. Remove the radiator fan shroud.
3. Remove the drive belt, if necessary.

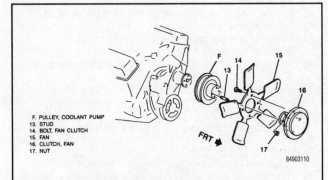

F. PULLEY, COOLANT PUMP
13. STUD
14. BOLT, FAN CLUTCH
15. FAN
16. CLUTCH, FAN
17. NUT

FRT

84903110

Fig. 58 Common engine fan and clutch assembly components

Fig. 59 Remove the four fan clutch-to-water pump pulley nuts and lift out the fan/clutch assembly

87983P48

4. Remove the four fan clutch-to-water pump pulley nuts and lift out the fan/clutch assembly.
5. Remove the fan clutch bolts and separate the fan from the clutch.

To install:

6. Install the fan on the fan clutch and tighten the bolts to 17 ft. lbs. (23 Nm).
7. Position the fan/clutch assembly on the water pump pulley. Tighten the nuts to 18 ft. lbs. (24 Nm).
8. Install the fan shroud.
9. Connect the battery cable.

7.4L Gasoline and All Diesel Engines

1. Disconnect the negative battery cable.
2. Remove the radiator shroud.
3. Locate the yellow dot on the fan clutch hub and matchmark the water pump pulley.
4. Remove the drive belt, if necessary.
5. Remove the fan clutch-to-water pump pulley nuts and lift out the fan/clutch assembly.
6. Remove the fan clutch bolts and separate the fan from the clutch.

To install:

7. Install the fan on the fan clutch and tighten the bolts to 18 ft. lbs. (24 Nm).
8. Position the fan/clutch assembly on the water pump pulley so that the reference marks on each hub align. Tighten the nuts to 18 ft. lbs. (24 Nm).
9. Install the fan shroud.
10. Connect the battery cable.

Auxiliary Cooling Fan

REMOVAL & INSTALLATION

1. Remove the grille.
2. Unplug the fan harness connector.
3. Remove the fan-to-brace bolts and lift out the fan.

4. Installation is the reverse of removal. Tighten the bolts to 53 ft. lbs. (72 Nm).

TESTING

♦ **See Figures 60 and 61**

For testing the auxiliary cooling fan, refer to the cooling fan circuit illustration and the diagnosis chart.

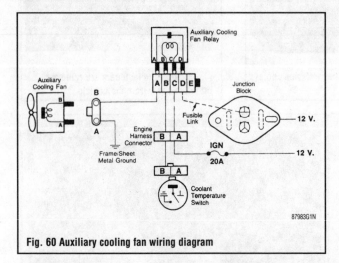

Fig. 60 Auxiliary cooling fan wiring diagram

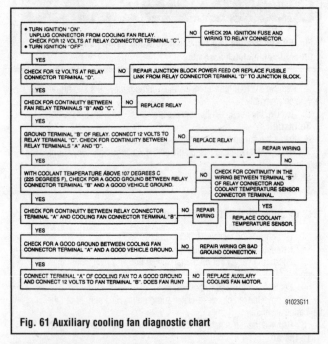

Fig. 61 Auxiliary cooling fan diagnostic chart

Water Pump

REMOVAL & INSTALLATION

4.8L Engines

♦ **See Figure 62**

>> **CAUTION**

Never open, service or drain the radiator or cooling system when hot; serious burns can occur from the steam and hot coolant. Also, when draining engine coolant, keep in mind that cats and dogs are

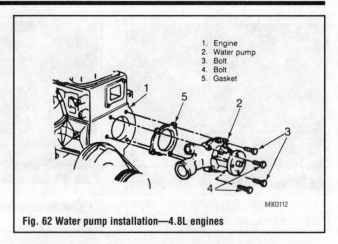

1. Engine
2. Water pump
3. Bolt
4. Bolt
5. Gasket

84903112

Fig. 62 Water pump installation—4.8L engines

attracted to ethylene glycol antifreeze and could drink any that is left in an uncovered container or in puddles on the ground. This will prove fatal in sufficient quantities. Always drain coolant into a sealable container. Coolant should be reused unless it is contaminated or is several years old.

1. Disconnect the negative battery cable.
2. Drain the radiator.
3. Loosen the alternator and other accessories at their adjusting points, and remove the fan belts from the fan pulley.
4. Remove the fan, fan clutch and pulley.
5. Remove any accessory brackets that might interfere with water pump removal.
6. Disconnect the hose from the water pump inlet and the heater hose from the nipple on the pump. Remove the bolts, pump assembly and old gasket from the timing chain cover.

To install:
7. Make sure the gasket surfaces on the pump and engine block are clean.
8. Install the pump assembly with a new gasket. Tighten the bolts to 15 ft. lbs. (20 Nm).
9. Installation of the remaining components is the reverse of removal.

4.3L, 5.0L, 5.7L and 7.4L Engines

♦ **See Figures 63, 64, 65, 66 and 67**

>> **CAUTION**

Never open, service or drain the radiator or cooling system when hot; serious burns can occur from the steam and hot coolant. Also, when draining engine coolant, keep in mind that cats and dogs are attracted to ethylene glycol antifreeze and could drink any that is left in an uncovered container or in puddles on the ground. This will prove fatal in sufficient quantities. Always drain coolant into a sealable container. Coolant should be reused unless it is contaminated or is several years old.

1. Disconnect the negative battery cable.
2. Drain the coolant from the radiator. Remove the upper fan shroud.
3. Remove the drive belt(s).
4. Remove the alternator and other accessories, if necessary.
5. Remove the fan, fan clutch and pulley.
6. Remove any accessory brackets that might interfere with water pump removal.
7. Disconnect the lower radiator hose from the water pump inlet and the heater hose from the nipple on the pump. On the 7.4L engine, remove the bypass hose.
8. Remove the bolts, then pull the water pump assembly away from the timing cover.

To install:
9. Clean all old gasket material from the timing chain cover.
10. Install the pump assembly with a new gasket. Tighten the bolts to 30 ft. lbs. (41 Nm).
11. Install the remaining components in the reverse of removal.

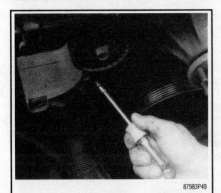

Fig. 63 Disconnect the lower radiator hose from the water pump inlet

Fig. 64 Remove the water pump attaching bolts

Fig. 65 Remove the water pump from the vehicle

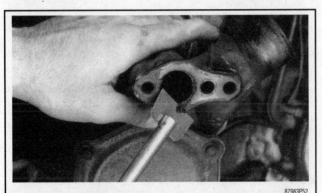

Fig. 66 Using a scraper, clean the old gasket from both mating surfaces of the water pump

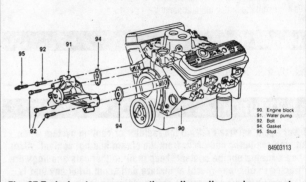

Fig. 67 Typical water pump mounting—all gasoline engines except 4.8L engine

6.2L and 6.5L Diesel Engines

▶ See Figure 68

✷✷ CAUTION

Never open, service or drain the radiator or cooling system when hot; serious burns can occur from the steam and hot coolant. Also, when draining engine coolant, keep in mind that cats and dogs are attracted to ethylene glycol antifreeze and could drink any that is left in an uncovered container or in puddles on the ground. This will prove fatal in sufficient quantities. Always drain coolant into a seal-able container. Coolant should be reused unless it is contaminated or is several years old.

1. Disconnect the batteries, negative cable first.
2. Drain the radiator.
3. Remove the fan shroud and fan.
4. Remove the drive belt(s).
5. On 6.2L diesel engines that are equipped with air conditioning, remove the air conditioning hose bracket nuts.
6. On early model diesel engines, remove the oil filler tube.
7. If necessary for access, unfasten the generator pivot bolt and remove the generator lower bracket.

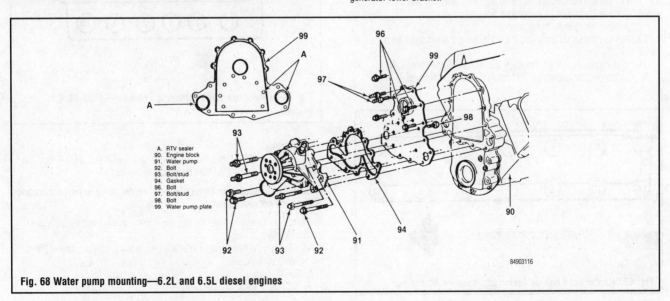

Fig. 68 Water pump mounting—6.2L and 6.5L diesel engines

8. On late model diesel engines, remove the vacuum pump and bracket.

9. On late model diesel engines, remove the power steering pump and lay it aside, then remove the pump bracket.

10. Disconnect the bypass hose and the lower radiator hose.

11. Remove the water pump bolts.

12. Remove the water pump plate and gasket and water pump.

13. If the pump gasket is to be replaced, unfasten the plate attaching bolts to the water pump and remove (and replace) the gasket.

To install:

14. Attach the water pump to the plate assembly. Tighten the bolts to 31 ft. lbs. (42 Nm).

15. When installing the pump, the flanges must be free of oil. Apply an anaerobic sealer (GM part #1052357 or equivalent) to the sealing surfaces **A** shown in the accompanying illustration.

➡The sealer must be wet to the touch when the bolts are tightened.

16. Install the pump and plate assembly to the engine and install the pump-to-engine bolts. Tighten the bolts to 17 ft. lbs. (23 Nm), except the three lower right side bolts. Tighten these bolts to 31 ft. lbs. (42 Nm).

17. Install the remaining components.

Cylinder Head

REMOVAL & INSTALLATION

✳ CAUTION

Never open, service or drain the radiator or cooling system when hot; serious burns can occur from the steam and hot coolant. Also, when draining engine coolant, keep in mind that cats and dogs are attracted to ethylene glycol antifreeze and could drink any that is left in an uncovered container or in puddles on the ground. This will prove fatal in sufficient quantities. Always drain coolant into a sealable container. Coolant should be reused unless it is contaminated or is several years old.

4.8L Engines

▶ See Figure 69

1. Disconnect the negative battery cable and unbolt it at the engine.

2. Drain the cooling system.

3. Remove the air cleaner assembly.

4. Disconnect the fuel line at the carburetor.

5. Disconnect the accelerator and transmission linkages.

6. Mark and disconnect all required electrical and vacuum lines.

7. Remove the combination manifold assembly retaining bolts.

8. Remove the combination manifold from the engine.

9. Remove the cylinder head cover.

10. Remove the rocker arms and pushrods. Keep them in order for re-installation.

11. If equipped, disconnect the AIR injection hose at the check valve.

12. Disconnect the upper radiator hose at the thermostat housing.

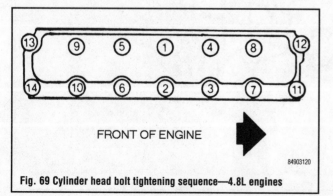

Fig. 69 Cylinder head bolt tightening sequence—4.8L engines

13. Remove the cylinder head retaining bolts.

14. With the aid of an assistant, lift the cylinder head from the engine.

To install:

15. Thoroughly clean both the head and block surfaces.

16. Install a new head gasket on the block. If an all steel gasket is used, coat both sides with sealer. If a composition gasket is used, do not use sealer. Position the gasket on the block with the bead up.

17. With the aid of an assistant, lower the cylinder head onto the engine.

18. Coat the threads of the head bolts with sealer and install them. Tighten the bolts, in 3 equal steps, in the sequence shown, to 95 ft. lbs. (129 Nm) for all but the left front (No. 12) bolt. Tighten that one to 85 ft. lbs. (115 Nm).

19. Installation of the remaining components is the reverse of removal.

4.3L Engines

▶ See Figure 70

1. Disconnect the negative battery cable.

2. Drain the coolant.

3. Remove the intake manifold.

4. Remove the exhaust manifold.

5. If equipped, remove the air pipe at the rear of the right cylinder head.

6. On models equipped, remove the air pump mounting bolt and spacer at the right side cylinder.

7. On 1996–98 models, remove the alternator and bracket.

8. On 1988–95 models, remove the engine accessory bracket bolts and studs at the cylinder head. If you are removing the left cylinder head, it may be necessary to loosen the remaining bracket bolts to provide clearance for head removal.

9. On 1996–98 models, remove the power steering pump and brackets from the left cylinder head, and lay them aside.

10. On 1996–98 models, remove the air conditioner compressor, and lay it aside.

11. Remove the spark plug wires at their brackets, the ground strap from the right side and the coolant sensor wire from the left head.

12. Remove the cylinder cover.

13. Remove the spark plugs.

14. Remove the pushrods.

15. Remove the cylinder head bolts in the reverse order of the tightening sequence.

16. Remove the cylinder head and gasket.

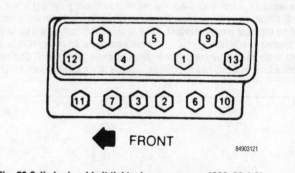

Fig. 70 Cylinder head bolt tightening sequence—1988–98 4.3L engines

To install:

17. Clean all gasket mating surfaces, install a new gasket and reinstall the cylinder head. Install the cylinder heads using new gaskets.

➡Coat a steel gasket on both sides with sealer. If a composition gasket is used, do not use sealer.

18. Clean the cylinder head bolts, apply sealer to the threads, and install them hand-tight.

19. Tighten the head bolts a little at a time in the sequence shown. Tighten the bolts in three stages:

1988–95 models:

• First pass: 25 ft. lbs. (34 Nm)

- Second pass: 45 ft. lbs. (61 Nm)
- Final pass: 65 ft. lbs. (90 Nm)

On 1996–98 models install the bolts in sequence to 22 ft. lbs. (30 Nm). The bolts must then be tightened again in sequence in the following order:

- Short length bolt: (Nos. 11, 7, 3, 2, 6 and 10) 55 degrees
- Medium length bolt: (Nos. 12 and 13) 65 degrees
- Long length bolts: (Nos. 1, 4, 8, 5 and 9) 75 degrees
20. Install the remaining components in the reverse of removal.

5.0L and 5.7L Engines

▶ **See Figures 71 thru 76**

1. Disconnect the negative battery cable and drain the coolant.
2. Remove the intake manifold.
3. Remove the exhaust manifolds and position them out of the way.
4. On 1988–95 models, if removing the right cylinder head, remove the following components.
   a. Remove the AIR pipe at the rear of the right cylinder head.
   b. Remove the AIR pump bolt and spacer
   c. Unfasten the nut and stud attaching to A/C compressor to the head and set the compressor aside with the hoses still attached.
   d. Remove the fuel pipe, plug wire and wiring harness brackets at the rear of the cylinder head.
   e. Remove the ground strap at the rear of the right side cylinder head.
5. On 1996–98 models, if removing the right cylinder head, remove the following components.
   a. Remove the alternator and bracket.
   b. Remove the ground strap at the rear of the right side cylinder head.
   c. Remove the oil dipstick tube.
   d. Remove the spark plug wire brackets from the rear of the head.
6. On 1988–95 models, if removing the left cylinder head, remove the following components.
   a. Remove the nut and stud attaching the main accessory bracket to the head. It also may be necessary to loosen the remaining bolts and studs

and move the bracket forward slightly for clearance to move the cylinder head.
   b. Unplug the coolant sensor wire and remove the spark plug wire brackets at the rear of the head.
7. On 1996–98 models, if removing the left cylinder head, remove the following components.
   a. Remove the A/C compressor and bracket and set the compressor aside with the hoses still attached.
   b. Remove the EGR inlet tube.
   c. Unplug the coolant sensor wire and remove the wiring harness brackets at the rear of the head.
8. Remove the cylinder head covers. Remove the spark plugs.
9. Back off the rocker arm nuts and pivot the rocker arms out of the way so that the pushrods can be removed. Identify the pushrods so that they can be installed in their original positions.
10. Remove the cylinder head bolts in the reverse order of the tightening sequence and then remove the heads.

To install:

11. Inspect the cylinder head and block mating surfaces. Clean all old gasket material.
12. Install the cylinder heads using new gaskets. Install the gaskets with the word **HEAD** up.

➡**Coat a steel gasket on both sides with sealer. If a composition gasket is used, do not use sealer.**

13. Clean the bolts, apply sealer to the threads, and install them hand-tight.
14. Tighten the cylinder head bolts a little at a time, in the sequence shown. Tighten the bolts in three stages:

- First pass: 25 ft. lbs. (34 Nm)
- Second pass: 45 ft. lbs. (61 Nm)
- Final pass: 65 ft. lbs. (90 Nm)

On 1996–98 models, install the bolts in sequence to 22 ft. lbs. (30 Nm). The bolts must then be tightened again in sequence in the following order:

- Short length bolt: (3, 4, 7, 8, 11, 12, 15, 16) 55 degrees

Fig. 71 Using a breaker bar, remove the cylinder head bolts in the reverse order of the tightening sequence

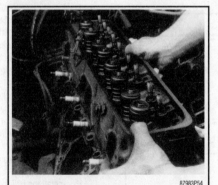

Fig. 72 After removing all the cylinder head bolts, remove the cylinder head

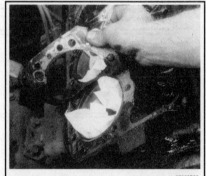

Fig. 73 Remove and discard the old cylinder head gasket

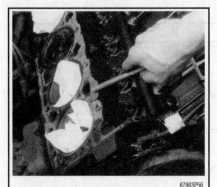

Fig. 74 Using a scraper, remove the old gasket residue from both mating surfaces

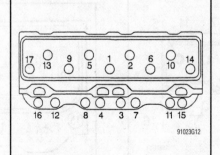

Fig. 75 Cylinder head bolt tightening sequence—1988–98 5.0L and 5.7L engines

Fig. 76 Using a torque wrench, tighten the cylinder head bolts in sequence

- Medium length bolt: (14, 17) 65 degrees
- Long length bolts: (1, 2, 5, 6, 9, 10, 13) 75 degrees
15. Installation of the remaining components is the reverse of removal.

6.2L and 6.5L Diesel Engines

▶ See Figures 77 and 78

1. Disconnect the negative battery cables. Drain the cooling system.
2. Remove the intake manifold.
3. Remove the fuel injection lines. Refer to Section 5 for this procedure.
4. Remove the cruise control transducer (if so equipped).
5. Remove the valve covers.
6. Drain the cooling system.
7. Raise the truck and support it with jack stands.
8. Remove the exhaust pipe from the exhaust manifold.
9. Lower the truck.
10. To remove the right cylinder head, remove the following components.
   a. Remove the A/C compressor and bracket. Set the compressor aside without disconnecting the lines.
   b. If equipped, remove the vacuum pump and bracket. Set the pump aside without disconnecting the lines.
   c. Disconnect the ground strap from the cowl.
   d. If equipped, remove the turbocharger.
11. To remove the left cylinder head, remove the following components.
   a. Remove the power steering pump. Set the pump aside without disconnecting the lines.
   b. Remove the alternator and the bracket.
   c. Remove the left side engine accessory bracket, the wiring harness at the clips, the glow plug relay and the dipstick tube.
12. Unplug the coolant sensor from the head.
13. Unplug the glow plug wires. If your vehicle equipped with a turbocharger, you may need tool J 39083 or its equivalent to unplug the connections as they cannot usually be reached by hand. Do not pull on the wires.

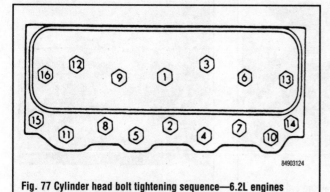

Fig. 77 Cylinder head bolt tightening sequence—6.2L engines

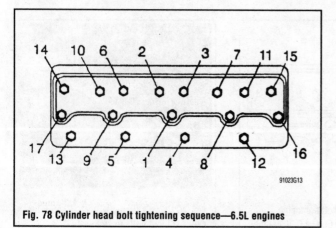

Fig. 78 Cylinder head bolt tightening sequence—6.5L engines

➡**Before removing the rocker arm assemblies, mark the location of the rocker arm and pushrods etc. As they must be installed in their original positions.**

14. Remove the rocker arm assemblies.
15. Remove the radiator, bypass and heater hoses.
16. Remove the ground straps and the coolant crossover pipe/thermostat housing assembly.
17. Remove the exhaust manifold.
18. Remove the head bolts.
19. Remove the cylinder head.

To install:
20. Clean the mating surfaces of the head and block thoroughly.
21. Install a new head gasket on the engine block. Do NOT coat the gaskets with any sealer on either engine. The gaskets have a special coating that eliminates the need for sealer. The use of sealer will interfere with this coating and cause leaks. Install the cylinder head onto the block.
22. Clean the head bolts thoroughly. The left rear head bolt must be installed into the head prior to head installation. Coat the threads and heads of the head bolts with sealing compound (GM part #1052080 or equivalent) before installation. On 1988–95 models, tighten the head bolts in three stages: 20 ft. lbs. (25 Nm); 50 ft. lbs. (68 Nm) and finally, ¼ or 90⁻ turn more. On 1996–98 models, tighten the head bolts in three stages: 20 ft. lbs. (25 Nm); 55 ft. lbs. (75 Nm) and finally, ¼ or 90⁻ turn more.
23. Install the coolant crossover pipe and thermostat. Tighten the bolts to 31 ft. lbs. (42 Nm).
24. Install the remaining components in the reverse of removal.

7.4L Engines

▶ See Figure 79

1. Disconnect the negative battery cable and drain the cooling system.
2. Remove the intake manifold.
3. If removing the right cylinder head, remove the alternator and bracket.
4. Remove the AIR pump, if equipped.
5. If the vehicle is equipped with air conditioning, remove the air conditioning compressor and the forward mounting bracket and lay the compressor aside. Do not disconnect any of the refrigerant lines.
6. Remove the exhaust manifold(s).
7. Remove the spark plugs.
8. Remove the rocker arm cover.
9. Remove the AIR pipes at the rear of the head, if equipped.
10. Disconnect the ground strap at the rear of the head.
11. Disconnect the temperature sensor wire.
12. Back off the rocker arm nuts and pivot the rocker arms out of the way so that the pushrods can be removed. Identify the pushrods so that they can be installed in their original positions.
13. Remove the cylinder head bolts and remove the heads.

To install:
14. Thoroughly clean the mating surfaces of the head and block. Clean the bolt holes thoroughly.
15. Install the cylinder heads using new gaskets. Install the gaskets with the word **HEAD** up.

➡**Coat a steel gasket on both sides with sealer. If a composition gasket is used, do not use sealer.**

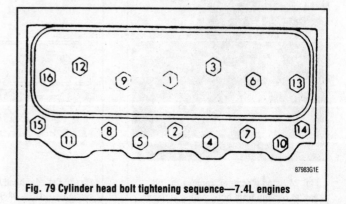

Fig. 79 Cylinder head bolt tightening sequence—7.4L engines

16. Clean the bolts, apply sealer to the threads, and install them hand-tight.

17. Tighten the head bolts a little at a time in the sequence shown. Tighten the bolts in three stages: 30 ft. lbs. (40 Nm), 60 ft. lbs. (80 Nm) and finally to 85 ft. lbs. (115 Nm).

18. Installation of the remaining components is the reverse of removal.

Oil Pan

REMOVAL & INSTALLATION

4.3L Engines

1988–95 MODELS

▶ See Figure 80

A one-piece oil pan gasket is used.

1. Disconnect the negative battery cable. Raise the vehicle, support it safely, and drain the engine oil.

2. Remove the exhaust crossover pipe.

3. Remove the torque converter cover (on models with automatic transmission).

4. If equipped, remove the strut rod brackets at the front engine mountings.

5. If equipped, remove the Strut rods at the flywheel cover, at the engine mounts and the flywheel cover.

6. Remove the starter motor.

7. Remove the front propeller shaft (K truck only).

8. Remove the underbody protection shield (K truck only).

9. Remove the front drive axle (K truck only).

10. Remove the oil pan bolts, nuts and reinforcements.

11. Remove the oil pan and gaskets.

※※ CAUTION

The EPA warns that prolonged contact with used engine oil may cause a number of skin disorders, including cancer! You should make every effort to minimize you exposure to used engine oil. Protective gloves should be worn when changing the oil. Wash your

hands and any other exposed skin areas as soon as possible after exposure to used engine oil. Soap and water, or waterless hand cleaner should be used.

To install:

12. Thoroughly clean all gasket surfaces. Use new gaskets and seals.

13. Apply a suitable sealant such as GM part number 1052080 or its equivalent to the front cover-to-block joint and to the rear crankshaft seal-to-block joint. Apply the sealant about 1 inch (25mm) in both directions from each of the four corners.

14. Tighten the pan bolts to 100 inch lbs. (11 Nm). Tighten the nuts at the corners to 17 ft. lbs. (23 Nm).

15. Install the remaining components in the reverse of removal.

1996–98 MODELS

▶ See Figure 81

1. Disconnect the negative battery cable. Raise the vehicle, support it safely, and drain the engine oil.

2. Remove the oil filter.

3. Remove the oil cooler lines from the oil pan and from the adapter.

4. Remove the oil filter adapter.

5. Remove the starter and starter opening shield, If equipped.

6. Disconnect the transmission oil cooler lines (on models with automatic transmission only).

7. Remove the front drive axle tube mount nuts and the lower drive axle bushing bolt.

8. Remove the rubber bell housing plugs.

9. Remove the oil pan bolts and nuts.

10. Remove the oil pan and gaskets.

※※ CAUTION

The EPA warns that prolonged contact with used engine oil may cause a number of skin disorders, including cancer! You should make every effort to minimize you exposure to used engine oil. Protective gloves should be worn when changing the oil. Wash your hands and any other exposed skin areas as soon as possible after exposure to used engine oil. Soap and water, or waterless hand cleaner should be used.

To install:

11. Thoroughly clean all gasket surfaces. Use new gaskets and seals.

12. Apply a suitable sealant such as GM part number 12346192 or its equivalent to the front cover-to-block joint and to the rear crankshaft seal-to-block joint. Apply the sealant about 1 inch (25mm) in both directions from each of the four corners.

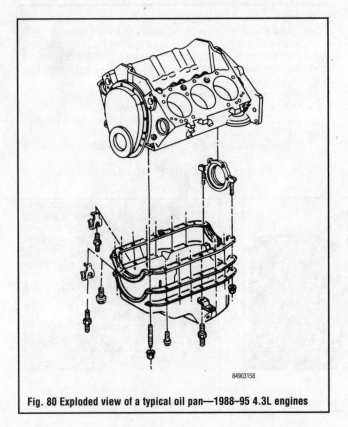

Fig. 80 Exploded view of a typical oil pan—1988-95 4.3L engines

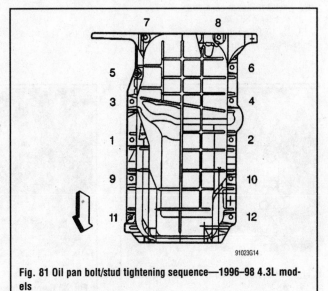

Fig. 81 Oil pan bolt/stud tightening sequence—1996–98 4.3L models

13. Use a feeler gauge to check the clearance between the three oil pan-to-transmission contact points. If the clearance exceeds 0.010 inch (0.254mm) at any of the points, adjust the pan until the clearance is within specifications.

14. Once the pan clearance is within specifications, tighten the oil pan retainers in sequence to 18 ft. lbs. (25 Nm).

15. Installation of the remaining components is the reverse of removal.

4.8L Engines

1. Disconnect the negative battery cable.
2. Raise and support the truck on jackstands.
3. Drain the engine oil.
4. Remove the flywheel cover.
5. Remove the starter assembly.
6. Remove the engine mount through-bolts from the engine front mounts.
7. Using a floor jack under the damper, raise the engine enough to remove the oil pan.
8. Remove the oil pan retaining bolts. Remove the oil pan from the engine. You may have to break loose the pan with a soft mallet.
9. Thoroughly clean the mating surfaces of the pan and block. If the lips of the pan are bent, straighten them.
10. Installation is the reverse of the removal procedure. Use new gaskets and seals. Tighten the pan-to-front cover bolts to 45 inch lbs. (5 Nm). Tighten the 1/4 in. pan-to-block bolts to 80 inch lbs. (9 Nm) and the 5/16 in. bolts to 14 ft. lbs. (19 Nm).
11. Fill the engine with the proper grade and viscosity of engine oil and check for leaks.

5.0L and 5.7L Engines

2WD MODELS

1. Disconnect the negative battery cable. Drain the engine oil.
2. Remove the oil dipstick.
3. If necessary remove the exhaust pipe crossover.
4. If equipped with automatic transmission, remove the converter housing pan and the transmission oil cooler line retainer from the bracket.
5. On 1996–98 models, remove the oil filter and if equipped, the oil filter adapter.
6. If necessary, remove the starter brace and bolt and swing the starter aside.
7. Remove the strut rods, if equipped.
8. Remove the oil pan and discard the gaskets.

To install:

9. Apply a suitable sealant such as GM part number 12346192 or its equivalent to the front cover-to-block joint and to the rear crankshaft seal-to-block joint. Apply the sealant about 1 inch (25mm) in both directions from each of the four corners.
10. Clean all gasket surfaces and use new gaskets to assemble.
11. Install new gasket and seals.
12. Install the oil pan.
13. On 1988–95 models, tighten the pan bolts to 100 inch lbs. (11 Nm). Tighten the pan nuts to 17 ft. lbs. (23 Nm).

14. On 1996–98 models, tighten the oil pan nuts and bolts to 18 ft. lbs. (25 Nm).
15. Install the strut rods, if equipped.
16. Install the remaining components.

4WD MODELS

▶ See Figures 82 thru 90

1. Disconnect the negative battery cable. Raise the vehicle, support it safely, and drain the engine oil.
2. On 1996–98 models, remove the engine oil dipstick.
3. Remove the underbody protection shield to access the axle bolts.
4. Remove the transmission oil cooler line bracket from the oil pan, if equipped (on models with automatic transmission only).
5. Remove the front propeller shaft.
6. On 1988–95 models, support the front axle, unfasten the axle mounting bolts and brackets. Rotate the axle to access the oil pan.
7. On 1996–98 models, unfasten the front axle two right side bolts and nuts, one upper bolt and nut. Rotate the drive axle forward and turn the front wheels to the left.
8. On 1988–95 models, remove the strut rods at the flywheel cover.
9. Remove the exhaust pipe crossover.
10. On 1988–95 models, remove the starter.
11. On 1996–98 models, remove the torque converter cover (on models with automatic transmission).
12. Oil cooler lines from the oil pan and from the adapter, if equipped.
13. Oil filter and oil filter adapter, if equipped.
14. Remove the oil pan bolts, nuts and reinforcements.
15. Remove the oil pan and gaskets.

✴✴ CAUTION

The EPA warns that prolonged contact with used engine oil may cause a number of skin disorders, including cancer! You should make every effort to minimize you exposure to used engine oil. Protective gloves should be worn when changing the oil. Wash your hands and any other exposed skin areas as soon as possible after exposure to used engine oil. Soap and water, or waterless hand cleaner should be used.

To install:

16. Thoroughly clean all gasket surfaces and install a new gasket.
17. Apply a suitable sealant such as GM part number 12346192 or its equivalent to the front cover-to-block joint and to the rear crankshaft seal-to-block joint. Apply the sealant about 1 inch (25mm) in both directions from each of the four corners.
18. Install the oil pan and new gaskets.
19. Install the oil pan bolts, nuts and reinforcements.
20. On 1988–95 models, tighten the pan bolts to 100 inch lbs. (11 Nm). Tighten the nuts at the corners to 17 ft. lbs. (23 Nm).
21. On 1996–98 models, tighten the oil pan nuts and bolts to 18 ft. lbs. (25 Nm).
22. Installation of the remaining components is the reverse of removal.

87983P58

Fig. 82 Remove the bolts from the oil filter adapter

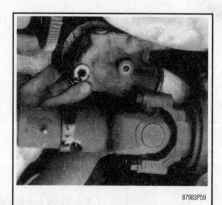

87983P59

Fig. 83 Remove the oil filter and adapter

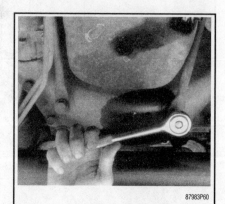

87983P60

Fig. 84 Remove the strut rod fasteners

Fig. 85 Remove the strut rods

Fig. 86 Remove the torque converter cover

Fig. 87 Remove the oil pan bolts and nuts

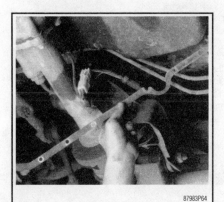

Fig. 88 Remove the oil pan reinforcements

Fig. 89 Remove the oil pan from the vehicle

Fig. 90 Remove the old gasket from both mating surfaces

7.4L Engines

1988–95 MODELS

▶ See Figure 91

1. Disconnect the battery.
2. Remove the fan shroud.
3. Remove the air cleaner.
4. Remove the distributor cap.
5. Raise and support the front end on jackstands.
6. Drain the engine oil.
7. Remove the converter housing pan. On 4WD vehicles with automatic transmission, remove the strut rods at the engine mounts.
8. Remove the oil filter.
9. Remove the oil pressure line.
10. Support the engine with a floor jack.

✳✳ WARNING

Do not place the jack under the pan, sheet metal or pulley!

11. Remove the engine mount through-bolts.
12. Raise the engine just enough to remove the pan.
13. Remove the oil pan and discard the gaskets.
To install:
14. Clean all mating surfaces thoroughly.
15. Apply RTV gasket material to the front and rear corners of the gaskets.
16. Coat the gaskets with adhesive sealer and position them on the block.
17. Install the rear pan seal in the pan with the seal ends mating with the gaskets.
18. Install the front seal on the bottom of the front cover, pressing the locating tabs into the holes in the cover.
19. Install the oil pan.

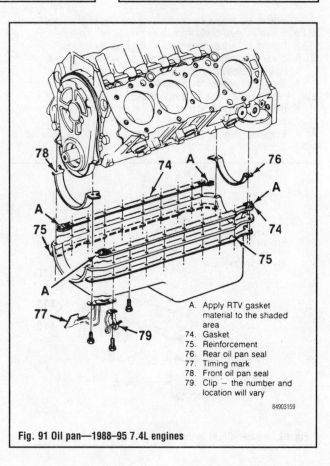

A. Apply RTV gasket material to the shaded area
74. Gasket
75. Reinforcement
76. Rear oil pan seal
77. Timing mark
78. Front oil pan seal
79. Clip — the number and location will vary

Fig. 91 Oil pan—1988–95 7.4L engines

20. Install the pan bolts, clips and reinforcements. Tighten the pan-to-cover bolts to 70 inch lbs. (8 Nm); the pan-to-block bolts to 13 ft. lbs. (18 Nm).

21. Install the remaining components in the reverse of removal.

1996–98 MODELS

1. Disconnect the negative battery cable and remove the oil level indicator and tube.

2. Raise the vehicle, support it safely with jackstands and drain the oil.

3. Remove the front propeller shaft (K truck only).

4. Remove the underbody protection shield (K truck only).

5. Unfasten the front axle two right side bolts and nuts, one upper bolt and nut. Rotate the drive axle forward and turn the front wheels to the left.

6. Remove the front drive axle (K truck only).

7. Remove the flywheel/torque converter cover.

8. Remove the exhaust crossover pipe.

9. Remove the oil filter and adapter, if equipped.

10. Remove the oil cooler line retainer from the bracket, if equipped.

11. Remove the transmission oil cooler line retainer from the bracket, if equipped.

12. Remove the oil pan bolts, nuts and strut rods, if equipped.

13. Remove the oil pan and gasket.

To install:

14. Thoroughly clean all gasket surfaces and install a new gasket.

15. Apply a suitable sealant such as GM part number 12345739 or its equivalent to the front cover-to-block joint and to the rear crankshaft seal-to-block joint. Apply the sealant about 1 inch (25mm) in both directions from each of the four corners.

16. Install the oil pan and new gaskets.

17. Install the oil pan bolts, nuts and strut rods. Tighten the pan bolts and nuts to 18 ft. lbs. (25 Nm).

18. Installation of the remaining components is the reverse of removal.

6.2L and 6.5L Diesel Engines

1988–95 MODELS

▶ See Figure 92

1. If necessary, remove the vacuum pump and drive (with air conditioning) or the oil pump drive (without air conditioning).

2. Disconnect the batteries and remove the engine oil dipstick.

3. If necessary, remove the upper radiator support and fan shroud.

4. Raise and support the truck. Drain the oil.

5. Remove the flywheel cover. On 4WD vehicles with automatic transmission, remove the strut rods at the engine mounts.

6. Disconnect the exhaust and crossover pipes, if necessary.

7. If necessary, remove the oil cooler lines at the filter base.

8. If necessary, remove the starter assembly and support the engine with a jack.

9. Remove the engine mount through-bolts.

10. Raise the front of the engine and remove the oil pan.

To install:

11. Apply a ³⁄₁₆ inch (5mm) bead of RTV sealant to the oil pan sealing surface, inboard of the bolt holes. The sealer must be wet to the touch when the oil pan is installed.

12. Install the oil pan rear seal, if equipped.

13. Position the oil pan on the block and install the bolts. Tighten the bolts to 89 inch lbs. (10 Nm), except for the two rear bolts. Tighten them to 17 ft. lbs. (23 Nm).

14. Install the remaining components.

1996–98 MODELS

1. Disconnect the batteries and remove the engine oil dipstick.

2. Raise the vehicle, support it with jackstands and drain the engine oil.

3. Remove the oil level tube.

4. Remove the flywheel cover.

5. Remove the oil cooler line clip.

6. If equipped, remove the propeller shaft.

7. Roll the front axle, if equipped.

8. Remove the oil pan bolts, pan and gasket.

To install:

9. Apply a ¹⁄₁₆ inch (2mm) bead of RTV sealant to the oil pan rear seal at the inside corners where the seal meets the rear main bearing cap on the block.

10. Install the oil pan rear seal before the sealer is dry.

11. Install the oil pan rear seal.

12. Position the oil pan on the block and install the bolts. Tighten the bolts to 89 inch lbs. (10 Nm), except for the two rear bolts. Tighten them to 17 ft. lbs. (23 Nm).

13. Installation of the remaining components is the reverse of removal.

Oil Pump

REMOVAL & INSTALLATION

4.3L, 5.0L, 5.7L and 7.4L Engines

▶ See Figures 93 and 94

1. Remove the oil pan.

2. Remove the bolt attaching the pump to the rear main bearing cap. Remove the pump and the extension shaft, which will come out behind it.

To install:

3. If the pump has been disassembled, is being replaced, or for any reason oil has been removed from it, it must be primed. It can either be filled with oil before installing the cover plate (and oil kept within the pump during handling), or the entire pump cavity can be filled with petroleum jelly.

→ If the pump is not primed, the engine could be damaged before it receives adequate lubrication when you start it.

4. Engage the extension shaft with the oil pump shaft. Align the slot on the

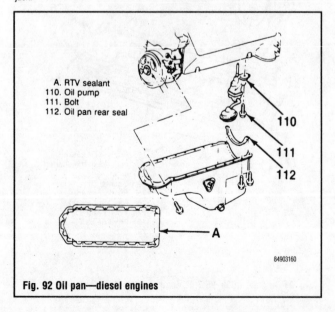

A. RTV sealant
110. Oil pump
111. Bolt
112. Oil pan rear seal

84903160

Fig. 92 Oil pan—diesel engines

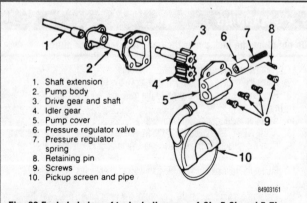

1. Shaft extension
2. Pump body
3. Drive gear and shaft
4. Idler gear
5. Pump cover
6. Pressure regulator valve
7. Pressure regulator spring
8. Retaining pin
9. Screws
10. Pickup screen and pipe

84903161

Fig. 93 Exploded view of typical oil pump—4.3L, 5.0L and 5.7L engines

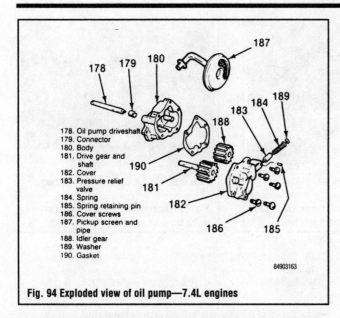

178. Oil pump driveshaft
179. Connector
180. Body
181. Drive gear and shaft
182. Cover
183. Pressure relief valve
184. Spring
185. Spring retaining pin
186. Cover screws
187. Pickup screen and pipe
188. Idler gear
189. Washer
190. Gasket

84903163

Fig. 94 Exploded view of oil pump—7.4L engines

top of the extension shaft with the drive tang on the lower end of the distributor driveshaft, and then position the pump at the rear main bearing cap so the mounting bolt can be installed. The installed position of the oil pump screen is with the bottom edge parallel to the oil pan rails. Install the bolt, tightening to 65 ft. lbs. (90 Nm).

5. Install the oil pan.

4.8L Engines

♦ See Figure 95

1. Raise and support the truck on jackstands.
2. Remove the oil pan.

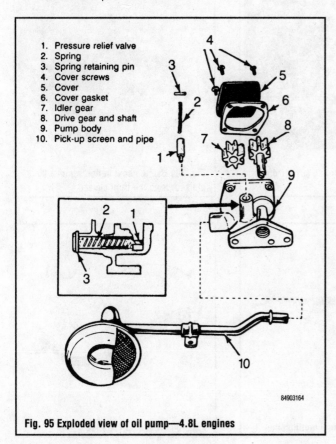

1. Pressure relief valve
2. Spring
3. Spring retaining pin
4. Cover screws
5. Cover
6. Cover gasket
7. Idler gear
8. Drive gear and shaft
9. Pump body
10. Pick-up screen and pipe

84903164

Fig. 95 Exploded view of oil pump—4.8L engines

3. Remove the oil pump tube bracket main bearing cap nut.
4. Remove the oil pump bolts and the oil pump.

To install:

5. Position the oil pump to the engine and align the slot in the oil pump shaft with the tang on the distributor shaft. The oil pump should slide easily in place.
6. Install the oil pump bolts and tighten to 115 inch lbs. (11 Nm).
7. Install the oil pump pick-up tube to the main bearing cap nut and tighten to 25 ft. lbs. (37 Nm).
8. Install the oil pan.

6.2L and 6.5L Diesel Engines

1. Drain the oil.
2. Lower the oil pan enough to gain access to the pump.
3. Rotate the crankshaft so that the forward crankshaft throw and No. 1 and No. 2 connecting rod journals are up.
4. Remove the bolt retaining the pump to the main bearing cap. Let the pump and extension shaft fall into the pan.
5. Remove the pan from the vehicle.

To install:

6. Maneuver the pan, pump and extension shaft into position.
7. Position the pump on the bearing cap.
8. Align the extension shaft hex with the drive hex on the oil pump drive or vacuum pump. The pump should push easily into place. Install the pump and tighten the bolt to 65 ft. lbs. (90 Nm).
9. Install the pan and fill the engine with oil.

Crankshaft Damper

REMOVAL & INSTALLATION

♦ See Figures 96, 97 and 98

➡A torsional damper puller tool is required to perform this procedure.

1. Disconnect the negative battery cable.
2. Remove the fan shroud assembly.
3. Remove the fan belts, fan and pulley.
4. If necessary, remove the radiator.
5. Remove the accessory drive pulley (crankshaft pulley on diesel engines).
6. Remove the torsional damper bolt.
7. Remove the torsional damper using tool J-39046 or its equivalent puller.

➡Make sure you do not lose the crankshaft key, if it has been removed.

To install:

8. Coat the crankshaft stub with engine oil.
9. Position the crankshaft key if one was used. If you pulled the crank seal, replace it with the open end facing in.

➡The inertial weight section of the damper is attached to the hub with a rubber-like material. The correct installation procedures, with the proper tools, MUST be followed or the resultant movement of the inertial weight will destroy the tuning of the damper!

10. Thread the stud on the tool into the end of the crankshaft.
11. Position the damper on the shaft and tap it into place with a plastic mallet (lightly!). Make sure the key is in place by securing it with a little RTV sealant.
12. Install the bearing, washer and nut and then turn the nut until the damper is pulled into position. Remove the tool.
13. Make sure the damper is all the way on, then install the bolt. Tighten the bolt to the specification outlined in the torque specification chart at the end of this section.
14. Install the remaining components and road test the truck.

Fig. 96 Remove the accessory drive pulley bolts

Fig. 97 Remove the accessory drive pulley and the damper bolt from the vehicle

Fig. 98 Remove the crankshaft damper using the puller tool

Timing Chain Cover

REMOVAL & INSTALLATION

4.3L, 5.0L and 5.7L Engines

▶ See Figures 99 thru 107

1. Drain the cooling system.
2. Drain the oil and lower the oil pan.
3. If equipped, remove the Crankshaft Position Sensor (CKP).
4. Remove the crankshaft pulley and damper. Remove the water pump.
5. Unfasten the retainers holding the timing case cover to the block and remove the cover and gaskets.

6. Use a suitable tool to pry the old seal out of the front face of the cover.
To install:
7. Install the new seal so that the open end is toward the inside of the cover.

➡ Coat the lip of the new seal with oil prior to installation.

8. Check that the timing chain oil slinger is in place against the crankshaft sprocket.
9. Apply sealer to the front cover as shown in the accompanying illustration. Install the cover carefully onto the locating dowels.
10. Tighten the attaching screws to 124 inch lbs. (14 Nm) on the 4.3L and 100 inch lbs. (11 Nm) on the 5.0L and 5.7L.
11. Install the remaining components and fill the engine with oil and coolant. Road test the truck.

Fig. 99 Remove the timing cover bolts

Fig. 100 Remove the timing cover from the engine

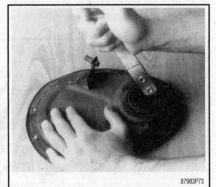

Fig. 101 Using a seal puller, remove the old seal from the front cover

Fig. 102 Installing the new seal in the front cover

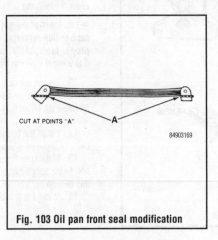

Fig. 103 Oil pan front seal modification

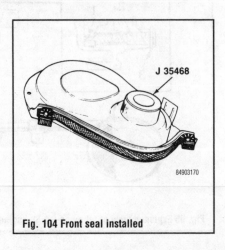

Fig. 104 Front seal installed

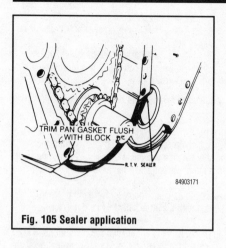

Fig. 105 Sealer application

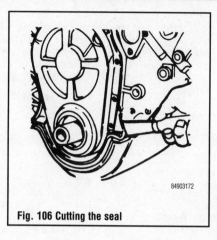

Fig. 106 Cutting the seal

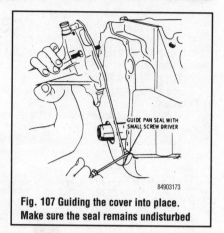

Fig. 107 Guiding the cover into place. Make sure the seal remains undisturbed

7.4L Engines

➡Special tool J-22102, or its equivalent seal driver, will be necessary for this job.

1. Disconnect the negative battery cable.
2. Drain the cooling system.
3. Remove the water pump.
4. Remove the crankshaft pulley and damper.
5. Remove the oil pan.
6. Remove the retainers holding the timing case cover to the block and pull off the cover and gaskets.
7. Use a suitable tool to pry the old seal out of the front face of the cover.

To install:

8. Install the remaining components in the reverse order of removal but please note the following steps.
9. Using seal driver J–22102, or equivalent, install the new seal so that the open end is toward the inside of the cover.

➡Coat the lip of the new seal with oil prior to installation.

10. Install a new front pan seal, cutting the tabs off.
11. Coat a new cover gasket with adhesive sealer and position it on the block.
12. Apply a ⅛ in. (bead of RTV gasket material to the front cover. Install the cover carefully onto the locating dowel.
13. Tighten the cover retainers to 106 inch lbs. (12 Nm).

6.2L and 6.5L Diesel Engines

♦ See Figure 108

1. Drain the cooling system.
2. Remove the water pump.
3. Rotate the crankshaft to align the marks on the injection pump driven gear and the camshaft gear as shown in the illustration.
4. Scribe a mark aligning the injection pump flange and the front cover.
5. Remove the crankshaft pulley and torsional damper.
6. If equipped, remove the Crankshaft Position sensor (CKP).
7. Remove the front cover-to-oil pan bolts.
8. Remove the two fuel return line clips.
9. Remove the injection pump gear.
10. Remove the injection pump retaining nuts from the front cover.
11. If equipped, remove the baffle.
12. Unfasten the remaining cover bolts, and remove the front cover.
13. If the front cover oil seal is to be replaced, it can now be pried out of the cover with a suitable prying tool. Press the new seal into the cover evenly.

➡The oil seal can also be replaced with the front cover installed. Remove the torsional damper first, then pry the old seal out of the cover using a suitable prying tool. Use care not to damage the surface of the crankshaft. Install the new seal evenly into the cover and install the damper.

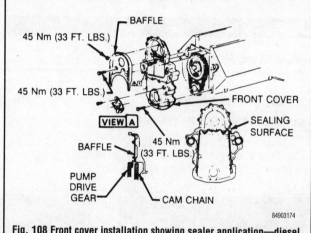

Fig. 108 Front cover installation showing sealer application—diesel engines

To install:

14. To install the front cover, first clean both sealing surfaces until all traces of old sealer are gone. Apply a ³⁄₃₂ in. (2mm) bead of sealant (GM sealant #1052357 or equivalent) to the sealing surface as shown in the illustration. Apply a bead of RTV type sealer to the bottom portion of the front cover which attached to the oil pan. Install the front cover.
15. Install the baffle.
16. Install the injection pump, making sure the scribe marks on the pump and front cover are aligned.
17. Install the injection pump driven gear, making sure the marks on the cam gear and pump are aligned. Be sure the dowel pin and the three holes on the pump flange are also aligned.
18. Install the fuel line clips, the front cover-to-oil bolts, and the torsional damper and crankshaft pulley.
19. Tighten the pan bolts to 89 inch lbs. (10 Nm), the cover-to-block bolts to 33 ft. lbs. (45 Nm), the baffle bolts and nut to 33 ft. lbs. (45 Nm), the injection pump nuts to 31 ft. lbs. (42 Nm) and the injection pump bolts to 17 ft. lbs. (23 Nm).

Timing Gear Cover and Seal

REMOVAL & INSTALLATION

4.8L Engines

1. Disconnect the negative battery cable.
2. Drain the cooling system.
3. Remove the water pump.

4. Remove the crankshaft pulley and damper.

5. Remove the oil pan-to-front cover bolts.

6. Remove the screws holding the timing case cover to the block, pull the cover forward enough to cut the front oil pan seal. Cut the seal flush with the block on both sides.

7. Pull off the cover and gaskets.

8. Use a suitable tool to pry the old seal out of the front face of the cover.

To install:

9. Install the remaining components in the reverse order of removal but please note the following steps.

10. Lubricate the new seal lip with engine oil and using a seal centering tool and installer J–23042, or equivalent, press the new seal into place. Leave the tool in position on the seal.

11. Install a new front pan seal, cutting the tabs off.

12. Coat a new cover gasket with adhesive sealer and position it on the block.

13. Apply a ⅛ in. (3.17mm) bead of RTV gasket material to the front cover. Install the cover carefully in place with the centering tool still attached.

14. Tighten the timing gear cover-to-block bolts to 80 inch lbs. (9 Nm).

15. Tighten the cover-to-pan bolts to 45 inch lbs. (6 Nm).

Timing Chain

REMOVAL & INSTALLATION

4.3L, 5.0L, 5.7L and 7.4L Engines

▸ See Figures 109, 110, 111, 112 and 113

1. Remove the timing cover. This will allow access to the timing chain.

2. Crank the engine until the timing marks on both sprockets are nearest each other and in line between the shaft centers.

3. On 1996–98 vehicles remove the crankshaft position sensor reluctor ring, if equipped. On 7.4L engines tool J-41371 or its equivalent puller must be used to remove the reluctor ring.

4. Take out the bolts that hold the camshaft gear to the camshaft. This gear is a light press fit on the camshaft and will come off easily. It is located by a dowel. The chain comes off with the camshaft gear.

➡A gear puller will be required to remove the crankshaft gear.

To install:

5. Without disturbing the position of the engine, mount the new crankshaft gear on the shaft, and mount the chain over the camshaft gear. Arrange the camshaft gear in such a way that the timing marks will line up between the shaft centers and the camshaft locating dowel will enter the dowel hole in the cam sprocket.

6. Place the cam sprocket, with its chain mounted over it, in position on the front of the truck and pull up with the three bolts that hold it to the camshaft.

7. After the gears are in place, turn the engine two full revolutions to make certain that the timing marks are in correct alignment between the shaft centers. Tighten the camshaft sprocket bolts (and nut on the 4.3L) to 21 ft. lbs. (28 Nm) on 1988–95 models. On 1996–98 models, tighten the bolts to 18 ft. Lbs. (25 Nm). On the 7.4L, tighten them to 20 ft. lbs. (26 Nm) on 1988–95 models. On 1996–98 models, tighten the bolts to 25 ft. Lbs. (34 Nm).

➡When installing the crankshaft position sensor you must use install a new oil ring seal onto the sensor.

8. Install the crankshaft position sensor reluctor ring (if equipped), onto the crankshaft until it is firmly seated against the crankshaft sprocket. On 1996–98 7.4L vehicles replace the reluctor ring with a new component.

9. Install the front cover, torsional damper, water pump and the radiator.

Fig. 109 Crank the engine until the timing marks on both sprockets are in line

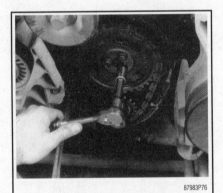

Fig. 110 Remove the camshaft gear retaining bolts

Fig. 111 Remove the camshaft gear and timing chain

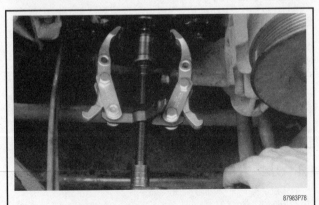

Fig. 112 A gear puller will be required to remove the crankshaft gear

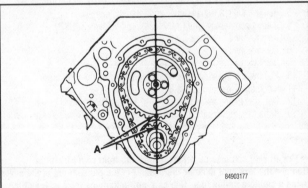

Fig. 113 Timing mark alignment—4.3L, 5.0L, 5.7L and 7.4L engines

6.2L and 6.5L Diesel Engines

▶ **See Figures 114 and 115**

1. Remove the front cover.
2. If applicable, remove the bolt and washer attaching the camshaft gear and the injection pump gear.
3. Crank the engine until the timing marks on both sprockets are nearest each other and in-line between the shaft centers.
4. Remove the camshaft sprocket, timing chain and crankshaft sprocket as a unit.

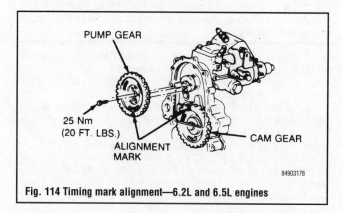

Fig. 114 Timing mark alignment—6.2L and 6.5L engines

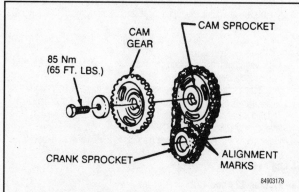

Fig. 115 Timing chain installation—6.2L and 6.5L engines

To install:

5. Install the camshaft sprocket, timing chain and crankshaft sprocket as a unit, aligning the timing marks on the sprockets as shown in the illustration. Tighten the camshaft gear bolt to 75 ft. lbs. (100 Nm) on 1988–95 models and 125 ft. Lbs. (171 Nm) on 1996–98 models.
6. Install the front cover as previously detailed. The injection pump must be re-timed since the timing chain assembly was removed.

Timing Gears

REMOVAL & INSTALLATION

4.8L Engines

▶ **See Figure 116**

The camshaft on these engines is gear driven, unlike the chain driven V6 and V8 engines. The camshaft must be removed to replace the gear.

1. Disconnect the negative battery cable. Remove the camshaft and place in an arbor press.

➡**Support the camshaft gear not the thrust plate.**

2. Press the gear off of the camshaft and remove the thrust plate and the spacer.

To install:

3. Support the camshaft at the front journal with tool J–22912–01 or equivalent, and mount the camshaft in a press.
4. Lubricate the thrust plate with engine oil.
5. Install the key if removed.
6. Install the spacer making sure the chamfer in the spacer faces toward the journal radius.
7. Install the thrust plate.
8. Install the camshaft gear on with the timing mark to the outside and press the gear on until it bottoms on the spacer.
9. Remove the camshaft from the press.

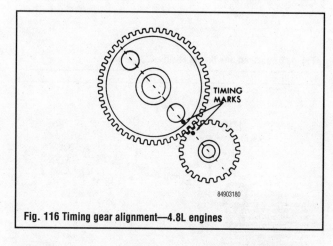

Fig. 116 Timing gear alignment—4.8L engines

➡**The clearance between the camshaft and thrust plate should be 0.003–0.008 in.**

Camshaft

REMOVAL & INSTALLATION

4.3L, 5.0L and 5.7L Engines

▶ **See Figures 117, 118, 119 and 120**

❈❈ CAUTION

Never open, service or drain the radiator or cooling system when hot; serious burns can occur from the steam and hot coolant. Also, when draining engine coolant, keep in mind that cats and dogs are attracted to ethylene glycol antifreeze and could drink any that is left in an uncovered container or in puddles on the ground. This will prove fatal in sufficient quantities. Always drain coolant into a sealable container. Coolant should be reused unless it is contaminated or is several years old.

1. Disconnect the negative battery cable.
2. Drain the coolant and remove the radiator.
3. If the vehicle is equipped with a mechanical fuel pump remove it.
4. Remove the drive belt(s).
5. If necessary, loosen the alternator bolts and move the alternator to one side.
6. Remove the valve covers.
7. Mark the lifters, pushrods, and rocker arms as to location so that they may be installed in the same position. Remove these parts.
8. If applicable, remove the air intake duct.
9. If necessary, remove the power steering pump from its brackets and move it out of the way.
10. If necessary, remove the air conditioning compressor from its brackets and move the compressor out of the way without disconnecting the lines.
11. Disconnect the hoses from the water pump.
12. Disengage and tag any electrical or vacuum connections that would interfere with camshaft removal.

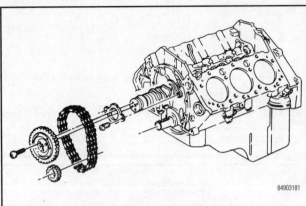

Fig. 117 Camshaft and timing chain—4.3L engines

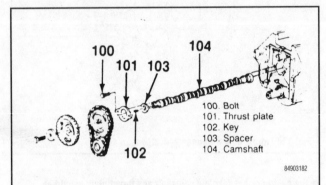

100. Bolt
101. Thrust plate
102. Key
103. Spacer
104. Camshaft

Fig. 118 Camshaft and related parts—5.0L, 5.7L, 6.2L, 6.5L and 7.4L engines

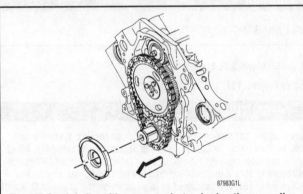

Fig. 119 Crankshaft position sensor reluctor ring location—gasoline engines

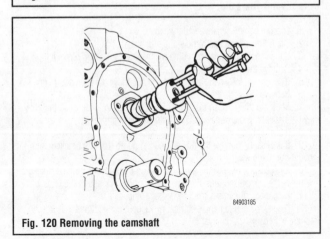

Fig. 120 Removing the camshaft

13. Mark the distributor as to location in the block. Remove the distributor.
14. If necessary, disconnect the hood release cable at the latch.
15. Remove the water pump.
16. Remove the front cover.

✳✳ CAUTION

Please refer to Section 1 before discharging the compressor or disconnecting air conditioning lines. Damage to the air conditioning system or personal injury could result. Consult your local laws concerning refrigerant discharge and recycling. In many areas it may be illegal for anyone but a certified technician to service the A/C system. Always use an approved recovery station when discharging the air conditioning.

17. If necessary, if the truck is equipped with air conditioning, discharge the air conditioning system and remove the condenser.
18. On carbureted engines remove the fuel pump eccentric, camshaft gear, oil slinger, and timing chain.
19. On 5.0L and 5.7L engines, remove the front engine mount through-bolts, place a piece of wood on a hydraulic jack, position the jack with the wood under the engine and raise the engine.
20. Remove the camshaft thrust plate (on front of camshaft) on the 4.3L.
21. Install 2 or 3 ⁵⁄₁₆–18 bolts, 4–5 in. (101–127mm) long, into the threaded holes in the end of the shaft. Carefully remove the camshaft from the engine.
22. Inspect the camshaft for signs of excessive wear or damage.

To install:
23. Liberally coat camshaft and bearing with heavy engine oil, engine assembly lubricant or engine oil supplement, and carefully insert the cam into the engine.
24. On 5.0L and 5.7L engines, lower the engine and install the front mount through-bolts.
25. Align the timing marks on the camshaft and crankshaft gears. (refer to timing chain removal and installation).
26. Install the distributor using the locating marks made during removal. If any problems are encountered, refer to distributor removal and installation.
27. Install the camshaft thrust plate (on front of camshaft) on the 4.3L. Tighten the bolts to 105 inch lbs. (12 Nm).
28. Installation of the remaining components is the reverse of removal.

4.8L Engines

▶ **See Figures 121 and 122**

1. Remove the grille. Remove the radiator hoses and remove the radiator.
2. Remove the hydraulic lifters.
3. Remove the timing gear cover.
4. Remove the fuel pump.
5. Remove the distributor.
6. Align the timing marks on the camshaft and crankshaft gears.
7. Remove the camshaft thrust plate bolts.
8. Support and carefully remove the camshaft.
9. If either the camshaft or the camshaft gear is being renewed, the gear must be pressed off the camshaft. The replacement parts must be assembled in the same way. When placing the gear on the camshaft, press the gear onto the shaft until it bottoms against the gear spacer ring. The end clearance of the thrust plate should be 0.003–0.008 in. –0.031mm)

To install:
10. Pre-lube the camshaft lobes with clean engine oil or engine oil supplement, and then install the camshaft assembly in the engine. Be careful not to damage the bearings.
11. Turn the crankshaft and the camshaft gears so that the timing marks align. Push the camshaft into position and install and tighten the thrust plate bolts to 80 inch lbs. (9 Nm).
12. Check camshaft and crankshaft gear run-out with a dial indicator. Camshaft gear run-out should not exceed 0.004 in. (0.012mm) and crankshaft gear run-out should not be above 0.003 in. (0.011mm).
13. Using a dial indicator, check the backlash at several points between the camshaft and crankshaft gear teeth. Backlash should be 0.004–0.006 inches. (0.015–0.023mm).
14. Install the remaining components.

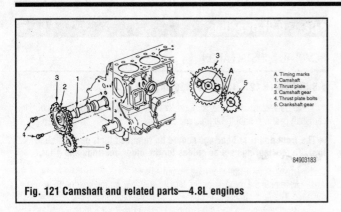

Fig. 121 Camshaft and related parts—4.8L engines

A. Timing marks
1. Camshaft
2. Thrust plate
3. Camshaft gear
4. Thrust plate bolts
5. Crankshaft gear

84903183

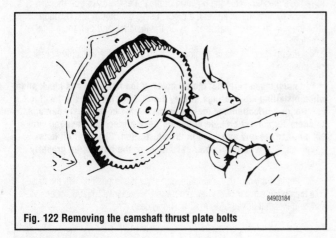

Fig. 122 Removing the camshaft thrust plate bolts

84903184

7.4L Engines

▶ **See Figures 118, 119 and 120**

1. Disconnect the negative battery cable.
2. Remove the air cleaner.
3. Remove the grille.
4. Remove the air conditioning compressor from its brackets and move the compressor out of the way without disconnecting the lines.
5. Drain the cooling system.
6. Remove the fan shroud and radiator.
7. Remove the drive belt(s), loosen the alternator bolts and move the alternator to one side.
8. Remove the cylinder head covers.
9. Disconnect the hoses from the water pump.
10. Remove the water pump.
11. Remove the torsional damper and pulley.
12. Remove the front cover.
13. Mark the distributor as to location in the block. Remove the distributor.
14. Remove the intake manifold.
15. Mark the lifters, pushrods, and rocker arms as to location so that they may be installed in the same position. Remove these parts.
16. Rotate the camshaft so that the timing marks align.
17. Remove the camshaft sprocket bolts.
18. Pull the camshaft sprocket and timing chain off. The sprocket is a tight fit, so you'll have to tap it loose with a plastic mallet.
19. If equipped, unfasten the camshaft retainer bolts and remove the retainer.
20. Install two 5/16 in.–18 bolts in the holes in the front of the camshaft and carefully pull the camshaft from the block.

To install:

21. Liberally coat camshaft and bearing with heavy engine oil or engine assembly lubricant and insert the cam into the engine.
22. If equipped, install the camshaft retainer and bolts. Tighten the bolts to 10 ft lbs. (14 Nm).

23. Install the distributor using the locating marks made during removal. (If any problems are encountered, refer to distributor removal and installation)
24. Install the camshaft sprocket bolts and tighten them to 20 ft. lbs. (27 Nm) on 1988–95 models and 25 ft. lbs. (34 Nm) on 1996–98 models.
25. Installation of the remaining components is the reverse of removal.

6.2L and 6.5L Diesel Engines

▶ **See Figures 118 and 120**

> **✳✳ CAUTION**
>
> **Please refer to Section 1 before discharging the compressor or disconnecting air conditioning lines. Damage to the air conditioning system or personal injury could result. Consult your local laws concerning refrigerant discharge and recycling. In many areas it may be illegal for anyone but a certified technician to service the A/C system. Always use an approved recovery station when discharging the air conditioning.**

1. Disconnect the negative battery cable.
2. If the truck is equipped with A/C, have the A/C system evacuated by a qualified technician using approved equipment.
3. Drain the cooling system.
4. Remove the radiator and condenser.
5. Remove the grille and the parking lamp assemblies.
6. Remove the hood latch and brace assembly.
7. If necessary, remove the power steering pump, alternator and air conditioning compressor and set them aside.
8. Remove the valve covers.
9. Mark the lifters, pushrods, and rocker arms as to location so that they may be installed in the same position. Remove these parts.
10. Remove the cylinder head and the oil pump drive.
11. Remove the timing chain.
12. If applicable, remove the fuel pump (lift pump).
13. Remove the front engine mount through-bolts, place a piece of wood on a hydraulic jack, position the jack with the wood under the engine and raise the engine.
14. Remove the camshaft retainer plate.
15. Remove the spacer, if equipped.
16. Remove the camshaft by carefully sliding it out of the block.

➡ **Whenever a new camshaft is installed, GM recommends replacing all the valve lifters, as well as the oil filter. The engine oil must be changed. These measures will help ensure proper wear characteristics of the new camshaft.**

To install:

17. Coat the camshaft lobes with Molykote® or an equivalent lube. Liberally tube the camshaft journals with clean engine oil and install the camshaft carefully.
18. Install the camshaft retainer plate and tighten the bolts to 17 ft. lbs. (23 Nm).
19. Lower the engine, install the front engine mount bolts and tighten them to 70 ft. lbs. (95 Nm). Tighten the nut to 50 ft. lbs. (70 Nm).
20. Installation of the remaining components is the reverse of removal.

INSPECTION

Run-Out

▶ **See Figure 123**

Camshaft run-out should be checked when the camshaft has been removed from the engine. An accurate dial indicator is needed for this procedure; engine specialists and most machine shops have this equipment. If you have access to a dial indicator, or can take your camshaft to someone who does, measure the camshaft bearing journal run-out. If the run-out exceeds the limit replace the camshaft.

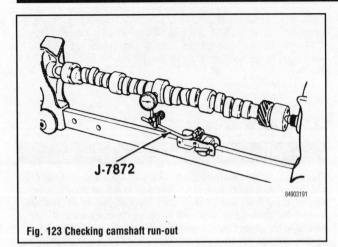

Fig. 123 Checking camshaft run-out

Lobe Height

♦ **See Figures 124 and 125**

Use a micrometer to check camshaft (lobe) height, making sure the anvil and the spindle of the micrometer are positioned directly on the heel and tip of the camshaft lobe as shown in the accompanying illustration.

End-Play

♦ **See Figure 126**

After the camshaft has been installed, end-play should be checked. The camshaft sprocket should be installed on the cam. Use a dial gauge to check the end-play, by moving the camshaft forward and backward. End-play specifications should be as noted in the Camshaft Specifications chart.

Camshaft Bearings

REMOVAL & INSTALLATION

♦ **See Figures 127, 128, 129, 130 and 131**

If excessive camshaft wear is found, or if the engine is completely rebuilt, the camshaft bearings should be replaced.

➡**The front and rear bearings should be removed last, and installed first. Those bearings act as guides for the other bearings and pilot.**

1. Drive the camshaft rear plug from the block.
2. Assemble the removal puller with its shoulder on the bearing to be removed. Gradually tighten the puller nut until the bearing is removed.
3. Remove the remaining bearings, leaving the front and rear for last. To remove these, reverse the position of the puller, so as to pull the bearings towards the center of the block. Leave the tool in this position, pilot the new front and rear bearings on the installer, and pull them into position.
4. Return the puller to its original position and pull the remaining bearings into position.

➡**You must make sure that the oil holes of the bearings and block align when installing the bearings. If they don't align, the camshaft will not get proper lubrication and may seize or at least be seriously damaged. To check for correct oil hole alignment, use a piece of brass rod with a 90° bend in the end as shown in the illustration. Check all oil hole openings. The wire must enter each hole, or the hole is not properly aligned.**

5. Replace the camshaft rear plug, and stake it into position. On the diesel, coat the outer diameter of the new plug with GM sealant #1052080 or equivalent, and install it flush to 1/32 in. (0.794mm) deep.

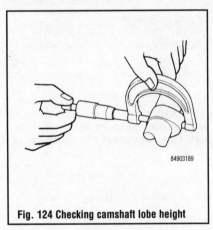

Fig. 124 Checking camshaft lobe height

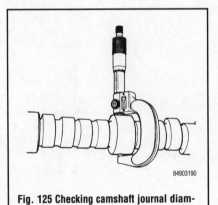

Fig. 125 Checking camshaft journal diameter

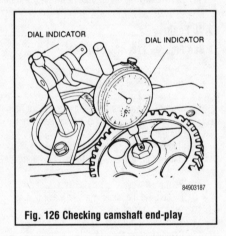

Fig. 126 Checking camshaft end-play

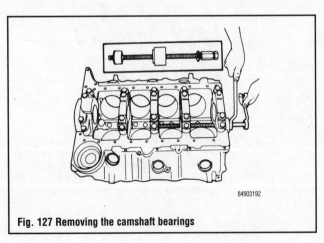

Fig. 127 Removing the camshaft bearings

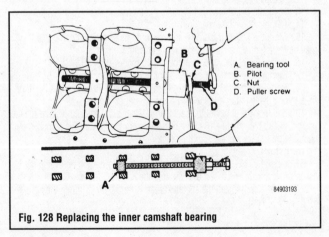

A. Bearing tool
B. Pilot
C. Nut
D. Puller screw

Fig. 128 Replacing the inner camshaft bearing

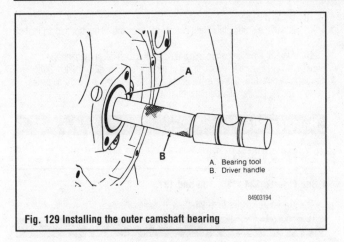

Fig. 129 Installing the outer camshaft bearing

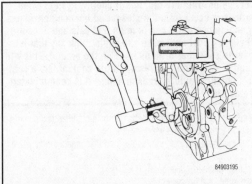

Fig. 130 Installing the front camshaft bearing on the diesel. The bearing tool is shown in the inset

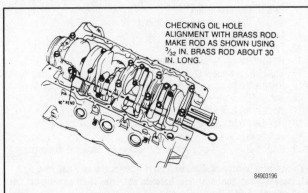

Fig. 131 Make this simple tool to check camshaft bearing oil hole alignment

Hydraulic Lifters

REMOVAL & INSTALLATION

4.8L Engines

▶ See Figure 132

1. Remove the rocker cover.
2. Remove the engine side cover.
3. Back off the rocker arm adjusting nuts and remove the pushrods. Keep them in order for installation.
4. Reaching through the side cover opening, lift out the hydraulic lifters. If your are going to re-use the lifters, remove them one at a time and mark each one for installation. They **must** be re-installed in the same locations.

Fig. 132 Stuck lifters must be freed using a slide hammer type lifter removal tool

If a lifter is stuck, it can be removed with a grasping-type lifter tool, available form most auto parts stores.
5. Inspect each lifter thoroughly. If any of them shows any signs of wear, heat bluing or damage, replace the whole set.

To install:

6. Install and coat each lifter with engine oil supplement.
7. Install the remaining components by reversing the removal procedure.
8. Once installation is complete, adjust the valves as described in the valve lash procedure.

4.3L, 5.0L, 5.7L and 7.4L Engines

1. Remove the cylinder head cover.
2. Remove the intake manifold.
3. Back off the rocker arm adjusting nuts and remove the pushrods. Keep them in order for installation.
4. Remove the lifter retainer bolts, retainer and restrictor.
5. Remove the lifters. If your are going to re-use the lifters, remove them one at a time and mark each one for installation. They **must** be re-installed in the same locations. If a lifter is stuck, it can be removed with a grasping-type lifter tool, available from most auto parts stores.
6. Inspect each lifter thoroughly. If any of them shows any signs of wear, heat bluing or damage, replace the whole set.
7. Coat each lifter with engine oil supplement prior to installation. Tighten the retainer bolts to 12 ft. lbs. (16 Nm). Adjust the valves as described in the valve lash procedure.

6.2L and 6.5L Diesel Engines

▶ See Figure 133

1. Remove the cylinder head cover.
2. Remove the rocker arm shaft, rocker arms and pushrods. Keep all parts in order and properly identified for installation.
3. Remove the clamps and lifter guide plates.
4. Remove the lifters by reaching through the access holes in the cylinder head with a magnetic lifter tool. If you are going to re-use the lifters, remove them one at a time and mark each one for installation. They **must** be re-installed in the same locations. If a lifter is stuck, it can be removed with a grasping-type lifter tool, available form most auto parts stores.

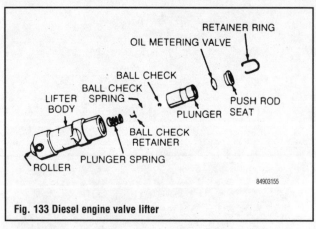

Fig. 133 Diesel engine valve lifter

To install:

5. Inspect each lifter thoroughly. If any of them shows any signs of wear, heat bluing or damage, replace the whole set.

➡Some engines will have both standard and 0.010 in. (.0039mm) over-size lifters. The oversized lifters will have "10" etched into the side. The block will be stamped "OS" on the cast pad next to the lifter bore. and on the top rail of the crankcase above the lifter bore.

✳✳ WARNING

New lifters must be primed before installation. Damage to the lifters and engine will result if new lifters are installed dry!

6. Prime new lifters by immersing them in clean kerosene, engine oil or diesel fuel and working the lifter plunger while the unit is submerged.

7. Prior to installation, coat the lifter roller with engine oil supplement. Re-used lifters must be installed in their original positions!

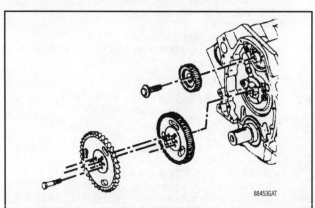

Fig. 134 View of the balance shaft drive and driven gears

8. Install the lifters.

9. Install the guide plates and clamps. Tighten the clamp bolts to 18 ft. lbs. (26 Nm).

10. After all the clamps are installed, turn the crankshaft by hand, 2 full turns (720°) to ensure free movement of the lifters in the guide plates. If the crankshaft won't turn, one or more lifters may be jamming in the guide plates.

11. The remainder of assembly the reverse of disassembly.

Balance Shaft

REMOVAL & INSTALLATION

▶ **See Figures 134, 135, 136 and 137**

The procedure applies to 1994–98 4.3L engines only.

✳✳ CAUTION

Never open, service or drain the radiator or cooling system when hot; serious burns can occur from the steam and hot coolant. Also, when draining engine coolant, keep in mind that cats and dogs are attracted to ethylene glycol antifreeze and could drink any that is left in an uncovered container or in puddles on the ground. This will prove fatal in sufficient quantities. Always drain coolant into a seal-able container. Coolant should be reused unless it is contaminated or is several years old.

1. Have the air conditioning system discharged by a qualified technician using a proper refrigerant recovery/recycling station.

2. Properly relieve the fuel system pressure, then disconnect the negative battery cable.

3. Remove the air cleaner intake duct.

4. Drain the engine cooling system.

5. Remove the A/C compressor and its brackets.

6. Remove the radiator and air conditioning condenser from the vehicle.

7. Remove the fan assembly.

8. Carefully release the belt tension, then remove the serpentine drive belt.

9. Remove the water pump.

10. Remove the crankshaft pulley and damper.

11. Drain the oil and remove the oil pan.

12. Remove the front cover.

13. Remove the timing chain and sprockets.

14. Unfasten the balance shaft gear bolt, then remove the gear.

15. Remove the balance shaft retainer.

16. Remove the intake manifold assembly.

17. Remove the hydraulic lifter retainer.

18. Remove the balance shaft and front bearing by gently driving them out using a soft faced mallet.

19. Using tool J–38834 or its equivalent, remove the balance shaft rear bearing.

➡The balance shaft and drive and driven gears are serviced only as a set, including the gear bolt. The balance shaft and front bearing are serviced as a package.

Fig. 135 View of the balance shaft location—1994–98 4.3L engine

Fig. 136 Unfasten the balance shaft gear bolt . . .

Fig. 137 . . . then remove the gear

✳✳ WARNING

The front bearing must not be removed from the balance shaft

To install:

20. Inspect the balance shaft gears for damage, such as nicks and burrs.

21. Using a suitable gasket scraper, clean the gasket mounting surfaces. Using solvent, clean the oil and grease from the gasket mounting surfaces.

22. Lubricate the balance shaft rear bearing with clean engine oil, then install the bearing using tool J–38834 or its equivalent.

23. Lubricate the balance shaft with clean engine oil, then install the balance shaft into the block.

24. Install the balance shaft bearing retainer and bolts. Tighten the bolts to 106 inch. lbs. (12 Nm).

25. Install the balance shaft driven gear and bolt. Tighten the bolt to 15 ft. lbs. (20 Nm) plus an additional 35¯ using a torque/angle meter.

26. Install the hydraulic lifter retainer, then rotate the balance shaft by hand and check that there is clearance between the balance shaft and the lifter retainer.

27. Temporarily install the balance shaft drive gear so that the timing mark on the gear points straight up, then remove the drive gear, turn the balance shaft so the timing mark on the driven gear is facing straight down.

28. Install the drive gear and make sure the timing marks on both gears line up (dot-to-dot).

29. Install the drive gear retaining bolt and tighten to 12 ft. lbs. (16 Nm).

30. Install the intake manifold assembly.

31. Install the timing chain and sprocket assemblies.

32. Install the front cover, seal, bolts and the oil pan assembly.

33. Using tool J–39046 or its equivalent engage the crankshaft pulley and damper.

34. Installation of the remaining components is the reverse of removal.

Rear Main Oil Seal

REMOVAL & INSTALLATION

4.8L Engines

▶ **See Figures 138, 139, 140, 141 and 142**

The rear main bearing oil seal, both halves, can be removed without removal of the crankshaft. Always replace the upper and lower halves together.

1. Raise and support the truck on jackstands.

2. Drain the oil.

3. Remove the oil pan.

4. Remove the rear main bearing cap.

5. Remove the old oil seal from its groove in the cap, prying from the bottom using a suitable tool.

6. Coat a new seal half completely with clean engine oil, and insert it into the bearing cap groove. Keep the oil off of the parting line surface, as this surface is treated with glue. Gradually push the seal with a hammer handle until the seal is rolled into place.

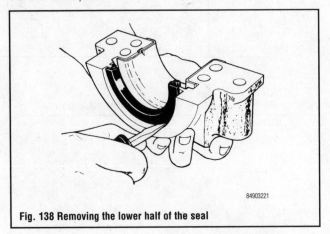
Fig. 138 Removing the lower half of the seal

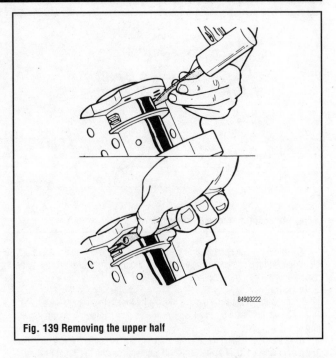
Fig. 139 Removing the upper half

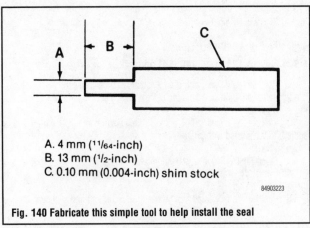
A. 4 mm (¹¹/₆₄-inch)
B. 13 mm (¹/₂-inch)
C. 0.10 mm (0.004-inch) shim stock

Fig. 140 Fabricate this simple tool to help install the seal

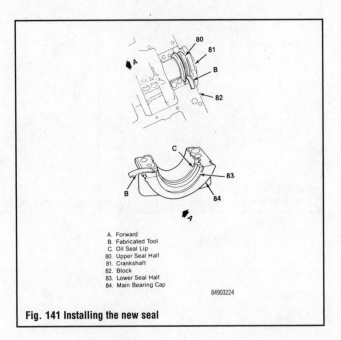
A. Forward
B. Fabricated Tool
C. Oil Seal Lip
80. Upper Seal Half
81. Crankshaft
82. Block
83. Lower Seal Half
84. Main Bearing Cap

Fig. 141 Installing the new seal

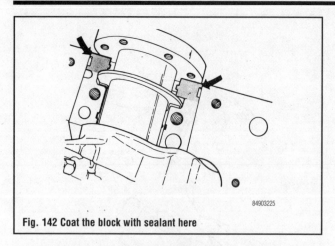

Fig. 142 Coat the block with sealant here

7. To remove the upper half of the old seal, use a small hammer and a soft, blunt punch to tap one end of the oil seal out until it protrudes far enough to be removed with needle-nosed pliers.

To install:

8. Push the new seal into place with the lip toward the front of the engine.

9. Install the bearing cap and tighten the bolts to a loose fit; do not final-torque.

10. With the cap fitted loosely, move the crankshaft first to the rear and then to the front with a rubber mallet. This will properly position the thrust bearing.

11. Tighten the bearing cap to a final torque of 65 ft. lbs. (90 Nm).

12. Install the oil pan.

1988–90 7.4L Engines

▶ See Figures 138, 139, 140, 141 and 142

1. Remove the oil pan, oil pump and rear main bearing cap.

2. Remove the oil seal from the bearing cap by prying it out with a suitable tool.

3. Remove the upper half of the seal with a small punch. Drive it around far enough to be gripped with pliers.

To install:

4. Clean the crankshaft and bearing cap.

5. Coat the lips and bead of the seal with light engine oil, keeping oil from the ends of the seal.

6. Position the fabricated tool between the crankshaft and seal seat.

7. Position the seal between the crankshaft and tip of the tool so that the seal bead contacts the tip of the tool. The oil seal lip should face forward.

8. Roll the seal around the crankshaft using the tool to protect the seal bead from the sharp corners of the crankcase.

9. The installation tool should be left installed until the seal is properly positioned with both ends flush with the block.

10. Remove the tool.

11. Install the other half of the seal in the bearing cap using the tool in the same manner as before. Light thumb pressure should install the seal.

12. Install the bearing cap with sealant applied to the mating areas of the cap and block. Keep sealant from the ends of the seal.

13. Tighten the main bearing cap retaining bolts to 10 ft. lbs. (14 Nm). Tap the end of the crankshaft first rearward, then forward with a lead hammer. This will line up the rear main bearing and the crankshaft thrust surfaces. Tighten the main bearing cap 110 ft. lbs. (150 Nm).

14. Install the oil pump.

15. Install the oil pan.

4.3L, 5.0L, 5.7L and 1991–98 7.4L Engines

▶ See Figures 143, 144 and 145

➡ Special tool J-35621 (or J-38841), or its equivalent seal installer, will be necessary for this job.

1. Remove the transmission.

2. With manual transmission, remove the clutch.

3. Remove the flywheel or flexplate.

4. Remove the oil pan.

5. Unfasten the oil seal retainer screws and nuts.

6. Remove the oil seal retainer and gasket.

7. Insert a small prying tool in the notches provided in the seal retainer and pry out the old seal. Be VERY CAREFUL to avoid nicking or scratching the sealing surfaces of the crankshaft.

To install:

8. Install a new gasket on the block and install the oil seal retainer. Tighten the screws and nuts to 11 ft. lbs. (15 Nm).

9. Install the oil pan.

10. Coat the inner and outer diameters of the new seal with clean engine oil.

11. Using seal tool J-35621, or equivalent, position the seal on the tool.

12. Thread the seal tool attaching screws into the holes in the crankshaft end and tighten them securely with a screwdriver.

13. Turn the installer handle until it bottoms.

14. Remove the tool.

15. Install the flywheel/flexplate, clutch (if applicable), and the transmission.

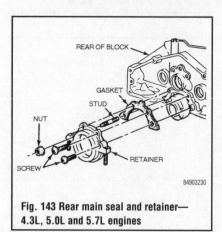

Fig. 143 Rear main seal and retainer—4.3L, 5.0L and 5.7L engines

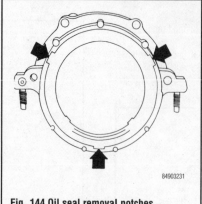

Fig. 144 Oil seal removal notches

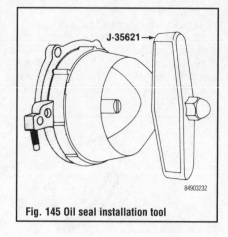

Fig. 145 Oil seal installation tool

6.2L Diesel Engines

ROPE SEAL

◢ **See Figures 146, 147 and 148**

The crankshaft need not be removed to replace the rear main bearing upper oil seal. The lower seal is installed in the bearing cap.

➥**Engines are originally equipped with a rope-type seal. This should be replaced with the lip-type seal available as a service replacement.**

1. Drain the crankcase oil and remove the oil pan and rear main bearing cap.

2. Using a special main seal tool or a tool that can be made from a dowel (see illustration), drive the upper seal into its groove on each side until it is tightly packed. This is usually ¼–¾ in. (6–19mm).

3. Measure the amount the seal was driven up on one side. Add ¹⁄₁₆ in. (2mm) and cut another length from the old seal. Use the main bearing cap as a holding fixture when cutting the seal as illustrated. Carefully trim the protruding seal.

4. Work these two pieces of seal up into the cylinder block on each side with two nailsets or small screwdrivers. Using the packing tool again, pack these pieces into the block, then trim the flush with a razor blade or hobby knife as shown. Do not scratch the bearing surface with the razor.

➥**It may help to use a bit of oil on the short pieces of the rope seal when packing it into the block.**

5. Apply Loctite® # 496 sealer or equivalent to the rear main bearing cap and install the rope seal. Cut the ends of the seal flush with the cap.

6. Check to see if the rear main cap with the new seal will seat properly on the block. Place a piece of Plastigage® on the rear main journal, install the cap and tighten to 70 ft. lbs. (94 Nm). Remove the cap and check the Plastigage® against specifications. If out of specs, recheck the end of the seal for fraying that may be preventing the cap from seating properly.

7. Make sure all traces of Plastigage® are removed from the crankshaft journal. Apply a thin film of sealer (GM part # 1052357 or equivalent) to the bearing cap. Keep the sealant off of both the seal and the bearing.

8. Just before assembly, apply a light coat of clean engine oil on the crankshaft surface that will contact the seal.

9. Install the bearing cap and tighten to specification.

10. Install the oil pump and oil pan.

TWO-PIECE LIP SEAL

◢ **See Figure 149**

1. Disconnect the negative battery cable. Drain the oil.

2. Remove the oil pan and oil pump.

3. Loosen the bolts and remove the rear main bearing cap. Pull out the old rope seal.

4. Clean the upper and lower seal grooves. Clean the main bearing cap and block mating surfaces and then check the bearing clearance.

5. Coat the inner side of the seal halves where they contact the crankshaft and slide them into position.

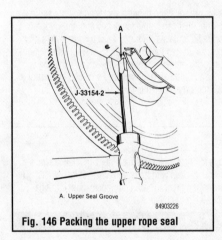

A. Upper Seal Groove

84903226

Fig. 146 Packing the upper rope seal

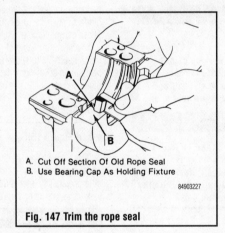

A. Cut Off Section Of Old Rope Seal
B. Use Bearing Cap As Holding Fixture

84903227

Fig. 147 Trim the rope seal

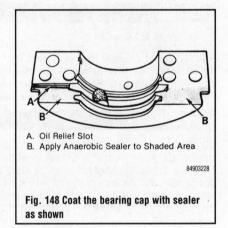

A. Oil Relief Slot
B. Apply Anaerobic Sealer to Shaded Area

84903228

Fig. 148 Coat the bearing cap with sealer as shown

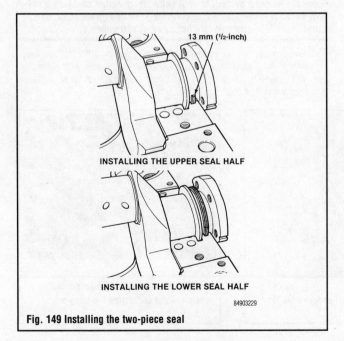

13 mm (½-inch)

INSTALLING THE UPPER SEAL HALF

INSTALLING THE LOWER SEAL HALF

84903229

Fig. 149 Installing the two-piece seal

6. Roll one seal half into the cylinder block groove until ½ in. (13mm) of the seal's end is protruding from the block.

7. Insert the other half into the opposite side of the groove. The ends of the seals (where they touch) should now be at either the 4 and 10 o'clock or the 8 and 2 o'clock positions. This is the only way you will be able to align the main bearing cap and seal lips properly!

8. Coat the seal groove in the bearing cap lightly with adhesive. Apply a thin film of anaerobic sealant to the cap (stay away from the oil hole!!), coat the bolts with oil and tap them into position. Tighten all bolts to specification, loosen and then retighten.

9. Install the oil pan and pump. Fill the engine with oil and connect the battery cable.

6.5L DIESEL ENGINES

◢ **See Figure 150**

1. Remove the transmission and flywheel.

2. Remove the oil seal using a suitable tool and discard the seal.

3. Clean the oil seal bore in the block and inspect the seal-to-engine contact surfaces.

To install:

4. Coat the crankshaft surface with clean engine oil and lightly coat the sealing area of the new oil seal.

5. Install the new seal with the spring cavity towards the engine, onto the crankshaft.

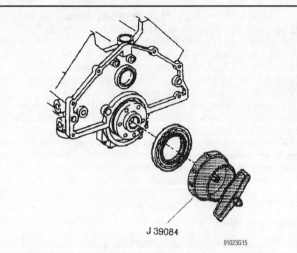

Fig. 150 Using tool J-39084 or equivalent, drive the seal in until tool bottoms out against the block and the crankshaft rear main bearing cap—6.5L engines

6. Using tool J–39084 or equivalent, drive the seal in until tool bottoms out against the block and the crankshaft rear main bearing cap.
7. Remove the tool.
8. Install the flywheel and transmission.

Flywheel and Ring Gear

REMOVAL & INSTALLATION

The ring gear is an integral part of the flywheel and is not replaceable. To remove the flywheel:
1. Remove the transmission.
2. Remove the six bolts attaching the flywheel to the crankshaft flange. Remove the flywheel.
3. Inspect the flywheel for cracks, and inspect the ring gear for burrs or worn teeth. Replace the flywheel if any damage is apparent. Remove burrs with a mill file.
4. Install the flywheel. The flywheel will only attach to the crankshaft in one position, as the bolt holes are unevenly spaced. Install the bolts and tighten to the following specifications.
- 4.3L, 5.0L and 5.7L engines: 75 ft. Lbs. (100 Nm).
- 6.2L, 6.5L and 7.4L engines: 65 ft. Lbs. (90 Nm).

EXHAUST SYSTEM

Inspection

▶ See Figures 151 thru 157

➡Safety glasses should be worn at all times when working on or near the exhaust system. Older exhaust systems will almost always be covered with loose rust particles which will shower you when disturbed. These particles are more than a nuisance and could injure your eye.

✳✳ CAUTION

DO NOT perform exhaust repairs or inspection with the engine or exhaust hot. Allow the system to cool completely before attempting any work. Exhaust systems are noted for sharp edges, flaking metal and rusted bolts. Gloves and eye protection are required. A healthy supply of penetrating oil and rags is highly recommended.

Your vehicle must be raised and supported safely to inspect the exhaust system properly. By placing 4 safety stands under the vehicle for support should provide enough room for you to slide under the vehicle and inspect the system completely. Start the inspection at the exhaust manifold or turbocharger pipe where the header pipe is attached and work your way to the back of the vehicle. On dual exhaust systems, remember to inspect both sides of the vehicle. Check the complete exhaust system for open seams, holes loose connections, or other deterioration which could permit exhaust fumes to seep into the passenger com-

partment. Inspect all mounting brackets and hangers for deterioration, some models may have rubber O-rings that can be overstretched and non-supportive. These components will need to be replaced if found. It has always been a practice to use a pointed tool to poke up into the exhaust system where the deterioration spots are to see whether or not they crumble. Some models may have heat shield covering certain parts of the exhaust system , it will be necessary to remove these shields to have the exhaust visible for inspection also.

REPLACEMENT

▶ See Figure 158

There are basically two types of exhaust systems. One is the flange type where the component ends are attached with bolts and a gasket in-between. The other exhaust system is the slip joint type. These components slip into one another using clamps to retain them together.

✳✳ CAUTION

Allow the exhaust system to cool sufficiently before spraying a solvent exhaust fasteners. Some solvents are highly flammable and could ignite when sprayed on hot exhaust components.

Before removing any component of the exhaust system, ALWAYS squirt a liquid rust dissolving agent onto the fasteners for ease of removal. A lot of knuckle skin will be saved by following this rule. It may even be wise to spray the fasteners and allow them to sit overnight.

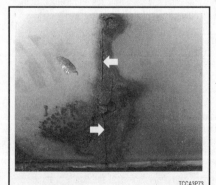

TCCA3P73

Fig. 151 Cracks in the muffler are a guaranteed leak

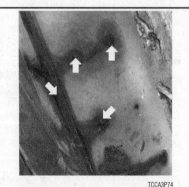

TCCA3P74

Fig. 152 Check the muffler for rotted spot welds and seams

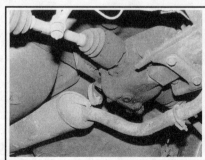

TCCA3P77

Fig. 153 Make sure the exhaust components are not contacting the body or suspension

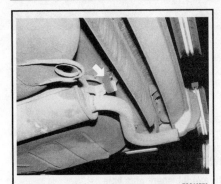

Fig. 154 Check for overstretched or torn exhaust hangers

Fig. 155 Example of a badly deteriorated exhaust pipe

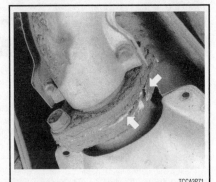

Fig. 156 Inspect flanges for gaskets that have deteriorated and need replacement

Flange Type

▶ See Figure 159

※ CAUTION

Do NOT perform exhaust repairs or inspection with the engine or exhaust hot. Allow the system to cool completely before attempting any work. Exhaust systems are noted for sharp edges, flaking metal and rusted bolts. Gloves and eye protection are required. A healthy supply of penetrating oil and rags is highly recommended. Never spray liquid rust dissolving agent onto a hot exhaust component.

Slip Joint Type

▶ See Figure 160

Before removing any component on the slip joint type exhaust system, ALWAYS squirt a liquid rust dissolving agent onto the fasteners for ease of removal. Start by unbolting the exhaust piece at both ends (if required). When unbolting the headpipe from the manifold, make sure that the bolts are free before trying to remove them. if you snap a stud in the exhaust manifold, the stud will have to be removed with a bolt extractor, which often means removal of the manifold itself. Next, remove the mounting U-bolts from around the exhaust pipe you are extracting from the vehicle. Don't be surprised if the U-bolts break while removing the nuts. Loosen the exhaust pipe from any mounting brackets retaining it to the floor pan and separate the components.

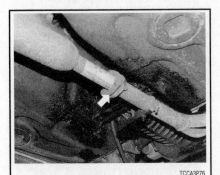

Fig. 157 Some systems, like this one, use large O-rings (donuts) in between the flanges

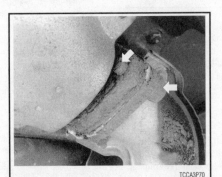

Fig. 158 Nuts and bolts will be extremely difficult to remove when deteriorated with rust

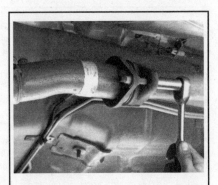

Fig. 159 Example of a flange type exhaust system joint

Before removing any component on a flange type system, ALWAYS squirt a liquid rust dissolving agent onto the fasteners for ease of removal. Start by unbolting the exhaust piece at both ends (if required). When unbolting the headpipe from the manifold, make sure that the bolts are free before trying to remove them. if you snap a stud in the exhaust manifold, the stud will have to be removed with a bolt extractor, which often means removal of the manifold itself. Next, disconnect the component from the mounting; slight twisting and turning may be required to remove the component completely from the vehicle. You may need to tap on the component with a rubber mallet to loosen the component. If all else fails, use a hacksaw to separate the parts. An oxy-acetylene cutting torch may be faster but the sparks are DANGEROUS near the fuel tank, and at the very least, accidents could happen, resulting in damage to the under-car parts, not to mention yourself.

Fig. 160 Example of a common slip joint type system

ENGINE RECONDITIONING

Determining Engine Condition

Anything that generates heat and/or friction will eventually burn or wear out (for example, a light bulb generates heat, therefore its life span is limited). With this in mind, a running engine generates tremendous amounts of both; friction is encountered by the moving and rotating parts inside the engine and heat is created by friction and combustion of the fuel. However, the engine has systems designed to help reduce the effects of heat and friction and provide added longevity. The oiling system reduces the amount of friction encountered by the moving parts inside the engine, while the cooling system reduces heat created by friction and combustion. If either system is not maintained, a break-down will be inevitable. Therefore, you can see how regular maintenance can affect the service life of your vehicle. If you do not drain, flush and refill your cooling system at the proper intervals, deposits will begin to accumulate in the radiator, thereby reducing the amount of heat it can extract from the coolant. The same applies to your oil and filter; if it is not changed often enough it becomes laden with contaminates and is unable to properly lubricate the engine. This increases friction and wear.

There are a number of methods for evaluating the condition of your engine. A compression test can reveal the condition of your pistons, piston rings, cylinder bores, head gasket(s), valves and valve seats. An oil pressure test can warn you of possible engine bearing, or oil pump failures. Excessive oil consumption, evidence of oil in the engine air intake area and/or bluish smoke from the tailpipe may indicate worn piston rings, worn valve guides and/or valve seals. As a general rule, an engine that uses no more than one quart of oil every 1000 miles is in good condition. Engines that use one quart of oil or more in less than 1000 miles should first be checked for oil leaks. If any oil leaks are present, have them fixed before determining how much oil is consumed by the engine, especially if blue smoke is not visible at the tailpipe.

COMPRESSION TEST

A noticeable lack of engine power, excessive oil consumption and/or poor fuel mileage measured over an extended period are all indicators of internal engine wear. Worn piston rings, scored or worn cylinder bores, blown head gaskets, sticking or burnt valves, and worn valve seats are all possible culprits. A check of each cylinder's compression will help locate the problem.

Gasoline Engines

▶ **See Figure 161**

➡A screw-in type compression gauge is more accurate than the type you simply hold against the spark plug hole. Although it takes slightly longer to use, it's worth the effort to obtain a more accurate reading.

1. Make sure that the proper amount and viscosity of engine oil is in the crankcase, then ensure the battery is fully charged.
2. Warm-up the engine to normal operating temperature, then shut the engine **OFF**.
3. Disable the ignition system.

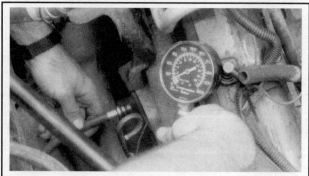

TCCS3801

Fig. 161 A screw-in type compression gauge is more accurate and easier to use without an assistant

4. Label and disconnect all of the spark plug wires from the plugs.
5. Thoroughly clean the cylinder head area around the spark plug ports, then remove the spark plugs.
6. Set the throttle plate to the fully open (wide-open throttle) position. You can block the accelerator linkage open for this, or you can have an assistant fully depress the accelerator pedal.
7. Install a screw-in type compression gauge into the No. 1 spark plug hole until the fitting is snug.

✳✳ WARNING

Be careful not to crossthread the spark plug hole.

8. According to the tool manufacturer's instructions, connect a remote starting switch to the starting circuit.
9. With the ignition switch in the **OFF** position, use the remote starting switch to crank the engine through at least five compression strokes (approximately 5 seconds of cranking) and record the highest reading on the gauge.
10. Repeat the test on each cylinder, cranking the engine approximately the same number of compression strokes and/or time as the first.
11. Compare the highest readings from each cylinder to that of the others. The indicated compression pressures are considered within specifications if the lowest reading cylinder is within 75 percent of the pressure recorded for the highest reading cylinder. For example, if your highest reading cylinder pressure was 150 psi (1034 kPa), then 75 percent of that would be 113 psi (779 kPa). So the lowest reading cylinder should be no less than 113 psi (779 kPa).
12. If a cylinder exhibits an unusually low compression reading, pour a tablespoon of clean engine oil into the cylinder through the spark plug hole and repeat the compression test. If the compression rises after adding oil, it means that the cylinder's piston rings and/or cylinder bore are damaged or worn. If the pressure remains low, the valves may not be seating properly (a valve job is needed), or the head gasket may be blown near that cylinder. If compression in any two adjacent cylinders is low, and if the addition of oil doesn't help raise compression, there is leakage past the head gasket. Oil and coolant in the combustion chamber, combined with blue or constant white smoke from the tailpipe, are symptoms of this problem. However, don't be alarmed by the normal white smoke emitted from the tailpipe during engine warm-up or from cold weather driving. There may be evidence of water droplets on the engine dipstick and/or oil droplets in the cooling system if a head gasket is blown.

Diesel Engines

Checking cylinder compression on diesel engines is basically the same procedure as on gasoline engines except for the following:
1. A special compression gauge adapter suitable for diesel engines (because these engines have much greater compression pressures) must be used.
2. Remove the injector tubes and remove the injectors from each cylinder.

✳✳ WARNING

Do not forget to remove the washer underneath each injector. Otherwise, it may get lost when the engine is cranked.

3. When fitting the compression gauge adapter to the cylinder head, make sure the bleeder of the gauge (if equipped) is closed.
4. When reinstalling the injector assemblies, install new washers underneath each injector.

OIL PRESSURE TEST

Check for proper oil pressure at the sending unit passage with an externally mounted mechanical oil pressure gauge (as opposed to relying on a factory installed dash-mounted gauge). A tachometer may also be needed, as some specifications may require running the engine at a specific rpm.
1. With the engine cold, locate and remove the oil pressure sending unit.
2. Following the manufacturer's instructions, connect a mechanical oil pressure gauge and, if necessary, a tachometer to the engine.
3. Start the engine and allow it to idle.
4. Check the oil pressure reading when cold and record the number. You

may need to run the engine at a specified rpm, so check the specifications chart located earlier in this section.

5. Run the engine until normal operating temperature is reached (upper radiator hose will feel warm).

6. Check the oil pressure reading again with the engine hot and record the number. Turn the engine **OFF**.

7. Compare your hot oil pressure reading to that given in the chart. If the reading is low, check the cold pressure reading against the chart. If the cold pressure is well above the specification, and the hot reading was lower than the specification, you may have the wrong viscosity oil in the engine. Change the oil, making sure to use the proper grade and quantity, then repeat the test.

Low oil pressure readings could be attributed to internal component wear, pump related problems, a low oil level, or oil viscosity that is too low. High oil pressure readings could be caused by an overfilled crankcase, too high of an oil viscosity or a faulty pressure relief valve.

Buy or Rebuild?

Now that you have determined that your engine is worn out, you must make some decisions. The question of whether or not an engine is worth rebuilding is largely a subjective matter and one of personal worth. Is the engine a popular one, or is it an obsolete model? Are parts available? Will it get acceptable gas mileage once it is rebuilt? Is the car it's being put into worth keeping? Would it be less expensive to buy a new engine, have your engine rebuilt by a pro, rebuild it yourself or buy a used engine from a salvage yard? Or would it be simpler and less expensive to buy another car? If you have considered all these matters and more, and have still decided to rebuild the engine, then it is time to decide how you will rebuild it.

➡**The editors at Chilton feel that most engine machining should be performed by a professional machine shop. Don't think of it as wasting money, rather, as an assurance that the job has been done right the first time. There are many expensive and specialized tools required to perform such tasks as boring and honing an engine block or having a valve job done on a cylinder head. Even inspecting the parts requires expensive micrometers and gauges to properly measure wear and clearances. Also, a machine shop can deliver to you clean, and ready to assemble parts, saving you time and aggravation. Your maximum savings will come from performing the removal, disassembly, assembly and installation of the engine and purchasing or renting only the tools required to perform the above tasks. Depending on the particular circumstances, you may save 40 to 60 percent of the cost doing these yourself.**

A complete rebuild or overhaul of an engine involves replacing all of the moving parts (pistons, rods, crankshaft, camshaft, etc.) with new ones and machining the non-moving wearing surfaces of the block and heads. Unfortunately, this may not be cost effective. For instance, your crankshaft may have been damaged or worn, but it can be machined undersize for a minimal fee.

So, as you can see, you can replace everything inside the engine, but, it is wiser to replace only those parts which are really needed, and, if possible, repair the more expensive ones. Later in this section, we will break the engine down into its two main components: the cylinder head and the engine block. We will discuss each component, and the recommended parts to replace during a rebuild on each.

Engine Overhaul Tips

Most engine overhaul procedures are fairly standard. In addition to specific parts replacement procedures and specifications for your individual engine, this section is also a guide to acceptable rebuilding procedures. Examples of standard rebuilding practice are given and should be used along with specific details concerning your particular engine.

Competent and accurate machine shop services will ensure maximum performance, reliability and engine life. In most instances it is more profitable for the do-it-yourself mechanic to remove, clean and inspect the component, buy the necessary parts and deliver these to a shop for actual machine work.

Much of the assembly work (crankshaft, bearings, piston rods, and other components) is well within the scope of the do-it-yourself mechanic's tools and abilities. You will have to decide for yourself the depth of involvement you desire in an engine repair or rebuild.

TOOLS

The tools required for an engine overhaul or parts replacement will depend on the depth of your involvement. With a few exceptions, they will be the tools found in a mechanic's tool kit (see Section 1 of this manual). More in-depth work will require some or all of the following:

*   A dial indicator (reading in thousandths) mounted on a universal base
*   Micrometers and telescope gauges
*   Jaw and screw-type pullers
*   Scraper
*   Valve spring compressor
*   Ring groove cleaner
*   Piston ring expander and compressor
*   Ridge reamer
*   Cylinder hone or glaze breaker
*   Plastigage
*   Engine stand

The use of most of these tools is illustrated in this section. Many can be rented for a one-time use from a local parts jobber or tool supply house specializing in automotive work.

Occasionally, the use of special tools is called for. See the information on Special Tools and the Safety Notice in the front of this book before substituting another tool.

OVERHAUL TIPS

Aluminum has become extremely popular for use in engines, due to its low weight. Observe the following precautions when handling aluminum parts:

*   Never hot tank aluminum parts (the caustic hot tank solution will eat the aluminum.
*   Remove all aluminum parts (identification tag, etc.) from engine parts prior to the tanking.
*   Always coat threads lightly with engine oil or anti-seize compounds before installation, to prevent seizure.
*   Never overtighten bolts or spark plugs especially in aluminum threads.

When assembling the engine, any parts that will be exposed to frictional contact must be prelubed to provide lubrication at initial start-up. Any product specifically formulated for this purpose can be used, but engine oil is not recommended as a prelube in most cases.

When semi-permanent (locked, but removable) installation of bolts or nuts is desired, threads should be cleaned and coated with Loctite® or another similar, commercial non-hardening sealant.

CLEANING

♦ **See Figures 162, 163, 164 and 165**

Before the engine and its components are inspected, they must be thoroughly cleaned. You will need to remove any engine varnish, oil sludge and/or carbon deposits from all of the components to insure an accurate inspection. A crack in the engine block or cylinder head can easily become overlooked if hidden by a layer of sludge or carbon.

Most of the cleaning process can be carried out with common hand tools and readily available solvents or solutions. Carbon deposits can be chipped away using a hammer and a hard wooden chisel. Old gasket material and varnish or sludge can usually be removed using a scraper and/or cleaning solvent. Extremely stubborn deposits may require the use of a power drill with a wire brush. If using a wire brush, use extreme care around any critical machined surfaces (such as the gasket surfaces, bearing saddles, cylinder bores, etc.). USE OF A WIRE BRUSH IS NOT RECOMMENDED ON ANY ALUMINUM COMPONENTS. Always follow any safety recommendations given by the manufacturer of the tool and/or solvent. You should always wear eye protection during any cleaning process involving scraping, chipping or spraying of solvents.

An alternative to the mess and hassle of cleaning the parts yourself is to drop them off at a local garage or machine shop. They will, more than likely, have the necessary equipment to properly clean all of the parts for a nominal fee.

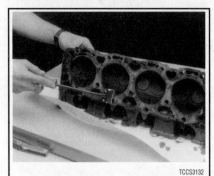

Fig. 162 Use a gasket scraper to remove the old gasket material from the mating surfaces

Fig. 163 Use a ring expander tool to remove the piston rings

Fig. 164 Clean the piston ring grooves using a ring groove cleaner tool, or . . .

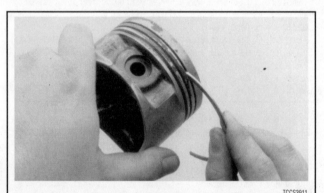

Fig. 165 . . . use a piece of an old ring to clean the grooves. Be careful, the ring can be quite sharp

✳✳ CAUTION

Always wear eye protection during any cleaning process involving scraping, chipping or spraying of solvents.

Remove any oil galley plugs, freeze plugs and/or pressed-in bearings and carefully wash and degrease all of the engine components including the fasteners and bolts. Small parts such as the valves, springs, etc., should be placed in a metal basket and allowed to soak. Use pipe cleaner type brushes, and clean all passageways in the components. Use a ring expander and remove the rings from the pistons. Clean the piston ring grooves with a special tool or a piece of broken ring. Scrape the carbon off of the top of the piston. You should never use a wire brush on the pistons. After preparing all of the piston assemblies in this manner, wash and degrease them again.

✳✳ WARNING

Use extreme care when cleaning around the cylinder head valve seats. A mistake or slip may cost you a new seat.

When cleaning the cylinder head, remove carbon from the combustion chamber with the valves installed. This will avoid damaging the valve seats.

REPAIRING DAMAGED THREADS

♦ See Figures 166, 167, 168, 169 and 170

Several methods of repairing damaged threads are available. Heli-Coil (shown here), Keenserts and Microdot are among the most widely used. All involve basically the same principle—drilling out stripped threads, tapping the hole and installing a prewound insert—making welding, plugging and oversize fasteners unnecessary.

Two types of thread repair inserts are usually supplied: a standard type for most inch coarse, inch fine, metric course and metric fine thread sizes and a spark lug type to fit most spark plug port sizes. Consult the individual tool manufacturer's catalog to determine exact applications. Typical thread repair kits will contain a selection of prewound threaded inserts, a tap (corresponding to the outside diameter threads of the insert) and an installation tool. Spark plug inserts usually differ because they require a tap equipped with pilot threads and a combined reamer/tap section. Most manufacturers also supply blister-packed thread repair inserts separately in addition to a master kit containing a variety of taps and inserts plus installation tools.

Before attempting to repair a threaded hole, remove any snapped, broken or damaged bolts or studs. Penetrating oil can be used to free frozen threads. The offending item can usually be removed with locking pliers or using a screw/stud extractor. After the hole is clear, the thread can be repaired, as shown in the series of accompanying illustrations and in the kit manufacturer's instructions.

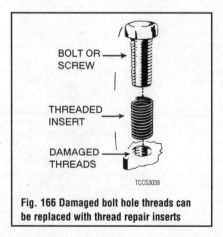

Fig. 166 Damaged bolt hole threads can be replaced with thread repair inserts

Fig. 167 Standard thread repair insert (left), and spark plug thread insert

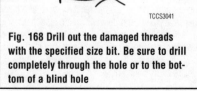

Fig. 168 Drill out the damaged threads with the specified size bit. Be sure to drill completely through the hole or to the bottom of a blind hole

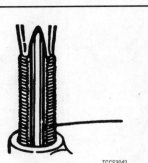

TCCS3042

Fig. 169 Using the kit, tap the hole in order to receive the thread insert. Keep the tap well oiled and back it out frequently to avoid clogging the threads

TCCS3043

Fig. 170 Screw the insert onto the installer tool until the tang engages the slot. Thread the insert into the hole until it is ¼–½ turn below the top surface, then remove the tool and break off the tang using a punch

Engine Preparation

To properly rebuild an engine, you must first remove it from the vehicle, then disassemble and diagnose it. Ideally you should place your engine on an engine stand. This affords you the best access to the engine components. Follow the manufacturer's directions for using the stand with your particular engine. Remove the flywheel or flexplate before installing the engine to the stand.

Now that you have the engine on a stand, and assuming that you have drained the oil and coolant from the engine, it's time to strip it of all but the necessary components. Before you start disassembling the engine, you may want to take a moment to draw some pictures, or fabricate some labels or containers to mark the locations of various components and the bolts and/or studs which fasten them. Modern day engines use a lot of little brackets and clips which hold wiring harnesses and such, and these holders are often mounted on studs and/or bolts that can be easily mixed up. The manufacturer spent a lot of time and money designing your vehicle, and they wouldn't have wasted any of it by haphazardly placing brackets, clips or fasteners on the vehicle. If it's present when you disassemble it, put it back when you assemble, you will regret not remembering that little bracket which holds a wire harness out of the path of a rotating part.

You should begin by unbolting any accessories still attached to the engine, such as the water pump, power steering pump, alternator, etc. Then, unfasten any manifolds (intake or exhaust) which were not removed during the engine removal procedure. Finally, remove any covers remaining on the engine such as the rocker arm, front or timing cover and oil pan. Some front covers may require the vibration damper and/or crank pulley to be removed beforehand. The idea is to reduce the engine to the bare necessities (cylinder head(s), valve train, engine block, crankshaft, pistons and connecting rods), plus any other `in block' components such as oil pumps, balance shafts and auxiliary shafts.

Finally, remove the cylinder head(s) from the engine block and carefully place on a bench. Disassembly instructions for each component follow later in this section.

Cylinder Head

There are two basic types of cylinder heads used on today's automobiles: the Overhead Valve (OHV) and the Overhead Camshaft (OHC). The latter can also be broken down into two subgroups: the Single Overhead Camshaft (SOHC) and the Dual Overhead Camshaft (DOHC). Generally, if there is only a single camshaft on a head, it is just referred to as an OHC head. Also, an engine with an OHV cylinder head is also known as a pushrod engine.

Most cylinder heads these days are made of an aluminum alloy due to its light weight, durability and heat transfer qualities. However, cast iron was the material of choice in the past, and is still used on many vehicles today. Whether made from aluminum or iron, all cylinder heads have valves and seats. Some use two valves per cylinder, while the more hi-tech engines will utilize a multi-valve configuration using 3, 4 and even 5 valves per cylinder. When the valve contacts the seat, it does so on precision machined surfaces, which seals the combustion chamber. All cylinder heads have a valve guide for each valve. The guide centers the valve to the seat and allows it to move up and down within it. The clearance between the valve and guide can be critical. Too much clearance and the engine may consume oil, lose vacuum and/or damage the seat. Too little, and the valve can stick in the guide causing the engine to run poorly if at all, and possibly causing severe damage. The last component all cylinder heads have are valve springs. The spring holds the valve against its seat. It also returns the valve to this position when the valve has been opened by the valve train or camshaft. The spring is fastened to the valve by a retainer and valve locks (sometimes called keepers). Aluminum heads will also have a valve spring shim to keep the spring from wearing away the aluminum.

An ideal method of rebuilding the cylinder head would involve replacing all of the valves, guides, seats, springs, etc. with new ones. However, depending on how the engine was maintained, often this is not necessary. A major cause of valve, guide and seat wear is an improperly tuned engine. An engine that is running too rich, will often wash the lubricating oil out of the guide with gasoline, causing it to wear rapidly. Conversely, an engine which is running too lean will place higher combustion temperatures on the valves and seats allowing them to wear or even burn. Springs fall victim to the driving habits of the individual. A driver who often runs the engine rpm to the redline will wear out or break the springs faster then one that stays well below it. Unfortunately, mileage takes it toll on all of the parts. Generally, the valves, guides, springs and seats in a cylinder head can be machined and re-used, saving you money. However, if a valve is burnt, it may be wise to replace all of the valves, since they were all operating in the same environment. The same goes for any other component on the cylinder head. Think of it as an insurance policy against future problems related to that component.

Unfortunately, the only way to find out which components need replacing, is to disassemble and carefully check each piece. After the cylinder head(s) are disassembled, thoroughly clean all of the components.

DISASSEMBLY

OHV Heads

♦ See Figures 171 thru 176

Before disassembling the cylinder head, you may want to fabricate some containers to hold the various parts, as some of them can be quite small (such as keepers) and easily lost. Also keeping yourself and the components organized will aid in assembly and reduce confusion. Where possible, try to maintain a components original location; this is especially important if there is not going to be any machine work performed on the components.

1. If you haven't already removed the rocker arms and/or shafts, do so now.
2. Position the head so that the springs are easily accessed.
3. Use a valve spring compressor tool, and relieve spring tension from the retainer.

➡ **Due to engine varnish, the retainer may stick to the valve locks. A gentle tap with a hammer may help to break it loose.**

4. Remove the valve locks from the valve tip and/or retainer. A small magnet may help in removing the locks.
5. Lift the valve spring, tool and all, off of the valve stem.
6. If equipped, remove the valve seal. If the seal is difficult to remove with the valve in place, try removing the valve first, then the seal. Follow the steps below for valve removal.
7. Position the head to allow access for withdrawing the valve.

Fig. 171 When removing an OHV valve spring, use a compressor tool to relieve the tension from the retainer

Fig. 172 A small magnet will help in removal of the valve locks

Fig. 173 Be careful not to lose the small valve locks (keepers)

Fig. 174 Remove the valve seal from the valve stem—O-ring type seal shown

Fig. 175 Removing an umbrella/positive type seal

Fig. 176 Invert the cylinder head and withdraw the valve from the valve guide bore

➡Cylinder heads that have seen a lot of miles and/or abuse may have mushroomed the valve lock grove and/or tip, causing difficulty in removal of the valve. If this has happened, use a metal file to carefully remove the high spots around the lock grooves and/or tip. Only file it enough to allow removal.

8. Remove the valve from the cylinder head.
9. If equipped, remove the valve spring shim. A small magnetic tool or screwdriver will aid in removal.
10. Repeat Steps 3 though 9 until all of the valves have been removed.

INSPECTION

Now that all of the cylinder head components are clean, it's time to inspect them for wear and/or damage. To accurately inspect them, you will need some specialized tools:

- A 0–1 in. micrometer for the valves
- A dial indicator or inside diameter gauge for the valve guides
- A spring pressure test gauge

If you do not have access to the proper tools, you may want to bring the components to a shop that does.

Valves

▶ **See Figures 177 and 178**

The first thing to inspect are the valve heads. Look closely at the head, margin and face for any cracks, excessive wear or burning. The margin is the best place to look for burning. It should have a squared edge with an even width all around the diameter. When a valve burns, the margin will look melted and the edges rounded. Also inspect the valve head for any signs of tulipping. This will show as a lifting of the edges or dishing in the center of the head and will usually not occur to all of the valves. All of the heads should look the same, any that seem dished more than others are probably bad. Next, inspect the valve lock grooves and valve tips. Check for any burrs around the lock grooves, especially if you had to file them to remove the valve. Valve tips should appear flat, although slight rounding with high mileage engines is normal. Slightly worn valve tips will need to be machined flat. Last, mea-

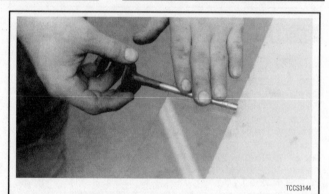

Fig. 177 Valve stems may be rolled on a flat surface to check for bends

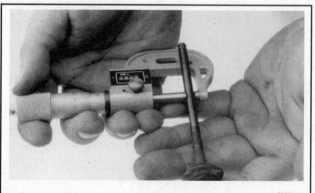

Fig. 178 Use a micrometer to check the valve stem diameter

sure the valve stem diameter with the micrometer. Measure the area that rides within the guide, especially towards the tip where most of the wear occurs. Take several measurements along its length and compare them to each other. Wear should be even along the length with little to no taper. If no minimum diameter is given in the specifications, then the stem should not read more than 0.001 in. (0.025mm) below the specification. Any valves that fail these inspections should be replaced.

Springs, Retainers and Valve Locks

▶ See Figures 179 and 180

The first thing to check is the most obvious, broken springs. Next check the free length and squareness of each spring. If applicable, insure to distinguish between intake and exhaust springs. Use a ruler and/or carpenter's square to measure the length. A carpenter's square should be used to check the springs for squareness. If a spring pressure test gauge is available, check each springs rating and compare to the specifications chart. Check the readings against the specifications given. Any springs that fail these inspections should be replaced.

The spring retainers rarely need replacing, however they should still be checked as a precaution. Inspect the spring mating surface and the valve lock retention area for any signs of excessive wear. Also check for any signs of cracking. Replace any retainers that are questionable.

Valve locks should be inspected for excessive wear on the outside contact area as well as on the inner notched surface. Any locks which appear worn or broken and its respective valve should be replaced.

Cylinder Head

There are several things to check on the cylinder head: valve guides, seats, cylinder head surface flatness, cracks and physical damage.

VALVE GUIDES

▶ See Figure 181

Now that you know the valves are good, you can use them to check the guides, although a new valve, if available, is preferred. Before you measure any-

thing, look at the guides carefully and inspect them for any cracks, chips or breakage. Also if the guide is a removable style (as in most aluminum heads), check them for any looseness or evidence of movement. All of the guides should appear to be at the same height from the spring seat. If any seem lower (or higher) from another, the guide has moved. Mount a dial indicator onto the spring side of the cylinder head. Lightly oil the valve stem and insert it into the cylinder head. Position the dial indicator against the valve stem near the tip and zero the gauge. Grasp the valve stem and wiggle towards and away from the dial indicator and observe the readings. Mount the dial indicator 90 degrees from the initial point and zero the gauge and again take a reading. Compare the two readings for a out of round condition. Check the readings against the specifications given. An Inside Diameter (I.D.) gauge designed for valve guides will give you an accurate valve guide bore measurement. If the I.D. gauge is used, compare the readings with the specifications given. Any guides that fail these inspections should be replaced or machined.

VALVE SEATS

A visual inspection of the valve seats should show a slightly worn and pitted surface where the valve face contacts the seat. Inspect the seat carefully for severe pitting or cracks. Also, a seat that is badly worn will be recessed into the cylinder head. A severely worn or recessed seat may need to be replaced. All cracked seats must be replaced. A seat concentricity gauge, if available, should be used to check the seat run-out. If run-out exceeds specifications the seat must be machined (if no specification is given use 0.002 in. or 0.051mm).

CYLINDER HEAD SURFACE FLATNESS

▶ See Figures 182 and 183

After you have cleaned the gasket surface of the cylinder head of any old gasket material, check the head for flatness.

Place a straightedge across the gasket surface. Using feeler gauges, determine the clearance at the center of the straightedge and across the cylinder head at several points. Check along the centerline and diagonally on the head surface. If the warpage exceeds 0.003 in. (0.076mm) within a 6.0 in. (15.2 cm) span, or 0.006 in. (0.152mm) over the total length of the head, the cylinder head must be resur-

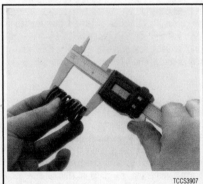

Fig. 179 Use a caliper to check the valve spring free-length

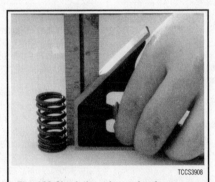

Fig. 180 Check the valve spring for squareness on a flat surface; a carpenter's square can be used

Fig. 181 A dial gauge may be used to check valve stem-to-guide clearance; read the gauge while moving the valve stem

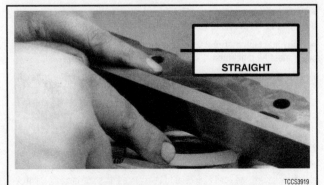

Fig. 182 Check the head for flatness across the center of the head surface using a straightedge and feeler gauge

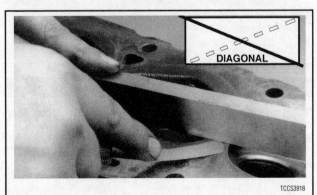

Fig. 183 Checks should also be made along both diagonals of the head surface

faced. After resurfacing the heads of a V-type engine, the intake manifold flange surface should be checked, and if necessary, milled proportionally to allow for the change in its mounting position.

CRACKS AND PHYSICAL DAMAGE

Generally, cracks are limited to the combustion chamber, however, it is not uncommon for the head to crack in a spark plug hole, port, outside of the head or in the valve spring/rocker arm area. The first area to inspect is always the hottest: the exhaust seat/port area.

A visual inspection should be performed, but just because you don't see a crack does not mean it is not there. Some more reliable methods for inspecting for cracks include Magnaflux, a magnetic process or Zyglo, a dye penetrant. Magnaflux is used only on ferrous metal (cast iron) heads. Zyglo uses a spray on fluorescent mixture along with a black light to reveal the cracks. It is strongly recommended to have your cylinder head checked professionally for cracks, especially if the engine was known to have overheated and/or leaked or consumed coolant. Contact a local shop for availability and pricing of these services.

Physical damage is usually very evident. For example, a broken mounting ear from dropping the head or a bent or broken stud and/or bolt. All of these defects should be fixed or, if unrepairable, the head should be replaced.

REFINISHING & REPAIRING

Many of the procedures given for refinishing and repairing the cylinder head components must be performed by a machine shop. Certain steps, if the inspected part is not worn, can be performed yourself inexpensively. However, you spent a lot of time and effort so far, why risk trying to save a couple bucks if you might have to do it all over again?

Valves

Any valves that were not replaced should be refaced and the tips ground flat. Unless you have access to a valve grinding machine, this should be done by a machine shop. If the valves are in extremely good condition, as well as the valve seats and guides, they may be lapped in without performing machine work.

It is a recommended practice to lap the valves even after machine work has been performed and/or new valves have been purchased. This insures a positive seal between the valve and seat.

LAPPING THE VALVES

➡ Before lapping the valves to the seats, read the rest of the cylinder head section to insure that any related parts are in acceptable enough condition to continue.

➡ Before any valve seat machining and/or lapping can be performed, the guides must be within factory recommended specifications.

1. Invert the cylinder head.
2. Lightly lubricate the valve stems and insert them into the cylinder head in their numbered order.
3. Raise the valve from the seat and apply a small amount of fine lapping compound to the seat.
4. Moisten the suction head of a hand-lapping tool and attach it to the head of the valve.
5. Rotate the tool between the palms of both hands, changing the position of the valve on the valve seat and lifting the tool often to prevent grooving.
6. Lap the valve until a smooth, polished circle is evident on the valve and seat.
7. Remove the tool and the valve. Wipe away all traces of the grinding compound and store the valve to maintain its lapped location.

❊❊ WARNING

Do not get the valves out of order after they have been lapped. They must be put back with the same valve seat with which they were lapped.

Springs, Retainers and Valve Locks

There is no repair or refinishing possible with the springs, retainers and valve locks. If they are found to be worn or defective, they must be replaced with new (or known good) parts.

Cylinder Head

Most refinishing procedures dealing with the cylinder head must be performed by a machine shop. Read the sections below and review your inspection data to determine whether or not machining is necessary.

VALVE GUIDE

➡ If any machining or replacements are made to the valve guides, the seats must be machined.

Unless the valve guides need machining or replacing, the only service to perform is to thoroughly clean them of any dirt or oil residue.

There are only two types of valve guides used on automobile engines: the replaceable-type (all aluminum heads) and the cast-in integral-type (most cast iron heads). There are four recommended methods for repairing worn guides.

- Knurling
- Inserts
- Reaming oversize
- Replacing

Knurling is a process in which metal is displaced and raised, thereby reducing clearance, giving a true center, and providing oil control. It is the least expensive way of repairing the valve guides. However, it is not necessarily the best, and in some cases, a knurled valve guide will not stand up for more than a short time. It requires a special knurlizer and precision reaming tools to obtain proper clearances. It would not be cost effective to purchase these tools, unless you plan on rebuilding several of the same cylinder head.

Installing a guide insert involves machining the guide to accept a bronze insert. One style is the coil-type which is installed into a threaded guide. Another is the thin-walled insert where the guide is reamed oversize to accept a split-sleeve insert. After the insert is installed, a special tool is then run through the guide to expand the insert, locking it to the guide. The insert is then reamed to the standard size for proper valve clearance.

Reaming for oversize valves restores normal clearances and provides a true valve seat. Most cast-in type guides can be reamed to accept an valve with an oversize stem. The cost factor for this can become quite high as you will need to purchase the reamer and new, oversize stem valves for all guides which were reamed. Oversizes are generally 0.003 to 0.030 in. (0.076 to 0.762mm), with 0.015 in. (0.381mm) being the most common.

To replace cast-in type valve guides, they must be drilled out, then reamed to accept replacement guides. This must be done on a fixture which will allow centering and leveling off of the original valve seat or guide, otherwise a serious guide-to-seat misalignment may occur making it impossible to properly machine the seat.

Replaceable-type guides are pressed into the cylinder head. A hammer and a stepped drift or punch may be used to install and remove the guides. Before removing the guides, measure the protrusion on the spring side of the head and record it for installation. Use the stepped drift to hammer out the old guide from the combustion chamber side of the head. When installing, determine whether or not the guide also seals a water jacket in the head, and if it does, use the recommended sealing agent. If there is no water jacket, grease the valve guide and its bore. Use the stepped drift, and hammer the new guide into the cylinder head from the spring side of the cylinder head. A stack of washers the same thickness as the measured protrusion may help the installation process.

VALVE SEATS

➡ Before any valve seat machining can be performed, the guides must be within factory recommended specifications.

➡ If any machining or replacements were made to the valve guides, the seats must be machined.

If the seats are in good condition, the valves can be lapped to the seats, and the cylinder head assembled. See the valves section for instructions on lapping.

If the valve seats are worn, cracked or damaged, they must be serviced by a machine shop. The valve seat must be perfectly centered to the valve guide, which requires very accurate machining.

CYLINDER HEAD SURFACE

If the cylinder head is warped, it must be machined flat. If the warpage is extremely severe, the head may need to be replaced. In some instances, it may be possible to straighten a warped head enough to allow machining. In either case, contact a professional machine shop for service.

CRACKS AND PHYSICAL DAMAGE

Certain cracks can be repaired in both cast iron and aluminum heads. For cast iron, a tapered threaded insert is installed along the length of the crack. Aluminum can also use the tapered inserts, however welding is the preferred method. Some physical damage can be repaired through brazing or welding. Contact a machine shop to get expert advice for your particular dilemma.

ASSEMBLY

The first step for any assembly job is to have a clean area in which to work. Next, thoroughly clean all of the parts and components that are to be assembled. Finally, place all of the components onto a suitable work space and, if necessary, arrange the parts to their respective positions.

OHV Engines

1. Lightly lubricate the valve stems and insert all of the valves into the cylinder head. If possible, maintain their original locations.
2. If equipped, install any valve spring shims which were removed.
3. If equipped, install the new valve seals, keeping the following in mind:
• If the valve seal presses over the guide, lightly lubricate the outer guide surfaces.
• If the seal is an O-ring type, it is installed just after compressing the spring but before the valve locks.
4. Place the valve spring and retainer over the stem.
5. Position the spring compressor tool and compress the spring.
6. Assemble the valve locks to the stem.
7. Relieve the spring pressure slowly and insure that neither valve lock becomes dislodged by the retainer.
8. Remove the spring compressor tool.
9. Repeat Steps 2 through 8 until all of the springs have been installed.

ROCKER ARM TYPE CAMSHAFT FOLLOWERS

1. Lightly lubricate the valve stems and insert all of the valves into the cylinder head. If possible, maintain their original locations.
2. If equipped, install any valve spring shims which were removed.
3. If equipped, install the new valve seals, keeping the following in mind:
• If the valve seal presses over the guide, lightly lubricate the outer guide surfaces.
• If the seal is an O-ring type, it is installed just after compressing the spring but before the valve locks.
4. Place the valve spring and retainer over the stem.
5. Position the spring compressor tool and compress the spring.
6. Assemble the valve locks to the stem.
7. Relieve the spring pressure slowly and insure that neither valve lock becomes dislodged by the retainer.
8. Remove the spring compressor tool.
9. Repeat Steps 2 through 8 until all of the springs have been installed.
10. Install the camshaft(s), rockers, shafts and any other components that were removed for disassembly.

Engine Block

GENERAL INFORMATION

A thorough overhaul or rebuild of an engine block would include replacing the pistons, rings, bearings, timing belt/chain assembly and oil pump. For OHV engines also include a new camshaft and lifters. The block would then have the cylinders bored and honed oversize (or if using removable cylinder sleeves, new sleeves installed) and the crankshaft would be cut undersize to provide new wearing surfaces and perfect clearances. However, your particular engine may not have everything worn out. What if only the piston rings have worn out and the clearances on everything else are still within factory specifications? Well, you could just replace the rings and put it back together, but this would be a very rare example. Chances are, if one component in your engine is worn, other components are sure to follow, and soon. At the very least, you should always replace the rings, bearings and oil pump. This is what is commonly called a "freshen up".

Cylinder Ridge Removal

Because the top piston ring does not travel to the very top of the cylinder, a ridge is built up between the end of the travel and the top of the cylinder bore.

Pushing the piston and connecting rod assembly past the ridge can be difficult, and damage to the piston ring lands could occur. If the ridge is not removed before installing a new piston or not removed at all, piston ring breakage and piston damage may occur.

➡It is always recommended that you remove any cylinder ridges before removing the piston and connecting rod assemblies. If you know that new pistons are going to be installed and the engine block will be bored oversize, you may be able to forego this step. However, some ridges may actually prevent the assemblies from being removed, necessitating its removal.

There are several different types of ridge reamers on the market, none of which are inexpensive. Unless a great deal of engine rebuilding is anticipated, borrow or rent a reamer.
1. Turn the crankshaft until the piston is at the bottom of its travel.
2. Cover the head of the piston with a rag.
3. Follow the tool manufacturers instructions and cut away the ridge, exercising extreme care to avoid cutting too deeply.
4. Remove the ridge reamer, the rag and as many of the cuttings as possible. Continue until all of the cylinder ridges have been removed.

DISASSEMBLY

▶ See Figures 184 and 185

The engine disassembly instructions following assume that you have the engine mounted on an engine stand. If not, it is easiest to disassemble the engine on a bench or the floor with it resting on the bell housing or transmission mounting surface. You must be able to access the connecting rod fasteners and turn the crankshaft during disassembly. Also, all engine covers (timing, front, side, oil pan, whatever) should have already been removed. Engines which are seized or locked up may not be able to be completely disassembled, and a core (salvage yard) engine should be purchased.

Pushrod Engines

If not done during the cylinder head removal, remove the pushrods and lifters, keeping them in order for assembly. Remove the timing gears and/or timing chain assembly, then remove the oil pump drive assembly and withdraw the camshaft from the engine block. Remove the oil pick-up and pump assembly. If equipped, remove any balance or auxiliary shafts. If necessary, remove the cylinder ridge from the top of the bore. See the cylinder ridge removal procedure earlier in this section.

All Engines

Rotate the engine over so that the crankshaft is exposed. Use a number punch or scribe and mark each connecting rod with its respective cylinder number. The cylinder closest to the front of the engine is always number 1. However, depending on the engine placement, the front of the engine could either be the

TCCS3803

Fig. 184 Place rubber hose over the connecting rod studs to protect the crankshaft and cylinder bores from damage

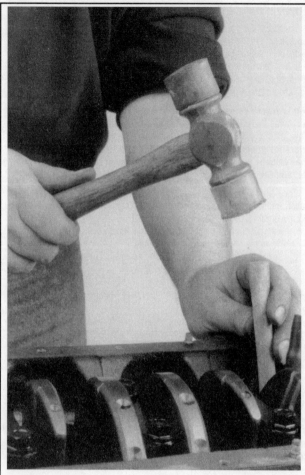

TCCS3804

Fig. 185 Carefully tap the piston out of the bore using a wooden dowel

flywheel or damper/pulley end. Generally the front of the engine faces the front of the vehicle. Use a number punch or scribe and also mark the main bearing caps from front to rear with the front most cap being number 1 (if there are five caps, mark them 1 through 5, front to rear).

✳✳ WARNING

Take special care when pushing the connecting rod up from the crankshaft because the sharp threads of the rod bolts/studs will score the crankshaft journal. Insure that special plastic caps are installed over them, or cut two pieces of rubber hose to do the same.

Again, rotate the engine, this time to position the number one cylinder bore (head surface) up. Turn the crankshaft until the number one piston is at the bottom of its travel, this should allow the maximum access to its connecting rod. Remove the number one connecting rods fasteners and cap and place two lengths of rubber hose over the rod bolts/studs to protect the crankshaft from damage. Using a sturdy wooden dowel and a hammer, push the connecting rod up about 1 in. (25mm) from the crankshaft and remove the upper bearing insert. Continue pushing or tapping the connecting rod up until the piston rings are out of the cylinder bore. Remove the piston and rod by hand, put the upper half of the bearing insert back into the rod, install the cap with its bearing insert installed, and hand-tighten the cap fasteners. If the parts are kept in order in this manner, they will not get lost and you will be able to tell which bearings came form what cylinder if any problems are discovered and diagnosis is necessary. Remove all the other piston assemblies in the same manner. On V-style engines, remove all of the pistons from one bank, then reposition the engine with the other cylinder bank head surface up, and remove that banks piston assemblies.

The only remaining component in the engine block should now be the crank-

shaft. Loosen the main bearing caps evenly until the fasteners can be turned by hand, then remove them and the caps. Remove the crankshaft from the engine block. Thoroughly clean all of the components.

INSPECTION

Now that the engine block and all of its components are clean, it's time to inspect them for wear and/or damage. To accurately inspect them, you will need some specialized tools:
- Two or three separate micrometers to measure the pistons and crankshaft journals
- A dial indicator
- Telescoping gauges for the cylinder bores
- A rod alignment fixture to check for bent connecting rods

If you do not have access to the proper tools, you may want to bring the components to a shop that does.

Generally, you shouldn't expect cracks in the engine block or its components unless it was known to leak, consume or mix engine fluids, it was severely overheated, or there was evidence of bad bearings and/or crankshaft damage. A visual inspection should be performed on all of the components, but just because you don't see a crack does not mean it is not there. Some more reliable methods for inspecting for cracks include Magnaflux˳, a magnetic process or Zyglo˳, a dye penetrant. Magnaflux˳ is used only on ferrous metal (cast iron). Zyglo˳ uses a spray on fluorescent mixture along with a black light to reveal the cracks. It is strongly recommended to have your engine block checked professionally for cracks, especially if the engine was known to have overheated and/or leaked or consumed coolant. Contact a local shop for availability and pricing of these services.

Engine Block

ENGINE BLOCK BEARING ALIGNMENT

Remove the main bearing caps and, if still installed, the main bearing inserts. Inspect all of the main bearing saddles and caps for damage, burrs or high spots. If damage is found, and it is caused from a spun main bearing, the block will need to be align-bored or, if severe enough, replacement. Any burrs or high spots should be carefully removed with a metal file.

Place a straightedge on the bearing saddles, in the engine block, along the centerline of the crankshaft. If any clearance exists between the straightedge and the saddles, the block must be align-bored.

Align-boring consists of machining the main bearing saddles and caps by means of a flycutter that runs through the bearing saddles.

DECK FLATNESS

The top of the engine block where the cylinder head mounts is called the deck. Insure that the deck surface is clean of dirt, carbon deposits and old gasket material. Place a straightedge across the surface of the deck along its centerline and, using feeler gauges, check the clearance along several points. Repeat the checking procedure with the straightedge placed along both diagonals of the deck surface. If the reading exceeds 0.003 in. (0.076mm) within a 6.0 in. (15.2cm) span, or 0.006 in. (0.152mm) over the total length of the deck, it must be machined.

CYLINDER BORES

♦ See Figure 186

The cylinder bores house the pistons and are slightly larger than the pistons themselves. A common piston-to-bore clearance is 0.0015–0.0025 in. (0.0381mm–0.0635mm). Inspect and measure the cylinder bores. The bore should be checked for out-of-roundness, taper and size. The results of this inspection will determine whether the cylinder can be used in its existing size and condition, or a rebore to the next oversize is required (or in the case of removable sleeves, have replacements installed).

The amount of cylinder wall wear is always greater at the top of the cylinder than at the bottom. This wear is known as taper. Any cylinder that has a taper of 0.0012 in. (0.305mm) or more, must be rebored. Measurements are taken at a number of positions in each cylinder: at the top, middle and bottom and at two points at each position; that is, at a point 90 degrees from the crankshaft centerline, as well as a point parallel to the crankshaft centerline. The measurements are made with either a special dial indicator or a telescopic gauge and micrometer. If the necessary precision tools to check the bore are not available, take the

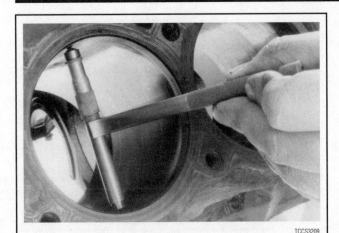

Fig. 186 Use a telescoping gauge to measure the cylinder bore diameter—take several readings within the same bore

block to a machine shop and have them mike it. Also if you don't have the tools to check the cylinder bores, chances are you will not have the necessary devices to check the pistons, connecting rods and crankshaft. Take these components with you and save yourself an extra trip.

For our procedures, we will use a telescopic gauge and a micrometer. You will need one of each, with a measuring range which covers your cylinder bore size.

1. Position the telescopic gauge in the cylinder bore, loosen the gauges lock and allow it to expand.

➡**Your first two readings will be at the top of the cylinder bore, then proceed to the middle and finally the bottom, making a total of six measurements.**

2. Hold the gauge square in the bore, 90 degrees from the crankshaft centerline, and gently tighten the lock. Tilt the gauge back to remove it from the bore.

3. Measure the gauge with the micrometer and record the reading.

4. Again, hold the gauge square in the bore, this time parallel to the crankshaft centerline, and gently tighten the lock. Again, you will tilt the gauge back to remove it from the bore.

5. Measure the gauge with the micrometer and record this reading. The difference between these two readings is the out-of-round measurement of the cylinder.

6. Repeat steps 1 through 5, each time going to the next lower position, until you reach the bottom of the cylinder. Then go to the next cylinder, and continue until all of the cylinders have been measured.

The difference between these measurements will tell you all about the wear in your cylinders. The measurements which were taken 90 degrees from the crankshaft centerline will always reflect the most wear. That is because at this position is where the engine power presses the piston against the cylinder bore the hardest. This is known as thrust wear. Take your top, 90 degree measurement and compare it to your bottom, 90 degree measurement. The difference between them is the taper. When you measure your pistons, you will compare these readings to your piston sizes and determine piston-to-wall clearance.

Crankshaft

Inspect the crankshaft for visible signs of wear or damage. All of the journals should be perfectly round and smooth. Slight scores are normal for a used crankshaft, but you should hardly feel them with your fingernail. When measuring the crankshaft with a micrometer, you will take readings at the front and rear of each journal, then turn the micrometer 90 degrees and take two more readings, front and rear. The difference between the front-to-rear readings is the journal taper and the first-to-90 degree reading is the out-of-round measurement. Generally, there should be no taper or out-of-roundness found, however, up to 0.0005 in. (0.0127mm) for either can be overlooked. Also, the readings should fall within the factory specifications for journal diameters.

If the crankshaft journals fall within specifications, it is recommended that it be polished before being returned to service. Polishing the crankshaft insures that any minor burrs or high spots are smoothed, thereby reducing the chance of scoring the new bearings.

Pistons and Connecting Rods

PISTONS

♦ **See Figure 187**

The piston should be visually inspected for any signs of cracking or burning (caused by hot spots or detonation), and scuffing or excessive wear on the skirts. The wrist pin attaches the piston to the connecting rod. The piston should move freely on the wrist pin, both sliding and pivoting. Grasp the connecting rod securely, or mount it in a vise, and try to rock the piston back and forth along the centerline of any wrist pin. There should not be any excessive play evident between the piston and the pin. If there are C-clips retaining the pin in the piston then you have wrist pin bushings in the rods. There should not be any excessive play between the wrist pin and the rod bushing. Normal clearance for the wrist pin is approx. 0.001–0.002 in. (0.025mm–0.051mm).

Use a micrometer and measure the diameter of the piston, perpendicular to the wrist pin, on the skirt. Compare the reading to its original cylinder measurement obtained earlier. The difference between the two readings is the piston-to-wall clearance. If the clearance is within specifications, the piston may be used as is. If the piston is out of specification, but the bore is not, you will need a new piston. If both are out of specification, you will need the cylinder rebored and oversize pistons installed. Generally if two or more pistons/bores are out of specification, it is best to rebore the entire block and purchase a complete set of oversize pistons.

Fig. 187 Measure the piston's outer diameter, perpendicular to the wrist pin, with a micrometer

CONNECTING ROD

You should have the connecting rod checked for straightness at a machine shop. If the connecting rod is bent, it will unevenly wear the bearing and piston, as well as place greater stress on these components. Any bent or twisted connecting rods must be replaced. If the rods are straight and the wrist pin clearance is within specifications, then only the bearing end of the rod need be checked. Place the connecting rod into a vice, with the bearing inserts in place, install the cap to the rod and torque the fasteners to specifications. Use a telescoping gauge and carefully measure the inside diameter of the bearings. Compare this reading to the rods original crankshaft journal diameter measurement. The difference is the oil clearance. If the oil clearance is not within specifications, install new bearings in the rod and take another measurement. If the clearance is still out of specifications, and the crankshaft is not, the rod will need to be reconditioned by a machine shop.

➡**You can also use Plastigage to check the bearing clearances. The assembling section has complete instructions on its use.**

Camshaft

Inspect the camshaft and lifters/followers as described earlier in this section.

Bearings

All of the engine bearings should be visually inspected for wear and/or damage. The bearing should look evenly worn all around with no deep scores or pits. If the bearing is severely worn, scored, pitted or heat blued, then the bearing, and the components that use it, should be brought to a machine shop for inspection. Full-circle bearings (used on most camshafts, auxiliary shafts, balance shafts, etc.) require specialized tools for removal and installation, and should be brought to a machine shop for service.

Oil Pump

➡**The oil pump is responsible for providing constant lubrication to the whole engine and so it is recommended that a new oil pump be installed when rebuilding the engine.**

Completely disassemble the oil pump and thoroughly clean all of the components. Inspect the oil pump gears and housing for wear and/or damage. Insure that the pressure relief valve operates properly and there is no binding or sticking due to varnish or debris. If all of the parts are in proper working condition, lubricate the gears and relief valve, and assemble the pump.

REFINISHING

▶ **See Figure 188**

Almost all engine block refinishing must be performed by a machine shop. If the cylinders are not to be rebored, then the cylinder glaze can be removed with a ball hone. When removing cylinder glaze with a ball hone, use a light or penetrating type oil to lubricate the hone. Do not allow the hone to run dry as this may cause excessive scoring of the cylinder bores and wear on the hone. If new pistons are required, they will need to be installed to the connecting rods. This should be performed by a machine shop as the pistons must be installed in the correct relationship to the rod or engine damage can occur.

Fig. 188 Use a ball type cylinder hone to remove any glaze and provide a new surface for seating the piston rings

Pistons and Connecting Rods

▶ **See Figure 189**

Only pistons with the wrist pin retained by C-clips are serviceable by the home-mechanic. Press fit pistons require special presses and/or heaters to remove/install the connecting rod and should only be performed by a machine shop.

All pistons will have a mark indicating the direction to the front of the engine and the must be installed into the engine in that manner. Usually it is a notch or arrow on the top of the piston, or it may be the letter F cast or stamped into the piston.

C-CLIP TYPE PISTONS

1. Note the location of the forward mark on the piston and mark the connecting rod in relation.
2. Remove the C-clips from the piston and withdraw the wrist pin.

➡**Varnish build-up or C-clip groove burrs may increase the difficulty of removing the wrist pin. If necessary, use a punch or drift to carefully tap the wrist pin out.**

3. Insure that the wrist pin bushing in the connecting rod is usable, and lubricate it with assembly lube.
4. Remove the wrist pin from the new piston and lubricate the pin bores on the piston.

Fig. 189 Most pistons are marked to indicate positioning in the engine (usually a mark means the side facing the front)

5. Align the forward marks on the piston and the connecting rod and install the wrist pin.
6. The new C-clips will have a flat and a rounded side to them. Install both C-clips with the flat side facing out.
7. Repeat all of the steps for each piston being replaced.

ASSEMBLY

Before you begin assembling the engine, first give yourself a clean, dirt free work area. Next, clean every engine component again. The key to a good assembly is cleanliness.

Mount the engine block into the engine stand and wash it one last time using water and detergent (dishwashing detergent works well). While washing it, scrub the cylinder bores with a soft bristle brush and thoroughly clean all of the oil passages. Completely dry the engine and spray the entire assembly down with an anti-rust solution such as WD-40 or similar product. Take a clean lint-free rag and wipe up any excess anti-rust solution from the bores, bearing saddles, etc. Repeat the final cleaning process on the crankshaft. Replace any freeze or oil galley plugs which were removed during disassembly.

Crankshaft

▶ **See Figures 190, 191, 192 and 193**

1. Remove the main bearing inserts from the block and bearing caps.
2. If the crankshaft main bearing journals have been refinished to a definite undersize, install the correct undersize bearing. Be sure that the bearing inserts and bearing bores are clean. Foreign material under inserts will distort bearing and cause failure.
3. Place the upper main bearing inserts in bores with tang in slot.

➡**The oil holes in the bearing inserts must be aligned with the oil holes in the cylinder block.**

4. Install the lower main bearing inserts in bearing caps.
5. Clean the mating surfaces of block and rear main bearing cap.
6. Carefully lower the crankshaft into place. Be careful not to damage bearing surfaces.
7. Check the clearance of each main bearing by using the following procedure:

   a. Place a piece of Plastigage, or its equivalent, on bearing surface across full width of bearing cap and about 1/4 in. off center.

   b. Install cap and tighten bolts to specifications. Do not turn crankshaft while Plastigage is in place.

   c. Remove the cap. Using the supplied Plastigage scale, check width of Plastigage at widest point to get maximum clearance. Difference between readings is taper of journal.

   d. If clearance exceeds specified limits, try a 0.001 in. or 0.002 in. undersize bearing in combination with the standard bearing. Bearing clearance must be within specified limits. If standard and 0.002 in. undersize bearing does not bring clearance within desired limits, refinish crankshaft journal, then install undersize bearings.

8. Install the rear main seal.
9. After the bearings have been fitted, apply a light coat of engine oil to the journals and bearings. Install the rear main bearing cap. Install all bearing caps

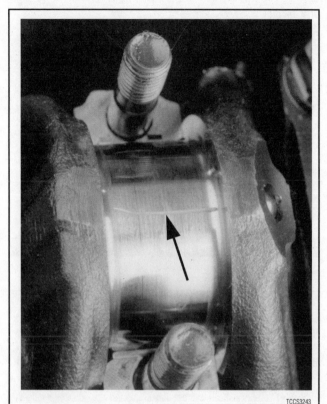

Fig. 190 Apply a strip of gauging material to the bearing journal, then install and torque the cap

except the thrust bearing cap. Be sure that main bearing caps are installed in original locations. Tighten the bearing cap bolts to specifications.

10. Install the thrust bearing cap with bolts finger-tight.

11. Pry the crankshaft forward against the thrust surface of upper half of bearing.

12. Hold the crankshaft forward and pry the thrust bearing cap to the rear. This aligns the thrust surfaces of both halves of the bearing.

13. Retain the forward pressure on the crankshaft. Tighten the cap bolts to specifications.

14. Measure the crankshaft end-play as follows:

a. Mount a dial gauge to the engine block and position the tip of the gauge to read from the crankshaft end.

b. Carefully pry the crankshaft toward the rear of the engine and hold it there while you zero the gauge.

c. Carefully pry the crankshaft toward the front of the engine and read the gauge.

d. Confirm that the reading is within specifications. If not, install a new thrust bearing and repeat the procedure. If the reading is still out of specifications with a new bearing, have a machine shop inspect the thrust surfaces of the crankshaft, and if possible, repair it.

15. Rotate the crankshaft so as to position the first rod journal to the bottom of its stroke.

Pistons and Connecting Rods

▶ See Figures 194, 195, 196 and 197

1. Before installing the piston/connecting rod assembly, oil the pistons, piston rings and the cylinder walls with light engine oil. Install connecting rod bolt protectors or rubber hose onto the connecting rod bolts/studs. Also perform the following:

a. Select the proper ring set for the size cylinder bore.

b. Position the ring in the bore in which it is going to be used.

c. Push the ring down into the bore area where normal ring wear is not encountered.

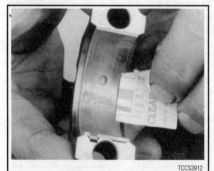
Fig. 191 After the cap is removed again, use the scale supplied with the gauging material to check the clearance

Fig. 192 A dial gauge may be used to check crankshaft end-play

Fig. 193 Carefully pry the crankshaft back and forth while reading the dial gauge for end-play

Fig. 194 Checking the piston ring-to-ring groove side clearance using the ring and a feeler gauge

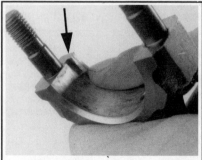
Fig. 195 The notch on the side of the bearing cap matches the tang on the bearing insert

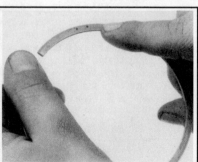
Fig. 196 Most rings are marked to show which side of the ring should face up when installed to the piston

d. Use the head of the piston to position the ring in the bore so that the ring is square with the cylinder wall. Use caution to avoid damage to the ring or cylinder bore.

e. Measure the gap between the ends of the ring with a feeler gauge. Ring gap in a worn cylinder is normally greater than specification. If the ring gap is greater than the specified limits, try an oversize ring set.

f. Check the ring side clearance of the compression rings with a feeler gauge inserted between the ring and its lower land according to specification. The gauge should slide freely around the entire ring circumference without binding. Any wear that occurs will form a step at the inner portion of the lower land. If the lower lands have high steps, the piston should be replaced.

2. Unless new pistons are installed, be sure to install the pistons in the cylinders from which they were removed. The numbers on the connecting rod and bearing cap must be on the same side when installed in the cylinder bore. If a connecting rod is ever transposed from one engine or cylinder to another, new bearings should be fitted and the connecting rod should be numbered to correspond with the new cylinder number. The notch on the piston head goes toward the front of the engine.

3. Install all of the rod bearing inserts into the rods and caps.

4. Install the rings to the pistons. Install the oil control ring first, then the second compression ring and finally the top compression ring. Use a piston ring expander tool to aid in installation and to help reduce the chance of breakage.

5. Make sure the ring gaps are properly spaced around the circumference of the piston. Fit a piston ring compressor around the piston and slide the piston and connecting rod assembly down into the cylinder bore, pushing it in with the wooden hammer handle. Push the piston down until it is only slightly below

TCCS3914

Fig. 197 Install the piston and rod assembly into the block using a ring compressor and the handle of a hammer

the top of the cylinder bore. Guide the connecting rod onto the crankshaft bearing journal carefully, to avoid damaging the crankshaft.

6. Check the bearing clearance of all the rod bearings, fitting them to the crankshaft bearing journals. Follow the procedure in the crankshaft installation above.

7. After the bearings have been fitted, apply a light coating of assembly oil to the journals and bearings.

8. Turn the crankshaft until the appropriate bearing journal is at the bottom of its stroke, then push the piston assembly all the way down until the connecting rod bearing seats on the crankshaft journal. Be careful not to allow the bearing cap screws to strike the crankshaft bearing journals and damage them.

9. After the piston and connecting rod assemblies have been installed, check the connecting rod side clearance on each crankshaft journal.

10. Prime and install the oil pump and the oil pump intake tube.

11. Install the auxiliary/balance shaft(s)/assembly(ies).

OHV Engines

CAMSHAFT, LIFTERS AND TIMING ASSEMBLY

1. Install the camshaft.
2. Install the lifters/followers into their bores.
3. Install the timing gears/chain assembly.

CYLINDER HEAD(S)

1. Install the cylinder head(s) using new gaskets.
2. Assemble the rest of the valve train (pushrods and rocker arms and/or shafts).

Engine Covers and Components

Install the timing cover(s) and oil pan. Refer to your notes and drawings made prior to disassembly and install all of the components that were removed. Install the engine into the vehicle.

Engine Start-up and Break-in

STARTING THE ENGINE

Now that the engine is installed and every wire and hose is properly connected, go back and double check that all coolant and vacuum hoses are connected. Check that you oil drain plug is installed and properly tightened. If not already done, install a new oil filter onto the engine. Fill the crankcase with the proper amount and grade of engine oil. Fill the cooling system with a 50/50 mixture of coolant/water.

1. Connect the vehicle battery.
2. Start the engine. Keep your eye on your oil pressure indicator; if it does not indicate oil pressure within 10 seconds of starting, turn the vehicle off.

✳✳ WARNING

Damage to the engine can result if it is allowed to run with no oil pressure. Check the engine oil level to make sure that it is full. Check for any leaks and if found, repair the leaks before continuing. If there is still no indication of oil pressure, you may need to prime the system.

3. Confirm that there are no fluid leaks (oil or other).
4. Allow the engine to reach normal operating temperature (the upper radiator hose will be hot to the touch).
5. If necessary, set the ignition timing.
6. Install any remaining components such as the air cleaner (if removed for ignition timing) or body panels which were removed.

BREAKING IT IN

Make the first miles on the new engine, easy ones. Vary the speed but do not accelerate hard. Most importantly, do not lug the engine, and avoid sustained high speeds until at least 100 miles. Check the engine oil and coolant levels frequently. Expect the engine to use a little oil until the rings seat. Change the oil and filter at 500 miles; 1500 miles, then every 3000 miles past that.

KEEP IT MAINTAINED

Now that you have just gone through all of that hard work, keep yourself from doing it all over again by thoroughly maintaining it. Not that you may not have maintained it before, heck you could have had one to two hundred thousand miles on it before doing this. However, you may have bought the vehicle used, and the previous owner did not keep up on maintenance. Which is why you just went through all of that hard work. See?

TORQUE SPECIFICATIONS

Components	Ft. Lbs.	Nm
Engine mounts		
4.8L engines		
Engine mount through-bolts	60	81
Exhaust pipe-to-exhaust manifold nuts	20	27
4.3L, 5.0L, and 5.7L engines		
1988-96 4.3L C/K series		
Front mount bolts	44	59
Front through-bolt	70	95
Front mount nut	50	68
Rear mount bolts	35	47
1997-98 4.3L C/K Series		
Mount-to-frame hollow bolts:		
Through-bolt	⊕ 74	⊕ 100
Nut	50	68
4.3L R/V series		
1988-91 4.3L R/V Series		
Front mount bolts	36	48
Front mount nut	33	45
Front through-bolt	70	95
Front through-bolt nut	50	68
Rear mount bolts	35	47
5.0L and 5.7L engines		
1988-91 models		
Front mount bolts	36	48
Front mount nut	30	40
Front through-bolt	85	115
Front through-bolt nut	55	75
Rear mount bolt/nut (R Series)	35	47
Rear mount bolt (V Series)	40	54
Rear mount nut (V Series)	36	48
1992-98 models		
Front mount frame bolt	44	59
Front mount frame nut	33	45
Front through-bolt	70	95
Front through-bolt nut	50	68
Front mount engine bolt	38	51
Rear mount bolts	35	47
Bell housing-to-engine bolts	35	47
Torque converter-to-flex bolts	46	63
7.4L engines		
1988-91 C/K Series		
Front mount frame bolt	36	48
Front mount engine bolt	45	60
Front through-bolt	70	95
Front through-bolt nut	50	68
Rear mount bolts	36	48

91023C30

TORQUE SPECIFICATIONS

Components	Ft. Lbs.	Nm
Engine mounts (cont.)		
1988-91 R/V Series		
Front mount bolts	36	48
Front mount nut	30	40
Front through-bolt	85	115
Front through-bolt nut	55	75
Rear mount bolt/nut (R Series)	35	47
Rear mount bolt (V Series)	40	54
Rear mount nut (V Series)	36	48
1992-98 4.3L C/K Series		
Front mount frame bolt	44	59
Front mount frame nut	33	45
Front through-bolt	70	95
Front through-bolt nut	50	68
Front mount engine bolt	38	51
Rear mount bolts	35	47
Bellhousing-to-engine bolts	35	47
Torque converter-to-flexplate bolts	46	63
6.2L and 6.5L engines		
Front mount bolt	44	59
Front mount nut	33	45
Bracket-to-block bolt	38	51
Through-bolt	70	95
Through-bolt nut	50	68
Bellhousing-to-engine bolts	30	40
Torque converter-to-flexplate bolts	46	63
Valve/Cylinder Head Cover		
Valve cover mounting bolts		
Gasoline engines		
4.3L and 4.8L engines		
1988-95 models	90 inch lbs.	10
1996-98 models	106 inch lbs.	12
5.0L and 5.7L engines		
1988 models	65 inch lbs.	7
1989-94 models	90 inch lbs.	10
1995 models	89 inch lbs.	10
1996-98 models	106 inch lbs.	12
7.4L engines		
1988-91 models	115 inch lbs.	13
1992-96 models	65 inch lbs.	7
1997-98 models		
Valve cover retainers	72 inch lbs.	8
Throttle body studs	108 inch lbs.	12
Diesel engines	16	22
Pushrod (Engine Side) Cover		
4.8L engines		
Pushrod (side cover) bolts	80 inch lbs.	9

91023C31

TORQUE SPECIFICATIONS

Components	Ft. Lbs.	Nm
Thermostat		
Gasoline engines		
Thermostat housing		
4.3L, 5.0L, 5.7L engines		
Bolts	20	28
Studs	21	28
7.4L engines		
Bolts	27	37
Diesel engines		
Thermostat housing bolts		
1988-91 models	35	47
1992-95 models	31	42
1996-98 models		
Thermostat housing bolt and stud	31	42
Thermostat Housing Crossover		
Cossover bolts		
1988-91 models	35	47
1992-98 models	31	42
Upper Intake Manifold		
4.3L engines		
1996-98 models		
Upper intake manifold mounting bolts and studs	88 inch lbs.	10
5.0 and 5.7L engines		
Upper intake manifold mounting bolts and studs	②	②
7.4L engines		
Upper intake manifold bolts		
1996 models	17	22
1997-98 models	③	③
Lower Intake Manifold		
4.3L engines		
1988-95 models		
Lower intake manifold bolts	35	48
1996-98 models		
Lower intake manifold bolts	④	④
5.0L and 5.7L engines		
1988-95 models		
Lower intake manifold bolts	35	48
1996-98 models		
Lower intake manifold bolts	⑤	⑤
Diesel engines		
1988-95 models		
Manifold bolts	32	42

91023C32

TORQUE SPECIFICATIONS

Components	Ft. Lbs.	Nm
Lower Intake Manifold (cont.)		
Diesel engines (cont.)		
1996-98 models		
Intake manifold studs	31	42
Turbocharger connector hose clamps	50 inch lbs.	6
Fuel filter bolts	31	42
7.4L engines		
Lower intake manifold bolts	30	40
Exhaust Manifold		
4.3L engines		
Exhaust manifold bolts		
Two center bolts	26	36
Outside bolts	20	28
5.0L and 5.7L engines		
1988-95 models		
Exhaust manifold bolts		
Two center bolts	26	36
Outside bolts	20	28
1996-98 models	⑥	⑥
7.4L engines		
1988-95 models		
Exhaust manifold bolts	40	54
1996-98 models		
Exhaust manifold nuts	22	30
Heat shields nuts	15	20
Oil level indicator tube	40	54
6.2L and 6.5L engines		
Manifold bolts	26	35
Combination Manifold		
4.8L engines		
Manifold-to-cylinder head bolts and nuts	38	52
Manifold center bolts and nuts	44	60
Turbocharger		
Turbocharger-to-exhaust manifold bolts	43	58
Turbocharger and the exhaust manifold assembly-to-engine bolts and studs	43	58
Oil return pipe bolt	19	26
Oil feed hose-to-turbocharger fitting	13	17
Exhaust pipe-to-turbocharger clamp	71 inch lbs.	8
Turbocharger braces		
Long brace		
Nut	26	34
Bolt	37	50
Short brace	19	25
Bolts	19	25
Intake manifold cover bolts	90 inch lbs.	11

91023C33

TORQUE SPECIFICATIONS

Components	Ft. Lbs.	Nm
Oil Pan (cont.)		
4.3L engines (cont.)		
1996-98 models		
Oil pan retainers (in sequence)	18	25
4.8L engines		
Oil pan-to-front cover bolts		
1/4 in. pan-to-block bolts	45 inch lbs.	5
5/16 in. bolts	80 inch lbs.	9
	14	19
5.0L and 5.7L engines		
1988-95 models		
Bolts	100 inch lbs.	11
Nuts	17	23
1996-98 models		
Oil pan nuts and bolts	18	25
7.4L engines		
1988-95 models		
Oil pan-to-cover bolts	70 inch lbs.	8
Oil pan-to-block bolts	13	18
1996-98 models		
Oil pan nuts and bolts	18	25
6.2L and 6.5L engines		
Oil pan bolts (except the two rear bolts)	89 inch lbs.	10
Two rear bolts	17	23
Connecting rods		
Cap nuts		
4.3L engines		
1988-95 models	20 plus 60°	27 plus 60°
1996-98 models	20 plus 55°	27 plus 55°
5.0L and 5.7L engines	45	60
6.2L and 6.5L engines	48	66
7.4L engines		
1988-95 models	48	66
1996-98 models	45	61
Crankshaft		
Main bearing cap bolts		
4.3L engines		
1988-95 models	81	110
1996-98 models	77	105
5.0L and 5.7L engines		
1988-95 models		
Outer bolts on caps 2, 3, and 4	70	95
All others	81	110
1996-98 models		
Bearing cap inboard bolt and stud		
Bearing cap (four bolt caps)	67	90
6.2L and 6.5L engines		
Inner	111	150
Outer	100	135
7.4L engines	100	135

91023C35

TORQUE SPECIFICATIONS

Components	Ft. Lbs.	Nm
Radiator		
Gasoline engines		
Lower fan shroud bolts	71 inch lbs.	9
Engine oil cooler pipe bolts	18	24
Transmission oil cooler bolts	19	26
Upper fan shroud bolts	71 inch lbs.	9
Diesel engines		
Early model vehicles		
Radiator retainers	71 inch lbs.	9
Late model vehicles		
Lower fan shroud bolts	71 inch lbs.	9
Engine oil cooler pipe bolts	18	24
Transmission oil cooler bolts	19	26
Upper fan shroud bolts	71 inch lbs.	9
Engine Fan		
Fan-to-fan clutch bolts	18	24
Fan/clutch assembly-to-water pump pulley nuts	18	24
Auxiliary Cooling Fan		
Fan-to-brace bolts	53	72
Water Pump		
4.8L engines		
Water pump bolts	15	20
4.3L, 5.0L, 5.7L and 7.4L engines		
Water pump bolts	30	41
6.2L and 6.5L Diesel engines		
Water pump-to- plate assembly bolts	31	42
Water pump-to-engine bolts		
Cylinder Head		
Cylinder head bolts		
4.8L engines		
4.3L engines		
1988-95 models		
1996-98 models		
5.0L and 5.7L engines		
1988-95 models		
1996-98 models		
6.2L and 6.5L engines		
1988-95 models		
1996-98 models		
7.4L engines		
Oil Pan		
4.3L engines		
1988-95 models		
Oil pan bolts	100 inch lbs.	11
Nuts at the corners	17	23

91023C34

TORQUE SPECIFICATIONS

Components	Ft. Lbs.	Nm
Oil Pump		
4.3L, 5.0L, 5.7L and 7.4L engines		
Oil pump bolt	65	90
4.8L engines		
Oil pump bolts	115 inch lbs.	11
6.2L and 6.5L engines		
Oil pump bolt	65	90
Crankshaft Damper		
Crankshaft damper bolt		
4.3L, 5.0L and 5.7L engines	74	100
4.8L engine	50	70
6.2L and 6.5L engine	200	270
7.4L engine		
1988-96 models	85	115
1997-98 models	110	149
Timing Chain Cover		
Timing cover retainers		
4.3L engine	124 inch lbs.	14
5.0L and 5.7L engines	100 inch lbs.	11
7.4L engines	106 inch lbs.	12
6.2L and 6.5L engines	30-33	40-45
Timing cover-to-block bolts	33	45
Baffle bolts and nut	31	42
Injection pump nuts	17	23
Timing Gear Cover and Seal		
4.3L engine		
Timing gear cover-to-block bolts	80 inch lbs.	9
Timing gear cover-to-pan bolts	45 inch lbs.	6
Camshaft sprocket bolts		
4.3L, 5.0L and 5.7L engines		
1988-95 models	21	28
1996-98 models	18	25
7.4L engines		
1988-95 models	20	26
1996-98 models	25	34
6.2L and 6.5L engines		
Camshaft gear bolt		
1988-95 models	75	100
1996-98 models	125	171
Camshaft thrust plate		
4.3L engine		
Bolts	105 inch lbs.	12
4.8L engines		
Bolts	80 inch lbs.	9
6.2L and 6.5L engines		
Camshaft retainer plate bolts	17	23

91023C36

TORQUE SPECIFICATIONS

Components	Ft. Lbs.	Nm
Hydraulic Lifters		
4.3L, 5.0L, 5.7L and 7.4L engines		
Lifter retainer bolts	12	16
6.2L and 6.5L engines		
Guide plates and clamps bolts	18	26
Balance Shaft	①	①
Rear Main Oil Seal		
7.4L engines		
1988-90 models		
Main bearing cap bolts	10	14
Main bearing cap	110	150
6.2L Diesel engines		
Rope type seal		
Main bearing cap	70	94
Flywheel and Ring Gear		
4.3L, 5.0L and 5.7L engines	75	100
6.2L, 6.5L and 7.4L engines	65	90

② Step 1: All bolts in sequence: 22 ft. lbs. (30 Nm)
Step 2: In a clockwise sequence to 7 ft. lbs. (10 Nm)
Step 1: Short length bolt: (11, 7, 3, 2, 6, 10) 55 degrees
Step 2: Medium length bolt: (12, 13) 65 degrees
Step 4: Long length bolts: (1, 4, 8, 5, 9) 75 degrees

① Step 1: 45 inch lbs. (5 Nm)
Final step: 83 inch lbs. (10 Nm)
② Step 1: 25 ft. lbs. (34 Nm)
Step 2: 45 ft. lbs. (61 Nm)
Final pass: 65 ft. lbs. (90 Nm)
③ Step 1: 72 ft. lbs. (8 Nm)
Final pass 10 ft. lbs. (14 Nm)
④ Step 1: 26 inch lbs. (3 Nm)
⑤ All bolts in sequence 22 ft. lbs. (30 Nm)
Step 2: 106 inch lbs. (12 Nm)
Step 1: Short length bolt: (3, 4, 7, 8, 11, 12, 15, 16) 55 degrees
⑥ Step 1: 71 ft. lbs. (8 Nm)
Step 2: Medium length bolts: (14, 17) 65 degrees
Step 2: 106 inch lbs. (12 Nm)
Step 3: Long length bolts: (1, 2, 5, 6, 9, 10, 13) 75 degrees
⑦ Step 1: 15 ft. lbs. (20 Nm)
① Step 1: 20 ft. lbs. (25 Nm)
Final step: 15 ft. lbs. (20 Nm)
Final Step: 1/4 or 90° turn more
⑧ Step 1: 50 ft. lbs. (68 Nm)
⑨ Step 1: 22 ft. lbs. (30 Nm)
① Step 1: 20 ft. lbs. (25 Nm)
Final pass: 22 ft. lbs. (30 Nm)
Step 2: 55 ft. lbs. (75 Nm)
The three lower right side bolts: 17 ft. lbs. (23 Nm)
Final Step: 1/4 or 90° turn more
① Step 1: 30 ft. lbs. (40 Nm)
Tighten bolts in three equal steps to 95 ft. lbs. (129 Nm) except the left front (No. 12) bolt
② Step 1: 20 ft. lbs. (60 Nm)
Number 12 bolt: 85 ft. lbs. (115 Nm)
⑬ First pass: 25 ft. lbs. (34 Nm)
Second pass: 45 ft. lbs. (61 Nm)
⑭ Balance shaft driven gear bolt 15 ft. lbs. (20 Nm)
Final pass: 65 ft. lbs. (90 Nm)
Balance shaft bearing retainer bolts 106 inch lbs. (12 Nm)
Plus an additional 35° using a torque/angle meter.
Drive gear retaining bolt 12 ft. lbs. (16 Nm)

91023C37

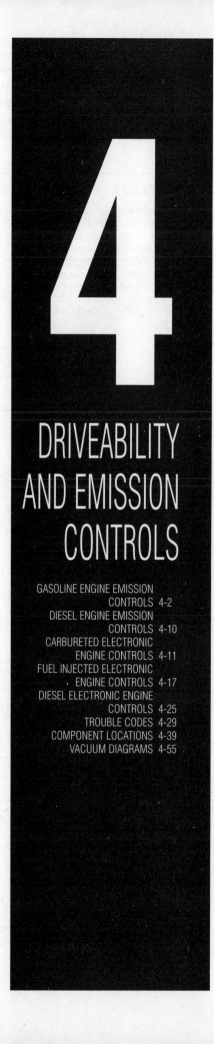

4

DRIVEABILITY AND EMISSION CONTROLS

GASOLINE ENGINE EMISSION CONTROLS

Crankcase Ventilation System

OPERATION

▶ **See Figures 1 and 2**

The Positive Crankcase Ventilation (PCV) system is used to evacuate the crankcase vapors. Outside vehicle air is routed through the air cleaner to the crankcase where it mixes with the blow-by gases and is passed through the PCV valve. It is then routed into the intake manifold. The PCV valve meters the air flow rate which varies under engine operation depending on manifold vacuum. In order to maintain idle quality, the PCV valve limits the air flow when intake manifold vacuum is high. If abnormal operating conditions occur, the system will allow excessive blow-by gases to back flow through the crankcase vent tube into the air cleaner. These blow-by gases will then be burned by normal combustion.

A plugged PCV valve or hose may cause rough idle, stalling or slow idle speed, oil leaks, oil in the air cleaner or sludge in the engine. A leaking PCV valve or hose could cause rough idle, stalling or high idle speed.

Other than checking and replacing the PCV valve and associated hoses, there is no service required.

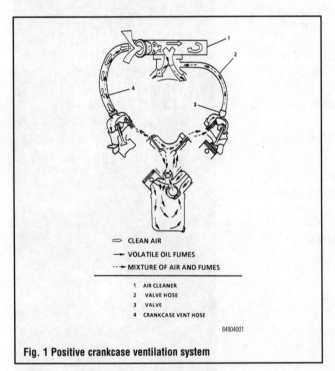

⇨ CLEAN AIR
→ VOLATILE OIL FUMES
--→ MIXTURE OF AIR AND FUMES

1 AIR CLEANER
2 VALVE HOSE
3 VALVE
4 CRANKCASE VENT HOSE

84904001

Fig. 1 Positive crankcase ventilation system

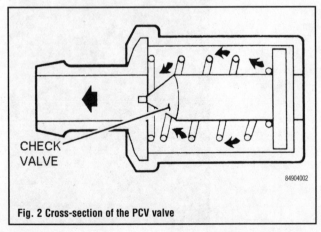

CHECK VALVE

84904002

Fig. 2 Cross-section of the PCV valve

TESTING

▶ **See Figure 3**

With the engine running, remove the PCV from the valve cover and place your thumb over the end of the valve. Check if vacuum is present at the valve. If vacuum is not present, check for plugged hoses, blockage of the manifold port at the throttle body/carburetor unit or a faulty PCV valve. Replace as necessary. With the engine not running, remove the PCV valve from the vehicle. Shake the valve and listen for the rattle of the check valve needle. If no rattle is heard, the valve is defective and must be replaced.

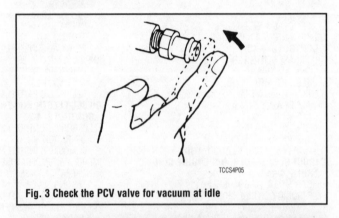

TCCS4P05

Fig. 3 Check the PCV valve for vacuum at idle

Evaporative Emission Control System

OPERATION

The Evaporative Emission Control System (EECS) is designed to prevent fuel tank vapors from being emitted into the atmosphere. Gasoline vapors are absorbed and stored by a fuel vapor charcoal canister. The charcoal canister absorbs the gasoline vapors and stores them until certain engine conditions are met and the vapors can be purged and burned by the engine.

The charcoal canister purge cycle is controlled either by a thermostatic vacuum switch or by a timed vacuum source. The thermostatic switch is installed in the coolant passage and prevents canister purge when engine operating temperature is below 115F (46C). The timed vacuum source uses a manifold vacuum-controlled diaphragm to control canister purge. When the engine is running, full manifold vacuum is applied to the top tube of the purge valve which lifts the valve diaphragm and opens the valve.

A vent located in the fuel tank, allows fuel vapors to flow to the charcoal canister. A tank pressure control valve, used on high altitude applications, prevents canister purge when the engine is not running. The fuel tank cap does not normally vent to the atmosphere but is designed to provide both vacuum and pressure relief.

Poor engine idle, stalling and poor driveability can be caused by a damaged canister or split, damaged or improperly connected hoses.

Evidence of fuel loss or fuel vapor odor can be caused by a liquid fuel leak:
• A cracked or damaged vapor canister
• A disconnected, misrouted, kinked or damaged vapor pipe or canister hoses
• A damaged air cleaner or improperly seated air cleaner gasket

TESTING

Vapor Canister

▶ **See Figure 4**

1. Apply a length of hose to the lower tube of the purge valve assembly and attempt to blow air through it. There should be little or no air should passing into the canister.

➡**If the canister is equipped with a constant purge hole, a small amount of air will pass into the canister.**

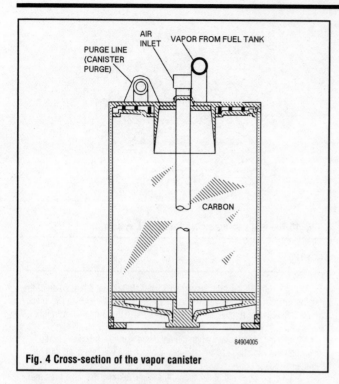

Fig. 4 Cross-section of the vapor canister

2. Using a hand-held vacuum pump, apply a vacuum of 15 in. Hg (51 kPa) to the control vacuum (upper) tube. If the vacuum does not hold for at least 20 seconds, the diaphragm is leaking. Replace the canister.

3. If the diaphragm holds vacuum, attempt to blow air through the hose connected to the PCV tube while vacuum is still being applied. An increase of air should be observed. If no increase is noted, the canister must be replaced.

Fuel Tank Pressure Control Valve

1. Attach a length of hose to the tank side of the valve assembly and try to blow air through it. Little or no air should pass into the canister.

2. Using a hand-held vacuum pump, apply vacuum equivalent to 15 in. Hg (51 kPa) to the control vacuum tube. If the diaphragm does not hold vacuum, the diaphragm is leaking. Replace the valve.

3. If the diaphragm holds vacuum, attempt to blow air through the hose connected to the valve while vacuum is still being applied. Air should pass. If no air is noted, the valve must be replaced.

Thermostatic Vacuum Switch

1. With engine temperature below 100F (38C), apply vacuum to the manifold side of the switch. The switch should hold vacuum.

2. Start and continue to run the engine until the engine temperature increases above 122F (50C). The vacuum should drop off.

3. Replace the switch if it fails either test.

REMOVAL & INSTALLATION

Vapor Canister

1. Tag and disconnect the hoses from the canister.
2. If equipped, unplug the electrical connector from the canister.
3. Remove the vapor canister retaining nut.
4. Remove the canister from the vehicle.

To install:

5. Install the canister. If necessary refer to the vehicle emission control label, located in the engine compartment for proper routing of the vacuum hoses.

6. If equipped, attach the canister electrical connection.

Thermostatic Vacuum Switch

1. Drain the cooling system to below the switch level.
2. Tag and disconnect the vacuum hoses from the switch.
3. Remove the thermostatic vacuum switch.

To install:

4. Install the thermostatic vacuum switch. Make sure to apply sealer to the switch threads.
5. Connect the vacuum hoses.
6. Refill the cooling system.

Canister Purge Solenoid

EXCEPT 1996–98 MODELS

▶ See Figure 5

1. Disconnect the negative battery cable.
2. Disconnect the electrical connectors and if equipped, the hoses from the solenoid.
3. Pull the solenoid away from the bracket and remove the assembly.

To install:

4. Install the solenoid to the bracket by sliding it into place.
5. Connect the electrical connectors and the hoses.
6. Connect the negative battery cable.

1996–98 MODELS

▶ See Figure 6

1. Disconnect the negative battery cable.
2. Unplug the solenoid electrical connection.
3. Unfasten the solenoid retaining bolts.
4. Remove the solenoid from its mounting on the intake manifold.
5. Installation is the reverse of removal.

EVAP Vacuum Switch

▶ See Figure 7

1. Disconnect the negative battery cable.
2. Unplug the vacuum switch electrical connection.
3. Tag and disconnect the hoses from the switch.

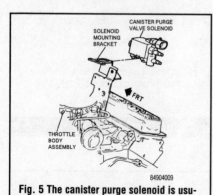

Fig. 5 The canister purge solenoid is usually mounted on a bracket—except 1996–98 models

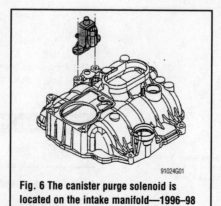

Fig. 6 The canister purge solenoid is located on the intake manifold—1996–98 models

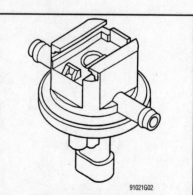

Fig. 7 View of the EVAP vacuum switch used on 1996–98 models

4. Remove the switch.
5. Installation is the reverse of removal.

Early Fuel Evaporation System

OPERATION

♦ **See Figures 8, 9 and 10**

The EFE system, used on some light duty models, consists of an EFE valve at the flange of the exhaust manifold, an actuator, and a thermal vacuum switch. The TVS is located in the coolant outlet housing and directly controls vacuum.

In both systems, manifold vacuum is applied to the actuator, which in turn, closes the EFE valve. This routes hot exhaust gases to the base of the carburetor. When coolant temperatures reach a set limit, vacuum is denied to the actuator allowing an internal spring to return the actuator to its normal position, opening the EFE valve.

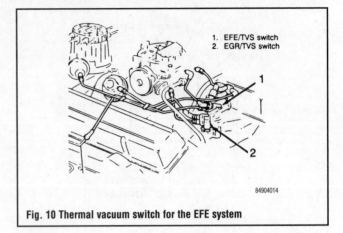

1. EFE/TVS switch
2. EGR/TVS switch

84904014

Fig. 10 Thermal vacuum switch for the EFE system

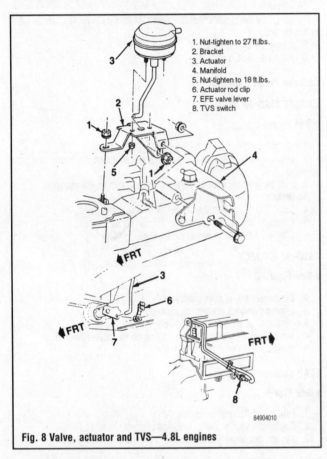

1. Nut-tighten to 27 ft.lbs.
2. Bracket
3. Actuator
4. Manifold
5. Nut-tighten to 18 ft.lbs.
6. Actuator rod clip
7. EFE valve lever
8. TVS switch

84904010

Fig. 8 Valve, actuator and TVS—4.8L engines

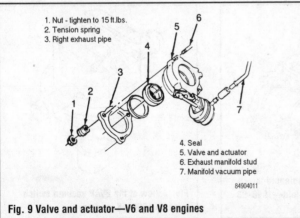

1. Nut - tighten to 15 ft.lbs.
2. Tension spring
3. Right exhaust pipe
4. Seal
5. Valve and actuator
6. Exhaust manifold stud
7. Manifold vacuum pipe

84904011

Fig. 9 Valve and actuator—V6 and V8 engines

TESTING

1. Locate the EFE valve on the exhaust manifold and not the position of the actuator arm. On some vehicles, the valve and arm are covered by a two-piece cover which must be removed for access. Make sure the engine is overnight cold.
2. Watch the actuator arm when the engine is started. The valve should close when the engine is started cold; the actuator link will be pulled into the diaphragm housing.
3. If the valve does not close, stop the engine. Remove the hose from the EFE valve and apply 10 in. Hg of vacuum by hand pump. The valve should close and stay closed for at least 20 seconds (you will hear it close). If the valve opens in less than 20 seconds, replace it. The valve could also be seized if it does not close; lubricate it with spray type manifold heat valve lube. If the valve does not close when vacuum is applied and when it is lubricated, replace the valve.
4. If the valve closes, the problem is not with the valve. Check for loose, cracked, pinched or plugged hoses, and replace as necessary. Test the EFE solenoid (located on the valve cover bracket); if it is working, the solenoid plunger will emit a noise when the current is applied.
5. Warm up the engine to operating temperature.
6. Watch the EFE valve to see if it has opened. It should now be open. If the valve is still closed, replace the solenoid if faulty, and/or check the engine thermostat; the engine coolant may not be reaching normal operating temperature.

REMOVAL & INSTALLATION

➡**If the vehicle is equipped with an oxygen sensor, it is located near the EFE valve. Use care when removing the EFE valve as not to damage the oxygen sensor.**

1. Disconnect the negative battery cable and vacuum hose at the EFE valve.
2. Remove the exhaust pipe-to-manifold nuts, and the washers and tension springs if used.
3. Lower the exhaust cross-over pipe. On some models, complete removal of the pipe is not necessary.
4. Remove the EFE valve.
To install:
5. Always install new seals and gaskets. Torque the exhaust nuts to 22 ft. lbs. (30 Nm). Connect the negative battery cable and vacuum hose to the valve.

Exhaust Gas Recirculation System

OPERATION

♦ **See Figures 11 and 12**

The EGR system's purpose is to control oxides of nitrogen which are formed during the peak combustion temperatures. The end products of combustion are

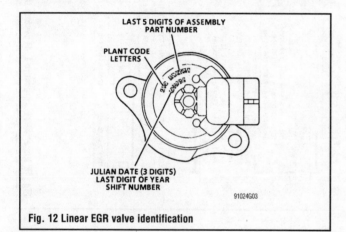

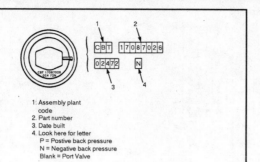

1: Assembly plant
   code
2. Part number
3. Date built
4. Look here for letter
   P = Postive back pressure
   N = Negative back pressure
   Blank = Port Valve

84904030

Fig. 11 Negative backpressure and positive backpressure EGR valve identification

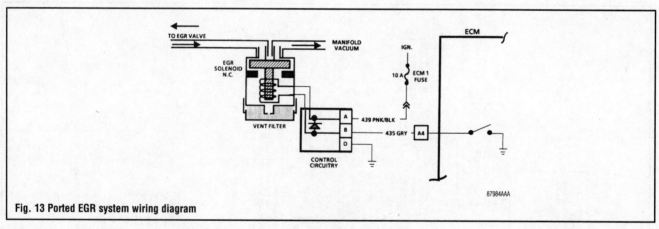

LAST 5 DIGITS OF ASSEMBLY PART NUMBER

PLANT CODE LETTERS

JULIAN DATE (3 DIGITS)
LAST DIGIT OF YEAR
SHIFT NUMBER

91024G03

Fig. 12 Linear EGR valve identification

relatively inert gases derived from the exhaust gases which are directed into the EGR valve to help lower peak combustion temperatures.

The port EGR valve is controlled by a flexible diaphragm which is spring loaded to hold the valve closed. Vacuum applied to the top side of the diaphragm overcomes the spring pressure and opens the valve which allows exhaust gas to be pulled into the intake manifold and enter the engine cylinders.

The negative backpressure EGR valve has bleed valve spring below the diaphragm, and the valve is normally closed. The valve varies the amount of exhaust flow into the manifold depending on manifold vacuum and variations in exhaust backpressure.

The diaphragm on this valve has an internal air bleed hole which is held closed by a small spring when there is no exhaust backpressure. Engine vacuum opens the EGR valve against the pressure of a large. When manifold vacuum combines with negative exhaust backpressure, the vacuum bleed hole opens and the EGR valve closes. This valve will open if vacuum is applied with the engine not running.

The linear EGR valve is operated exclusively by the control module command. The control module monitors various engine parameters:

- Throttle Position Sensor (TPS)
- Manifold Absolute Pressure (MAP)
- Engine Coolant Temperature (ECT) sensor
- Pintle position sensor

Output messages are then sent to the EGR system indicating the proper amount of exhaust gas recirculation necessary to lower combustion temperatures.

Refer to the accompanying illustrations to identify the EGR valve used in your vehicle.

TESTING

▶ **See Figures 13 thru 18**

Refer to the appropriate chart for diagnosis the EGR system. On linear EGR systems, an OBD-II compliant scan tool will be needed.

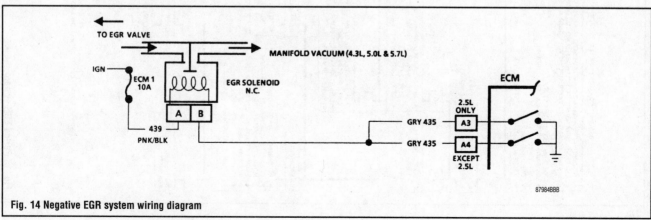

87984AAA

Fig. 13 Ported EGR system wiring diagram

87984BBB

Fig. 14 Negative EGR system wiring diagram

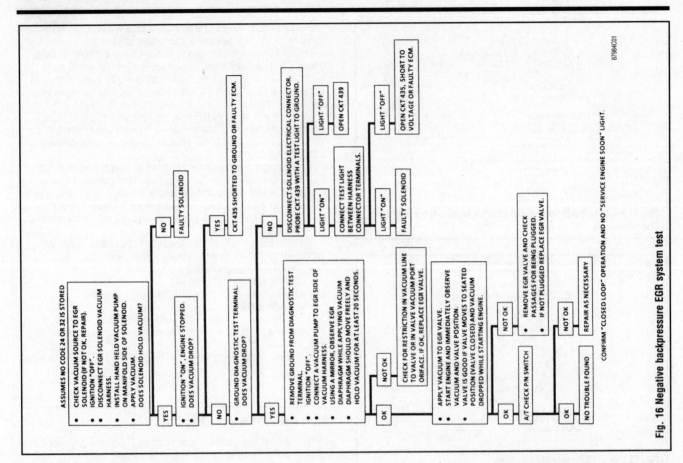

Fig. 16 Negative backpressure EGR system test

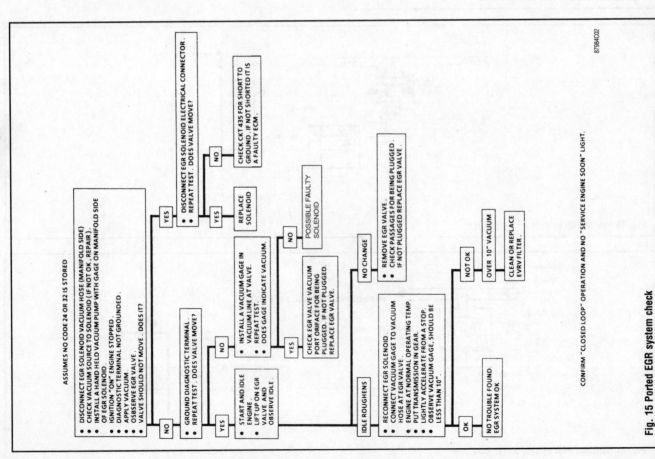

Fig. 15 Ported EGR system check

Step	Action	Value(s)	Yes	No
1	Was the system checked for trouble codes?	—	Go to Step 2	Check for trouble codes
2	1. Set parking brake and block drive wheels. 2. Install scan tool. 3. Check Transmission Range (TR) switch position 4. Have engine idling at normal operating temperature. 5. With scan tool command EGR pintle position to specified value. 6. Increase RPM to specified value. Is actual EGR pintle position greater than the specified value?	0% 2000 3%	Go to Step 15	Go to Step 3
3	1. With scan tool command a 25% position step increase (0% To 25%, 25% To 50%, 50% To 75%, 75% To 100%). 2. Observe MAP and actual EGR pintle position for specified value. EGR should increase by about 25% of position, and MAP should also increase. Is actual EGR pintle position stable, and within 10% of position of desired EGR pintle position command after the specified value?	3 seconds 2 seconds	Go to Step 4	Go to Step 6
4	Set EGR pintle position to specified value. Did MAP increase when actual pintle responded?	25%	Go to Step 5	Go to Step 13

87984C04

Fig. 17 Linear EGR system test

Step	Action	Value(s)	Yes	No
5	Set desired EGR pintle position to specified value. Is desired EGR pintle position at the specified value?	100%	Intermittent problem	Go to Step 14
6	Check and replace fuse if necessary. Is the action complete?	—	Go to Step 16	Go to Step 7
7	Check for any open circuits in wiring to EGR valve coil and repair if necessary. Is the action complete?	—	Go to Step 16	Go to Step 8
8	Check for any faulty connections to EGR valve coil and repair if necessary. Is the action complete?	—	Go to Step 16	Go to Step 9
9	1. Connect J 39200 DVOM or equivalent. 2. Check for reference voltage at EGR valve. Is the voltage at the specified value?	5V	Go to Step 10	Go to Step 11
10	1. Turn ignition "ON," engine "OFF." 2. Remove EGR valve, leaving connector on. 3. Push and hold in pintle of EGR valve. 4. Check for voltage at position sensor signal from valve. Is any voltage present?	—	Go to Step 11	Go to Step 14
11	Check for an open in circuit from control module to EGR valve in the pintle position circuit and repair if necessary. Is the action complete?	—	Go to Step 16	Go to Step 12
12	Replace control module. Is the action complete?	—	Go to Step 16	—
13	Check and repair EGR valve passages for blockages if necessary. Is the action complete?	—	Go to Step 16	—
14	Replace EGR valve. Is the action complete?	—	Go to Step 16	—
15	EGR valve is stuck open. Replace EGR valve. Is the action complete?	—	Go to Step 16	—
16	1. Turn the ignition "ON," engine "OFF." 2. Using the scan tool, command the component "ON" and "OFF." Does the component operate properly?	—	System OK	Go to Step 2

87984C05

Fig. 18 Linear EGR system test (continued)

REMOVAL & INSTALLATION

EGR Valve

EXCEPT 1996–98 MODELS

◆ See Figures 19, 20 and 21

1. Disconnect the negative battery cable.
2. Remove the air cleaner assembly from the engine.
3. Remove the EGR valve vacuum tube from the valve.
4. Remove the EGR bolts and/or nuts, then remove the EGR valve and gasket.

To install:

5. Using a new gasket place the EGR valve in position manifold. Install the nuts and/or bolts. Tighten the bolts to 17 ft. lbs. (24 Nm) and the nuts to 15 ft. lbs. (20 Nm).
6. Install the remaining components.

1996–98 MODELS

◆ See Figures 22 and 23

➡Do not try to disassemble the EGR valve.

1. Matchmark the location of the position of the EGR valve in location to its mounting. Do not rotate the EGR valve 180.
2. Unplug the EGR valve electrical connection.
3. Unfasten the valve retaining bolts and remove the valve.
4. Remove EGR valve gasket and clean the gasket mating surfaces.

To install:

5. Install a new EGR flange gasket.
6. Install the EGR valve and its retaining bolts. Make sure the marks made prior to valve removal are aligned.

7. Tighten the EGR valve bolts in two steps, fist tighten the bolts to 89 inch lbs. (10 Nm), then tighten the bolts to 18 ft. lbs. (25 Nm).
8. Attach the valve electrical connection.

EGR Solenoid

◆ See Figures 24 and 25

1. Disconnect the negative battery cable.
2. Remove the air cleaner, as required.
3. Unplug the electrical connector at the solenoid.
4. Disconnect the vacuum hoses.
5. Remove the retaining bolts and the solenoid.
6. Remove the filter, as required.

To install:

7. If removed, install the filter.
8. Install the remaining components.

Air Injector Reactor System

OPERATION

The Air Injector Reactor (AIR) system injects compressed air into the exhaust system, near enough to the exhaust valves to continue the burning of the normally unburned segment of the exhaust gases. To do this, it employs an air injection pump and a system of hoses, valves, tubes, etc., necessary to carry the compressed air from the pump to the exhaust manifolds.

A diverter valve is used to prevent backfiring. The valve senses sudden increases in manifold vacuum and ceases the injection of air during rich periods. During coasting, this valve diverts the entire air flow through a muffler and during high engine speeds, expels it through a relief valve. Check valves in the system prevent exhaust gases from entering the pump.

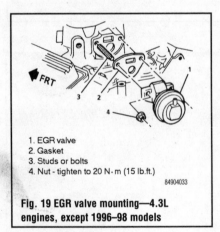

1. EGR valve
2. Gasket
3. Studs or bolts
4. Nut - tighten to 20 N·m (15 lb.ft.)

84904033

Fig. 19 EGR valve mounting—4.3L engines, except 1996–98 models

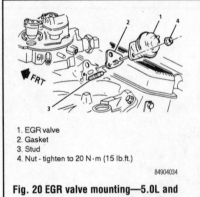

1. EGR valve
2. Gasket
3. Stud
4. Nut - tighten to 20 N·m (15 lb.ft.)

84904034

Fig. 20 EGR valve mounting—5.0L and 5.7L engines, except 1996–98 models

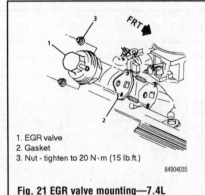

1. EGR valve
2. Gasket
3. Nut - tighten to 20 N·m (15 lb.ft.)

84904035

Fig. 21 EGR valve mounting—7.4L engines, except 1996–98 models

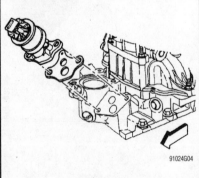

91024G04

Fig. 22 Linear EGR valve mounting— 1996–98 4.3L, 5.0L and 5.7L engines

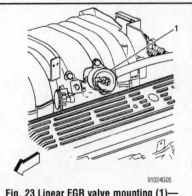

91024G05

Fig. 23 Linear EGR valve mounting (1)— 1996–98 7.4L engines

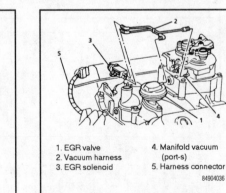

1. EGR valve
2. Vacuum harness
3. EGR solenoid
4. Manifold vacuum (port-s)
5. Harness connector

84904036

Fig. 24 EGR valve and solenoid mounting—7.4L engine shown, others similar

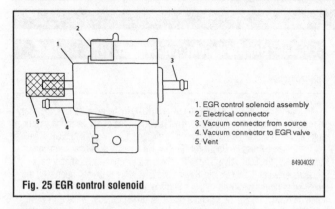

1. EGR control solenoid assembly
2. Electrical connector
3. Vacuum connector from source
4. Vacuum connector to EGR valve
5. Vent

84904037

Fig. 25 EGR control solenoid

TESTING

→The AIR system is not completely silent under normal conditions. Noises will rise in pitch as engine speed increases. If the noise is excessive, eliminate the air pump itself by disconnecting the drive belt. If the noise disappears, the air pump is not at fault.

Check Valve

To test the check valve, disconnect the hose at the diverter valve. Place your hand over the check valve and check for exhaust pulses. If exhaust pulses are present, the check valve must be replaced.

Diverter Valve

Pull off the vacuum line to the top of the valve with the engine running. There should be vacuum in the line, if not replace the line. No air should be escaping with the engine running at a steady idle. Open and quickly close the throttle. A blast of air should come out of the valve muffler for at least one second.

Air Pump

Disconnect the hose from the diverter valve. Start the engine and accelerate it to about 1500 rpm. The air flow should increase as the engine is accelerated. If no air flow is noted or it remains constant, check the following:
1. Drive belt tension.
2. Listen for a leaking pressure relief valve. If it is defective, replace the whole relief/diverter valve.
3. Foreign matter in pump filter openings. If the pump is defective or excessively noisy, it must be replaced.

REMOVAL & INSTALLATION

▶ **See Figure 26**

All hoses and fittings should be inspected for condition and tightness of connections. Check the drive belt for wear and tension periodically.

Air Pump

1. Disconnect the output hose.
2. Hold the pump from turning by squeezing the drive belt.
3. Loosen, but do not remove, the pulley bolts.
4. Loosen the alternator so the belt can be removed.
5. Remove the pulley.
6. Remove the pump mounting bolts and the pump.
To install:
7. Install the pump with the mounting bolts loose.
8. Install the pulley and tighten the bolts finger-tight.
9. Install the drive belt.
10. Squeeze the drive belt to prevent the pump from turning.
11. Tighten the pulley bolts to 25 ft. lbs. (33 Nm). Tighten the pump mountings.
12. Check and adjust the belt tension.
13. Connect the hose.
14. If any hose leaks are suspected, pour soapy water over the suspected area with the engine running. Bubbles will form wherever air is escaping.

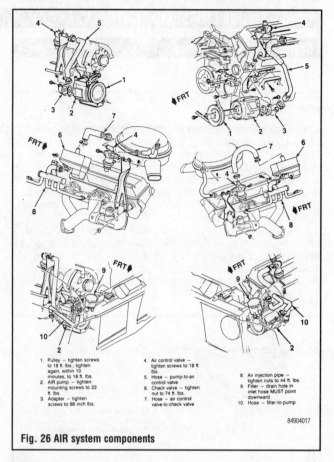

1. Pulley — tighten screws to 18 ft. lbs.; tighten again, within 10 minutes, to 18 ft. lbs.
2. AIR pump — tighten mounting screws to 22 ft. lbs.
3. Adapter — tighten screws to 98 inch lbs.
4. Air control valve — tighten screws to 18 ft. lbs.
5. Hose — pump-to-air control valve
6. Check valve — tighten nut to 74 ft. lbs.
7. Hose — air control valve-to-check valve
8. Air injection pipe — tighten nuts to 44 ft. lbs.
9. Filter — drain hole in inlet hose MUST point downward
10. Hose — filter-to-pump

84904017

Fig. 26 AIR system components

Filter

▶ **See Figure 27**

1. Remove the pump and the diverter valve as an assembly.

❊❊ WARNING

Do not clamp the pump in a vise or use a hammer or pry bar on the pump housing! Damage to the housing may result.

2. To change the filter, break the plastic fan from the hub. It is seldom possible to remove the fan without breaking it. Wear safety glasses.
3. Remove the remaining portion of the fan filter from the pump hub. Be careful that filter fragments do not enter the air intake hole.
To install:
4. Position the new centrifugal fan filter on the pump hub. Place the pump pulley against the fan filter and install the securing screws. Tighten the screws alternately to 95 inch lbs. (10 Nm). The fan filter will be pressed onto the pump hub.
5. Install the pump on the engine and adjust the drive belt.

84904018

Fig. 27 Air pump filter removal

DIESEL ENGINE EMISSIONS CONTROLS

Crankcase Ventilation

OPERATION

▶ **See Figure 28**

A Crankcase Depression Regulator Valve (CDRV) is used to regulate (meter) the flow of crankcase gases back into the engine to be burned. The CDRV is designed to limit vacuum in the crankcase as the gases are drawn from the valve covers through the CDRV and into the intake manifold (air crossover).

Fresh air enters the engine through the combination filter, check valve and oil fill cap. The fresh air mixes with blow-by gases and enters both valve covers. The gases pass through a filter installed on the valve covers and are drawn into connecting tubing.

Intake manifold vacuum acts against a spring loaded diaphragm to control the flow of crankcase gases. Higher intake vacuum levels pull the diaphragm closer to the top of the outlet tube. This reduces the amount of gases being drawn from the crankcase and decreases the vacuum level in the crankcase. As the intake vacuum decreases, the spring pushes the diaphragm away from the top of the outlet tube allowing more gases to flow to the intake manifold.

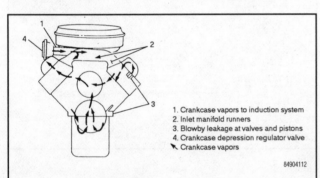

1. Crankcase vapors to induction system
2. Inlet manifold runners
3. Blowby leakage at valves and pistons
4. Crankcase depression regulator valve
↖ Crankcase vapors

84904112

Fig. 28 Crankcase vapor flow

TESTING

Do not attempt to test the valve. If you suspect problems with the system, clean the filter and vent pipes with solvent. Be sure to dry the components before installing them.

REMOVAL & INSTALLATION

▶ **See Figures 29 and 30**

The components of this system can be removed by disconnecting the hoses and pulling the component from its mounting grommet. Be careful not to damage the grommet; replace if necessary.

Exhaust Gas Recirculation System

OPERATION

To lower the formation of nitrogen oxides (NOx) in the exhaust, it is necessary to reduce combustion temperatures. This is done in the diesel, as in the gasoline engine, by introducing exhaust gases into the cylinders through the EGR valve.

The Exhaust Pressure Regulator (EPR) valve and solenoid operate in conjunction with the EGR valve. The EPR valve's job is to increase exhaust back-pressure in order to increase EGR flow. The EPR valve is usually open, and the solenoid is normally closed. When energized by the **B+** wire from the Throttle Position Switch (TPS), the solenoid opens, allowing vacuum to the EPR valve, closing it. This occurs at idle. As the throttle is opened, at a calibrated throttle angle, the TPS de-energizes the EPR solenoid, cutting off vacuum to the EPR valve, closing the valve. Two other solenoids are used for EGR valve control. The EGR solenoid allows vacuum to reach the EGR vent solenoid under certain conditions. The vent solenoid then controls the EGR valve to regulate the flow of gasses into the intake manifold.

TESTING

Exhaust Gas Recirculation (EGR) Valve

▶ **See Figure 31**

Apply vacuum to the EGR valve with a hand vacuum pump. The valve should be fully open at 11 in. Hg (75 kPa) and closed below 6 in. Hg (41 kPa).

EPR Valve

1. Apply 11 in. Hg (75 kPa) vacuum to the EPR valve tube with a hand vacuum pump. Observe the valve actuator lever for movement.
2. If it does not move, spray a penetrating lubricant on the lever and try to free the valve.

✳✳ CAUTION

Make sure the valve is not hot.

3. If the lubricant will not free the valve, it must be replaced.

REMOVAL & INSTALLATION

EGR Valve

NON-TURBO MODELS

▶ **See Figure 32**

1. Remove the air cleaner assembly and air intake tube.
2. Unplug the vacuum hose from the valve.

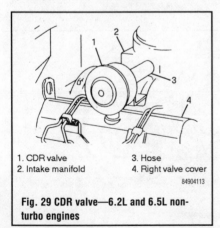

1. CDR valve
2. Intake manifold
3. Hose
4. Right valve cover

84904113

Fig. 29 CDR valve—6.2L and 6.5L non-turbo engines

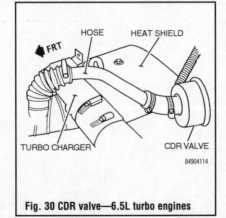

HOSE   HEAT SHIELD
↖ FRT
TURBO CHARGER   CDR VALVE

84904114

Fig. 30 CDR valve—6.5L turbo engines

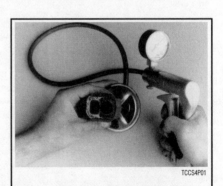

TCCS4P01

Fig. 31 Some EGR valves may be tested using a vacuum pump by watching for diaphragm movement

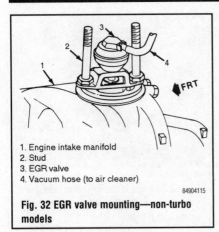

1. Engine intake manifold
2. Stud
3. EGR valve
4. Vacuum hose (to air cleaner)

84904115

Fig. 32 EGR valve mounting—non-turbo models

1	INTAKE MANIFOLD
2	EGR VALVE
3	UPPER INTAKE MANIFOLD

91024G06

Fig. 33 Remove the upper intake manifold cover to access the EGR valve—turbo models

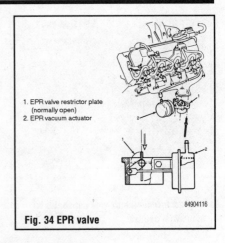

1. EPR valve restrictor plate (normally open)
2. EPR vacuum actuator

84904116

Fig. 34 EPR valve

3. Remove the studs securing the valve to the intake manifold.
4. Installation is the reverse of removal. Tighten the studs until snug.

TURBO MODELS

▶ See Figure 33

1. Remove the upper intake manifold cover.
2. Unplug the vacuum hose from the valve.
3. Remove the bolts securing the valve to the intake manifold.
4. Installation is the reverse of removal. Tighten the bolts to 18 ft. lbs. (25 Nm).

EPR Valve

▶ See Figure 34

1. Raise and safely support the vehicle.
2. Unplug the vacuum hose from the actuator.

3. Disconnect the exhaust pipe from the valve.
4. Remove the studs securing the valve to the exhaust manifold.
5. Installation is the reverse of removal.

EGR/EPR Solenoid Assembly

▶ See Figures 35 and 36

1. Disconnect the negative battery cable.
2. Label and disconnect the vacuum hoses from the assembly.
3. Unplug the solenoid electrical connectors.
4. Remove the retainers securing the solenoid assembly.
5. Installation is the reverse of removal.

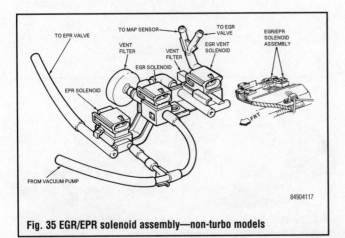

84904117

Fig. 35 EGR/EPR solenoid assembly—non-turbo models

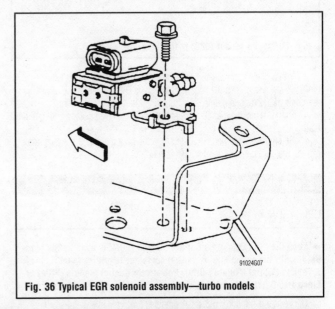

91024G07

Fig. 36 Typical EGR solenoid assembly—turbo models

CARBURETED ELECTRONIC ENGINE CONTROLS

Electrostatic Discharge

▶ See Figure 37

Many of the electrical components in today's vehicles are Electrostatic Discharge (ESD) sensitive and may be damaged if the following precautions are not followed. Even if you think the component you are working on is not ESD sensitive its better to follow the procedures just to be safe.

1. Always touch a good known ground before handling the part. This should be repeated while handling the part and should be done more frequently if you are sliding back and forward across a seat, sitting down or walking a distance.
2. Avoid touching the terminals of the component unless you are instructed to.

91024G18

Fig. 37 Look for the ESD symbol on all electrical components. This will let you know it is ESD sensitive

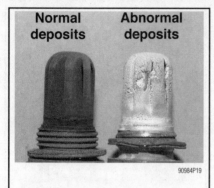

Fig. 38 Inspect the oxygen sensor tip for abnormal deposits

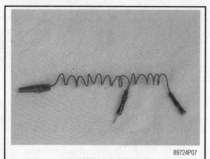

Fig. 39 Jumper wires that will make sensor testing easier and safer (for the sensor) are available from your local auto parts store

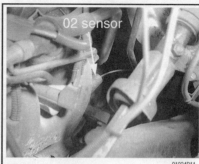

Fig. 40 On older model vehicles, the oxygen sensor is usually located in the exhaust manifold

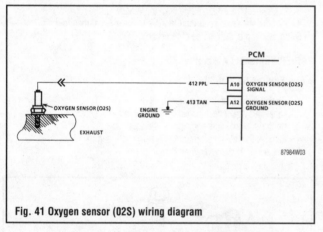

Fig. 41 Oxygen sensor (02S) wiring diagram

3. When diagnosing the component using a Digital Volt Ohm Meter (DVOM), always connect the negative lead of the DVOM first. Never probe the terminals of a component unless instructed to in a testing procedure.

4. Do not remove the a component from its protective package until you are ready to install it.

5. Before removing the component from the package, it is a good idea to ground the package on a good known ground.

Electronic Control Module

OPERATION

➡When the term Electronic Control Module (ECM) is used in this manual it will refer to the engine control computer regardless that it may be a Vehicle Control Module (VCM), Powertrain Control Module (PCM) or Electronic Control Module (ECM).

The ECM is a reliable solid state computer, protected in a metal box. It is used to monitor and control all the functions of the Computer Command Control (CCC) system and is usually located in the engine compartment, though it can also be located in one of several places in the passenger compartment (refer to the component location diagrams in this section). The ECM can perform several on-vehicle functions at the same time and has the ability to diagnose itself as well as other CCC system circuits.

REMOVAL & INSTALLATION

1. Disconnect the negative battery cable.
2. Disengage the connectors from the ECM.
3. Remove the ECM mounting hardware.
4. Remove the ECM from the passenger compartment.
5. Installation is the reverse of removal.

Oxygen Sensor

OPERATION

The oxygen sensor is a spark plug shaped device that is screwed into the exhaust manifold on V6 and V8 engines, and into the exhaust pipe on the 4.8L. It monitors the oxygen content of the exhaust gases and sends a voltage signal to the ECM. The ECM monitors this voltage and, depending on the value of the received signal, issues a command to the mixture control solenoid on the carburetor to adjust for rich or lean conditions.

The proper operation of the oxygen sensor depends upon four basic conditions:

1. Good electrical connections. Since the sensor generates low currents, good clean electrical connections at the sensor are a must.

2. Outside air supply. Air must circulate to the internal portion of the sensor. When servicing the sensor, do not restrict the air passages.

3. Proper operating temperatures. The ECM will not recognize the sensor's signals until the sensor reaches approximately 600F (316C).

4. Non-leaded fuel. The use of leaded gasoline will damage the sensor very quickly.

TESTING

▶ See Figures 38, 39, 40 and 41

1. Perform a visual inspection on the sensor as follows:
   a. Remove the sensor from the exhaust.
   b. If the sensor tip has a black/sooty deposit, this may indicate a rich fuel mixture.
   c. If the sensor tip has a white gritty deposit, this may indicate an internal anti-freeze leak.
   d. If the sensor tip has a brown deposit, this could indicate oil consumption.

➡All these contaminates can destroy the sensor, if the problem is not repaired the new sensor will also be damaged.

2. Reinstall the sensor.

3. Start the engine and bring it to normal operating temperature, then run the engine above 1200 rpm for two minutes.

4. Backprobe with a high impedance averaging voltmeter (set to the DC voltage scale) between the oxygen sensor (02S) and battery ground.

5. Verify that the 02S voltage fluctuates rapidly between 0.40–0.60 volts.

6. If the 02S voltage is stabilized at the middle of the specified range (approximately 0.45–0.55 volts) or if the 02S voltage fluctuates very slowly between the specified range (02S signal crosses 0.5 volts less than 5 times in ten seconds), the 02S may be faulty.

7. If the 02S voltage stabilizes at either end of the specified range, the ECM is probably not able to compensate for a mechanical problem such as a vacuum leak or a faulty pressure regulator. These types of mechanical problems will cause the 02S to sense a constant lean or constant rich mixture. The mechanical problem will first have to be repaired and then the 02S test repeated.

8. Pull a vacuum hose located after the throttle plate. Voltage should drop to approximately 0.12 volts (while still fluctuating rapidly). This tests the ability of the 02S to detect a lean mixture condition. Reattach the vacuum hose.

9. Richen the mixture using a propane enrichment tool. Voltage should rise to approximately 0.90 volts (while still fluctuating rapidly). This tests the ability of the 02S to detect a rich mixture condition.

10. If the 02S voltage is above or below the specified range, the 02S and/or the 02S wiring may be faulty. Check the wiring for any breaks, repair as necessary and repeat the test.

REMOVAL & INSTALLATION

▶ See Figure 42

✳✳ WARNING

The sensor uses a permanently attached pigtail and connector. This pigtail should not be removed from the sensor. Damage or removal of the pigtail or connector could affect the proper operation of the sensor. Keep the electrical connector and louvered end of the sensor clean and free of grease. NEVER use cleaning solvents of any type on the sensor!

➡ **The oxygen sensor may be difficult to remove when the temperature of the engine is below 120F (49C). Excessive force may damage the threads in the exhaust manifold or exhaust pipe.**

1. Unplug the electrical connector and any attaching hardware.
2. Remove the sensor using an appropriate sized wrench or special socket.
To install:
3. Coat the threads of the sensor with a GM anti-seize compound, part number 5613695, or its equivalent, before installation. New sensors are usually precoated with this compound.

➡ **The GM anti-seize compound is NOT a conventional anti-seize paste. The use of a regular paste may electrically insulate the sensor, render-**

ing it useless. The threads MUST be coated with the proper electrically conductive anti-seize compound.

4. Install the sensor and tighten to 30 ft. lbs. (40 Nm). Use care in making sure the silicone boot is in the correct position to avoid melting it during operation.
5. Engage the electrical connector and attaching hardware if used.

Coolant Temperature Sensor/Engine Coolant Temperature Sensor

OPERATION

▶ See Figure 43

The Coolant Temperature Sensor (CTS)/Engine Coolant Temperature Sensor (ECT) is a thermistor (a resistor which changes value based on temperature). The sensor is mounted in the coolant stream and the ECM supplies a 5 volt signal to the sensor through a resistor in the ECM and measures the voltage. The voltage will be high when the engine is cold, and low when the engine is hot. By measuring the voltage, the ECM knows the engine coolant temperature.

TESTING

▶ See Figures 44, 45, 46, 47 and 48

1. Remove the ECT sensor from the vehicle.
2. Immerse the tip of the sensor in container of water.
3. Connect a digital ohmmeter to the two terminals of the sensor.
4. Using a calibrated thermometer, compare the resistance of the sensor to the temperature of the water. Refer to the engine coolant sensor temperature vs. resistance illustration.
5. Repeat the test at two other temperature points, heating or cooling the water as necessary.

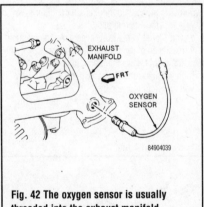

Fig. 42 The oxygen sensor is usually threaded into the exhaust manifold

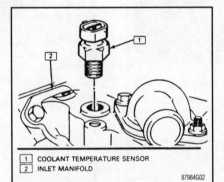

1 COOLANT TEMPERATURE SENSOR
2 INLET MANIFOLD

Fig. 43 Coolant temperature sensor location—carbureted engines

Fig. 44 Submerge the end of the coolant temperature sensor in cold or hot water and check the resistance

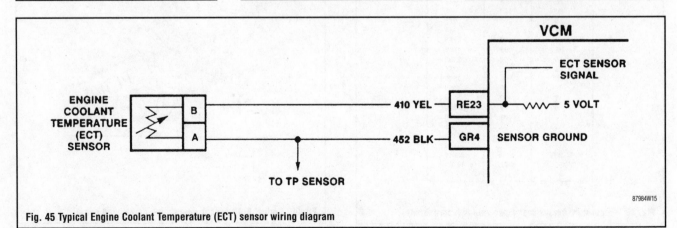

Fig. 45 Typical Engine Coolant Temperature (ECT) sensor wiring diagram

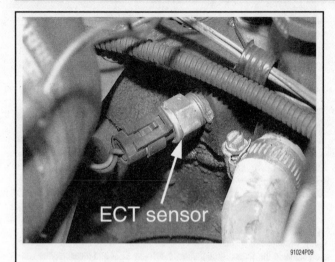

Fig. 46 The ECT sensor is usually located near the thermostat housing

Fig. 47 Using a thermometer, a DVOM and some jumper leads, check the resistance of the ECT sensor and compare your readings to those in the chart

6. If the sensor does not met specification shown in the temperature versus resistance chart, it must be replaced.

7. The sensor may also be checked in the vehicle. Unplug the sensor and attach a digital ohmmeter to the two terminals of the sensor.

8. Using a calibrated thermometer, compare the resistance of the sensor to the ambient air temperature.

9. Repeat the test at two other temperature points, heating or cooling the water as necessary.

10. If the sensor does not met specification shown in the temperature versus resistance chart, it must be replaced.

REMOVAL & INSTALLATION

1. Disconnect the negative battery cable.
2. Drain the cooling system below the level of the sensor and disengage the sensor electrical connection.
3. Remove the coolant sensor.
To install:
4. Install the sensor and engage the electrical connector.
5. Refill the cooling system and connect the negative battery cable.

Manifold Absolute Pressure Sensor

OPERATION

▶ **See Figures 49, 50 and 51**

The Manifold Absolute Pressure (MAP) sensor measures the changes in intake manifold pressure, which result from the engine load and speed changes, and converts this to a voltage output.

A closed throttle on engine coastdown will produce a low MAP output, while a wide-open throttle will produce a high output. This high output is produced because the pressure inside the manifold is the same as outside the manifold, so 100 percent of the outside air pressure is measured.

The MAP sensor reading is the opposite of what you would measure on a vacuum gauge. When manifold pressure is high, vacuum is low. The MAP sensor is also used to measure barometric pressure under certain conditions, which allows the ECM to automatically adjust for different altitudes.

The ECM sends a 5 volt reference signal to the MAP sensor. As the manifold pressure changes, the electrical resistance of the sensor also changes. By monitoring the sensor output voltage, the ECM knows the manifold pressure. A higher pressure, low vacuum (high voltage) requires more fuel, while a lower pressure, higher vacuum (low voltage) requires less fuel.

The ECM uses the MAP sensor to control fuel delivery and ignition timing.

TEMPERATURE VS. RESISTANCE VALUES (APPROXIMATE)		
°C	°F	OHMS
100	212	177
90	194	241
80	176	332
70	158	467
60	140	667
50	122	973
45	113	1188
40	104	1459
35	95	1802
30	86	2238
25	77	2796
20	68	3520
15	59	4450
10	50	5670
5	41	7280
0	32	9420
-5	23	12300
-10	14	16180
-15	5	21450
-20	-4	28680
-30	-22	52700
-40	-40	100700

Fig. 48 Temperature versus resistance values (approximate)

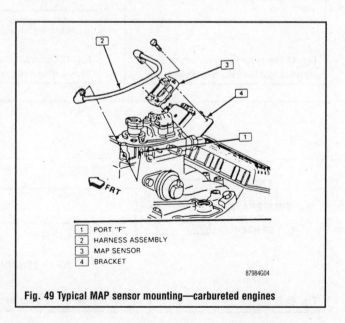

1	PORT "F"
2	HARNESS ASSEMBLY
3	MAP SENSOR
4	BRACKET

Fig. 49 Typical MAP sensor mounting—carbureted engines

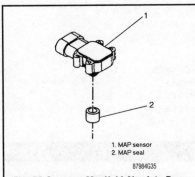

Fig. 50 Common Manifold Absolute Pressure (MAP) sensor used on 4.3L, 5.0L and 5.7L fuel injected engines

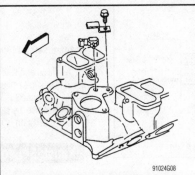

Fig. 51 Common Manifold Absolute Pressure (MAP) sensor used on 7.4L fuel injected engines

Fig. 52 Location of the MAP sensor—TBI system shown

Fig. 53 Probe the terminals of the MAP sensor to check for proper reference voltage

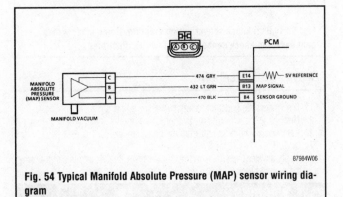

Fig. 54 Typical Manifold Absolute Pressure (MAP) sensor wiring diagram

TESTING

▶ **See Figures 52, 53 and 54**

1. Backprobe with a high impedance voltmeter at MAP sensor terminals A and C.
2. With the key **ON** and engine off, the voltmeter reading should be approximately 5.0 volts.
3. If the voltage is not as specified, either the wiring to the MAP sensor or the ECM may be faulty. Correct any wiring or ECM faults before continuing test.
4. Backprobe with the high impedance voltmeter at MAP sensor terminals B and A.

5. Verify that the sensor voltage is approximately 0.5 volts with the engine not running (at sea level).
6. Record MAP sensor voltage with the key **ON** and engine off.
7. Start the vehicle.
8. Verify that the sensor voltage is greater than 1.5 volts (above the recorded reading) at idle.
9. Verify that the sensor voltage increases to approximately 4.5. volts (above the recorded reading) at Wide Open Throttle (WOT).
10. If the sensor voltage is as specified, the sensor is functioning properly.
11. If the sensor voltage is not as specified, check the sensor and the sensor vacuum source for a leak or a restriction. If no leaks or restrictions are found, the sensor may be defective and should be replaced.

REMOVAL & INSTALLATION

1. Disconnect the negative battery cable.
2. Tag and disconnect the vacuum harness assembly.
3. Disengage the electrical connector.
4. Release the locktabs, unfasten the bolts and remove the sensor.
5. Installation is the reverse of removal.

Throttle Position Sensor

OPERATION

The Throttle Position Sensor (TPS) is located inside the carburetor. It is a potentiometer with one wire connected to 5 volts from the ECM and the other to ground. A third wire is connected to the ECM to measure the voltage from the TPS.

As the accelerator pedal is moved, the output of the TPS also changes. At a closed throttle position, the output of the TPS is low (approximately 0.5 volts). As the throttle valve opens, the output increases so that, at wide-open throttle, the output voltage should be approximately 4.5 volts.

By monitoring the output voltage from the TPS, the ECM can determine fuel delivery based on throttle valve angle (driver demand).

TESTING

▶ **See Figure 55**

1. Backprobe with a high impedance voltmeter at TPS terminals A and B.
2. With the key **ON** and engine off, the voltmeter reading should be approximately 5.0 volts.
3. If the voltage is not as specified, either the wiring to the TPS or the ECM may be faulty. Correct any wiring or ECM faults before continuing test.
4. Backprobe with a high impedance voltmeter at terminals C and B.
5. With the key **ON** and engine off and the throttle closed, the TPS voltage should be approximately 0.5–1.2 volts.
6. Verify that the TPS voltage increases or decreases smoothly as the throttle is opened or closed. Make sure to open and close the throttle very slowly in order to detect any abnormalities in the TPS voltage reading.
7. If the sensor voltage is not as specified, replace the sensor.

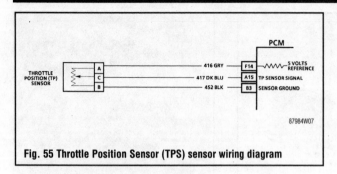

Fig. 55 Throttle Position Sensor (TPS) sensor wiring diagram

REMOVAL & INSTALLATION

The throttle position sensor is located in the carburetor. Please refer to Section 5 for the carburetor disassembly procedures to remove the TPS.

Vehicle Speed Sensor

OPERATION

The Vehicle Speed Sensor (VSS) is sometimes located behind the speedometer or more commonly on the transmission. It sends a pulsing voltage signal to the ECM, which the ECM converts to vehicle speed. This sensor mainly controls the operation of the Torque Converter Clutch (TCC) system, shift light and cruise control.

TESTING

▶ **See Figure 56**

1. Backprobe the VSS terminals with a high impedance voltmeter (set at the AC voltage scale).
2. Safely raise and support the entire vehicle using jackstands. Make absolutely sure the vehicle is secure.
3. Start the vehicle and place it in gear.
4. Verify that the VSS voltage increases as the speed increases.
5. If the VSS voltage is not as specified the VSS may be faulty.

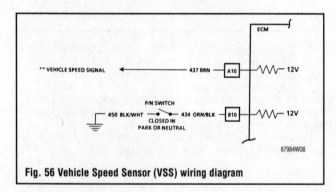

Fig. 56 Vehicle Speed Sensor (VSS) wiring diagram

REMOVAL & INSTALLATION

Speedometer Mounted

1. Disconnect the negative battery cable.
2. Remove the instrument cluster.

3. Remove the screws securing the sensor assembly.
4. Installation is the reverse of removal.

Transmission Mounted

1. Raise and safely support the vehicle.
2. Unplug the electrical connector.
3. Disconnect the speedometer cable from the sensor.
4. Remove the sensor from the transmission.
5. Installation is the reverse of removal.

Knock Sensor

OPERATION

Located in the engine block, the Knock Sensor (KS) retards ignition timing during a spark knock condition to allow the ECM to maintain maximum timing advance under most conditions.

TESTING

▶ **See Figure 57**

1. Connect a timing light to the vehicle and start the engine.
2. Check that the timing is correct before testing knock sensor operation.
3. If timing is correct, tap on the front of the engine block with a metal object while observing the timing to see if the timing retards.
4. If the timing does not retard, the knock sensor may be defective.

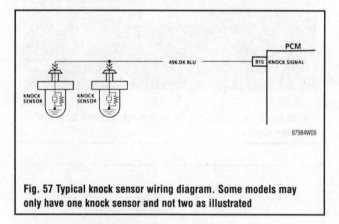

Fig. 57 Typical knock sensor wiring diagram. Some models may only have one knock sensor and not two as illustrated

REMOVAL & INSTALLATION

1. Disconnect the negative battery cable.
2. Disengage the wiring harness connector from the knock sensor.
3. Remove the knock sensor from the engine block.
To install:
4. Apply a water base caulk to the knock sensor threads and install the sensor in the engine block.

❊❊ WARNING

Do not use silicone tape to coat the knock sensor threads, as this will insulate the sensor from the engine block.

5. Engage the wiring harness connector.
6. Connect the negative battery cable.

FUEL INJECTED ELECTRONIC ENGINE CONTROLS

EMISSION AND ELECTRONIC ENGINE CONTROL COMPONENT LOCATIONS—TYPICAL TBI SYSTEM

1. Throttle Position (TP) sensor
2. Manifold Absolute Pressure (MAP) sensor
3. Idle Air Control (IAC) valve
4. Engine Coolant Temperature (ECT) sensor
5. Fuel injector
6. Oxygen sensor (at end of exhaust manifold)
7. EGR valve

EMISSION AND ELECTRONIC ENGINE CONTROL COMPONENT LOCATIONS—TYPICAL CSFI SYSTEM

1. Mass Air Flow (MAF) sensor
2. Throttle Position (TP) sensor
3. Engine Coolant Temperature (ECT) sensor
4. Linear EGR valve

5. Intake Air Temperature (IAT) sensor
6. PCV valve
7. Idle Air Control (IAC) valve
8. Manifold Absolute Pressure (MAP) sensor (under resonance cover)

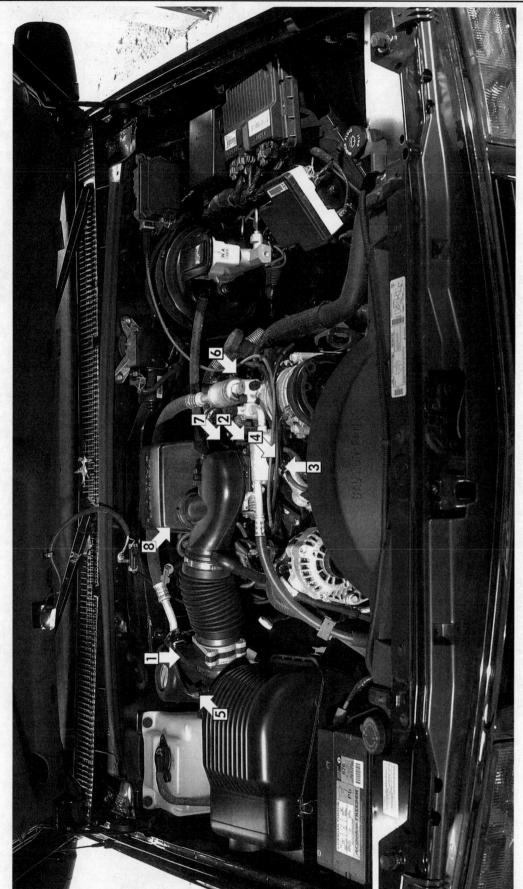

91021P02

Electrostatic Discharge

♦ **See Figure 58**

Many of the electrical components in today's vehicles are Electrostatic Discharge (ESD) sensitive and may be damaged if the following precautions are not followed. Even if you think the component you are working on is not ESD sensitive its better to follow the procedures just to be safe.

1. Always touch a good known ground before handling the part. This should be repeated while handling the part and should be done more frequently if you are sliding back and forward across a seat, sitting down or walking a distance.

2. Avoid touching the terminals of the component unless you are instructed to.

3. When diagnosing the component using a Digital Volt Ohm Meter (DVOM), always connect the negative lead of the DVOM first.

4. Do not remove the a component from its protective package until you are ready to install it.

5. Before removing the component from the package, it is a good idea to ground the package on a good known ground.

91024G18

Fig. 58 Look for the ESD symbol on all electrical components. This will let you know it is ESD sensitive

Electronic Control Module

OPERATION

➡ **When the term Electronic Control Module (ECM) is used in this manual it will refer to the engine control computer, regardless of whether it be a Vehicle Control Module (VCM), Powertrain Control Module (PCM) or Electronic Control Module (ECM).**

The Electronic Control Module (ECM) is required to maintain the exhaust emissions at acceptable levels. The module is a small, solid state computer which receives signals from many sources and sensors; it uses these data to make judgments about operating conditions and then control output signals to the fuel and emission systems to match the current requirements.

Engines coupled to electronically controlled transmissions employ a Powertrain Control Module (PCM) or Vehicle Control Module (VCM) to oversee both engine and transmission operation. The integrated functions of engine and transmission control allow accurate gear selection and improved fuel economy.

In the event of an ECM failure, the system will default to a pre-programmed set of values. These are compromise values which allow the engine to operate, although at a reduced efficiency. This is variously known as the default, limp-in or back-up mode. Driveability is almost always affected when the ECM enters this mode.

REMOVAL & INSTALLATION

1. Disconnect the negative battery cable.
2. Disengage the connectors from the ECM.
3. Remove the spring retainer off and over the rail of the ECM.
4. Slide the ECM out of the bracket at an angle.
5. Remove the ECM.

To install:
6. Install the ECM into the bracket.
7. Install the spring retainer and engage the electrical connectors.
8. Connect the negative battery cable.

Oxygen Sensor

OPERATION

♦ **See Figure 59**

There are two types of oxygen sensor's used in these vehicles. They are the single wire oxygen sensor (02S) and the heated oxygen sensor (H02S). The oxygen sensor is a spark plug shaped device that is screwed into the exhaust manifold. It monitors the oxygen content of the exhaust gases and sends a voltage signal to the Electronic Control Module (ECM). The ECM monitors this voltage and, depending on the value of the received signal, issues a command to the mixture control solenoid on the carburetor to adjust for rich or lean conditions.

The heated oxygen sensor has a heating element incorporated into the sensor to aid in the warm up to the proper operating temperature and to maintain that temperature.

The proper operation of the oxygen sensor depends upon four basic conditions:

1. Good electrical connections. Since the sensor generates low currents, good clean electrical connections at the sensor are a must.

2. Outside air supply. Air must circulate to the internal portion of the sensor. When servicing the sensor, do not restrict the air passages.

3. Proper operating temperatures. The ECM will not recognize the sensor's signals until the sensor reaches approximately 600°F (316°C).

4. Non-leaded fuel. The use of leaded gasoline will damage the sensor very quickly.

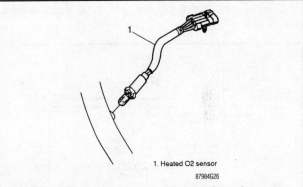

1. Heated O2 sensor

87984G26

Fig. 59 The heated oxygen sensor usually has a three wire connector

TESTING

Single Wire Sensor

Refer to the oxygen sensor procedures in the carbureted electronic engine control section of this manual for testing of the signal wire sensor.

Heated Oxygen Sensor

♦ **See Figures 38 and 60**

1. Perform a visual inspection on the sensor as follows:
    a. Remove the sensor from the exhaust.
    b. If the sensor tip has a black/sooty deposit, this may indicate a rich fuel mixture.
    c. If the sensor tip has a white gritty deposit, this may indicate an internal anti-freeze leak.
    d. If the sensor tip has a brown deposit, this could indicate oil consumption.

➡️**All these contaminates can destroy the sensor, if the problem is not repaired the new sensor will also be damaged.**

2. Reinstall the sensor.

3. Start the engine and bring it to normal operating temperature, then run the engine above 1200 rpm for two minutes.

4. Turn the ignition **OFF** disengage the H02S harness connector.

5. Connect a test light between harness terminals A and B. With the ignition switch **ON** and the engine off, verify that the test light is lit. If the test light is not lit, either the supply voltage to the H02S heater or the ground circuit of the H02S heater is faulty. Check the H02S wiring and the fuse.

6. Next, connect a high impedance ohmmeter between the H02S terminals B and A and verify that the resistance is 3.5–14.0 ohms.

7. If the H02S heater resistance is not as specified, the H02S may be faulty.

8. Start the engine and bring it to normal operating temperature, then run the engine above 1200 rpm for two minutes.

9. Backprobe with a high impedance averaging voltmeter (set to the DC voltage scale) between the oxygen sensor (02S) and battery ground.

10. Verify that the 02S voltage fluctuates rapidly between 0.40–0.60 volts.

11. If the 02S voltage is stabilized at the middle of the specified range (approximately 0.45–0.55 volts) or if the 02S voltage fluctuates very slowly between the specified range (02S signal crosses 0.5 volts less than 5 times in ten seconds), the 02S may be faulty.

12. If the 02S voltage stabilizes at either end of the specified range, the ECM is probably not able to compensate for a mechanical problem such as a vacuum leak or a faulty fuel pressure regulator. These types of mechanical problems will cause the 02S to sense a constant lean or constant rich mixture. The mechanical problem will first have to be repaired and then the 02S test repeated.

13. Pull a vacuum hose located after the throttle plate. Voltage should drop to approximately 0.12 volts (while still fluctuating rapidly). This tests the ability of the 02S to detect a lean mixture condition. Reattach the vacuum hose.

14. Richen the mixture using a propane enrichment tool. Voltage should rise to approximately 0.90 volts (while still fluctuating rapidly). This tests the ability of the 02S to detect a rich mixture condition.

15. If the 02S voltage is above or below the specified range, the 02S and/or the 02S wiring may be faulty. Check the wiring for any breaks, repair as necessary and repeat the test.

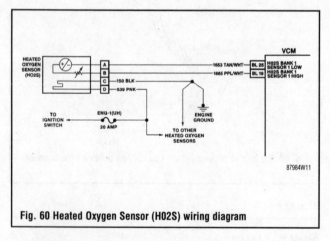

Fig. 60 Heated Oxygen Sensor (H02S) wiring diagram

REMOVAL & INSTALLATION

Refer to the oxygen sensor procedures in the carbureted electronic engine control section of this manual for the removal and installation of the oxygen sensor.

Crankshaft Position Sensor

OPERATION

♦ **See Figure 61**

The Crankshaft Position (CKP) Sensor provides a signal through the ignition module which the ECM uses as a reference to calculate rpm and crankshaft position.

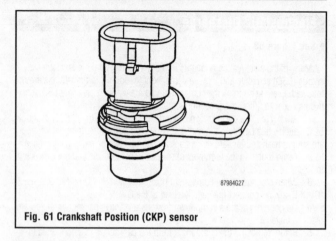

Fig. 61 Crankshaft Position (CKP) sensor

TESTING

♦ **See Figure 62**

1. Disconnect the CKP sensor harness. Connect an LED test light between battery ground and CKP harness terminal A.

2. With the ignition **ON** and the engine off, verify that the test light illuminates.

3. If not as specified, repair or replace the fuse and/or wiring.

4. Carefully connect the test light between CKP harness terminal A and B. Verify that the test light illuminates.

5. If not as specified, repair the CKP harness ground circuit (terminal B).

6. Turn the ignition **OFF** and disconnect the test light.

7. Next, connect suitable jumper wires between the CKP sensor and CKP sensor harness. Connect a duty cycle meter to the jumper wire corresponding to CKP terminal C and battery ground.

8. Crank the engine and verify that the duty cycle signal is between 40–60%.

9. If it is not as specified, the CKP sensor may be faulty.

10. Next, connect a AC volt meter to the jumper wire corresponding to CKP terminal C and battery ground.

11. Crank the engine and verify that the AC voltage signal is at least 10.0 volts.

12. If not as specified the CKP sensor may be faulty.

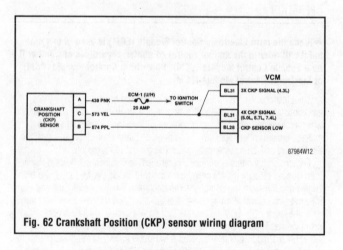

Fig. 62 Crankshaft Position (CKP) sensor wiring diagram

REMOVAL & INSTALLATION

1. Disconnect the negative battery cable.

2. Detach the sensor harness connector at the sensor.

3. Unfasten the retaining bolt, then remove the sensor from the front cover. Inspect the sensor O-ring for wear, cracks or leakage and replace if necessary.

To install:

4. Lubricate the O-ring with clean engine oil, then place on the sensor. Install the sensor into the front cover.

5. Install the sensor and tighten the retaining bolt.
6. Attach the sensor harness connector.
7. Connect the negative battery cable.

Camshaft Position Sensor

OPERATION

▶ **See Figure 63**

The ECM uses the camshaft signal to determine the position of the No. 1 cylinder piston during its power stroke. The signal is used by the ECM to calculate fuel injection mode of operation.

If the cam signal is lost while the engine is running, the fuel injection system will shift to a calculated fuel injected mode based on the last fuel injection pulse, and the engine will continue to run.

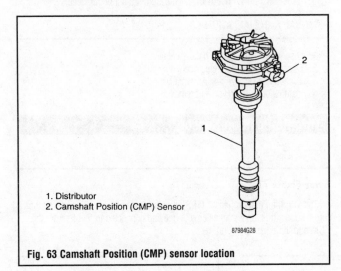

1. Distributor
2. Camshaft Position (CMP) Sensor

87984G28

Fig. 63 Camshaft Position (CMP) sensor location

TESTING

▶ **See Figure 64**

1. Disconnect the CMP sensor wiring harness and connect an LED test light between CMP harness terminal C and battery ground.
2. With the ignition **ON** and the engine off, verify that the test light illuminates.
3. If not as specified, repair or replace the fuse and/or wiring.
4. Carefully connect the test light between CMP harness terminal A and C and verify that the test light illuminates.
5. If not as specified, repair the CMP harness ground circuit (terminal A).
6. Turn the ignition **OFF** and disconnect the test light.
7. Next, connect suitable jumper wires between the CMP sensor and CMP sensor harness. Connect a DC volt meter to the jumper wire corresponding to CMP terminal B and battery ground.
8. Start the engine and verify that the voltage signal is 5–7 volts.
9. If it is not as specified, the CMP sensor may be faulty.

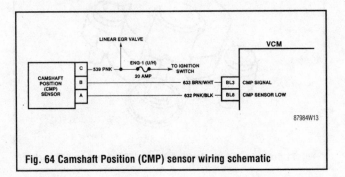

87984W13

Fig. 64 Camshaft Position (CMP) sensor wiring schematic

REMOVAL & INSTALLATION

1. Disconnect the negative battery cable.
2. Detach the sensor harness connector at the sensor.
3. Unfasten the retaining bolt, then remove the sensor from the camshaft housing. Inspect the sensor O-ring for wear, cracks or leakage and replace if necessary.
   To install:
4. Lubricate the O-ring with clean engine oil, then place on the sensor. Install the sensor into the camshaft housing.
5. Install the CMP sensor retaining bolt, then tighten to 88 inch lbs. (10 Nm).
6. Attach the sensor harness connector.
7. Connect the negative battery cable.

Mass Air Flow Sensor

OPERATION

▶ **See Figure 65**

The Mass Air Flow (MAF) Sensor measures the amount of air entering the engine during a given time. The ECM uses the mass airflow information for fuel delivery calculations. A large quantity of air entering the engine indicates an acceleration or high load situation, while a small quantity of air indicates deceleration or idle.

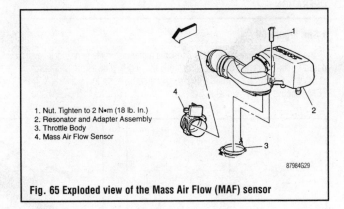

1. Nut. Tighten to 2 N•m (18 lb. In.)
2. Resonator and Adapter Assembly
3. Throttle Body
4. Mass Air Flow Sensor

87984G29

Fig. 65 Exploded view of the Mass Air Flow (MAF) sensor

TESTING

▶ **See Figure 66**

1. Backprobe with a high impedance voltmeter between MAF sensor terminals C and B.
2. With the ignition **ON** engine off, verify that battery voltage is present.
3. If the voltage is not as specified, either the wiring to the MAF sensor, fuse or the ECM may be faulty. Correct any wiring or ECM faults before continuing test.
4. Disconnect the voltmeter and backprobe with a frequency meter between MAF sensor terminals A and B.

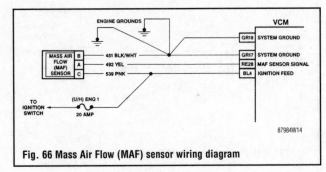

87984W14

Fig. 66 Mass Air Flow (MAF) sensor wiring diagram

5. Start the engine and wait until it reaches normal idle speed and verify that the MAF sensor output is approximately 2000 Hz.

6. Slowly raise engine speed up to maximum recommended rpm and verify that the MAF sensor output rises smoothly to approximately 8000 Hz.

7. If MAF sensor output is not as specified the sensor may be faulty.

REMOVAL & INSTALLATION

1. Disconnect the negative battery cable.
2. Unplug the electrical connector.
3. Remove the air intake hoses from the sensor, then remove its attaching bolts.
4. Installation is the reverse of removal.

Engine Coolant Temperature Sensor

LOCATION

▶ **See Figures 67 and 68**

Refer to the Engine Coolant Temperature (ECT) sensor procedures in the carbureted electronic engine control portion of this section for operation, testing and the removal and installation of the ECT.

Intake Air Temperature Sensor

OPERATION

▶ **See Figure 69**

the Intake Air Temperature (IAT) Sensor is a thermistor which changes value based on the temperature of the air entering the engine. Low temperature produces a high resistance, while a high temperature causes a low resistance. The ECM supplies a 5 volt signal to the sensor through a resistor in the ECM and measures the voltage. The voltage will be high when the incoming air is cold, and low when the air is hot. By measuring the voltage, the ECM calculates the incoming air temperature.

The IAT sensor signal is used to adjust spark timing according to incoming air density.

TESTING

▶ **See Figures 48 and 70**

1. Remove the Intake Air Temperature (IAT) sensor.
2. Connect a digital ohmmeter to the two terminals of the sensor.
3. Using a calibrated thermometer, compare the resistance of the sensor to the temperature of the ambient air. Refer to the temperature vs. resistance illustration.
4. Repeat the test at two other temperature points, heating or cooling the air as necessary with a hair dryer or other suitable tool.
5. If the sensor does not meet specification, it must be replaced.

REMOVAL & INSTALLATION

1. Disconnect the negative battery cable.
2. Disengage the sensor electrical connection.
3. Loosen and remove the IAT sensor.
4. Installation is the reverse of removal.

Throttle Position Sensor

OPERATION

▶ **See Figure 71**

The Throttle Position Sensor (TPS) is connected to the throttle shaft on the throttle body. It is a potentiometer with one end connected to 5 volts from the ECM and the other to ground.

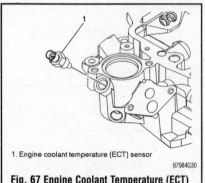

1. Engine coolant temperature (ECT) sensor

87984G30

Fig. 67 Engine Coolant Temperature (ECT) sensor location—4.3L, 5.0L and 5.7L fuel injected engines

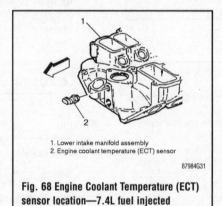

1. Lower intake manifold assembly
2. Engine coolant temperature (ECT) sensor

87984G31

Fig. 68 Engine Coolant Temperature (ECT) sensor location—7.4L fuel injected engines

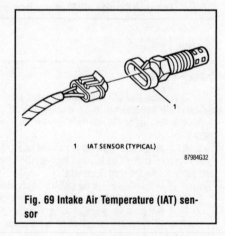

1   IAT SENSOR (TYPICAL)

87984G32

Fig. 69 Intake Air Temperature (IAT) sensor

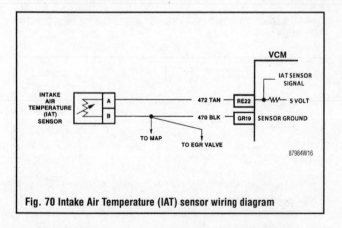

87984W16

Fig. 70 Intake Air Temperature (IAT) sensor wiring diagram

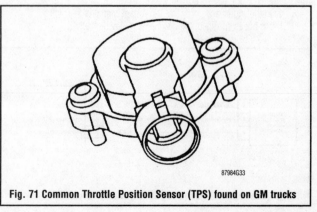

87984G33

Fig. 71 Common Throttle Position Sensor (TPS) found on GM trucks

A third wire is connected to the ECM to measure the voltage from the TPS. As the throttle valve angle is changed (accelerator pedal moved), the output of the TPS also changes. At a closed throttle position, the output of the TPS is low (approximately .5 volts). As the throttle valve opens, the output increases so that, at wide-open throttle, the output voltage should be approximately 4.5 volts.

By monitoring the output voltage from the TPS, the ECM can determine fuel delivery based on throttle valve angle (driver demand).

TESTING

▶ **See Figures 72, 73 and 74**

1. Backprobe with a high impedance voltmeter at TPS terminals A and B.
2. With the key **ON** and engine off, the voltmeter reading should be approximately 5.0 volts.
3. If the voltage is not as specified, either the wiring to the TPS or the ECM may be faulty. Correct any wiring or ECM faults before continuing test.
4. Backprobe with a high impedance voltmeter at terminals C and B.
5. With the key **ON** and engine off and the throttle closed, the TPS voltage should be approximately 0.5–1.2 volts.
6. Verify that the TPS voltage increases or decreases smoothly as the throttle is opened or closed. Make sure to open and close the throttle very slowly in order to detect any abnormalities in the TPS voltage reading.
7. If the sensor voltage is not as specified, replace the sensor.

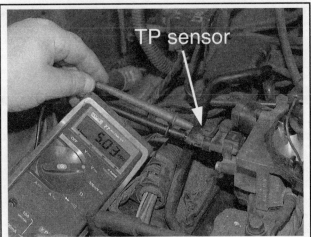

Fig. 72 Using a DVOM, backprobe terminals A and B of the TPS sensor to check for proper reference voltage

Fig. 73 Using the DVOM, backprobe terminals C and B of the TPS sensor, open and close the throttle and make sure the voltage changes smoothly

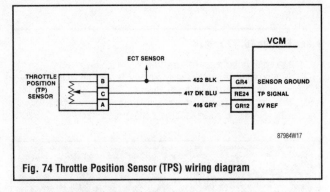

Fig. 74 Throttle Position Sensor (TPS) wiring diagram

REMOVAL & INSTALLATION

1. Disconnect the negative battery cable and remove the air cleaner and gasket.
2. Disengage the electrical connector.
3. Unfasten the two TPS attaching screw assemblies.
4. Remove the TPS from the throttle body assembly.
5. Remove the TPS seal.
To install:
6. Install the TPS seal over the throttle shaft.
7. With the throttle valve closed, install the TPS on the throttle shaft. Rotate it counterclockwise, to align the mounting holes.
8. Install the two TPS attaching screw assemblies.
9. Engage the electrical connector.
10. Install the air cleaner and gasket.
11. Connect the negative battery cable.

Idle Air Control Valve

OPERATION

▶ **See Figure 75**

The engine idle speed is controlled by the ECM through the Idle Air Control (IAC) valve mounted on the throttle body. The ECM sends voltage pulses to the IAC motor causing the IAC motor shaft and pintle to move in or out a given distance (number of steps) for each pulse, (called counts).

This movement controls air flow around the throttle plate, which in turn, controls engine idle speed, either cold or hot. IAC valve pintle position counts can be seen using a scan tool. Zero counts corresponds to a fully closed passage, while 140 or more counts (depending on the application) corresponds to full flow.

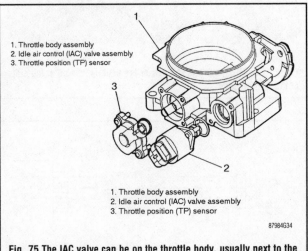

1. Throttle body assembly
2. Idle air control (IAC) valve assembly
3. Throttle position (TP) sensor

Fig. 75 The IAC valve can be on the throttle body, usually next to the throttle position sensor

TESTING

♦ See Figures 76, 77 and 78

1. Disengage the IAC electrical connector.
2. Using an ohmmeter, measure the resistance between IAC terminals A and B. Next measure the resistance between terminals C and D.
3. Verify that the resistance between both sets of IAC terminals is 20–80 ohms. If the resistance is not as specified, the IAC may be faulty.

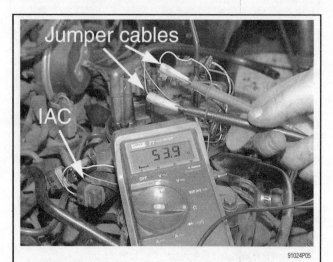

Fig. 76 Using an ohmmeter, backprobe terminals of the TPS sensor to check for the resistance reading

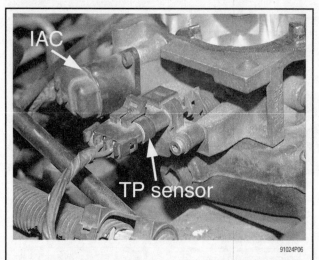

Fig. 77 The TP sensor and IAC sensor are usually located at the side of the throttle body

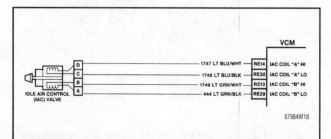

Fig. 78 Idle Air Control (IAC) valve wiring and terminal identification

4. Measure the resistance between IAC terminals B and C. Next measure the resistance between terminals A and D.
5. Verify that the resistance between both sets of IAC terminals is infinite. If the resistance is not infinite, the IAC may be faulty.
6. Also, with a small mirror, inspect IAC air inlet passage and pintle for debris. Clean as necessary, as this can cause IAC malfunction.

REMOVAL & INSTALLATION

1. Disconnect the negative battery cable.
2. Disengage the electrical connection.
3. Remove the IAC valve. On thread-mounted units, use 1¼ in. (32mm) wrench and on flange-mounted units, remove the screw assemblies.
4. Remove the IAC valve gasket or O-ring and discard it.
   To install:
5. Clean the old gasket material from the surface of the throttle body assembly on the thread mounted valve. On the flange-mounted valve clean the surface to ensure proper O-ring sealing
6. Install the valve with a new gasket or O-ring. Tighten the thread mounted assembly 13 ft. lbs. (18 Nm) and tighten the flange mounted attaching screws to 28 inch. lbs. (3 Nm).
7. Engage the electrical connector to the IAC valve.
8. Connect the negative battery cable.

Manifold Absolute Pressure Sensor

Refer to the Manifold Absolute Pressure (MAP) sensor procedures in the carbureted electronic engine control section of this manual for operation, testing and the removal and installation of the MAP sensor.

Vehicle Speed Sensor

OPERATION

The vehicle speed sensor is made up of a coil mounted on the transmission and a tooth rotor mounted to the output shaft of the transmission. As each tooth nears the coil, the coil produces an AC voltage pulse. As the vehicle speed increases the number of voltage pulses per second increases.

TESTING

♦ See Figure 79

1. To test the VSS, backprobe the VSS terminals with a high impedance voltmeter (set at the AC voltage scale).
2. Safely raise and support the entire vehicle using jackstands. Make absolutely sure the vehicle is stable.
3. Start the vehicle and place it in gear.

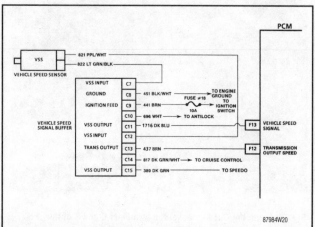

Fig. 79 Typical Vehicle Speed Sensor (VSS) and vehicle speed signal buffer wiring diagram

4. Verify that the VSS voltage increases as the drive shaft speed increases.
5. If the VSS voltage is not as specified the VSS may be faulty.

REMOVAL & INSTALLATION

▶ **See Figure 80**

1. Disconnect the negative battery cable.
2. Disengage the electrical connection.
3. Unfasten the sensor retainers.
4. Remove the sensor and gasket or O-ring.

To install:

5. Install the sensor with a new gasket or O-ring.
6. Fasten the sensor retainers.
7. Engage the electrical connections.
8. Connect the negative battery cable.

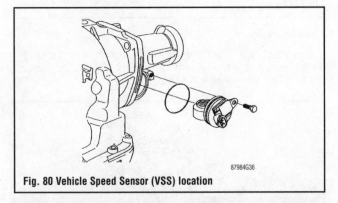

Fig. 80 Vehicle Speed Sensor (VSS) location

Knock Sensor

OPERATION

▶ **See Figures 81 and 82**

Located in the engine block, the knock sensor retards ignition timing during a spark knock condition to allow the ECM to maintain maximum timing advance under most conditions.

TESTING

▶ **See Figure 57**

1. Connect a timing light to the vehicle and start the engine.
2. Check that the timing is correct before testing knock sensor operation.
3. If timing is correct, tap on the front of the engine block with a metal object while observing the timing to see if the timing retards.
4. If the timing does not retard the knock sensor may be defective.

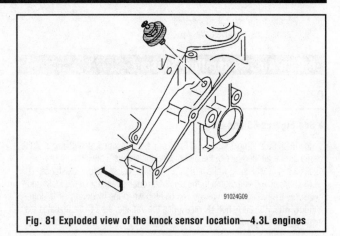

Fig. 81 Exploded view of the knock sensor location—4.3L engines

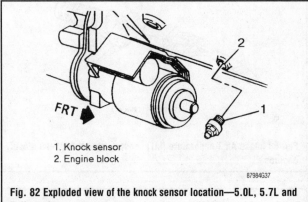

1. Knock sensor
2. Engine block

Fig. 82 Exploded view of the knock sensor location—5.0L, 5.7L and 7.4L engines

REMOVAL & INSTALLATION

1. Disconnect the negative battery cable.
2. Disengage the wiring harness connector from the knock sensor.
3. Remove the knock sensor from the engine block.

To install:

4. Apply a water base caulk to the knock sensor threads and install the sensor in the engine block.

❊❊ WARNING

Do not use silicone tape to coat the knock sensor threads, as this will insulate the sensor from the engine block.

5. Engage the wiring harness connector.
6. Connect the negative battery cable.

DIESEL ELECTRONIC ENGINE CONTROLS

Electronic Control Module

OPERATION

➡ **When the term Electronic Control Module (ECM) is used in this manual it will refer to the engine control computer regardless that it may be a Vehicle Control Module (VCM), Powertrain Control Module (PCM) or Electronic Control Module (ECM).**

The Electronic Control Module (ECM) is required to maintain the exhaust emissions at acceptable levels. The module is a small, solid state computer which receives signals from many sources and sensors. It uses this data to make judgments about operating conditions and then controls the emission systems to match the current requirements.

REMOVAL & INSTALLATION

1. Disconnect the negative battery cable.
2. Disengage the connectors from the ECM.
3. Remove the ECM mounting hardware.
4. Remove the ECM.
5. Remove the ECM.

To install:

6. Install the ECM and its mounting hardware.

7. Engage the electrical connectors.
8. Connect the negative battery cable.

Intake Air Temperature Sensor

OPERATION

▶ **See Figures 83 and 84**

the Intake Air Temperature (IAT) Sensor is a thermistor which changes value based on the temperature of the air entering the engine. Low temperature produces a high resistance, while a high temperature causes a low resistance. The ECM supplies a 5 volt signal to the sensor through a resistor in the ECM and measures the voltage. The voltage will be high when the incoming air is cold, and low when the air is hot. By measuring the voltage, the ECM calculates the incoming air temperature.

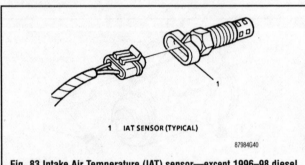

| 1 | IAT SENSOR (TYPICAL) |

87984G40

Fig. 83 Intake Air Temperature (IAT) sensor—except 1996–98 diesel engines

91024G10

Fig. 84 Intake Air Temperature (IAT) sensor—1996–98 6.5L diesel engines

TESTING

▶ **See Figures 48 and 85**

1. Remove the Intake Air Temperature (IAT) sensor.
2. Connect a digital ohmmeter to the two terminals of the sensor.

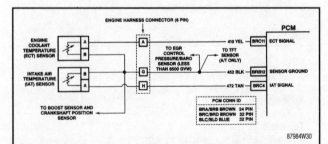

87984W30

Fig. 85 Intake Air Temperature (IAT) and Engine Coolant Temperature (ECT) sensor wiring diagram

3. Using a calibrated thermometer, compare the resistance of the sensor to the temperature of the ambient air. Refer to the temperature vs. resistance illustration.
4. Repeat the test at two other temperature points, heating or cooling the air as necessary with a hair dryer or other suitable tool.
5. If the sensor does not meet specification, it must be replaced.

REMOVAL & INSTALLATION

1. Unplug the sensor electrical connection.
2. Loosen and remove the sensor from the vehicle.
3. Installation is the reverse of removal.

Engine Coolant Temperature Sensor

LOCATION

▶ **See Figure 86**

Refer to the Engine Coolant Temperature (ECT) sensor procedures in the carbureted electronic engine control portion of this section for operation, testing and the removal and installation of the ECT.

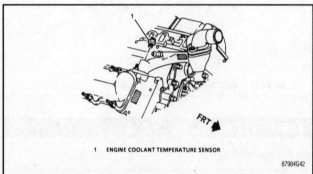

| 1 | ENGINE COOLANT TEMPERATURE SENSOR |

87984G42

Fig. 86 Engine Coolant Temperature (ECT) sensor location on diesel engines

Crankshaft Position Sensor

OPERATION

The Crankshaft Position (CKP) sensor is a hall-effect type sensor that monitors crankshaft position and speed. There are four teeth 90 apart on the front crankshaft sprocket that induce a pulse in the sensor which is transmitted to the ECM.

TESTING

▶ **See Figure 87**

1. Check the sensor wiring, the wiring harness and the terminals for damage and repair as necessary.
2. Disconnect the CKP sensor harness. Connect an Digital Volt Ohm Meter (DVOM) attach the negative lead of the meter to battery ground and the positive lead to CKP harness terminal C. The voltage should be between 4.8–5.2 volts.
3. If not as specified, repair or replace the fuse and/or wiring.
4. Connect an LED test light between the battery positive terminal and CKP terminal B.
5. With the ignition **ON** and the engine off, verify that the test light illuminates.
6. If not as specified, repair or replace the wiring.
7. Turn the ignition **OFF** and disconnect the test light.
8. Next, connect suitable jumper wires between the CKP sensor and CKP sensor harness. Connect a DVOM to the jumper wire corresponding to CKP terminal A and battery ground.

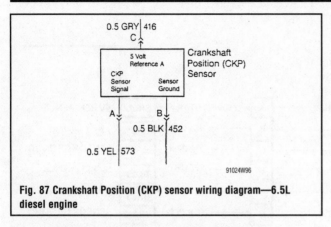

Fig. 87 Crankshaft Position (CKP) sensor wiring diagram—6.5L diesel engine

9. Crank the engine and verify that the voltage is 4 volts or more.
10. If it is not as specified, the CKP sensor may be faulty.

REMOVAL & INSTALLATION

♦ **See Figure 88**

1. Disconnect the negative battery cable.
2. Detach the sensor harness connector at the sensor.
3. Unfasten the retaining bolt, then remove the sensor from the front cover. Inspect the sensor O-ring for wear, cracks or leakage and replace if necessary.

To install:

4. Lubricate the O-ring with clean engine oil, then place on the sensor. Install the sensor into the front cover.
5. Install the sensor retaining bolt. Tighten the bolt to 17 ft. lbs. (25 Nm).
6. Attach the sensor harness connector.
7. Connect the negative battery cable.

Vehicle Speed Sensor

OPERATION

The vehicle speed sensor is made up of a coil mounted on the transmission and a tooth rotor mounted to the output shaft of the transmission. As each tooth nears the coil, the coil produces an AC voltage pulse. As the vehicle speed increases the number of voltage pulses per second increases.

TESTING

♦ **See Figure 79**

1. To test the VSS, backprobe the VSS terminals with a high impedance voltmeter (set at the AC voltage scale).
2. Safely raise and support the entire vehicle using jackstands. Make absolutely sure the vehicle is stable.
3. Start the vehicle and place it in gear.
4. Verify that the VSS voltage increases as the drive shaft speed increases.
5. If the VSS voltage is not as specified the VSS may be faulty.

REMOVAL & INSTALLATION

♦ **See Figure 80**

1. Disconnect the negative battery cable.
2. Disengage the electrical connection.
3. Unfasten the sensor retainers.
4. Remove the sensor and gasket or O-ring.

To install:

5. Install the sensor with a new gasket or O-ring.
6. Fasten the sensor retainers.
7. Engage the electrical connections.
8. Connect the negative battery cable.

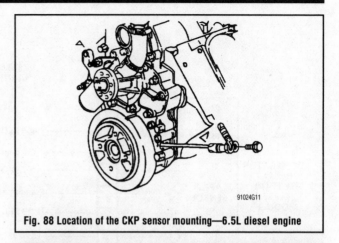

Fig. 88 Location of the CKP sensor mounting—6.5L diesel engine

Accelerator Pedal Position Sensor Module

OPERATION

The Accelerator Pedal Position (APP) sensor module contains three potentiometers (a device for measuring unknown voltage or potential difference by comparison to a standard voltage). Each of the APP sensors send a varying voltage to the ECM. By monitoring the output voltage from the Accelerator Pedal Position (APP) module, the ECM can determine fuel delivery based on the accelerator pedal position (driver demand).

TESTING

♦ **See Figure 89**

1. Backprobe with a high impedance voltmeter at APP sensor terminals G and A.
2. With the key **ON** and engine off, the voltmeter reading should be approximately 5.0 volts.
3. If the voltage is not as specified, either the wiring to the APP sensor or the ECM may be faulty. Correct any wiring or ECM faults before continuing test.
4. Backprobe with a high impedance voltmeter at terminals F and A.
5. With the key **ON** and engine idling, the APP sensor voltage should be approximately 0.5 volts.
6. Verify that the APP voltage increases or decreases smoothly as the throttle is opened or closed. Make sure to open and close the throttle very slowly in order to detect any abnormalities in the APP sensor voltage reading.
7. If the APP sensor voltage is not as specified, replace the APP sensor.
8. Backprobe with a high impedance voltmeter at APP sensor terminals D and B.
9. With the key **ON** and engine off, the voltmeter reading should be approximately 5.0 volts.
10. If the voltage is not as specified, either the wiring to the APP sensor or the ECM may be faulty. Correct any wiring or ECM faults before continuing test.
11. Backprobe with a high impedance voltmeter at terminals C and B.
12. With the key **ON** and engine idling, the APP sensor voltage should be approximately 4.5 volts.
13. Verify that the APP voltage decreases smoothly as the throttle is opened. Make sure to open and close the throttle very slowly in order to detect any abnormalities in the APP sensor voltage reading.
14. If the APP sensor voltage is not as specified, replace the APP sensor.
15. Backprobe with a high impedance voltmeter at APP sensor terminals E and J.
16. With the key **ON** and engine off, the voltmeter reading should be approximately 5.0 volts.
17. If the voltage is not as specified, either the wiring to the APP sensor or the ECM may be faulty. Correct any wiring or ECM faults before continuing test.

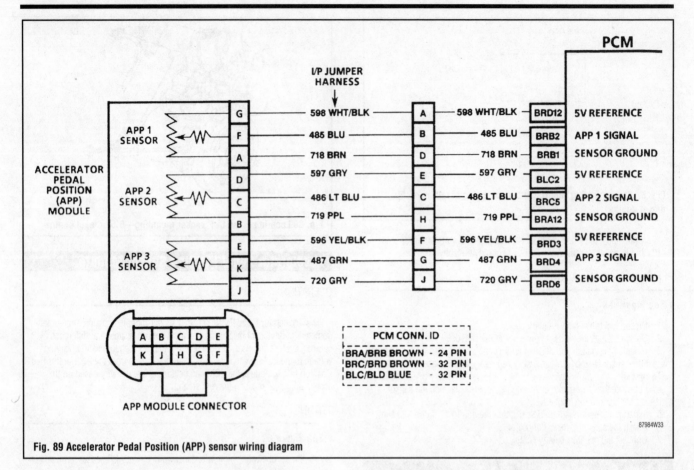

Fig. 89 Accelerator Pedal Position (APP) sensor wiring diagram

18. Backprobe with a high impedance voltmeter at terminals K and J.
19. With the key **ON** and engine idling, the APP sensor voltage should be approximately 4.0 volts.
20. Verify that the APP voltage decreases smoothly to about 2.0 volts as the throttle is opened. Make sure to open and close the throttle very slowly in order to detect any abnormalities in the APP sensor voltage reading.
21. If the APP sensor voltage is not as specified, replace the APP sensor module.

REMOVAL & INSTALLATION

▶ **See Figure 90**

1. Disconnect the negative battery cable.
2. Unplug the APP module electrical connection.
3. Unfasten the module retaining bolts.
4. Remove the module.

To install:

5. Place the module in position and install the mounting bolts. Tighten the bolts to 10 inch lbs. (1 Nm).
6. Attach the module electrical connection.
7. Connect the negative battery cable.

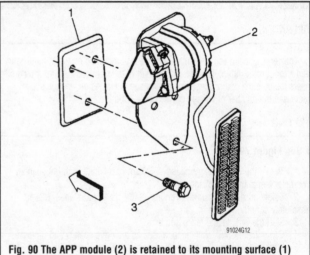

Fig. 90 The APP module (2) is retained to its mounting surface (1) by three bolts (3)—1996–98 diesel engines shown, others similar

TROUBLE CODES

DIAGNOSTIC CODE IDENTIFICATION

The "Service Engine Soon" light will only be "ON" if the malfunction exists under the conditions listed below. If the malfunction clears, the light will go out and the code will be stored in the ECM/PCM. Any codes stored will be erased if no problem reoccurs within 50 engine starts.

CODE AND CIRCUIT	PROBABLE CAUSE	CODE AND CIRCUIT	PROBABLE CAUSE
Code 13 - Oxygen O₂ Sensor Circuit (Open Circuit)	Indicates that the oxygen sensor circuit or sensor was open for one minute while off idle.	Code 33 - Manifold Absolute Pressure (MAP) Sensor Circuit (Signal Voltage High - Low Vacuum)	MAP sensor output to high for 5 seconds or an open signal circuit.
Code 14 - Coolant Temperature Sensor (CTS) Circuit (High Temperature Indicated)	Sets if the sensor or signal line becomes grounded for 3 seconds.	Code 34 - Manifold Absolute Pressure (MAP) Sensor Circuit (Signal Voltage Low-High Vacuum)	Low or no output from sensor with engine running.
Code 15 - Coolant Temperature Sensor (CTS) Circuit (Low Temperature Indicated)	Sets if the sensor, connections, or wires open for 3 seconds.	Code 35 - Idle Air Control (IAC) System	IAC error
Code 21 - Throttle Position Sensor (TPS) Circuit (Signal Voltage High)	TPS voltage greater than 2.5 volts for 3 seconds with less than 1200 RPM.	Code 42 - Electronic Spark Timing (EST)	ECM/PCM has seen an open or grounded EST or bypass circuit.
Code 22 - Throttle Position Sensor (TPS) Circuit (Signal Voltage Low)	A shorted to ground or open signal circuit will set code in 3 seconds.	Code 43 - Electronic Spark Control (ESC) Circuit	Signal to the ECM/PCM has remained low for too long or the system has failed a functional check.
Code 23 - Intake Air Temperature (IAT) Sensor Circuit (Low Temperature Indicated)	Sets if the sensor, connections, or wires open for 3 seconds.	Code 44 - Oxygen (O₂) Sensor Circuit (Lean Exhaust Indicated)	Sets if oxygen sensor voltage remains below .2 volt for about 20 seconds.
Code 24 - Vehicle Speed Sensor (VSS)	No vehicle speed present during a road load decel.	Code 45 - Oxygen (O₂) Sensor Circuit (Rich Exhaust Indicated)	Sets if oxygen sensor voltage remains above .7 volt for about 1 minute.
Code 25 - Intake Air Temperature (IAT) Sensor Circuit (High Temperature Indicated)	Sets if the sensor or signal line becomes grounded for 3 seconds.	Code 51 - Faulty MEM-CAL or ECM/PCM Problem	Faulty MEM-CAL, PROM, or ECM/PCM.
Code 32 - Exhaust Gas Recirculation (EGR) System	Vacuum switch shorted to ground on start up OR Switch not closed after the ECM/PCM has commanded EGR for a specified period of time. OR EGR solenoid circuit open for a specified period of time.	Code 52 - Fuel CALPAK Missing	Fuel CAL-PAK missing or faulty.
		Code 53 - System Over Voltage	System overvoltage. Indicates a basic generator problem.
		Code 54 - Fuel Pump Circuit (Low Voltage)	Sets when the fuel pump voltage is less than 2 volts when reference pulses are being received.
		Code 55 - Faulty ECM/PCM	Faulty ECM/PCM

84904064

Fig. 92 Fuel injected engine trouble codes through 1995, except with 4L60E and 4L80E transmissions

CODE IDENTIFICATION

The "Service Engine Soon" light will only be "ON" if the malfunction exists under the conditions listed below. If the malfunction clears, the light will go out and the code will be stored in the ECM. Any Codes stored will be erased if no problem reoccurs within 50 engine starts.

CODE AND CIRCUIT	PROBABLE CAUSE	CODE AND CIRCUIT	PROBABLE CAUSE
Code 12 - No engine speed reference pulse.	No engine speed sensor reference pulses to the ECM. This code is not stored in memory and will only flash while the fault is present. Normal code with ignition "ON," engine not running.	Code 31 - MAP Sensor Too Low	Absolute Pressure (MAP) circuit signal voltage too low. Engine must run at curb idle for 10 seconds before this code will set.
Code 14 - Coolant Sensor High Temperature Indication	Sets if the sensor or signal line becomes grounded for 10 seconds.	Code 32 - EGR Loop Error	Exhaust Gas Recirculation (EGR) vacuum circuit has seen improper EGR vacuum. Vehicle must be running at road speed approximately 30 mph (48 Km/h) for 10 seconds before this code will set.
Code 15 - Coolant Sensor Low Temperature Indication	Sets if the sensor, connections, or wires open for 10 seconds.	Code 33 - MAP Sensor Too High	Absolute Pressure (MAP) circuit signal voltage too high. Engine must run at curb idle for 10 seconds before this code will set.
Code 21 - TPS Signal Voltage High	Throttle Position Sensor (TPS) circuit voltage high (open circuit or misadjusted TPS). Engine must run 30 seconds, at curb idle speed, before this code will set.	Code 51 - PROM	Faulty or improperly installed PROM. It takes approximately 10 seconds before this code will set.
Code 22 - TPS Signal Voltage Low	Throttle Position Sensor (TPS) circuit voltage low (grounded circuit). Engine must run 2 minutes at 1250 rpm or above before this code will set.	Code 52 - ECM	Fault in ECM circuit. It takes 10 seconds before this code will set.
Code 23 - TPS Not Calibrated	Throttle Position Sensor (TPS) circuit. Voltage not between .25 and 1.3 volts at curb idle speed. Engine must run for 30 seconds, at curb idle, before this code will set.	Code 53 - Five volt Reference Overload	5 volt reference (Vref) circuit overloaded (grounded circuit). It takes 10 seconds before this Code will set.
Code 24 - VSS No Vehicle Speed Indication	Vehicle speed sensor (VSS) circuit (open or grounded circuit). Vehicle must operate at road speed for 10 seconds before this code will set.		

84904119

Fig. 91 Carbureted engine trouble codes

DIAGNOSTIC TROUBLE CODE (DTC) IDENTIFICATION

The MIL (Service Engine Soon) will only be "ON" if the malfunction exists with the conditions listed below. If the malfunction clears, the lamp will go out and the DTC will be stored in the PCM. Any DTCs stored will be erased if no problem reoccurs within 50 engine starts.

DTC AND CIRCUIT	PROBABLE CAUSE	DTC AND CIRCUIT	PROBABLE CAUSE
DTC 13 - Oxygen O2S Sensor Circuit (Open Circuit)	Indicates that the oxygen sensor circuit or sensor was open for one minute while off idle.	DTC 33 - Manifold Absolute Pressure (MAP) Sensor Circuit (Signal Voltage High - Low Vacuum)	MAP sensor output high for 5 seconds or an open signal circuit.
DTC 14 - Engine Coolant Temperature (ECT) Sensor Circuit (High Temperature Indicated)	Sets if the sensor or signal line becomes grounded or greater than 145°C (294°F) for 0.5 seconds.	DTC 34 - Manifold Absolute Pressure (MAP) Sensor Circuit (Signal Voltage Low - High Vacuum)	Low or no output from MAP sensor with engine operating.
DTC 15 - Engine Coolant Temperature (ECT) Sensor Circuit (Low Temperature Indicated)	Sets if the sensor, connections, or wires open or less than -33°C (-27°F) for 0.5 seconds.	DTC 35 - IAC	IAC error
DTC 16 - Transmission Output Speed Low	Open in CKT 1697/1716 or power loss to VSS buffer	• DTC 37 - Brake Switch Stuck On	With no voltage and vehicle speed is less than 5 mph for 6 seconds, then vehicle speed is 5 - 20 MPH for 6 seconds, then vehicle speed is greater than 20 MPH for 6 seconds, this must occur for 7 times.
DTC 21 - Throttle Position (TP) Sensor Circuit (Signal Voltage High)	TP voltage greater than 4.88 volts 4 seconds with less than 1200 RPM.	• DTC 38 - Brake Switch Stuck Off	With voltage and vehicle speed is greater than 20 MPH for 6 seconds, then vehicle speed is 5 - 20 MPH for 6 seconds. This must occur 7 times.
DTC 22 - Throttle Position (TP) Sensor Circuit (Signal Voltage Low)	A short to ground, open signal circuit, or TP voltage less than 0.16 volts for 4 seconds.	DTC 42 - Ignition Control (IC)	PCM detects an open or grounded IC or bypass circuit.
DTC 24 - Vehicle Speed Sensor (VSS) Signal Low	No vehicle speed sensor signal present during a road load decel.	DTC 43 - Knock Sensor (KS) Circuit	Signal to the PCM has remained low for too long, or the system has failed a functional system check.
DTC 28 - Fluid Pressure Switch Assembly	PCM detects 1 of 2 invalid combinations of the fluid pressure switch range signals	DTC 44 - Oxygen Sensor (O2S) Circuit (Lean Exhaust Indicated)	Sets if oxygen sensor voltage remains less than 0.2 volt for 20 seconds.
DTC 32 - Exhaust Gas Recirculation (EGR) System	Vacuum switch shorted to ground on start up OR Switch not closed after the PCM has commanded EGR for a specified period of time. OR EGR solenoid circuit open for a specified period of time.	DTC 45 - Oxygen Sensor (O2S) Circuit (Rich Exhaust Indicated)	Sets if oxygen sensor voltage remains greater than 0.7 volt for about 1 minute.

84904066

Fig. 93 Fuel injected engine trouble codes through 1995 with 4L60E transmissions

DIAGNOSTIC TROUBLE CODE (DTC) IDENTIFICATION

The MIL (Service Engine Soon) will only be "ON" if the malfunction exists with the conditions listed below. If the malfunction clears, the lamp will go out and the DTC will be stored in the PCM. Any DTCs stored will be erased if no problem reoccurs within 50 engine starts.

DTC AND CIRCUIT	PROBABLE CAUSE	DTC AND CIRCUIT	PROBABLE CAUSE
DTC 51 - Faulty PROM (MEM-CAL) Problem	Faulty PROM (MEM-CAL) or PCM.	• DTC 69 - TCC Stuck "ON"	Slip > -20 and slip 20 TCC is not locked gear = 2, 3 or 4 TPS > 25%, not in P/N for 4 seconds.
DTC 53 - System Voltage High	System overvoltage of 19.5 volts for 2 seconds	• DTC 72 - Vehicle Speed Sensor Loss	Not in P/N - Output speed changes greater than 1000 RPM • P/N - Output speed changes greater than 2050 RPM • For 2 seconds
DTC 54 - Fuel Pump Circuit (Low Voltage)	Sets when the fuel pump voltage is less than 2 volts when reference pulses are being received.	• DTC 73 - Pressure Control Solenoid	If return amperage varies more than 0.16 amps from commanded amperage
DTC 55 - Faulty PCM	Faulty PCM.	• DTC 75 - System Voltage Low	System voltage < 7.3 at low temperature or < 11.7 at high temperature for 4 seconds.
• DTC 58 - Transmission Fluid Temperature High	Transmission fluid temperature greater than 154°C (309°F) for one second	• DTC 79 - Transmission Fluid Over Temperature	Transmission fluid Temperature > 150°C and < 154°C for 15 minutes.
• DTC 59 - Transmission Fluid Temperature Low	Transmission fluid temperature greater than -33°C (-27°F) for one second	• DTC 81 - 2-3 Shift Solenoid Circuit Fault	2-3 shift solenoid is command "ON", and circuit voltage is low for two seconds OR 2-3 shift solenoid is command "OFF", and circuit voltage is high for two seconds
• DTC 66 - 3-2 Control Solenoid Circuit Fault	At High Duty Cycle the circuit voltage is high OR at Low Duty Cycle the Circuit Voltage is low for four seconds.	• DTC 82 - 1-2 Shift Solenoid Circuit Fault	1-2 shift solenoid is command "ON", and circuit voltage is high for two seconds OR 1-2 shift solenoid is command "OFF" and circuit voltage is low for two seconds
• DTC 67 Torque Converter Clutch Circuit	TCC is commanded "ON" and circuit voltage remains high for two seconds OR TCC is commanded "OFF" and circuit voltage remains low for two seconds.		

84904067

Fig. 94 Fuel injected engine trouble codes through 1995 with 4L60E transmissions (continued)

DIAGNOSTIC TROUBLE CODE IDENTIFICATION (Continued)

The MIL (Service Engine Soon) will only be "ON" if the malfunction exists with the conditions listed below. If the malfunction clears, the lamp will go out and the DTC will be stored in the PCM. Any DTCs stored will be erased if no problem reoccurs within 50 engine starts. Note: All DTC(S) with the sign * are transmission related DTC(S).

Remember, always start with the lowest numerical DTC first, when diagnosing some engine DTC(S) trigger other transmission DTC(S).

DTC AND CIRCUIT	PROBABLE CAUSE	DTC AND CIRCUIT	PROBABLE CAUSE
DTC 58 - Transmission Fluid Temperature High*		DTC 82 - 1-2 Shift Solenoid Circuit Fault*	
DTC 59 - Transmission Fluid Temperature Low*		DTC 83 - TCC Solenoid Circuit Fault*	
DTC 68 - Overdrive Ratio Error*		DTC 85 - Undefined Ratio*	
DTC 73 - Pressure Control Solenoid*		DTC 86 - Low Ratio*	
DTC 75 - System Voltage Low*		DTC 87 - High Ratio*	
DTC 81 - 2-3 Shift Solenoid Circuit Fault*			

84904069

Fig. 96 Fuel injected engine trouble codes through 1995 with 4L80E transmissions (continued)

DIAGNOSTIC TROUBLE CODE IDENTIFICATION

The MIL (Service Engine Soon) will only be "ON" if the malfunction exists with the conditions listed below. If the malfunction clears, the lamp will go out and the DTC will be stored in the PCM. Any DTCs stored will be erased if no problem reoccurs within 50 engine starts. Note: All DTC(S) with the sign * are transmission related DTC(S).

Remember, always start with the lowest numerical DTC first, when diagnosing some engine DTC(S) trigger other transmission DTC(S).

DTC AND CIRCUIT	PROBABLE CAUSE	DTC AND CIRCUIT	PROBABLE CAUSE
DTC 13 - Oxygen Sensor O2S Circuit (Open Circuit)	Indicates that the oxygen sensor circuit or sensor was open for one minute while off idle.	DTC 33 - Manifold Absolute Pressure (MAP) Sensor Circuit (Signal Voltage High - Low Vacuum)	MAP sensor output to high for 5 seconds or an open signal circuit.
DTC 14 - Engine Coolant Temperature (ECT) Sensor Circuit (High Temperature Indicated)	Signal voltage has been greater than 151°C (304°F) for 1 second.	DTC 34 - Manifold Absolute Pressure (MAP) Sensor Circuit (Signal Voltage Low - High Vacuum)	Low or no output from sensor with engine operating.
DTC 15 - Engine Coolant Temperature (ECT) Sensor Circuit (Low Temperature Indicated)	Signal voltage has been less than -37°C (-34°F) for 1 second.	DTC 39 - TCC Stuck "OFF"	
DTC 21 - Throttle Position (TP) Sensor Circuit. (Signal Voltage High)	If signal voltage has been greater than 4.9 volts for 1 second.	DTC 42 - Ignition Control (IC)	PCM has an open or grounded IC or bypass circuit.
DTC 22 - Throttle Position (TP) Sensor Circuit (Signal Voltage Low)	DTC 22 will set if TP signal voltage is less than 2 volt for more than 1 second.	DTC 43 - Knock Sensor (KS) Circuit	Signal to the PCM has remained low for too long or the system has failed a functional check.
DTC 24 - Vehicle Speed Sensor (VSS)	With input speed at least 3000 RPM, output speed must read less than 200 RPM for 1.5 seconds.	DTC 44 - Oxygen Sensor O2S Circuit (Lean Exhaust Indicated)	Sets if oxygen sensor voltage remains less than .2 volt for 20 seconds.
DTC 28 - Fluid Pressure Switch Assembly*		DTC 45 - Oxygen Sensor O2S Circuit (Rich Exhaust Indicated)	Sets if oxygen sensor voltage remains greater than .7 volt for 1 minute.
DTC 32 - Exhaust Gas Recirculation (EGR) System	Vacuum switch shorted to ground on start up OR Switch not closed after the PCM has commanded EGR for a specified period of time OR EGR solenoid circuit open for a specified period of time.	DTC 51 - Faulty PROM (MEM-CAL) Problem	Faulty PROM or PCM.
		DTC 53 - System Over Voltage	Generator voltage is greater than 19.5 volts for 2 seconds.
		DTC 54 - Fuel Pump Circuit (Low Voltage)	Sets when the fuel pump voltage is less than 2 volts when reference pulses are being received.
		DTC 55 - Faulty PCM	Faulty PCM.

84904068

Fig. 95 Fuel injected engine trouble codes through 1995 with 4L80E transmissions

87984G51

P1133 - Heated Oxygen Sensor (HO2S) Insufficient Switching Bank 1, Sensor 1
P1134 - Heated Oxygen Sensor (HO2S) Transition Time Ratio Bank 1, Sensor 1
P1153 - Heated Oxygen Sensor (HO2S) Insufficient Switching Bank 2, Sensor 1
P1154 - Heated Oxygen Sensor (HO2S) Transition Time Ratio Bank 2, Sensor 1
P1345 - Crankshaft Position/Camshaft Position (CKP/CMP) Correlation
P1351 - Ignition Control (IC) Circuit High Voltage
P1361 - Ignition Control (IC) Circuit Low Voltage
P1380 - Electronic Brake Control Module (EBCM) DTC Detected - Rough Road Data Unusable
P1381 - Misfire Detected - No Electronic Brake Control Module (EBCM) VCM Serial Data
P1406 - Exhaust Gas Recirculation (EGR) Valve Pintle Position Circuit
P1415 - AIR System Bank 1
P1416 - AIR System Bank 2
P1441 - Evaporative Emission (EVAP) System Flow During Non-Purge
P1508 - Idle Air Control (IAC) System Low RPM
P1509 - Idle Air Control (IAC; System High RPM

P0500 - Vehicle Speed Sensor (VSS) Circuit
P0506 - Idle System Low - Idle Air Control (IAC) Responding
P0507 - Idle System High - Idle Air Control (IAC) Responding
P1106 - Manifold Absolute Pressure (MAP) Sensor Circuit Intermittent High Voltage
P1107 - Manifold Absolute Pressure (MAP) Sensor Circuit Intermittent Low Voltage
P1111 - Intake Air Temperature (IAT) Sensor Circuit Intermittent High Voltage
P1112 - Intake Air Temperature (IAT) Sensor Circuit Intermittent Low Voltage
P1114 - Engine Coolant Temperature (ECT) Sensor Circuit Intermittent Low Voltage
P1115 - Engine Coolant Temperature (ECT) Sensor Circuit Intermittent High Voltage
P1121 - Throttle Position (TP) Sensor Circuit Intermittent High Voltage
P1122 - Throttle Position (TP) Sensor Circuit Intermittent Low Voltage

Fig. 98 Trouble code list for 1996-98 gasoline engines (continued)

87984G50

DTC P0101 - Mass Air Flow (MAF) System Performance
DTC P0102 - Mass Air Flow (MAF) Sensor Circuit Low Frequency
DTC P0103 - Mass Air Flow (MAF) Sensor Circuit High Frequency
DTC P0106 - Manifold Absolute Pressure (MAP) Sensor System Performance
DTC P0107 - Manifold Absolute Pressure (MAP) Sensor Circuit Low Voltage
DTC P0108 - Manifold Absolute Pressure (MAP) Sensor Circuit High Voltage
P0112 - Intake Air Temperature (IAT) Sensor Circuit Low Voltage
P0113 - Intake Air Temperature (IAT) Sensor Circuit High Voltage
P0117 - Engine Coolant Temperature (ECT) Sensor Circuit Low Voltage
P0118 - Engine Coolant Temperature (ECT) Sensor Circuit High Voltage
P0121 - Throttle Position (TP) System Performance
P0122 - Throttle Position (TP) Sensor Circuit Low Voltage
P0123 - Throttle Position (TP) Sensor Circuit High Voltage
P0125 - Engine Coolant Temperature (ECT) Excessive Time to Closed Loop Fuel Control
P0131 - Heated Oxygen Sensor (HO2S) Circuit Low Voltage Bank 1, Sensor 1
P0132 - Heated Oxygen Sensor (HO2S) Circuit High Voltage Bank 1, Sensor 1
P0133 - Heated Oxygen Sensor (HO2S) Circuit Slow Response Bank 1, Sensor 1
P0134 - Heated Oxygen Sensor (HO2S) Circuit Insufficient Activity Bank 1, Sensor 1
P0135 - Heated Oxygen Sensor (HO2S) Heater Circuit Bank 1, Sensor 1
P0137 - Heated Oxygen Sensor (HO2S) Circuit Low Voltage Bank 1, Sensor 2
P0138 - Heated Oxygen Sensor (HO2S) Circuit High Voltage Bank 1, Sensor 2
P0140 - Heated Oxygen Sensor (HO2S) Circuit Insufficient Activity Bank 1, Sensor 2
P0141 - Heated Oxygen Sensor (HO2S) Heater Circuit Bank 1, Sensor 2
P0143 - Heated Oxygen Sensor (HO2S) Circuit Low Voltage Bank 1, Sensor 3
P0144 - Heated Oxygen Sensor (HO2S) Circuit High Voltage Bank 1, Sensor 3

P0146 - Heated Oxygen Sensor (HO2S) Circuit Insufficient Activity Bank 1, Sensor 3
P0147 - Heated Oxygen Sensor (HO2S) Heater Circuit Bank 1, Sensor 3
P0151 - Heated Oxygen Sensor (HO2S) Circuit Low Voltage Bank 2, Sensor 1
P0152 - Heated Oxygen Sensor (HO2S) Circuit High Voltage Bank 2, Sensor 1
P0153 - Heated Oxygen Sensor (HO2S) Circuit Slow Response Bank 2, Sensor 1
P0154 - Heated Oxygen Sensor (HO2S) Circuit Insufficient Activity Bank 2, Sensor 1
P0155 - Heated Oxygen Sensor (HO2S) Heater Circuit Bank 2, Sensor 1
P0157 - Heated Oxygen Sensor (HO2S) Circuit Low Voltage Bank 2, Sensor 2
P0158 - Heated Oxygen Sensor (HO2S) Circuit High Voltage Bank 2, Sensor 2
P0160 - Heated Oxygen Sensor (HO2S) Circuit Insufficient Activity Bank 2, Sensor 2
P0161 - Heated Oxygen Sensor (HO2S) Heater Circuit Bank 2, Sensor 2
P0171 - Fuel Trim System Lean Bank 1
P0172 - Fuel Trim System Rich Bank 1
P0174 - Fuel Trim System Lean Bank 2
P0175 - Fuel Trim System Rich Bank 2
P0300 - Engine Misfire Detected
P0301 - Cylinder 1 Misfire Detected
P0302 - Cylinder 2 Misfire Detected
P0303 - Cylinder 3 Misfire Detected
P0304 - Cylinder 4 Misfire Detected
P0305 - Cylinder 5 Misfire Detected
P0306 - Cylinder 6 Misfire Detected
P0307 - Cylinder 7 Misfire Detected
P0308 - Cylinder 8 Misfire Detected
P0325 - Knock Sensor (KS) Module Circuit
P0327 - Knock Sensor (KS) Circuit Low Voltage
P0336 - Crankshaft Position (CKP) Sensor Circuit Performance
P0337 - Crankshaft Position (CKP) Sensor Circuit Performance
P0338 - Crankshaft Position (CKP) Sensor Circuit High Frequency
P0339 - Crankshaft Position (CKP) Sensor Circuit Intermittent
P0340 - Camshaft Position (CMP) Sensor Circuit
P0341 - Camshaft Position (CMP) Sensor Circuit Performance
P0401 - Exhaust Gas Recirculation (EGR) System
P0410 - AIR System
P0420 - Three Way Catalytic Converter (TWC) System Low Efficiency Bank 1
P0430 - Three Way Catalytic Converter (TWC) System Low Efficiency Bank 2
P0441 - Evaporative Emission (EVAP) System No Flow During Purge

Fig. 97 Trouble code list for 1996-98 gasoline engines

DIAGNOSTIC TROUBLE CODE (DTC) IDENTIFICATION

The MIL (Service Engine Soon) will only be "ON" if the malfunction exists under the conditions listed below. If the malfunction clears, the lamp will go out and the DTC will be stored in the PCM. Any DTCs stored will be erased if no problem reoccurs within 50 engine starts. Note: All DTCs with the sign * are transmission related DTCs.

Remember, always start with the lowest numerical DTC first, when diagnosing some engine DTCs trigger other transmission DTCs.

DTC AND CIRCUIT	PROBABLE CAUSE	DTC AND CIRCUIT	PROBABLE CAUSE
DTC 14 - Engine Coolant Temperature (ECT) Sensor Circuit (High Temperature Indicated)	Sets if the sensor or signal line becomes grounded or greater than 145°C (294°F) for 0.5 seconds.	DTC 32 - Exhaust Gas Recirculation (EGR) System Error	Exhaust Gas Recirculation (EGR) vacuum circuit has seen improper EGR vacuum. Vehicle must be running at road speed approximately 30 mph (48 Km/h) for 10 seconds before this DTC will set.
DTC 15 - Engine Coolant Temperature (ECT) Sensor Circuit (Low Temperature Indicated)	Sets if the sensor, connections, or wires open or less than -33°C (-27°F) for 0.5 seconds.	DTC 33 - Manifold Absolute Pressure (MAP) Sensor Circuit (Signal Voltage High - Low Vacuum)	MAP sensor output high for 5 seconds or an open signal circuit.
DTC 16 - Transmission Output Speed Signal Low	Open in CKT 1716 or power loss to VSS buffer module.		
DTC 21 - Throttle Position (TP) Sensor Circuit (Signal Voltage High)	TP voltage greater than 4.88 volts 4 seconds with less than 1200 RPM.	*DTC 37 - Brake Switch Stuck On	With no voltage and vehicle speed is less than 5 mph for 6 seconds, then vehicle speed is 5 - 20 MPH for 6 seconds, then vehicle speed is greater than 20 MPH for 6 seconds, this must occur for 7 times.
DTC 22 - Throttle Position (TP) Sensor Circuit (Signal Voltage Low)	A short to ground, open signal circuit, or TP voltage less than 0.16 volts for 4 seconds.	*DTC 38 - Brake Switch Stuck Off	With voltage and vehicle speed is greater than 20 MPH for 6 seconds, then vehicle speed is 5 - 20 MPH for 6 seconds. This must occur 7 times.
DTC 23 - Throttle Position (TP) Sensor Not Calibrated	Throttle Position TP sensor circuit voltage not between 25 and 1.3 volts at curb idle speed. Engine must run for 30 seconds, at curb idle, before this DTC will set.		
*DTC 24 - Vehicle Speed Sensor (VSS) Signal Low	No vehicle speed sensor signal present during a road load decel.		
*DTC 28 - Fluid Pressure Switch Assembly	PCM detects 1 of 2 invalid combinations of the fluid pressure switch range signals.		
DTC 31 - MAP Sensor too low	MAP Sensor signal voltage too low. Engine must run at curb idle for 10 seconds before this DTC will set.		

Fig. 100 Trouble code list for 1991–93 diesel engines with 4L60E automatic transmissions

CODE IDENTIFICATION

The "Service Engine Soon" light will only be "ON" if the malfunction exists under the conditions listed below. If the malfunction clears, the light will go out and the code will be stored in the ECM. Any Codes stored will be erased if no problem reoccurs within 50 engine starts.

CODE AND CIRCUIT	PROBABLE CAUSE	CODE AND CIRCUIT	PROBABLE CAUSE
Code 12 - No engine speed reference pulse.	No engine speed sensor reference pulses to the ECM. This code is not stored in memory and will only flash while the fault is present. Normal code with ignition "ON." engine not running	Code 31 - MAP Sensor Too Low	Absolute Pressure (MAP) circuit signal voltage too low. Engine must run at curb idle for 10 seconds before this code will set
Code 14 - Coolant Sensor High Temperature Indication	Sets if the sensor or signal line becomes grounded for 5 minutes.	Code 32 - EGR Loop Error	Exhaust Gas Recirculation (EGR) vacuum circuit has seen improper EGR vacuum. Vehicle must be running at road speed approximately 30 mph (48 Km/h) for 10 seconds before this code will set.
Code 15 - Coolant Sensor Low Temperature Indication	Sets if the sensor, connections, or wires open for 5 minutes.	Code 33 - MAP Sensor Too High	Absolute Pressure (MAP) circuit signal voltage too high. Engine must run for 10 seconds at curb idle speed, before this code will set.
Code 21 - TPS Signal Voltage High	Throttle Position Sensor (TPS) circuit voltage high (open circuit or misadjusted TPS). Engine must run 30 seconds, at curb idle speed, before this code will set	Code 51 - PROM	Faulty or improperly installed PROM. It takes approximately 10 seconds before this code will set.
Code 22 - TPS Signal Voltage Low	Throttle Position Sensor (TPS) circuit voltage low (grounded circuit). Engine must run 2 minutes at 1250 rpm or above before this code will set.	Code 52 - ECM	Fault in ECM circuit. It takes 10 seconds before this code will set.
Code 23 - TPS Not Calibrated	Throttle Position Sensor (TPS) circuit. Voltage not between 25 and 1 3 volts at curb idle speed. Engine must run for 30 seconds, at curb idle, before this code will set.	Code 53 - Five volt Reference Overload	5 volt reference (Vref) circuit overloaded (grounded circuit). It takes 10 seconds before this Code will set.
Code 24 - VSS No Vehicle Speed Indication	Vehicle speed sensor (VSS) circuit (open or grounded circuit). Vehicle must operate at road speed for 10 seconds before this code will set.		

Fig. 99 Trouble code list for 1988–93 diesel engines with manual transmissions and 1988–90 diesel engines with automatic transmissions

DIAGNOSTIC TROUBLE CODE (DTC) IDENTIFICATION

The MIL (Malfunction Indicator Lamp) will be "ON" if an emission malfunction exists. If the malfunction clears, the lamp will go "OFF" and the DTC will be stored in the PCM. Any DTC(s) stored will be cleared if no problem reoccurs within 50 engine starts.

! Important

All DTC(s) with the sign * are transmission related DTC(s).
Remember, always start with the lowest numerical engine DTC first. When diagnosing some engine DTC(s), other transmission symptoms can occur.

DTC NUMBER AND NAME	DTC NUMBER AND NAME
DTC 13 - Engine Shutoff Solenoid Circuit Fault	* DTC 28 - Trans Range Pressure Switch Circuit
DTC 14 - Engine Coolant Temperature (ECT) Sensor Circuit Low (High Temperature Indicated)	DTC 29 - Glow Plug Relay Fault
DTC 15 - Engine Coolant Temperature (ETC) Sensor Circuit High (Low Temperature Indicated)	DTC 31 - EGR Control Pressure/Baro Sensor Circuit Low (High Vacuum)
DTC 16 - Vehicle Speed Sensor Buffer Fault	DTC 32 - EGR Circuit Error
DTC 17 - High Resolution Circuit Fault	DTC 33 - EGR Control Pressure/Baro Sensor Circuit High
DTC 18 - Pump Cam Reference Pulse Error	DTC 34 - Injection Timing Stepper Motor Fault
DTC 19 - Crankshaft Position Reference Error	DTC 35 - Injection Pulse Width Error (Response Time Short)
DTC 21 - Accelerator Pedal Position 1 Circuit High	DTC 36 - Injection Pulse Width Error (Response Time Long)
DTC 22 - Accelerator Pedal Position 1 Circuit Low	* DTC 37 - TCC Brake Switch Stuck "ON"
DTC 23 - Accelerator Pedal Position 1 Circuit Range Fault	* DTC 38 - TCC Brake Switch Stuck "OFF"
* DTC 24 - Vehicle Speed Sensor Circuit Low (Output Speed Signal)	DTC 41 - Brake Switch Circuit Fault
DTC 25 - Accelerator Pedal Position 2 Circuit High	DTC 42 - Fuel Temperature Circuit Low (High Temp Indicated)
DTC 26 - Accelerator Pedal Position 2 Circuit Low	DTC 43 - Fuel Temperature Circuit High (Low Temp Indicated)
DTC 27 - Accelerator Pedal Position 2 Circuit Range Fault	DTC 44 - EGR Pulse Width Error
	DTC 45 - EGR Vent Error
	DTC 46 - Malfunction Indicator Lamp Circuit Fault

Fig. 102 Trouble code list for 1994-95 diesel engines

DIAGNOSTIC TROUBLE CODE (DTC) IDENTIFICATION

The MIL (Service Engine Soon) will only be "ON" if the malfunction exists with the conditions listed below. If the malfunction clears, the lamp will go out and the DTC will be stored in the PCM. Any DTCs stored will be erased if no problem reoccurs within 50 engine starts. Note: All DTCs with the sign * are transmission related DTCs.
Remember, always start with the lowest numerical DTC first, when diagnosing some engine DTCs trigger other transmission DTCs.

DTC AND CIRCUIT	PROBABLE CAUSE	DTC AND CIRCUIT	PROBABLE CAUSE
DTC 51 - Faulty PROM Problem	Faulty PROM or PCM.	*DTC 69 - TCC Stuck "ON"	Slip >-20 and slip 20 TCC is not locked gear =2,3 or 4 TPS >25%, not in P/N for 4 seconds.
*DTC 52 - Long System Voltage High	Generator Voltage is greater than 16V for 109 minutes.	*DTC 72 - Vehicle Speed Sensor Loss	Not in P/N - Output speed changes greater than 1000 RPM
*DTC 53 - System Voltage High	System overvoltage of 19.5 volts for 2 seconds		• P/N - Output speed changes greater than 2050 RPM
DTC 55 - Faulty PCM	Faulty PCM.		• For 2 seconds
*DTC 58 - Transmission Fluid Temperature High	Transmission fluid temperature greater than 154°C (309°F) for one second.	*DTC 73 - Pressure Control Solenoid	If return amperage varies more than 0.16 amps. from commanded amperage
*DTC 59 - Transmission Fluid Temperature Low	Transmission fluid temperature greater than -33°C (-27°F) for one second.	*DTC 75 - System Voltage Low	System voltage <7.3 at low temperature or <11.7 at high temperature for 4 seconds.
*DTC 66 - 3-2 Control Solenoid Circuit Fault	At High Duty Cycle the circuit voltage is high OR at Low Duty Cycle the Circuit Voltage is low for four seconds.	*DTC 79 - Transmission Fluid Over Temperature	Transmission fluid Temperature >150C and <154C for 15 minutes.
		*DTC 81 - 2-3 Shift Solenoid Circuit Fault	2-3 shift solenoid is command "ON", and circuit voltage is high for two seconds OR 2-3 shift solenoid is command "OFF", and circuit voltage is low for two seconds.
*DTC 67 Torque Converter Clutch Circuit	TCC is commanded "ON" and circuit voltage remains high for two seconds OR "TCC is commanded "OFF" and circuit voltage remains low for two seconds.	*DTC 82 - 1-2 Shift Solenoid Circuit Fault	1-2 shift solenoid is command "ON," and circuit voltage is high for two seconds OR 1-2 shift solenoid is command "OFF" and circuit voltage is low for two seconds.

Fig. 101 Trouble code list for 1991-93 diesel engines with 4L60E automatic transmissions (continued)

DTC	Description	Illuminate MIL
P0112	IAT Sensor Circuit Low Voltage	Yes
P0113	IAT Sensor Circuit High Voltage	Yes
P0117	ECT Sensor Circuit Low Voltage	Yes
P0118	ECT Sensor Circuit High Voltage	Yes
P0121	APP Sensor 1 Circuit Performance	No
P0122	APP Sensor 1 Circuit Low Voltage	No
P0123	APP Sensor 1 Circuit High Voltage	No
P0182	Fuel Temperature Sensor Circuit Low Voltage	Yes
P0183	Fuel Temperature Sensor Circuit High Voltage	Yes
P0215	Engine Shutoff Control Circuit	No
P0216	Injection Timing Control System	Yes
P0219	Engine Overspeed Condition	No
P0220	APP Sensor 2 Circuit	No
P0221	APP Sensor 2 Circuit Performance	No
P0222	APP Sensor 2 Circuit Low Voltage	No
P0223	APP Sensor 2 Circuit High Voltage	No
P0225	APP Sensor 3 Circuit	No
P0226	APP Sensor 3 Circuit Performance	No
P0227	APP Sensor 3 Circuit Low Voltage	No
P0228	APP Sensor 3 Circuit High Voltage	No
P0231	Lift Pump Secondary Circuit Low Voltage	No
P0236	TC Boost System	Yes
P0237	TC Boost Sensor Circuit Low Voltage	Yes
P0238	TC Boost Sensor Circuit High Voltage	Yes
P0251	Injection Pump Cam System	Yes
P0263	Cylinder 8 Balance System	No
P0266	Cylinder 7 Balance System	No
P0269	Cylinder 2 Balance System	No
P0272	Cylinder 6 Balance System	No
P0275	Cylinder 5 Balance System	No
P0278	Cylinder 4 Balance System	No
P0281	Cylinder 3 Balance System	No
P0284	Cylinder 1 Balance System	No
P0335	CKP Sensor Circuit Performance	Yes
P0370	Timing Reference High Resolution	Yes
P0380	Glow plug Circuit Performance	Yes
P0404	EGR System	Yes
P0405	EGR Sensor Circuit Low Voltage	Yes

87984G52

Fig. 104 Trouble code list for 1996-98 diesel engines

DIAGNOSTIC TROUBLE CODE (DTC) IDENTIFICATION

The MIL (Malfunction Indicator Lamp) will be "ON" if an emission malfunction exists. If the malfunction clears, the lamp will go "OFF" and the DTC will be stored in the PCM. Any DTC(s) stored will be cleared if no problem recurs within 50 engine starts.

🔲 Important

All DTC(s) with the sign * are transmission related DTC(s).
Remember, always start with the lowest numerical engine DTC first. When diagnosing some engine DTC(s), other transmission symptoms can occur.

DTC NUMBER AND NAME

DTC 47 - Intake Air Temperature Sensor Circuit Low (High Temp Indicated)

DTC 48 - Intake Air Temperature Sensor Circuit High (Low Temp Indicated)

DTC 49 - Service Throttle Soon Lamp Circuit Fault

* **DTC 51** - PROM Error

* **DTC 52** - System Voltage High Long

* **DTC 53** - System Voltage High

* **DTC 56** - Injection Pump Calibration Resistor Error

* **DTC 57** - PCM 5 Volt Shorted

* **DTC 58** - Trans Fluid Temp Circuit Low

* **DTC 59** - Trans Fluid Temp Circuit High

* **DTC 63** - Accelerator Pedal Position 3 Circuit High

* **DTC 64** - Accelerator Pedal Position 3 Circuit Low

* **DTC 65** - Accelerator Pedal Position 3 Circuit Range Fault

* **DTC 66** - 3-2 Control Solenoid Circuit

* **DTC 67** - TCC Solenoid Circuit

* **DTC 69** - TCC Stuck "ON"

* **DTC 71** - Set/Coast Switch Fault

DTC NUMBER AND NAME

* **DTC 72** - Vehicle Speed Sensor Circuit Loss (Output Speed Signal)

* **DTC 73** - Pressure Control Solenoid Circuit

* **DTC 75** - System Voltage Low

* **DTC 76** - Resume/Accel Switch Fault

* **DTC 79** - Trans Fluid Overtemp

* **DTC 81** - 2-3 Shift Solenoid Circuit

* **DTC 82** - 1-2 Shift Solenoid Circuit

* **DTC 88** - TDC Offset Error

DTC 91 - Cylinder Balance Fault #1 Cyl

DTC 92 - Cylinder Balance Fault #2 Cyl

DTC 93 - Cylinder Balance Fault #3 Cyl

DTC 94 - Cylinder Balance Fault #4 Cyl

DTC 95 - Cylinder Balance Fault #5 Cyl

DTC 96 - Cylinder Balance Fault #6 Cyl

DTC 97 - Cylinder Balance Fault #7 Cyl

DTC 98 - Cylinder Balance Fault #8 Cyl

DTC 99 - Accelerator Pedal Position 2 (5 Bolt Reference Fault)

87984G59

Fig. 103 Trouble code list for 1994-95 diesel engines (continued)

DTC	Description	Illuminate MIL
P0406	EGR Sensor Circuit High Voltage	Yes
P0501	Vehicle Speed Sensor Circuit	No
P0567	Cruise Resume Circuit	No
P0568	Cruise Set Circuit	No
P0571	Cruise Brake Switch Circuit	No
P0601	PCM Memory	No
P0602	PCM Not Programmed	No
P0606	PCM Internal Communication Interrupted	Yes
P1125	APP System	No
P1214	Injection Pump Timing Offset	Yes
P1216	Fuel Solenoid Response Time Too Short	No
P1217	Fuel Solenoid Response Time Too Long	No
P1218	Injection Pump Calibration Circuit	Yes
P1627	A/D Performance	Yes
P1635	5 Volt Reference Low	No
P1641	Malfunction Indicator Lamp (MIL) Control Circuit	No
P1653	EGR Vent Solenoid Control Circuit	Yes
P1654	Service Throttle Soon (STS) Lamp Control Circuit	No
P1655	EGR Solenoid Control Circuit	Yes
P1656	Wastegate Solenoid Control Circuit	Yes

Fig. 105 Trouble code list for 1996–98 diesel engines (continued)

87984G53

General Information

Since the control module is programmed to recognize the presence and value of electrical inputs, it will also note the lack of a signal or a radical change in values. It will, for example, react to the loss of signal from the vehicle speed sensor or note that engine coolant temperature has risen beyond acceptable (programmed) limits. Once a fault is recognized, a numeric code is assigned and held in memory. The dashboard warning lamp: CHECK ENGINE or SERVICE ENGINE SOON (SES), will illuminate to advise the operator that the system has detected a fault. This lamp is also known as the Malfunction Indicator Lamp (MIL).

More than one code may be stored. Keep in mind not every engine uses every code. Additionally, the same code may carry different meanings relative to each engine or engine family.

In the event of an computer control module failure, the system will default to a pre-programmed set of values. These are compromise values which allow the engine to operate, although possibly at reduced efficiency. This is variously known as the default, limp-in or back-up mode. Driveability is almost always affected when the ECM enters this mode.

SCAN TOOLS

♦ See Figures 106

On most models, the stored codes may be read with only the use of a small jumper wire, however the use of a hand-held scan tool such as GM's TECH-1 or equivalent is recommended. On 1996–98 models, an OBD-II compliant scan tool must be used. There are many manufacturers of these tools; a purchaser must be certain that the tool is proper for the intended use. If you own a scan type tool, it probably came with comprehensive instructions on proper use. Be sure to follow the instructions that came with your unit if they differ from what is given here; this is a general guide with useful information included.

The scan tool allows any stored codes to be read from the ECM or PCM memory. The tool also allows the operator to view the data being sent to the computer control module while the engine is running. This ability has obvious diagnostic advantages; the use of the scan tool is frequently required for component testing. The scan tool makes collecting information easier; the data must be correctly interpreted by an operator familiar with the system.

An example of the usefulness of the scan tool may be seen in the case of a temperature sensor which has changed its electrical characteristics. The ECM is reacting to an apparently warmer engine (causing a driveability problem), but the sensor's voltage has not changed enough to set a fault code. Connecting the scan tool, the voltage signal being sent to the ECM may be viewed; comparison to normal values or a known good vehicle reveals the problem quickly.

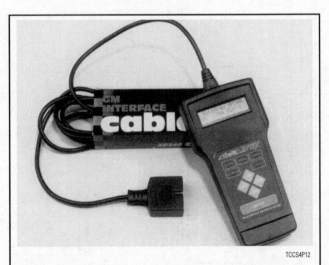

TCCS4P12

Fig. 106 Inexpensive scan tools, such as this Auto Xray®, are available to interface with your General Motors vehicle

ELECTRICAL TOOLS

The most commonly required electrical diagnostic tool is the digital multimeter, allowing voltage, ohmage (resistance) and amperage to be read by one instrument. The multimeter must be a high-impedance unit, with 10 megohms of impedance in the voltmeter. This type of meter will not place an additional load on the circuit it is testing; this is extremely important in low voltage circuits. The multimeter must be of high quality in all respects. It should be handled carefully and protected from impact or damage. Replace batteries frequently in the unit.

Other necessary tools include an unpowered test light, a quality tachometer with an inductive (clip-on) pick up, and the proper tools for releasing GM's Metri-Pack, Weather Pack and Micro-Pack terminals as necessary. The Micro-Pack connectors are used at the ECM electrical connector. A vacuum pump/gauge may also be required for checking sensors, solenoids and valves.

Diagnosis and Testing

Diagnosis of a driveability and/or emissions problems requires attention to detail and following the diagnostic procedures in the correct order. Resist the temptation to perform any repairs before performing the preliminary diagnostic steps. In many cases this will shorten diagnostic time and often cure the problem without electronic testing.

The proper troubleshooting procedure for these vehicles is as follows:

VISUAL/PHYSICAL INSPECTION

This is possibly the most critical step of diagnosis and should be performed immediately after retrieving any codes. A detailed examination of connectors, wiring and vacuum hoses can often lead to a repair without further diagnosis. Performance of this step relies on the skill of the technician performing it; a careful inspector will check the undersides of hoses as well as the integrity of hard-to-reach hoses blocked by the air cleaner or other component. Wiring should be checked carefully for any sign of strain, burning, crimping, or terminal pull-out from a connector. Checking connectors at components or in harnesses is required; usually, pushing them together will reveal a loose fit.

INTERMITTENTS

If a fault occurs intermittently, such as a loose connector pin breaking contact as the vehicle hits a bump, the ECM will note the fault as it occurs and energize the dash warning lamp. If the problem self-corrects, as with the terminal pin again making contact, the dash lamp will extinguish after 10 seconds but a code will remain stored in the computer control module's memory.

When an unexpected code appears during diagnostics, it may have been set during an intermittent failure that self-corrected; the codes are still useful in diagnosis and should not be discounted.

CIRCUIT/COMPONENT REPAIR

The fault codes and the scan tool data will lead to diagnosis and checking of a particular circuit. It is important to note that the fault code indicates a fault or loss of signal in an ECM-controlled system, not necessarily in the specific component.

Refer to the appropriate Diagnostic Code chart to determine the codes meaning. The component may then be tested following the appropriate component test procedures found in this section. If the component is OK, check the wiring for shorts or opens. Further diagnoses should be left to an experienced driveability technician.

If a code indicates the ECM to be faulty and the ECM is replaced, but does not correct the problem, one of the following may be the reason:

• There is a problem with the ECM terminal connections: The terminals may have to be removed from the connector in order to check them properly.

• The ECM or PROM is not correct for the application: The incorrect ECM or PROM may cause a malfunction and may or may not set a code.

• The problem is intermittent: This means that the problem is not present at the time the system is being checked. In this case, make a careful physical inspection of all portions of the system involved.

• Shorted solenoid, relay coil or harness: Solenoids and relays are turned on and off by the ECM using internal electronic switches called drivers. Each driver is part of a group of four called Quad-Drivers. A shorted solenoid, relay coil or harness may cause an ECM to fail, and a replacement ECM to fail when it is installed. Use a short tester, J34696, BT 8405, or equivalent, as a fast, accurate means of checking for a short circuit.

• The Programmable Read Only Memory (PROM) may be faulty: Although the PROM rarely fails, it operates as part of the ECM. Therefore, it could be the cause of the problem. Substitute a known good PROM.

• The replacement ECM may be faulty: After the ECM is replaced, the system should be rechecked for proper operation. If the diagnostic code again indicates the ECM is the problem, substitute a known good ECM. Although this is a very rare condition, it could happen.

Reading Codes

1988–95 MODELS

▶ See Figures 107 and 108

Listings of the trouble for the various engine control system covered in this manual are located in this section. Remember that a code only points to the faulty circuit NOT necessarily to a faulty component. Loose, damaged or corroded connections may contribute to a fault code on a circuit when the sensor or component is operating properly. Be sure that the components are faulty before replacing them, especially the expensive ones.

The Assembly Line Diagnostic Link (ALDL) connector or Data Link Connector (DLC) may be located under the dash and sometimes covered with a plastic cover labeled DIAGNOSTIC CONNECTOR.

1. The diagnostic trouble codes can be read by grounding test terminal B. The terminal is most easily grounded by connecting it to terminal A (internal ECM ground). This is the terminal to the right of terminal B on the top row of the ALDL connector.

2. Once the terminals have been connected, the ignition switch must be moved to the **ON** position with the engine not running.

3. The Service Engine Soon or Check Engine light should be flashing. If it isn't, turn the ignition **OFF** and remove the jumper wire. Turn the ignition **ON** and confirm that light is now on. If it is not, replace the bulb and try again. If the bulb still will not light, or if it does not flash with the test terminal grounded, the system should be diagnosed by an experienced driveability technician. If the light is OK, proceed as follows.

4. The code(s) stored in memory may be read through counting the flashes of the dashboard warning lamp. The dash warning lamp should begin to flash Code 12. The code will display as one flash, a pause and two flashes. Code 12 is not a fault code. It is used as a system acknowledgment or handshake code; its presence indicates that the ECM can communicate as requested. Code 12 is used to begin every diagnostic sequence. Some vehicles also use Code 12 after all diagnostic codes have been sent.

5. After Code 12 has been transmitted 3 times, the fault codes, if any, will each be transmitted 3 times. The codes are stored and transmitted in numeric order from lowest to highest.

➡The order of codes in the memory does not indicate the order of occurrence.

6. If there are no codes stored, but a driveability or emissions problem is evident, the system should be diagnosed by an experienced driveability technician.

7. If one or more codes are stored, record them. Refer to the applicable Diagnostic Code chart in this section.

8. Switch the ignition **OFF** when finished with code retrieval or scan tool readings.

➡After making repairs, clear the trouble codes and operate the vehicle to see if it will reset, indicating further problems.

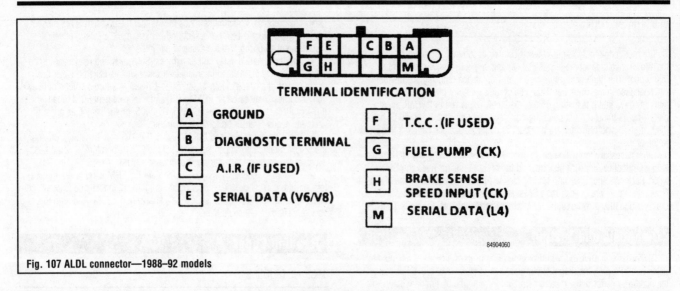

TERMINAL IDENTIFICATION

A	GROUND	F	T.C.C. (IF USED)
B	DIAGNOSTIC TERMINAL	G	FUEL PUMP (CK)
C	A.I.R. (IF USED)	H	BRAKE SENSE SPEED INPUT (CK)
E	SERIAL DATA (V6/V8)	M	SERIAL DATA (L4)

84904060

Fig. 107 ALDL connector—1988–92 models

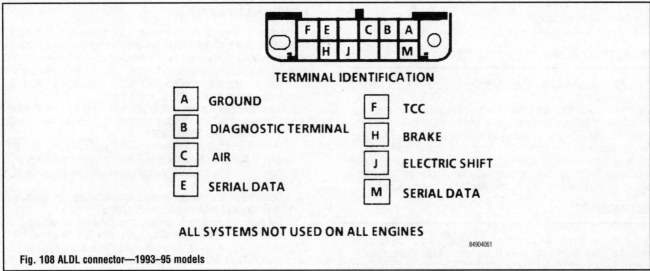

TERMINAL IDENTIFICATION

A	GROUND	F	TCC
B	DIAGNOSTIC TERMINAL	H	BRAKE
C	AIR	J	ELECTRIC SHIFT
E	SERIAL DATA	M	SERIAL DATA

ALL SYSTEMS NOT USED ON ALL ENGINES

84904061

Fig. 108 ALDL connector—1993–95 models

1996–98 MODELS

▶ See Figure 109

On 1996–98 models, an OBD-II compliant scan tool must be used to retrieve the trouble codes. Follow the scan tool manufacturer's instructions on how to connect the scan tool to the vehicle and how to retrieve the codes.

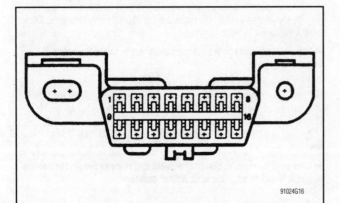

91024G16

Fig. 109 The Data Link Connector (DLC) is located under the left-hand side of the instrument panel—1996–98 models

Clearing Codes

Stored fault codes may be erased from memory at any time by removing power from the ECM for at least 30 seconds. It may be necessary to clear stored codes during diagnosis to check for any recurrence during a test drive, but the stored codes must be written down when retrieved. The codes may still be required for subsequent troubleshooting. Whenever a repair is complete, the stored codes must be erased and the vehicle test driven to confirm correct operation and repair.

✷✷ WARNING

The ignition switch must be OFF any time power is disconnected or restored to the ECM. Severe damage may result if this precaution is not observed.

Depending on the electrical distribution of the particular vehicle, power to the ECM may be disconnected by removing the ECM fuse in the fusebox, disconnecting the in-line fuse holder near the positive battery terminal or disconnecting the ECM power lead at the battery terminal. Disconnecting the negative battery cable to clear codes is not recommended as this will also clear other memory data in the vehicle such as radio presets.

COMPONENT LOCATIONS

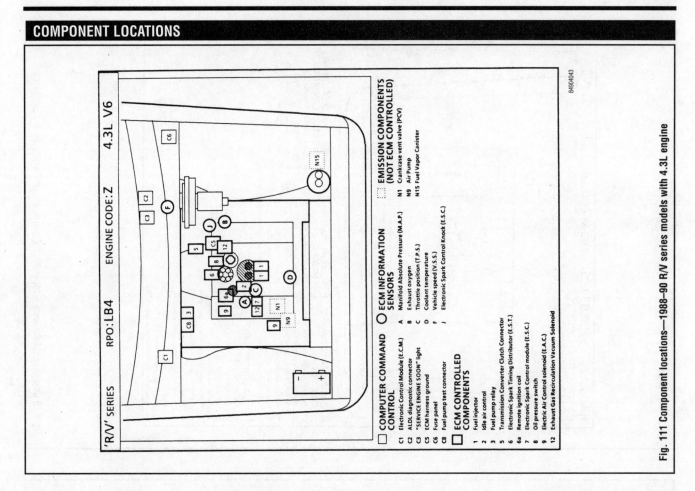

Fig. 111 Component locations—1988–90 R/V series models with 4.3L engine

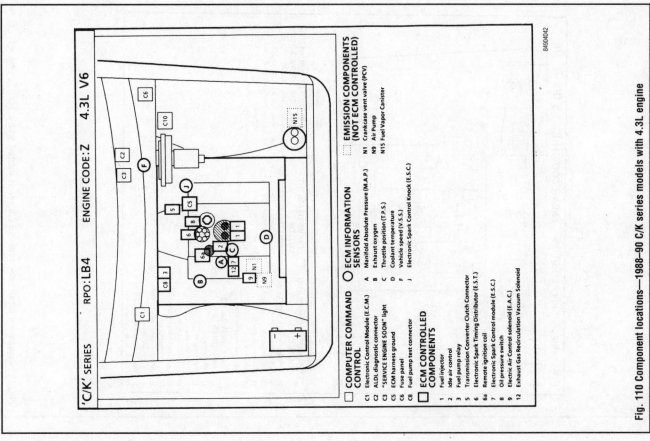

Fig. 110 Component locations—1988–90 C/K series models with 4.3L engine

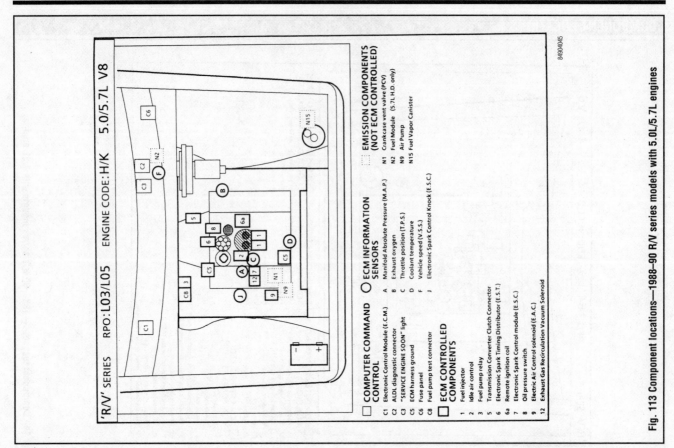

COMPUTER COMMAND CONTROL

C1 Electronic Control Module (E.C.M.)
C2 ALDL diagnostic connector
C5 "SERVICE ENGINE SOON" light
C6 ECM harness ground
C6 Fuse panel
C8 Fuel pump test connector

ECM CONTROLLED COMPONENTS

1 Fuel injector
2 Idle air control
3 Fuel pump relay
5 Transmission Converter Clutch Connector
6 Electronic Spark Timing Distributor (E.S.T.)
6a Remote ignition coil
7 Electronic Spark Control module (E.S.C.)
8 Oil pressure switch
9 Electric Air Control solenoid (E.A.C.)
12 Exhaust Gas Recirculation Vacuum Solenoid

ECM INFORMATION SENSORS

A Manifold Absolute Pressure (M.A.P.)
B Exhaust oxygen
C Throttle position (T.P.S.)
D Coolant temperature
F Vehicle speed (V.S.S.)
J Electronic Spark Control Knock (E.S.C.)

EMISSION COMPONENTS (NOT ECM CONTROLLED)

N1 Crankcase vent valve (PCV)
N2 Fuel Module (5.7L H.D. only)
N9 Air Pump
N15 Fuel Vapor Canister

Fig. 113 Component locations—1988-90 R/V series models with 5.0L/5.7L engines

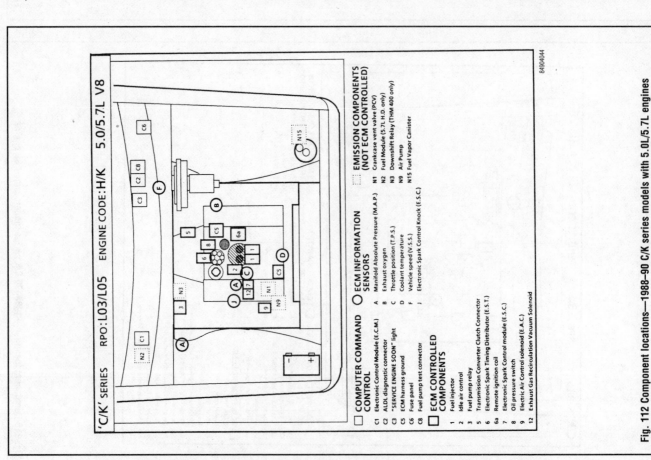

COMPUTER COMMAND CONTROL

C1 Electronic Control Module (E.C.M.)
C2 ALDL diagnostic connector
C5 "SERVICE ENGINE SOON" light
C6 ECM harness ground
C6 Fuse panel
C8 Fuel pump test connector

ECM CONTROLLED COMPONENTS

1 Fuel injector
2 Idle air control
3 Fuel pump relay
5 Transmission Converter Clutch Connector
6 Electronic Spark Timing Distributor (E.S.T.)
6a Remote ignition coil
7 Electronic Spark Control module (E.S.C.)
8 Oil pressure switch
9 Electric Air Control solenoid (E.A.C.)
12 Exhaust Gas Recirculation Vacuum Solenoid

ECM INFORMATION SENSORS

A Manifold Absolute Pressure (M.A.P.)
B Exhaust oxygen
C Throttle position (T.P.S.)
D Coolant temperature
F Vehicle speed (V.S.S.)
J Electronic Spark Control Knock (E.S.C.)

EMISSION COMPONENTS (NOT ECM CONTROLLED)

N1 Crankcase vent valve (PCV)
N2 Fuel Module (5.7L H.D. only)
N3 Downshift Relay (THM 400 only)
N9 Air Pump
N15 Fuel Vapor Canister

Fig. 112 Component locations—1988-90 C/K series models with 5.0L/5.7L engines

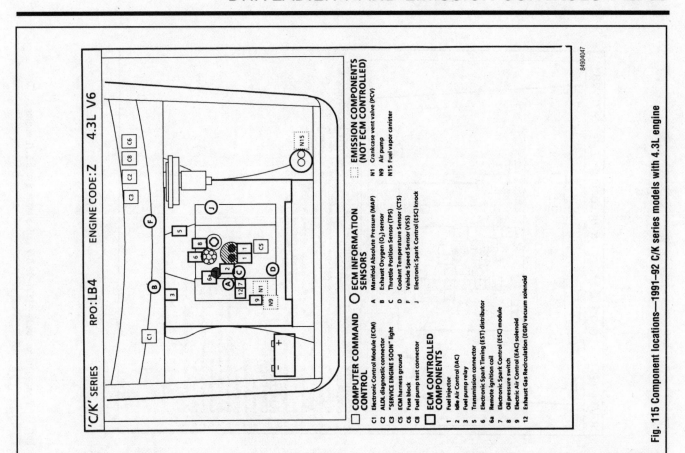

Fig. 115 Component locations—1991–92 C/K series models with 4.3L engine

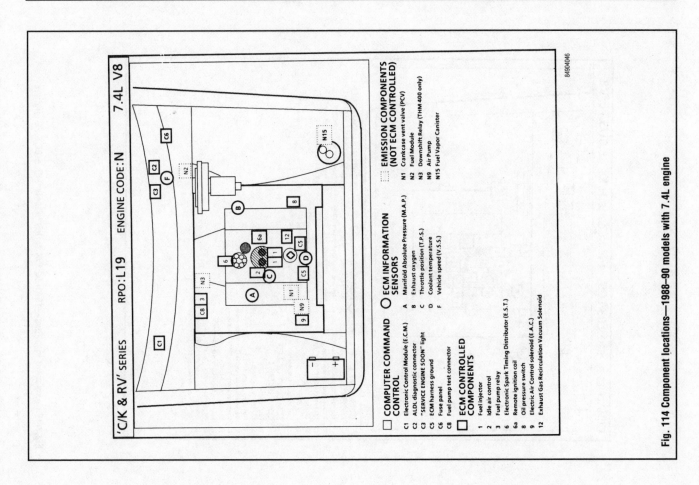

Fig. 114 Component locations—1988–90 models with 7.4L engine

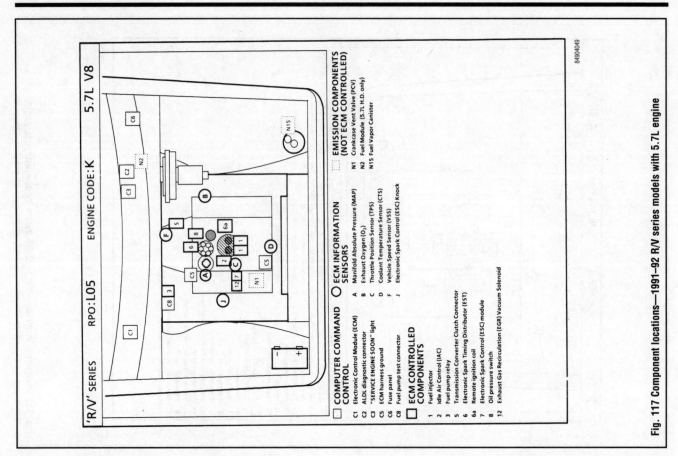

Fig. 117 Component locations—1991-92 R/V series models with 5.7L engine

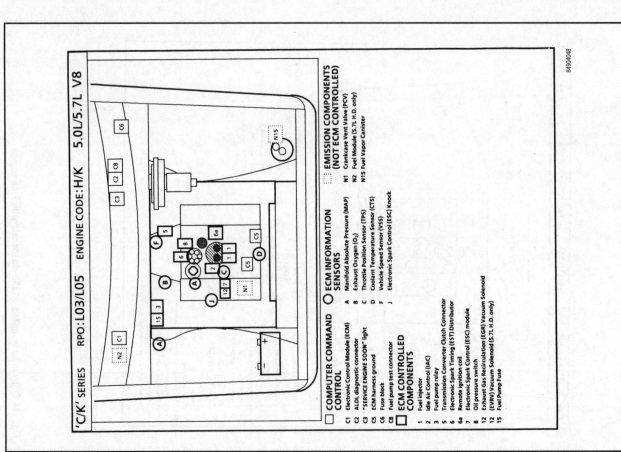

Fig. 116 Component locations—1991-92 C/K series models with 5.0L/5.7L engines

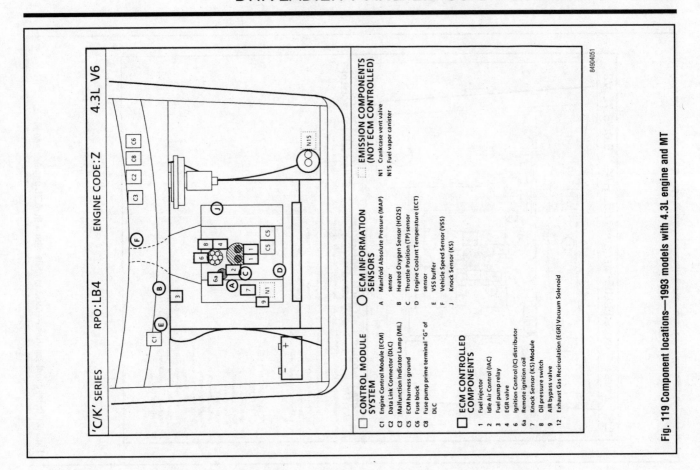

'C/K' SERIES   RPO: LB4   ENGINE CODE: Z   4.3L V6

□ CONTROL MODULE SYSTEM

C1 Engine Control Module (ECM)
C2 Data Link Connector (DLC)
C3 Malfunction Indicator Lamp (MIL)
C6 ECM harness ground
C6 Fuse block
C8 Fuse pump prime terminal "G" of DLC

○ ECM INFORMATION SENSORS

A Manifold Absolute Pressure (MAP) sensor
B Heated Oxygen Sensor (HO2S)
C Throttle Position (TP) sensor
D Engine Coolant Temperature (ECT) sensor
E VSS buffer
F Vehicle Speed Sensor (VSS)
J Knock Sensor (KS)

□ ECM CONTROLLED COMPONENTS

1 Fuel injector
2 Idle Air Control (IAC)
3 Fuel pump relay
4 EGR valve
6 Ignition Control (IC) distributor
6a Remote ignition coil
8 Oil pressure switch
9 AIR bypass valve
12 Exhaust Gas Recirculation (EGR) Vacuum Solenoid

⋮ EMISSION COMPONENTS (NOT ECM CONTROLLED)

N1 Crankcase vent valve
N15 Fuel vapor canister

Fig. 119 Component locations—1993 models with 4.3L engine and MT

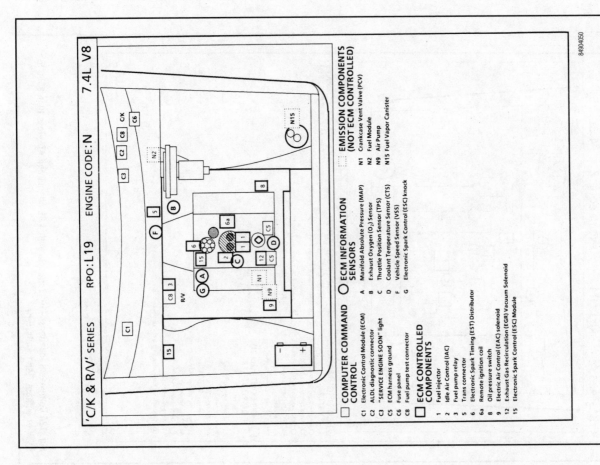

'C/K & R/V' SERIES   RPO: L19   ENGINE CODE: N   7.4L V8

□ COMPUTER COMMAND CONTROL

C1 Electronic Control Module (ECM)
C2 ALDL diagnostic connector
C3 "SERVICE ENGINE SOON" light
C5 ECM harness ground
C6 Fuse panel
C8 Fuel pump test connector

□ ECM CONTROLLED COMPONENTS

1 Fuel injector
2 Idle Air Control (IAC)
3 Fuel pump relay
5 Trans connector
6 Electronic Spark Timing (EST) Distributor
6a Remote ignition coil
8 Oil pressure switch
9 Electric Air Control (EAC) solenoid
12 Exhaust Gas Recirculation (EGR) Vacuum Solenoid
15 Electronic Spark Control (ESC) Module

○ ECM INFORMATION SENSORS

A Manifold Absolute Pressure (MAP)
B Exhaust Oxygen (O2) Sensor
C Throttle Position Sensor (TPS)
D Coolant Temperature Sensor (CTS)
F Vehicle Speed Sensor (VSS)
G Electronic Spark Control (ESC) knock

⋮ EMISSION COMPONENTS (NOT ECM CONTROLLED)

N1 Crankcase Vent Valve (PCV)
N2 Fuel Module
N9 Air Pump
N15 Fuel Vapor Canister

Fig. 118 Component locations—1991–92 models with 7.4L engine

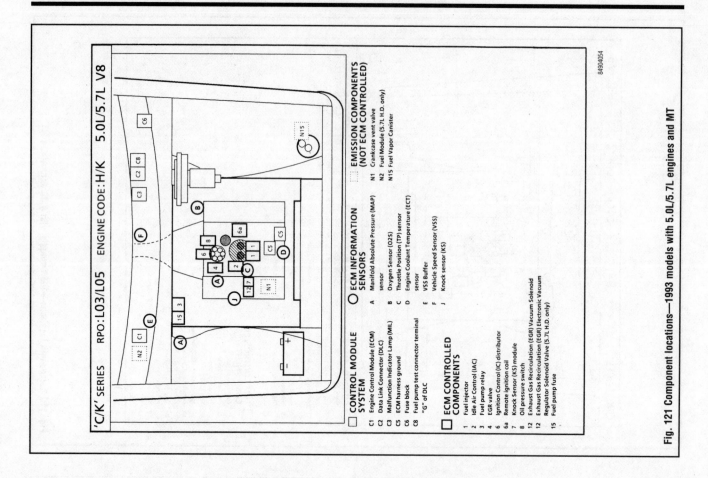

'C/K' SERIES   RPO: L03/L05   ENGINE CODE: H/K   5.0L/5.7L V8

□ **CONTROL MODULE SYSTEM**
C1 Engine Control Module (ECM)
C2 Data Link Connector (DLC)
C3 Malfunction Indicator Lamp (MIL)
C5 ECM harness ground
C6 Fuse block
C8 Fuel pump test connector terminal "G" of DLC

○ **ECM INFORMATION SENSORS**
A Manifold Absolute Pressure (MAP) sensor
B Oxygen Sensor (O2S)
C Throttle Position (TP) sensor
D Engine Coolant Temperature (ECT) sensor
E VSS Buffer
F Vehicle Speed Sensor (VSS)
J Knock sensor (KS)

□ **ECM CONTROLLED COMPONENTS**
1 Fuel injector
2 Idle Air Control (IAC)
3 Fuel pump relay
4 EGR valve
6 Ignition Control (IC) distributor
6a Remote ignition coil
7 Knock Sensor (KS) module
8 Oil pressure switch
12 Exhaust Gas Recirculation (EGR) Vacuum Solenoid
12 Exhaust Gas Recirculation (EGR) Electronic Vacuum Regulator Solenoid Valve (5.7L H.D. only)
15 Fuel pump fuse

▒ **EMISSION COMPONENTS (NOT ECM CONTROLLED)**
N1 Crankcase vent valve
N2 Fuel Module (5.7L H.D. only)
N15 Fuel Vapor Canister

Fig. 121 Component locations—1993 models with 5.0L/5.7L engines and MT

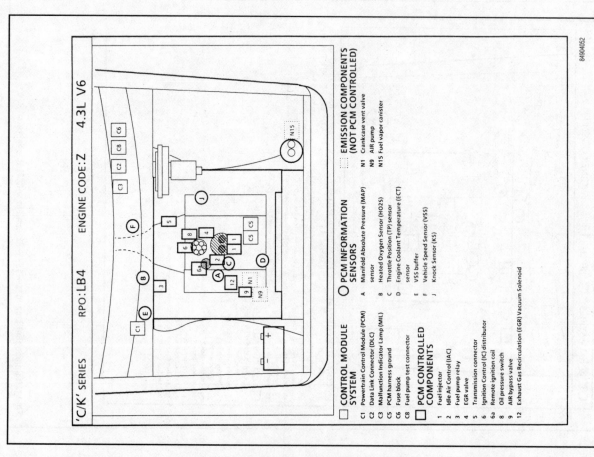

'C/K' SERIES   RPO: LB4   ENGINE CODE: Z   4.3L V6

□ **CONTROL MODULE SYSTEM**
C1 Powertrain Control Module (PCM)
C2 Data Link Connector (DLC)
C3 Malfunction Indicator Lamp (MIL)
C5 PCM harness ground
C6 Fuse block
C8 Fuel pump test connector

○ **PCM INFORMATION SENSORS**
A Manifold Absolute Pressure (MAP) sensor
B Heated Oxygen Sensor (HO2S) sensor
C Throttle Position (TP) sensor
D Engine Coolant Temperature (ECT) sensor
E VSS buffer
F Vehicle Speed Sensor (VSS)
J Knock Sensor (KS)

□ **PCM CONTROLLED COMPONENTS**
1 Fuel injector
2 Idle Air Control (IAC)
3 Fuel pump relay
4 EGR valve
5 Transmission connector
6a Remote ignition coil
6 Ignition Control (IC) distributor
8 Oil pressure switch
9 Air bypass valve
12 Exhaust Gas Recirculation (EGR) Vacuum Solenoid

▒ **EMISSION COMPONENTS (NOT PCM CONTROLLED)**
N1 Crankcase vent valve
N9 Air pump
N15 Fuel vapor canister

Fig. 120 Component locations—1993 models with 4.3L engine and AT—less than 8500 lbs. GVW or without Tier 1 emissions

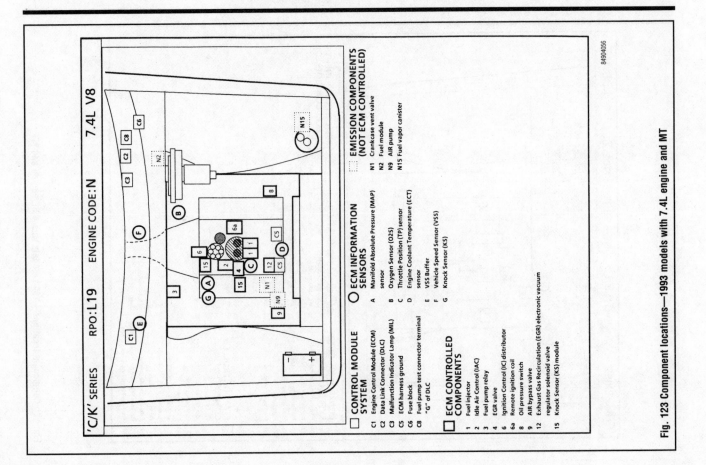

'C/K' SERIES   RPO: L19   ENGINE CODE: N   7.4L V8

CONTROL MODULE SYSTEM
C1 Engine Control Module (ECM)
C2 Data Link Connector (DLC)
C3 Malfunction Indicator Lamp (MIL)
C5 ECM harness ground
C6 Fuse block
C8 Fuel pump test connector terminal "G" of DLC

ECM INFORMATION SENSORS
A Manifold Absolute Pressure (MAP) sensor
B Oxygen Sensor (O2S)
C Throttle Position (TP) sensor
D Engine Coolant Temperature (ECT) sensor
E VSS Buffer
F Vehicle Speed Sensor (VSS)
G Knock Sensor (KS)

EMISSION COMPONENTS (NOT ECM CONTROLLED)
N1 Crankcase vent valve
N2 Fuel module
N9 AIR pump
N15 Fuel vapor canister

ECM CONTROLLED COMPONENTS
1 Fuel injector
2 Idle Air Control (IAC)
3 Fuel pump relay
4 EGR valve
6 Ignition Control (IC) distributor
6a Remote ignition coil
8 Oil pressure switch
9 AIR bypass valve
12 Exhaust Gas Recirculation (EGR) electronic vacuum regulator solenoid valve
15 Knock Sensor (KS) module

Fig. 123 Component locations—1993 models with 7.4L engine and MT

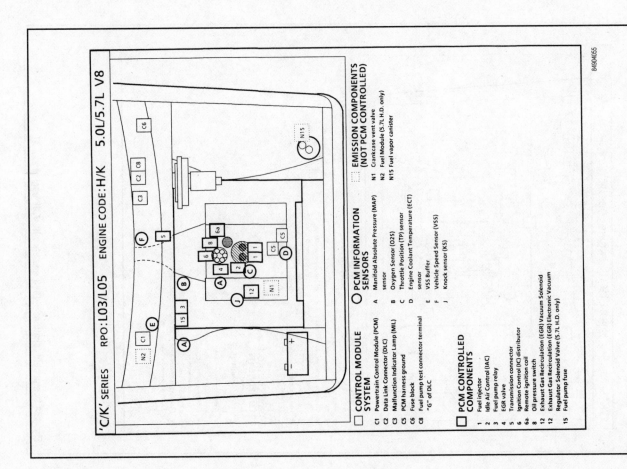

'C/K' SERIES   RPO: L03/L05   ENGINE CODE: H/K   5.0L/5.7L V8

CONTROL MODULE SYSTEM
C1 Powertrain Control Module (PCM)
C2 Data Link Connector (DLC)
C3 Malfunction Indicator Lamp (MIL)
C5 PCM harness ground
C6 Fuse block
C8 Fuel pump test connector terminal "G" of DLC

PCM INFORMATION SENSORS
A Manifold Absolute Pressure (MAP) sensor
B Oxygen Sensor (O2S)
C Throttle Position (TP) sensor
D Engine Coolant Temperature (ECT) sensor
E VSS Buffer
F Vehicle Speed Sensor (VSS)
J Knock sensor (KS)

EMISSION COMPONENTS (NOT PCM CONTROLLED)
N1 Crankcase vent valve
N2 Fuel Module (5.7L H.D. only)
N15 Fuel vapor canister

PCM CONTROLLED COMPONENTS
1 Fuel injector
2 Idle Air Control (IAC)
3 Fuel pump relay
4 EGR valve
5 Transmission connector
6 Ignition Control (IC) distributor
6a Remote ignition coil
8 Oil pressure switch
12 Exhaust Gas Recirculation (EGR) Vacuum Solenoid
12 Exhaust Gas Recirculation (EGR) Electronic Vacuum
15 Regulator Solenoid Valve (5.7L H.D. only)
15 Fuel pump fuse

Fig. 122 Component locations—1993 models with 5.0L/5.7L engines and AT

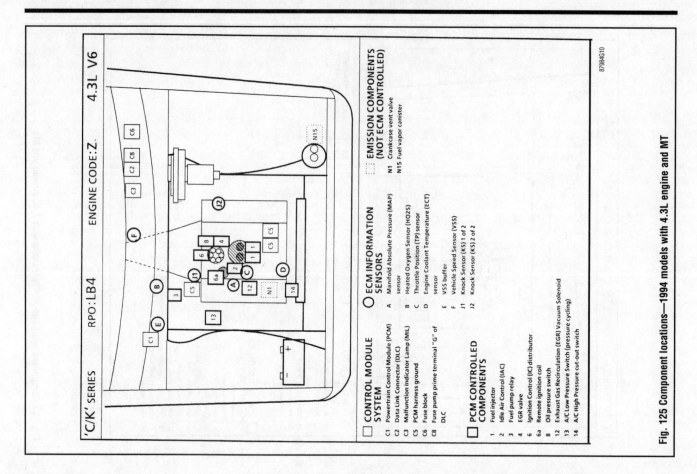

'C/K' SERIES   RPO:LB4   ENGINE CODE:Z   4.3L V6

CONTROL MODULE SYSTEM

C1 Powertrain Control Module (PCM)
C2 Data Link Connector (DLC)
C3 Malfunction Indicator Lamp (MIL)
C5 PCM harness ground
C6 Fuse block
C8 Fuse pump prime terminal "G" of DLC

PCM CONTROLLED COMPONENTS

1   Fuel injector
2   Idle Air Control (IAC)
3   Fuel pump relay
4   EGR valve
6   Ignition Control (IC) distributor
6a Remote ignition coil
8   Oil pressure switch
12 Exhaust Gas Recirculation (EGR) Vacuum Solenoid
13 A/C Low Pressure Switch (pressure cycling)
14 A/C High Pressure cut-out switch

ECM INFORMATION SENSORS

A   Manifold Absolute Pressure (MAP) sensor
B   Heated Oxygen Sensor (HO2S)
C   Throttle Position (TP) sensor
D   Engine Coolant Temperature (ECT) sensor
E   VSS buffer
F   Vehicle Speed Sensor (VSS)
J1 Knock Sensor (KS) 1 of 2
J2 Knock Sensor (KS) 2 of 2

EMISSION COMPONENTS (NOT ECM CONTROLLED)

N1   Crankcase vent valve
N15 Fuel vapor canister

87984G10

Fig. 125 Component locations—1994 models with 4.3L engine and MT

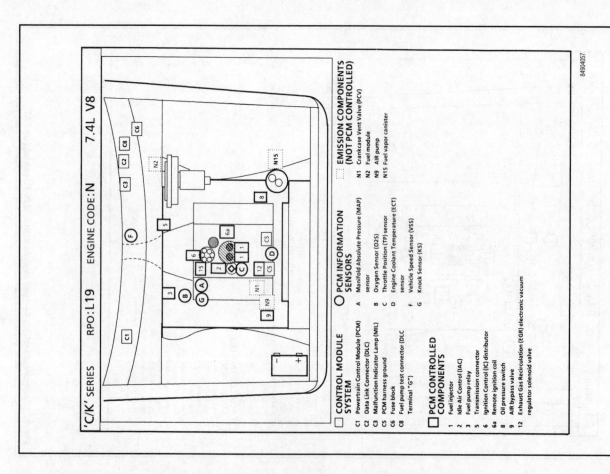

'C/K' SERIES   RPO:L19   ENGINE CODE:N   7.4L V8

CONTROL MODULE SYSTEM

C1 Powertrain Control Module (PCM)
C2 Data Link Connector (DLC)
C3 Malfunction Indicator Lamp (MIL)
C5 PCM harness ground
C6 Fuse block
C8 Fuse pump test connector (DLC Terminal "G")

PCM CONTROLLED COMPONENTS

1   Fuel injector
2   Idle Air Control (IAC)
3   Fuel pump relay
5   Transmission connector
6   Ignition Control (IC) distributor
6a Remote ignition coil
8   Oil pressure switch
9   AIR bypass valve
12 Exhaust Gas Recirculation (EGR) electronic vacuum regulator solenoid valve

PCM INFORMATION SENSORS

A   Manifold Absolute Pressure (MAP) sensor
B   Oxygen Sensor (O2S)
C   Throttle Position (TP) sensor
D   Engine Coolant Temperature (ECT) sensor
F   Vehicle Speed Sensor (VSS)
G   Knock Sensor (KS)

EMISSION COMPONENTS (NOT PCM CONTROLLED)

N1   Crankcase Vent Valve (PCV)
N2   Fuel module
N9   AIR pump
N15 Fuel vapor canister

8494057

Fig. 124 Component locations—1993 models with 7.4L engine and AT

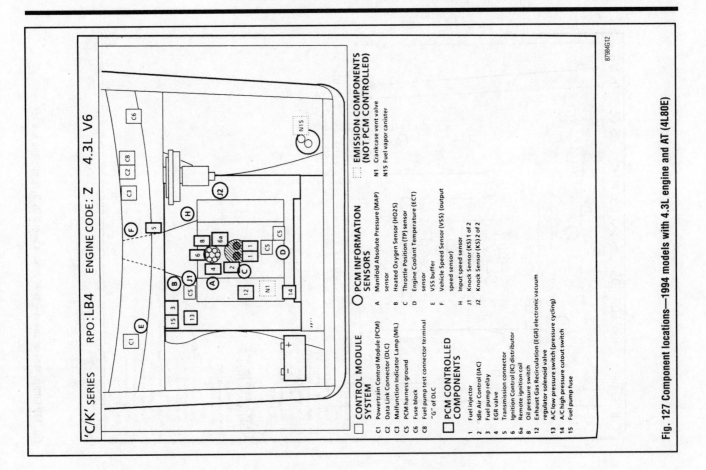

Fig. 127 Component locations—1994 models with 4.3L engine and AT (4L80E)

'C/K' SERIES   RPO:LB4   ENGINE CODE: Z   4.3L V6

CONTROL MODULE SYSTEM

C1 Powertrain Control Module (PCM)
C2 Data Link Connector (DLC)
C3 Malfunction Indicator Lamp (MIL)
C5 PCM harness ground
C6 Fuse block
C8 Fuel pump test connector terminal "G" of DLC

PCM CONTROLLED COMPONENTS

1 Fuel injector
2 Idle Air Control (IAC)
3 Fuel pump relay
4 EGR valve
5 Ignition Control (IC) distributor
6 Remote ignition coil
6a Ignition Control (IC) distributor
8 Oil pressure switch
12 Exhaust Gas Recirculation (EGR) electronic vacuum regulator solenoid valve
13 A/C low pressure switch (pressure cycling)
14 A/C high pressure cutout switch
15 Fuel pump fuse

PCM INFORMATION SENSORS

A Manifold Absolute Pressure (MAP) sensor
B Heated Oxygen Sensor (HO2S)
C Throttle Position (TP) sensor
D Engine Coolant Temperature (ECT) sensor
E VSS buffer
F Vehicle Speed Sensor (VSS) (output speed sensor)
H Input speed sensor
J1 Knock Sensor (KS) 1 of 2
J2 Knock Sensor (KS) 2 of 2

EMISSION COMPONENTS (NOT PCM CONTROLLED)

N1 Crankcase vent valve
N15 Fuel vapor canister

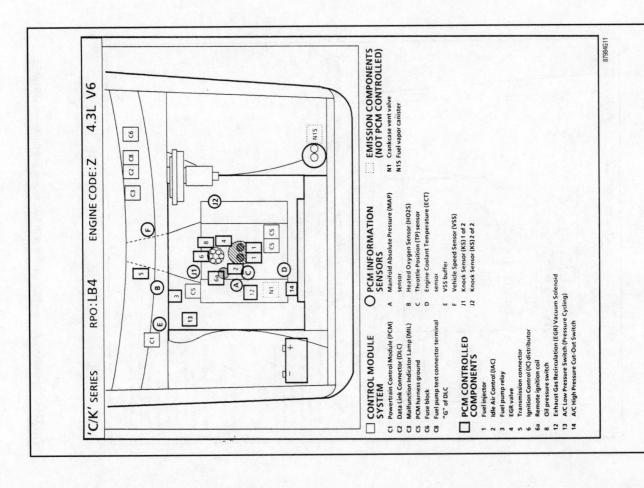

Fig. 126 Component locations—1994 models with 4.3L engine and AT

'C/K' SERIES   RPO:LB4   ENGINE CODE: Z   4.3L V6

CONTROL MODULE SYSTEM

C1 Powertrain Control Module (PCM)
C2 Data Link Connector (DLC)
C3 Malfunction Indicator Lamp (MIL)
C5 PCM harness ground
C6 Fuse block
C8 Fuel pump test connector terminal "G" of DLC

PCM CONTROLLED COMPONENTS

1 Fuel injector
2 Idle Air Control (IAC)
3 Fuel pump relay
4 EGR valve
5 Ignition Control (IC) distributor
6 Remote ignition coil
6a Ignition Control (IC) distributor
8 Oil pressure switch
13 Exhaust Gas Recirculation (EGR) Vacuum Solenoid
14 A/C Low Pressure Switch (Pressure Cycling)
A/C High Pressure Cut-Out Switch

PCM INFORMATION SENSORS

A Manifold Absolute Pressure (MAP) sensor
B Heated Oxygen Sensor (HO2S)
C Throttle Position (TP) sensor
D Engine Coolant Temperature (ECT) sensor
E VSS buffer
F Vehicle Speed Sensor (VSS)
J1 Knock Sensor (KS) 1 of 2
J2 Knock Sensor (KS) 2 of 2

EMISSION COMPONENTS (NOT PCM CONTROLLED)

N1 Crankcase vent valve
N15 Fuel vapor canister

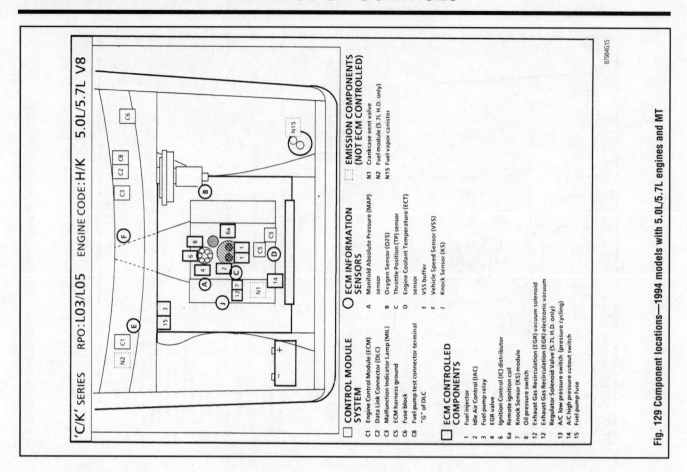

Fig. 129 Component locations—1994 models with 5.0L/5.7L engines and MT

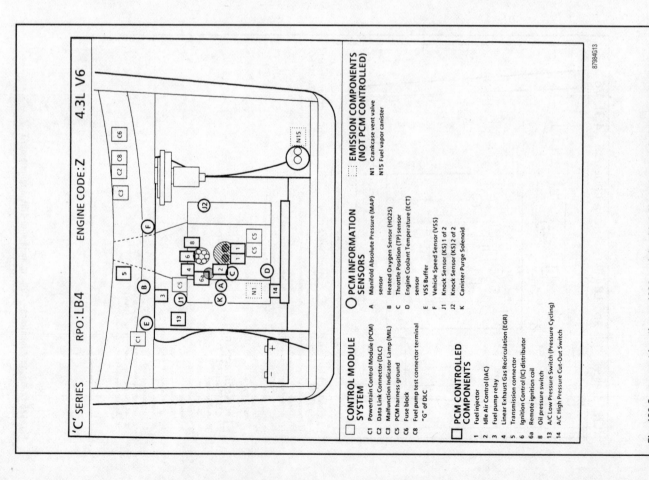

Fig. 128 Component locations—1994 models with 4.3L engine and California emissions

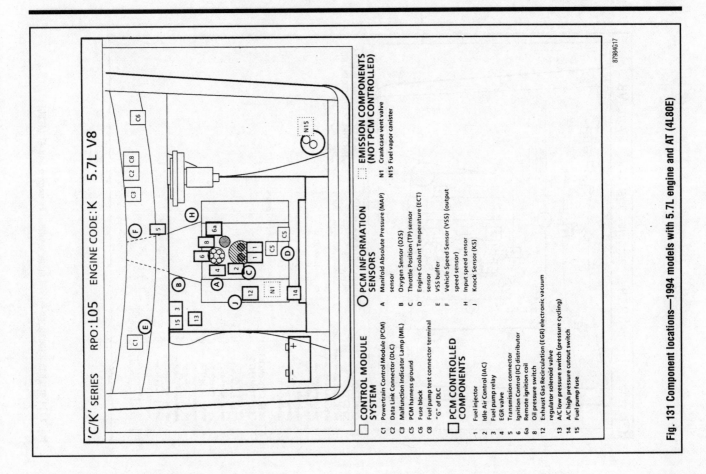

87984G17

'C/K' SERIES   RPO: L05   ENGINE CODE: K   5.7L V8

CONTROL MODULE SYSTEM

C1 Powertrain Control Module (PCM)
C2 Data Link Connector (DLC)
C3 Malfunction Indicator Lamp (MIL)
C5 PCM harness ground
C6 Fuse block
C8 Fuel pump test connector terminal
"G" of DLC

PCM CONTROLLED COMPONENTS

1 Fuel injector
2 Idle Air Control (IAC)
3 Fuel pump relay
4 EGR valve
5 Transmission connector
6 Ignition Control (IC) distributor
6a Remote ignition coil
8 Oil pressure switch
12 Exhaust Gas Recirculation (EGR) electronic vacuum regulator solenoid valve
13 A/C low pressure switch (pressure cycling)
14 A/C high pressure cutout switch
15 Fuel pump fuse

PCM INFORMATION SENSORS

A Manifold Absolute Pressure (MAP) sensor
B Oxygen Sensor (O2S)
C Throttle Position (TP) sensor
D Engine Coolant Temperature (ECT) sensor
E VSS buffer
F Vehicle Speed Sensor (VSS) (output speed sensor)
H Input speed sensor
J Knock Sensor (KS)

EMISSION COMPONENTS (NOT PCM CONTROLLED)

N1 Crankcase vent valve
N15 Fuel vapor canister

Fig. 131 Component locations—1994 models with 5.7L engine and AT (4L80E)

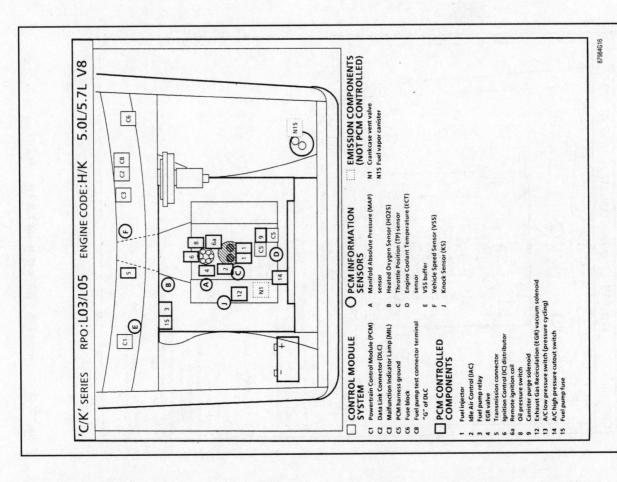

87984G16

'C/K' SERIES   RPO: L03/L05   ENGINE CODE: H/K   5.0L/5.7L V8

CONTROL MODULE SYSTEM

C1 Powertrain Control Module (PCM)
C2 Data Link Connector (DLC)
C3 Malfunction Indicator Lamp (MIL)
C5 PCM harness ground
C6 Fuse block
C8 Fuel pump test connector terminal
"G" of DLC

PCM CONTROLLED COMPONENTS

1 Fuel injector
2 Idle Air Control (IAC)
3 Fuel pump relay
4 EGR valve
5 Transmission connector
6 Ignition Control (IC) distributor
6a Remote ignition coil
8 Oil pressure switch
9 Canister purge solenoid
12 Exhaust Gas Recirculation (EGR) vacuum solenoid
13 A/C low pressure switch (pressure cycling)
14 A/C high pressure cutout switch
15 Fuel pump fuse

PCM INFORMATION SENSORS

A Manifold Absolute Pressure (MAP) sensor
B Heated Oxygen Sensor (HO2S) sensor
C Throttle Position (TP) sensor
D Engine Coolant Temperature (ECT) sensor
E VSS buffer
F Vehicle Speed Sensor (VSS)
J Knock Sensor (KS)

EMISSION COMPONENTS (NOT PCM CONTROLLED)

N1 Crankcase vent valve
N15 Fuel vapor canister

Fig. 130 Component locations—1994 models with 5.0L/5.7L engines and AT (4L80E)

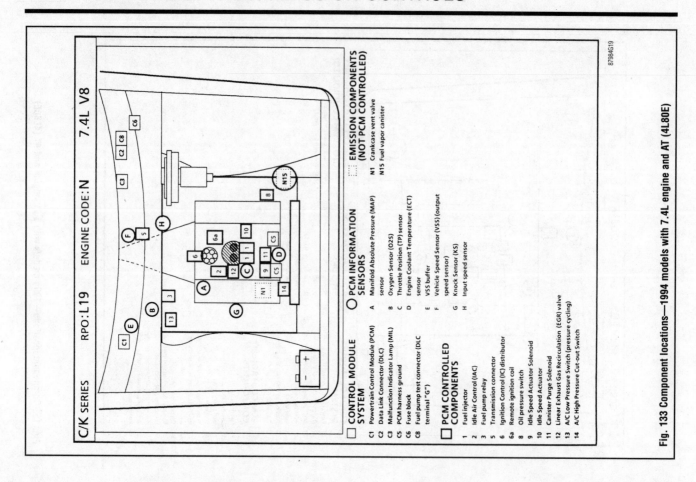

CONTROL MODULE SYSTEM

C1 Powertrain Control Module (PCM)
C2 Data Link Connector (DLC)
C3 Malfunction Indicator Lamp (MIL)
C5 PCM harness ground
C6 Fuse block
C8 Fuel pump test connector (DLC terminal "G")

PCM CONTROLLED COMPONENTS

1 Fuel injector
2 Idle Air Control (IAC)
3 Fuel pump relay
5 Transmission connector
6 Ignition Control (IC) distributor
6a Remote ignition coil
8 Oil pressure switch
9 Idle Speed Actuator Solenoid
10 Idle Speed Actuator
11 Canister Purge Solenoid
12 Linear Exhaust Gas Recirculation (EGR) valve
13 A/C Low Pressure Switch (pressure cycling)
14 A/C High Pressure Cut-out Switch

PCM INFORMATION SENSORS

A Manifold Absolute Pressure (MAP) sensor
B Oxygen Sensor (O2S)
C Throttle Position (TP) sensor
D Engine Coolant Temperature (ECT) sensor
E VSS buffer
F Vehicle Speed Sensor (VSS) (output speed sensor)
G Knock Sensor (KS)
H Input speed sensor

EMISSION COMPONENTS (NOT PCM CONTROLLED)

N1 Crankcase vent valve
N15 Fuel vapor canister

Fig. 133 Component locations—1994 models with 7.4L engine and AT (4L80E)

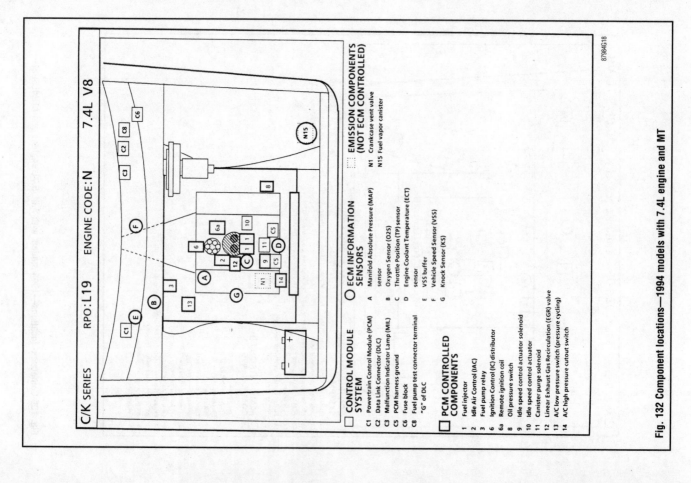

CONTROL MODULE SYSTEM

C1 Powertrain Control Module (PCM)
C2 Data Link Connector (DLC)
C3 Malfunction Indicator Lamp (MIL)
C5 PCM harness ground
C6 Fuse block
C8 Fuel pump test connector terminal "G" of DLC

PCM CONTROLLED COMPONENTS

1 Fuel injector
2 Idle Air Control (IAC)
3 Fuel pump relay
6 Ignition Control (IC) distributor
6a Remote ignition coil
8 Oil pressure switch
9 Idle speed control actuator solenoid
10 Idle speed control actuator
11 Canister purge solenoid
12 Linear Exhaust Gas Recirculation (EGR) valve
13 A/C low pressure switch (pressure cycling)
14 A/C high pressure cutout switch

ECM INFORMATION SENSORS

A Manifold Absolute Pressure (MAP) sensor
B Oxygen Sensor (O2S)
C Throttle Position (TP) sensor
D Engine Coolant Temperature (ECT) sensor
E VSS buffer
F Vehicle Speed Sensor (VSS)
G Knock Sensor (KS)

EMISSION COMPONENTS (NOT ECM CONTROLLED)

N1 Crankcase vent valve
N15 Fuel vapor canister

Fig. 132 Component locations—1994 models with 7.4L engine and MT

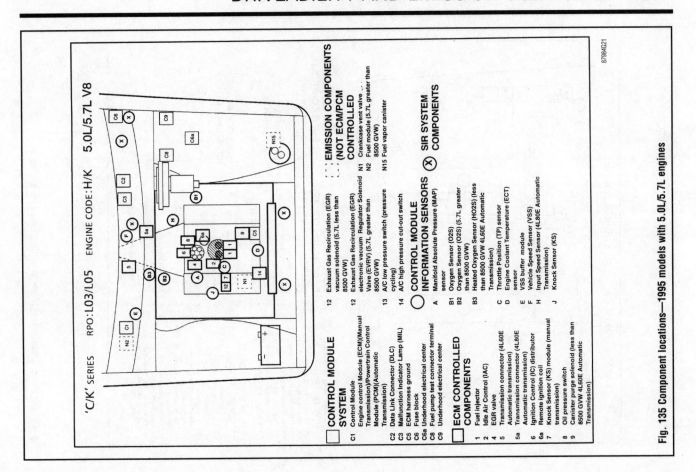

'C/K' SERIES   RPO: L03/L05   ENGINE CODE: H/K   5.0L/5.7L V8

CONTROL MODULE SYSTEM

C1 Control Module
Engine control Module (ECM)(Manual Transmission)/Powertrain Control Module (PCM)(Automatic Transmission)
C2 Data Link Connector (DLC)
C3 Malfunction Indicator Lamp (MIL)
C5 ECM harness ground
C6 Fuse block
C6a Underhood electrical center
C8 Fuel pump test connector terminal
C9 Underhood electrical center

ECM CONTROLLED COMPONENTS

1 Fuel injector
2 Idle Air Control (IAC)
4 EGR valve
5 Transmission connector (4L60E Automatic transmission)
5a Transmission connector (4L60E Automatic transmission)
6 Ignition Control (IC) distributor
6a Remote ignition coil
7 Knock Sensor (KS) module (manual transmission)
8 Oil pressure switch
9 Canister purge solenoid (less than 8500 GVW 4L60E Automatic Transmission)

12 Exhaust Gas Recirculation (EGR) vacuum solenoid (5.7L less than 8500 GVW)
12 Exhaust Gas Recirculation (EGR) electronic vacuum Regulator Solenoid Valve (EVRV) (5.7L greater than 8500 GVW)
13 A/C low pressure switch (pressure cycling)
14 A/C high pressure cut-out switch

CONTROL MODULE INFORMATION SENSORS

A Manifold Absolute Pressure (MAP) sensor
B1 Oxygen Sensor (O2S)
B2 Oxygen Sensor (O2S) (5.7L greater than 8500 GVW)
B3 Heated Oxygen Sensor (HO2S) (less than 8500 GVW 4L60E Automatic Transmission)
C Throttle Position (TP) sensor
D Engine Coolant Temperature (ECT) sensor
E VSS buffer module
H Vehicle Speed Sensor (VSS)
H Input Speed Sensor (4L80E Automatic Transmission)
J Knock Sensor (KS)

EMISSION COMPONENTS (NOT ECM/PCM CONTROLLED)

N1 Crankcase vent valve
N2 Fuel module (5.7L greater than 8500 GVW)
N15 Fuel vapor canister

SIR SYSTEM COMPONENTS

Fig. 135 Component locations—1995 models with 5.0L/5.7L engines

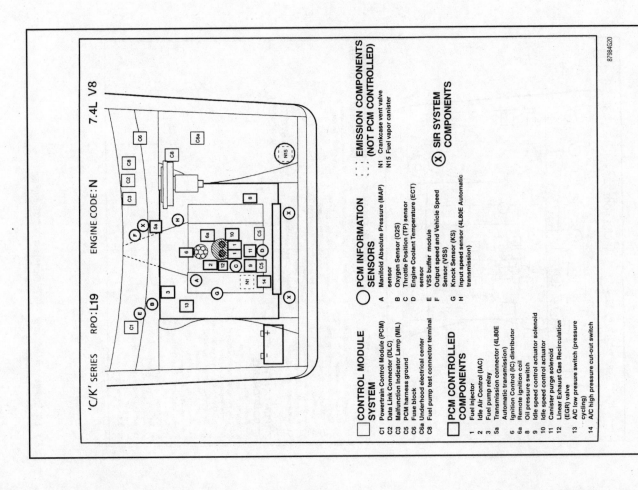

'C/K' SERIES   RPO: L19   ENGINE CODE: N   7.4L V8

CONTROL MODULE SYSTEM

C1 Powertrain Control Module (PCM)
C2 Data Link Connector (DLC)
C3 Malfunction Indicator Lamp (MIL)
C5 PCM harness ground
C6 Fuse block
C6a Underhood electrical center
C8 Fuel pump test connector terminal

PCM CONTROLLED COMPONENTS

1 Fuel injector
2 Idle Air Control (IAC)
3 Fuel pump relay
5a Transmission connector (4L80E Automatic transmission)
6 Ignition Control (IC) distributor
6a Remote ignition coil
8 Oil pressure switch
9 Idle speed control actuator solenoid
10 Idle speed control actuator
11 Canister purge solenoid
12 Linear Exhaust Gas Recirculation (EGR) valve
13 A/C low pressure switch (pressure cycling)
14 A/C high pressure cut-out switch

PCM INFORMATION SENSORS

A Manifold Absolute Pressure (MAP) sensor
B Oxygen Sensor (O2S)
C Throttle Position (TP) sensor
D Engine Coolant Temperature (ECT) sensor
E VSS buffer module
F Output speed and Vehicle Speed Sensor (VSS)
G Knock Sensor (KS)
H Input speed sensor (4L80E Automatic transmission)

EMISSION COMPONENTS (NOT PCM CONTROLLED)

N1 Crankcase vent valve
N15 Fuel vapor canister

SIR SYSTEM COMPONENTS

Fig. 134 Component locations—1995 models with 7.4L engine

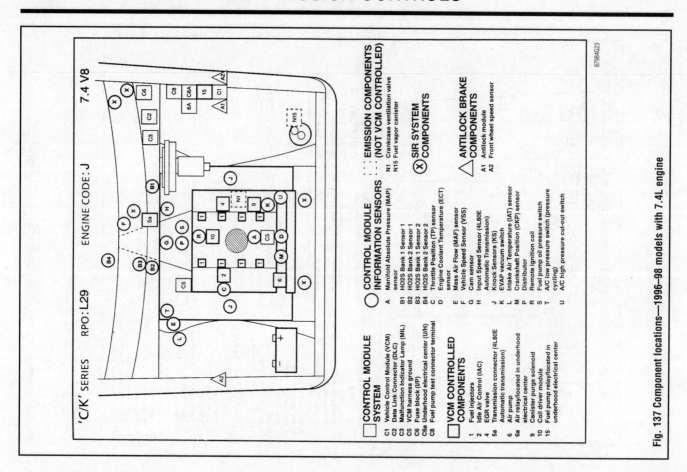

Fig. 137 Component locations—1996–98 models with 7.4L engine

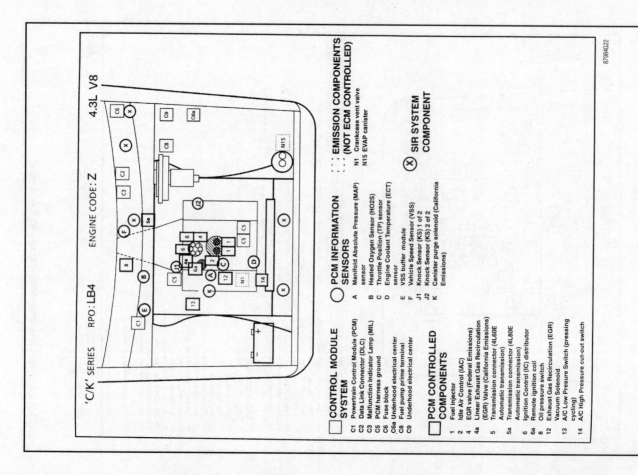

Fig. 136 Component locations—1995 models with 4.3L engine

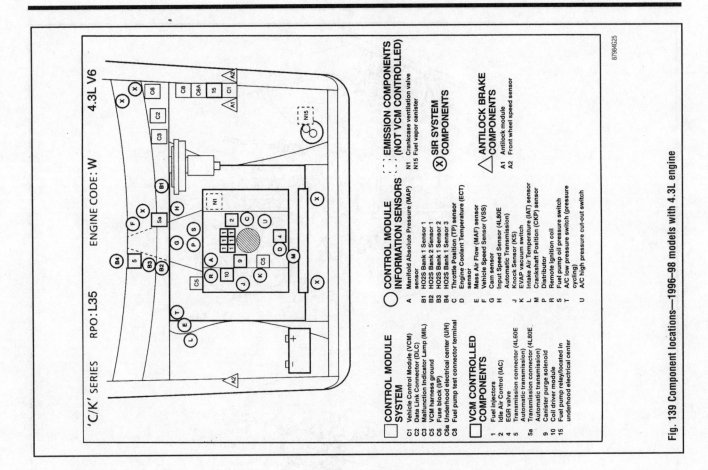

'C/K' SERIES   RPO: L35   ENGINE CODE: W   4.3L V6

□ **CONTROL MODULE SYSTEM**

C1 Vehicle Control Module (VCM)
C2 Data Link Connector (DLC)
C3 Malfunction Indicator Lamp (MIL)
C5 VCM harness ground
C6 Fuse block (I/P)
C6a Underhood electrical center (U/H)
C8 Fuel pump test connector terminal

□ **VCM CONTROLLED COMPONENTS**

1   Fuel injectors
2   Idle Air Control (IAC)
4   EGR valve
5   Transmission connector (4L60E Automatic transmission)
5a Transmission connector (4L80E Automatic transmission)
9   Canister purge solenoid
10 Coil driver module
15 Fuel pump relay/located in underhood electrical center

○ **CONTROL MODULE INFORMATION SENSORS**

A   Manifold Absolute Pressure (MAP) sensor
B1 HO2S Bank 1 Sensor 1
B2 HO2S Bank 2 Sensor 1
B3 HO2S Bank 1 Sensor 2
B4 HO2S Bank 1 Sensor 3
C   Throttle Position (TP) sensor
D   Engine Coolant Temperature (ECT) sensor
E   Mass Air Flow (MAF) sensor
F   Vehicle Speed Sensor (VSS)
G   Cam sensor
H   Input Speed Sensor (4L80E Automatic Transmission)
J   EVAP vacuum switch
K   Knock sensor (KS)
L   Intake Air Temperature (IAT) sensor
M   Crankshaft Position (CKP) sensor
P   Distributor
R   Remote ignition coil
S   Fuel pump oil pressure switch
T   A/C low pressure switch (pressure cycling)
U   A/C high pressure switch cut-out switch

┆ **EMISSION COMPONENTS (NOT VCM CONTROLLED)**

N1   Crankcase ventilation valve
N15 Fuel vapor canister

Ⓧ **SIR SYSTEM COMPONENTS**

△ **ANTILOCK BRAKE COMPONENTS**

A1 Antilock module
A2 Front wheel speed sensor

87984G25

Fig. 139 Component locations—1996-98 models with 4.3L engine

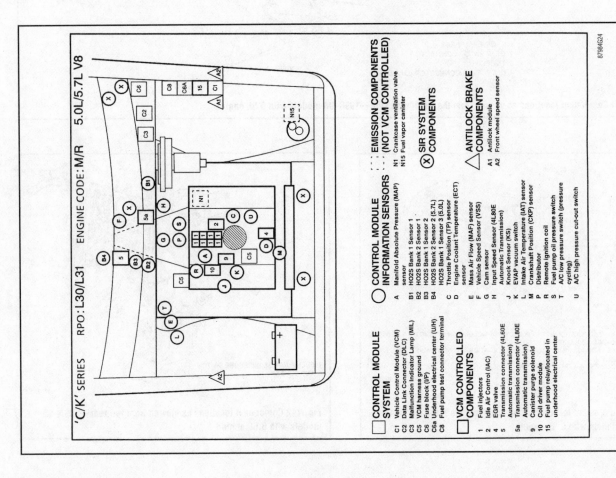

'C/K' SERIES   RPO: L30/L31   ENGINE CODE: M/R   5.0L/5.7L V8

□ **CONTROL MODULE SYSTEM**

C1 Vehicle Control Module (VCM)
C2 Data Link Connector (DLC)
C3 Malfunction Indicator Lamp (MIL)
C5 VCM harness ground
C6 Fuse block (I/P)
C6a Underhood electrical center (U/H)
C8 Fuel pump test connector terminal

□ **VCM CONTROLLED COMPONENTS**

1   Fuel injectors
2   Idle Air Control (IAC)
4   EGR valve
5   Transmission connector (4L60E Automatic transmission)
5a Transmission connector (4L80E Automatic transmission)
9   Canister purge solenoid
10 Coil driver module
15 Fuel pump relay/located in underhood electrical center

○ **CONTROL MODULE INFORMATION SENSORS**

A   Manifold Absolute Pressure (MAP) sensor
B1 HO2S Bank 1 Sensor 1
B2 HO2S Bank 2 Sensor 1
B3 HO2S Bank 1 Sensor 2 (5.7L)
B4 HO2S Bank 1 Sensor 3 (5.0L)
C   Throttle Position (TP) sensor
D   Engine Coolant Temperature (ECT) sensor
E   Mass Air Flow (MAF) sensor
F   Vehicle Speed Sensor (VSS)
G   Cam sensor
H   Input Speed Sensor (4L80E Automatic Transmission)
K   Knock Sensor (KS)
K   EVAP vacuum switch
L   Intake Air Temperature (IAT) sensor
M   Crankshaft Position (CKP) sensor
P   Distributor
R   Remote ignition coil
S   Fuel pump oil pressure switch
T   A/C low pressure switch (pressure cycling)
U   A/C high pressure switch cut-out switch

┆ **EMISSION COMPONENTS (NOT VCM CONTROLLED)**

N1   Crankcase ventilation valve
N15 Fuel vapor canister

Ⓧ **SIR SYSTEM COMPONENTS**

△ **ANTILOCK BRAKE COMPONENTS**

A1 Antilock module
A2 Front wheel speed sensor

87984G24

Fig. 138 Component locations—1996-98 models with 5.0L/5.7L engines

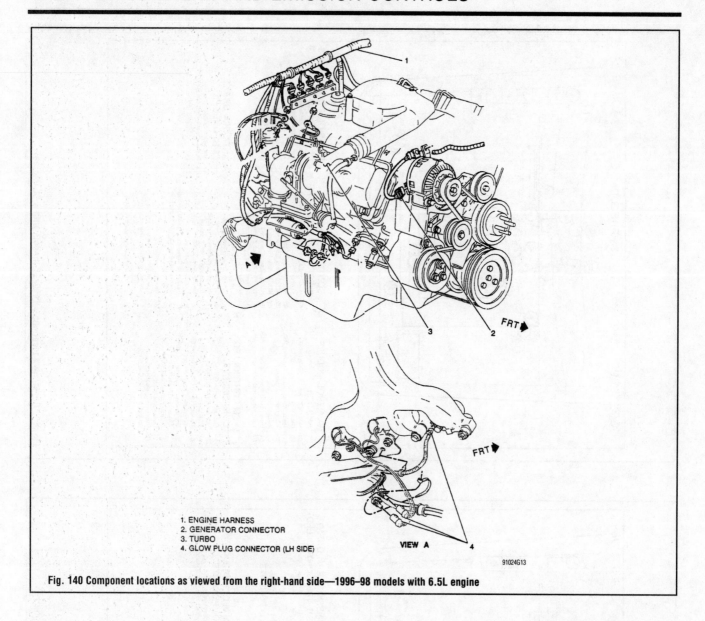

1. ENGINE HARNESS
2. GENERATOR CONNECTOR
3. TURBO
4. GLOW PLUG CONNECTOR (LH SIDE)

Fig. 140 Component locations as viewed from the right-hand side—1996–98 models with 6.5L engine

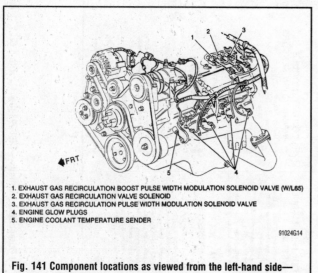

1. EXHAUST GAS RECIRCULATION BOOST PULSE WIDTH MODULATION SOLENOID VALVE (W/L65)
2. EXHAUST GAS RECIRCULATION VALVE SOLENOID
3. EXHAUST GAS RECIRCULATION PULSE WIDTH MODULATION SOLENOID VALVE
4. ENGINE GLOW PLUGS
5. ENGINE COOLANT TEMPERATURE SENDER

Fig. 141 Component locations as viewed from the left-hand side—1996–98 models with 6.5L engine

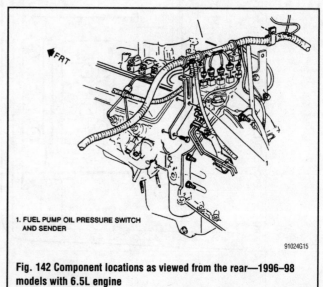

1. FUEL PUMP OIL PRESSURE SWITCH AND SENDER

Fig. 142 Component locations as viewed from the rear—1996–98 models with 6.5L engine

VACUUM DIAGRAMS

Following are vacuum diagrams for most of the engine and emissions package combinations covered by this manual. Because vacuum circuits will vary based on various engine and vehicle options, always refer first to the vehicle emission control information label, if present. Should the label be missing, or should the vehicle be equipped with a different engine from the vehicle's original equipment, refer to the diagrams below for the same or similar configuration.

If you wish to obtain a replacement emissions label, most manufacturers make the labels available for purchase. The labels can usually be ordered from a local dealer.

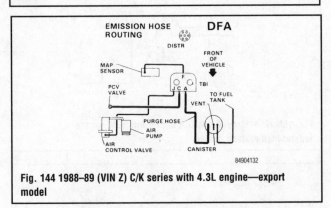

Fig. 143 1988–89 (VIN Z) C/K series with 4.3L engine—domestic model

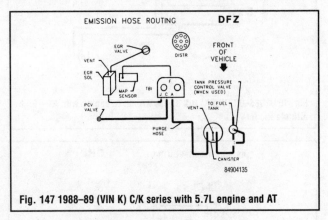

Fig. 147 1988–89 (VIN K) C/K series with 5.7L engine and AT

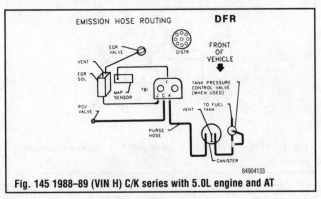

Fig. 144 1988–89 (VIN Z) C/K series with 4.3L engine—export model

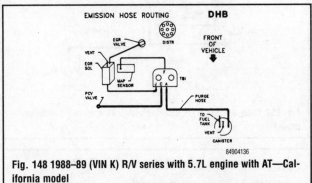

Fig. 148 1988–89 (VIN K) R/V series with 5.7L engine with AT—California model

Fig. 145 1988–89 (VIN H) C/K series with 5.0L engine and AT

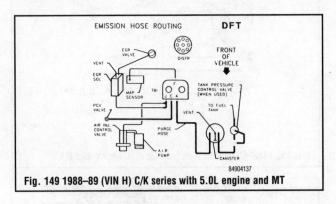

Fig. 149 1988–89 (VIN H) C/K series with 5.0L engine and MT

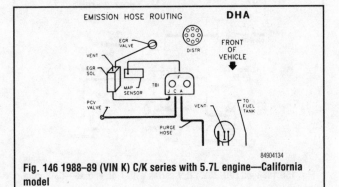

Fig. 146 1988–89 (VIN K) C/K series with 5.7L engine—California model

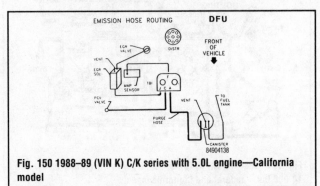

Fig. 150 1988–89 (VIN K) C/K series with 5.0L engine—California model

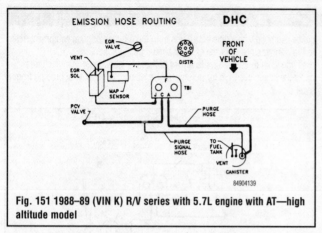

Fig. 151 1988–89 (VIN K) R/V series with 5.7L engine with AT—high altitude model

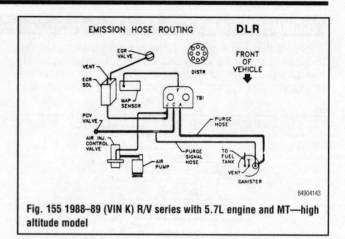

Fig. 155 1988–89 (VIN K) R/V series with 5.7L engine and MT—high altitude model

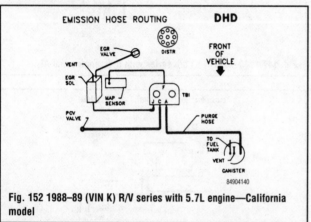

Fig. 152 1988–89 (VIN K) R/V series with 5.7L engine—California model

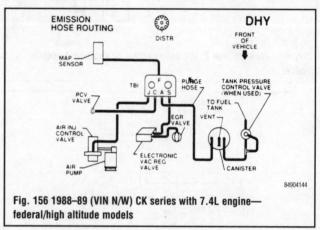

Fig. 156 1988–89 (VIN N/W) CK series with 7.4L engine—federal/high altitude models

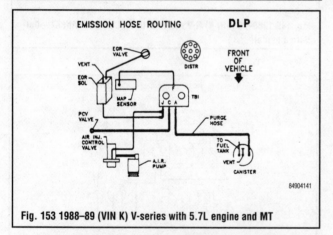

Fig. 153 1988–89 (VIN K) V-series with 5.7L engine and MT

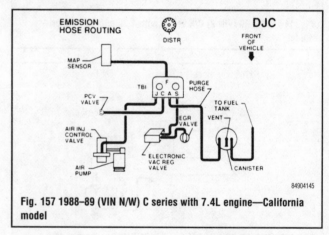

Fig. 157 1988–89 (VIN N/W) C series with 7.4L engine—California model

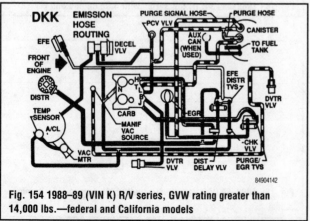

Fig. 154 1988–89 (VIN K) R/V series, GVW rating greater than 14,000 lbs.—federal and California models

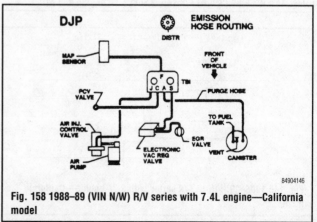

Fig. 158 1988–89 (VIN N/W) R/V series with 7.4L engine—California model

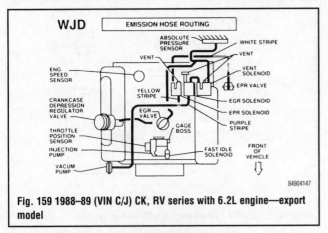

Fig. 159 1988–89 (VIN C/J) CK, RV series with 6.2L engine—export model

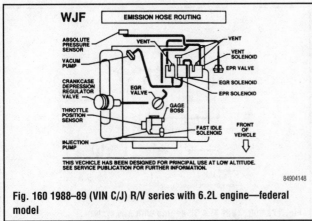

Fig. 160 1988–89 (VIN C/J) R/V series with 6.2L engine—federal model

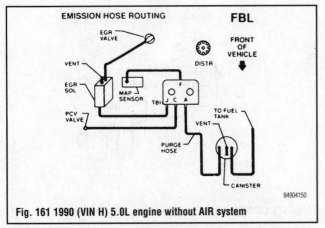

Fig. 161 1990 (VIN H) 5.0L engine without AIR system

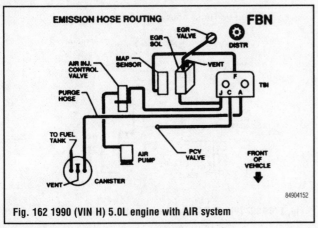

Fig. 162 1990 (VIN H) 5.0L engine with AIR system

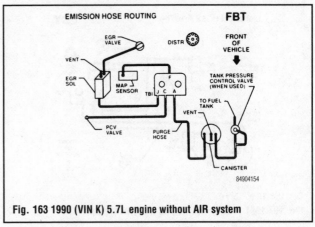

Fig. 163 1990 (VIN K) 5.7L engine without AIR system

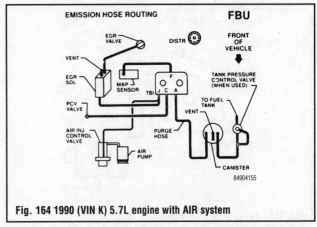

Fig. 164 1990 (VIN K) 5.7L engine with AIR system

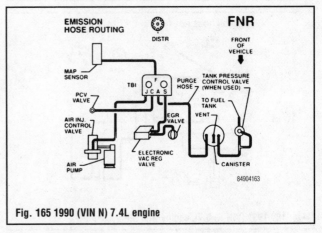

Fig. 165 1990 (VIN N) 7.4L engine

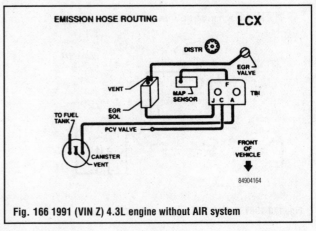

Fig. 166 1991 (VIN Z) 4.3L engine without AIR system

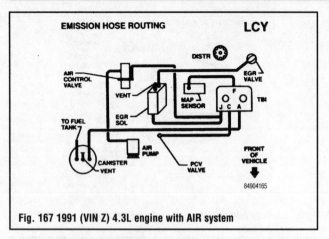

Fig. 167 1991 (VIN Z) 4.3L engine with AIR system

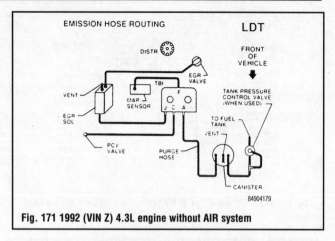

Fig. 171 1992 (VIN Z) 4.3L engine without AIR system

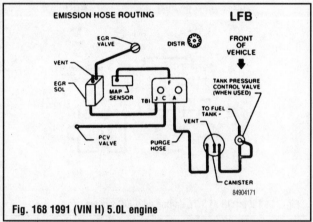

Fig. 168 1991 (VIN H) 5.0L engine

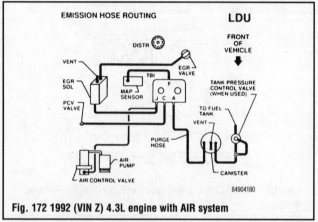

Fig. 172 1992 (VIN Z) 4.3L engine with AIR system

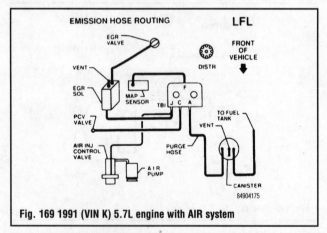

Fig. 169 1991 (VIN K) 5.7L engine with AIR system

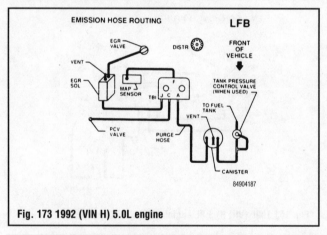

Fig. 173 1992 (VIN H) 5.0L engine

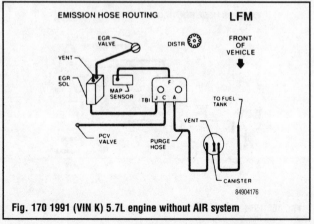

Fig. 170 1991 (VIN K) 5.7L engine without AIR system

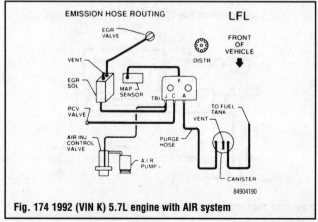

Fig. 174 1992 (VIN K) 5.7L engine with AIR system

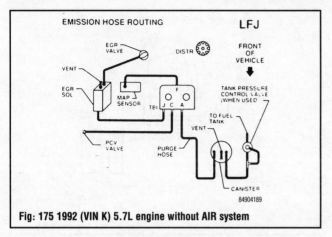

Fig. 175 1992 (VIN K) 5.7L engine without AIR system

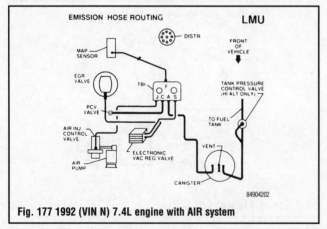

Fig. 176 1992 (VIN N) 7.4L engine without AIR system

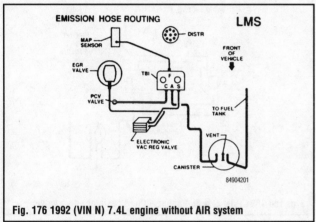

Fig. 177 1992 (VIN N) 7.4L engine with AIR system

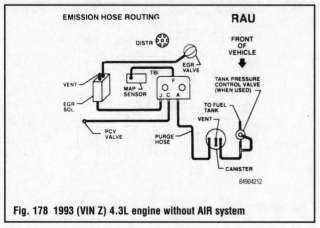

Fig. 178 1993 (VIN Z) 4.3L engine without AIR system

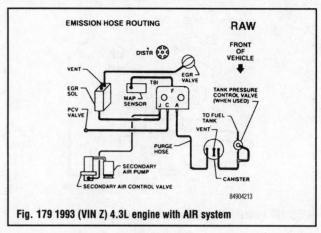

Fig. 179 1993 (VIN Z) 4.3L engine with AIR system

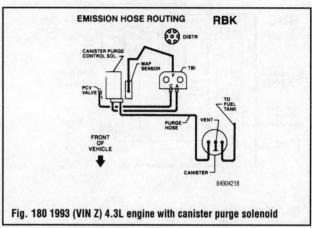

Fig. 180 1993 (VIN Z) 4.3L engine with canister purge solenoid

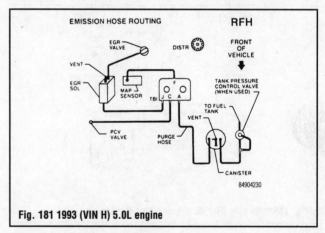

Fig. 181 1993 (VIN H) 5.0L engine

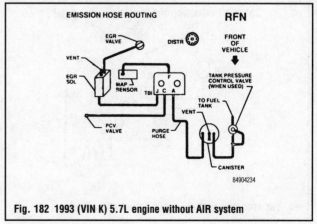

Fig. 182 1993 (VIN K) 5.7L engine without AIR system

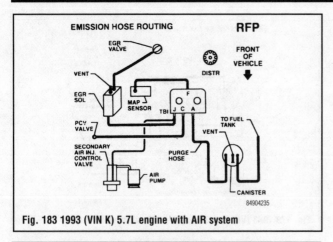

Fig. 183 1993 (VIN K) 5.7L engine with AIR system

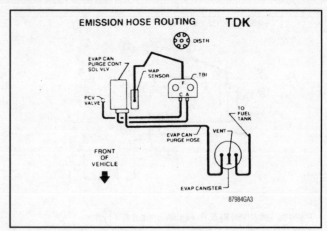

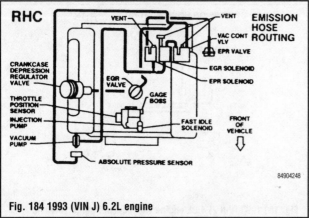

Fig. 184 1993 (VIN J) 6.2L engine

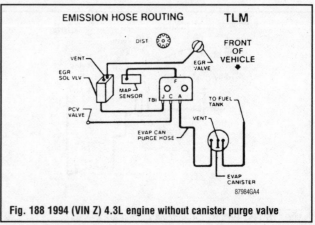

Fig. 188 1994 (VIN Z) 4.3L engine without canister purge valve

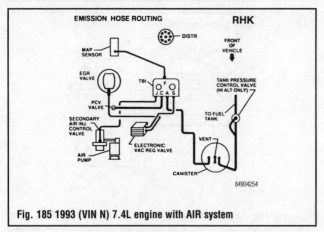

Fig. 185 1993 (VIN N) 7.4L engine with AIR system

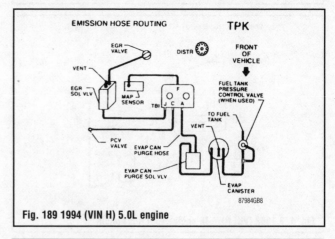

Fig. 189 1994 (VIN H) 5.0L engine

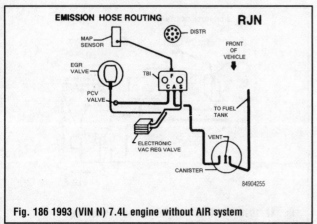

Fig. 186 1993 (VIN N) 7.4L engine without AIR system

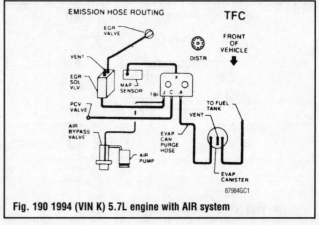

Fig. 190 1994 (VIN K) 5.7L engine with AIR system

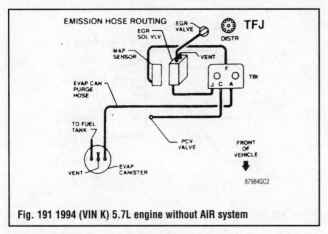

Fig. 191 1994 (VIN K) 5.7L engine without AIR system

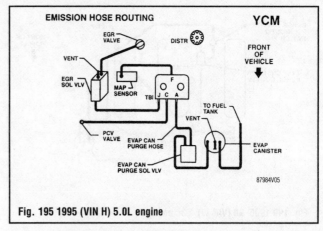

Fig. 195 1995 (VIN H) 5.0L engine

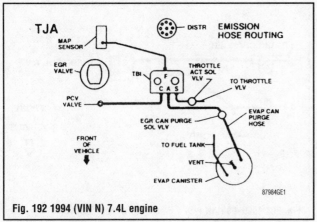

Fig. 192 1994 (VIN N) 7.4L engine

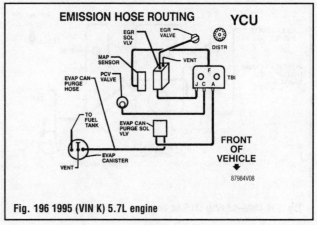

Fig. 196 1995 (VIN K) 5.7L engine

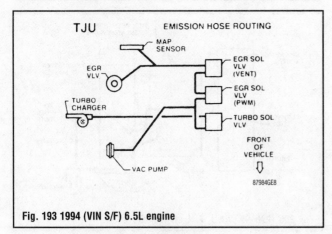

Fig. 193 1994 (VIN S/F) 6.5L engine

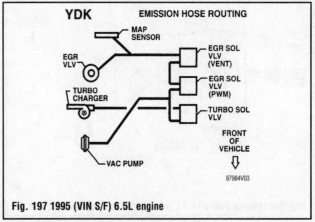

Fig. 197 1995 (VIN S/F) 6.5L engine

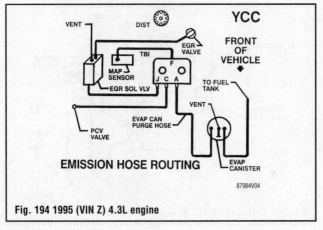

Fig. 194 1995 (VIN Z) 4.3L engine

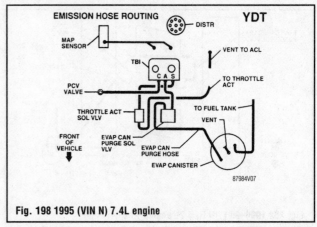

Fig. 198 1995 (VIN N) 7.4L engine

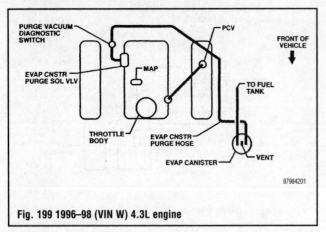

Fig. 199 1996–98 (VIN W) 4.3L engine

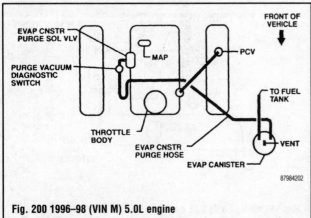

Fig. 200 1996–98 (VIN M) 5.0L engine

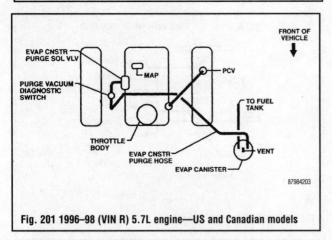

Fig. 201 1996–98 (VIN R) 5.7L engine—US and Canadian models

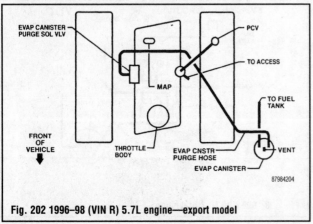

Fig. 202 1996–98 (VIN R) 5.7L engine—export model

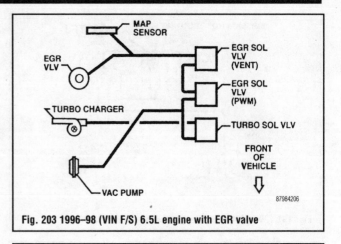

Fig. 203 1996–98 (VIN F/S) 6.5L engine with EGR valve

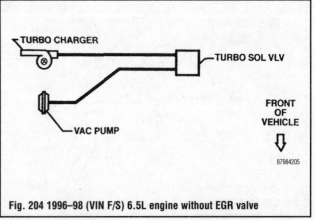

Fig. 204 1996–98 (VIN F/S) 6.5L engine without EGR valve

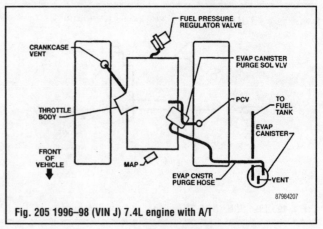

Fig. 205 1996–98 (VIN J) 7.4L engine with A/T

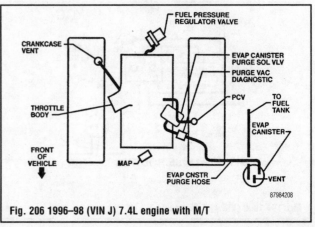

Fig. 206 1996–98 (VIN J) 7.4L engine with M/T

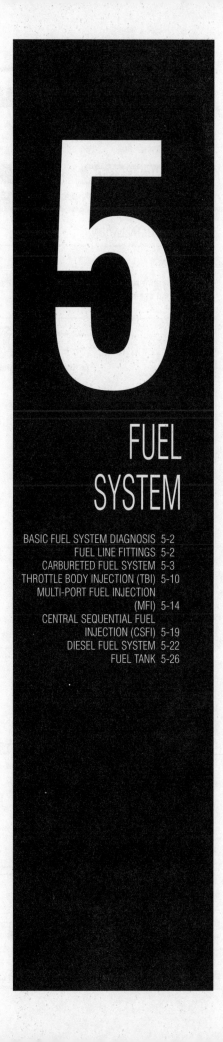

5

FUEL
SYSTEM

BASIC FUEL SYSTEM DIAGNOSIS

When there is a problem starting or driving a vehicle, two of the most important checks involve the ignition and the fuel systems. The two questions that mechanics attempt to answer first, ``is there spark?'' and ``is there fuel?'' will often lead to solving most basic problems. For ignition system diagnosis and testing, please refer to Section 2 of this manual. If the ignition system checks out (there is spark), then you must determine if the fuel system is operating properly (is there fuel?).

FUEL LINE FITTINGS

Quick-Connect Fittings

REMOVAL & INSTALLATION

♦ See Figure 1

➡This procedure requires Tool Set J37088-A or its equivalent fuel line quick-connect separator.

1. Grasp both sides of the fitting. Twist the female connector ¼ turn in each direction to loosen any dirt within the fittings. Using compressed air, blow out the dirt from the quick-connect fittings at the end of the fittings.

❋❋ CAUTION

Safety glasses MUST be worn when using compressed air to avoid eye injury due to flying dirt particles!

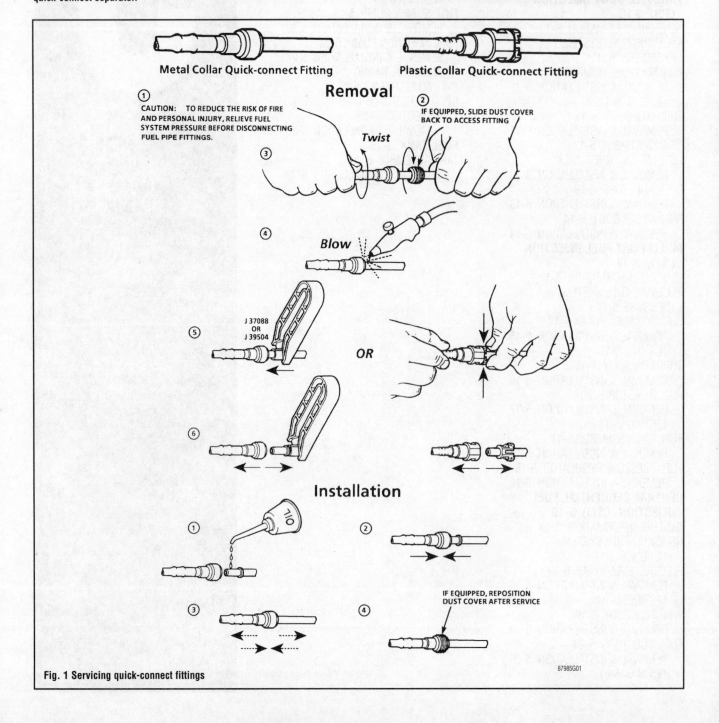

Fig. 1 Servicing quick-connect fittings

87985G01

2. For plastic (hand releasable) fittings, squeeze the plastic retainer release tabs, then pull the connection apart.

3. For metal fittings, choose the correct tool from kit J37088-A or its equivalent for the size of the fitting to be disconnected. Insert the proper tool into the female connector, then push inward to release the locking tabs. Pull the connection apart.

4. If it is necessary to remove rust or burrs from the male tube end of a quick-connect fitting, use emery cloth in a radial motion with the tube end to prevent damage to the O-ring sealing surfaces. Using a clean shop towel, wipe off the male tube ends. Inspect all connectors for dirt and burrs. Clean and/or replace if required.

To install:

5. Apply a few drops of clean engine oil to the male tube end of the fitting.

6. Push the connectors together to cause the retaining tabs/fingers to snap into place.

7. Once installed, pull on both ends of each connection to make sure they are secure and check for leaks.

CARBURETED FUEL SYSTEM

Only the 4.8L, 5.7L and 7.4L engines are equipped with a carburetor. The 4.8L uses a Rochester 1MEF 1-bbl. model; the 5.7L and 7.4L use the Rochester M4MEF 4-bbl. model.

Mechanical Fuel Pump

REMOVAL & INSTALLATION

♦ See Figures 2, 3 and 4

✳✳ CAUTION

Observe all applicable safety precautions when working around fuel. Whenever servicing the fuel system, always work in a well ventilated area. Do not allow fuel spray or vapors to come in contact with a spark or open flame. Keep a dry chemical fire extinguisher near the work area. Always keep fuel in a container specifically designed for fuel storage; also, always properly seal fuel containers to avoid the possibility of fire or explosion.

➡ When you connect the fuel pump outlet fitting, always use two wrenches to avoid damaging the pump.

1. Disconnect the fuel intake and outlet lines at the pump and plug the pump intake line.

2. You can remove the upper bolt from the right front engine mounting boss (on the front of the block) and insert a long bolt to hold the fuel pump pushrod on the 5.7L engine.

3. Remove the two pump mounting bolts and lockwashers; remove the pump and its gasket. The 5.7L utilizes a mounting plate between the pump and gasket.

4. If the rocker arm pushrod is to be removed, unfasten the two adapter bolts and lockwashers and remove the adapter and its gasket.

To install:

5. Install the fuel pump with a new gasket. Tighten the mounting bolts to 17 ft. lbs. (23 Nm) on the 4.8L engine, 27 ft. lbs. (34 Nm) on the 7.4L engine and

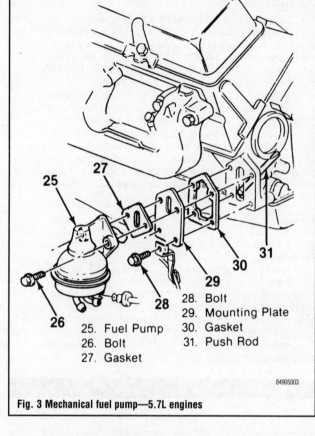

25. Fuel Pump
26. Bolt
27. Gasket
28. Bolt
29. Mounting Plate
30. Gasket
31. Push Rod

Fig. 3 Mechanical fuel pump—5.7L engines

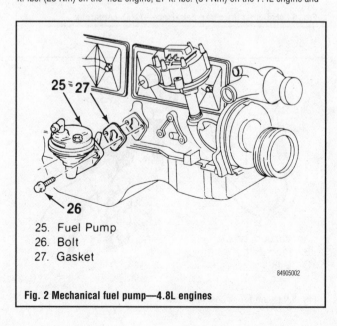

25. Fuel Pump
26. Bolt
27. Gasket

Fig. 2 Mechanical fuel pump—4.8L engines

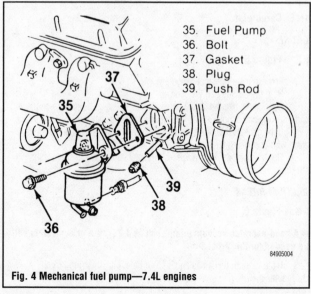

35. Fuel Pump
36. Bolt
37. Gasket
38. Plug
39. Push Rod

Fig. 4 Mechanical fuel pump—7.4L engines

the top bolt on the 5.7L engine, and 3 ft. lbs. (4 Nm) on the 5.7L engine's lower bolt. Heavy grease can be used to hold the fuel pump pushrod up when installing the pump. Coat the mating surfaces with sealer.

6. Connect the fuel lines an check for leaks.

TESTING

Pressure

Fuel pumps should always be tested on the vehicle. The larger line between the pump and tank is the suction side of the system and the smaller line, between the pump and carburetor, is the pressure side. A leak in the pressure side would be apparent because of dripping fuel. A leak in the suction side is usually only apparent because of a reduced volume of fuel delivered to the pressure side.

1. Tighten any loose line connections and look for any kinks or restrictions.

2. Disconnect the fuel line at the carburetor. Disengage the distributor-to-coil primary wire. Place a container at the end of the fuel line and crank the engine a few revolutions. If little or no fuel flows from the line, either the fuel pump is inoperative or the line is plugged. Blow through the lines with compressed air and try the test again. Reconnect the line.

3. If fuel flows in good volume, check the fuel pump pressure to be sure.

4. Attach a low pressure gauge to the pressure side of the fuel line. On trucks equipped with a vapor return system, squeeze off the return hose.

5. Run the engine at idle and note the reading on the gauge. Stop the engine and compare the reading with the specifications listed in the tune-up specifications chart located in Section 1. If the pump is operating properly, the pressure will be as specified and will be constant at idle speed. If pressure varies sporadically or is too high or low, the pump should be replaced.

6. Remove the pressure gauge.

Volume

1. Disconnect the fuel line from the carburetor. Run the fuel line into a suitable measuring container.

2. Run the engine at idle until there is one pint of fuel in the container. One pint should be pumped in 30 seconds or less.

3. If the flow is below minimum, check for a restriction in the line. The only way to check fuel pump pressure is by connecting an accurate pressure gauge to the fuel line at the carburetor level. Never replace a fuel pump without performing this simple test. If the engine seems to be starving out, check the ignition system first. Also check for a plugged fuel filter or a restricted fuel line before replacing the pump.

Carburetor

PRELIMINARY CHECKS

1MEF Carburetor

CHOKE

▶ See Figure 5

1. Remove the air cleaner assembly.
2. Hold the throttle half way down.
3. Open and close the choke several times. Be sure all links are connected and not damaged. Choke valve, linkage and fast idle cam must operate freely.
4. If the choke valve, linkage or fast idle cam is sticking due to varnish, clean with choke cleaner.
5. Do not lubricate the linkage, as lubricant will collect dust and cause sticking.

VACUUM BREAK

▶ See Figure 6

➡A hand-operated vacuum pump such as J-23738-A or equivalent will be needed for this procedure.

1. If the vacuum break has an air bleed hole, plug it during this checking procedure.

2. Apply 15 in. Hg (103 kPa) of vacuum to the vacuum break with the hand pump.

   a. Apply finger pressure to see if the plunger has moved through full travel. If not, replace the vacuum break.

   b. Observe the vacuum gauge. Vacuum should hold for at least twenty seconds. If not, replace the vacuum break.

3. Replace vacuum break hoses that are cracked, cut or hardened.

IDLE STOP SOLENOID (ISS)

A non-functioning idle stop solenoid (if equipped) could cause stalling or rough idle.

1. Turn the ignition **ON**, but do not start the engine.

2. Open the throttle momentarily to allow the solenoid plunger to extend.

3. Disconnect the wire at the solenoid. The plunger should drop back from the throttle lever. If not, back out (counterclockwise) the 1/8 in. (3mm) hex screw 1 full turn. Reconnect the wire and repeat this step.

4. Connect the solenoid wire. The plunger should move out and contact the throttle lever.

5. If the plunger does not move in and out as the wire is disengaged and connected, or, if the plunger can be pushed back and forth with light finger pressure when the wire is engaged, check the voltage across the feed wire:

   a. If 12–15 volts are present in the feed wire, replace the solenoid.

   b. If the voltage is low, locate the cause of the open circuit in the solenoid feed wire and repair as necessary.

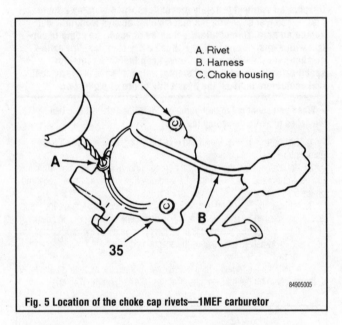

A. Rivet
B. Harness
C. Choke housing

Fig. 5 Location of the choke cap rivets—1MEF carburetor

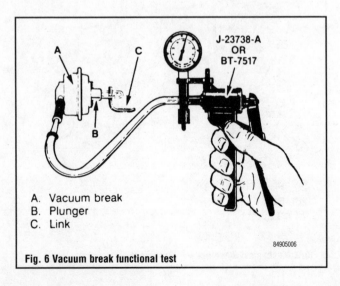

J-23738-A OR BT-7517

A. Vacuum break
B. Plunger
C. Link

Fig. 6 Vacuum break functional test

M4MEF Carburetor

FLOAT LEVEL

♦ See Figure 7

➡This procedure requires the use of an external float level gauge tool No. J-34935-1 or equivalent.

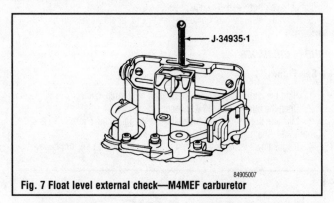

Fig. 7 Float level external check—M4MEF carburetor

1. With the engine idling and the choke valve wide open, insert tool J-34935-1 or equivalent in the vent slot or vent hole. Allow the gauge to float freely.

➡Do not press down on the gauge. Flooding or float damage could result.

2. Observe the mark on the gauge that lines up with the top of the casting. The setting should be within 1/16 in. (1.6mm) of the specified float level setting. Incorrect fuel pressure will adversely affect the fuel level.

3. If not within specification, remove the air horn and adjust the float.

CHOKE VALVE

1. Remove the air cleaner assembly.
2. Hold the throttle half way down.
3. Open and close the choke several times. Be sure all links are connected and not damaged. Choke valve, linkage and fast idle cam must operate freely.
4. If the choke valve, linkage or fast idle cam is sticking due to varnish, clean with choke cleaner.
5. Do not lubricate linkage, as lubricant will collect dust and cause sticking.

ELECTRIC CHOKE ELEMENT

1. Allow the choke thermostat to stabilize at about 70°F (21°C).
2. Open the throttle to allow the choke valve to close.
3. Start the engine and determine the length of time for the choke valve to reach full open position:
   a. If longer than five minutes, check the voltage at the choke thermostat connector with the engine running.
   b. If voltage is between 12–15 volts, check for proper ground between choke cover and choke housing. If correct, replace choke cover assembly.
   c. If the voltage is low or zero, check all wires and connections.

VACUUM BREAK

➡A hand-operated vacuum pump such as J-23738-A or equivalent will be needed for this procedure.

1. If the vacuum break has an air bleed hole, plug it during this checking procedure.
2. Apply 15 in. Hg (103 kPa) of vacuum to the vacuum break with the hand pump.
   a. Apply finger pressure to see if the plunger has moved through full travel. If not, replace the vacuum break.
   b. Observe the vacuum gauge. Vacuum should hold vacuum for at least twenty seconds. If not, replace the vacuum break.
3. Replace vacuum break hoses that are cracked, cut or hardened.

IDLE STOP SOLENOID (ISS)

A non-functioning idle stop solenoid (if equipped) could cause stalling or rough idle.

1. Turn the ignition **ON**, but do not start the engine.
2. Open the throttle momentarily to allow the solenoid plunger to extend.
3. Disconnect the wire at the solenoid. The plunger should drop back from the throttle lever.
4. Connect the solenoid wire. The plunger should move out and contact the throttle lever.
5. If the plunger does not move in and out as the wire is disconnected and connected, check the voltage across the feed wire:
   a. If 12–15 volts are present in the feed wire, replace the solenoid.
   b. If the voltage is low, locate the cause of the open circuit in the solenoid feed wire and repair as necessary.

THROTTLE KICKER

➡A hand-operated vacuum pump such as J-23738-A or equivalent will be needed for this procedure.

1. Hold the throttle half way open to allow the plunger to extend fully.
2. Apply 20 in. Hg (68 kPa) of vacuum to the throttle kicker with the hand vacuum pump.
   a. Apply finger pressure to the plunger to see if it has extended fully. If not, replace the throttle kicker.
   b. Observe the vacuum gauge. Vacuum should hold for at least twenty seconds. If not, replace the throttle kicker.
3. Release the vacuum to the throttle kicker.
4. If the plunger does not retract to its starting position, replace kicker.

ADJUSTMENTS

1MEF Carburetor

IDLE MIXTURE

♦ See Figure 8

1. Set the parking brake and block the drive wheels.
2. Remove the carburetor from the engine.
3. Drain the fuel from the carburetor into an approved container.
4. Remove the idle mixture needle plug as follows:
   a. Invert the carburetor and support it to avoid damaging external components.
   b. Make two parallel hacksaw cuts in the throttle body, between the locator points near one idle mixture needle plug. The distance between the cuts depends on the size of the punch to be used.
   c. Cut down to the plug, but not more than 1/8 in. (3mm) beyond the locator point.

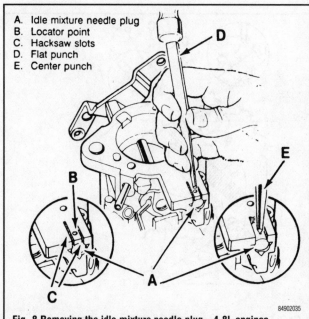

A. Idle mixture needle plug
B. Locator point
C. Hacksaw slots
D. Flat punch
E. Center punch

Fig. 8 Removing the idle mixture needle plug—4.8L engines

d. Place a flat punch at a point near the ends of the saw marks. Hold the punch at a 45° angle and drive it into the throttle body until the casting breaks away, exposing the steel plate.

e. Use a center punch to break the plug apart, uncover idle mixture needle. Remove all loose pieces of plug.

f. Repeat the previous steps for the other needle plug.

5. Use idle mixture needle socket J-29030-B or equivalent to lightly seat the idle mixture needle, then back it out 3 full turns.

6. Reinstall the carburetor on the engine.

7. Reinstall the air cleaner.

8. Place the transmission in Park (automatic transmission) or Neutral (manual transmission).

9. Start the engine and bring it to a normal operating temperature, choke valve open, and air conditioning off.

10. Connect a known, accurate tachometer to the engine.

11. Check ignition timing, and adjust if necessary, by following the procedure described on the Emission Control Information Label located under the hood on the vehicle.

12. Use idle mixture needle socket J-29030-B or equivalent to turn the mixture needle an ⅛ in. (3mm) turn at a time, in or out, to obtain the highest rpm (best idle).

13. Adjust the idle speed solenoid to obtain the curb idle speed specified on the underhood emission control information label.

14. Again try to readjust mixture needle to obtain the highest idle rpm. The adjustment is correct when the highest rpm (best idle) is reached with the minimum number of mixture needle turns from the seated position.

15. If necessary, readjust the idle stop solenoid to obtain the specified curb idle speed.

16. Check (and if necessary adjust) the base idle speed and fast idle speed. Refer to the underhood emission control information label.

17. Turn off the engine, remove all test equipment.

18. Remove the block from the drive wheels.

FAST IDLE

▶ See Figure 9

1. Check and adjust the idle speed.

2. With the engine at normal operating temperature, air cleaner installed, EGR valve signal line disconnected and plugged and the air conditioning off, connect a tachometer.

3. Disconnect the vacuum advance hose at the distributor and plug the line.

4. With the transmission in Neutral, start the engine and set the fast idle cam follower on the high step of the cam.

5. Bend the tank in or out to obtain the fast idle speed shown on your underhood sticker.

FAST IDLE CAM

▶ See Figure 10

1. Check and adjust the fast idle speed.

2. Set the fast idle cam follower on the second step of the cam.

3. Apply force to the choke coil rod and hold the choke valve toward the closed position.

4. Measure the clearance between the lower edge of the choke valve and the inside of the air horn wall. The gap should be 0.275 in. (7mm).

5. Bend the fast idle cam link at the upper end, to obtain the correct clearance.

CHOKE UNLOADER

▶ See Figure 11

1. Hold the choke valve down by applying light force to the choke coil lever.

2. Open the throttle valve to wide open.

3. Measure the clearance between the lower edge of the choke valve and the air horn wall. The gap should be 0.52 in. (13mm).

4. If adjustment is necessary, bend the unloader tang on the throttle lever.

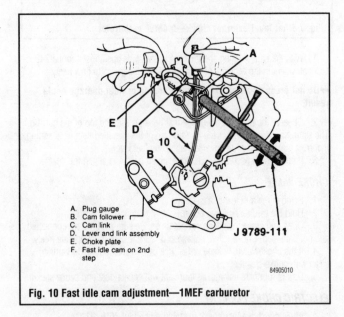

A. Plug gauge
B. Cam follower
C. Cam link
D. Lever and link assembly
E. Choke plate
F. Fast idle cam on 2nd step

J 9789-111

84905010

Fig. 10 Fast idle cam adjustment—1MEF carburetor

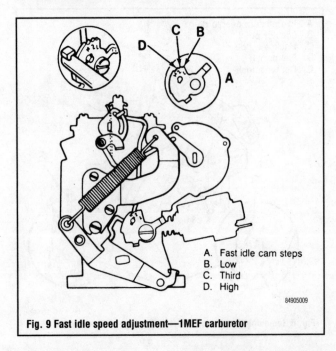

A. Fast idle cam steps
B. Low
C. Third
D. High

84905009

Fig. 9 Fast idle speed adjustment—1MEF carburetor

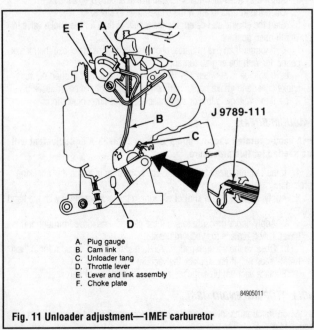

A. Plug gauge
B. Cam link
C. Unloader tang
D. Throttle lever
E. Lever and link assembly
F. Choke plate

J 9789-111

84905011

Fig. 11 Unloader adjustment—1MEF carburetor

CHOKE COIL ROD

1. Place the cam follower on the highest step of the fast idle cam.
2. Hold the choke valve completely closed.
3. A 0.120 in. (3mm) plug gauge must pass through the hole in the lever attached to the choke coil housing and enter the hole in the casting.
4. Bend the choke link to adjust.

PRIMARY VACUUM BREAK

♦ See Figure 12

1. Place the fast idle cam follower on highest step of the fast idle cam.
2. Plug purge bleed hole in the vacuum break with masking tape. Not all models will have this hole.
3. Using an outside vacuum source, apply 15 in. Hg (103 kPa) of vacuum to the primary vacuum break diaphragm. Push down on the choke valve. Make sure the plunger is fully extended.
4. Insert a 0.2 in. (5mm) gauge between the lower edge of the choke valve and the air horn wall.
5. Bend vacuum break rod for adjustment.
6. After adjustment, check for binding or interference. Remove tape.

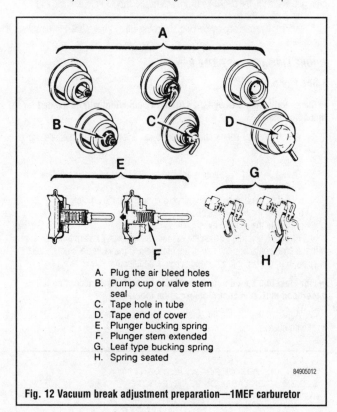

A. Plug the air bleed holes
B. Pump cup or valve stem seal
C. Tape hole in tube
D. Tape end of cover
E. Plunger bucking spring
F. Plunger stem extended
G. Leaf type bucking spring
H. Spring seated

84905012

Fig. 12 Vacuum break adjustment preparation—1MEF carburetor

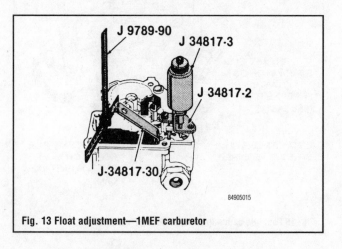

84905015

Fig. 13 Float adjustment—1MEF carburetor

FLOAT LEVEL

♦ See Figure 13

1. Remove the air horn and gasket.
2. Hold the float retainer in place, and hold the float arm against the top of the float needle by pushing down on the float arm at the outer end toward the float bowl casting.

➡A special tool is available to make this job a little easier, but it's not absolutely necessary.

3. Using an adjustable T-scale, measure the distance from the toe of the float to the float bowl gasket surface. The distance should be $FR9/32–$FR13/32 in. (7.1–10.3mm).

➡The gauge should be held on the index point on the float for accurate measurement.

4. Adjust the float level by bending the float lever up or down at the float arm junction.

M4MEF Carburetor

FLOAT

♦ See Figure 14

➡A float level T-scale such as J-9789-90 or equivalent and float positioning tool kit J-34817 or equivalent will be needed for this adjustment.

1. Remove the air horn, gasket, power piston and metering rod assembly, and the float bowl insert.
2. Attach float adjustment tool J-34817-1 or equivalent to the float bowl.
3. Place float adjustment tool J-34817-3 or equivalent into float adjustment tool J-34817-1 or equivalent, with the contact pin resting on the outer edge of the float lever.
4. Measure the distance from the top of the casting to the top of the float at a point 3/16 (4.8mm) from the large end of the float using the float adjustment tool J-9789-90 or equivalent.
5. If more than 1/16 in. (1.6mm) from specification, use the float gauge adjusting tool J-34817-25 or equivalent to bend the lever up or down.
6. Remove the gauge adjusting tool and measure, repeating until within specifications.
7. Check the float alignment and reassemble the carburetor.

PUMP

♦ See Figure 15

➡Float Level T-scale J-9789-90 or equivalent will be needed for this adjustment.

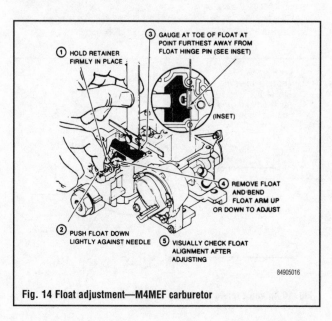

1. HOLD RETAINER FIRMLY IN PLACE
2. PUSH FLOAT DOWN LIGHTLY AGAINST NEEDLE
3. GAUGE AT TOE OF FLOAT AT POINT FURTHEST AWAY FROM FLOAT HINGE PIN (SEE INSET)
   (INSET)
4. REMOVE FLOAT AND BEND FLOAT ARM UP OR DOWN TO ADJUST
5. VISUALLY CHECK FLOAT ALIGNMENT AFTER ADJUSTING

84905016

Fig. 14 Float adjustment—M4MEF carburetor

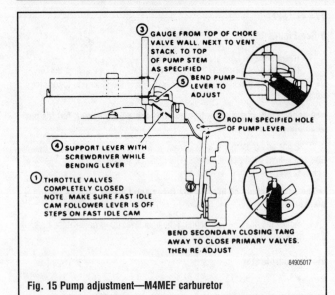

Fig. 15 Pump adjustment—M4MEF carburetor

1. The pump link must be in the specified hole to make this adjustment.
2. With the fast idle cam off the cam follower lever, turn the throttle stop screw out so it does not touch the throttle lever.
3. Measure the distance from the top of the choke valve wall to the top of the pump stem.
4. Adjust, if necessary, by supporting the pump lever with a screwdriver and bending it at the notch.

AIR VALVE RETURN SPRING

♦ **See Figure 16**

1. Loosen the setscrew.
2. Turn spring fulcrum pin counterclockwise until the air valves open.
3. Turn the pin clockwise until the air valves close, then the additional turns specified.
4. Tighten the setscrew. Apply lithium grease to the spring contact area.

CHOKE STAT LEVER

♦ **See Figure 17**

➡**Linkage Bending Tool J-9789-111 or equivalent will be needed for this adjustment.**

1. Drill out and remove the choke cover attaching rivets. Remove choke cover and thermostat assembly.
2. Place fast idle cam on high step against the cam follower lever.
3. Push up on the choke stat lever to close the choke valve.

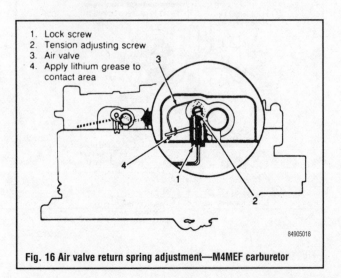

1. Lock screw
2. Tension adjusting screw
3. Air valve
4. Apply lithium grease to contact area

Fig. 16 Air valve return spring adjustment—M4MEF carburetor

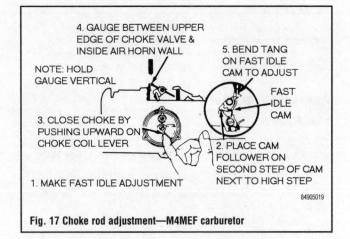

Fig. 17 Choke rod adjustment—M4MEF carburetor

4. Check the stat lever for correct orientation by inserting a 0.120 in. (3mm) plug gauge hole in the choke housing. The gauge should fit in the hole and touch the edge of the lever.
5. Adjust, if necessary, by bending the choke link with J-9789-111 or equivalent.

CHOKE LINK AND FAST IDLE CAM

♦ **See Figure 18**

➡**Choke Valve Angle Gauge J-26701-A or equivalent will be needed for this adjustment.**

1. Attach a rubber band to the vacuum break lever of the intermediate choke shaft.
2. Open the throttle to allow the choke valve to close.
3. Set up J-26701-A or equivalent and set the angle to specification as follows:
    a. Rotate the degree scale until zero is opposite the pointer.
    b. Center the leveling bubble.
    c. Rotate the scale to the specified angle.
4. Place the fast idle cam on the second step against the cam follower lever, with the lever contacting the rise of the high step. If the lever does not contact the cam, turn the fast idle adjusting screw in additional turn(s).

➡**Final fast idle speed adjustment must be performed according to the underhood emission control information label.**

5. Adjust, if bubble is not re-centered, by bending the fast idle cam kick lever with pliers.

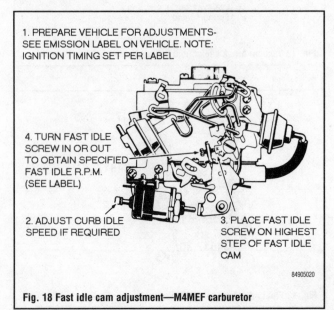

Fig. 18 Fast idle cam adjustment—M4MEF carburetor

PRIMARY SIDE VACUUM BREAK

▶ **See Figure 19**

➡ **Choke Valve Angle Gauge J-26701-A and Hand Operated Vacuum Pump J-23738-A or equivalents, will be needed for this adjustment.**

1. Attach rubber band to the vacuum break lever of the intermediate choke shaft.
2. Open the throttle to allow the choke valve to close.
3. Set up J-26701-A or equivalent and set angle to specifications.
4. Plug the vacuum break bleed holes, if applicable. Apply 15 in. Hg (103 kPa) of vacuum to seat the vacuum break plunger.
5. Seat the bucking spring, if so equipped. If necessary, bend the air valve link to permit full plunger travel, then re-apply vacuum to fully retract plunger.
6. Adjust, if bubble is not re-centered, by turning the vacuum break adjusting screw.

SECONDARY SIDE VACUUM BREAK

➡ **Choke Valve Angle Gauge J-6701-A, Hand Operated Vacuum Pump J-23738-A and Linkage Bending Tool J-9789-111 or equivalents will be needed for this adjustment.**

1. Attach a rubber band to the vacuum break lever of the intermediate choke shaft.
2. Open the throttle to allow the choke valve to close.
3. Set up J-26701-A or equivalent and set angle to specification.
4. Plug vacuum break bleed holes, if so equipped. Apply 15 in. Hg (103 kPa) of vacuum to seat the vacuum break plunger.
5. Compress the plunger bucking spring, if so equipped. If necessary, bend the air valve link to permit full plunger travel, then re-apply vacuum to fully retract the plunger.
6. Adjust, if bubble is not re-centered, by either supporting the link where shown and bending it with J-9789-111 or equivalent, or by turning the screw with a ⅛ in. (3mm) hex wrench.

AIR VALVE LINK

▶ **See Figures 20 and 21**

➡ **Hand Operated Vacuum Pump J-23738-A and Linkage Bending Tool J-9789-111 or equivalents will be needed for this adjustment.**

1. Plug vacuum break bleed holes, if applicable. With the air valves closed, apply 15 in. Hg (103 kPa) of vacuum to seat the vacuum break plunger.
2. Gauge the clearance between the air valve link and the end of the slot in the air valve lever. Clearance should be 0.025 in. (0.6mm).
3. Adjust, if necessary, by bending the link with J-9789-111 or equivalent.

UNLOADER

➡ **Choke Valve Angle Gauge J-26701-A and Linkage Bending Tool J-9789-111 or equivalents will be needed for this adjustment.**

1. Attach rubber band to the vacuum break lever of the intermediate choke shaft.

2. Open the throttle to allow the choke valve to close.
3. Set up J-26701-A or equivalent and set angle to specifications.
4. Hold the secondary lockout lever away from the pin.
5. Hold the throttle lever in wide open position.
6. Adjust, if bubble is not re-centered, by bending fast idle lever with J-9789-111 or equivalent.

SECONDARY THROTTLE LOCKOUT

1. Place the fast idle cam on the high step against the cam follower lever.
2. Hold the throttle lever closed.
3. Gauge the clearance between the lockout lever and pin. It must be 0.015 inch plus or minus 0.005 in. (0.38mm plus or minus 0.13mm).
4. Adjust, if necessary, by bending pin.
5. Push down on tail of fast idle cam to move lockout lever away from pin.
6. Rotate the throttle lever to bring the lockout pin to the position of minimum clearance with the lockout lever.
7. Gauge the clearance between the lockout lever and pin. The minimum must be 0.015 in. (0.38mm).
8. Adjust, if necessary, by filing the end of the pin.

IDLE MIXTURE

▶ **See Figure 22**

1. Set the parking brake and block the drive wheels.
2. Remove the carburetor from the engine.
3. Drain the fuel from the carburetor into an approved container.
4. Remove the idle mixture needle plug as follows:
   a. Invert the carburetor and support it to avoid damaging external components.
   b. Make two parallel hacksaw cuts in the throttle body, between the locator points near one idle mixture needle plug. The distance between the cuts depends on the size of the punch to be used.

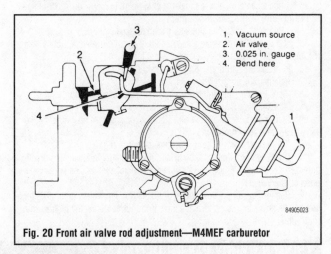

1. Vacuum source
2. Air valve
3. 0.025 in. gauge
4. Bend here

84905023

Fig. 20 Front air valve rod adjustment—M4MEF carburetor

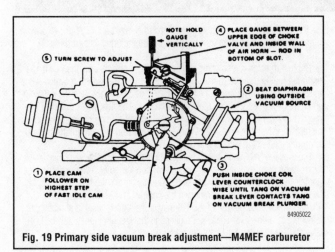

84905022

Fig. 19 Primary side vacuum break adjustment—M4MEF carburetor

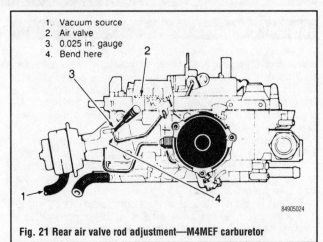

1. Vacuum source
2. Air valve
3. 0.025 in. gauge
4. Bend here

84905024

Fig. 21 Rear air valve rod adjustment—M4MEF carburetor

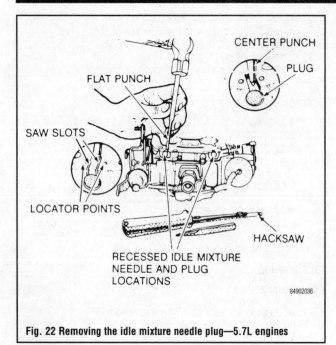

FLAT PUNCH
CENTER PUNCH
PLUG
SAW SLOTS
LOCATOR POINTS
HACKSAW
RECESSED IDLE MIXTURE
NEEDLE AND PLUG
LOCATIONS

84902036

Fig. 22 Removing the idle mixture needle plug—5.7L engines

c. Cut down to the plug, but not more than ⅛ in. (3mm) beyond the locator point.

d. Place a flat punch at a point near the ends of the saw marks. Hold the punch at a 45° angle and drive it into the throttle body until the casting breaks away, exposing the steel plate.

e. Use a center punch to break the plug apart, uncover idle mixture needle. Remove all loose pieces of plug.

f. Repeat the previous steps for the other needle plug.

5. Use idle mixture needle socket J-29030-B or equivalent to lightly seat the idle mixture needle, then back it out 3 full turns.

6. Reinstall the carburetor on the engine.

7. Reinstall the air cleaner.

8. Place the transmission in Park (automatic transmission) or Neutral (manual transmission).

9. Start the engine and bring it to a normal operating temperature, choke valve open, and air conditioning off.

10. Connect a known, accurate tachometer to the engine.

11. Check ignition timing, and adjust if necessary, by following the procedure described on the Emission Control Information Label located under the hood on the vehicle.

12. Use idle mixture needle socket J-29030-B or equivalent to turn the mixture needle an ⅛ in. (3mm) turn at a time, in or out, to obtain the highest rpm (best idle).

13. Adjust the idle speed solenoid to obtain the curb idle speed specified on the underhood emission control information label.

14. Again try to readjust mixture needle to obtain the highest idle rpm. The adjustment is correct when the highest rpm (best idle) is reached with the minimum number of mixture needle turns from the seated position.

15. If necessary, readjust the idle stop solenoid to obtain the specified curb idle speed.

16. Check (and if necessary adjust) the base idle speed and fast idle speed. Refer to the underhood emission control information label.

17. Turn off the engine, remove all test equipment.

18. Remove the block from the drive wheels.

REMOVAL & INSTALLATION

1. Disconnect the negative battery terminal.

2. Remove the air cleaner assembly and gasket.

3. Disengage the electrical connectors from the choke and idle stop solenoid.

4. Disconnect and tag the vacuum hoses.

5. Disconnect the accelerator linkage and the downshift cable (automatic transmission only).

6. Disconnect the cruise control linkage (if equipped).

7. Disengage the fuel line connection at the fuel inlet nut.

8. Remove the carburetor attaching nuts and the carburetor with the mounting insulator and gaskets.

To install:

9. Installation is the reverse of removal but please note the following important steps.

✷✷ CAUTION

Clean the sealing surfaces on the intake manifold and carburetor. Be sure to extinguish all open flames while filling and testing carburetor with gasoline to avoid the risk of fire.

10. Install the carburetor with a new flange gasket. It is good shop practice to fill the carburetor float bowl before installing the carburetor. This reduces the strain on starting motor and battery and reduces the possibility of backfiring while attempting to start the engine. Operate the throttle several times and check the discharge from pump jets before installing the carburetor.

11. On models equipped with the 1MEF carburetor, install the assembly attaching bolts and tighten them to 36 inch lbs. (4 Nm) and then to 16 ft. lbs. (22 Nm). Be sure to tighten the bolts in a crisscross pattern.

12. On models equipped with the M4MEF carburetor, install the carburetor attaching bolts and tighten them to 12 ft. lbs. (16 Nm). Be sure to torque the bolts in a crisscross pattern.

➡**On models equipped with the M4MEF carburetor, when tightening the carburetor at recommended maintenance intervals, check the bolt torque. If less than 5 ft. lbs. (7 Nm), retighten to 8 ft. lbs. (11 Nm); but if greater than 5 ft. lbs. (7 Nm), do not retighten.**

THROTTLE BODY INJECTION (TBI)

General Information

The electronic fuel injection system is a fuel metering system with the amount of fuel delivered by the Throttle Body Injectors (TBI) determined by an electronic signal supplied by the Electronic Control Module (ECM). The ECM monitors various engine and vehicle conditions to calculate the fuel delivery time (pulse width) of the injectors. The fuel pulse may be modified by the ECM to account for special operating conditions, such as cranking, cold starting, altitude, acceleration and deceleration.

The ECM controls the exhaust emissions by modifying fuel delivery to achieve, as near as possible, an air/fuel ratio of 14.7:1. The injector ``on'' time is determined by various inputs to the ECM. By increasing the injector pulse, more fuel is delivered, enriching the air/fuel ratio. Decreasing the injector pulse, leans the air/fuel ratio.

The basic TBI unit is made up of two major casting assemblies: (1) a throttle body with a valve to control airflow and (2) a fuel body assembly with an integral pressure regulator and fuel injector to supply the required fuel. An electronically operated device to control the idle speed and a device to provide information regarding throttle valve position are included as part of the TBI unit.

The fuel injector is a solenoid-operated device controlled by the ECM. The incoming fuel is directed to the lower end of the injector assembly which has a fine screen filter surrounding the injector inlet. The ECM actuates the solenoid, which lifts a normally closed ball valve off a seat. The fuel under pressure is injected in a conical spray pattern at the walls of the throttle body bore above the throttle valve. The excess fuel passes through a pressure regulator before being returned to the vehicle fuel tank.

The pressure regulator is a diaphragm-operated relief valve with injector pressure on one side and air cleaner pressure on the other. The function of the regulator is to maintain a constant pressure drop across the injector throughout the operating load and speed range of the engine.

The throttle body portion of the TBI may contain ports located at, above, or below the throttle valve. These ports generate the vacuum signals for the EGR valve, MAP sensor and the canister purge system.

Relieving Fuel System Pressure

The pressure regulator utilizes a constant bleed feature when the engine is turned off, but follow these general tips:
1. Always disconnect the negative battery terminal.
2. Loosen the fuel filler cap to relive the vapor pressure in the fuel tank.

Electric Fuel Pump

REMOVAL & INSTALLATION

♦ See Figure 23

✳✳ CAUTION

The 220 TBI unit has a bleed in the pressure regulator to relieve pressure any time the engine is turned off, however a small amount of fuel may be released when the fuel line is disconnected. As a precaution, cover the fuel line with a cloth and dispose of properly.

1. With the engine turned **OFF**, relieve the fuel pressure at the pressure regulator. Refer to the fuel relief procedure in this section.
2. Disconnect the negative battery cable.
3. Raise and support the rear of the vehicle on jackstands.
4. Drain the fuel tank, then remove it.
5. Using a hammer and a drift punch, drive the fuel lever sending device and pump assembly locking ring (located on top of the fuel tank) counterclockwise. Lift the assembly from the tank and remove the pump from the fuel lever sending device.
6. Pull the pump up into the attaching hose while pulling it outward away from the bottom support. Be careful not to damage the rubber insulator and strainer during removal. After the pump assembly is clear of the bottom support, pull it out of the rubber connector.
To install:
7. Connect the fuel pump to the hose.

➡**Be careful that you don't fold or twist the strainer when installing the sending unit, or you'll restrict fuel flow.**

8. Install a new O-ring on the pump assembly and then position them into the fuel tank.
9. Turn the locking ring clockwise until its tight.
10. Install the fuel tank and connect the battery cable.

TESTING

➡**Special tools J-29658-82 and J-29658, or their equivalents, will be necessary for this procedure.**

1. Disconnect the negative battery cable.
2. Secure two sections of ⅜ in. x 10 in. (9.5mm x 254mm) steel tubing, with a double-flare on one end of each section.
3. Install a flare nut on each section of tubing, then connect each of the sections into the flare nut-to-flare nut adapter, while care included in the gauge adapter tool No. J-29658-82 or equivalent.
4. Attach the pipe and the adapter assembly to the gauge tool No. J-29658 or equivalent.
5. Raise and support the vehicle on jackstands.
6. Remove the air cleaner and plug the THERMAC vacuum port on the TBI.
7. Disconnect the fuel feed hose between the fuel tank and the filter, then secure the other ends of the ⅜ in. (9.5mm) tubing into the fuel hoses with hose clamps.
8. Reconnect the battery cable.
9. Start the engine, check for leaks and observe the fuel pressure, it should be 9–13 psi (62–89 kPa).
10. Depressurize the fuel system, remove the testing tool, remove the plug from the THERMAC vacuum port, reconnect the fuel line, start the engine and check for fuel leaks.

Throttle Body

REMOVAL & INSTALLATION

♦ See Figures 24 thru 29

1. Release the fuel pressure. Refer to the fuel relief procedure in this section.
2. Disconnect the THERMAC hose from the engine fitting and remove the air cleaner.
3. Unplug the electrical connectors at the idle air control, throttle position sensor and the injector. Squeeze the plastic tabs on the injector connections and pull straight up.
4. Disconnect the grommet with wires from the throttle body.
5. Disconnect the throttle linkage, return spring, transmission control cable and cruise control (if equipped).
6. Unplug the throttle body vacuum hoses, the fuel supply and fuel return lines.
7. Disconnect the bolts securing the throttle body, then remove it.
To install:
8. Installation is the reverse of removal but please pay special attention to the following steps.
9. Replace the manifold gaskets and O-rings.
10. Install the TBI unit and tighten the bolts to 12 ft. lbs. (16 Nm).
11. Install new O-rings into the fuel line nuts and then screw them on by hand. Tighten them to 20 ft. lbs. (26 Nm).
12. Turn the ignition switch **ON** (but don't start the engine!) and check for leaks around the fuel line nuts.

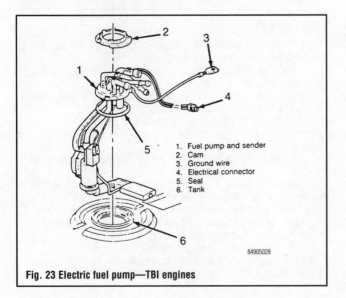

1. Fuel pump and sender
2. Cam
3. Ground wire
4. Electrical connector
5. Seal
6. Tank

84905028

Fig. 23 Electric fuel pump—TBI engines

87985P20

Fig. 24 Tag and disconnect the vacuum lines from the throttle body

Fig. 25 Tag and unplug all electrical connections from the throttle body

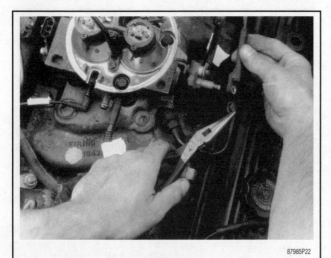

Fig. 26 A pair of needlenose pliers can be used to disconnect the linkages from the throttle body assembly

Fig. 27 A flare nut wrench can be used to disconnect the fuel lines. Make sure the wrench fits snugly on the fuel line nut, so as not to round off the nut edges

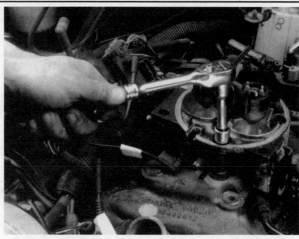

Fig. 28 A ratchet and the correct size socket can be used to remove the bolts securing the throttle body to the intake manifold

Fig. 29 Remove the throttle body from the intake manifold

ADJUSTMENT

▶ **See Figure 30**

Only if parts of the throttle body have been replaced should this procedure be performed; the engine should be at operating temperature.

1. Remove the air cleaner, adapter and gaskets. Discard the gaskets. Plug any vacuum line ports, as necessary.

2. Leave the Idle Air Control (IAC) valve connected and ground the Assembly Link Diagnostic (ALDL) connector terminal.

3. Turn the ignition switch to the **ON** position, do not start the engine. Wait for at least 30 seconds (this allows the IAC valve pintle to extend and seat in the throttle body).

4. With the ignition switch still in the **ON** position, unplug the IAC electrical connector.

5. Remove the ground from the diagnostic terminal and start the engine. Let the engine reach normal operating temperature.

6. Apply the parking brake and block the drive wheels. Remove the plug from the idle stop screw by piercing it first with a suitable tool, then applying leverage to the tool to lift the plug out.

7. Adjust the idle stop screw to the proper specifications

8. Turn the ignition **OFF** and reconnect the IAC valve connector. Unplug any plugged vacuum line ports and install the air cleaner, adapter and new gaskets.

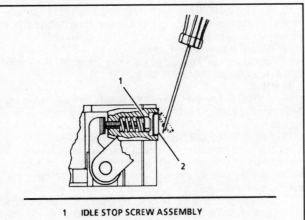

1   IDLE STOP SCREW ASSEMBLY
2   IDLE STOP SCREW PLUG

84905046

Fig. 30 Use a suitable tool to remove the idle stop screw plug to access the screw

Fuel Meter Cover

REMOVAL & INSTALLATION

▶ **See Figure 31**

1. Relieve the fuel system pressure. Refer to the fuel relief procedure in this section.
2. Raise the hood, install fender covers and remove the air cleaner assembly.
3. Disconnect the negative battery cable.
4. Unplug electrical connector at the injector by squeezing the two tabs and pulling straight up.
5. Remove the five screws securing the fuel meter cover to the fuel meter body. Notice the location of the two short screws during removal.

✳✳ CAUTION

Do not remove the four screws securing the pressure regulator to the fuel meter cover! The fuel pressure regulator includes a large spring under heavy tension which, if accidentally released, could cause personal injury! The fuel meter cover is serviced only as a complete assembly and includes the fuel pressure regulator preset and plugged at the factor.

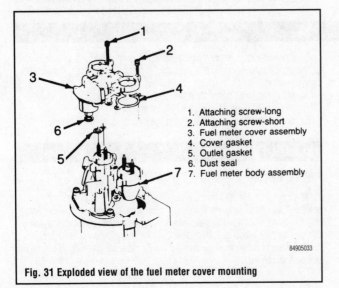

1. Attaching screw-long
2. Attaching screw-short
3. Fuel meter cover assembly
4. Cover gasket
5. Outlet gasket
6. Dust seal
7. Fuel meter body assembly

84905033

Fig. 31 Exploded view of the fuel meter cover mounting

6. Remove the fuel meter cover assembly from the throttle body.

✳✳ WARNING

DO NOT immerse the fuel meter cover (with pressure regulator) in any type of cleaner! Immersion of cleaner will damage the internal fuel pressure regulator diaphragms and gaskets.

To install:

7. Be sure to use new gaskets and then install the fuel meter cover. Tighten the attaching screws to 28 inch lbs. (3 Nm).

➡ The service kits may include a small vial of thread locking compound with directions for use. If the material is not available, use part number 1054.3L4, Loctite® or equivalent. Do not use a higher strength locking compound than recommended, as this may prevent attaching screw removal or breakage of the screw head if removal is again required.

8. Attach all the fuel injectors connectors, start the engine and check for leaks.

Fuel Injectors

REMOVAL & INSTALLATION

▶ **See Figures 32, 33 and 34**

✳✳ WARNING

When removing the injectors, be careful not to damage the electrical connector pins (on top of the injector), the injector fuel filter and the nozzle. The fuel injector is serviced as a complete assembly ONLY. The injector is an electrical component and should not be immersed in any kind of cleaner.

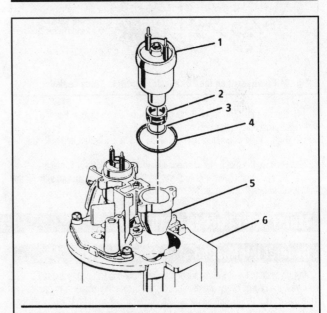

1   FUEL INJECTOR ASSEMBLY

2   FUEL INJECTOR INLET FILTER

3   FUEL INJECTOR LOWER "O" RING

4   FUEL INJECTOR UPPER "O" RING

5   FUEL METER BODY ASSEMBLY

6   THROTTLE BODY ASSEMBLY

84905034

Fig. 32 Fuel injectors and related components

Fig. 33 Remove the TBI fuel injector by carefully lifting the injector up until it is free from the fuel meter body

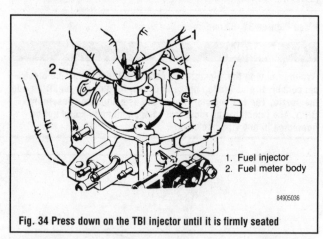

1. Fuel injector
2. Fuel meter body

84905036

Fig. 34 Press down on the TBI injector until it is firmly seated

1. Remove the air cleaner. Relieve the fuel system pressure. Refer to the fuel relief procedure in this section.
2. At the injector connector, squeeze the two tabs together and pull straight up.
3. Remove the fuel meter cover and leave the cover gasket in place.
4. Using a small pry bar or tool No. J-26868 or equivalent, carefully lift the injector until it is free from the fuel meter body.

MULTI-PORT FUEL INJECTION (MFI)

General Information

In this system, the injectors are controlled individually. Each cylinder receives one charge every two revolutions just before the intake valve opens. This means that the mixture is never static in the intake manifold along with the mixture adjustments that can be made almost simultaneously between the firing of one injector and the next. A camshaft signal sensor or a special distributor reference pulse informs the ECM when the No. 1 cylinder is on the compression stroke. If the sensor fails or the distributor reference pulse is interrupted in any way, the system reverts to pulsing all the injectors simultaneously.

Relieving Fuel System Pressure

➡**Fuel pressure gauge J 34730-1A or its equivalent is required to perform this procedure.**

1. Disconnect the negative battery cable.
2. Loosen the fuel filler cap to relieve fuel tank pressure.

5. Remove the small O-ring from the nozzle end of the injector. Carefully rotate the injector's fuel filter back and forth to remove it from the base of the injector.
6. Discard the fuel meter cover gasket.
7. Remove the large O-ring and backup washer from the top of the counterbore of the fuel meter body injector cavity.

To install:

8. Lubricate the new lower O-rings with automatic transmission fluid and then push on the nozzle end of the injector until it presses against the injector fuel filter.
9. Position the injector backup washer into the fuel meter bore.
10. Lubricate the new upper O-rings with automatic transmission fluid and then position it over the backup washer so that it seats properly and is flush with the top of the meter body. Positioning must be correct or the injector will leak after installation.
11. Install the injector so that the raised lug on the injector base is aligned with the notch in the fuel meter body cavity. Press down on the injector until it is fully seated. The electrical terminals should be parallel with the throttle shaft.
12. Install the cover gasket and the meter cover.
13. Reconnect the electrical leads, start the engine and check for leaks.

Fuel Meter Body

REMOVAL & INSTALLATION

1. Relieve the fuel system pressure. Refer to the fuel relief procedure in this section.
2. Raise the hood, install fender covers and remove the air cleaner assembly.
3. Disconnect the negative battery cable.
4. Remove the fuel meter cover assembly.
5. Remove the fuel meter cover gasket, fuel meter outlet gasket and pressure regulator seal.
6. Remove the fuel injectors.
7. Remove the fuel inlet and outlet nuts and gaskets from the fuel meter body.
8. Remove the three screws and lockwashers.
9. Remove the fuel meter body from the throttle assembly.

➡**DO not remove the center screw and staking at each end holding the fuel distribution skirt in the throttle body. The skirt is an integral part of the throttle body and is not serviced separately.**

10. Remove the fuel meter body insulator gasket.

To install:

11. Be sure to install new gaskets and O-rings wherever necessary. Apply a threadlocking compound to the fuel meter retaining screws prior to tightening.
12. Install the remaining components in the reverse order of removal.

3. Connect fuel pressure gauge J-34730-1A or its equivalent to the pressure connection. Wrap a shop towel around the fitting while connecting the gauge to prevent spillage.
4. Install the bleed hose into an approved container and open the valve to bleed the system. The system is now safe for servicing.
5. Drain any fuel remaining in the gauge into an approved container.

Electric Fuel Pump

♦ **See Figure 35**

All Chevrolet/GMC fuel-injected vehicles that use the MFI system are equipped with an electric fuel pump. For a fuel injection system to work properly, the pump must develop pressures well above those of a mechanical fuel pump. This high pressure is maintained within the lines even when the engine is off. Extreme caution must be used to safely release the pressurized fuel before any work is begun.

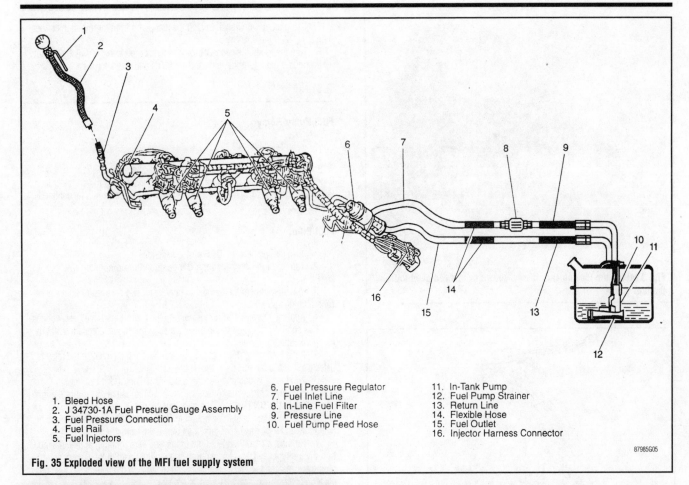

1. Bleed Hose
2. J 34730-1A Fuel Presure Gauge Assembly
3. Fuel Pressure Connection
4. Fuel Rail
5. Fuel Injectors
6. Fuel Pressure Regulator
7. Fuel Inlet Line
8. In-Line Fuel Filter
9. Pressure Line
10. Fuel Pump Feed Hose
11. In-Tank Pump
12. Fuel Pump Strainer
13. Return Line
14. Flexible Hose
15. Fuel Outlet
16. Injector Harness Connector

87985G05

Fig. 35 Exploded view of the MFI fuel supply system

✳✳ CAUTION

Always relieve the fuel pressure within the system before any work is begun on any fuel component. Failure to safely relieve the pressure may result in fire and/or serious injury.

REMOVAL & INSTALLATION

Single Tank

▶ **See Figures 36, 37, 38 and 39**

1. Disconnect the negative battery cable.
2. Relieve the fuel system pressure. Refer to the fuel system relief procedure in this section.

3. Raise the vehicle and support it safely with jackstands.
4. Drain the fuel system and remove the fuel tank. Refer to the fuel tank removal procedure in this section.
5. Remove the fuel sender assembly turning it counterclockwise using tool J-39765 or its equivalent.
6. Remove the assembly from the tank.
7. Pull the pump up into the attaching hose while pulling outward from the bottom support. Do not damage the rubber insulator or the strainer.
8. Inspect the fuel pump attaching hose and the rubber sound insulation for signs of deterioration.
9. Inspect the strainer for blockage and damage.

TCCS5P06

Fig. 36 A special tool is usually available to remove or install the fuel pump locking cam

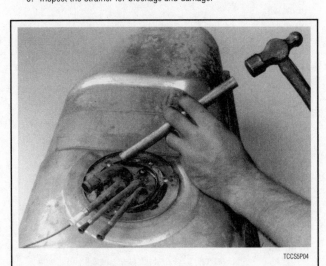

TCCS5P04

Fig. 37 A brass drift and a hammer can also be used to loosen the fuel pump locking cam

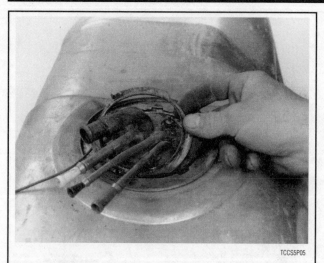

Fig. 38 Once the locking cam is released, it can be removed to free the fuel pump

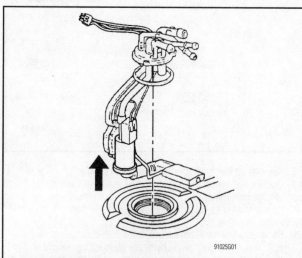

Fig. 39 Once the locking cam is removed, the fuel pump assembly can be lifted straight up and out of the tank

To install:
10. Installation is the reverse of removal but please pay special attention to the following steps.
11. Install the fuel pump assembly into the attaching hose.

➥Be careful not to bend or fold over the fuel strainer when installing the fuel sender as this will restrict fuel flow.

12. When installing the fuel sender into the fuel tank use a new O-ring seal.
13. Install the camlock assembly turning it clockwise to lock it.
14. Turn the ignition switch **ON** for 2 seconds then turn the switch **OFF** for 10 seconds. Again, turn the ignition switch **ON** and check for leaks.

Dual Tanks

1. Disconnect the negative battery cable.
2. Loosen the filler cap(s) to relieve fuel tank pressure.
3. Disconnect the fuel pipes from the pump.
4. Slide the pump out of the bracket.
To install:
5. Installation is the reverse of removal but please note the following steps.
6. Install new fuel pipe O-rings.

7. Using a backup wrench to stop the fuel pump from turning, tighten the fittings to 22 ft. lbs. (30 Nm).
8. Turn the ignition switch **ON** for 2 seconds then turn the switch **OFF** for 10 seconds. Again, turn the ignition switch **ON** and check for leaks.

TESTING

Fuel Pump Relay

1. Turn the ignition **OFF**.
2. Remove the relay.
3. Locate the two terminals on the relay, which are connected to the coil windings. Check the relay coil for continuity. Connect the common meter lead to terminal 85 and positive meter lead to terminal 86. There should be continuity. If not, replace the relay.

Fuel Pump

1. Turn the ignition key **OFF** for ten seconds.
2. Turn the ignition key to the **ON** position but do not start the engine.
3. You should here the fuel pump operate for two seconds (a light electrical humming sound).
4. Apply a 12 volt fused jumper wire to the fuel pump prime (test) connector. This should be located in the driver's side of the engine compartment. The fuel pump should operate.
5. If the fuel pump does operate, remove and test the relay. If the relay is defective, replace the relay and repeat the test.
6. If the relay is operating properly, connect a grounded test light to the fuel pump relay control wire (green with white stripe) at the relay. Turn the ignition switch to the **ON** position. The test light should illuminate for two seconds and go out. If the test light does not illuminate, check the relay control wire for continuity and repair as necessary, then repeat the test.
7. Connect a grounded test light to the feed wire (orange) at the relay and turn the ignition key **ON**. The test light should illuminate. If the light does not illuminate, test feed wire for continuity and the fuse in the underhood fuse relay center. Repair as necessary and repeat the test.
8. If the fuel pump is still not functioning, connect a fused jumper wire between the feed (orange) wire and the fuel pump motor (gray) wire at the relay. The pump should operate.
9. If the pump does not operate, check the fuel pump motor wire for continuity and repair as necessary.
10. If the pump will still not operate, replace the pump.
11. If the pump does operate, start the vehicle and remove the relay. The vehicle should continue to run. If the vehicle stalls, check the fuel pump/oil pressure switch and its wiring. Repair as necessary and repeat the test.

Throttle Body

REMOVAL & INSTALLATION

▶ See Figure 40

1. Disconnect the negative battery cable.
2. Remove the air inlet duct.
3. Unplug the Idle Air Control (IAC) valve and the Throttle Position Sensor (TPS) electrical connectors.
4. Disconnect the throttle and cruise control cables.
5. Unfasten the throttle body retaining nuts and remove the throttle body.
6. Remove and discard the flange gasket.
7. Clean both gasket mating surfaces.

➥When cleaning the old gasket from the machined aluminum surfaces be careful as sharp tools may damage the sealing surfaces

To install:
8. Install the new flange gasket and the throttle body assembly.
9. Tighten the throttle body attaching nuts to 18 ft. lbs. (25 Nm).
10. Install the remaining components.

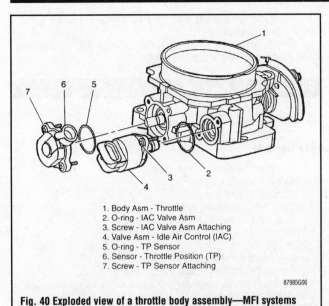

1. Body Asm - Throttle
2. O-ring - IAC Valve Asm
3. Screw - IAC Valve Asm Attaching
4. Valve Asm - Idle Air Control (IAC)
5. O-ring - TP Sensor
6. Sensor - Throttle Position (TP)
7. Screw - TP Sensor Attaching

87985G06

Fig. 40 Exploded view of a throttle body assembly—MFI systems

Fuel Injectors

REMOVAL & INSTALLATION

▶ See Figure 41

➡Use care when removing the injectors to prevent damage to the electrical connector pins on the injector and the nozzle. The fuel injector is serviced as a complete assembly only. Since the injector is an electrical component, it should not be immersed in any type of cleaner.

1. Disconnect the negative battery cable.
2. Relieve the fuel system pressure. Refer to the fuel system relief procedure in this section.
3. Remove the intake manifold plenum.
4. Remove the fuel rail assembly.

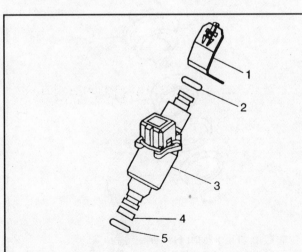

1. Clip - SFI Fuel Injector Retainer
2. O-ring - SFI Fuel Injector Upper
3. Injector Asm - SFI Fuel
4. O-ring - Backup
5. O-ring - SFI Fuel Injector Lower

87985G08

Fig. 41 Exploded view of the fuel injector assembly—MFI systems

5. Unplug the electrical wiring harness.
6. Disassemble the injector clip and discard it.
7. Remove the injector o-ring seals from both ends of the injector. Save the o-ring backups for use on reassembly.
   To install:
8. Install the o-ring backups before installing the O-rings.
9. Lubricate the new injector O-rings with clean engine oil and install them on the injector assembly.
10. Install the fuel injector into the fuel rail injector socket with the electrical connectors facing outward.
11. Install new injector retaining clips on the injector fuel rail assembly by sliding the clip into the injector groove as it snaps onto the fuel rail.
12. Install the remaining components in the reverse order of removal.

TESTING

▶ See Figure 42

➡This test requires the use of fuel injector tester J 34730-3 or its equivalent.

1. With the engine cool and the ignition turned **OFF**, install the fuel pressure gauge to the fuel pressure connection. Wrap a shop towel around the fitting while connecting the gauge to prevent spillage.
2. Disengage all the fuel injector electrical connectors. Engage the tester to one fuel injector.
3. Turn **ON** the ignition and bleed the air from the pressure gauge.
4. Turn **OFF** the ignition for ten seconds and then turn it **ON** again. This will bring the fuel pressure to its maximum pressure. Record this reading.
5. Press the tester button and record the lowest pressure reading. Subtract this reading from the initial reading obtained and record the result.
6. Connect the tester to each injector and repeat Steps 4 and 5.
7. Pressure should fall between 56–62 psi (386–427 kPa). Replace any injector that does not meet these specifications.

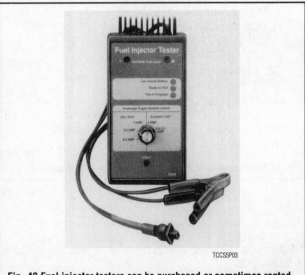

TCCS5P03

Fig. 42 Fuel injector testers can be purchased or sometimes rented

Fuel Rail Assembly

REMOVAL & INSTALLATION

▶ See Figure 43

➡Clean the fuel rail assembly before removal. The fittings should be capped to prevent dirt from entering open lines.

1. Disconnect the negative battery cable.
2. Relieve fuel system pressure.
3. Remove the intake manifold plenum.

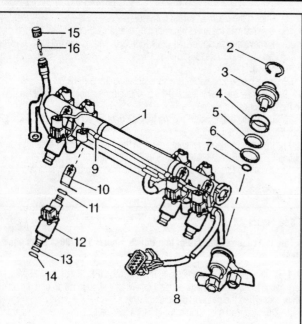

1. Rail Asm - Fuel
2. Clip - Regulator Retainer
3. Cartridge Regulator Asm - Fuel Pressure
4. Ring - Backup
5. O-ring - Regulator Seal
6. Filter - Regulator
7. O-ring - Regulator Seal
8. Wiring Harness - Fuel Injector
9. Retainer Clip - Wiring Harness
10. Clip - SFI Fuel Injector Retainer
11. O-ring - SFI Fuel Injector Upper
12. Injector Asm - SFI Fuel
13. O-ring - Backup
14. O-ring - SFI Fuel Injector Lower
15. Cap - Fuel Pressure Connection
16. Core Asm - Fuel Pressure Connection

87985G10

Fig. 43 Exploded view of the fuel rail assembly—MFI systems

4. Remove the distributor.
5. Disconnect the fuel lines at the rail.
6. Unfasten the fuel pipe bracket bolt.
7. Remove the fuel inlet and return line O-rings and discard them.
8. Unplug the fuel injector electrical connectors and remove them from the coil bracket.
9. Unfasten the fuel rail retaining bolts.
10. Disconnect the vacuum line to the fuel pressure regulator.
11. Remove the fuel rail.
12. Remove the O-rings seals and backups from the injectors. Discard the old seals, but retain the backups for reuse.
To install:
13. Installation is the reverse of removal but please pay special attention to the following steps.

➡Ensure that the O-ring backups are on the injectors before installing the O-rings. Lubricate the O-rings with clean engine oil before installation.

14. Install the fuel rail in the intake manifold. Tilt the fuel rail assembly to install the injectors. Tighten the fuel rail retaining bolts to 89 inch. lbs. (10 Nm).
15. Install new O-rings on the fuel pipes.

16. Tighten the fuel pipe nuts to 20 ft. lbs. (27 Nm) using a backup wrench to prevent the fittings from turning.
17. Turn the ignition **ON** for 2 seconds and then turn it **OFF** for 10 seconds. Again turn the ignition **ON** and check for leaks.

Fuel Pressure Regulator

REMOVAL & INSTALLATION

▶ **See Figure 44**

1. Disconnect the negative battery cable.
2. Relieve fuel system pressure.
3. Disconnect the ignition coil.
4. Remove the upper intake manifold.
5. Disconnect the vacuum line to the regulator.
6. Remove the snapring from the regulator housing.
7. Place a towel under the regulator to absorb any spilled fuel and remove the pressure regulator from the fuel rail socket.
8. Remove the pressure regulator from the fuel rail.
9. Remove the pressure regulator O-ring filter, O-ring backup and O-ring and discard them.
To install:
10. Before installing the O-rings, lubricate them with clean engine oil and install them on the regulator inlet as a complete assembly.
11. Install the snapring retainer into the slot on the regulator housing.
12. Connect the vacuum line to the regulator.

➡Ensure that the retainer is properly seated in the slot in the regulator housing. Pull on the regulator to make sure that it is properly seated.

13. Connect the negative battery cable.
14. Turn the ignition **ON** for 2 seconds and then turn it **OFF** for 10 seconds. Again turn the ignition **ON** and check for leaks.
15. Install the manifold plenum.

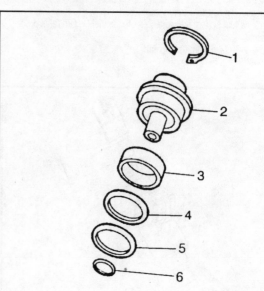

1. Clip - Regulator Retainer
2. Cartridge Regulator Asm - Fuel Pressure
3. Ring - Backup
4. O-ring - Regulator Seal
5. Filter - Regulator
6. O-ring - Regulator Seal

87985G09

Fig. 44 Exploded view of the pressure regulator assembly—MFI systems

CENTRAL SEQUENTIAL FUEL INJECTION (CSFI)

General Information

Most 1996–98 trucks are equipped with the Central Sequential Fuel Injection (CSFI) system. Fuel is delivered to the engine by individual fuel injectors and poppet nozzles mounted in the intake manifold near each cylinder. Each is fired sequentially for accuracy and precise metering control.

Relieving Fuel System Pressure

➡**Fuel pressure gauge J 34730-1A or its equivalent is required to perform this procedure.**

1. Disconnect the negative battery cable.
2. Loosen the fuel filler cap to relieve fuel tank pressure.
3. Engage the fuel pressure gauge to the fuel pressure connection. Wrap a shop towel around the fitting while connecting the gauge to prevent spillage.
4. Install the bleed hose into an approved container and open the valve to bleed the system. The system is now safe for servicing.
5. Drain any fuel remaining in the gauge into an approved container.

Electric Fuel Pump

◆ **See Figure 45**

All Chevrolet/GMC Central Sequential Fuel Injection (CSFI) fuel-injected vehicles are equipped with an electric fuel pump. For a fuel injection system to work properly, the pump must develop pressures well above those of a mechanical fuel pump. This high pressure is maintained within the lines even when the engine is **OFF**. Extreme caution must be used to safely release the pressurized fuel before any work is begun.

✳✳ CAUTION

Always relieve the fuel pressure within the system before any work is begun on any fuel component. Failure to safely relieve the pressure may result in fire and/or serious injury.

REMOVAL & INSTALLATION

The removal and installation of the fuel pump for trucks equipped with the CSFI system is the same as trucks equipped with the MFI system. Please refer to the MFI system procedures earlier in this section for fuel pump removal and installation.

TESTING

The testing of the fuel pump and its circuit for trucks equipped with the CSFI system is the same as trucks equipped with the MFI system. Please refer to the MFI system procedures earlier in this section for fuel pump testing.

Throttle Body

REMOVAL & INSTALLATION

◆ **See Figure 46**

1. Disconnect the negative battery cable.
2. Remove the air inlet fastener and duct.
3. Unplug the Idle Air Control (IAC) valve and the Throttle Position Sensor (TPS) electrical connectors.

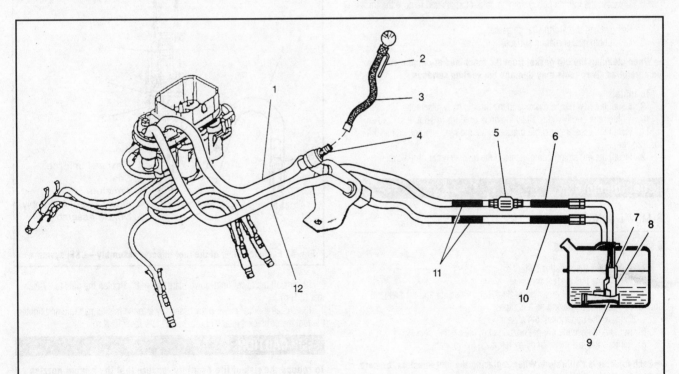

1. Fuel Inlet
2. Bleed Hose
3. J 34730-1A Fuel Pressure Gauge Assembly
4. Fuel Pressure Connection
5. In-Line Fuel Filter
6. Pressure Line
7. Fuel pump Feed Hose
8. In-Tank Fuel Pump
9. Fuel Pump Strainer
10. Return Line
11. Flexible Hose
12. Fuel Outlet

87985G11

Fig. 45 Exploded view of the fuel supply system—CSFI system

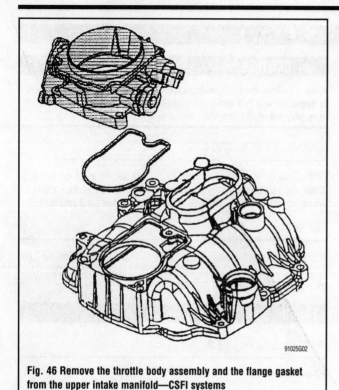

Fig. 46 Remove the throttle body assembly and the flange gasket from the upper intake manifold—CSFI systems

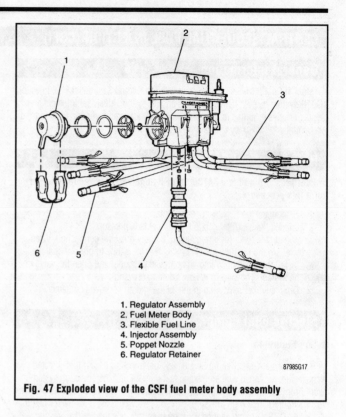

1. Regulator Assembly
2. Fuel Meter Body
3. Flexible Fuel Line
4. Injector Assembly
5. Poppet Nozzle
6. Regulator Retainer

Fig. 47 Exploded view of the CSFI fuel meter body assembly

4. Disconnect the throttle and cruise control cables.
5. Remove the accelerator cable bracket nuts and bracket.
6. Unfasten the throttle body retaining bolts or studs and remove the throttle body.
7. Remove and discard the flange gasket.
8. Clean both gasket mating surfaces.

➡**When cleaning the old gasket from the machined aluminum surfaces be careful as sharp tools may damage the sealing surfaces**

To install:
9. Install the new flange gasket and the throttle body assembly.
10. Tighten the throttle body attaching bolts or studs to 18 ft. lbs. (25 Nm).
11. Install the accelerator cable bracket bolts and nuts and tighten to 18 ft. lbs. (25 Nm).
12. Install the remaining components in the reverse order of removal.

Fuel Injectors

REMOVAL & INSTALLATION

▶ **See Figures 47 and 48**

1. Disconnect the negative battery cable.
2. Relieve the fuel system pressure.
3. Disengage the fuel meter body electrical connection and the fuel feed and return hoses from the engine fuel pipes.
4. Remove the upper manifold assembly.
5. Tag and remove the poppet nozzle out of the casting socket.
6. Remove the fuel meter body by releasing the locktabs.

➡**Each injector is calibrated. When replacing the fuel injectors, be sure to replace it with the correct injector.**

7. Disassemble the lower hold-down plate and nuts.
8. While pulling the poppet nozzle tube downward, push with a small pry-tool down between the injector terminals and remove the injectors.

To install:
9. Lubricate the new injector O-ring seats with engine oil.
10. Install the O-rings on the injector.
11. Install the fuel injector into the fuel meter body injector socket.

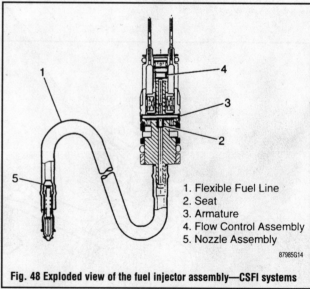

1. Flexible Fuel Line
2. Seat
3. Armature
4. Flow Control Assembly
5. Nozzle Assembly

Fig. 48 Exploded view of the fuel injector assembly—CSFI systems

12. Install the lower hold-down plate and nuts. Tighten the nuts to 27 inch lbs. (3 Nm).
13. Install the fuel meter body assembly into the intake manifold and tighten the fuel meter bracket retainer bolts to 88 inch. lbs. (10 Nm).

✳✳ CAUTION

To reduce the risk of fire or injury, ensure that the poppet nozzles are properly seated and locked in their casting sockets.

14. Install the fuel meter body into the bracket and lock all the tabs in place.
15. Install the poppet nozzles into the casting sockets.
16. Engage the electrical connections and install new o-ring seals on the fuel return and feed hoses.
17. Install the fuel feed and return hoses and tighten the fuel pipe nuts to 22 ft. lbs. (30 Nm).

18. Connect the negative battery cable.
19. Turn the ignition **ON** for 2 seconds and then turn it **OFF** for 10 seconds. Again turn the ignition **ON** and check for leaks.
20. Install the manifold plenum.

TESTING

▶ **See Figure 42**

➡ **This test requires the use of fuel injector tester J 39021 or its equivalent.**

1. Disconnect the fuel injector harness and attach a noid light in order to test for injector pulse.
2. With the engine cool and the ignition turned **OFF**, install the fuel pressure gauge to the fuel pressure connection. Wrap a shop towel around the fitting while connecting the gauge to prevent spillage.
3. Turn **ON** the ignition and record the fuel gauge pressure with the pump running.
4. Turn **OFF** the ignition. Pressure should drop and hold steady at this point.
5. To perform this test, set the selector switch to the balance test 2.5 amp position.
6. Turn the injector **ON** by depressing the button on the injector tester. Note this pressure reading the instant the gauge needle stops.
7. Repeat the balance test on the remaining injectors and record the pressure drop on each.
8. Start the engine to clear fuel from the intake. Retest the injectors that appear faulty. Any injector that has a plus or minus 1.5 psi (10 kPa) difference from the other injectors is suspect.

Fuel Meter Body Assembly

REMOVAL & INSTALLATION

▶ **See Figure 49**

1. Disconnect the negative battery cable.
2. Relieve the fuel system pressure.
3. Unplug the electrical connector from the fuel meter body.
4. Disconnect the fuel feed and return lines from the engine fuel pipes.
5. Remove the upper manifold assembly.

➡ **When disconnecting the poppet nozzles, tag the nozzles sequence in order of removal to ensure the attached in their original positions during installation.**

6. Squeeze the poppet nozzle locking tabs together while lifting the nozzle out of the casting socket.

7. Remove the fuel meter body attaching bolts.
8. Release the lock tabs on the fuel meter body bracket and remove the fuel meter body assembly.

To install:

9. Installation is the reverse of removal but please pay special attention to the following steps.
10. Place the fuel meter body into position and install its retaining bolts. Tighten the bolts to 88 inch lbs. (10 Nm).

✳✳ WARNING

In order to reduce the risk of fire and personal injury, make sure the poppet nozzles are firmly seated and locked in their casting sockets. An unlocked poppet nozzle could work loose from its socket resulting in a fuel leak.

11. Install new O-rings on the fuel feed and return lines.
12. Attach the fuel feed and return lines to the engine fuel pipes. Tighten the fuel pipe nuts to 22 ft. lbs. (30 Nm).
13. Turn the ignition **ON** for 2 seconds and then turn it **OFF** for 10 seconds. Again turn the ignition **ON** and check for leaks.

Engine Fuel Pipes

REMOVAL & INSTALLATION

▶ **See Figure 50**

1. Disconnect the negative battery cable.
2. Relieve the fuel system pressure. Refer to the fuel system relief procedure in this section.
3. Remove the fuel lines at the rear of the intake manifold.
4. Remove the nuts and the retainer.
5. Loosen the injector fuel inlet and outlet pipes.
6. Remove the rear fuel line bracket.
7. Pull straight up on the fuel pipe to remove the pipes from the injector assembly.

➡ **Check the injector assembly to make sure the O-rings have been removed.**

8. Remove the O-rings from both ends of the fuel feed and return pipes.

To install:

9. Apply a few drops of clean engine oil to the male tube ends.
10. Install the inlet and outlet of the fuel injector assembly.
11. Install the fuel pipes to the fuel injector assembly.

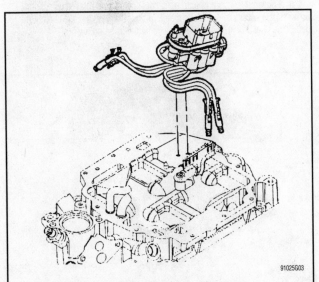

91025G03

Fig. 49 Release the lock tabs on the fuel meter body bracket and remove the fuel meter body assembly—CSFI systems

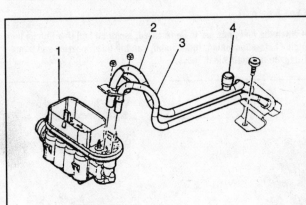

1. Fuel Meter Body
2. Fuel Inlet
3. Fuel Outlet
4. Fuel Pressure Connection

87985G16

Fig. 50 Exploded view of the engine fuel pipes and related components—CSFI systems

12. Install the fuel pipe retainer and attaching nuts. After the pipes are secured, pull up on them gently to ensure that they are properly secured. Tighten the rear fuel line bracket bolt to 53 inch. lbs. (6 Nm) and the fuel pipe retainer nuts to 27 inch. lbs. (3 Nm).

13. Tighten the fuel pipe nuts to 22 ft. lbs. (30 Nm) and connect the negative battery cable.

14. Turn the ignition **ON** for 2 seconds and then turn it **OFF** for 10 seconds. Again turn the ignition **ON** and check for leaks.

Fuel Pressure Regulator

REMOVAL & INSTALLATION

▶ **See Figure 51**

1. Disconnect the negative battery cable.
2. Relieve the fuel system pressure.
3. Remove the upper manifold assembly.
4. Remove the fuel pressure regulator vacuum tube.
5. Disassemble the fuel pressure regulator snapring retainer.
6. Remove the fuel pressure regulator assembly and the O-rings. Discard the O-rings, filter and backup O-rings.

To install:

7. Lubricate the O-rings with clean engine oil and install as an assembly.
8. Install the remaining components in the reverse order of their removal.

Fuel Pressure Connection

The fuel pressure connection is non-replaceable, but is serviceable.

SERVICE

▶ **See Figure 52**

1. Disconnect the negative battery cable.
2. Relieve the fuel system pressure.
3. Remove the fuel pressure connection cap.

DIESEL FUEL SYSTEM

Fuel Injection Lines

REMOVAL & INSTALLATION

▶ **See Figure 53**

➡ **When the fuel lines are to be removed, clean all fuel line fittings thoroughly before loosening. Immediately cap the lines, nozzles and pump fittings to maintain cleanliness.**

4. Using a valve core removal tool remove the valve core assembly and discard it.

To install:

5. Install a new valve core assembly using a valve core tool.
6. Connect the negative battery cable.
7. Turn the ignition **ON** for 2 seconds and then turn it **OFF** for 10 seconds. Again turn the ignition **ON** and check for leaks.
8. Install the fuel pressure connection cap.

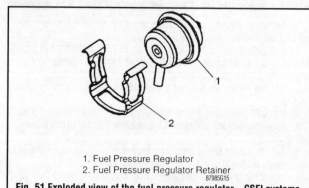

1. Fuel Pressure Regulator
2. Fuel Pressure Regulator Retainer

87985G15

Fig. 51 Exploded view of the fuel pressure regulator—CSFI systems

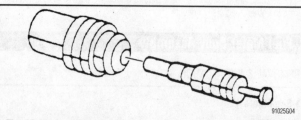

91025G04

Fig. 52 A valve core removal tool is used to remove the valve core assembly—CSFI systems

1. Disconnect both batteries.
2. Disconnect the air cleaner bracket at the valve cover.
3. Remove the crankcase ventilator bracket and move it aside.
4. Disconnect the secondary filter lines.
5. Remove the secondary filter adapter.
6. Loosen the vacuum pump hold-down clamp and rotate the pump in order to gain access to the intake manifold bolt. Remove the intake manifold bolts. The injection line clips are retained by the same bolts.

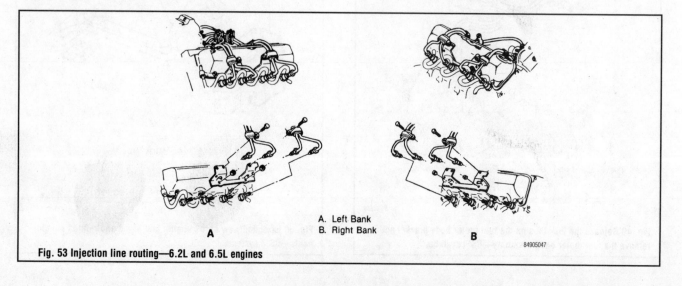

A. Left Bank
B. Right Bank

84905047

Fig. 53 Injection line routing—6.2L and 6.5L engines

7. Remove the intake manifold. Install a protective cover (GM part no. J-29664-1 or equivalent) so no foreign material falls into the engine.

8. Remove the injection line clips at the loom brackets.

9. Remove the injection lines at the nozzles and cover the nozzles with protective caps.

10. Remove the injection lines at the pump and tag the lines for later installation.

11. Remove the fuel line from the injection pump.

To install:

12. Installation is the reverse of removal but please pay special attention to the following steps.

13. Install the injection lines at the pump and nozzles. Tighten all fittings to 20 ft. lbs. (25 Nm).

14. Install the fuel lines at the filter. Tighten the bolts to 9 inch lbs. (1 Nm).

15. Install the filter to the manifold and tighten the bolts to 30 ft. lbs. (40 Nm).

Fuel Injectors

REMOVAL & INSTALLATION

▶ **See Figure 54**

➡ **Special tool J-29873, or its equivalent, an injection nozzle socket, will be necessary for this procedure.**

1. Disconnect the batteries.
2. Disconnect the fuel line clip, and remove the fuel return hose.
3. Remove the fuel injection lines as previously detailed.
4. Using GM special tool J-29873, remove the injector. Always remove the injector by turning the 30mm hex portion of the injector; turning the round portion will damage the injector. Always cap the injector and fuel lines when disconnected, to prevent contamination.

To install:

5. Always install the injector by turning the 30mm hex portion of the injector; turning the round portion will damage the injector.

6. Install the injector with a new gasket and tighten to 50 ft. lbs. (70 Nm). Connect the injection line and tighten the nut to 20 ft. lbs. (25 Nm). Install the fuel return hose, fuel line clips, and connect the batteries.

TESTING

1. Install a suitable pressure gauge.
2. Open the shut-off valve on the gauge a ¼ turn.

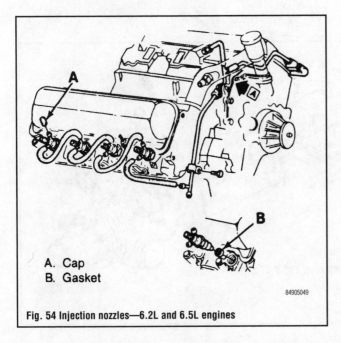

A. Cap
B. Gasket

84905049

Fig. 54 Injection nozzles—6.2L and 6.5L engines

❋❋ **CAUTION**

When testing nozzle opening pressure, always keep your hands (or any exposed skin!) away from the nozzle. Diesel injectors have sufficient pressure to penetrate your skin!

3. Slowly depress the lever on the gauge. Note when the needle on the gauge stops—the maximum pressure is the opening pressure. Pressure should never fall below 1500 psi (10,342 kPa) on the 6.2L engine or 1700 psi (11,721 kPa) on the 6.5L engine.

4. Replace any injector which does not meets these pressures.

Fuel Supply Pump

REMOVAL & INSTALLATION

1988–90 6.2L Engines

▶ **See Figure 55**

❋❋ **CAUTION**

Never smoke when working around diesel fuel! Avoid all sources of sparks or ignition.

1. Disconnect the fuel intake and outlet lines at the pump and plug the pump intake line.

2. You can insert a long bolt to hold the fuel pump pushrod.

3. Remove the two pump mounting bolts and lockwashers; remove the pump and its gasket. The 6.2L utilizes a mounting plate between the pump and gasket.

4. If the rocker arm pushrod is to be removed, remove the two adapter bolts and lockwashers and remove the adapter and its gasket.

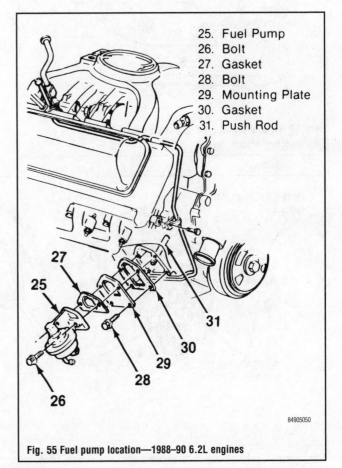

25. Fuel Pump
26. Bolt
27. Gasket
28. Bolt
29. Mounting Plate
30. Gasket
31. Push Rod

84905050

Fig. 55 Fuel pump location—1988–90 6.2L engines

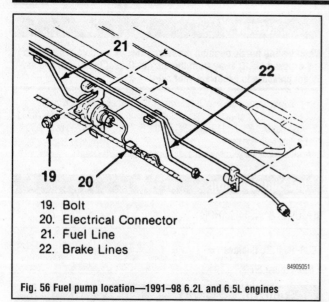

19. Bolt
20. Electrical Connector
21. Fuel Line
22. Brake Lines

84905051

Fig. 56 Fuel pump location—1991–98 6.2L and 6.5L engines

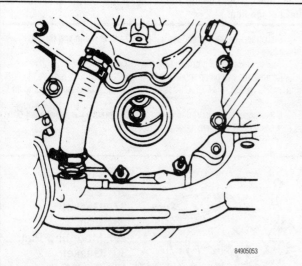

84905053

Fig. 57 Rotate the crankshaft so that the injection pump drive gear bolts become visible through the hole

To install:

5. Install the fuel pump with a new gasket. Tighten the upper mounting bolts to 24 ft. lbs. (33 Nm) and the lower bolt to 6 ft. lbs. (8 Nm). Heavy grease can be used to hold the fuel pump pushrod up when installing the pump. Coat the mating surfaces with sealant.

6. Connect the fuel lines an check for leaks.

1991–98 6.2L and 6.5L Engines

▶ See Figure 56

1. Disconnect the negative battery cables.
2. Locate the pump on the left frame rail and disconnect the electrical lead from the pump and the harness from the pump support bracket.
3. Use two open end wrenches and disconnect the fuel lines at the pump.
4. Remove the pump support bracket screws and remove it from the brake lines.
5. Remove the pump and bracket.

To install:

6. Installation of the components is the reverse of removal.

Fuel Injection Pump

REMOVAL & INSTALLATION

▶ See Figures 57 and 58

1. Disconnect both batteries.
2. If necessary, remove the fan and fan shroud.
3. Remove the intake manifold.
4. Remove the fuel injection lines.
5. If applicable, disconnect the accelerator cable at the injection pump, and the detent cable where applicable.
6. Disconnect the fuel inlet line from the pump.
7. Tag and disconnect the necessary wires and hoses at the injection pump.
8. Disconnect the fuel return line at the top of the injection pump.
9. If necessary for access, remove the air conditioning hose retainer bracket if equipped with A/C.
10. Remove the oil fill tube, including the crankcase depression valve vent hose assembly.
11. Remove the grommet for the oil filler tube.
12. Scribe or paint a matchmark on the front cover and on the injection pump flange.
13. The crankshaft must be rotated in order to gain access to the injection pump drive gear bolts through the oil filler neck hole.
14. Remove the injection pump-to-front cover attaching nuts. Remove the pump and cap all open lines and nozzles.

To install:

15. Replace the gasket.

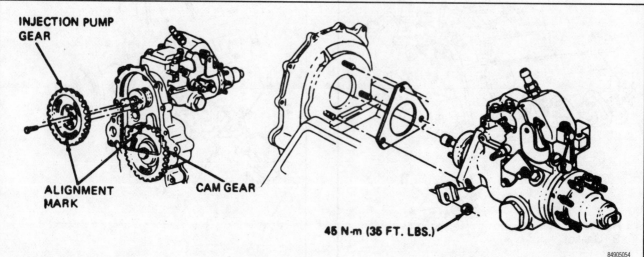

INJECTION PUMP GEAR

ALIGNMENT MARK

CAM GEAR

45 N·m (35 FT. LBS.)

84905054

Fig. 58 Injection pump mounting

→Make sure the locating pin on the pump hub goes into the slotted hole on the driven gear and not the hole in the gear.

16. Align the locating pin on the pump hub with the slot in the injection pump driven gear. At the same time, align the timing marks.

17. Attach the injection pump to the front cover, aligning the timing marks before tightening the nuts to 30 ft. lbs. (40 Nm).

18. Install the drive gear-to-injection pump bolts. Tighten the bolts to 20 ft. lbs. (25 Nm).

19. Install the grommet for the oil filler tube and the tube.

20. Install and tighten the fuel feed line at the injection pump to 20 ft. lbs. (25 Nm).

21. Install the remaining components in the reverse order of removal.

INJECTION TIMING ADJUSTMENT

1988–94 Models

▸ **See Figures 59 and 60**

→**Special tool J-26987, or its equivalent, will be necessary for this procedure.**

For the engine to be properly timed, the lines on the top of the injection pump adapter and the flange of the injection pump must be aligned.

1. The engine must be **OFF** for resetting the timing.

2. Loosen the three pump retaining nuts with tool J-26987, an injection pump intake manifold wrench, or its equivalent.

3. Align the mark on the injection pump with the marks on the adapter and tighten the nuts. Tighten to 30 ft. lbs. (40 Nm). Use a ¾ in. (19.05mm) open-end wrench on the boss at the front of the injection pump to aid in rotating the pump to align the marks.

4. Adjust the throttle rod.

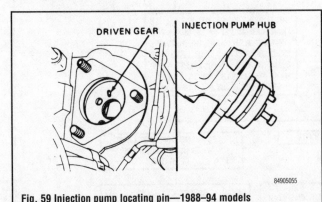

Fig. 59 Injection pump locating pin—1988–94 models

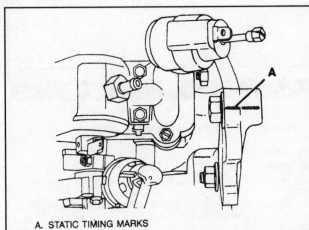

A. STATIC TIMING MARKS

Fig. 60 Injection pump timing alignment marks—1988–94 models

1995–98 Models

The use of a suitable scan tool is required to check or adjust the injection timing.

1. Start the engine and bring it to operating temperature.

2. Attach the scan tool and activate the time set. (If the time set function is activated properly the diesel injection time on the scan tool will read 0.0 degrees.

→**The actual injection time on the scan tool will fluctuate. The average reading should be 3.5 degrees.**

3. Read the actual injection time using the scan tool functions. The reading should be 3.5 degrees.

→**If the engine stalls during time set activation, slightly rotate the injection pump (1mm = 2degrres) towards the drivers side of the vehicle, tighten the flange nuts and repeat time set.**

4. If the injection timing is correct, the adjustment is complete. If the timing is incorrect continue with the procedure.

5. On 1997–98 models, move the A/C compressor to the side to improve access to the injection pump lower mounting bolts.

6. With the engine **OFF**, loosen the pump flange nuts.

7. Slightly rotate the injection pump in the desired direction (towards the drivers or passenger side of the vehicle) until the set injection time is 3.5 degrees.

→**It is normal for the actual injection time shown on the scan tool screen to fluctuate. Average fluctuation should be 3.5 degrees.**

8. Tighten the pump bolts.

9. If moved, install the A/C compressor and remove the scan tool.

10. Road test the vehicle.

Glow Plugs

INSPECTION

▸ **See Figure 61**

1. Check all connections on the controller.

2. Check the upper copper stud nuts on the controller. Do not tighten them.

3. Check the engine harness ground connection and the wiring harness nuts. Tighten them to 44 inch lbs. (5 Nm).

4. Check that the four-wire connector at the controller is seated properly and latched.

5. Tighten the controller mounting nuts to 25 ft. lbs. (35 Nm).

REMOVAL & INSTALLATION

1. Disconnect the negative battery cables.

2. On the 6.2L engine and the left side only of the 6.5L, disconnect the glow plug lead wires and then remove the plugs. You'll need a 3/8 in. (9.525mm) deep-well socket.

3. On the right side of the 6.5L engine, raise the truck and support it with safety stands. Remove the right front tire.

4. Remove the inner splash shield from the fender well.

5. Remove the lead wire from the plug at the No. 2 cylinder. Remove the lead wires from plugs in the Nos. 4 and 6 cylinders at the harness connectors.

6. Remove the heat shroud for the plug in the No. 4 cylinder. Remove the heat shroud for the plug in the No. 6 cylinder. Slide the shrouds back just far enough to allow access so you can unplug the wires.

7. Remove the plugs in cylinders No. 2, 4 and 6.

8. Reach up under the vehicle and disconnect the lead wire at No. 8. Remove the glow plug. You may find that removing the exhaust down pipe make this a bit easier when working on Nos. 6 and 8.

9. Installation is the reverse of removal. Install all glow plugs and carefully tighten them to 13 ft. lbs. (17 Nm) for the right side on the 6.5L; 17 ft. lbs. (23 Nm) on all others.

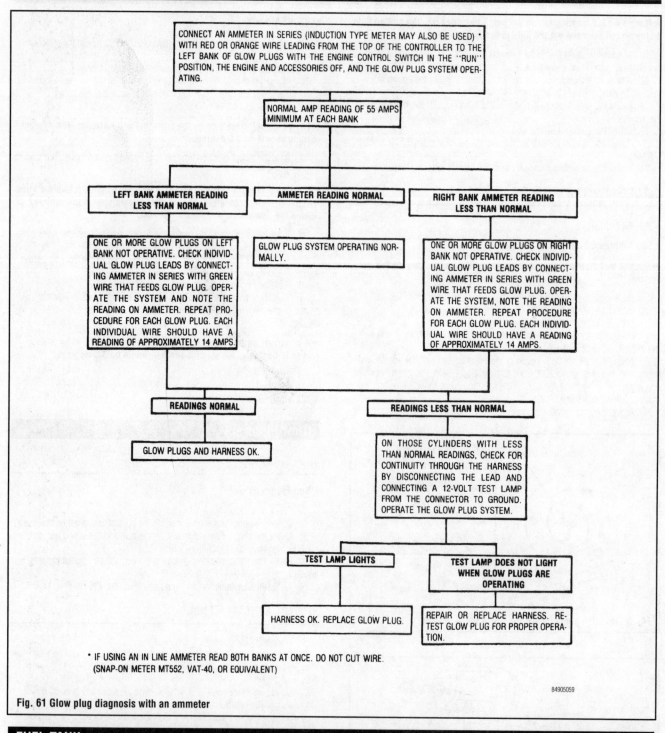

CONNECT AN AMMETER IN SERIES (INDUCTION TYPE METER MAY ALSO BE USED) * WITH RED OR ORANGE WIRE LEADING FROM THE TOP OF THE CONTROLLER TO THE LEFT BANK OF GLOW PLUGS WITH THE ENGINE CONTROL SWITCH IN THE "RUN" POSITION, THE ENGINE AND ACCESSORIES OFF, AND THE GLOW PLUG SYSTEM OPERATING.

NORMAL AMP READING OF 55 AMPS MINIMUM AT EACH BANK

LEFT BANK AMMETER READING LESS THAN NORMAL

AMMETER READING NORMAL

RIGHT BANK AMMETER READING LESS THAN NORMAL

ONE OR MORE GLOW PLUGS ON LEFT BANK NOT OPERATIVE. CHECK INDIVIDUAL GLOW PLUG LEADS BY CONNECTING AMMETER IN SERIES WITH GREEN WIRE THAT FEEDS GLOW PLUG. OPERATE THE SYSTEM AND NOTE THE READING ON AMMETER. REPEAT PROCEDURE FOR EACH GLOW PLUG. EACH INDIVIDUAL WIRE SHOULD HAVE A READING OF APPROXIMATELY 14 AMPS.

GLOW PLUG SYSTEM OPERATING NORMALLY.

ONE OR MORE GLOW PLUGS ON RIGHT BANK NOT OPERATIVE. CHECK INDIVIDUAL GLOW PLUG LEADS BY CONNECTING AMMETER IN SERIES WITH GREEN WIRE THAT FEEDS GLOW PLUG. OPERATE THE SYSTEM, NOTE THE READING ON AMMETER. REPEAT PROCEDURE FOR EACH GLOW PLUG. EACH INDIVIDUAL WIRE SHOULD HAVE A READING OF APPROXIMATELY 14 AMPS.

READINGS NORMAL

READINGS LESS THAN NORMAL

GLOW PLUGS AND HARNESS OK.

ON THOSE CYLINDERS WITH LESS THAN NORMAL READINGS, CHECK FOR CONTINUITY THROUGH THE HARNESS BY DISCONNECTING THE LEAD AND CONNECTING A 12-VOLT TEST LAMP FROM THE CONNECTOR TO GROUND. OPERATE THE GLOW PLUG SYSTEM.

TEST LAMP LIGHTS

TEST LAMP DOES NOT LIGHT WHEN GLOW PLUGS ARE OPERATING

HARNESS OK. REPLACE GLOW PLUG.

REPAIR OR REPLACE HARNESS. RETEST GLOW PLUG FOR PROPER OPERATION.

* IF USING AN IN LINE AMMETER READ BOTH BANKS AT ONCE. DO NOT CUT WIRE. (SNAP-ON METER MT552, VAT-40, OR EQUIVALENT)

84905059

Fig. 61 Glow plug diagnosis with an ammeter

FUEL TANK

Tank Assembly

REMOVAL & INSTALLATION

1. Disconnect the negative battery cable.
2. Drain the tank.
3. Raise the rear of your vehicle and support it with jackstands.
4. Remove the clamp on the filler neck and the vent tube hose.
5. If equipped, remove the gauge hose which is attached to the frame.
6. While supporting the tank securely, remove the support straps and insulators.

7. If equipped, remove the fuel tank shield.
8. Lower the tank until the gauge wiring, electrical connections and all hoses can be removed.
9. Remove the tank.
   To install:
10. Raise the tank until all hoses, electrical connections and wiring can be attached.
11. Raise the tank into position, and If equipped, install the tank shield.
12. Install the tank retaining straps. Tighten the strap retainers to 33 ft. lbs. (45 Nm). Make certain that any anti-squeak material is replaced during installation.
13. Install the remaining components in the reverse order of removal.

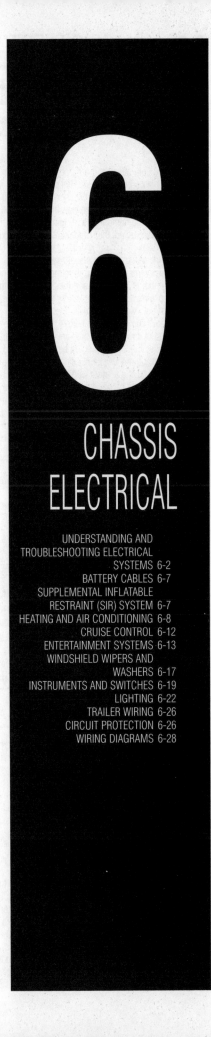

6

CHASSIS ELECTRICAL

UNDERSTANDING AND TROUBLESHOOTING ELECTRICAL SYSTEMS

Basic Electrical Theory

♦ See Figure 1

For any 12 volt, negative ground, electrical system to operate, the electricity must travel in a complete circuit. This simply means that current (power) from the positive (+) terminal of the battery must eventually return to the negative (-) terminal of the battery. Along the way, this current will travel through wires, fuses, switches and components. If, for any reason, the flow of current through the circuit is interrupted, the component fed by that circuit will cease to function properly.

Perhaps the easiest way to visualize a circuit is to think of connecting a light bulb (with two wires attached to it) to the battery—one wire attached to the negative (-) terminal of the battery and the other wire to the positive (+) terminal. With the two wires touching the battery terminals, the circuit would be complete and the light bulb would illuminate. Electricity would follow a path from the battery to the bulb and back to the battery. It's easy to see that with longer wires on our light bulb, it could be mounted anywhere. Further, one wire could be fitted with a switch so that the light could be turned on and off.

The normal automotive circuit differs from this simple example in two ways. First, instead of having a return wire from the bulb to the battery, the current travels through the frame of the vehicle. Since the negative (-) battery cable is attached to the frame (made of electrically conductive metal), the frame of the vehicle can serve as a ground wire to complete the circuit. Secondly, most automotive circuits contain multiple components which receive power from a single circuit. This lessens the amount of wire needed to power components on the vehicle.

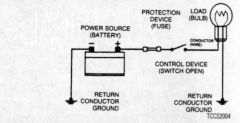

Fig. 1 This example illustrates a simple circuit. When the switch is closed, power from the positive (+) battery terminal flows through the fuse and the switch, and then to the light bulb. The light illuminates and the circuit is completed through the ground wire back to the negative (-) battery terminal. In reality, the two ground points shown in the illustration are attached to the metal frame of the vehicle, which completes the circuit back to the battery

HOW DOES ELECTRICITY WORK: THE WATER ANALOGY

Electricity is the flow of electrons—the subatomic particles that constitute the outer shell of an atom. Electrons spin in an orbit around the center core of an atom. The center core is comprised of protons (positive charge) and neutrons (neutral charge). Electrons have a negative charge and balance out the positive charge of the protons. When an outside force causes the number of electrons to unbalance the charge of the protons, the electrons will split off the atom and look for another atom to balance out. If this imbalance is kept up, electrons will continue to move and an electrical flow will exist.

Many people have been taught electrical theory using an analogy with water. In a comparison with water flowing through a pipe, the electrons would be the water and the wire is the pipe.

The flow of electricity can be measured much like the flow of water through a pipe. The unit of measurement used is amperes, frequently abbreviated as amps (a). You can compare amperage to the volume of water flowing through a pipe. When connected to a circuit, an ammeter will measure the actual amount of current flowing through the circuit. When relatively few electrons flow through a circuit, the amperage is low. When many electrons flow, the amperage is high.

Water pressure is measured in units such as pounds per square inch (psi); The electrical pressure is measured in units called volts (v). When a voltmeter is connected to a circuit, it is measuring the electrical pressure.

The actual flow of electricity depends not only on voltage and amperage, but also on the resistance of the circuit. The higher the resistance, the higher the force necessary to push the current through the circuit. The standard unit for measuring resistance is an ohm. Resistance in a circuit varies depending on the amount and type of components used in the circuit. The main factors which determine resistance are:

• Material—some materials have more resistance than others. Those with high resistance are said to be insulators. Rubber materials (or rubber-like plastics) are some of the most common insulators used in vehicles as they have a very high resistance to electricity. Very low resistance materials are said to be conductors. Copper wire is among the best conductors. Silver is actually a superior conductor to copper and is used in some relay contacts, but its high cost prohibits its use as common wiring. Most automotive wiring is made of copper.

• Size—the larger the wire size being used, the less resistance the wire will have. This is why components which use large amounts of electricity usually have large wires supplying current to them.

• Length—for a given thickness of wire, the longer the wire, the greater the resistance. The shorter the wire, the less the resistance. When determining the proper wire for a circuit, both size and length must be considered to design a circuit that can handle the current needs of the component.

• Temperature—with many materials, the higher the temperature, the greater the resistance (positive temperature coefficient). Some materials exhibit the opposite trait of lower resistance with higher temperatures (negative temperature coefficient). These principles are used in many of the sensors on the engine.

OHM'S LAW

There is a direct relationship between current, voltage and resistance. The relationship between current, voltage and resistance can be summed up by a statement known as Ohm's law.

Voltage (E) is equal to amperage (I) times resistance (R): $E = I \times R$

Other forms of the formula are $R = E/I$ and $I = E/R$

In each of these formulas, E is the voltage in volts, I is the current in amps and R is the resistance in ohms. The basic point to remember is that as the resistance of a circuit goes up, the amount of current that flows in the circuit will go down, if voltage remains the same.

The amount of work that the electricity can perform is expressed as power. The unit of power is the watt (w). The relationship between power, voltage and current is expressed as:

Power (w) is equal to amperage (I) times voltage (E): $W = I \times E$

This is only true for direct current (DC) circuits; The alternating current formula is a tad different, but since the electrical circuits in most vehicles are DC type, we need not get into AC circuit theory.

Electrical Components

POWER SOURCE

Power is supplied to the vehicle by two devices: The battery and the alternator. The battery supplies electrical power during starting or during periods when the current demand of the vehicle's electrical system exceeds the output capacity of the alternator. The alternator supplies electrical current when the engine is running. Just not does the alternator supply the current needs of the vehicle, but it recharges the battery.

The Battery

In most modern vehicles, the battery is a lead/acid electrochemical device consisting of six 2 volt subsections (cells) connected in series, so that the unit is capable of producing approximately 12 volts of electrical pressure. Each subsection consists of a series of positive and negative plates held a short distance apart in a solution of sulfuric acid and water.

The two types of plates are of dissimilar metals. This sets up a chemical reaction, and it is this reaction which produces current flow from the battery when its positive and negative terminals are connected to an electrical load . The power removed from the battery is replaced by the alternator, restoring the battery to its original chemical state.

The Alternator

On some vehicles there isn't an alternator, but a generator. The difference is that an alternator supplies alternating current which is then changed to direct current for use on the vehicle, while a generator produces direct current. Alternators tend to be more efficient and that is why they are used.

Alternators and generators are devices that consist of coils of wires wound together making big electromagnets. One group of coils spins within another set and the interaction of the magnetic fields causes a current to flow. This current is then drawn off the coils and fed into the vehicles electrical system.

GROUND

Two types of grounds are used in automotive electric circuits. Direct ground components are grounded to the frame through their mounting points. All other components use some sort of ground wire which is attached to the frame or chassis of the vehicle. The electrical current runs through the chassis of the vehicle and returns to the battery through the ground (-) cable; if you look, you'll see that the battery ground cable connects between the battery and the frame or chassis of the vehicle.

➡**It should be noted that a good percentage of electrical problems can be traced to bad grounds.**

PROTECTIVE DEVICES

▶ **See Figure 2**

It is possible for large surges of current to pass through the electrical system of your vehicle. If this surge of current were to reach the load in the circuit, the surge could burn it out or severely damage it. It can also overload the wiring, causing the harness to get hot and melt the insulation. To prevent this, fuses, circuit breakers and/or fusible links are connected into the supply wires of the electrical system. These items are nothing more than a built-in weak spot in the system. When an abnormal amount of current flows through the system, these protective devices work as follows to protect the circuit:

• Fuse—when an excessive electrical current passes through a fuse, the fuse "blows" (the conductor melts) and opens the circuit, preventing the passage of current.

• Circuit Breaker—a circuit breaker is basically a self-repairing fuse. It will open the circuit in the same fashion as a fuse, but when the surge subsides, the circuit breaker can be reset and does not need replacement.

• Fusible Link—a fusible link (fuse link or main link) is a short length of special, high temperature insulated wire that acts as a fuse. When an excessive electrical current passes through a fusible link, the thin gauge wire inside the link melts, creating an intentional open to protect the circuit. To repair the circuit, the link must be replaced. Some newer type fusible links are housed in plug-in modules, which are simply replaced like a fuse, while older type fusible links must be cut and spliced if they melt. Since this link is very early in the electrical path, it's the first place to look if nothing on the vehicle works, yet the battery seems to be charged and is properly connected.

Always replace fuses, circuit breakers and fusible links with identically rated components. Under no circumstances should a component of higher or lower amperage rating be substituted.

SWITCHES & RELAYS

▶ **See Figures 3 and 4**

Switches are used in electrical circuits to control the passage of current. The most common use is to open and close circuits between the battery and the various electric devices in the system. Switches are rated according to the amount of amperage they can handle. If a sufficient amperage rated switch is not used in a circuit, the switch could overload and cause damage.

Some electrical components which require a large amount of current to operate use a special switch called a relay. Since these circuits carry a large amount of current, the thickness of the wire in the circuit is also greater. If this large wire were connected from the load to the control switch, the switch would have to carry the high amperage load and the fairing or dash would be twice as large to accommodate the increased size of the wiring harness. To prevent these problems, a relay is used.

Relays are composed of a coil and a set of contacts. When the coil has a current passed though it, a magnetic field is formed and this field causes the contacts to move together, completing the circuit. Most relays are normally open, preventing current from passing through the circuit, but they can take any electrical form depending on the job they are intended to do. Relays can be considered "remote control switches." They allow a smaller current to operate devices that require higher amperages. When a small current operates the coil, a larger current is allowed to pass by the contacts. Some common circuits which may use relays are the horn, headlights, starter, electric fuel pump and other high draw circuits.

LOAD

Every electrical circuit must include a "load" (something to use the electricity coming from the source). Without this load, the battery would attempt to deliver its entire power supply from one pole to another. This is called a "short circuit." All this electricity would take a short cut to ground and cause a great amount of damage to other components in the circuit by developing a tremendous amount of heat. This condition could develop sufficient heat to melt the insulation on all the surrounding wires and reduce a multiple wire cable to a lump of plastic and copper.

WIRING & HARNESSES

The average vehicle contains meters and meters of wiring, with hundreds of individual connections. To protect the many wires from damage and to keep them from becoming a confusing tangle, they are organized into bundles,

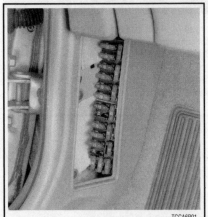

Fig. 2 Most vehicles use one or more fuse panels. This one is located on the driver's side kick panel

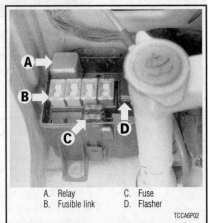

A. Relay   C. Fuse
B. Fusible link   D. Flasher

Fig. 3 The underhood fuse and relay panel usually contains fuses, relays, flashers and fusible links

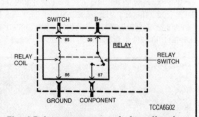

Fig. 4 Relays are composed of a coil and a switch. These two components are linked together so that when one operates, the other operates at the same time. The large wires in the circuit are connected from the battery to one side of the relay switch (B+) and from the opposite side of the relay switch to the load (component). Smaller wires are connected from the relay coil to the control switch for the circuit and from the opposite side of the relay coil to ground

enclosed in plastic or taped together and called wiring harnesses. Different harnesses serve different parts of the vehicle. Individual wires are color coded to help trace them through a harness where sections are hidden from view.

Automotive wiring or circuit conductors can be either single strand wire, multi-strand wire or printed circuitry. Single strand wire has a solid metal core and is usually used inside such components as alternators, motors, relays and other devices. Multi-strand wire has a core made of many small strands of wire twisted together into a single conductor. Most of the wiring in an automotive electrical system is made up of multi-strand wire, either as a single conductor or grouped together in a harness. All wiring is color coded on the insulator, either as a solid color or as a colored wire with an identification stripe. A printed circuit is a thin film of copper or other conductor that is printed on an insulator backing. Occasionally, a printed circuit is sandwiched between two sheets of plastic for more protection and flexibility. A complete printed circuit, consisting of conductors, insulating material and connectors for lamps or other components is called a printed circuit board. Printed circuitry is used in place of individual wires or harnesses in places where space is limited, such as behind instrument panels.

Since automotive electrical systems are very sensitive to changes in resistance, the selection of properly sized wires is critical when systems are repaired. A loose or corroded connection or a replacement wire that is too small for the circuit will add extra resistance and an additional voltage drop to the circuit.

The wire gauge number is an expression of the cross-section area of the conductor. Vehicles from countries that use the metric system will typically describe the wire size as its cross-sectional area in square millimeters. In this method, the larger the wire, the greater the number. Another common system for expressing wire size is the American Wire Gauge (AWG) system. As gauge number increases, area decreases and the wire becomes smaller. An 18 gauge wire is smaller than a 4 gauge wire. A wire with a higher gauge number will carry less current than a wire with a lower gauge number. Gauge wire size refers to the size of the strands of the conductor, not the size of the complete wire with insulator. It is possible, therefore, to have two wires of the same gauge with different diameters because one may have thicker insulation than the other.

It is essential to understand how a circuit works before trying to figure out why it doesn't. An electrical schematic shows the electrical current paths when a circuit is operating properly. Schematics break the entire electrical system down into individual circuits. In a schematic, usually no attempt is made to represent wiring and components as they physically appear on the vehicle; switches and other components are shown as simply as possible. Face views of harness connectors show the cavity or terminal locations in all multi-pin connectors to help locate test points.

CONNECTORS

▶ See Figures 5 and 6

Three types of connectors are commonly used in automotive applications—weatherproof, molded and hard shell.

• Weatherproof—these connectors are most commonly used where the connector is exposed to the elements. Terminals are protected against moisture and dirt by sealing rings which provide a weathertight seal. All repairs require the use of a special terminal and the tool required to service it. Unlike standard blade type terminals, these weatherproof terminals cannot be straightened once they are bent. Make certain that the connectors are properly seated and all of the sealing rings are in place when connecting leads.

Fig. 5 Hard shell (left) and weatherproof (right) connectors have replaceable terminals

TCCA6P03

TCCA6P04

Fig. 6 Weatherproof connectors are most commonly used in the engine compartment or where the connector is exposed to the elements

• Molded—these connectors require complete replacement of the connector if found to be defective. This means splicing a new connector assembly into the harness. All splices should be soldered to insure proper contact. Use care when probing the connections or replacing terminals in them, as it is possible to create a short circuit between opposite terminals. If this happens to the wrong terminal pair, it is possible to damage certain components. Always use jumper wires between connectors for circuit checking and NEVER probe through weatherproof seals.

• Hard Shell—unlike molded connectors, the terminal contacts in hard-shell connectors can be replaced. Replacement usually involves the use of a special terminal removal tool that depresses the locking tangs (barbs) on the connector terminal and allows the connector to be removed from the rear of the shell. The connector shell should be replaced if it shows any evidence of burning, melting, cracks, or breaks. Replace individual terminals that are burnt, corroded, distorted or loose.

Test Equipment

Pinpointing the exact cause of trouble in an electrical circuit is most times accomplished by the use of special test equipment. The following describes different types of commonly used test equipment and briefly explains how to use them in diagnosis. In addition to the information covered below, the tool manufacturer's instructions booklet (provided with the tester) should be read and clearly understood before attempting any test procedures.

JUMPER WIRES

✳✳ CAUTION

Never use jumper wires made from a thinner gauge wire than the circuit being tested. If the jumper wire is of too small a gauge, it may overheat and possibly melt. Never use jumpers to bypass high resistance loads in a circuit. Bypassing resistances, in effect, creates a short circuit. This may, in turn, cause damage and fire. Jumper wires should only be used to bypass lengths of wire or to simulate switches.

Jumper wires are simple, yet extremely valuable, pieces of test equipment. They are basically test wires which are used to bypass sections of a circuit. Although jumper wires can be purchased, they are usually fabricated from lengths of standard automotive wire and whatever type of connector (alligator clip, spade connector or pin connector) that is required for the particular application being tested. In cramped, hard-to-reach areas, it is advisable to have insulated boots over the jumper wire terminals in order to prevent accidental grounding. It is also advisable to include a standard automotive fuse in any jumper wire. This is commonly referred to as a "fused jumper". By inserting an in-line fuse holder between a set of test leads, a fused jumper wire can be used for bypassing open circuits. Use a 5 amp fuse to provide protection against voltage spikes.

Jumper wires are used primarily to locate open electrical circuits, on either the ground (-) side of the circuit or on the power (+) side. If an electrical component fails to operate, connect the jumper wire between the component and a good ground. If the component operates only with the jumper installed, the ground circuit is open. If the ground circuit is good, but the component does not operate, the circuit between the power feed and component may be open. By moving the jumper wire successively back from the component toward the power source, you can isolate the area of the circuit where the open is located. When the component stops functioning, or the power is cut off, the open is in the segment of wire between the jumper and the point previously tested.

You can sometimes connect the jumper wire directly from the battery to the "hot" terminal of the component, but first make sure the component uses 12 volts in operation. Some electrical components, such as fuel injectors or sensors, are designed to operate on about 4 to 5 volts, and running 12 volts directly to these components will cause damage.

TEST LIGHTS

▶ **See Figure 7**

The test light is used to check circuits and components while electrical current is flowing through them. It is used for voltage and ground tests. To use a 12 volt test light, connect the ground clip to a good ground and probe wherever necessary with the pick. The test light will illuminate when voltage is detected. This does not necessarily mean that 12 volts (or any particular amount of voltage) is present; it only means that some voltage is present. It is advisable before using the test light to touch its ground clip and probe across the battery posts or terminals to make sure the light is operating properly.

※ WARNING

Do not use a test light to probe electronic ignition, spark plug or coil wires. Never use a pick-type test light to probe wiring on computer controlled systems unless specifically instructed to do so. Any wire insulation that is pierced by the test light probe should be taped and sealed with silicone after testing.

Like the jumper wire, the 12 volt test light is used to isolate opens in circuits. But, whereas the jumper wire is used to bypass the open to operate the load, the 12 volt test light is used to locate the presence of voltage in a circuit. If the test light illuminates, there is power up to that point in the circuit; if the test light does not illuminate, there is an open circuit (no power). Move the test light in successive steps back toward the power source until the light in the handle illuminates. The open is between the probe and a point which was previously probed.

The self-powered test light is similar in design to the 12 volt test light, but contains a 1.5 volt penlight battery in the handle. It is most often used in place of a multimeter to check for open or short circuits when power is isolated from the circuit (continuity test).

The battery in a self-powered test light does not provide much current. A weak battery may not provide enough power to illuminate the test light even

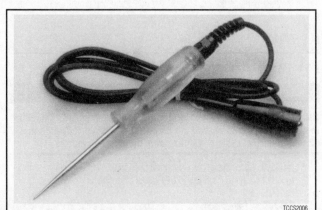

TCCS2006

Fig. 7 A 12 volt test light is used to detect the presence of voltage in a circuit

when a complete circuit is made (especially if there is high resistance in the circuit). Always make sure that the test battery is strong. To check the battery, briefly touch the ground clip to the probe; if the light glows brightly, the battery is strong enough for testing.

➡**A self-powered test light should not be used on any computer controlled system or component. The small amount of electricity transmitted by the test light is enough to damage many electronic automotive components.**

MULTIMETERS

Multimeters are an extremely useful tool for troubleshooting electrical problems. They can be purchased in either analog or digital form and have a price range to suit any budget. A multimeter is a voltmeter, ammeter and ohmmeter (along with other features) combined into one instrument. It is often used when testing solid state circuits because of its high input impedance (usually 10 megaohms or more). A brief description of the multimeter main test functions follows:

• Voltmeter—the voltmeter is used to measure voltage at any point in a circuit, or to measure the voltage drop across any part of a circuit. Voltmeters usually have various scales and a selector switch to allow the reading of different voltage ranges. The voltmeter has a positive and a negative lead. To avoid damage to the meter, always connect the negative lead to the negative (-) side of the circuit (to ground or nearest the ground side of the circuit) and connect the positive lead to the positive (+) side of the circuit (to the power source or the nearest power source). Note that the negative voltmeter lead will always be black and that the positive voltmeter will always be some color other than black (usually red).

• Ohmmeter—the ohmmeter is designed to read resistance (measured in ohms) in a circuit or component. Most ohmmeters will have a selector switch which permits the measurement of different ranges of resistance (usually the selector switch allows the multiplication of the meter reading by 10, 100, 1,000 and 10,000). Some ohmmeters are "auto-ranging" which means the meter itself will determine which scale to use. Since the meters are powered by an internal battery, the ohmmeter can be used like a self-powered test light. When the ohmmeter is connected, current from the ohmmeter flows through the circuit or component being tested. Since the ohmmeter's internal resistance and voltage are known values, the amount of current flow through the meter depends on the resistance of the circuit or component being tested. The ohmmeter can also be used to perform a continuity test for suspected open circuits. In using the meter for making continuity checks, do not be concerned with the actual resistance readings. Zero resistance, or any ohm reading, indicates continuity in the circuit. Infinite resistance indicates an opening in the circuit. A high resistance reading where there should be none indicates a problem in the circuit. Checks for short circuits are made in the same manner as checks for open circuits, except that the circuit must be isolated from both power and normal ground. Infinite resistance indicates no continuity, while zero resistance indicates a dead short.

※ WARNING

Never use an ohmmeter to check the resistance of a component or wire while there is voltage applied to the circuit.

• Ammeter—an ammeter measures the amount of current flowing through a circuit in units called amperes or amps. At normal operating voltage, most circuits have a characteristic amount of amperes, called "current draw" which can be measured using an ammeter. By referring to a specified current draw rating, then measuring the amperes and comparing the two values, one can determine what is happening within the circuit to aid in diagnosis. An open circuit, for example, will not allow any current to flow, so the ammeter reading will be zero. A damaged component or circuit will have an increased current draw, so the reading will be high. The ammeter is always connected in series with the circuit being tested. All of the current that normally flows through the circuit must also flow through the ammeter; if there is any other path for the current to follow, the ammeter reading will not be accurate. The ammeter itself has very little resistance to current flow and, therefore, will not affect the circuit, but it will measure current draw only when the circuit is closed and electricity is flowing. Excessive current draw can blow fuses and drain the battery, while a reduced current draw can cause motors to run slowly, lights to dim and other components to not operate properly.

Troubleshooting Electrical Systems

When diagnosing a specific problem, organized troubleshooting is a must. The complexity of a modern automotive vehicle demands that you approach any problem in a logical, organized manner. There are certain troubleshooting techniques, however, which are standard:

• Establish when the problem occurs. Does the problem appear only under certain conditions? Were there any noises, odors or other unusual symptoms? Isolate the problem area. To do this, make some simple tests and observations, then eliminate the systems that are working properly. Check for obvious problems, such as broken wires and loose or dirty connections. Always check the obvious before assuming something complicated is the cause.

• Test for problems systematically to determine the cause once the problem area is isolated. Are all the components functioning properly? Is there power going to electrical switches and motors. Performing careful, systematic checks will often turn up most causes on the first inspection, without wasting time checking components that have little or no relationship to the problem.

• Test all repairs after the work is done to make sure that the problem is fixed. Some causes can be traced to more than one component, so a careful verification of repair work is important in order to pick up additional malfunctions that may cause a problem to reappear or a different problem to arise. A blown fuse, for example, is a simple problem that may require more than another fuse to repair. If you don't look for a problem that caused a fuse to blow, a shorted wire (for example) may go undetected.

Experience has shown that most problems tend to be the result of a fairly simple and obvious cause, such as loose or corroded connectors, bad grounds or damaged wire insulation which causes a short. This makes careful visual inspection of components during testing essential to quick and accurate troubleshooting.

Testing

OPEN CIRCUITS

▶ See Figure 8

This test already assumes the existence of an open in the circuit and it is used to help locate the open portion.

1. Isolate the circuit from power and ground.
2. Connect the self-powered test light or ohmmeter ground clip to the ground side of the circuit and probe sections of the circuit sequentially.
3. If the light is out or there is infinite resistance, the open is between the probe and the circuit ground.
4. If the light is on or the meter shows continuity, the open is between the probe and the end of the circuit toward the power source.

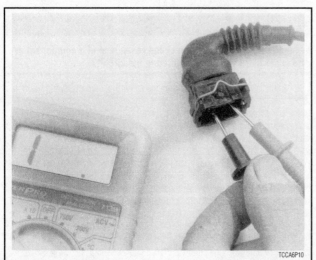

TCCA6P10

Fig. 8 The infinite reading on this multimeter indicates that the circuit is open

SHORT CIRCUITS

➡**Never use a self-powered test light to perform checks for opens or shorts when power is applied to the circuit under test. The test light can be damaged by outside power.**

1. Isolate the circuit from power and ground.
2. Connect the self-powered test light or ohmmeter ground clip to a good ground and probe any easy-to-reach point in the circuit.
3. If the light comes on or there is continuity, there is a short somewhere in the circuit.
4. To isolate the short, probe a test point at either end of the isolated circuit (the light should be on or the meter should indicate continuity).
5. Leave the test light probe engaged and sequentially open connectors or switches, remove parts, etc. until the light goes out or continuity is broken.
6. When the light goes out, the short is between the last two circuit components which were opened.

VOLTAGE

This test determines voltage available from the battery and should be the first step in any electrical troubleshooting procedure after visual inspection. Many electrical problems, especially on computer controlled systems, can be caused by a low state of charge in the battery. Excessive corrosion at the battery cable terminals can cause poor contact that will prevent proper charging and full battery current flow.

1. Set the voltmeter selector switch to the 20V position.
2. Connect the multimeter negative lead to the battery's negative (-) post or terminal and the positive lead to the battery's positive (+) post or terminal.
3. Turn the ignition switch **ON** to provide a load.
4. A well charged battery should register over 12 volts. If the meter reads below 11.5 volts, the battery power may be insufficient to operate the electrical system properly.

VOLTAGE DROP

▶ See Figure 9

When current flows through a load, the voltage beyond the load drops. This voltage drop is due to the resistance created by the load and also by small resistances created by corrosion at the connectors and damaged insulation on the wires. The maximum allowable voltage drop under load is critical, especially if there is more than one load in the circuit, since all voltage drops are cumulative.

1. Set the voltmeter selector switch to the 20 volt position.
2. Connect the multimeter negative lead to a good ground.
3. Operate the circuit and check the voltage prior to the first component (load).
4. There should be little or no voltage drop in the circuit prior to the first component. If a voltage drop exists, the wire or connectors in the circuit are suspect.
5. While operating the first component in the circuit, probe the ground side of the component with the positive meter lead and observe the voltage readings. A small voltage drop should be noticed. This voltage drop is caused by the resistance of the component.
6. Repeat the test for each component (load) down the circuit.
7. If a large voltage drop is noticed, the preceding component, wire or connector is suspect.

RESISTANCE

▶ See Figures 10 and 11

✳✳ WARNING

Never use an ohmmeter with power applied to the circuit. The ohmmeter is designed to operate on its own power supply. The normal 12 volt electrical system voltage could damage the meter!

1. Isolate the circuit from the vehicle's power source.
2. Ensure that the ignition key is **OFF** when disconnecting any components or the battery.
3. Where necessary, also isolate at least one side of the circuit to be checked, in order to avoid reading parallel resistances. Parallel circuit resistances will always give a lower reading than the actual resistance of either of the branches.

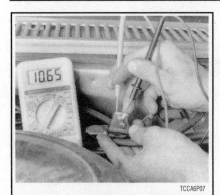

Fig. 9 This voltage drop test revealed high resistance (low voltage) in the circuit

Fig. 10 Checking the resistance of a coolant temperature sensor with an ohmmeter. Reading is 1.04 kilohms

Fig. 11 Spark plug wires can be checked for excessive resistance using an ohmmeter

4. Connect the meter leads to both sides of the circuit (wire or component) and read the actual measured ohms on the meter scale. Make sure the selector switch is set to the proper ohm scale for the circuit being tested, to avoid misreading the ohmmeter test value.

Wire and Connector Repair

Almost anyone can replace damaged wires, as long as the proper tools and parts are available. Wire and terminals are available to fit almost any need. Even the specialized weatherproof, molded and hard shell connectors are now available from aftermarket suppliers.

BATTERY CABLES

Disconnecting the Cables

When working on any electrical component on the vehicle, it is always a good idea to disconnect the negative (-) battery cable. This will prevent potential damage to many sensitive electrical components such as the Engine Control Module (ECM), radio, alternator, etc.

➡**Any time you disengage the battery cables, it is recommended that you disconnect the negative (-) battery cable first. This will prevent your accidentally grounding the positive (+) terminal to the body of the vehicle when disconnecting it, thereby preventing damage to the above mentioned components.**

Be sure the ends of all the wires are fitted with the proper terminal hardware and connectors. Wrapping a wire around a stud is never a permanent solution and will only cause trouble later. Replace wires one at a time to avoid confusion. Always route wires exactly the same as the factory.

➡**If connector repair is necessary, only attempt it if you have the proper tools. Weatherproof and hard shell connectors require special tools to release the pins inside the connector. Attempting to repair these connectors with conventional hand tools will damage them.**

Before you disconnect the cable(s), first turn the ignition to the **OFF** position. This will prevent a draw on the battery which could cause arcing (electricity trying to ground itself to the body of a vehicle, just like a spark plug jumping the gap) and, of course, damaging some components such as the alternator diodes.

When the battery cable(s) are reconnected (negative cable last), be sure to check that your lights, windshield wipers and other electrically operated safety components are all working correctly. If your vehicle contains an Electronically Tuned Radio (ETR), don't forget to also reset your radio stations. Ditto for the clock.

SUPPLEMENTAL INFLATABLE RESTRAINT (SIR) SYSTEM

General Information

The Supplemental Inflatable Restraint (SIR) system offers protection in addition to that provided by the seat belt by deploying an air bag from the center of the steering wheel or dash panel. The air bag deploys when the vehicle is involved in a frontal crash of sufficient force up to 30° off the centerline of the vehicle. To further absorb the crash energy, there is also a knee bolster located beneath the instrument panel in the driver's area and the steering column is collapsible.

The system has an energy reserve, which can store a large enough electrical charge to deploy the air bag(s) for up to ten minutes after the battery has been disconnected or damaged. The system **MUST** be disabled before any service is performed on or around SIR components or SIR wiring.

SERVICE PRECAUTIONS

When performing service around the SIR system components or wiring, the SIR system **MUST** be disabled. Failure to do so could result in possible air bag deployment, personal injury or unneeded SIR system repairs.
- When carrying a live inflator module, make sure that the bag and trim cover are pointed away from you. Never carry the inflator module by the wires

or connector on the underside of the module. In case of accidental deployment, the bag will then deploy with minimal chance of injury.
- When placing a live inflator module on a bench or other surface, always face the bag and trim cover up, away from the surface.

DISARMING THE SYSTEM

▶ See Figure 12

➡**With the AIR BAG fuse removed and the ignition switch ON, the AIR BAG warning lamp will be on. This is normal and does not indicate any system malfunction.**

1. Turn the steering wheel so that the vehicle's wheels are pointing straight ahead.
2. Turn the ignition switch to **LOCK**, remove the key, then disconnect the negative battery cable.
3. Remove the AIR BAG fuse from the fuse block.
4. Remove the steering column filler panel.
5. Disengage the Connector Position Assurance (CPA) and the yellow two way connector located at the base of the steering column.
6. Connect the negative battery cable.

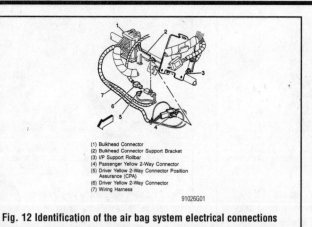

(1) Bulkhead Connector
(2) Bulkhead Connector Support Bracket
(3) I/P Support Rollbar
(4) Passenger Yellow 2-Way Connector
(5) Driver Yellow 2-Way Connector Position Assurance (CPA)
(6) Driver Yellow 2-Way Connector
(7) Wiring Harness

91026G01

Fig. 12 Identification of the air bag system electrical connections

ARMING THE SYSTEM

1. Disconnect the negative battery cable.
2. Turn the ignition switch to **LOCK**, then remove the key.
3. Engage the yellow SIR connector and CPA located at the base of the steering column.
4. Install the steering column filler panel.
5. Install the AIR BAG fuse to the fuse block.
6. Connect the negative battery cable.
7. Turn the ignition switch to **RUN** and make sure that the AIR BAG warning lamp flashes seven times and then shuts off. If the warning lamp does not shut off, make sure that the wiring is properly connected. If the light remains on, take the vehicle to a reputable repair facility for service.

HEATING AND AIR CONDITIONING

Blower Motor

REMOVAL & INSTALLATION

Front

1988–90 C/K SERIES AND 1988–91 R/V SERIES

♦ See Figure 13

1. Disconnect the negative battery terminal.
2. If equipped, unfasten the attaching bolts and nuts and remove the insulating shield from the case.
3. Mark the position of the blower motor in relation to its case.
4. Unplug the electrical connection at the motor.
5. If equipped, disconnect the blower motor cooling tube.
6. Unfasten the blower attaching screws and remove the assembly. Pry gently on the flange if the sealer sticks.
7. The blower wheel can be removed from the motor shaft by unfastening the nut at the center.
To install:
8. Install the blower wheel to the motor shaft and tighten the nut at the center.
9. Apply a bead of sealer to the blower mounting flange. Position the blower so that the marks are aligned and install the screws.
10. If equipped, connect the motor cooling tube.
11. Install the remaining components.

1991–92 R/V SERIES AND 1991–98 C/K SERIES

1. Disconnect the negative battery cable.
2. Remove the instrument panel storage compartment.

1. Stud	12. Core
2. Screw	13. Shaft
3. Connector	14. Valve
4. Screw	15. Valve
5. Motor	16. Case
6. Case	17. Shaft
7. Fan	18. Shroud
8. Nut	19. Plate
9. Bolt	20. Bolts
10. Clamp	21. Elbow
11. Clamp	22. Tube

84906002

Fig. 13 Typical heater case and related parts

3. Unfasten the forward-most screw in the right side door sill plate. Remove the trim panel from the right hinge pillar.
4. If necessary for access, unplug the ECM wiring and remove the ECM.
5. Unplug the electrical lead at the blower motor and if equipped, remove the underdash courtesy lamp.
6. Remove the bolt from the right side lower instrument panel support. Remove the blower cover and the cooling tube.
7. Unfasten the flange screws and pull out the blower motor. You may have to pry back the right side of the instrument panel slightly. Be careful!
To install:
8. Installation is the reverse of removal.

Rear

1988–91 MODELS WITHOUT AIR CONDITIONING

1. Disconnect the negative battery cable.
2. Disconnect the blower motor wiring harness.
3. Remove the blower motor clamp.
4. Remove the motor attaching screws and lift out the motor.
To install:
5. Installation is the reverse of removal.

1988–91 MODELS WITH AIR CONDITIONING

1. Disconnect the negative battery cable.
2. Remove the drain tube from the rear duct.
3. Unfasten the attaching screws and remove the rear duct from the roof panel.
4. Disconnect the blower motor wiring and remove the ground strap and wire.
5. Support the case and remove the lower-to-upper case half screws and lower the case and motor assemblies.
6. Remove the motor retaining strap and remove the motor and wheels.
To install:
7. Install the components in the reverse order of removal.

1992–98 MODELS

♦ See Figure 14

1. Disconnect the negative battery cable.
2. Remove the right rear quarter panel trim.
3. Disconnect the electrical lead at the fan.
4. Remove the screws and if equipped, the cooling tube.
5. If necessary, remove the fan retaining nut and lift out the blower fan.
6. Remove the blower motor.
To install:
7. Install the blower motor and then position the fan.
8. Install the retaining nut and then tighten the mounting screws to 12 inch lbs. (2 Nm).
9. Install the remaining components.

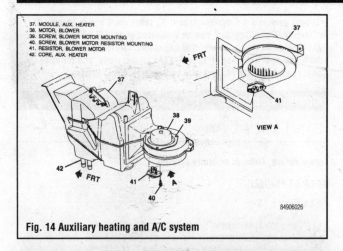

37. MODULE, AUX. HEATER
38. MOTOR, BLOWER
39. SCREW, BLOWER MOTOR MOUNTING
40. SCREW, BLOWER MOTOR RESISTOR MOUNTING
41. RESISTOR, BLOWER MOTOR
42. CORE, AUX. HEATER

FRT

VIEW A

FRT

84906026

Fig. 14 Auxiliary heating and A/C system

Heater Core

REMOVAL & INSTALLATION

✷✷ CAUTION

Never open, service or drain the radiator or cooling system when hot; serious burns can occur from the steam and hot coolant. Also, when draining engine coolant, keep in mind that cats and dogs are attracted to ethylene glycol antifreeze and could drink any that is left in an uncovered container or in puddles on the ground. This will prove fatal in sufficient quantities. Always drain coolant into a sealable container. Coolant should be reused unless it is contaminated or is several years old.

Front

1988–91 R/V SERIES WITHOUT AIR CONDITIONING

1. Disconnect the negative battery cable.
2. Disconnect the heater hoses at the core tubes and drain the engine coolant. Plug the core tubes to prevent spillage.
3. Remove the nuts from the distributor air ducts in the engine compartment.
4. Remove the glove compartment and door.
5. Disconnect the air-defrost and temperature door cables.
6. Remove the floor outlet and unfasten the defroster duct-to-heater distributor screw.
7. Remove the heater distributor-to-instrument panel screws. Pull the assembly rearward to gain access to the wiring harness and disconnect the wires attached to the unit.
8. Remove the heater distributor from the truck.
9. Remove the heater core retaining straps and remove the core from the truck.
To install:
10. Installation is the reverse of removal but please note the following important step.
11. When placing the heater core in position. Be sure that the case-to-core and case-to-dash panel sealer is intact.

1988–91 R/V SERIES WITH AIR CONDITIONING

1. Disconnect the negative battery cable.
2. Disconnect the heater hoses at the core tubes and drain the engine coolant. Plug the core tubes to prevent spillage.
3. Remove the glove compartment and door.
4. Disconnect the center duct from the defroster outlet duct.
5. Disconnect the center, lower air distributor and the center air outlet ducts.
6. Disconnect the temperature door cable.
7. Remove the nuts from the 3 selector duct studs that project into the engine compartment.
8. Remove the outlet duct-to-instrument panel screws. Pull the assembly rearward to gain access to the wiring harness and disconnect the wires and vacuum tubes attached to the unit.

9. Remove the heater distributor from the truck.
10. Remove the heater core retaining straps and remove the core from the case.
To install:
11. Installation is the reverse of removal but please note the following important step.
12. When placing the heater core in position. Be sure that the case-to-core and case-to-dash panel sealer is intact.

1988–90 C/K SERIES

1. Disconnect the negative battery cable.
2. Remove the coolant overflow bottle.
3. Drain the cooling system.
4. Disconnect the heater hoses at the core tubes.
5. In the engine compartment, remove the heater case-to-firewall screws.
6. Disconnect the antenna cable at the mast.
7. Remove the glove box.
8. Disconnect the wiring harness at the engine's Electronic Control Module (ECM).
9. Remove the ECM and bracket.
10. Remove the right side kick panel.
11. Remove the right side lower dash panel bolt and nut.
12. Remove the heater case mounting bolts.
13. While lifting the instrument panel slightly, remove the case assembly.
14. Lift the core from the case.
To install:
15. Install the components in the reverse order of removal.

1991–92 R/V AND 1991–98 C/K SERIES

1. Disconnect the negative battery cable.
2. Drain the cooling system.
3. Remove the instrument panel glove compartment.
4. Tag and unplug all electrical leads as necessary.
5. Remove the center air distribution duct from the floor.
6. If necessary, remove the ECM and mounting tray.
7. Remove the hinge pillar trim panels.
8. Remove the blower motor cover and then remove the motor.
9. Remove the steering wheel and tilt back the instrument panel slightly.
10. Remove the coolant overflow tank. Disengage the heater hoses at the core connections.
11. Unfasten the attaching screws and nut and then remove the heater case.
12. Remove the seven screws and lift off the heater case cover.
13. Remove the fasteners and brackets that hold the heater core to the case and lift the core from the case.
To install:
14. Installation is the reverse of removal but please note the following important step.
15. After placing the heater case into position. Tighten the 4 lower screws to 17 inch lbs. (2 Nm); the upper screw to 97 inch lbs. (11 Nm); and the nuts to 25 inch lbs. (2.8 Nm).

Rear

1988–91 MODELS

1. Disconnect the negative battery cable.
2. Drain the cooling system.
3. Disconnect the heater hoses at the core tubes.
4. Disconnect the blower motor wiring harness.
5. Remove the blower motor clamp.
6. Remove the motor attaching screws and lift out the motor.
7. Unfasten the upper-to-lower case half screws and remove the upper case half.
8. Remove the core seal.
9. Lift out the core.
To install:
10. Installation of the components is the reverse of removal.

1992–98 MODELS

1. Disconnect the negative battery cable and drain the engine coolant.
2. Remove the right rear quarter panel trim and then remove the panel itself.
3. Remove the right rear wheelhousing liner.
4. Disconnect the heater hoses from the core.

5. Unplug the electrical lead. Remove the drain valve.
6. Remove the heater module.
7. If necessary, remove the blower motor.
8. Remove the heater case cover.
9. Remove the heater case cover and then remove the heater core.

To install:
10. Install the heater core and then install the heater case cover.
11. Install the remaining components in the reverse order of removal.

Heater Water Control Valve

REMOVAL & INSTALLATION

♦ See Figure 15

✳✳ CAUTION

Never open, service or drain the radiator or cooling system when hot; serious burns can occur from the steam and hot coolant. Also, when draining engine coolant, keep in mind that cats and dogs are attracted to ethylene glycol antifreeze and could drink any that is left in an uncovered container or in puddles on the ground. This will prove fatal in sufficient quantities. Always drain coolant into a sealable container. Coolant should be reused unless it is contaminated or is several years old.

1. Drain the cooling system.
2. Loosen the hose clamps at the valve enough to slide the clamps away from the fittings on the valve.
3. Disconnect the hoses and the vacuum line from the valve.
4. Remove the valve.
5. Installation is the reverse of removal.

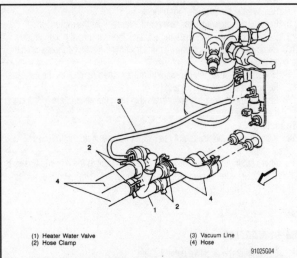

(1) Heater Water Valve   (3) Vacuum Line
(2) Hose Clamp   (4) Hose

91025G04

Fig. 15 Location of the heater water control and its related components (on models equipped)

Air Conditioning Components

REMOVAL & INSTALLATION

Repair or service of air conditioning components is not covered by this manual, because of the risk of personal injury or death, and because of the legal ramifications of servicing these components without the proper EPA certification and experience. Cost, personal injury or death, environmental damage, and legal considerations (such as the fact that it is a federal crime to vent refrigerant into the atmosphere), dictate that the A/C components on your vehicle should be serviced only by a Motor Vehicle Air Conditioning (MVAC) trained, and EPA certified automotive technician.

➡If your vehicle's A/C system uses R-12 refrigerant and is in need of recharging, the A/C system can be converted over to R-134a refrigerant (less environmentally harmful and expensive). Refer to Section 1 for additional information on R-12 to R-134a conversions, and for additional considerations dealing with your vehicle's A/C system.

Control Cables

REMOVAL & INSTALLATION

Temperature, Defrost or Mode Cables

1988–94 MODELS

♦ See Figure 16

1. Disconnect the negative battery cable.
2. Remove the instrument panel trim plate and then remove the control assembly.
3. Disconnect the cables at the control head.
4. If necessary, remove the instrument panel glove compartment.
5. Disconnect the cables from the heater case.

To install:
6. Attach the cables to the heater case. Make sure the cable(s) are routed properly.
7. Install the remaining components.

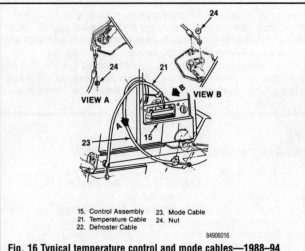

15. Control Assembly   23. Mode Cable
21. Temperature Cable   24. Nut
22. Defroster Cable

84906016

Fig. 16 Typical temperature control and mode cables—1988–94 models

Vent Cable

1988–91 MODELS

1. Disconnect the negative battery cable.
2. Remove the glove box. Remove the ash tray and let it hang.
3. Lower the steering column access panel and let it hang.
4. Remove the cable mounting bracket and disconnect the cable from the vent door.
5. Remove the cable from the access panel, then remove the cable from the vehicle.

To install:
6. Installation is the reverse of removal.

LEFT VENT CABLE—1992–94 MODELS

See Figure 17

1. Remove the steering column opening filler.
2. Disconnect the cable from the opening filler and from the air inlet valve.
3. Remove the cable from the vehicle.

To install:
4. Attach the cable to the to the air inlet valve and the steering column opening filler.
5. Install the steering column opening filler.

RIGHT VENT CABLE—1992–94 MODELS

▶ **See Figure 17**

1. Remove the glove box and the steering column opening filler.
2. Loosen the cable attaching screw and disconnect the cable from the heater module.
3. Disconnect the cable from the opening filler.
4. Remove the cable from the vehicle.

To install:

5. Attach the cable to the to the heater module and the steering column opening filler.
6. Install the cable attaching screw and the steering column opening filler.
7. Install the instrument panel compartment.

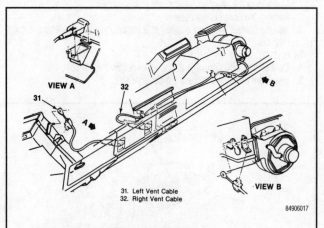

31. Left Vent Cable
32. Right Vent Cable

84906017

Fig. 17 Vent control cables—1992–94 models

Temperature Control Cable

1995–98 MODELS

▶ **See Figure 18**

1. Disconnect the negative battery cable.
2. Roll the instrument panel back and then remove the control assembly.
3. Unplug the control assembly electrical connection.
4. Disconnect the cables at the control assembly.
5. If necessary, remove the instrument panel glove compartment.
6. Note the routing of the cables. Squeeze the retainer that attaches the cable to the temperature valve, squeeze the post and lift the cable end to remove it.

To install:

7. Cycle the temperature control to the full cold position.
8. Make sure the temperature door is closed.
9. Snap the cable onto the temperature valve and secure the cable by snapping it into the heater case.

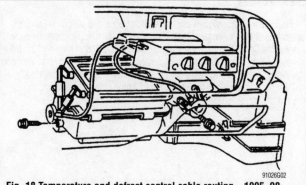

91026G02

Fig. 18 Temperature and defrost control cable routing—1995–98 models

10. Attach the cable to the control assembly making sure the cable is properly routed.
11. Attach the control assembly electrical connection.
12. Install the control assembly and roll the panel forward. Connect the battery cable.

Defrost Control Cable

1995–98 MODELS

1. Remove the instrument cluster trim plate.
2. Remove the control assembly.
3. Unplug the control assembly electrical connection.
4. Disconnect the cables at the control assembly.
5. Disconnect the cable from the defroster valve.

To install:

6. Cycle the mode control to the heater position.
7. Make sure the defrost door is closed.
8. Snap the cable onto the temperature valve and secure the cable by snapping it into the heater case.
9. Attach the cable to the control assembly making sure the cable is properly routed.
10. Attach the control assembly electrical connection.
11. Install the control assembly and the instrument cluster trim plate.

ADJUSTMENT

1988–94 Temperature Cable

1. Remove the instrument panel compartment and door.
2. Loosen the cable attaching bolt at the heater case assembly.

➡ **Ensure that the cable is installed in the bracket on the defroster duct assembly**

3. Place the temperature lever in the full **COLD** position and hold while tightening the cable attaching screw.
4. Install the instrument panel compartment and door.

Control Panel

REMOVAL & INSTALLATION

Front

▶ **See Figures 19, 20 and 21**

1. Disconnect the negative battery cable.
2. If necessary for access, remove the radio.
3. Remove the instrument panel bezel.
4. Remove the control panel-to-dash screws or release the snap-fit retainers using a small prytool.
5. Lower the control panel from the dash, without kinking the cable, and disconnect the cable, vacuum harness (if equipped) and electrical harness.

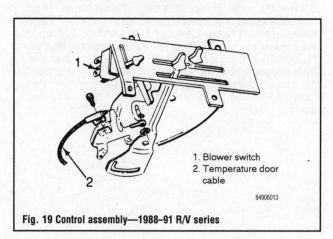

1. Blower switch
2. Temperature door cable

84906013

Fig. 19 Control assembly—1988–91 R/V series

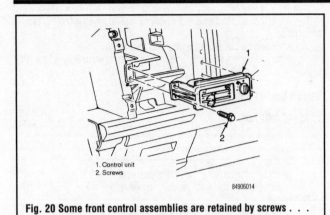

Fig. 20 Some front control assemblies are retained by screws . . .

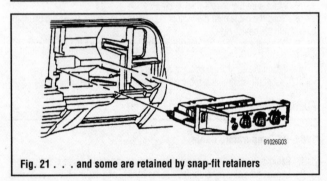

Fig. 21 . . . and some are retained by snap-fit retainers

To install:

6. Connect the control cable, vacuum harness (if equipped) and electrical harness to the rear of the control assembly and position it into the dash.

7. If equipped, install the screws and tighten them to 17 inch lbs. (2 Nm).

8. If equipped with the snap-fit retainers, slide the assembly into the dash until the retainers engage.

9. Install the instrument panel bezel and if removed, the radio.

10. Connect the negative battery cable.

CRUISE CONTROL

General Information

1988-95 MODELS

The electro-motor cruise control system maintains a desired speed under normal driving conditions. The main components of the system are the multi-function lever, cruise control module, vehicle speed sensor, vehicle speed sensor calibrator module, release switches and electrical harness.

The module contains a stepper motor and a electronic controller. The controller monitors the vehicle speed and operates the stepper motor. The motor operates a band and throttle cable to maintain the desired speed. The module also contains a low speed limit that will prevent system operation below 25 mph (40 km/h). The controller is activated by the signals from the multi-function lever located on the turn signal lever. A release switch which is either mounted on the brake or clutch pedal (if equipped with a manual transmission), disengages the system when the brake or clutch pedal is depressed and the throttle then returns to idle.

Rear

FRONT OVERHEAD

♦ See Figure 22

1. Disconnect the negative battery cable.
2. Remove the roof console.
3. Pull the control panel out slightly, disconnect the electrical lead and then remove the control head.

To install:

4. Connect the lead and slide the panel back into the console.
5. Install the roof console and connect the battery cable.

CENTER OVERHEAD

1. Disconnect the negative battery cable.
2. Remove the control panel bezel.
3. Pull the control panel out slightly, disconnect the electrical lead and then remove the control panel.

To install:

4. Connect the lead and slide the panel back into the console.
5. Install the bezel and connect the battery cable.

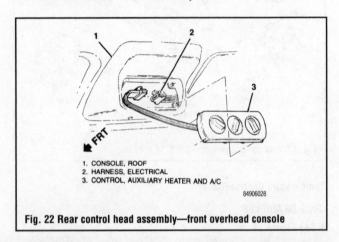

1. CONSOLE, ROOF
2. HARNESS, ELECTRICAL
3. CONTROL, AUXILIARY HEATER AND A/C

Fig. 22 Rear control head assembly—front overhead console

1996-98 MODELS

Gasoline Engines

The cruise control system used on vehicles equipped with gasoline engines comprises of the Vehicle Control Module (VCM), cruise control module, the multi-function lever and the brake release switch. The cruise control module contains a stepper motor which is used to vary throttle position. The cruise control module receives its commands from the multi-function lever and the vehicle speed from the VCM. Based on these commands the cruise control module will control vehicle speed.

Diesel Engines

The cruise control system used on vehicles equipped with diesel engines comprises of the Powertrain Control Module (PCM), electronic throttle system, the Vehicle Speed Sensor Buffer (VSSB), the multi-function lever and the brake release switch. The PCM receives commands from the multi-function lever and the vehicle speed information from the VSSB. Based on the commands from the multi-function switch and the VSSB, the PCM the uses the electronic throttle system to control vehicle speed.

CRUISE CONTROL TROUBLESHOOTING

Problem	Possible Cause
Will not hold proper speed	Incorrect cable adjustment
	Binding throttle linkage
	Leaking vacuum servo diaphragm
	Leaking vacuum tank
	Faulty vacuum or vent valve
	Faulty stepper motor
	Faulty transducer
	Faulty speed sensor
	Faulty cruise control module
Cruise intermittently cuts out	Clutch or brake switch adjustment too tight
	Short or open in the cruise control circuit
	Faulty transducer
	Faulty cruise control module
Vehicle surges	Kinked speedometer cable or casing
	Binding throttle linkage
	Faulty speed sensor
	Faulty cruise control module
Cruise control inoperative	Blown fuse
	Short or open in the cruise control circuit
	Faulty brake or clutch switch
	Leaking vacuum circuit
	Faulty cruise control switch
	Faulty stepper motor
	Faulty transducer
	Faulty speed sensor
	Faulty cruise control module

Note: Use this chart as a guide. Not all systems will use the components listed.

TCCA6C01

ENTERTAINMENT SYSTEMS

Radio

REMOVAL & INSTALLATION

❉❉ WARNING

Make certain that the speaker is attached to the radio before the unit is turned ON. If it is not, the output transistors may be damaged.

1988–91 R/V Series

▶ See Figure 23

1. Disconnect the negative battery cable.
2. Remove the control knobs and the bezels from the radio control shafts.
3. Remove the nuts from the support shafts.
4. Remove the support bracket retaining screws.
5. Lifting the rear edge of the radio, push the radio forward until the control shafts clear the instrument panel. Then, lower the radio far enough so that the electrical connections can be unplugged.
6. Remove the power lead, speaker, and antenna wires and then pull out the unit.
To install:
7. Install the components in the reverse order of removal.

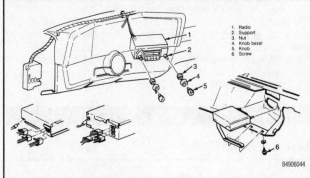

1. Radio
2. Support
3. Nut
4. Knob bezel
5. Knob
6. Screw

84906044

Fig. 23 Radio installation—1988–91 R/V series

1988–94 C/K Models

▶ See Figures 24, 25, 26, 27 and 28

1. Disconnect the negative battery cable.
2. Remove the instrument cluster trim and bezel.
3. Remove the retainers or screws.
4. Pull the unit towards you just far enough to disconnect the wiring. Then, remove the unit.
To install:
5. Install the components in the reverse order of removal.

1995–98 C/K Models

1. Disconnect the negative battery cable.
2. Remove the accessory trim plate.
3. If the unit is retained with screws, unfasten the screws.
4. If the unit is not retained by screws, release the retainers using a small screwdriver and pull out the unit.
5. Unplug all electrical connections and remove the unit.
To install:
6. Installation is the reverse of removal.

Radio Receiver

REMOVAL & INSTALLATION

▶ See Figure 29

➥ **Some models contain a radio receiver, which is mounted separately from the control head.**

1. Disconnect the negative battery cable.
2. Remove the steering column filler panel and the ashtray.
3. Unplug any electrical leads.
4. Unfasten the screw from the receiver bracket and then remove the nut from the center support.
5. Remove the receiver.
6. Unfasten the nut on the bracket and remove the bracket and clip from the receiver.

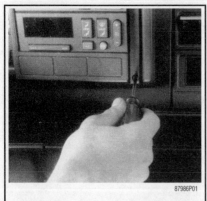
Fig. 24 Remove the trim retaining screws

Fig. 25 Remove the trim plate

Fig. 26 Remove the audio component retaining fasteners

Fig. 27 Remove the tape player from the instrument panel and disengage the electrical connections

Fig. 28 Remove the radio from the instrument panel and disengage the electrical connections

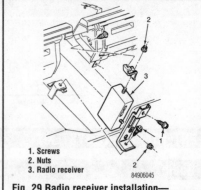
1. Screws
2. Nuts
3. Radio receiver
Fig. 29 Radio receiver installation—1988–94 models

To install:
7. Attach the clip and bracket to the receiver. Tighten the nut to 22 inch lbs. (3 Nm).
8. Attach the receiver to the center support and tighten that nut to 22 inch lbs. (3 Nm).
9. Tighten the screw on the bracket to 17 inch lbs. (2 Nm). Attach the electrical lead.
10. Install the ashtray and steering column panel.
11. Connect the battery cable.

Tape Player

REMOVAL & INSTALLATION

1988–94 Models

1. Disconnect the negative battery cable.
2. Remove the accessory trim panel.
3. Unplug the unit electrical connections.
4. Remove the retainers or screws and remove the unit.
5. Remove the bumper and clip from the unit.
To install:
6. Install the components in the reverse order of removal but please note the following steps.
7. Attach the bumper and clip to the unit.
8. Install the unit making sure the bumper goes into the hole on the bracket.

1995–98 C/K Models

▶ **See Figure 30**

1. Disconnect the negative battery cable.
2. Remove the accessory trim plate.
3. If the unit is retained with screws, unfasten the screws.

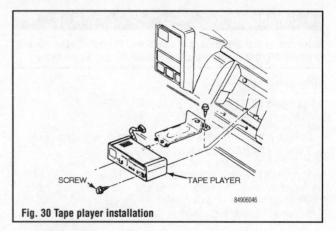
SCREW   TAPE PLAYER
Fig. 30 Tape player installation

4. If the unit is not retained by screws, release the retainers using a small screwdriver and pull out the unit.
5. Unplug all electrical connections and remove the unit.
To install:
6. Install the components in the reverse order of removal but please note the following steps.
7. If the unit is not retained by screws, push the unit in until the retainers are fully engaged.
8. If the unit is retained with screws, install and tighten the screws.

CD Player

REMOVAL & INSTALLATION

1. Disconnect the negative battery cable.
2. Remove the accessory trim plate.

3. Disconnect any electrical leads.
4. Release the retainers using a small screwdriver and pull out the unit.
5. Unplug all electrical connections and remove the unit.
To install:
6. Install the components in the reverse order of removal but please note the following steps.
7. If the unit is not retained by screws, push the unit in until the retainers are fully engaged.
8. If the unit is retained with screws, install and tighten the screws.

Amplifier

REMOVAL & INSTALLATION

♦ **See Figure 31**

1. Disconnect the negative battery cable.
2. Locate the amplifier, disconnect the wires and unbolt it from the bracket.
3. To install, mount the amplifier in the bracket and connect the wires.
4. Connect the battery cable.

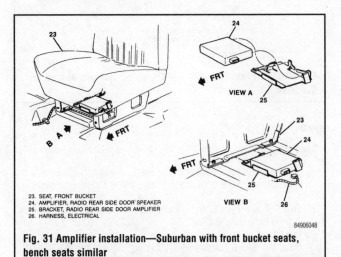

23. SEAT, FRONT BUCKET
24. AMPLIFIER, RADIO REAR SIDE DOOR SPEAKER
25. BRACKET, RADIO REAR SIDE DOOR AMPLIFIER
26. HARNESS, ELECTRICAL

84906048

Fig. 31 Amplifier installation—Suburban with front bucket seats, bench seats similar

Speakers

REMOVAL & INSTALLATION

1988–91 R/V Series

FRONT

♦ **See Figure 32**

1. Disconnect the negative battery cable.
2. Remove the four upper screws on the instrument panel bezel.
3. Unfasten the instrument panel pad screws and remove the pad.
4. Unfasten the speaker screws, lift up the speaker until you can disconnect the wiring and remove the speaker.
To install:
5. Installation is the reverse of removal.

REAR

♦ **See Figure 33**

1. Disconnect the negative battery cable.
2. Unfasten the speaker grille retaining screws and remove the grille.
3. Unfasten the speaker screws, lift up the speaker until you can disconnect the wiring and remove the speaker.
To install:
4. Install the assembly in the reverse order of removal.

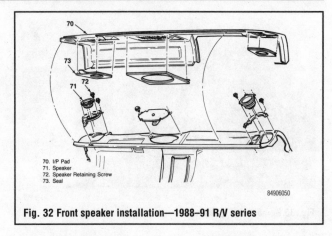

70. I/P Pad
71. Speaker
72. Speaker Retaining Screw
73. Seal

84906050

Fig. 32 Front speaker installation—1988–91 R/V series

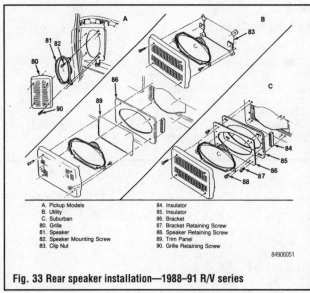

A. Pickup Models
B. Utility
C. Suburban
80. Grille
81. Speaker
82. Speaker Mounting Screw
83. Clip Nut
84. Insulator
85. Insulator
86. Bracket
87. Bracket Retaining Screw
88. Speaker Retaining Screw
89. Trim Panel
90. Grille Retaining Screw

84906051

Fig. 33 Rear speaker installation—1988–91 R/V series

1988–94 Models

FRONT

♦ **See Figures 34 and 35**

1. Disconnect the negative battery cable.
2. Unfasten the speaker grille retaining fasteners and remove the grille.
3. Unfasten the speaker screws, lift up the speaker until you can disconnect the wiring and remove the speaker.
To install:
4. Installation is the reverse of removal. Tighten the speaker screws to 17 inch lbs. (2 Nm).

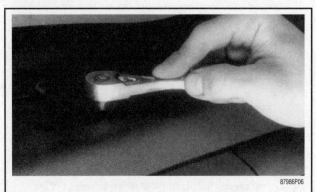

87986P06

Fig. 34 Remove the speaker grille retaining fasteners

Fig. 35 Remove the speakers and disconnect the wiring

REAR

♦ See Figures 36 and 37

1. Disconnect the negative battery cable.
2. Unfasten the speaker grille or trim panel retaining screws and remove the grille.
3. Unfasten the speaker screws, lift up the speaker until you can disconnect the wiring and remove the speaker.

To install:

4. Install the components in the reverse order of removal. Tighten the speaker screws to 17 inch lbs. (2 Nm).

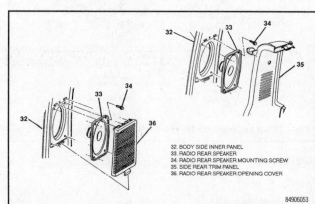

32. BODY SIDE INNER PANEL
33. RADIO REAR SPEAKER
34. RADIO REAR SPEAKER MOUNTING SCREW
35. SIDE REAR TRIM PANEL
36. RADIO REAR SPEAKER OPENING COVER

84906053

Fig. 36 Rear speaker installation—C/K series; Pick-Up and Cab Chassis

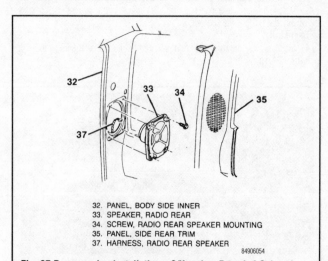

32. PANEL, BODY SIDE INNER
33. SPEAKER, RADIO REAR
34. SCREW, RADIO REAR SPEAKER MOUNTING
35. PANEL, SIDE REAR TRIM
37. HARNESS, RADIO REAR SPEAKER

84906054

Fig. 37 Rear speaker installation—C/K series; Extended Cab and Crew Cab

SIDE DOOR PANEL

♦ See Figure 38

1. Disconnect the negative battery cable.
2. Disconnect the speaker wiring.
3. Remove the side door map pocket.
4. Unfasten the speaker screws and remove the speaker.

To install:

5. Installation is the reverse of removal. Tighten the speaker screws to 14 inch lbs. (2 Nm).

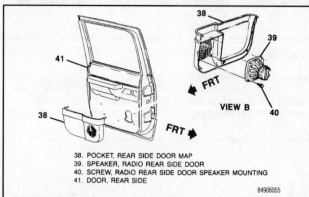

38. POCKET, REAR SIDE DOOR MAP
39. SPEAKER, RADIO REAR SIDE DOOR
40. SCREW, RADIO REAR SIDE DOOR SPEAKER MOUNTING
41. DOOR, REAR SIDE

84906055

Fig. 38 Rear speaker installation—C/K series; rear side door on the Suburban

REAR OVERHEAD

♦ See Figure 39

1. Disconnect the negative battery cable.
2. Unfasten the speaker grille or trim panel retaining screws and remove the grille.
3. Unfasten the speaker screws, lift up the speaker until you can disconnect the wiring and remove the speaker.

To install:

4. Install the speaker components in the reverse order of removal. Tighten the speaker screws to 17 inch lbs. (2 Nm).

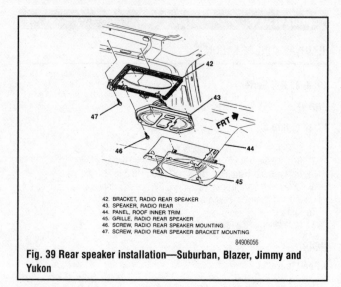

42. BRACKET, RADIO REAR SPEAKER
43. SPEAKER, RADIO REAR
44. PANEL, ROOF INNER TRIM
45. GRILLE, RADIO REAR SPEAKER
46. SCREW, RADIO REAR SPEAKER MOUNTING
47. SCREW, RADIO REAR SPEAKER BRACKET MOUNTING

84906056

Fig. 39 Rear speaker installation—Suburban, Blazer, Jimmy and Yukon

1995–96 Models

FRONT SIDE DOOR

1. Remove the trim panel and the speaker retainer screws.
2. Using a small screwdriver release the speaker retainer.

3. Remove the speaker and disengage the electrical connector.

To install:

4. Engage the electrical connector and install the speaker. The speaker should snap into the retainer when fully seated.

5. Tighten the speaker screws to 18 inch lbs. (2 Nm), and install the trim panel.

FRONT DOOR ARMREST

1. Lift the armrest speaker cover at the rear edge and slide the cover back to disengage the front retainer.

2. Disengage the electrical connector and rotate the speaker to release it.

To install:

3. Install the speaker to the cover by rotating it into position. The speaker should snap into position when fully seated.

4. Engage the electrical connector and slide the cover into the front slots.

5. Lower the armrest speaker cover to engage the retainers.

REAR SPEAKERS

1. Remove the speaker grille or rear trim panel.
2. Remove the speaker screws and the speaker.
3. Disengage the electrical connectors.

To install:

4. Engage the electrical connectors and install the speakers.
5. Fasten the speaker screws to 18 inch lbs. (2 Nm).
6. Install the speaker grille or rear trim panel.

SIDE DOOR

▶ **See Figures 37 and 40**

1. Remove the speaker grille and retainers.
2. Remove the speaker and disengage the electrical connectors.

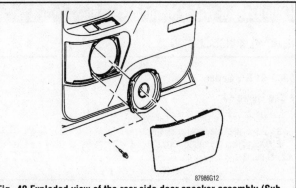

Fig. 40 Exploded view of the rear side door speaker assembly (Suburban models)

To install:

3. Engage the electrical connectors and install the speakers.
4. Install the speaker retainers and grille.

REAR OVERHEAD SPEAKERS

▶ **See Figure 39**

1. Remove the speaker grille.
2. Remove the roof inner trim panel, if necessary.
3. Remove the speaker screws and the speaker.
4. Disengage the electrical connectors, as necessary.

To install:

5. Installation is the reverse of removal. Tighten the speaker screws to 17 inch lbs. (2 Nm).

WINDSHIELD WIPERS AND WASHERS

Windshield Wiper Blade and Arm

REMOVAL & INSTALLATION

Wiper Blade

1988–95 MODELS

▶ **See Figure 41**

1. Insert a small prytool into the blade retaining slot over the spring.
2. Pivot the prytool so the blade tip presses downward on the retainer spring, releasing the pin of the wiper arm.
3. Remove the wiper blade.
4. Install the wiper blade by pressing the pin of the wiper assembly into the blade retainer until the blade is engaged.

1996–98 MODELS

▶ **See Figure 42**

1. Push in the button on the wiper blade assembly clip and remove the blade from the inside radius of the wiper arm.
2. Bring the wiper arm out through the opening in the blade.
3. Install the blade assembly onto the arm making sure it firmly engages.

Wiper Arm

▶ **See Figure 43**

Before removing either or both of the wiper arm(s), mark their position on the windshield to indicate the proper park position. This will aid during installation.

1. Disconnect the washer hose.
2. Lift the wiper arm from the glass and pull the retaining latch.
3. Remove the wiper arm assembly.

To install:

4. Installation is the reverse of removal.

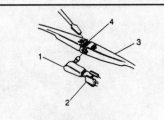

1. ASSEMBLY, WIPER ARM
2. NOZZLE, WASHER
3. ASSEMBLY, BLADE
4. SPRING, BLADE RETAINER

91026G05

Fig. 41 Press the blade of the prytool onto the wiper blade retaining spring—1988–95 models

1. WIPER ARM ASSEMBLY
2. WIPER BLADE
3. RETAINING SPRING
4. SCREWDRIVER
5. WIPER ARM PIN

91026G06

Fig. 42 Use a prytool to push in the button on the wiper blade assembly clip—1996–98 models

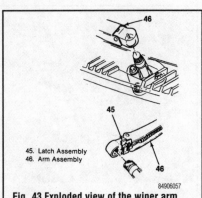

45. Latch Assembly
46. Arm Assembly

84906057

Fig. 43 Exploded view of the wiper arm mounting

Windshield Wiper Motor

REMOVAL & INSTALLATION

1988–91 R/V Series

♦ **See Figure 44**

1. Make sure the wipers are parked.
2. Disconnect the negative battery cable.
3. Disconnect the wiring harness at the wiper motor and the hoses from the washer pump.

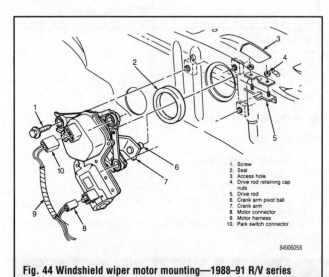

1. Screw
2. Seal
3. Access hole
4. Drive rod retaining cap nuts
5. Drive rod
6. Crank arm pivot ball
7. Crank arm
8. Motor connector
9. Motor harness
10. Park switch connector

84906058

Fig. 44 Windshield wiper motor mounting—1988–91 R/V series

4. Reach down through the access hole in the plenum and loosen the wiper drive rod attaching screws. Remove the drive rod from the wiper motor crank arm.
5. Remove the wiper motor attaching screws and the motor assembly and linkage.
6. To install, reverse the removal procedure.

➡ **Lubricate the wiper motor crank arm pivot before reinstallation.**

Except 1988–91 R/V Series

♦ **See Figures 45 thru 50**

1. Disconnect the negative battery cable.
2. Pivot the wiper arm away from the windshield, move the latch to the open position and lift the wiper arm off of the driveshaft.
3. Remove the cowl vent grille.
4. Unplug the wiring connector from the motor.
5. Remove the drive link-to-crank arm fasteners and slide the links from the arm. Do not remove the arm!
6. Remove the motor mounting bolts and lift the motor out.

To install:

7. Install the motor and tighten the bolts to 62 inch lbs. (7 Nm).
8. Install the drive link-to-crank arm fasteners and slide the links onto the arm.
9. Install the remaining components in the reverse order of removal.

Rear Window Wiper Motor

REMOVAL & INSTALLATION

♦ **See Figure 51**

1. Disconnect the negative battery cable.
2. Remove the rear wiper arm.

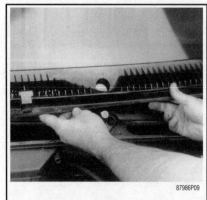

87986P09

Fig. 45 Remove the cowl vent grille

87986P10

Fig. 46 Disengage the wiring connector from the motor

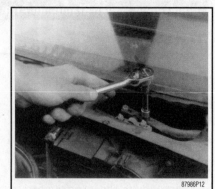

87986P12

Fig. 47 Remove the drive link-to-crank arm fasteners

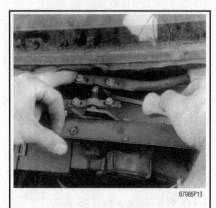

87986P13

Fig. 48 Slide the links from the arm

87986P14

Fig. 49 Remove the motor mounting bolts

87986P15

Fig. 50 Remove the motor from the vehicle

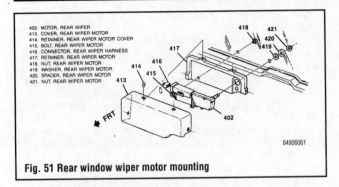

402. MOTOR, REAR WIPER
413. COVER, REAR WIPER MOTOR
414. RETAINER, REAR WIPER MOTOR COVER
415. BOLT, REAR WIPER MOTOR
416. CONNECTOR, REAR WIPER HARNESS
417. RETAINER, REAR WIPER MOTOR
418. NUT, REAR WIPER MOTOR
419. WASHER, REAR WIPER MOTOR
420. SPACER, REAR WIPER MOTOR
421. NUT, REAR WIPER MOTOR

84906061

Fig. 51 Rear window wiper motor mounting

3. Remove the motor cover as follows:

   a. Push the retainer pin into the cover using a punch. There are four retainers.

   b. Unfasten the cover retainers and remove the cover.

4. Unplug the motor wiring.

5. Remove the mounting bolts, nuts, spacers and washers, then lift out the motor.

To install:

6. Install the components in the reverse order of removal but please note the following steps.

7. Install the motor, washers, spacers, bolts and nut. Tighten the bolt to 53 inch lbs. (6 Nm).

8. When installing the cover and the retainers, push the pins into the retainers until the top of the pin is flush with the top of the retainer.

Windshield Washer Motor

REMOVAL & INSTALLATION

1988–91 R/V Series

1. Disconnect the negative battery cable.
2. Remove the two attaching screws and remove the reservoir.

INSTRUMENTS AND SWITCHES

Instrument Cluster

❊❊ WARNING

When replacing cluster components there are several steps which should be taken to avoid damage to Electrostatic Discharge Sensitive (EDS) parts. They are:

- Do not open the package until it is time to install the part
- Avoid touching the electrical terminals on the part
- Before removing the part from the package, ground the package to a known good ground on the truck
- Always touch a known good ground before handling the part. You should ground yourself occasionally while installing the part, especially after sliding across the seat, sitting down or walking a short distance

REMOVAL & INSTALLATION

1988–91 R/V Series

▸ See Figure 52

1. Disconnect the negative battery cable.
2. Remove the headlamp switch control knob.
3. Remove the radio control knobs.
4. Remove the steering column cover (4 screws).
5. Unfasten the eight instrument bezel screws and remove instrument bezel.

3. Unplug the wiring at the motor.
4. Disconnect the fluid tube at the motor.
5. Remove the motor from the reservoir.

To install:

6. Installation of the assembly is the reverse of removal.

1988–96 C/K Models

1. Disconnect the negative battery cable.
2. Unplug the wiring harness connector(s) from the pump.
3. Disconnect the hose(s) from the pump.
4. Remove the attaching fasteners and lift off the reservoir.
5. Remove the pump from the reservoir.

To install:

6. Installation the components in the reverse order of removal.

1997–98 C/K Models

1. Disconnect the negative battery cable.
2. Remove the storage compartment and tray.
3. Unfasten the reservoir bolts.
4. Disconnect the hoses from the reservoir.
5. Unplug the electrical connections from the reservoir and remove the reservoir from the vehicle.
6. Remove the cover from the reservoirs.
7. Remove the hoses and connectors from the motors.
8. Remove the motors and the seals from the reservoir.

To install:

9. Install the components in the reverse order of removal but please note the following steps.

➡The front and rear motors are different sizes and are not interchangeable. The rear motor has a bigger electrical harness connection.

10. Install the motor seals and the motor in the reservoir. If the motor is hard to install, lubricate it with washer solvent and reinstall it.

11. Tighten the reservoir retaining bolts to 53 inch lbs. (6 Nm).

➡Washer pump hose connectors are color coded. Attach the gray connector to the rear motor and the black connector to the front motor.

6. Reach under the dash, depress the speedometer cable tang, and remove the cable.

7. Pull instrument cluster out just far enough to disconnect all lines and wires.

8. Remove the cluster.

To install:

9. Install the cluster.

10. Connect all lines and wires.

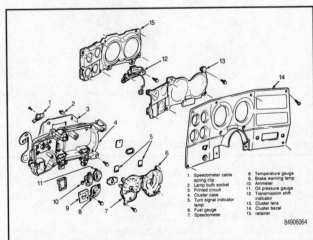

1. Speedometer cable spring clip
2. Lamp bulb socket
3. Printed circuit
4. Cluster case
5. Turn signal indicator lamp
6. Fuel gauge
7. Speedometer
8. Temperature gauge
9. Brake warning lamp
10. Ammeter
11. Oil pressure gauge
12. Transmission shift indicator
13. Cluster lens
14. Cluster bezel
15. retainer

84906064

Fig. 52 Instrument cluster assembly—1988–91 R/V series

11. Depress the speedometer cable tang, and reattach the cable.
12. Install the remaining components in the reverse order of removal.

1988–91 C/K Models

▶ **See Figures 53 and 54**

1. Disconnect the negative battery cable.
2. Remove the radio control head.
3. Remove the heater control panel.
4. Momentarily ground the cluster assembly by jumping from the metal retaining plate to a good ground.
5. On trucks with automatic transmission, remove the cluster trim plate.
6. Remove the four cluster retaining screws.
7. Carefully pull the cluster towards you until you can reach the electrical connector. Unplug the connector. Avoid touching the connector pins.

To install:
8. Carefully position the cluster until you can reach the electrical connector. Plug in the connector. Avoid touching the connector pins.
9. Install the cluster retaining screws.
10. Install the remaining components.

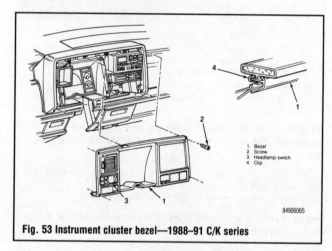

Fig. 53 Instrument cluster bezel—1988–91 C/K series

1. Bezel
2. Screw
3. Headlamp switch
4. Clip

84906065

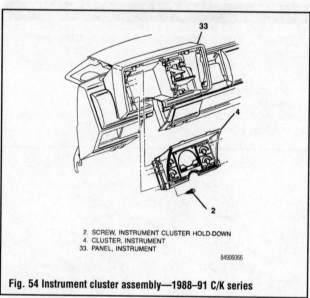

2. SCREW, INSTRUMENT CLUSTER HOLD-DOWN
4. CLUSTER, INSTRUMENT
33. PANEL, INSTRUMENT

84906066

Fig. 54 Instrument cluster assembly—1988–91 C/K series

1992–94 C/K Models

1. Disconnect the negative battery cable.
2. Remove the instrument panel cluster bezel.
3. Unplug the electrical connections for the headlamp switch and the dimmer control.
4. Remove the radio control head.

5. Remove the heater control panel. On air conditioned vehicles, disengage the A/C harness.
6. Remove the cluster retaining screws.
7. Disconnect the gear shift indicator cable from the steering column shift bowl.
8. Carefully pull the cluster towards you until you can reach the electrical connector. Unplug the connector. Avoid touching the connector pins.
9. If replacing the bulbs, turn the bulb assembly ½ turn to the left to remove.

To install:
10. Install the bulb assembly. Carefully position the cluster until you can reach the electrical connector. Plug in the connector. Avoid touching the connector pins.
11. Install the cluster retaining screws.
12. Connect the gear shift indicator cable.
13. Install the heater control panel and A/C harness (if removed).
14. Install the remaining components in the reverse order of removal.

1995–98 Models

1. Disconnect the negative battery cable.
2. If your vehicle is equipped with a tilt steering wheel, move the wheel to the lowest position. If the vehicle does not have a tilt wheel, it may be necessary to lower the column.
3. Unfasten the eight clips that retain the instrument cluster bezel and remove the bezel. There are four clips on the top of the cluster bezel and four clips on the bottom of the cluster bezel.
4. Unplug the electrical connections from the headlamp switch, dimmer control and any other accessory switches that would interfere cluster removal.
5. Unfasten the four cluster retaining screws and remove the cluster making sure nothing contacts the circuit connections.
6. If replacing the bulbs, turn the bulb assembly ½ turn to the left to remove.

To install:
7. Install the bulb assembly.
8. Place the cluster into position without touching the connector pins. Install and tighten the cluster retainers.
9. Install the remaining components in the reverse order of removal.

Gauges

REMOVAL & INSTALLATION

Except 1988–91 R/V Series

1. Remove the cluster.
2. Remove the gauge mounting screws.
3. Carefully pull the gauge from the circuit board. Avoid touching any of the circuit board pins.
4. Installation is the reverse of removal.

1988–91 R/V Series

1. Disconnect the negative battery cable.
2. Remove the headlamp switch control knob.
3. Remove the radio control knobs.
4. Remove the clock adjuster stem.
5. Remove the steering column cover (4 screws).
6. Unfasten eight screws and remove instrument bezel.
7. Remove the cluster lens.
8. Remove the shift indicator.
9. Remove the gauge retainer plate.
10. Unfasten the gauge retaining screws and lift out the gauge.

To install:
11. Install the remaining components in the reverse order of removal.

Windshield Wiper Switch

REMOVAL & INSTALLATION

The wiper switch assembly is part of the steering column assembly. To gain access to the switch, the steering wheel, turn signal switch and ignition lock will have to be removed. Refer to Section 8 for these procedures.

Rear Wiper Switch

REMOVAL & INSTALLATION

1. Remove the instrument cluster bezel.
2. Disconnect the switch wiring.
3. Remove the wiper switch retaining screws.
4. Pull the switch away from the bezel.
5. Installation is the reverse of removal.

Headlight Switch

REMOVAL & INSTALLATION

Except 1988–91 R/V Series

▶ See Figures 55 and 56

1. Remove the instrument cluster bezel.
2. Disconnect the switch wiring.
3. The headlamp switch is either retained by screws or is of the snap-in type. Remove the headlamp switch by unfastening the retaining screws or unsnap the switch from the bezel.
4. Installation is the reverse of removal.

Fig. 55 The headlight switch is mounted behind a bezel on the instrument panel—1988–95 model shown, others similar

1. Bezel
2. Switch
3. Screw

84906070

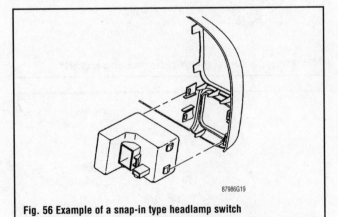

87986G19

Fig. 56 Example of a snap-in type headlamp switch

1988–91 R/V Series

▶ See Figure 57

1. Disconnect negative battery cable.
2. Reaching up behind instrument cluster, depress shaft retaining button and remove switch knob and rod.
3. Remove instrument cluster bezel screws on left end. Pull out on bezel and hold switch nut with a wrench.
4. Attach multiple wiring connectors at switch terminals.

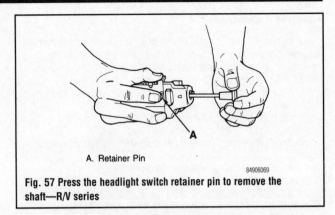

A. Retainer Pin

84906069

Fig. 57 Press the headlight switch retainer pin to remove the shaft—R/V series

5. Remove switch by rotating while holding switch nut.
6. Installation is the reverse of removal.

Back-Up Light Switch

REMOVAL & INSTALLATION

Manual Transmission

▶ See Figures 58 and 59

1. Disconnect the negative battery cable.
2. Raise the vehicle and support it safely.
3. Unplug the electrical connector at the switch.
4. Unscrew the switch from the transmission case.
5. Installation is the reverse of removal. Tighten the switch to 21 ft. lbs. (28 Nm).

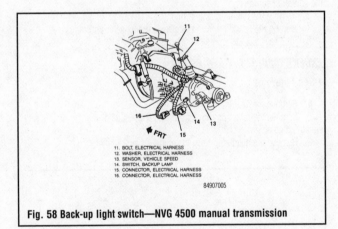

11. BOLT, ELECTRICAL HARNESS
12. WASHER, ELECTRICAL HARNESS
13. SENSOR, VEHICLE SPEED
14. SWITCH, BACKUP LAMP
15. CONNECTOR, ELECTRICAL HARNESS
16. CONNECTOR, ELECTRICAL HARNESS

84907005

Fig. 58 Back-up light switch—NVG 4500 manual transmission

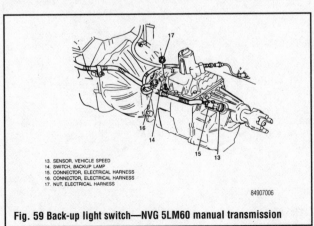

13. SENSOR, VEHICLE SPEED
14. SWITCH, BACKUP LAMP
15. CONNECTOR, ELECTRICAL HARNESS
16. CONNECTOR, ELECTRICAL HARNESS
17. NUT, ELECTRICAL HARNESS

84907006

Fig. 59 Back-up light switch—NVG 5LM60 manual transmission

Automatic Transmission

The back-up light switch on 1995–98 models is incorporated into the neutral/park safety switch. The back-up light switch on 1988–94 models is mounted in the steering column and is covered in Section 8 of this manual. This procedure applies to 1995–98 models only.

1. Place the transmission in park and disconnect the negative battery cable.
2. Raise the vehicle and support it with jackstands.
3. Disconnect the shift cable end from the shift control lever and remove the nut securing the shift control lever to the manual shaft.
4. Unplug the electrical connector from the switch and remove the switch retainers.
5. Remove the switch from the transmission.

To install:

This adjustment is performed with the switch removed from the vehicle. Neutral position tool J 41364-A or its equivalent is required for this procedure.

6. Position tool J 41364-A or its equivalent onto the park/neutral switch. make sure that the slots on the switch are lined up with the lower tabs on the tool.
7. Rotate the tool until the upper locator pin on the tool is lined with the slot on the top of the switch. Do not remove the tool from the switch

➡**Before sliding the switch onto the shaft, it may be necessary to lightly file the outer edge of the shafts to remove any burrs.**

8. Align the switch hub flats with the manual shaft flats, then slide the switch onto the shaft until the switch mounting bracket contacts the mounting bosses on the transmission.
9. Install the switch and tighten the switch retainers. Tighten the switch retainers to 20 ft. lbs. (27 Nm).
10. Remove the adjustment tool.
11. Engage the electrical connector and install the control lever to the manual shaft.
12. Install the control lever nut and tighten to 20 ft. lbs. (27 Nm).
13. Lower the vehicle and connect the negative battery cable.
14. Check the switch for proper operation. The vehicle should start in **P** or **N** only.
15. If adjustment is required, loosen the switch retaining bolts and rotate the switch slightly, tighten the bolts and check switch operation.

LIGHTING

Headlights

REMOVAL & INSTALLATION

Sealed Beam Headlights

1988–91 R/V SERIES

▶ **See Figures 60 and 61**

1. Remove the headlight bezel.
2. Remove the retaining ring screws and the retaining ring. Do not disturb the adjusting screws.
3. Remove the retaining ring spring.
4. Unplug the headlight from the electrical connector and remove it.
5. Installation is the reverse of removal.

EXCEPT 1988–91 R/V SERIES

▶ **See Figure 62**

1. Remove the headlight bezel.
2. Remove the retaining ring screws and the retaining ring. Do not disturb the adjusting screws.
3. Remove the headlamp from the mounting bracket.

4. Unplug the headlamp wiring connector.
5. Installation is the reverse of removal.

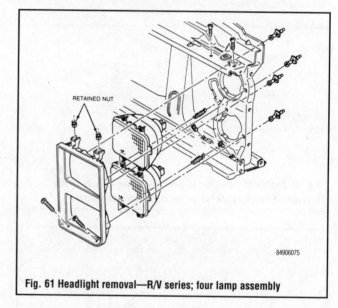

Fig. 61 Headlight removal—R/V series; four lamp assembly

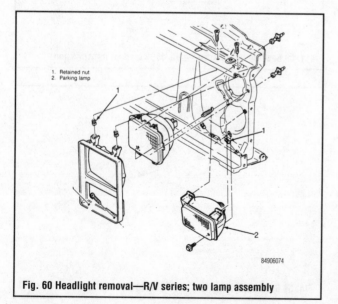

Fig. 60 Headlight removal—R/V series; two lamp assembly

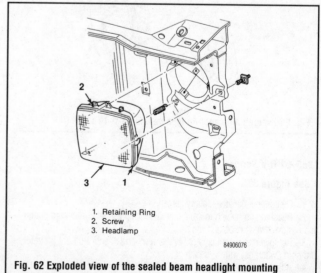

1. Retaining Ring
2. Screw
3. Headlamp

Fig. 62 Exploded view of the sealed beam headlight mounting

Composite Headlights

▶ **See Figure 63**

1. Disconnect the negative battery cable and make certain that the headlight switch is off.
2. Raise the hood.
3. Unfasten the two long screws from the top of the radiator support and pull the headlight assembly forward.
4. Unplug the wiring connector.
5. Twist the bulb or, if equipped the retaining ring, to the left, then pull the bulb assembly from the unit.

To install:

6. Position the new bulb assembly into the unit and twist it to the right. The connector end should be facing down.

➥Always replace a high beam with a high beam, or a low beam with a low beam! The low beam should have a gray tip and a yellow gasket, while the high beam bulb uses a red gasket.

7. Install the remaining components in the reverse order of removal.

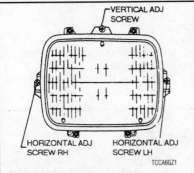

Fig. 63 Twist the bulb or, if equipped, the retaining ring to the left, then pull to remove the bulb assembly from the lens

AIMING THE HEADLIGHTS

▶ **See Figures 64, 65, 66, 67 and 68**

The headlights must be properly aimed to provide the best, safest road illumination. The lights should be checked for proper aim and adjusted as necessary. Certain state and local authorities have requirements for headlight aiming; these should be checked before adjustment is made.

✳✳ CAUTION

About once a year, when the headlights are replaced or any time front end work is performed on your vehicle, the headlight should be accurately aimed by a reputable repair shop using the proper equipment. Headlights not properly aimed can make it virtually impossible to see and may blind other drivers on the road, possibly causing an accident. Note that the following procedure is a temporary fix, until you can take your vehicle to a repair shop for a proper adjustment.

Headlight adjustment may be temporarily made using a wall, as described below, or on the rear of another vehicle. When adjusted, the lights should not glare in oncoming car or truck windshields, nor should they illuminate the passenger compartment of vehicles driving in front of you. These adjustments are rough and should always be fine-tuned by a repair shop which is equipped with headlight aiming tools. Improper adjustments may be both dangerous and illegal.

For most of the vehicles covered by this manual, horizontal and vertical aiming of each sealed beam unit is provided by two adjusting screws which move the retaining ring and adjusting plate against the tension of a coil spring. There is no adjustment for focus; this is done during headlight manufacturing.

➥Because the composite headlight assembly is bolted into position, no adjustment should be necessary or possible. Some applications, however, may be bolted to an adjuster plate or may be retained by adjusting screws. If so, follow this procedure when adjusting the lights, BUT always have the adjustment checked by a reputable shop.

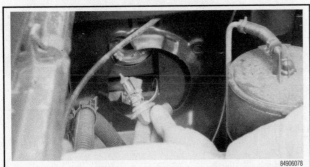

Fig. 64 Location of the aiming screws on most vehicles with sealed beam headlights

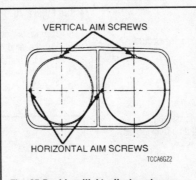

Fig. 65 Dual headlight adjustment screw locations—one side shown here (other side should be mirror image)

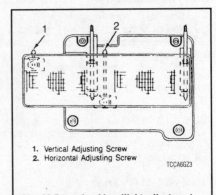

1. Vertical Adjusting Screw
2. Horizontal Adjusting Screw

Fig. 66 Example of headlight adjustment screw location for composite headlamps

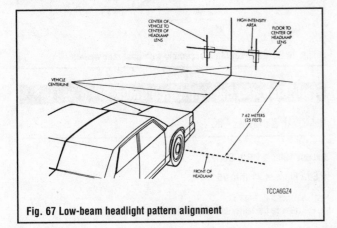

Fig. 67 Low-beam headlight pattern alignment

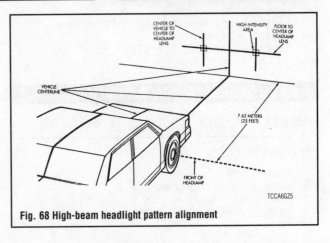

Fig. 68 High-beam headlight pattern alignment

Before removing the headlight bulb or disturbing the headlamp in any way, note the current settings in order to ease headlight adjustment upon reassembly. If the high or low beam setting of the old lamp still works, this can be done using the wall of a garage or a building:

1. Park the vehicle on a level surface, with the fuel tank about ½ full and with the vehicle empty of all extra cargo (unless normally carried). The vehicle should be facing a wall which is no less than 6 feet (1.8m) high and 12 feet (3.7m) wide. The front of the vehicle should be about 25 feet from the wall.

2. If aiming is to be performed outdoors, it is advisable to wait until dusk in order to properly see the headlight beams on the wall. If done in a garage, darken the area around the wall as much as possible by closing shades or hanging cloth over the windows.

3. Turn the headlights **ON** and mark the wall at the center of each light's low beam, then switch on the brights and mark the center of each light's high beam. A short length of masking tape which is visible from the front of the vehicle may be used. Although marking all four positions is advisable, marking one position from each light should be sufficient.

4. If neither beam on one side is working, and if another like-sized vehicle is available, park the second one in the exact spot where the vehicle was and mark the beams using the same-side light. Then switch the vehicles so the one to be aimed is back in the original spot. It must be parked no closer to or farther away from the wall than the second vehicle.

5. Perform any necessary repairs, but make sure the vehicle is not moved, or is returned to the exact spot from which the lights were marked. Turn the headlights **ON** and adjust the beams to match the marks on the wall.

6. Have the headlight adjustment checked as soon as possible by a reputable repair shop.

Front Parking Lamp Assembly

REMOVAL & INSTALLATION

1988–91 R/V Series

WITH TWO HEADLIGHTS

1. Disconnect the negative battery cable.
2. Remove the four bezel retaining screws and remove the bezel.
3. Remove the three parking lamp retaining screws. Unplug the electrical connector and remove the parking lamp. Remove the bulb.
4. Installation is the reverse of removal.

WITH FOUR HEADLIGHTS

1. Remove the radiator grille.
2. Unplug the electrical connector from the parking lamp assembly.
3. Remove the two nuts at the top of the housing and lift it up from the radiator grille. Remove the bulb.
4. Installation is the reverse of removal.

Except 1988–91 R/V Series

▶ See Figure 69

1. Remove the parking lamp assembly retaining screws.
2. Remove the parking lamp assembly.
3. Twist the bulb holder and pull the bulb and holder from the lamp.
4. Twist the bulb and remove it from the holder.
5. To install, twist the new bulb into the lamp and tighten the retaining screws.

Front Side Marker Lamp Bulb and/or Housing

REMOVAL & INSTALLATION

▶ See Figure 69

1. Remove the grille
2. Remove the nuts and the side marker lamp.
3. Remove the bulb from the lamp.
4. To install, twist the new bulb into the lamp and tighten the retaining nuts.

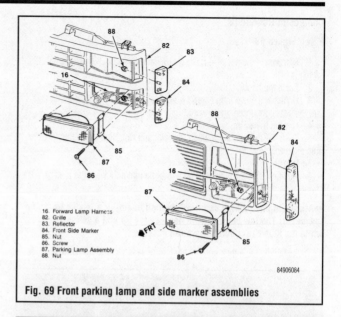

16. Forward Lamp Harness
82. Grille
83. Reflector
84. Front Side Marker
85. Nut
86. Screw
87. Parking Lamp Assembly
88. Nut

84906084

Fig. 69 Front parking lamp and side marker assemblies

Rear Side Marker Lamp Bulb and/or Housing

REMOVAL & INSTALLATION

1988–91 R/V Series

1. Remove the lens-to-housing screws. Remove the lens.
2. Replace the bulb.
3. Installation is the reverse of removal.

Except 1988–91 R/V Series

▶ See Figure 70

1. Remove the lamp attaching screws.
2. Pull the lamp from the fender.
3. Twist the bulb holder and remove the holder and bulb from the lamp.
4. Twist the bulb and remove it from the holder.
5. To install, twist in a new bulb, replace the lamp and tighten the retaining screws.

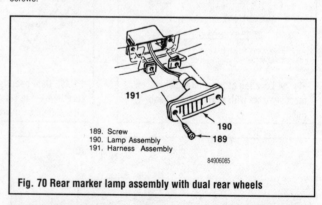

189. Screw
190. Lamp Assembly
191. Harness Assembly

84906085

Fig. 70 Rear marker lamp assembly with dual rear wheels

Tail, Stop and Back-up Lamp Bulbs

REMOVAL & INSTALLATION

Except 1988–91 R/V Series

▶ See Figures 71 thru 76

1. Lower the tailgate.
2. Remove the lamp assembly retaining screws.

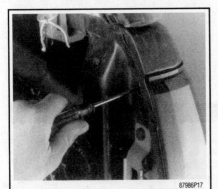

Fig. 71 Remove the lamp assembly retaining screws

Fig. 72 Pull the lamp assembly from the truck

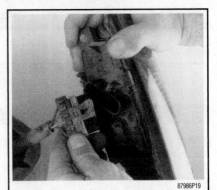

Fig. 73 Disengage the electrical connection

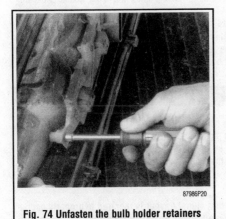

Fig. 74 Unfasten the bulb holder retainers

Fig. 75 Remove the bulb holder

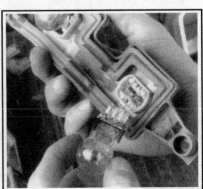

Fig. 76 Pull this type of bulb from the socket

3. Pull the lamp assembly from the truck and disconnect the wiring.
4. Remove the bulb holder fasteners.
5. Remove the bulb(s) from the lamp.
6. Install the bulb, connect the wiring and install the lamp.

1988–91 R/V Series

1. Remove the lens-to-housing attaching screws. Remove the lens.
2. Replace the bulb(s).
3. Installation is the reverse of removal.

Roof Marker Lamps

REMOVAL & INSTALLATION

1. Remove the lens screws.
2. Remove the lens.
3. Remove the insulator.
4. Remove the bulb.
5. Install the bulb and the insulator, position the lens and tighten the retaining screws.

Dome Light

REMOVAL & INSTALLATION

▶ See Figures 77 and 78

1. Remove the lens screws, if equipped.
2. Remove the lens.
3. Remove the bulb.
4. Installation is the reverse of removal.

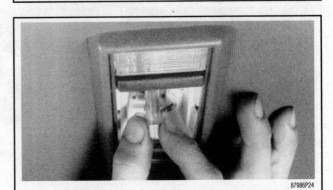

Fig. 77 Remove the lens cover from the dome light

Fig. 78 Remove the bulb from the dome light

License Plate Light

REMOVAL & INSTALLATION

1. Remove the lamp housing retaining screws or bolts.

2. Remove the lens.
3. Replace the bulb.
4. Installation is the reverse of removal.

TRAILER WIRING

Wiring the vehicle for towing is fairly easy. There are a number of good wiring kits available and these should be used, rather than trying to design your own.

All trailers will need brake lights and turn signals as well as tail lights and side marker lights. Most areas require extra marker lights for overwide trailers. Also, most areas have recently required back-up lights for trailers, and most trailer manufacturers have been building trailers with back-up lights for several years.

Additionally, some Class I, most Class II and just about all Class III and IV trailers will have electric brakes. Add to this number an accessories wire, to operate trailer internal equipment or to charge the trailer's battery, and you can have as many as seven wires in the harness.

Determine the equipment on your trailer and buy the wiring kit necessary. The kit will contain all the wires needed, plus a plug adapter set which includes the female plug, mounted on the bumper or hitch, and the male plug, wired into, or plugged into the trailer harness.

When installing the kit, follow the manufacturer's instructions. The color coding of the wires is usually standard throughout the industry. One point to note: some domestic vehicles, and most imported vehicles, have separate turn signals. On most domestic vehicles, the brake lights and rear turn signals operate with the same bulb. For those vehicles without separate turn signals, you can purchase an isolation unit so that the brake lights won't blink whenever the turn signals are operated.

One, final point, the best kits are those with a spring loaded cover on the vehicle mounted socket. This cover prevents dirt and moisture from corroding the terminals. Never let the vehicle socket hang loosely; always mount it securely to the bumper or hitch.

CIRCUIT PROTECTION

Fuse Block and Convenience Center

▶ See Figures 79, 80, 81, 82 and 83

➡For 1988–93 models, refer to the wiring diagrams for fuse application and amperage ratings.

Fuses protect all the major electrical systems in the car. In case of an electrical overload, the fuse melts, breaking the circuit and stopping the flow of electricity.

The fuse block on most models covered by this manual is located under the instrument panel to the left of the steering column. The fuse block should be visible from underneath the steering column, near the pedal bracket.

If the panel is not visible, check for a removable compartment door or trim panel which may used on later models to hide the block. This panel is usually located on the left end of the instrument panel.

The convenience center is located just below the instrument panel on the drivers side. It contains individual relays such as the seat belt and ignition key alarm, and flasher.

On newer model vehicles there is an underhood fuse/relay center that contains both mini and maxi fuses, as well as some relays.

Each fuse block uses miniature fuses (normally plug-in blade terminal-type for these vehicles) which are designed for increased circuit protection and greater reliability. The compact plug-in or blade terminal design allows for fingertip removal and replacement.

Although most fuses are interchangeable in size, the amperage values are not. Should you install a fuse with too high a value, damaging current could be allowed to destroy the component you were attempting to protect by using a fuse in the first place. The plug-in type fuses have a volt number molded on them and are color coded for easy identification. Be sure to only replace a fuse with the proper amperage rated substitute.

A blown fuse can easily be checked by visual inspection or by checking for continuity with a tester.

➡A special heavy duty turn signal flasher is required to properly operate the turn signals when a trailer's lights are connected to the system.

REPLACEMENT

1. Locate the fuse for the circuit in question.

➡When replacing the fuse, DO NOT use one with a higher amperage rating.

2. Check the fuse by pulling it from the fuse block and observing the element. If it is broken, install a replacement fuse the same amperage rating. If the fuse blows again, check the circuit for a short to ground or faulty device in the circuit protected by the fuse.

Fusible Link

The fuse link is a short length of wire, integral with the engine compartment wiring harness and should not be confused with standard wire. The fusible link wire gauge is smaller than the circuit which it protects. Under no circumstances

Fig. 79 Some models may use an underhood fuse/relay panel

Fig. 80 Fuse panel cover—1991 model shown

Fig. 81 The fuse panel cover is located at the driver's side of the instrument panel. Remove the panel to access the fuses—1996–98 models shown

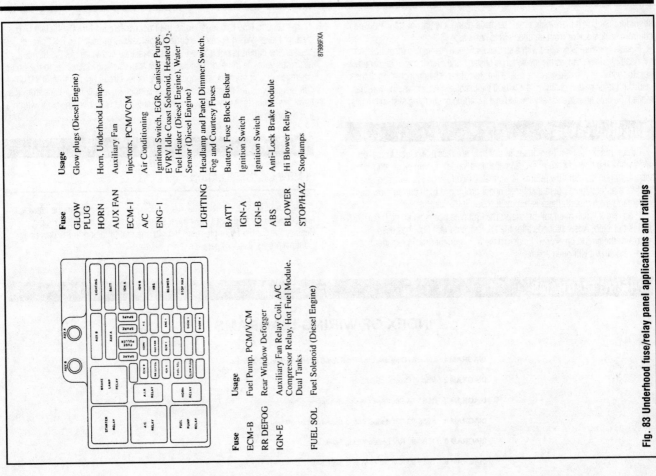

Fuse	Usage
GLOW PLUG	Glow plugs (Diesel Engine)
HORN	Horn, Underhood Lamps
AUX FAN	Auxiliary Fan
ECM-I	Injectors, PCM/VCM
A/C	Air Conditioning
ENG-1	Ignition Switch, EGR, Canister Purge, EVRV Idle Coast Solenoid, Heated O$_2$, Fuel Heater (Diesel Engine), Water Sensor (Diesel Engine)
LIGHTING	Headlamp and Panel Dimmer Switch, Fog and Courtesy Fuses
BATT	Battery, Fuse Block Busbar
IGN-A	Ignition Switch
IGN-B	Ignition Switch
ABS	Anti-Lock Brake Module
BLOWER	Hi Blower Relay
STOP/HAZ	Stoplamps

Fuse	Usage
ECM-B	Fuel Pump, PCM/VCM
RR DEFOG	Rear Window Defogger
IGN-E	Auxiliary Fan Relay Coil, A/C Compressor Relay, Hot Fuel Module, Dual Tanks
FUEL SOL	Fuel Solenoid (Diesel Engine)

Fig. 83 Underhood fuse/relay panel applications and ratings

Fuse	Usage
1	Stop/TCC Switch, Buzzer, CHMSL, Hazard Lamps, Stoplamps
2	Transfer Case
3	Courtesy Lamps, Cargo Lamp, Glove Box Lamp, Dome/Reading Lamps, Vanity Mirrors, Power Mirrors
4	Instrument Cluster, DRL Relay, Lamp Switch, Keyless Entry, Low Coolant Module, Illuminated Entry Module, DRAC (Diesel Engine)
5	Not Used
6	Cruise Control
7	Auxiliary Power Outlet
8	Air Bag System
9	License Lamp, Parking Lamps, Taillamps, Roof Marker Lamps, Tailgate Lamps, Front Sidemarkers, Fog Lamp Relay, Door Switch Illumination, Fender Lamps, Headlamp Switch Illumination
10	Air Bag System
11	Wiper Motor, Washer Pump
12	A/C, A/C Blower, High Blower Relay
13	Power Amp, Cigarette Lighter, Door Lock Relay, Power Lumbar Seat
14	4WD Indicator, Cluster, Comfort Controls, Instrument Switches, Radio Illumination, Chime Module

Fuse	Usage
15	DRL Relay, Fog Lamp Relay
16	Front and Rear Turn Signals, Back-Up Lamps, BTSI Solenoid
17	Radio (Ignition)
18	4WAL/VCM, ABS, Cruise Control
19	Radio (Battery)
20	PRNDL, Automatic Transmission, Speedometer, Check Gages Warning Light
21	Not Used
22	Not Used
23	Not Used
24	Front Axle, 4WD Indicator Lamp, TP2 Relay (Gasoline Engine)
A	Power Door Lock, Six-Way Power Seat, Keyless Entry Module
B	Power Windows

Fig. 82 Fuse application and amperage ratings—1994–98 models. Refer to the wiring diagrams for 1988–93 models

should a fuse link replacement repair be made using a length of standard wire cut from bulk stock or from another wiring harness.

Fusible link wire is covered with a special thick, non-flammable insulation. An overload condition causes the insulation to blister. If the overall condition continues, the wire will melt. To check a fusible link, look for blistering insulation. If the insulation is okay, pull gently on the wire. If the fusible link stretches, the wire has melted. Fusible links are usually located in the starting or charging system circuits.

Circuit Breakers

Circuit breakers differ from fuses in that they are reusable. Circuit breakers open when the flow of current exceeds specified value and will close after a few seconds when current flow returns to normal. Circuits breakers are used due to the fact that they must operate at times under prolonged high current flow due to demand even though there is not malfunction in the circuit.

There are 2 types of circuit breakers. The first type opens when high current flow is detected. A few seconds after the excessive current flow has been removed, the circuit breaker will close. If the high current flow is experienced again, the circuit will open again.

The second type is referred to as the Positive Temperature Coefficient (PTC) circuit breaker. When excessive current flow passes through the PTC circuit breaker, the circuit is not opened but its resistance increases. As the device heats ups with the increase in current flow, the resistance increases to the point where the circuit is effectively open. Unlike other circuit breakers, the PTC circuit breaker will not reset until the circuit is opened, removing voltage from the terminals. Once the voltage is removed, the circuit breaker will re-close within a few seconds.

Flashers

REMOVAL & INSTALLATION

The turn signal and hazard flasher units are usually located in the convenience center located just below the instrument panel on the drivers side. Replace the flasher by unplugging the old one and plugging in the new one. Confirm proper flasher operation.

WIRING DIAGRAMS

INDEX OF WIRING DIAGRAMS

91026W00

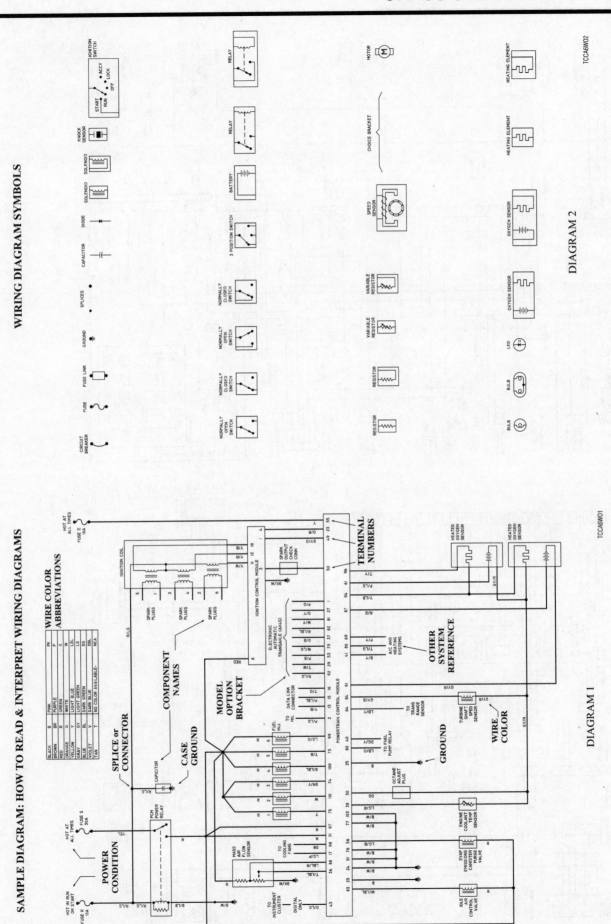

WIRING DIAGRAM SYMBOLS

SAMPLE DIAGRAM: HOW TO READ & INTERPRET WIRING DIAGRAMS

DIAGRAM 1

DIAGRAM 2

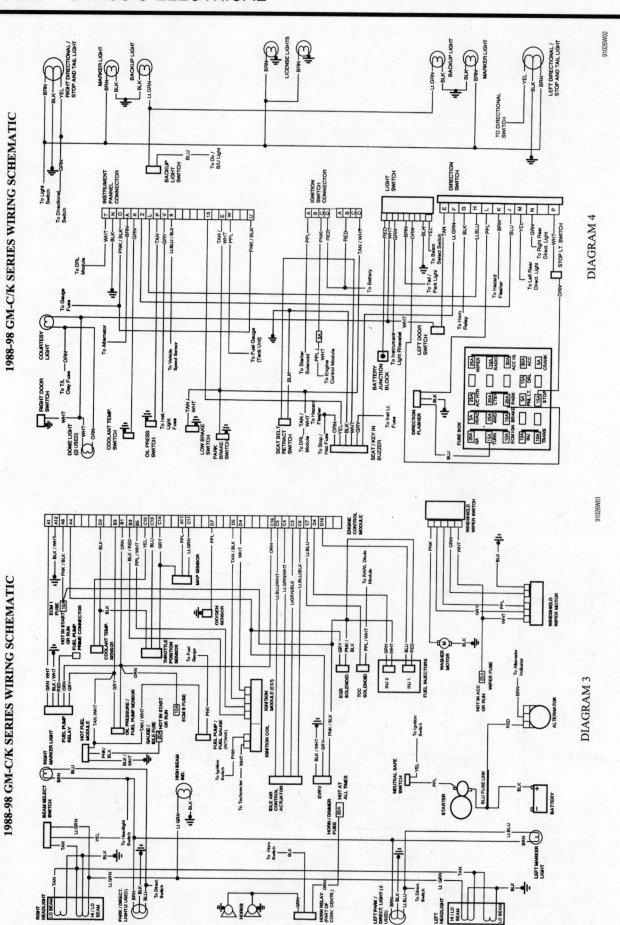

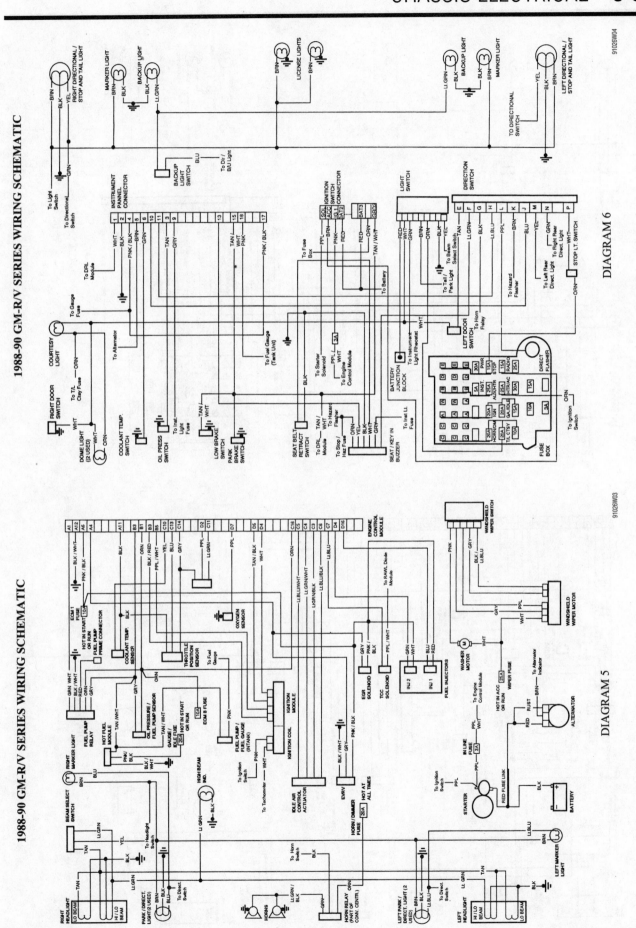

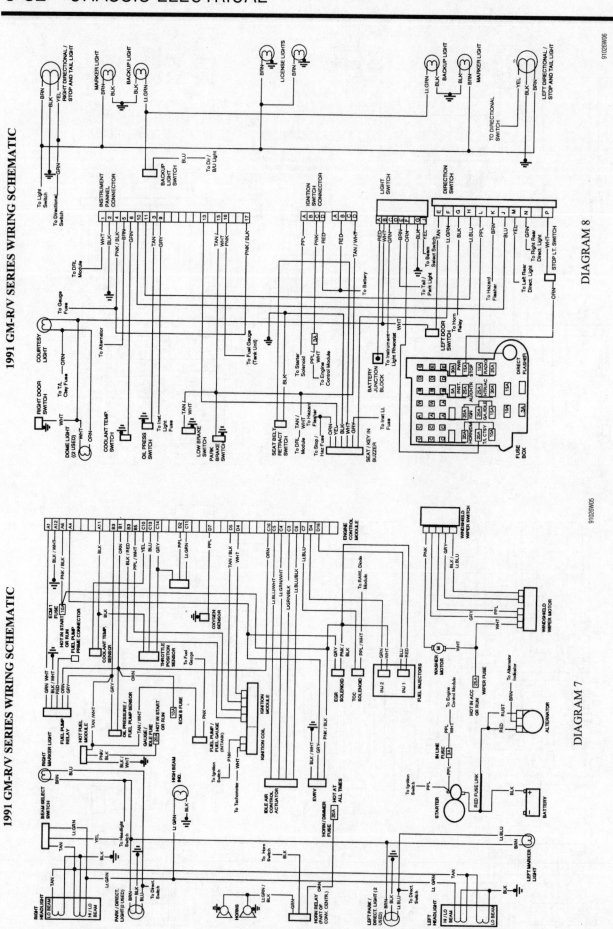

1991 GM-R/V SERIES WIRING SCHEMATIC

DIAGRAM 8

1991 GM-R/V SERIES WIRING SCHEMATIC

DIAGRAM 7

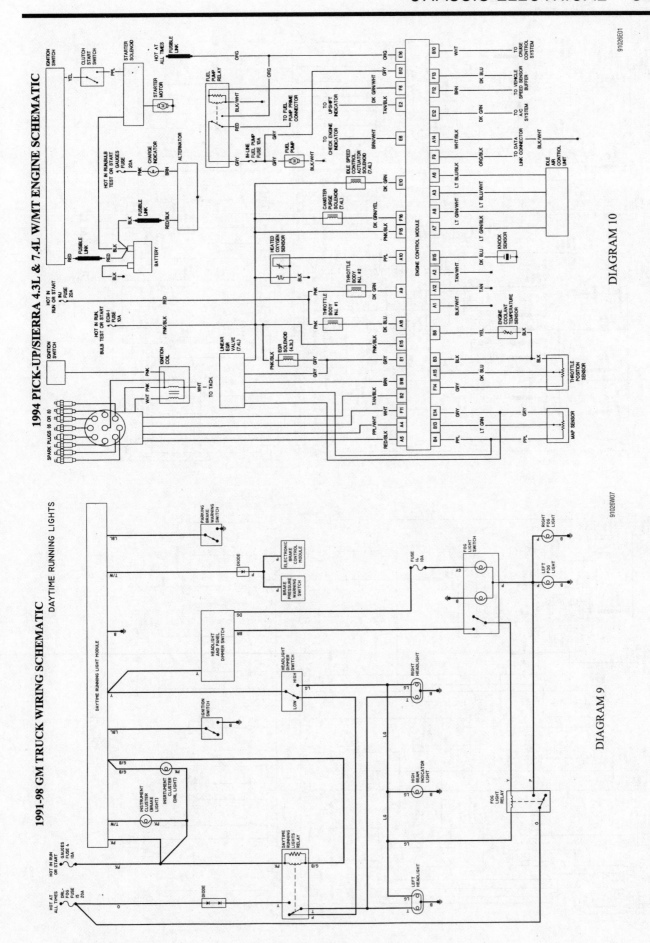

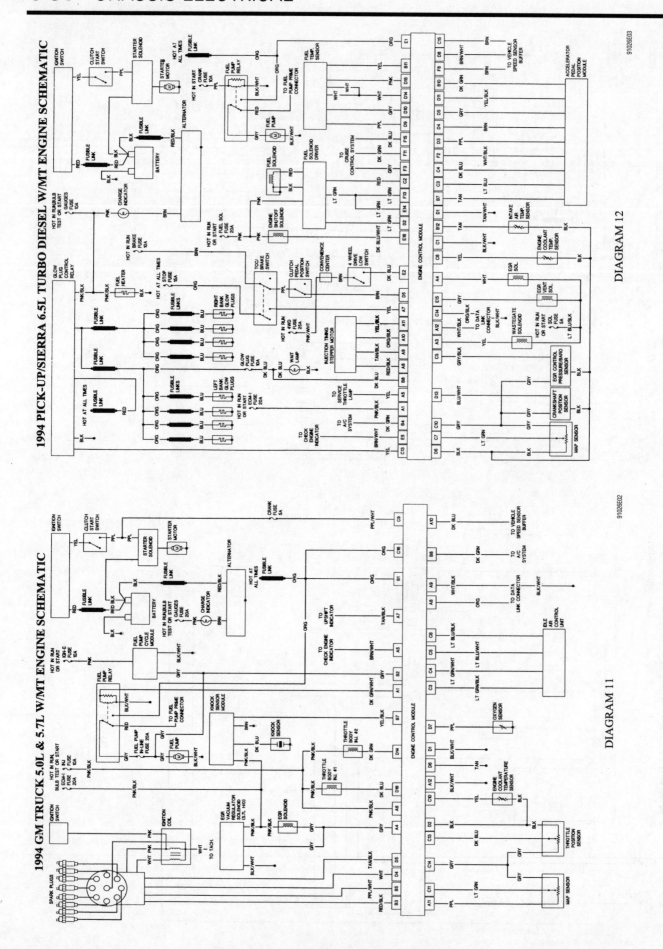

1994 PICK-UP/SIERRA 6.5L TURBO DIESEL W/MT ENGINE SCHEMATIC

DIAGRAM 12

1994 GM TRUCK 5.0L & 5.7L W/MT ENGINE SCHEMATIC

DIAGRAM 11

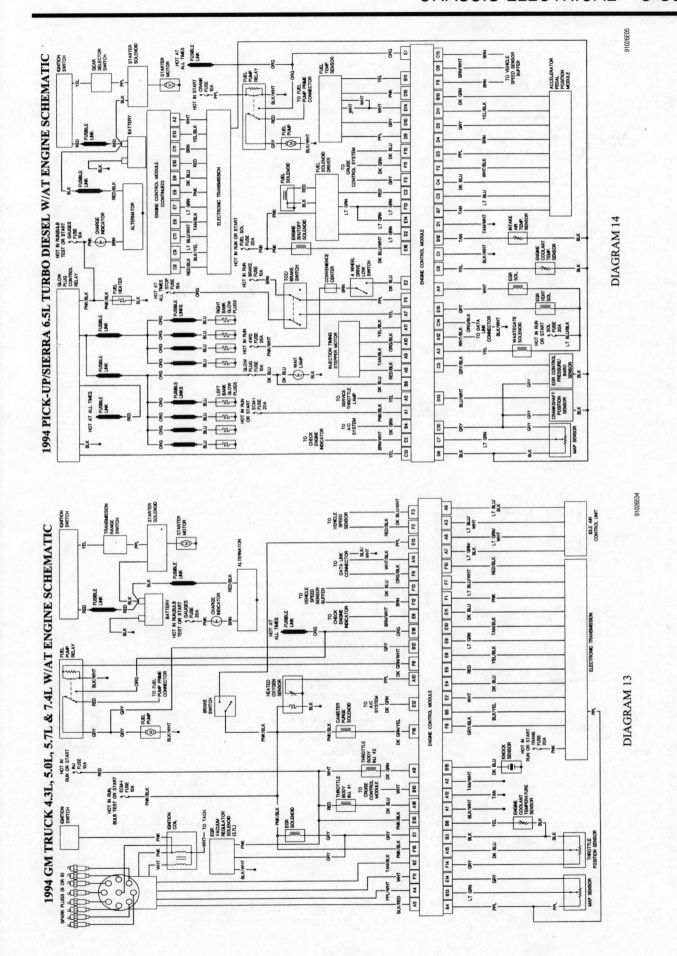

1994 PICK-UP/SIERRA 6.5L TURBO DIESEL W/AT ENGINE SCHEMATIC

DIAGRAM 14

1994 GM TRUCK 4.3L, 5.0L, 5.7L & 7.4L W/AT ENGINE SCHEMATIC

DIAGRAM 13

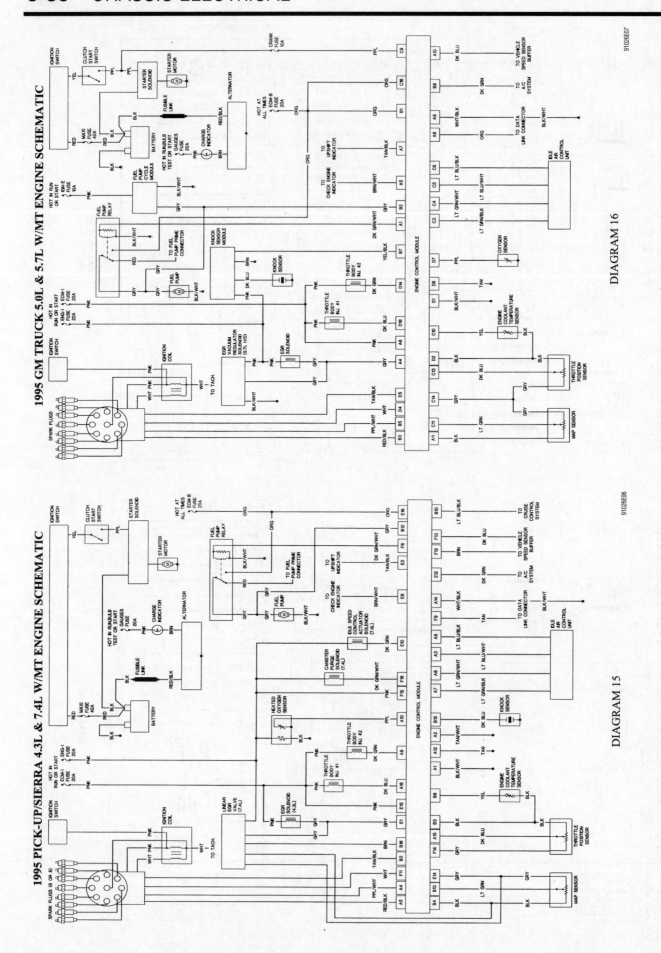

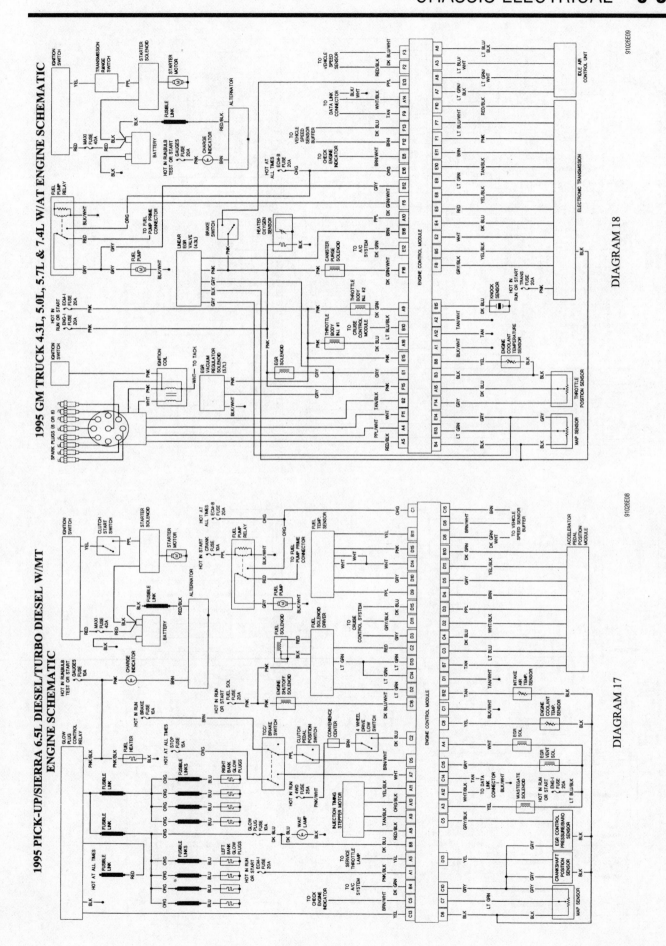

1995 GM TRUCK 4.3L, 5.0L, 5.7L & 7.4L W/AT ENGINE SCHEMATIC

DIAGRAM 18

1995 PICK-UP/SIERRA 6.5L DIESEL/TURBO DIESEL W/MT ENGINE SCHEMATIC

DIAGRAM 17

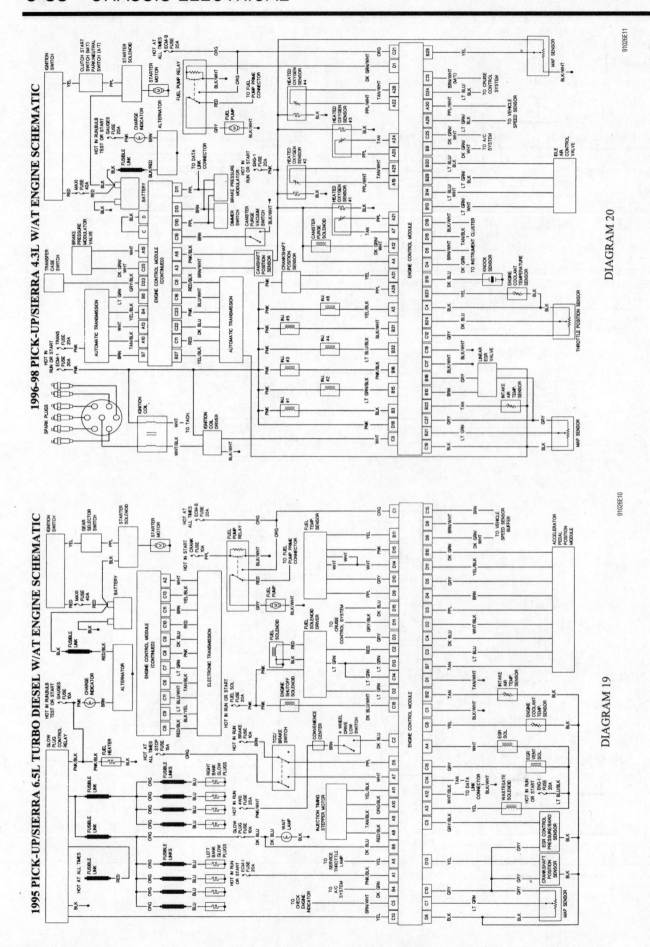

1996-98 PICK-UP/SIERRA 4.3L W/AT ENGINE SCHEMATIC

DIAGRAM 20

1995 PICK-UP/SIERRA 6.5L TURBO DIESEL W/AT ENGINE SCHEMATIC

DIAGRAM 19

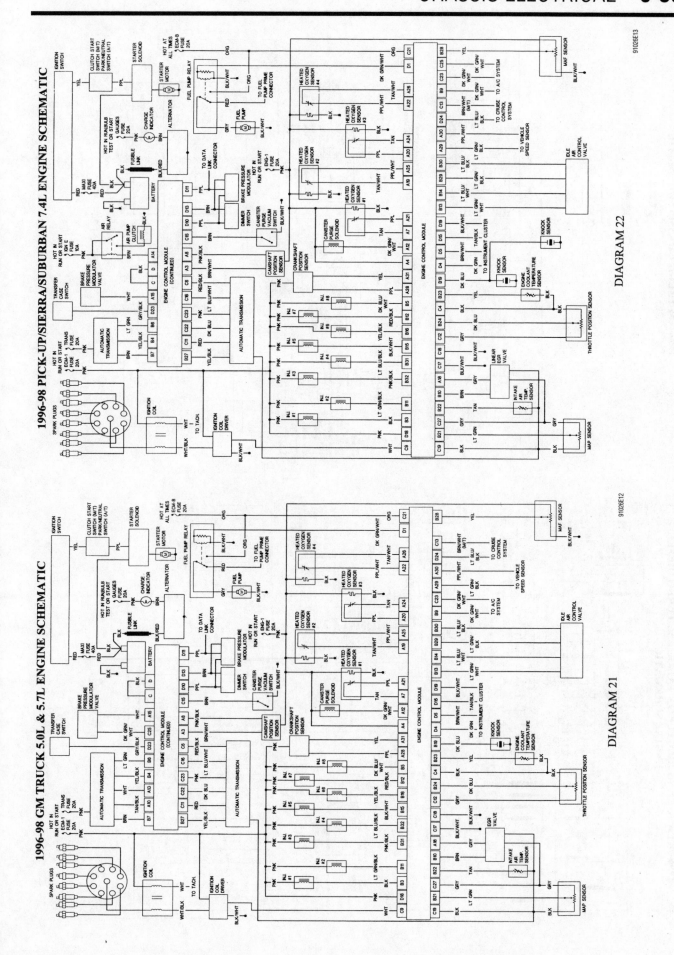

1996-98 PICK-UP/SIERRA/SUBURBAN 7.4L ENGINE SCHEMATIC

DIAGRAM 22

1996-98 GM TRUCK 5.0L & 5.7L ENGINE SCHEMATIC

DIAGRAM 21

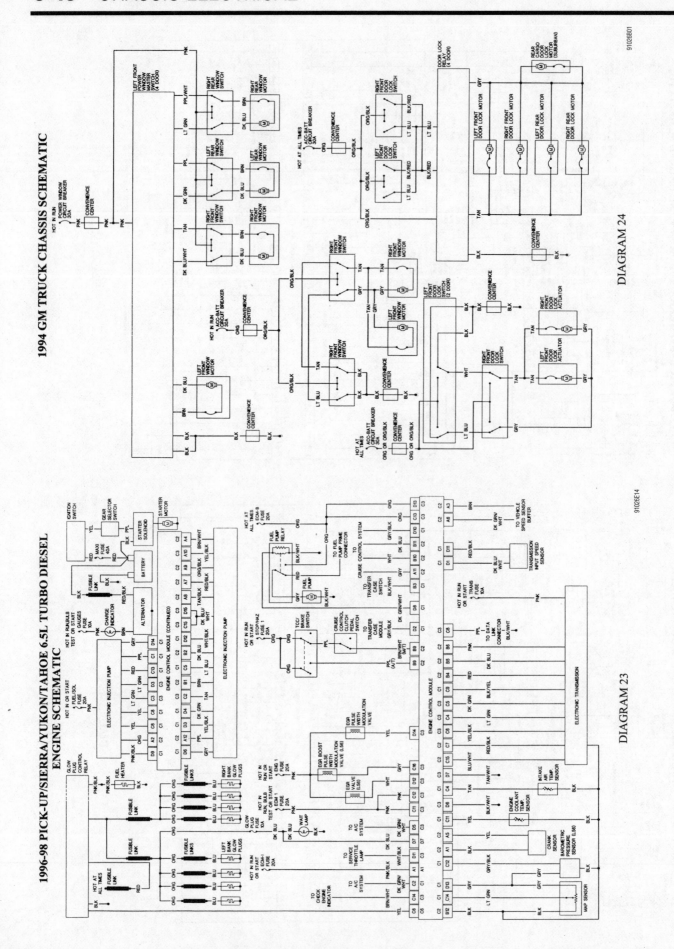

1994 GM TRUCK CHASSIS SCHEMATIC

DIAGRAM 24

1996-98 PICK-UP/SIERRA/YUKON/TAHOE 6.5L TURBO DIESEL ENGINE SCHEMATIC

DIAGRAM 23

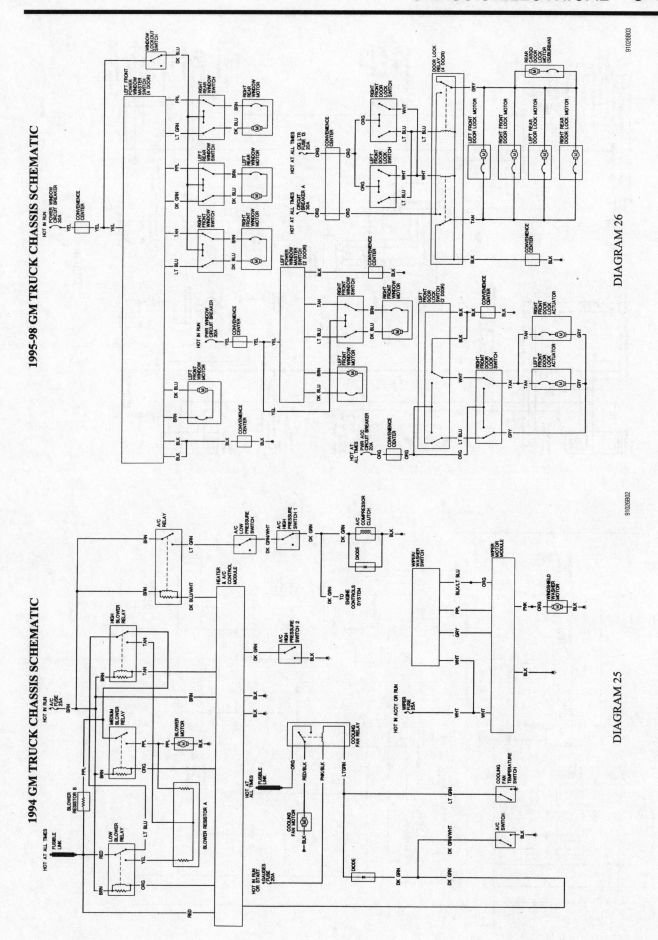

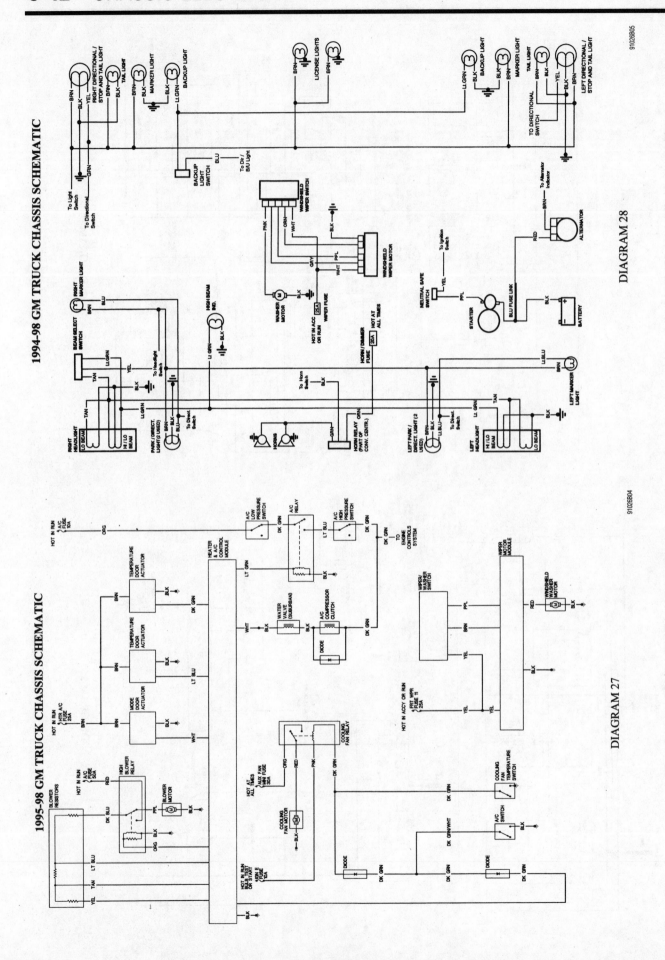

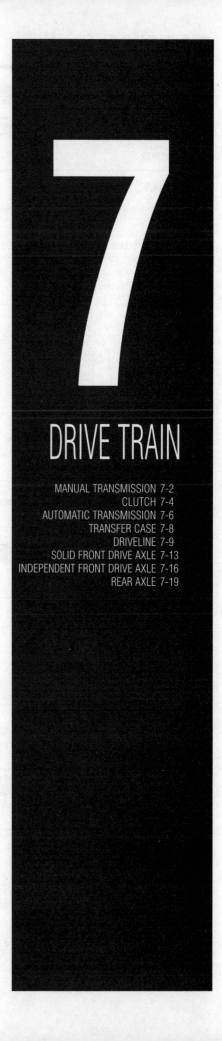

7

DRIVE TRAIN

MANUAL TRANSMISSION

Adjustments

SHIFT LINKAGE

▶ **See Figure 1**

1. Loosen the nuts on either side of the swivel. Refer to the illustration of the floor shift linkage for component location.
2. Move the shift control lever to neutral and move the control levers to the front detent and then back one. This will place the transmission in neutral.
3. Place a 0.249–0.250 in. (6–7mm) gauge pin through the control levers and hold the shift rod levers forward tightly and tighten the nuts.
4. Remove the gauge pin and lubricate the levers.

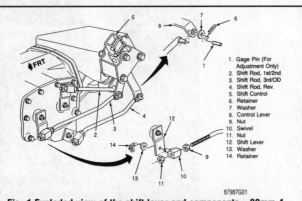

1. Gage Pin (For Adjustment Only)
2. Shift Rod, 1st/2nd
3. Shift Rod, 3rd/OD
4. Shift Rod, Rev.
5. Shift Control
6. Retainer
7. Washer
8. Control Lever
9. Nut
10. Swivel
11. Nut
12. Shift Lever
13. Washer
14. Retainer

87987G01

Fig. 1 Exploded view of the shift lever and components—89mm 4-speed overdrive

Shift Linkage

REMOVAL & INSTALLATION

1. Remove the cotter pin and the washer.
2. Disconnect the shift rod from the control lever and remove the retainer and washer.
3. Disconnect the shift rod from the shift lever and remove the nuts and swivel.

To install:
4. Install but do not tighten the nuts and swivel.
5. Connect the shift rod to the shift lever.
6. Install the washer and new retainer.
7. Connect the shift rod to the control lever and install the washer and new retainer.
8. Adjust the shift linkage as outlined in this section.

Shift Lever

REMOVAL & INSTALLATION

117mm 4-Speed

▶ **See Figure 2**

1. On 4WD models, remove the transfer case lever boot.
2. Remove the transmission lever boot retaining ring.
3. Remove the boot retaining screws.
4. Remove the boot.
5. Push downward on the cap at the bottom of the lever and turn it counter-clockwise. Pull the lever from the transmission.
6. Installation is the reverse of removal.

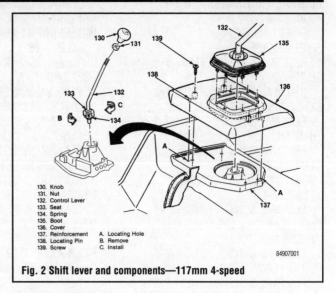

130. Knob
131. Nut
132. Control Lever
133. Seat
134. Spring
135. Boot
136. Cover
137. Reinforcement
138. Locating Pin
139. Screw

A. Locating Hole
B. Remove
C. Install

84907001

Fig. 2 Shift lever and components—117mm 4-speed

NVG 4500/NVG 5LM60

▶ **See Figure 3**

1. Remove the boot retaining screws and lift off the boot.
2. Loosen the jam nut and unscrew the lever.
3. If removing the shifter housing, place the shift lever in third or fourth gear.

➡ **Do not disassemble shift housing, internal parts for the housing are not available.**

4. Unfasten the shift housing-to-transmission bolts and remove the housing.
5. Installation is the reverse of removal. Tighten the housing bolts to 89 inch lbs. (10 Nm).

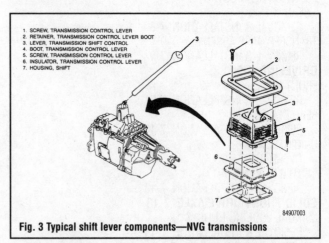

1. SCREW, TRANSMISSION CONTROL LEVER
2. RETAINER, TRANSMISSION CONTROL LEVER BOOT
3. LEVER, TRANSMISSION SHIFT CONTROL
4. BOOT, TRANSMISSION CONTROL LEVER
5. SCREW, TRANSMISSION CONTROL LEVER
6. INSULATOR, TRANSMISSION CONTROL LEVER
7. HOUSING, SHIFT

84907003

Fig. 3 Typical shift lever components—NVG transmissions

Extension Housing Rear Seal

REMOVAL & INSTALLATION

Except NVG 4500 Transmission

1. Raise and support the truck on jackstands.
2. Drain the transmission oil.
3. Matchmark and disconnect the driveshaft.
4. Deform the seal with a punch and pull it from the housing using a suitable seal puller.

5. Coat the outside of the new seal with locking compound and fill the gap between the seal lips with chassis grease. Install the seal using an appropriate seal driver (installer) tool.

NVG 4500 Transmission

▶ **See Figure 4**

1. Raise and support the truck on jackstands.
2. Drain the transmission oil.
3. Matchmark and disconnect the driveshaft.
4. If necessary, remove the parking brake.
5. Unfasten the yoke nut and washers, then remove the yoke.
6. Deform the seal with a punch and pull it from the housing using a suitable seal puller.

To install:

7. Install a new seal using a suitable seal driver (installer).
8. Install the yoke, washers and nut. Tighten the nut to 325 ft. lbs. (441 Nm).
9. Install the remaining components in the reverse order of removal.

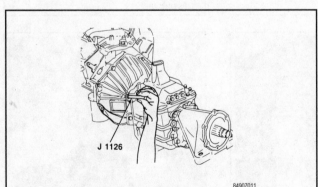

Fig. 4 Installing the extension housing oil seal—85mm and NVG 4500

Transmission

REMOVAL & INSTALLATION

▶ **See Figures 5 and 6**

1. Place the transmission in third or fourth gear.
2. Jack up your vehicle and support it with jackstands.
3. Drain the transmission.
4. Unplug the speedometer cable or Vehicle Speed Sensor (VSS) connector, back-up lamp wire and any other wires that would interfere with transmission removal.

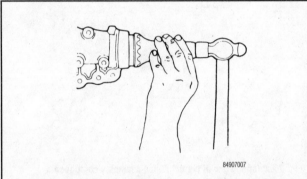

J 1126

Fig. 5 Use guide pins when removing and installing the transmission

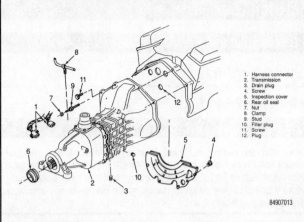

1.	Harness connector
2.	Transmission
3.	Drain plug
4.	Screw
5.	Inspection cover
6.	Rear oil seal
7.	Nut
8.	Clamp
9.	Stud
10.	Filler plug
11.	Screw
12.	Plug

84907013

Fig. 6 Exploded view of the transmission mounting—85mm 5-speed shown, others similar

5. Remove the gearshift lever. Plug the opening to keep out dirt.
6. Remove driveshaft after making the position of the shaft to the flange.
7. On 4WD models, remove the transfer case.
8. If necessary, remove the parking brake and controls.
9. Remove the exhaust pipes.
10. If equipped, remove the clutch slave cylinder and position it aside.
11. Position a transmission jack or its equivalent under the transmission to support it.
12. Remove the crossmember. Visually inspect to see if other equipment, brackets or lines must be removed to permit removal of transmission.

➡ **Mark position of crossmember when removing to prevent incorrect installation. The tapered surface should face the rear.**

13. Remove the flywheel housing underpan.
14. On NVG 4500 models, unbolt the transmission-to-bell housing bolts.
15. On all except the NVG 4500 models, remove the top two transmission-to-housing bolts and insert two guide pins.

➡ **The use of guide pins will not only support the transmission but will prevent damage to the clutch disc. Guide pins can be made by taking two bolts, the same as those just removed only longer, and cutting off the heads. Cut a slot in the head that will receive a screwdriver. Be sure to support the clutch release bearing and support assembly during removal of the transmission. This will prevent the release bearing from falling out of the flywheel housing.**

16. On all except the NVG 4500 models, remove the remaining bolts and slide transmission straight back from engine. Use care to keep the transmission drive gear straight in line with clutch disc hub.
17. Remove the transmission from beneath your vehicle.

To install:

Installation is the reverse of removal but please note the following important steps.

18. Make sure the transmission is in third or fourth gear. On NVG transmissions, place the transmission in Neutral.
19. Coat the input shaft splines with high temperature grease.
20. On all except the NVG 4500 models, install the guide pins in the top 2 bolt holes.
21. On NVG 4500 models, install the transmission-to-housing bolts.

✳✳ WARNING

Do not force the transmission into the clutch disc hub. Do not let the transmission hang unsupported in the splined portion of the clutch disc.

22. On all except the NVG 4500 models, tighten the transmission-to-engine bolts to 35 ft. lbs. (47 Nm). On NVG 4500 models tighten transmission-to-housing bolts to 74 ft. lbs. (100 Nm).

CLUTCH

Driven Disc and Pressure Plate

REMOVAL & INSTALLATION

♦ **See Figures 7 thru 15**

❋❋ CAUTION

The clutch driven disc may contain asbestos, which has been determined to be a cancer causing agent. Never clean clutch surfaces with compressed air! Avoid inhaling any dust from any clutch surface! When cleaning clutch surfaces, use a commercially available brake cleaning fluid.

➡Before removing the bellhousing, the engine must be supported. This can be done by placing a hydraulic jack, with a board on top, under the oil pan.

1. Remove the slave cylinder.
2. Remove the transmission.
3. If equipped, remove the inspection cover from the clutch.
4. On all NVG 4500 models, remove the bellhousing.
5. Remove the throwout spring and fork.
6. Remove the ballstud from the bellhousing.
7. Install a pilot tool (an old input shaft makes a good pilot tool) to hold the clutch while you are removing it.

➡**Before removing the clutch from the flywheel, mark the flywheel, clutch cover and one pressure plate lug, so that these parts may be assembled in their same relative positions. They were balanced as an assembly.**

8. Loosen the clutch attaching bolts one turn at a time to prevent distortion of the clutch cover until the tension is released.

9. Remove the clutch pilot tool and the clutch from the vehicle.
10. Check the pressure plate and flywheel for signs of wear, scoring, overheating, etc. If the clutch plate, flywheel, or pressure plate is oil-soaked, inspect the engine rear main seal and the transmission input shaft seal, and correct leakage as required. Replace any damaged parts.

To install:

11. On vehicles equipped with a gasoline engine, lubricate the pilot bearing with a few drops of machine oil. On vehicles equipped with diesel engines, the bearing is sealed and does not require lubrication.
12. Install a new pilot bearing. A brass drift or equivalent may be used to drive the bearing into place on vehicles equipped with a gasoline engine. On vehicles equipped with diesel engines, use a suitable pilot bearing driver.
13. Install the pressure plate in the cover assembly, aligning the notch in the pressure plate with the notch in the cover flange. Install pressure plate

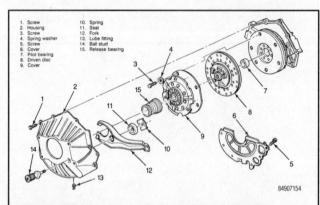

1. Screw	10. Spring
2. Housing	11. Seat
3. Screw	12. Fork
4. Spring washer	13. Lube fitting
5. Screw	14. Ball stud
6. Cover	15. Release bearing
7. Pilot bearing	
8. Driven disc	
9. Cover	

84907154

Fig. 7 Exploded view of typical clutch assembly components

Fig. 8 Remove the clutch and pressure plate bolts

Fig. 9 Remove the clutch and pressure plate assembly . . .

Fig. 10 . . . then separate the clutch and pressure plate

Fig. 11 Be sure that the flywheel surface is clean, before installing the clutch

Fig. 12 Install a clutch alignment arbor, to align the clutch assembly during installation

Fig. 13 Apply a thread locking agent to clutch assembly bolts

Fig. 14 Be sure to use a torque wrench to tighten the bolts

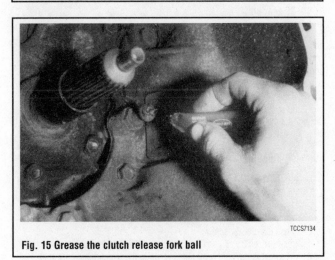

Fig. 15 Grease the clutch release fork ball

retracting springs, lockwashers and drive strap-to-pressure plate bolts. Tighten to 11 ft. lbs. (15 Nm). The clutch is now ready to be installed.

➡The manufacturer recommends that new pressure plate bolts and washers be used.

14. Turn the flywheel until the **X** mark is at the bottom.

15. Install the clutch disc, pressure plate and cover, using an old input shaft as an aligning tool.

16. Turn the clutch until the **X** mark or painted white letter on the clutch cover aligns with the **X** mark on the flywheel.

17. Install the attaching bolts and tighten them a little at a time in a crossing pattern until the spring pressure is taken up. On 1988–94 models, tighten the bolts to 22 ft. lbs. (30 Nm) on 4.3L, 5.0L and 5.7L engines; 32 ft. lbs. (43 Nm) on 6.2L and 6.5L engines; and 24 ft. lbs. (33 Nm) on 7.4L engines. On 1995–98 gasoline models tighten the bolts to 30 ft. lbs. (41 Nm). On 1995–98 diesel models, tighten the bolts to 25 ft. lbs. (34 Nm).

18. Remove the alignment tool.

19. Coat the rounded end of the ballstud with high temperature wheel bearing grease.

20. Install the ballstud in the bellhousing. Pack the ballstud from the lubrication fitting. Coat the rounded end of the ballstud with grease.

21. Pack the inside recess and the outside groove of the release bearing with high temperature wheel bearing grease and install the release bearing and fork.

22. Install the release bearing seat and spring.

23. Install the clutch housing. Tighten the bolts to the specifications outlined in the torque specification cart at the end of this section.

24. Install the transmission.

25. Install the inspection cover.

26. Install the slave cylinder. Tighten the bolt to 13 ft. lbs. (18 Nm).

27. Bleed the hydraulic system.

Clutch Master Cylinder and Reservoir

REMOVAL & INSTALLATION

▶ See Figures 16 and 17

1. Disconnect the negative battery cable.

2. Remove the lower steering column covers.

3. Remove the lower left side air conditioning duct, if so equipped.

4. Disconnect the pushrod from the clutch pedal.

5. Disconnect the reservoir hose.

6. Disconnect the secondary cylinder hydraulic line to the master cylinder.

7. Unfasten the master cylinder retaining nuts and remove the master cylinder.

8. To install, using a new gasket, reverse the removal procedure. After installation, bleed the clutch system.

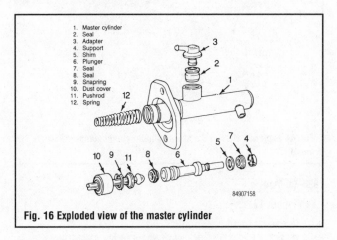

```
1. Master cylinder
2. Seal
3. Adapter
4. Support
5. Shim
6. Plunger
7. Seal
8. Seal
9. Snapring
10. Dust cover
11. Pushrod
12. Spring
```

Fig. 16 Exploded view of the master cylinder

```
1. Hydraulic line
2. Speedometer cable
3. Secondary cylinder line
4. master cylinder
5. Nut
6. Nut
7. Bleeder screw
8. Secondary cylinder
```

Fig. 17 Clutch hydraulic system

Clutch Slave Cylinder

REMOVAL & INSTALLATION

1988–95 Models

▶ See Figures 17 and 18

1. Disconnect the negative battery cable.

2. Raise the vehicle and support it safely.

3. Disconnect the hydraulic line from the slave cylinder.
4. Disconnect the hydraulic line from the master cylinder.
5. If necessary on 1988–91 R/V models, remove the nut retaining the hydraulic line and the speedometer cable to the cowl, then install the nut to hold the speedometer cable in place.
6. Cover all hydraulic lines to prevent dirt and moisture from entering the system.
7. Remove the bolts securing the cylinder and remove it from the transmission.
8. Installation is the reverse of removal. Tighten the cylinder retainer to 13 ft. lbs. (18 Nm) Bleed the clutch hydraulic system.

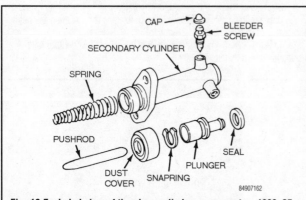

Fig. 18 Exploded view of the slave cylinder components—1988–95 models

1996–98 Models

▶ **See Figure 19**

1. Remove the transmission.
2. Unfasten the bolts that attach the slave cylinder to the clutch housing shaft.
3. Remove the cylinder from the transmission input shaft and the bearing from the cylinder.

To install:
4. Install the bearing on the cylinder.
5. Install the cylinder on the input shaft and make sure the bleed screw and the coupling are positioned with the transmission ports. Install the cylinder bolts and tighten them to 71 inch lbs. (8 Nm).
6. Install the transmission.

AUTOMATIC TRANSMISSION

Vacuum Modulator

REMOVAL & INSTALLATION

➡ **This applies to the THM 400 only.**

1. Raise and support the front end on jackstands.
2. Disconnect the vacuum line at the modulator.
3. Remove the screw and retaining clamp.
4. Remove the modulator. Be careful, some fluid may run out.

To install:
5. Install the modulator.
6. Install the vacuum line. Be careful not to kink the vacuum line during installation. Replace any lost fluid.

Neutral Safety Switch

REMOVAL & INSTALLATION

The back-up light switch is incorporated into the neutral/park safety switch. The neutral safety switch on 1988–94 models is mounted in the steering col-

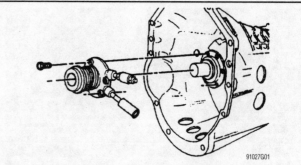

Fig. 19 The slave cylinder is attached to the clutch housing shaft— 1996–98 models

HYDRAULIC SYSTEM BLEEDING

1988–95 Models

1. Fill the clutch master cylinder with the proper grade and type fluid. Raise and support the vehicle safely.
2. Remove the slave cylinder retaining bolts. Hold the cylinder at about 45° angle with the bleeder at the highest point.
3. Have and assistant fully depress the clutch pedal. Open the bleeder screw. Repeat until all air is expelled from the system.
4. Be sure that the fluid level remains full in the clutch master cylinder throughout the bleeding procedure.
5. Install the slave cylinder.

1996–98 Models

1. Fill the clutch master cylinder with the proper grade and type fluid. Raise and support the vehicle safely.
2. Have an assistant, fully depress the clutch pedal. Open the bleeder screw located on the side of the transmission to expel air.
3. Close the bleeder screw.
4. Repeat steps 2 and 3 until all air is expelled from the system.
5. Be sure that the fluid level remains full in the clutch master cylinder throughout the bleeding procedure.
6. If the previous procedure fails to work, perform the following steps.
   a. Remove the clutch master cylinder reservoir cap.
   b. Pump the clutch pedal quickly for about 30 seconds.
   c. Stop and let the air escape. Repeat as necessary.

umn and is covered in Section 8 of this manual. The neutral safety switch on 1995–98 models only is covered under the back-up light switch removal & installation procedure in Section 6 of this manual.

Extension Housing Rear Seal

REMOVAL & INSTALLATION

▶ **See Figure 20**

1. Raise and support the truck on jackstands.
2. Matchmark and remove the driveshaft. Be careful! Some fluid may run out. You can avoid this by raising only the rear of the truck.
3. Centerpunch the seal to distort it and carefully pry it out.

To install:
4. Coat the outer edge of the new seal with non-hardening sealer.
5. Place the seal in the bore and carefully drive it into place. A seal installer makes this job easier.
6. Install the driveshaft. It's a good idea to coat the driveshaft end with grease to avoid damaging the seal.
7. Lower the truck and replace any lost fluid.

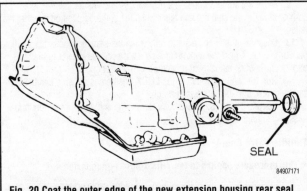

Fig. 20 Coat the outer edge of the new extension housing rear seal with non-hardening sealer before installation

Transmission

REMOVAL & INSTALLATION

♦ See Figure 21

➡ It would be best to drain the transmission before starting.

1. Disconnect the battery ground cable.
2. Remove the air cleaner.
3. If equipped, disconnect the detent or TV cable at the throttle lever.
4. On 4WD models, remove the transfer case shift lever knob and boot.
5. Raise and support the truck on jackstands.
6. Disconnect the shift linkage from the transmission.
7. If it is necessary to disconnect the fuel line, relieve the fuel system pressure. Disconnect the fuel lines.
8. Remove any skid plates that would interfere with transmission removal.
9. Drain the transmission fluid.
10. Remove the driveshaft(s), after matchmarking its/their flanges.
11. Detach the speedometer cable or Vehicle Speed Sensor (VSS) connector, downshift cable, vacuum modulator cable, shift linkage, throttle linkage, electrical wiring, the fluid cooler lines, or any other component that would interfere with transmission removal.
12. Remove the dipstick tube.
13. If necessary, remove the starter motor.
14. If necessary, disconnect the support bracket at the catalytic converter.
15. Support the transmission on a transmission jack and unbolt the transmission rear mount or the transfer case adapter from the crossmember.
16. Remove the crossmember.
17. Remove any transmission support braces. Note their exact positions for installation.
18. Remove the torque converter underpan, matchmark the flywheel and converter, and remove the converter bolts.
19. If necessary for clearance, move the exhaust system aside.
20. If necessary for clearance, disconnect the parking brake cable.
21. Remove the transfer case and the adapter.
22. Support the engine on a jack and lower the transmission slightly for access to the upper transmission-to-engine bolts.
23. Remove the transmission-to-engine bolts and pull the transmission back. Rig up a strap or keep the front of the transmission up so the converter doesn't fall out.

To install:

Installation is the reverse of removal but please note the following important steps.

24. Tighten the transmission-to-engine bolts to 35 ft. lbs. (47 Nm).

➡ Make sure that the torque converter-to-flexplate matchmarks are aligned, the torque converter is flush with the flywheel and the converter turns freely by hand.

25. On all except 1996–98 models, tighten the converter bolts to 50 ft. lbs. (68 Nm).
26. On 1996–98 models, tighten the converter bolts to 46 ft. lbs. (63 Nm).
27. Tighten the transmission support brace bolts to 35 ft. lbs. (47 Nm).

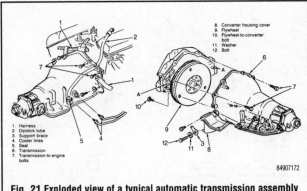

Fig. 21 Exploded view of a typical automatic transmission assembly and its related components

28. On all except 1991–98 models, tighten the crossmember retainers to 35 ft. lbs. (47 Nm).
29. On 1991–98 models tighten the crossmember retainers to 56 ft. lbs. (77 Nm).
30. On 1988–94 4WD models, tighten the transfer case-to-transmission attaching bolts to 24 ft. lbs. (32 Nm) and the transfer case-to-frame bracket bolts to 35 ft. lbs. (47 Nm).
31. On 1995–98 4WD models, tighten the adapter-to-transfer case and adapter-to-transmission bolts to 33 ft. lbs. (45 Nm).

ADJUSTMENTS

Shift Linkage

♦ See Figures 22 and 23

1. Raise and support the front end on jackstands. Block the rear wheels.
2. Loosen the shift lever bolt or nut at the transmission lever so that the lever is free to move on the rod.
3. Set the column shift lever to the neutral gate notch, by rotating it until the shift lever drops into the Neutral gate. Do not use the indicator pointer as a reference to position the shift lever, as this will not be accurate.
4. Set the transmission lever in the neutral position by moving it clockwise to the park detent, then counterclockwise 2 detents to neutral.
5. Hold the rod tightly in the swivel and tighten the nut or bolt to 17 ft. lbs. (23 Nm) on all but the 4L80E transmission. On the 4L80E transmission, tighten the bolt to 20 ft. lbs. (30 Nm).
6. Lower the vehicle.
7. Move the column shifter to park and check that the engine starts. Check the adjustment by moving the selector to each gear position.

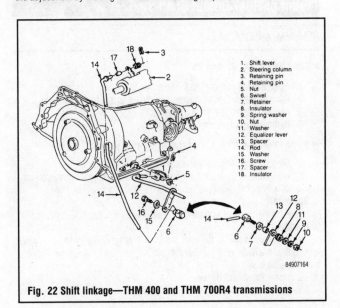

Fig. 22 Shift linkage—THM 400 and THM 700R4 transmissions

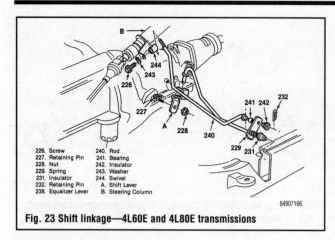

226. Screw	240. Rod
227. Retaining Pin	241. Bearing
228. Nut	242. Insulator
229. Spring	243. Washer
231. Insulator	244. Swivel
232. Retaining Pin	A. Shift Lever
238. Equalizer Lever	B. Steering Column

84907166

Fig. 23 Shift linkage—4L60E and 4L80E transmissions

Shift Cable

➡**This procedure applies to 4L60-E and 4L80-E transmissions.**

1. Place the transmission in park and apply the parking brake.
2. Raise and support the vehicle on jackstands.
3. On the shift cable end slide the black retaining clip forward just enough to allow the white lock button to be out.

➡**Do not push the white lock button completely out.**

4. Push the white lock button out just far enough to free the metal core adjust body inside the core.
5. Inspect the core adjust body for dirt or debris that may restrict its travel.
6. If there are any restrictions found the shift cable end should be washed with soap and water. If after cleaning the cable the travel of the core adjust body is still restricted the shift cable assembly must be replaced.
7. Lower the vehicle, turn the ignition switch **ON** and move the transmission lever from park to one-to-ten times.
8. Place the shift lever in park and turn the ignition switch **OFF**. Raise and support the vehicle on jackstands.
9. Make sure the transmission is in mechanical park by rotating the control lever clockwise until it stops.
10. Push the white lock button in to secure the core adjuster body adjuster and slide the black retainer clip rearward until it covers the white lock button and locks in place over the shift cable end.
11. Lower the vehicle and turn the ignition switch **ON**.

12. Move the shifter through the gear ranges and ensure that the light comes on under the shift column letter when the shifter is positioned under that letter.
13. Ensure that the engine starts only when the transmission is placed in park or neutral. Adjust the park/neutral switch if necessary. Refer to the park/neutral switch adjustment procedure in this section.
14. Turn the ignition switch to the **LOCK** position and ensure that the key can be removed in the park position only.
15. Release the parking brake, start the engine and check for proper transmission shift operation.

Throttle Valve Cable

➡**This procedure applies to the THM 700R4 transmission.**

The adjustment is made at the engine end of the cable with the engine off, by rotating the throttle lever by hand. DO NOT use the accelerator pedal to rotate the throttle lever.

1. Remove the air cleaner.
2. Depress and hold down the metal adjusting tab at the end of the cable.
3. Move the slider until it stops against the fitting.
4. Release the adjusting tab.
5. Rotate the throttle lever to the full extent of it travel.
6. The slider must move towards the lever when the lever is at full travel. Make sure that the cable moves freely.

➡**The cable may appear to function properly with the engine cold. Recheck it with the engine hot.**

7. Road test the truck.

Neutral Start/Back-Up Switch

The procedure is for switches that are mounted on the transmission only.

This adjustment is performed with the switch removed from the vehicle. Neutral position tool J 41364–A or its equivalent is required for this procedure.

1. Position tool J 41364–A or its equivalent onto the park/neutral switch. make sure that the slots on the switch are lined up with the lower tabs on the tool.
2. Rotate the tool until the upper locator pin on the tool is lined with the slot on the top of the switch.

➡**Do not remove the tool from the switch.**

3. Install the switch and remove the tool.

TRANSFER CASE

Front or Rear Output Shaft Seal

REMOVAL & INSTALLATION

▶ **See Figures 24, 25 and 26**

1. Raise and support the truck on jackstands.
2. Remove the skid plate if necessary to gain access to the front seal.
3. Matchmark and remove the driveshaft.
4. Remove the nut, washer and yoke.

➡**Some models don't use a washer at the rear yoke nut.**

5. Some models employ a shield around the seal. Remove it.
6. Using a hammer and a punch, carefully distort the seal so that you can pull it out with a pliers. Be careful to avoid damage to the seal bore!

To install:

7. Coat the seal lips with clean oil fluid. Coat the outer edge of the seal with gasket sealer.
8. Position the seal in the bore and drive it into place by carefully tapping around it with a hammer. If you have access to one, a seal installer will make the job a little easier.
9. Install the shield, if used.
10. Coat the outer surface of the yoke neck with clean oil and slide it into place.

11. Install the nut and washer. Tighten the nut to the specification shown in the torque specification chart at the end of this section.
12. Install the driveshaft.
13. Install the skid plate.

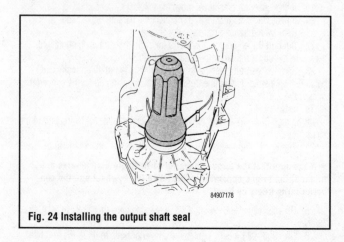

84907178

Fig. 24 Installing the output shaft seal

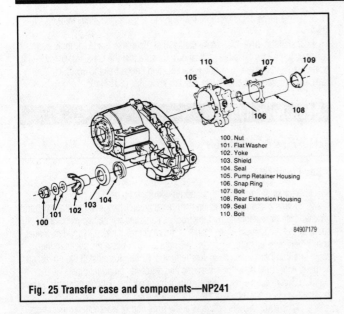

Fig. 25 Transfer case and components—NP241

100. Nut
101. Flat Washer
102. Yoke
103. Shield
104. Seal
105. Pump Retainer Housing
106. Snap Ring
107. Bolt
108. Rear Extension Housing
109. Seal
110. Bolt

84907179

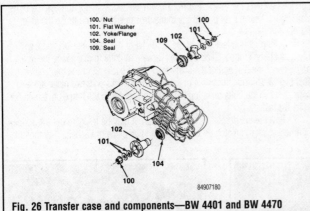

Fig. 26 Transfer case and components—BW 4401 and BW 4470

100. Nut
101. Flat Washer
102. Yoke/Flange
104. Seal
109. Seal

84907180

Transfer Case Assembly

REMOVAL & INSTALLATION

♦ **See Figures 25, 26 and 27**

1. Raise and support the truck on jackstands.
2. Drain the transfer case.
3. Disconnect the speedometer cable.
4. On models equipped with the NP208 transfer case, place the case in the 4H position.
5. Remove the skid plate and if necessary, the crossmember support.
6. If necessary, on trucks with automatic transmission, disconnect the strut rod.

DRIVELINE

Front Driveshaft

REMOVAL & INSTALLATION

Solid Axle

♦ **See Figure 28**

Chevrolet and GMC use U-bolts or straps to secure the driveshaft to the pinion flange. Use the following procedure to remove the driveshaft.

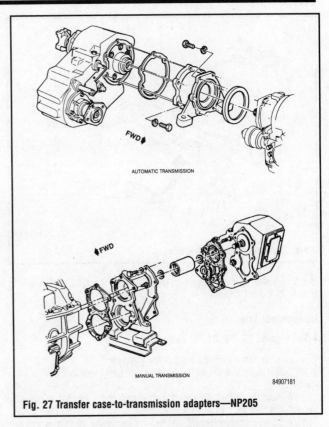

Fig. 27 Transfer case-to-transmission adapters—NP205

84907181

7. Tag and unplug all electrical connections and hoses from the transfer case.
8. On models equipped with the NP208 transfer case, remove the parking brake cable guide from the pivot on the right frame rail.
9. Matchmark the driveshafts, disconnect them, and remove them.
10. Disconnect the shift lever rod.
11. Support the transfer case and remove the bolts attaching the transfer case to transmission adapter.
12. Move the transfer case to the rear until the input shaft clears the adapter and lower the transfer case from the truck.

To install:
Installation is the reverse of removal. Please note the following steps.
13. On models equipped with the NP208 transfer case, when installing the transfer case, make sure its in the 4H position.
14. On models except those equipped with the NP208 transfer case and all 1996–98 models, tighten the transfer case-to-transmission adapter bolts to 24 ft. lbs. (32 Nm).
15. On models equipped with the NP208 transfer case, tighten the transfer case-to-transmission adapter bolts to 30 ft. lbs. (40 Nm).
16. On 1996–98 models, tighten the transfer case-to-transmission adapter bolts to 33 ft. lbs. (45 Nm).
17. If necessary, tighten the transmission end bolts to 129 ft. lbs. (175 Nm); the transfer case end bolts to 35 ft. lbs. (47 Nm).

1. Jack up your vehicle and support it with jackstands.
2. Scribe aligning marks on the driveshaft and the pinion flange to aid in reassembly.
3. Remove the U-bolts or straps at the axle end of the shaft. Compress the shaft slightly and tape the bearings into place to avoid losing them.
4. Remove the U-bolts or flange bolts at the transfer case end of the shaft. Tape the bearings into place.
5. Remove the driveshaft.

To install:
6. Install the driveshaft. Make certain that the marks made earlier line up correctly to prevent possible imbalances. Be sure that the constant velocity joint

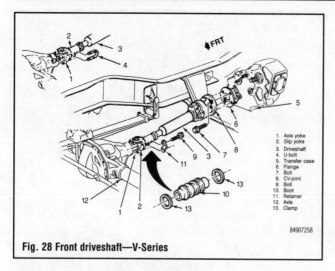

Fig. 28 Front driveshaft—V-Series

is at the transfer case end. Tighten the U-bolts to 15 ft. lbs. (20 Nm); flange bolts to 75 ft. lbs. (101 Nm).

Independent Axle

◆ **See Figures 29, 30, 31, 32 and 33**

1. Jack up your vehicle and support it with jackstands.
2. Scribe aligning marks on the driveshaft and each flange to aid in reassembly.
3. Remove the flange bolts and retainers at each end of the shaft. Remove the slip yoke from the front axle.
4. Push the driveshaft forward until it clears the transfer case flange and remove it. If the shaft is difficult to disengage from either flange, pry it loose; never hammer it loose!

5. Use a piece of tape to hold the U-joint caps in place. Remove the driveshaft.
6. Install the driveshaft. Make certain that the marks made earlier line up correctly to prevent possible imbalances. Be sure that the constant velocity joint is at the transfer case end. Tighten the axle end flange bolts to 15 ft. lbs. (20 Nm); the transfer case end flange bolts to 75 ft. lbs. (101 Nm).

Rear Driveshaft

REMOVAL & INSTALLATION

◆ **See Figures 34 thru 40**

1. Jack up your truck and support it with jackstands.
2. Scribe alignment marks on the driveshaft and flange of the rear axle, and transfer case or transmission. If the truck is equipped with a two piece driveshaft, be certain to also scribe marks at the center joint near the splined connection. When reinstalling driveshafts, it is necessary to place the shafts in the same position from which they were removed. Failure to reinstall the driveshaft properly will cause driveline vibrations and reduced component life.
3. Disconnect the rear universal joint by removing U-bolts or straps. Tape the bearings into place to avoid losing them.
4. If there are U-bolts or straps at the front end of the shaft, remove them. Tape the bearings into place. For trucks with two piece shafts, remove the bolts retaining the bearing support to the frame crossmember. Compress the shaft slightly and remove it.
5. If there are no fasteners at the front end of the transmission, there will only be a splined fitting. Slide the shaft forward slightly to disengage the axle flange, lower the rear end of the shaft, then pull it back out of the transmission. Most two wheel drive trucks are of this type. For trucks with two piece driveshafts, remove the bolts retaining the bearing support to the frame crossmember.
To install:
6. Reverse the procedure for installation. It may be tricky to get the scribed alignment marks to match up on trucks with two piece driveshafts. For those

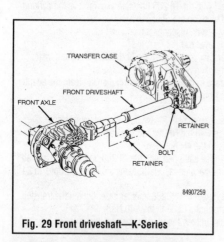

Fig. 29 Front driveshaft—K-Series

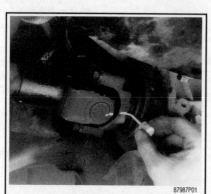

Fig. 30 Scribe aligning marks on the driveshaft and each flange to aid in reassembly

Fig. 31 Remove the flange bolts and retainers at each end of the shaft

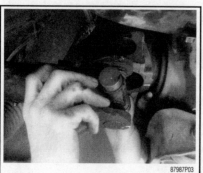

Fig. 32 Push the driveshaft forward until it clears the transfer case flange and remove it

Fig. 33 Use a piece of tape to hold the U-joint caps in place

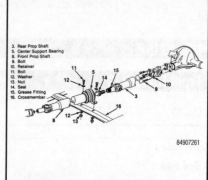

Fig. 34 Two-piece rear driveshaft with center bearing

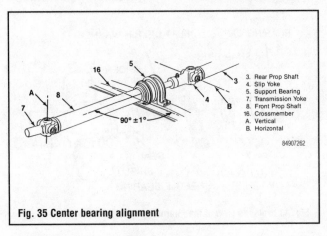

Fig. 35 Center bearing alignment

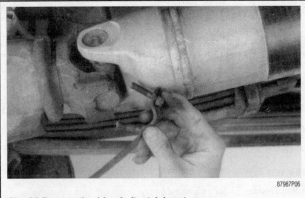

Fig. 38 Remove the driveshaft retaining straps

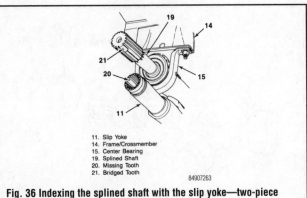

Fig. 36 Indexing the splined shaft with the slip yoke—two-piece shafts

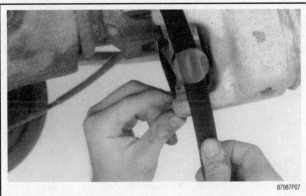

Fig. 39 Tape the bearings into place to avoid losing them

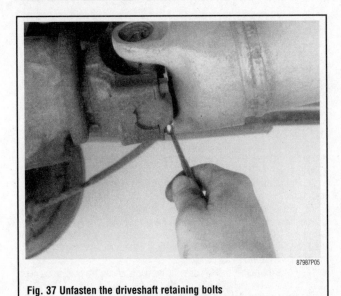

Fig. 37 Unfasten the driveshaft retaining bolts

Fig. 40 Lower the rear end of the shaft, then pull it back out of the transmission

models only, the following instructions may be of some help. First, slide the grease cap and gasket onto the rear splines.

• K models with 16 splines, after installing the front shaft to the transmission and bolting the support to the crossmember, arrange the front trunnion vertically and the second trunnion horizontally.

• Models with 32 splines have an alignment key. The driveshaft cannot be replaced incorrectly. Simply match up the key with the keyway.

7. On two wheel drive automatic transmission models, lubricate the internal yoke splines at the transmission end of the shaft with lithium base grease. The grease should seep out through the vent hole.

➡A thump in the rear driveshaft sometimes occurs when releasing the brakes after braking to a stop, especially on a downgrade. This is most common with automatic transmission. It is often caused by the driveshaft splines binding and can be cured by removing the driveshaft, inspecting the splines for rough edges, and carefully lubricating. A similar thump may be caused by the clutch plates in Positraction limited slip rear axles binding. If this isn't caused by wear, it can be cured by draining and refilling the rear axle with the special lubricant and adding Positraction additive, both of which are available from dealers.

8. On all except C 3500 HD models, tighten the U-bolt or strap retainers to 15 ft. lbs. (20 Nm).

9. On C3500 HD models, tighten the U-bolt or strap retainers to 27 ft. lbs. (37 Nm).

10. If equipped, tighten the center bearing retainers to 26 ft. lbs. (35 Nm).

U-Joints

OVERHAUL

There are three types of U-joints used in these trucks. The first is held together by wire snaprings in the yokes. The second type is held together with injection molded plastic retainer rings. This type cannot be reassembled with the same parts, once disassembled. However, repair kits are available. The third type (4WD models only) is the large constant velocity joint which looks like a double U-joint, located at the transfer case end of the front driveshaft on V-Series trucks.

Snapring Type

▶ **See Figures 41, 42, 43 and 44**

1. Remove the driveshaft(s) from the truck.
2. Remove the lockrings from the yoke and remove the lubrication fitting.
3. Support the yoke in a bench vise. Never clamp the driveshaft tube.
4. Use a soft drift pin and hammer to drive against one trunnion bearing to drive the opposite bearing from the yoke.

➡ **The bearing cap cannot be driven completely out.**

5. Grasp the cap and work it out.
6. Support the other side of the yoke and drive the other bearing cap from the yoke and remove as in Steps 4 and 5.
7. Remove the trunnion from the driveshaft yoke.
8. If equipped with a sliding sleeve, remove the trunnions bearings from the sleeve yoke in the same manner as above. Remove the seal retainer from the end of the sleeve and pull the seal and washer from the retainer.

To remove the bearing support:

9. Remove the dust shield, or, if equipped with a flange, remove the cotter pin and nut and pull the flange and deflector assembly from the shaft.

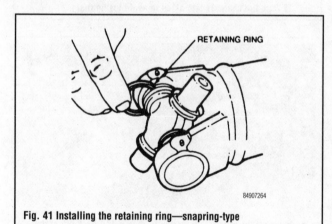

Fig. 41 Installing the retaining ring—snapring-type

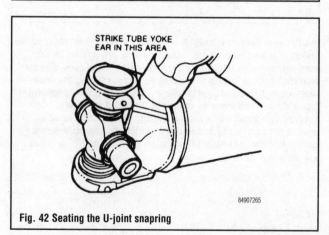

Fig. 42 Seating the U-joint snapring

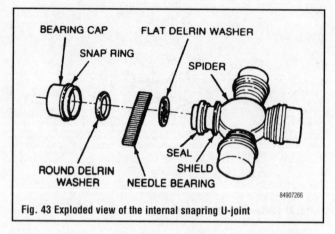

Fig. 43 Exploded view of the internal snapring U-joint

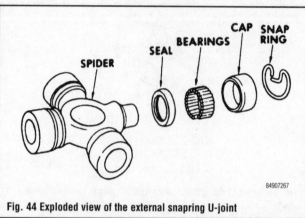

Fig. 44 Exploded view of the external snapring U-joint

10. Remove the support bracket from the rubber cushion and pull the cushion away from the bearing.
11. Pull the bearing assembly from the shaft. If equipped, remove the grease retainers and slingers from the bearing.

Assemble the bearing support as follows:

12. Install the inner deflector on the driveshaft and punch the deflector on 2 opposite sides to be sure that it is tight.
13. Pack the retainers with special high melting grease. Insert a slinger (if used) inside one retainer and press this retainer over the bearing outer race.
14. Start the bearing and slinger on the shaft journal. Support the driveshaft and press the bearing and inner slinger against the shoulder of the shaft with a suitable pipe.
15. Install the second slinger on the shaft and press the second retainer on the shaft.
16. Install the dust shield over the shaft (small diameter first) and depress it into position against the outer slinger or, if equipped with a flange, install the flange and deflector. Align the centerline of the flange yoke with the centerline of the driveshaft yoke and start the flange straight on the splines of the shaft with the end of the flange against the slinger.
17. Force the rubber cushion onto the bearing and coat the outside diameter of the cushion with clean brake fluid.
18. Force the bracket onto the cushion.

Assemble the trunnion bearings:

19. Repack the bearings with grease and replace the trunnion dust seals after any operation that requires disassembly of the U-joint. But be sure that the lubricant reservoir at the end of the trunnion is full of lubricant. Fill the reservoirs with lubricant from the bottom.
20. Install the trunnion into the driveshaft yoke and press the bearings into the yoke over the trunnion hubs as far as it will go.
21. Install the lockrings.
22. Hold the trunnion in one hand and tap the yoke slightly to seat the bearings against the lockrings.
23. On the rear driveshafts, install the sleeve yoke over the trunnion hubs and install the bearings in the same manner as above.

Molded Retainer Type

▶ **See Figures 45, 46, 47 and 48**

1. Remove the driveshaft.
2. Support the driveshaft in a horizontal position. Place the U-joint so that the lower ear of the shaft yoke is supported by a 1⅛ in. socket. Press the lower bearing cup out of the yoke ear. This will shear the plastic retaining the lower bearing cup.

➡**Never clamp the driveshaft tubing in a vise.**

3. If the bearing cup is not completely removed, lift the cross, insert a spacer and press the cup completely out.
4. Rotate the driveshaft, shear the opposite plastic retainer, and press the other bearing cup out in the same manner.
5. Remove the cross from the yoke. Production U-joints cannot be reassembled. There are no bearing retainer grooves in the cups. Discard all parts that we removed and substitute those in the overhaul kit.
6. Remove the sheared plastic bearing retainer. Drive a small pin or punch through the injection holes to aid in removal.
7. If the front U-joint is serviced, remove the bearing cups from the slip yoke in the manner previously described.

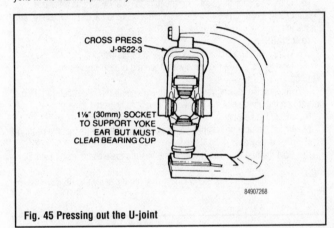

Fig. 45 Pressing out the U-joint

8. Be sure that the seals are installed on the service bearing cups to hold the needle bearings in place for handling. Grease the bearings if they aren't pre-greased.
9. Install one bearing cup partway into one side of the yoke and turn this ear to the bottom.
10. Insert the opposite bearing cup partway. Be sure that both trunnions are started straight into the bearing cups.
11. Press against opposite bearing cups, working the cross constantly to be sure that it is free in the cups. If binding occurs, check the needle rollers to be sure that one needle has not become lodged under an end of the trunnion.
12. As soon as one bearing retainer groove is exposed, stop pressing and install the bearing retainer snapring.
13. Continue to press until the opposite bearing retainer can be installed. If difficulty installing the snaprings is encountered, tap the yoke with a hammer to spring the yoke ears slightly.
14. Assemble the other half of the U-joint in the same manner.

Center Bearing

REMOVAL & INSTALLATION

1. Raise the vehicle and support it wit safety stands.
2. Remove the rear and front driveshafts.
3. Remove the center bearing as follows:
   a. Stand the driveshaft in a press on its end with the center bearing supported by the press bars.
   b. Use the press to remove the center bearing.

To install:

4. Install the center bearing on the driveshaft using a press.
5. Install the front driveshaft.

➡**The center bearing must be aligned to prevent damage to the driveshaft assembly. When bolting the center bearing in place, be sure that it is perpendicular (90⁻) to the driveshaft.**

6. Install the rear driveshaft. Tighten the center bearing retainers to 26 ft. lbs. (35 Nm).
7. Lower the vehicle and road test to ensure proper operation.

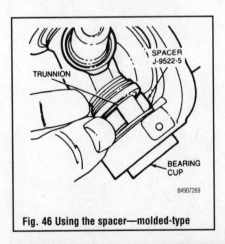

Fig. 46 Using the spacer—molded-type

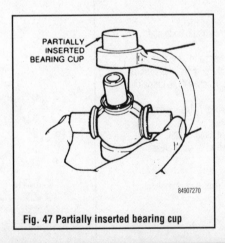

Fig. 47 Partially inserted bearing cup

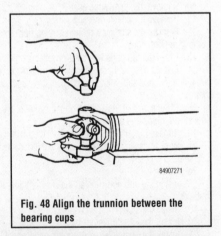

Fig. 48 Align the trunnion between the bearing cups

SOLID FRONT DRIVE AXLE

The 10/15 series and 20/25 series trucks use a GMC 8½ in. ring gear axle. The 30/35 series trucks use a Dana 60, 9¾ in. ring gear axle.

Manual Locking Hubs

The engagement and disengagement of the hubs is a manual operation which must be performed at each hub assembly. The hubs should be placed FULLY in either Lock or Free position or damage will result.

❋❋ WARNING

Do not place the transfer case in either 4-wheel mode unless the hubs are in the Lock position!

Locking hubs should be run in the Lock position periodically for a few miles to assure proper differential lubrication.

REMOVAL & INSTALLATION

▶ **See Figure 49**

➡ **This procedure requires snapring pliers. It cannot be performed properly without them!**

1. Raise and support the front end on jackstands.
2. Remove the wheels.
3. Lock the hubs. Remove the outer retaining plate, Allen head bolts and take off the plate, O-ring, and knob assembly.

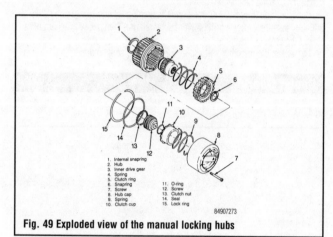

1. Internal snapring
2. Hub
3. Inner drive gear
4. Spring
5. Clutch ring
6. Snapring
7. Screw
8. Hub cap
9. Spring
10. Clutch cup
11. O-ring
12. Screw
13. Clutch nut
14. Seal
15. Lock ring

84907273

Fig. 49 Exploded view of the manual locking hubs

➡ **These bolts may have washers. Don't lose them!**

4. Remove the external snapring from the axle shaft.
5. Remove the compression spring.
6. Remove the clutch cup.
7. Remove the O-ring and dial screw.
8. Remove the clutch nut and seal.
9. Remove the large internal snapring from the wheel hub.
10. Remove the inner drive gear.
11. Remove the clutch ring and spring.
12. Remove the smaller internal snapring from the clutch hub body and remove the hub body.
13. Clean all hub parts in a safe, non-flammable solvent and wipe them dry.
14. Inspect each component for wear or damage. Make sure that the springs are functional and stiff. Make sure that all gear teeth are intact, with no chips or burrs.
15. Make sure that the splines on the inside of the wheel hub are clean and free of dirt, chips and burrs.
16. Surface irregularities can be cleaned up with light filing or emery paper.
17. Prior to assembly, coat all parts with the same wheel bearing grease you've used on the wheel bearings.

To install:
18. Install the hub body. Install the smaller internal snapring in the clutch hub body.
19. Install the clutch ring and spring.
20. Install the inner drive gear.
21. Install the large internal snapring in the wheel hub.
22. Install the external snapring on the axle shaft. If the snapring groove is not completely visible, reach around, inside the knuckle and push the axle shaft outwards.
23. Install the clutch nut and seal.
24. Install the O-ring and dial screw.
25. Install the clutch cup.
26. Install the compression spring.
27. Place the hub dial in the Lock position.
28. Coat the hub dial assembly O-ring with wheel bearing grease and position the hub dial and retainer on the hub.
29. Install the Allen head bolts. Make sure that you used any washers that were there originally. Tighten these bolts to 45 inch lbs. (5 Nm).

30. Rotate the hub dial to the free position and turn the wheel hubs to make sure that the axle is free.
31. Install the wheels.

Automatic Locking Hubs

REMOVAL & INSTALLATION

▶ **See Figure 50**

The following procedure covers removal & installation only, for the hub assembly. The hub should be disassembled ONLY if overhaul is necessary. In that event, an overhaul kit will be required. Follow the instructions in the overhaul kit to rebuild the hub.

1. Remove the capscrews and washer from the hub cap.
2. Remove the hub cap and spring.
3. Remove the bearing race, bearing and retainer.
4. Remove the keeper from the outer clutch housing.
5. Remove the large snapring to release the locking unit. The snapring is removed by squeezing the ears of the snapring with needle-nose pliers.
6. Remove the locking unit from the hub. You can make this job easier by threading 2 hub cap screws into the outer clutch housing and hold these to pull out the unit.

To install:
7. Wipe clean all parts and check for wear or damage.
8. Coat all parts with the same wheel bearing grease you've used on the bearings.
9. Position the locking unit in the hub and install the large snapring. Pull outward on the unit to make sure the snapring is fully seated in its groove.
10. Install the keepers.
11. Install the bearing retainer, bearing and race. Make sure that the bearing is fully pack with grease.
12. Coat the hub cap O-ring with wheel bearing grease and install the hub cap.
13. Install the capscrews and washers. Tighten the screws to 45 inch lbs. (5 Nm).

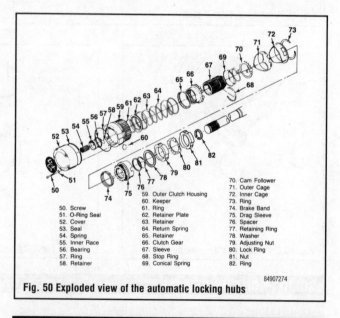

50. Screw
51. O-Ring Seal
52. Cover
53. Seal
54. Spring
55. Inner Race
56. Bearing
57. Ring
58. Retainer
59. Outer Clutch Housing
60. Keeper
61. Ring
62. Retainer Plate
63. Retainer
64. Return Spring
65. Retainer
66. Clutch Gear
67. Sleeve
68. Stop Ring
69. Conical Spring
70. Cam Follower
71. Outer Cage
72. Inner Cage
73. Ring
74. Brake Band
75. Drag Sleeve
76. Spacer
77. Retaining Ring
78. Washer
79. Adjusting Nut
80. Lock Ring
81. Nut
82. Ring

84907274

Fig. 50 Exploded view of the automatic locking hubs

Axle Shaft

REMOVAL & INSTALLATION

▶ **See Figures 51 and 52**

1. Raise and support the front end on jackstands.
2. Remove the wheel.

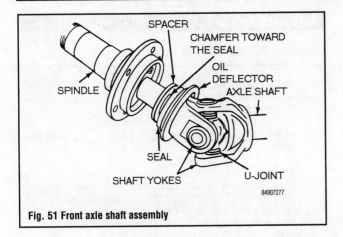

Fig. 51 Front axle shaft assembly

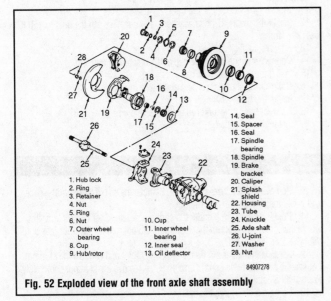

14. Seal
15. Spacer
16. Seal
17. Spindle bearing
18. Spindle
19. Brake bracket
20. Caliper
21. Splash shield
22. Housing
23. Tube
24. Knuckle
25. Axle shaft
26. U-joint
27. Washer
28. Nut

1. Hub lock
2. Ring
3. Retainer
4. Nut
5. Ring
6. Nut
7. Outer wheel bearing
8. Cup
9. Hub/rotor
10. Cup
11. Inner wheel bearing
12. Inner seal
13. Oil deflector

Fig. 52 Exploded view of the front axle shaft assembly

3. Remove the locking hub.
4. Remove the hub and bearing assembly. Refer to the procedures in this section.
5. Remove the nuts and remove the caliper mounting bracket and splash shield.
6. Tap the end of the spindle with a plastic mallet to break it loose from the knuckle. If tapping won't break it loose, you'll have to do the following:
   a. Thread the bearing locknut part way onto the spindle.
   b. Position a 2 or 3-jawed pull with the jaws grabbing the locknut and the screw bearing in the end of the axle shaft.
   c. Tighten the puller until the spindle breaks free. It will be very helpful to

spray Liquid Wrench®, WD-40® or similar solvent around the spindle mating area and around the bolt holes. As the puller is tightened, tap the spindle with the plastic mallet. This often helps break the spindle loose.
7. Pull out the axle shaft assembly.

To install:
8. Place the spacer and a new seal on the axle shaft.

➡ **The spacer's chamfer points towards the oil deflector.**

9. Pack the spindle bearing with wheel bearing grease.
10. Slide the axle shaft into the housing. When installing the axle shaft, turn the shaft slowly to align the splines with the differential.
11. Place the spindle on the knuckle. Be sure the seal and oil deflector are in place.
12. Install the caliper bracket and splash shield.
13. Using new washers, install the nuts and tighten them to 65 ft. lbs. (88 Nm).
14. Install the hub and rotor assembly. Adjust the wheel bearings.
15. Install the locking hubs.
16. Install the caliper and then install the wheel.

AXLE SHAFT U-JOINT OVERHAUL

◆ **See Figures 51 and 52**

1. Remove the axle shaft.
2. Squeeze the ends of the trunnion bearings in a vise to relieve the load on the snaprings. Remove the snaprings.
3. Support the yoke in a vise and drive on one end of the trunnion bearing with a brass drift enough to drive the opposite bearing from the yoke.
4. Support the other side of the yoke and drive the other bearing out.
5. Remove the trunnion.
6. Clean and check all parts. You can buy U-joint repair kits to replace all the worn parts.
7. Lubricate the bearings with wheel bearing grease.
8. Replace the trunnion and press the bearings into the yoke and over the trunnion hubs far enough to install the lock rings.
9. Hold the trunnion in one hand and tap the yoke lightly to seat the bearings against the lock rings.
10. The axle slingers can be pressed off the shaft.

➡ **Always replace the slingers if the spindle seals are replaced.**

11. Replace the shaft.

Pinion Seal

REMOVAL & INSTALLATION

◆ **See Figures 53, 54, 55 and 56**

➡ **The following special tools, or their equivalents, are required for this procedure: J–8614–1, J–8614–2, J–8614–3, and J–22804.**

1. Raise the vehicle and support it with jackstands.
2. Remove the driveshaft.

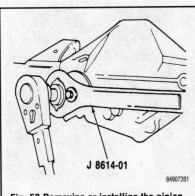

Fig. 53 Removing or installing the pinion nut

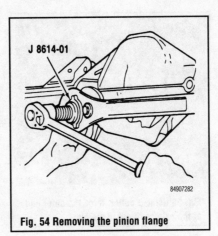

Fig. 54 Removing the pinion flange

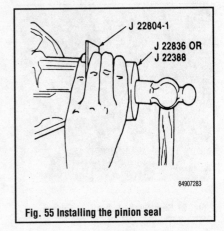

Fig. 55 Installing the pinion seal

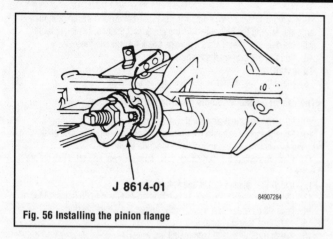

J 8614-01

84907284

Fig. 56 Installing the pinion flange

3. Using a Holding Bar Tool J–8614–1, attached to the pinion shaft flange, remove the self locking nut and washer from the pinion shaft.

4. Install Tool J–8614–2, and 3 into the holding bar and remove the flange from the drive pinion. Remove the drive pinion from the carrier.

5. With a long drift, tap on the inner race of the outer pinion bearing to remove the seal.

To install:

6. Install the oil seal, gasket and using Tool J–22804 install the oil seal.

7. Install the flange, washer and nut and tighten the nut to 270 ft. lbs. (366 Nm) for the GMC axle; 255 ft. lbs. (346 Nm) for the Dana axle.

8. Install the driveshaft and lower the vehicle.

INDEPENDENT FRONT DRIVE AXLE

Drive Axle Shaft, Hub and Bearing

REMOVAL & INSTALLATION

♦ **See Figures 57 thru 66**

1. Raise and support the front end on jackstands.
2. Remove the wheel.
3. Remove the skid plate.
4. Remove the hub nut and washer. Insert a long drift or dowel through the vanes in the brake rotor to hold the rotor in place. Be careful!
5. Loosen, but do not remove (yet!) the axle shaft inner flange bolts.
6. Remove the brake pipe and wire support brackets from the upper control arm.
7. If equipped, unplug the wheel speed sensor electrical connection.
8. Disconnect the tie rod end from the steering knuckle. Push the linkage to the other side of the truck and secure it out of the way.
9. Disconnect the lower shock absorber mounting bolt and swivel it out of the way.

Axle Housing

REMOVAL & INSTALLATION

1. Raise and support the vehicle safely.
2. Support the axle with a hydraulic jack.
3. Matchmark and remove the driveshaft.
4. Disconnect the connecting rod from the steering arm.
5. Disconnect the brake caliper and position it out of the way, without disconnecting the brake line.
6. Disconnect the shock absorbers from the axle brackets.
7. Remove the front stabilizer bar.
8. Disconnect the axle vent tube clip at the differential housing.
9. Take up the weight of the axle assembly using a suitable jack.
10. Remove the nuts, washers, U-bolts and plates from the axle and separate the axle from the springs. Remove the axle assembly from the vehicle.

To install:

11. Position the axle under the truck.
12. Install the plates, U-bolts, washers, and nuts. Tighten the nuts to 150 ft. lbs. (203 Nm).
13. Remove the jack.
14. Connect the axle vent tube clip at the differential housing.
15. Install the front stabilizer bar.
16. Connect the shock absorbers at the axle brackets.
17. Install the brake caliper
18. Connect the connecting rod at the steering arm.
19. Install the driveshaft.

10. Remove the stabilizer bar clamp. Remove the stabilizer bar bolt, spacer and bushings at the lower control arm.

11. Position a floor jack under the spring seat and lower control arm, this will relieve spring tension on the upper arm. Do not remove the floor jack until the drive axle is reinstalled.

12. Remove the cotter pin on the upper ball joint and **loosen** the stud nut. Loosen the stud from the control arm and then remove the stud nut completely. Press the ball stud out of the knuckle.

13. Using a puller, force the outer end of the axle shaft out of the hub. Remove the inboard flange bolts and the remove the drive axle.

❊❊ WARNING

Never allow the vehicle to rest on the wheels with the axle shaft removed!

To install:

14. Position the shaft in the hub and install the washer and hub nut finger tight. Install the inner flange bolts finger tight.

15. Connect the upper ball joint to the knuckle and tighten the stud nut to 75 ft. lbs. (100 Nm). Install a new cotter pin.

87987P09

Fig. 57 Remove the hub nut and washer

87987P10

Fig. 58 Using a puller, force the outer end of the axle shaft out of the hub

87987P11

Fig. 59 Matchmark the flange

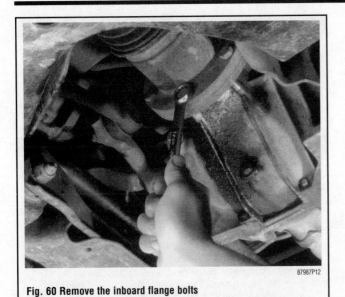

Fig. 60 Remove the inboard flange bolts

Fig. 61 Remove the drive axle from the vehicle

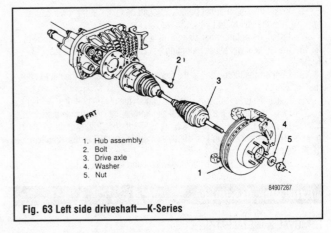

1. Hub assembly
2. Bolt
3. Drive axle
4. Washer
5. Nut

Fig. 63 Left side driveshaft—K-Series

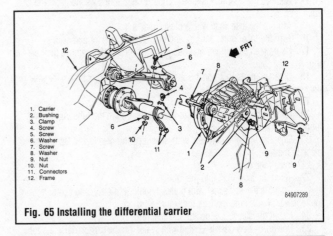

Fig. 64 Installing the shaft seal

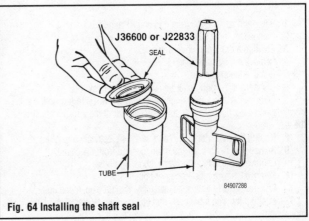

1. Carrier
2. Bushing
3. Clamp
4. Screw
5. Screw
6. Washer
7. Screw
8. Washer
9. Nut
10. Nut
11. Connectors
12. Frame

Fig. 65 Installing the differential carrier

1. Axle shaft
2. Deflector
3. Seal
4. Bearing
5. Axle tube
6. Bolt
7. Thrust washer
8. Connector
9. Snapring
10. Sleeve
11. Indicator switch
12. Thermal actuator
13. Spring
14. Clip
15. Shift fork
16. Damper spring
17. Shift shaft
18. Bolt
19. Shim
20. Pilot bearing
21. Output shaft
22. Carrier case
23. Carrier bushing
24. Fill plug
25. Drain plug
26. Washer
27. Seal
28. Snapring
29. Deflector
30. Output shaft

Fig. 62 Exploded view of the front axle—K-Series

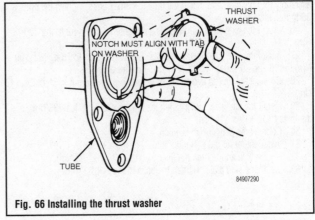

NOTCH MUST ALIGN WITH TAB ON WASHER

THRUST WASHER

TUBE

Fig. 66 Installing the thrust washer

16. Install the stabilizer bar bolt, spacer and bushings at the lower control arm. Tighten the bolt to 24 ft. lbs. (33 Nm).

17. Install the stabilizer bar clamp. Tighten the bolts to 12 ft. lbs. (16 Nm).

18. Install the lower shock mounting bolt and tighten it to 54 ft. lbs. (73 Nm).

19. Connect the tie rod end at the steering knuckle. Tighten the nut to 35 ft. lbs. (47 Nm).

20. Install the brake support pipe and tighten the nut to 13 ft. lbs. (17 Nm).

21. Insert a drift into the brake rotor and tighten the inner flange bolts to 59 ft. lbs. (80 Nm). Tighten the outer hub nut to 173 ft. lbs. (235 Nm) on 1988–91 models, 180 ft. lbs. (245 Nm) on 1992–95 models and 165 ft. lbs. (225 Nm) on 1996–98 models. Remove the drift.

22. Install the skid plate. Install the wheels and lower the truck.

Axle Tube Assembly

REMOVAL & INSTALLATION

1. Raise and support the front end on jackstands.
2. Remove the right wheel.
3. Position a drain pan under the axle.
4. Remove the stabilizer bar.
5. Remove the skid plate.
6. Disconnect the right inner tie rod end at the relay rod.
7. Remove the axle shaft flange bolts, turn the wheel to loosen the axle from the axle tube, push the axle towards the front of the truck and tie it out of the way.
8. Unplug the indicator switch and actuator electrical connectors.
9. Remove the drain plug and drain the fluid from the case.
10. Remove the axle tube-to-frame mounting bolts.
11. Remove the axle tube-to-carrier bolts.
12. Remove the axle tube/shaft assembly. Keep the open end up.
13. Position the axle tube, open end up, in a vise by clamping on the mounting flange.
14. Remove the snapring, sleeve, connector and thrust washer from the shaft end.
15. Tap out the axle shaft with a plastic mallet.
16. Turn the tube, outer end up, and pry out the deflector and seal.
17. Using a slide hammer and bearing remover adapter, remove the bearing.
18. Clean all parts in a non-flammable solvent and inspect them for wear or damage. Clean off all old gasket material.
To install:
19. Using a bearing driver, install the new bearing in the tube. Apply axle lubricant to the bearing.
20. Coat the lips of a new seal with wheel bearing grease and tap it into place in the tube.
21. Install the deflector.
22. Insert the axle shaft into the tube.
23. Coat the thrust washer with grease to hold it in place and position it on the tube end. Make sure the tabs index the slots.
24. Install the sleeve, connector and snapring.
25. Position a new gasket, coated with sealer, on the carrier. Raise the tube assembly into position and install the tube-to-carrier bolts. Tighten the bolts to 30 ft. lbs. (40 Nm).
26. Install the axle shaft flange bolts and tighten them to 59 ft. lbs. (80 Nm).
27. Install the axle tube-to-frame bolts. Tighten the nuts to 75 ft. lbs. (100 Nm) for 15 and 25 series; 107 ft. lbs. (145 Nm) for 35 series.
28. Connect the tie rod end to the relay rod. Tighten the nut to 35 ft. lbs. (47 Nm).
29. Install the stabilizer bar. Tighten the brackets to 24 ft. lbs. (33 Nm), and the links to 12 ft. lbs. (16 Nm).
30. Connect the actuator and switch.
31. Install the drain plug. Tighten it to 24 ft. lbs. (33 Nm).
32. Fill the axle and tighten the filler plug to 24 ft. lbs. (33 Nm).
33. Install the skid plate. Tighten the bolts to 25 ft. lbs. (34 Nm).

Differential Pilot Bearing

REMOVAL & INSTALLATION

1. Remove the right side axle shaft tube/shaft assembly.
2. Remove the shim and pilot bearing from the carrier.
3. Dip the new bearing in axle fluid. Installation is the reverse of removal.

Output Shaft

REMOVAL & INSTALLATION

1. Raise and support the front end on jackstands.
2. Drain the axle.
3. Remove the left side axle shaft.
4. Remove the lower carrier mounting bolt.
5. CAREFULLY pry against the lower part of the carrier to provide clearance for the output shaft removal. While prying, insert a prybar between the output shaft flange and the carrier case. Pry the output shaft free. BE CAREFUL! It's possible to damage the carrier if you pry too hard.
6. Remove the deflector and seal from the carrier.
To install:
7. Lubricate the lips of a new seal with wheel bearing grease and drive it into place.
8. Install the deflector.
9. Pry against the case and position the output shaft in the carrier. Tap it into place with a plastic mallet.
10. Install the lower carrier mounting bolt, washer and nut. Tighten the bolt to 80 ft. lbs. (110 Nm).
11. Install the left axle shaft.
12. Fill the axle.

Pinion Seal

REMOVAL & INSTALLATION

▶ See Figures 67 and 68

1. Raise and support the front end on jackstands.
2. Matchmark and disconnect the front driveshaft at the carrier.
3. Remove the wheels.
4. Dismount the calipers and wire them up, out of the way.
5. Position an inch pound torque wrench on the pinion nut. Measure the torque needed to rotate the pinion one full revolution. Record the figure.
6. Matchmark the pinion flange, shaft and nut. Count and record the number of exposed threads on the pinion shaft.
7. Hold the flange and remove the nut and washer.

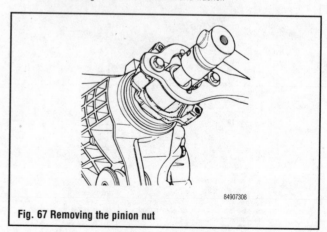

84907308

Fig. 67 Removing the pinion nut

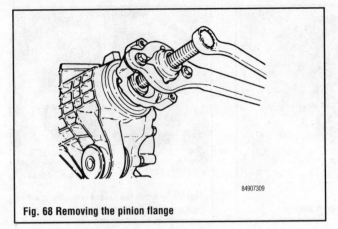

84907309

Fig. 68 Removing the pinion flange

8. Using a puller, remove the flange.

9. Carefully pry the seal from its bore. Be careful to avoid scratching the seal bore.

10. Remove the deflector from the flange.

To install:

11. Clean the seal bore thoroughly.

12. Remove any burrs from the deflector staking on the flange.

13. Tap the deflector onto the flange and stake it in three places.

14. Position the new seal in the carrier bore and drive it into place until flush. Coat the seal lips with wheel bearing grease.

15. Coat the outer edge of the flange neck with wheel bearing grease and slide it onto the pinion shaft.

16. Place a new nut and washer onto the pinion shaft and tighten it to the position originally recorded. That is, the alignment marks are aligned, and the recorded number of threads are exposed on the pinion shaft.

✳✳ WARNING

Never hammer the flange onto the pinion!

17. Measure the rotating torque of the pinion. Compare this to the original torque. Tighten the pinion nut, in small increments, until the rotating torque is 3 inch lbs. (0.35 Nm) GREATER than the original torque.

18. Install the driveshaft.

19. Install the calipers and install the wheels.

REAR AXLE

Axle Shaft, Bearing, and Seal

REMOVAL & INSTALLATION

Semi-Floating Axles

EXCEPT LOCKING DIFFERENTIAL

▶ **See Figures 69 thru 74**

1. Support the axle on jackstands.

2. Remove the wheels and brake drums.

3. Clean off the differential cover area, loosen the cover to drain the lubricant, and remove the cover.

4. Turn the differential until you can reach the differential pinion shaft lockscrew. Remove the lockscrew and the pinion shaft.

5. Push in on the axle end. Remove the C-lock from the inner (button) end of the shaft.

6. Remove the shaft, being careful of the oil seal.

7. You can pry the oil seal out of the housing by placing the inner end of the axle shaft behind the steel case of the seal, then prying it out carefully.

8. A puller or a slide hammer is required to remove the bearing from the housing.

Differential Carrier

REMOVAL & INSTALLATION

1. Raise and support the front end on jackstands.

2. Remove the wheels.

3. Remove the skid plate.

4. Drain the carrier.

5. Matchmark and remove the front driveshaft.

6. Disconnect the right axle shaft at the tube flange.

7. Disconnect the left axle shaft at the carrier flange.

8. Wire both axle shafts out of the way.

9. Unplug the connectors at the indicator switch and actuator.

10. Disconnect the carrier vent hose.

11. Remove the axle tube-to-frame bolts, washers and nuts.

12. Remove the lower carrier mounting bolt.

13. Disconnect the right side inner tie rod end at the relay rod.

14. Depending on the model, it may be necessary to remove the engine oil filter.

15. Support the carrier on a floor jack

16. Remove the upper carrier mounting bolt.

17. Lower the carrier assembly from the truck.

To install:

18. Raise the carrier into position.

19. Install the upper carrier mounting bolt, washers and nut. Then, install the lower carrier mounting bolt, washers and nut. Tighten the bolts to 80 ft. lbs. (110 Nm).

20. Remove the jack.

21. Install the oil filter.

22. Connect the tie rod end. Tighten the nut to 35 ft. lbs. (47 Nm).

23. Install the axle tube-to-frame bolts, washers and nuts. Tighten the nuts to 75 ft. lbs. (100 Nm) for 15 and 25 series; 107 ft. lbs. (145 Nm) for 35 series.

24. Connect the vent hose.

25. Connect the wiring.

26. Connect the axle shafts at the flanges. Tighten the bolts to 59 ft. lbs. (80 Nm).

27. Connect the driveshaft. Tighten the bolts to 15 ft. lbs. (20 Nm).

28. Fill the carrier with gear oil.

29. Install the wheels.

30. Add any engine oil lost when the filter was removed.

To install:

9. Pack the new or reused bearing with wheel bearing grease and lubricate the cavity between the seal lips with the same grease.

10. The bearing has to be driven into the housing. Don't use a drift, you might cock the bearing in its bore. Use a piece of pipe or a large socket instead. Drive only on the outer bearing race. In a similar manner, drive the seal in flush with the end of the tube.

11. Slide the shaft into place, turning it slowly until the splines are engaged with the differential. Be careful of the oil seal.

12. Install the C-lock on the inner axle end. Pull the shaft out so that the C-lock seats in the counterbore of the differential side gear.

13. Position the differential pinion shaft through the case and the pinion gears, aligning the lockscrew hole. Install the lockscrew.

14. Install the cover with a new gasket and tighten the bolts evenly in a criss-cross pattern.

15. Fill the axle with lubricant.

16. Replace the brake drums and wheels.

LOCKING DIFFERENTIAL

▶ **See Figures 75 and 76**

This axle uses a thrust block on the differential pinion shaft.

1. Support the axle on jackstands.

2. Remove the wheels and brake drums.

Fig. 69 Remove the differential pinion shaft lockscrew

Fig. 70 Remove the pinion shaft

Fig. 71 Remove the C-lock from the inner (button) end of the shaft

Fig. 72 Remove the axle shaft from the vehicle

Fig. 73 Use a puller to remove the oil seal

Fig. 74 Install the oil seal using a seal installer

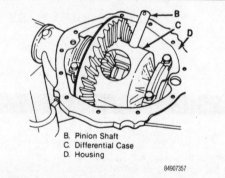

B. Pinion Shaft
C. Differential Case
D. Housing

Fig. 75 Positioning the case for the best clearance—semi-floating axle w/locking differential

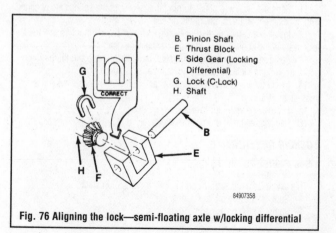

B. Pinion Shaft
E. Thrust Block
F. Side Gear (Locking Differential)
G. Lock (C-Lock)
H. Shaft

Fig. 76 Aligning the lock—semi-floating axle w/locking differential

3. Clean off the differential cover area, loosen the cover to drain the lubricant, and remove the cover.

4. Rotate the differential case so that you can remove the lockscrew and support the pinion shaft so it can't fall into the housing. Remove the differential pinion shaft lockscrew.

5. Carefully pull the pinion shaft partway out and rotate the differential case until the shaft touches the housing at the top.

6. Use a screwdriver to position the C-lock with its open end directly inward. You can't push in the axle shaft till you do this.

7. Push the axle shaft in and remove the C-lock.

8. Remove the shaft, being careful of the oil seal.

9. You can pry the oil seal out of the housing by placing the inner end of the axle shaft behind the steel case of the seal, then prying it out carefully.

10. A puller or a slide hammer is required to remove the bearing from the housing.

To install:

11. Pack the new or reused bearing with wheel bearing grease and lubricate the cavity between the seal lips with the same grease.

12. The bearing has to be driven into the housing. Don't use a drift, you might cock the bearing in its bore. Use a piece of pipe or a large socket instead. Drive only on the outer bearing race. In a similar manner, drive the seal in flush with the end of the tube.

13. Slide the shaft into place, turning it slowly until the splines are engaged with the differential. Be careful of the oil seal.

14. Keep the pinion shaft partway out of the differential case while installing the C-lock on the axle shaft. Put the C-lock on the axle shaft and carefully pull out on the axle shaft until the C-lock is clear of the thrust block.

15. Position the differential pinion shaft through the case and the pinion gears, aligning the lockscrew hole. Install the lockscrew.

16. Install the cover with a new gasket and tighten the bolts evenly in a criss-cross pattern.

17. Fill the axle with lubricant.

18. Replace the brake drums and wheels.

Full-Floating Axles

◗ **See Figures 77 thru 83**

The procedures are the same for locking and non-locking axles.

The best way to remove the bearings from the wheel hub is with an arbor press. Use of a press reduces the chances of damaging the bearing races, cocking the bearing in its bore, or scoring the hub walls. A local machine shop is probably equipped with the tools to remove and install bearings and seals. However, if one is not available, the hammer and drift method outlined can be used.

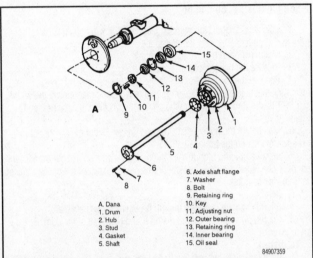

A. Dana
1. Drum
2. Hub
3. Stud
4. Gasket
5. Shaft
6. Axle shaft flange
7. Washer
8. Bolt
9. Retaining ring
10. Key
11. Adjusting nut
12. Outer bearing
13. Retaining ring
14. Inner bearing
15. Oil seal

84907359

Fig. 77 Exploded view of the axle, hub and drum assembly—full-floating axle, 9¾ and 10½ in.

1. Support the axles on jackstands.
2. Remove the wheels.
3. Remove the bolts and lock washers that attach the axle shaft flange to the hub.
4. Rap on the flange with a soft faced hammer to loosen the shaft. Grip the rib on the end of the flange with a pair of locking pliers and twist to start shaft removal. Remove the shaft from the axle tube.
5. The hub and drum assembly must be removed to remove the bearings and oil seals. You will need a large socket to remove and later adjust the bearing adjustment nut. There are also special tools available.
6. Disengage the tang of the locknut retainer from the slot or slat of the locknut, then remove the locknut from the housing tube.
7. Disengage the tang of the retainer from the slot or flat of the adjusting nut and remove the retainer from the housing tube.
8. Remove the adjusting nut from the housing tube.
9. Remove the thrust washer from the housing tube.
10. Pull the hub and drum straight off the axle housing.
11. Remove the oil seal and discard.
12. Use a hammer and a long drift to knock the inner bearing, cup, and oil seal from the hub assembly.
13. Remove the outer bearing snapring with a pair of pliers. It may be necessary to tap the bearing outer race away from the retaining ring slightly by tapping on the ring to remove the ring.
14. Drive the outer bearing from the hub with a hammer and drift.

To install:

15. Place the outer bearing into the hub. The larger outside diameter of the bearing should face the outer end of the hub. Drive the bearing into the hub using a washer that will cover both the inner and outer races of the bearing. Place a socket on top of this washer, then drive the bearing into place with a series of light taps. If available, an arbor press should be used for this job.
16. Drive the bearing past the snapring groove, and install the snapring. Then, turning the hub assembly over, drive the bearing back against the snapring. Protect the bearing by placing a washer on top of it. You can use the thrust washer that fits between the bearing and the adjusting nut for the job.

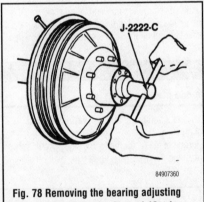

J-2222-C

84907360

Fig. 78 Removing the bearing adjusting nut—full-floating axle, 9¾ and 10½ in.

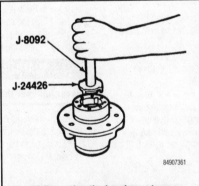

J-8092

J-24426

84907361

Fig. 79 Removing the bearing outer cup—full-floating axle, 9¾ and 10½ in.

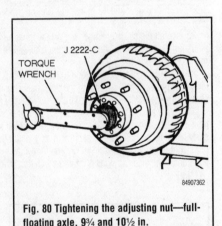

TORQUE WRENCH

J 2222-C

84907362

Fig. 80 Tightening the adjusting nut—full-floating axle, 9¾ and 10½ in.

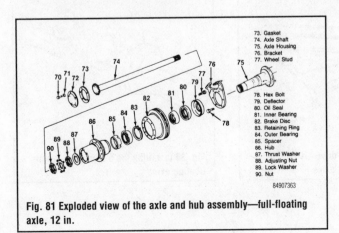

73. Gasket
74. Axle Shaft
75. Axle Housing
76. Bracket
77. Wheel Stud
78. Hex Bolt
79. Deflector
80. Oil Seal
81. Inner Bearing
82. Brake Disc
83. Retaining Ring
84. Outer Bearing
85. Spacer
86. Hub
87. Thrust Washer
88. Adjusting Nut
89. Lock Washer
90. Nut

84907363

Fig. 81 Exploded view of the axle and hub assembly—full-floating axle, 12 in.

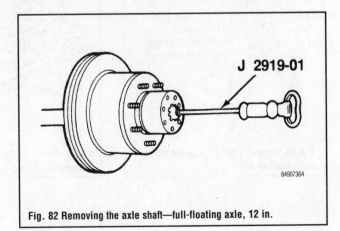

J 2919-01

84907364

Fig. 82 Removing the axle shaft—full-floating axle, 12 in.

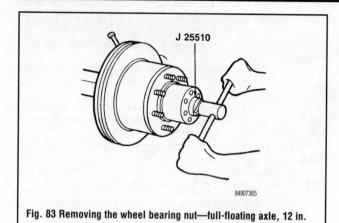

Fig. 83 Removing the wheel bearing nut—full-floating axle, 12 in.

17. Place the inner bearing into the hub. The thick edge should be toward the shoulder in the hub. Press the bearing into the hub until it seats against the shoulder, using a washer and socket as outlined earlier. Make certain that the bearing is not cocked and that it is fully seated on the shoulder.

18. Pack the cavity between the oil seal lips with wheel bearing grease, and position it in the hub bore. Carefully press it into place on top of the inner bearing.

19. Pack the wheel bearings with grease, and lightly coat the inside diameter of the hub bearing contact surface and the outside diameter of the axle housing tube.

20. Make sure that the inner bearing, oil seal, axle housing oil deflector, and outer bearing are properly positioned. Install the hub and drum assembly on the axle housing, being careful so as not to damage the oil seal or dislocate other internal components.

21. Install the thrust washer so that the tang on the inside diameter of the washer is in the keyway on the axle housing.

22. Install the adjusting nut. Tighten to 50 ft. lbs. (68 Nm) while rotating the hub. Back off the nut ¼ turn and retighten to 35 ft. lbs. (47 Nm) on models with the 11 inch ring gear and 13 ft. lbs. (17 Nm) on models with the 10 ½ inch ring gear.

23. Install the tanged retainer against the inner adjusting nut. Align the adjusting nut so that the short tang of the retainer will engage the nearest slot on the adjusting nut.

24. Install the outer locknut and tighten to 65 ft. lbs. (88 Nm). Bend the long tang of the retainer into the slot of the outer nut. This method of adjustment should provide 0.001–0.010 in. (0.0254–0.254mm) end-play.

25. Place a new gasket over the axle shaft and position the axle shaft in the housing so that the shaft splines enter the differential side gear. Position the gasket so that the holes are in alignment, and install the flange-to-hub attaching bolts. Tighten to 115 ft. lbs. (156 Nm) on models with the 10 ½ inch ring gear and tighten the axle cap bolts on models with the 11 inch ring gear to 15 ft. lbs. (20 Nm).

➡ To prevent lubricant from leaking through the flange holes, apply a non-hardening sealer to the bolt threads. Use the sealer sparingly.

26. Replace the wheels.

Pinion Seal

REMOVAL & INSTALLATION

Semi-Floating Axles

♦ See Figures 84, 85 and 86

1. Raise and support the truck on jackstands. It would help to have the front end slightly higher than the rear to avoid fluid loss.

2. Matchmark and remove the driveshaft.

3. Release the parking brake.

4. Remove the rear wheels. Rotate the rear wheels by hand to make sure that there is absolutely no brake drag. If there is brake drag, remove the drums.

5. Using a torque wrench on the pinion nut, record the force needed to rotate the pinion.

6. Matchmark the pinion shaft, nut and flange. Count the number of exposed threads on the pinion shaft.

7. Install a holding tool on the pinion. A very large adjustable wrench will do, or, if one is not available, put the drums back on and set the parking brake as tightly as possible.

8. Remove the pinion nut.

9. Slide the flange off of the pinion. A puller may be necessary.

10. Centerpunch the oil seal to distort it and pry it out of the bore. Be careful to avoid scratching the bore.

To install:

11. Pack the cavity between the lips of the seal with lithium-based chassis lube.

12. Position the seal in the bore and carefully drive it into place. A seal installer is VERY helpful in doing this.

13. Pack the cavity between the end of the pinion splines and the pinion flange with Permatex No.2₂ sealer, or equivalent non-hardening sealer.

14. Place the flange on the pinion and push it on as far as it will go.

15. Install the pinion washer and nut on the shaft and force the pinion into place by turning the nut.

✳✳ WARNING

Never hammer the flange into place!

16. Tighten the nut until the exact number of threads previously noted appear and the matchmarks align.

17. Measure the rotating torque of the pinion under the same circumstances as before. Compare the two readings. As necessary, tighten the pinion nut in

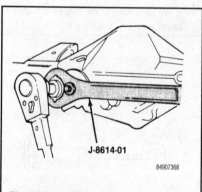

Fig. 84 Removing the drive pinion nut—semi-floating axles

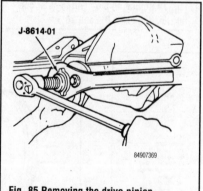

Fig. 85 Removing the drive pinion flange—semi-floating axles

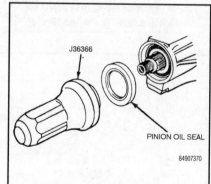

Fig. 86 Installing the pinion seal—semi-floating axles

VERY small increments until the torque necessary to rotate the pinion is 3 inch lbs. (0.35 Nm) higher than the originally recorded torque.

18. Install the driveshaft.

Full-Floating Axles

1. Raise and support the truck on jackstands. It would help to have the front end slightly higher than the rear to avoid fluid loss.
2. Matchmark and remove the driveshaft.
3. Matchmark the pinion shaft, nut and flange. Count the number of exposed threads on the pinion shaft.
4. Install a holding tool on the pinion. A very large adjustable wrench will do, or, if one is not available, set the parking brake as tightly as possible.
5. Remove the pinion nut.
6. Slide the flange off of the pinion. A puller may be necessary.
7. Centerpunch the oil seal to distort it and pry it out of the bore. Be careful to avoid scratching the bore.

To install:
8. Pack the cavity between the lips of the seal with lithium-based chassis lube.
9. Position the seal in the bore and carefully drive it into place. A seal installer is VERY helpful in doing this.
10. Place the flange on the pinion and push it on as far as it will go.

✳✳ WARNING

Never hammer the flange into place!

11. Install the pinion washer and nut on the shaft and force the pinion into place by turning the nut.
12. On models with the 11 inch ring gear, tighten the nut to 440–500 ft. lbs. (596–678 Nm).
13. On models with the 10 ½ inch ring gear Tighten the nut until the exact number of threads previously noted appear and the matchmarks align.
14. Install the driveshaft.

Axle Housing

REMOVAL & INSTALLATION

1. Raise and support the rear end on jackstands.
2. For the 9 ¾ in. ring gear and the 10 ½ in. ring gear axles, place jackstands under the frame side rails for support.
3. Drain the lubricant from the axle housing and remove the driveshaft.
4. Remove the wheel, the brake drum or hub and the drum assembly.
5. Disconnect the parking brake cable from the lever and at the brake flange plate.
6. Disconnect the hydraulic brake lines from the connectors.
7. Disconnect the shock absorbers from the axle brackets.
8. Remove the vent hose from the axle vent fitting (if used).
9. Disconnect the height sensing and brake proportional valve linkage (if used).
10. If used, remove the stabilizer shaft.
11. Support the axle assembly with a hydraulic jack.
12. Remove the nuts and washers from the U-bolts.
13. Remove the U-bolts, spring plates and spacers from the axle assembly.
14. Lower the jack and remove the axle assembly.

To install:
15. Raise the axle assembly into position.
16. Install the U-bolts, spring plates and spacers.
17. Install the nuts and washers on the U-bolts. Tighten the nuts to the specifications shown in the torque specification chart at the end of this section.
18. Install the remaining components in the reverse order of removal.
19. Fill the axle housing.

TORQUE SPECIFICATIONS

Components	Ft. Lbs.	Nm
Manual transmission		
Shifter housing bolts	89 inch lbs.	10
Transmission		
Except the NVG 4500 models transmission-to-engine bolts	35	47
NVG 4500 models transmission-to-housing bolts	74	100
Clutch		
Clutch bolts		
1988-94 models		
4.3L, 5.0L and 5.7L engines	22	30
6.2L and 6.5L engines	32	43
7.4L engines	24	33
1995-98 models		
Gasoline engines	30	41
Diesel engines	25	34
Clutch housing bolts		
1988-90 models		
R/V Series	40	54
C/K Series	55	75
1991 Models	31	43
1992-94 models	29	39
1995-98 models	23	31
Clutch Slave Cylinder		
Slave cylinder retainer		
1988-95 Models	13	18
1996-98 Models	71 inch lbs.	8
Automatic Transmission		
Transmission-to-engine bolts	35	47
Converter bolts		
Except 1996-98 models	50	68
1996-98 models	46	63
Transmission support brace bolts	35	47
Crossmember retainers		
Except 1991-98 models	35	47
1991-98 models	56	77
Transfer case-to-transmission attaching bolts	24	32
1988-94 4WD models		
Transfer case-to-frame bracket bolts	35	47
1988-94 4WD models		
Adapter-to-transfer case bolts		
1995-98 4WD models	33	45
Adapter-to-transmission bolts		
1995-98 4WD models	33	45
Shift Linkage		
Shift lever bolt or nut		
Except 4L80E	17	23
4L80E	20	30
Transfer case		
Front or Rear Output Shaft Seal		
Yoke nut		
NP205	150	203
NP208	120	163

TORQUE SPECIFICATIONS

Components	Ft. Lbs.	Nm
Transfer case (cont.)		
NP241	110	149
NVG243	110	149
BW 1370, BW 4401, BW 4470 front	165	225
BW 1370, BW 4401, BW 4470 rear	125	170
Transfer case-to-transmission adapter bolts		
Except NP208 transfer case and all 1996-98 models	24	32
NP208 transfer case	30	40
1996-98 models	33	45
Transmission end bolts (if equipped)	129	175
Transfer case end bolts (if equipped)	35	47
Driveline		
Front Driveshaft		
Solid Axle		
U-bolts	15	20
Flange bolts	75	101
Independent Axle		
Axle end flange bolts	15	20
Transfer case end flange bolts	75	101
Rear Driveshaft		
Except C 3500 HD models U-bolt or strap retainers	15	20
C3500 HD models U-bolt or strap retainers	27	37
Center Bearing retainers	26	35
Solid front drive axle		
Manual Locking Hubs		
Outer retaining plate Allen head bolts	45 inch lbs.	5
Automatic Locking Hubs		
Capscrews	45 inch lbs.	5
Pinion Seal nut		
GMC axle	270	366
Dana axle	255	346
Axle Housing		
U-bolt nuts	150	203
Independent front drive axle		
Drive Axle Shaft, Hub and Bearing		
Upper ball joint-to-knuckle stud nut	75	100
Stabilizer bar-to-lower control arm	24	33
Stabilizer bar clamp bolts	12	16
Lower shock absorber mounting bolt	54	73
Tie rod end-to-steering knuckle nut	35	47
Brake support pipe nut	13	17
Inner flange bolts	59	60
Outer hub nut		
1988-91 models	173	235
1992-95 models	180	245
1996-98 models	165	225
Axle Tube Assembly		

91027C02

TORQUE SPECIFICATIONS

Components	Ft. Lbs.	Nm
Driveline (cont.)		
Tie rod end-to-relay rod nut	35	47
Stabilizer bar		
Bracket retainers	24	33
Link retainers	12	16
Skid plate bolts	25	34
Differential Carrier		
Carrier mounting bolts	80	110
Axle tube-to-frame nuts		
15 and 25 series	75	100
35 series	107	145
Axle shafts-to-flange bolts	59	80
Driveshaft bolts	15	20
Rear axle		
Axle Shaft, Bearing, and Seal		
Adjusting nut	①	①
Outer locknut	65	88
Axle Housing		
U-bolt nuts		
R series		
Bolts facing up	125	170
Bolts facing down	147	200
C/K series		
100 and 200 models	81	110
300 models without dual rear wheels or 7.4L engine	81	110
300 models with dual rear wheels or 7.4L engine without dual rear wheels	109	148
3500 heavy duty models	207	280

① Tighten to 50 ft. lbs.(**68 Nm**) while rotating the hub, then back off the nut 1/4 turn

Models with the 10 1/2 inch ring gear retighten nut to 13 ft. lbs. 17 Nm

Models with the 11 inch ring gear models retighten nut to 35 ft. lbs. 47 Nm

91027C03

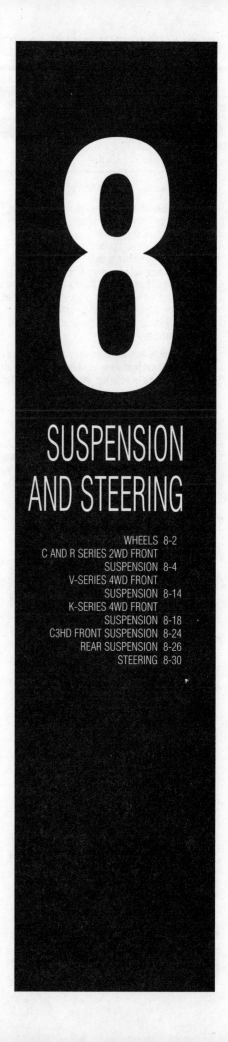

8

SUSPENSION AND STEERING

WHEELS

Wheels

REMOVAL & INSTALLATION

▶ **See Figures 1, 2, 3, 4, 5 and 6**

1. Park the vehicle on a level surface.
2. Remove the jack, tire iron and, if necessary, the spare tire from their storage compartments.
3. Refer to Section 1 of this manual for the jacking points on your vehicle. Then, place the jack in the proper position.
4. If equipped with an automatic transmission, place the selector lever in **P**; with a manual transmission, place the shifter in Reverse.
5. If equipped with a wheel cover or hub cap, insert the tapered end of the tire iron in the groove and pry off the cover.
6. Apply the parking brake and block the diagonally opposite wheel with a wheel chock or two.

➡ **Wheel chocks may be purchased at your local auto parts store, or a block of wood cut into wedges may be used. If possible, keep one or two of the chocks in your tire storage compartment, in case any of the tires has to be removed on the side of the road.**

7. With the tires still on the ground, use the tire iron/wrench to break the lug nuts loose.

➡ **If a nut is stuck, never use heat to loosen it or damage to the wheel and bearings may occur. If the nuts are seized, one or two heavy hammer blows directly on the end of the bolt usually loosens the rust. Be careful, as continued pounding will likely damage the brake drum or rotor.**

8. Using the jack, raise the vehicle until the tire is clear of the ground. Support the vehicle safely using jackstands.
9. Unfasten the lug nuts, then remove the tire and wheel assembly.

To install:
10. On models with single wheels perform the following steps for installation.
   a. Lift the wheel onto the lugs.
   b. Snug down the topmost nut, then snug down the rest of the nuts in a crisscross pattern.
   c. When all nuts are snugged, torque them, in a crisscross pattern, to the specifications listed at the end of this procedure.
11. On models with dual wheels perform the following steps for installation.
   a. Install the inner and outer wheels, and clamp ring. Be sure that the pins on the clamp ring face outwards.
   b. Install the nuts snugly, in a crisscross pattern. When all the lugs are snugged, tighten them in the sequence shown to the specifications listed in the specifications chart at the end of this section..

INSPECTION

Inspect the tires for lacerations, puncture marks, nails and other sharp objects. Repair or replace as necessary. Also check the tires for treadwear and air pressure as outlined in Section 1 of this manual. Check the wheel assemblies for dents, cracks, rust and metal fatigue. Repair or replace as necessary.

Wheel Lug Studs

REMOVAL & INSTALLATION

With Disc Brakes

▶ **See Figures 7, 8 and 9**

1. Raise and support the appropriate end of the vehicle safely using jackstands, then remove the wheel.

Fig. 1 The jack is sometimes stored under the hood on the inner fender. There may also be a decal showing jack operation and lifting point locations

Fig. 2 Use the tire iron to loosen the wheel trim cover

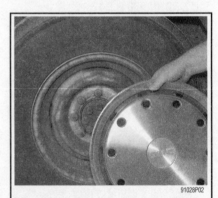

Fig. 3 Once loosened, remove the wheel trim cover from the wheel

Fig. 4 Use the tire iron to loosen the wheel lug nuts before raising the vehicle with the jack

Fig. 5 Place the jack at a suitable lifting point and raise the vehicle

A. Eight Stud Wheel
B. Ten Stud Wheel
C. Five Stud Wheel
D. Six Stud Wheel

Fig. 6 Wheel lug nut tightening sequence—all models

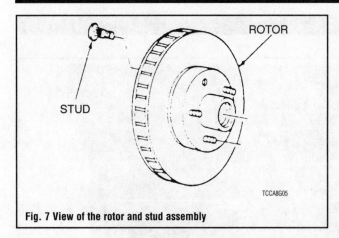

Fig. 7 View of the rotor and stud assembly

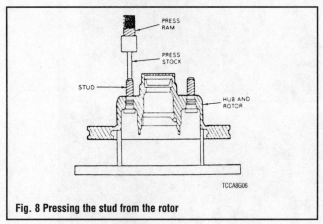

Fig. 8 Pressing the stud from the rotor

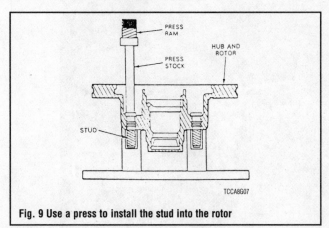

Fig. 9 Use a press to install the stud into the rotor

2. Remove the brake pads and caliper. Support the caliper aside using wire or a coat hanger. For details, please refer to Section 9 of this manual.

3. Remove the outer wheel bearing and lift off the rotor. For details on wheel bearing removal, installation and adjustment, please refer to Section 1 of this manual.

4. Properly support the rotor using press bars, then drive the stud out using an arbor press.

➡ **If a press is not available, CAREFULLY drive the old stud out using a blunt drift. MAKE SURE the rotor is properly and evenly supported or it may be damaged.**

To install:

5. Clean the stud hole with a wire brush and start the new stud with a hammer and drift pin. Do not use any lubricant or thread sealer.

6. Finish installing the stud with the press.

➡ **If a press is not available, start the lug stud through the bore in the hub, then position about 4 flat washers over the stud and thread the lug nut. Hold the hub/rotor while tightening the lug nut, and the stud should be drawn into position. MAKE SURE THE STUD IS FULLY SEATED, then remove the lug nut and washers.**

7. Install the rotor and adjust the wheel bearings.
8. Install the brake caliper and pads.
9. Install the remaining components.

With Drum Brakes

▶ **See Figures 10, 11 and 12**

1. Raise the vehicle and safely support it with jackstands, then remove the wheel.

2. Remove the brake drum.

3. If necessary to provide clearance, remove the brake shoes, as outlined in Section 9 of this manual.

4. Using a large C-clamp and socket, press the stud from the axle flange.

5. Coat the serrated part of the stud with liquid soap and place it into the hole.

To install:

6. Position about 4 flat washers over the stud and thread the lug nut. Hold the flange while tightening the lug nut, and the stud should be drawn into position. MAKE SURE THE STUD IS FULLY SEATED, then remove the lug nut and washers.

7. Install the remaining components.

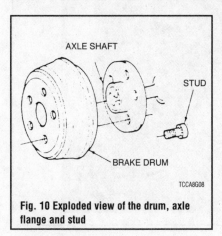

Fig. 10 Exploded view of the drum, axle flange and stud

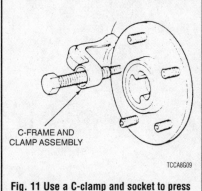

Fig. 11 Use a C-clamp and socket to press out the stud

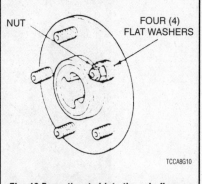

Fig. 12 Force the stud into the axle flange using washers and a lug nut

C AND R-SERIES 2WD FRONT SUSPENSION

STEERING AND FRONT SUSPENSION COMPONENT LOCATIONS—R-SERIES

1. Sway bar
2. Steering gear
3. Coil spring
4. Center link
5. Tie rod end
6. Steering knuckle
7. Lower ball joint
8. Lower control arm
9. Pitman arm
10. Upper control arm
11. Idler arm

STEERING AND FRONT SUSPENSION COMPONENT LOCATIONS—C SERIES

1. Steering gear
2. Sway bar
3. Pitman arm
4. Tie rod end
5. Lower ball joint
6. Lower control arm
7. Coil spring
8. Shock ab sorber
9. Upper control arm
10. Idler arm
11. Center link (relay rod)
12. Steering knuckle

Coil Spring

> ✳✳ **CAUTION**
>
> **Coil springs are under considerable tension. Be very careful when removing and installing them; they can exert enough force to cause serious injury. Always use spring compressors or a safety chain when removing a coil spring or releasing spring tension!**

REMOVAL & INSTALLATION

R-Series

♦ See Figure 13

1. Raise and support the truck under the frame rails. The control arms should hang freely.
2. Remove the wheel.
3. Disconnect the shock absorber at the lower end and move it aside.
4. Disconnect the stabilizer bar from the lower control arm.
5. Support the lower control arm with a jack and install a spring compressor on the spring, or chain the spring to the control arm as a safety precaution.

➡On trucks with an air cylinder inside the spring, remove the valve core from the cylinder and expel the air by compressing the cylinder with a prybar. With the cylinder compressed, replace the valve core so that the cylinder will stay in the compressed position. Push the cylinder as far as possible towards the top of the spring.

6. Raise the jack to remove the tension from the lower control arm cross-shaft and remove the two U-bolts securing the cross-shaft to the crossmember.

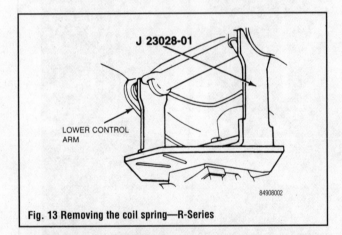

Fig. 13 Removing the coil spring—R-Series

> ✳✳ **CAUTION**
>
> **The cross-shaft and lower control arm keeps the coil spring compressed. Use care when you lower the assembly.**

7. Slowly release the jack and lower the control arm until the spring can be removed. Be sure that all compression is relieved from the spring.
8. If the spring was chained, remove the chain and spring. If you used spring compressors, remove the spring and slowly release the compressors.
9. Remove the air cylinder, if so equipped.

To install:

Installation is the reverse of removal but please note the following important steps.

10. Install the air cylinder so that the protector plate is towards the upper control arm. The schrader valve should protrude through the hole in the lower control arm.
11. Tighten the two U-bolts securing the cross-shaft to the crossmember to 85 ft. lbs. (115 Nm).
12. Tighten the stabilizer bar-to-lower control arm nuts to 24 ft. lbs. (32 Nm).

13. Tighten the shock absorber bolt to 59 ft. lbs. (80 Nm).
14. If equipped with air cylinders, inflate the cylinder to 60 psi (413 kPa).
15. Lower the truck. Once the weight of the truck is on the wheels, reduce the air cylinder pressure to 50 psi (344 kPa). Have the alignment checked.

C-Series

♦ See Figure 14

1. Raise and support the truck under the frame rails. The control arms should hang freely.
2. Remove the wheel.
3. Remove the shock absorber.
4. Disconnect the stabilizer bar from the lower control arm.
5. Support the lower control arm and install a spring compressor on the spring, or chain the spring to the control arm as a safety precaution.
6. Raise the jack to remove the tension from the lower control arm pivot bolts. Remove the rear, then the front pivot bolts.

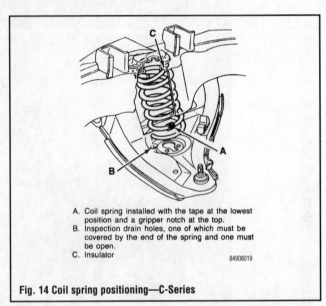

A. Coil spring installed with the tape at the lowest position and a gripper notch at the top.
B. Inspection drain holes, one of which must be covered by the end of the spring and one must be open.
C. Insulator

Fig. 14 Coil spring positioning—C-Series

> ✳✳ **CAUTION**
>
> **The lower control arm keeps the coil spring compressed. Use care when you lower the assembly.**

7. Slowly release the jack and lower the control arm until the spring can be removed. Be sure that all compression is relieved from the spring.
8. Place a piece of tape on one of the lower coil so you can tell the top from the bottom during installation. If the spring was chained, remove the chain and spring. If you used spring compressors, remove the spring and slowly release the compressors.

To install:

Installation is the reverse of removal but please note the following important steps.

9. Install the chain and spring. If you used spring compressors, install the spring and compressors.
- Make sure that the insulator is in place.
- Make sure that the tape is at the lower end. New springs will have an identifying tape.
- Make sure that the gripper notch on the top coil is in the frame bracket.
- Make sure that on drain hole in the lower arm is covered by the bottom coil and the other is open.

10. Install the pivot shaft bolts, front one first. The bolts **must** be installed with the heads towards the front of the truck! Remove the safety chain or spring compressors.

➡**Do not tighten the bolts while the vehicle is raised. The bolts must be torqued with the truck at its proper ride height.**

11. Lower the truck. Once the weight of the truck is on the wheels perform the **Z** height adjustment as outlined in this section.

 a. If the figure is correct, tighten the control arm pivot nuts to 96 ft. lbs. (130 Nm) on 1988–90 models; 121 ft. lbs. (165 Nm) on 1991–95 models and 101 ft. lbs. (137 Nm) on 1996–98 models.

 b. If the figure is not correct, tighten the bolts to specification and have the front end alignment corrected.

Shock Absorbers

REMOVAL & INSTALLATION

R-Series

1. Raise and support the front end on jackstands.
2. Remove the lower end nut, bolt and washer. Separate the shock absorber from the lower control arm.
3. Remove the upper end nut and washer.
4. Remove the shock absorber.
5. When installing the shock, tighten the upper end nut to 140 ft. lbs. (190 Nm) and the lower end bolt to 59 ft. lbs. (80 Nm).

C-Series

▶ **See Figure 15**

1. Raise and support the front end on jackstands.
2. Remove the wheel.
3. Hold the stem with a wrench and back off the shock absorber upper nut.
4. Remove the nut, retainer and upper grommet.
5. Remove the lower mounting bolts and pull the shock absorber out through the lower control arm.
6. If the shock absorber is being reused, check the grommets for wear and damage. Replace them as needed.

To install:

7. Install the shock absorber onto the vehicle.
8. Tighten the upper nut to 100 inch. lbs. (11 Nm) and the lower mounting bolts to 20 ft. lbs. (27 Nm).

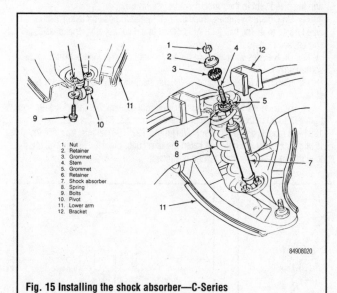

1. Nut
2. Retainer
3. Grommet
4. Stem
5. Grommet
6. Retainer
7. Shock absorber
8. Spring
9. Bolts
10. Pivot
11. Lower arm
12. Bracket

84908020

Fig. 15 Installing the shock absorber—C-Series

TESTING

▶ **See Figure 16**

The purpose of the shock absorber is simply to limit the motion of the spring during compression and rebound cycles. If the vehicle is not equipped with these motion dampers, the up and down motion would multiply until the vehicle

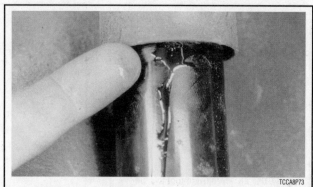

TCCA8P73

Fig. 16 When fluid is seeping out of the shock absorber, it's time to replace the shock

was alternately trying to leap off the ground and to pound itself into the pavement.

Contrary to popular rumor, the shocks do not affect the ride height of the vehicle. This is controlled by other suspension components such as springs and tires. Worn shock absorbers can affect handling; if the front of the vehicle is rising or falling excessively, the "footprint" of the tires changes on the pavement and steering is affected.

The simplest test of the shock absorber is simply push down on one corner of the unladen vehicle and release it. Observe the motion of the body as it is released. In most cases, it will come up beyond it original rest position, dip back below it and settle quickly to rest. This shows that the damper is controlling the spring action. Any tendency to excessive pitch (up-and-down) motion or failure to return to rest within 2-3 cycles is a sign of poor function within the shock absorber. Oil-filled shocks may have a light film of oil around the seal, resulting from normal breathing and air exchange. This should NOT be taken as a sign of failure, but any sign of thick or running oil definitely indicates failure. Gas filled shocks may also show some film at the shaft; if the gas has leaked out, the shock will have almost no resistance to motion.

While each shock absorber can be replaced individually, it is recommended that they be changed as a pair (both front or both rear) to maintain equal response on both sides of the vehicle. Chances are quite good that if one has failed, its mate is weak also.

Upper Ball Joint

INSPECTION

1. Raise and support the front end on jackstands so that the control arms hang freely.
2. Remove the wheel.
3. The upper ball joint is spring-loaded. Replace the ball joint if there is any lateral movement, if it can be twisted in its socket with your fingers or the seals are cut and torn.

REMOVAL & INSTALLATION

▶ **See Figures 17 and 18**

1. Raise and support the truck with jackstands. Remove wheel.
2. Support the lower control arm with a floor jack.
3. Remove the cotter pin from the upper ball stud and loosen, but do not remove the stud nut.
4. Using a forcing-type ball joint separator tool, loosen the ball stud in the steering knuckle. When the stud is loose, remove the tool and the stud nut. It may be necessary to remove the brake caliper and wire it to the frame to gain clearance.
5. On R-series trucks, drill out the rivets using a ⅛ in. drill bit. Remove the ball joint assembly.
6. On C-series trucks, drill out the rivets using a ⅛ in. drill bit to start a pilot hole. Drill out the rivets with a ½ in. bit. Remove the ball joint assembly using a screw-type forcing tool.

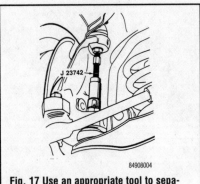

Fig. 17 Use an appropriate tool to separate the upper ball joint from the steering knuckle—C and R-Series

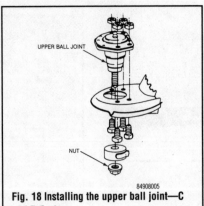

Fig. 18 Installing the upper ball joint—C and R-Series

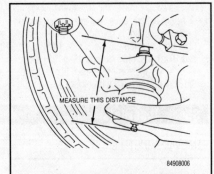

Fig. 19 Measure the distance between the tip of the lower ball joint stud and the grease fitting below the ball joint as shown

To install:

Installation is the reverse of removal but please note the following important steps.

7. On R-series vehicles, tighten the ball joint nuts to 18 ft. lbs. (24 Nm).
8. On R-series vehicles, tighten the ball stud nut as follows:
• ½ ton trucks: 50 ft. lbs. (68 Nm), plus the additional torque to align the cotter pin. Do not exceed 90 ft. lbs. (122 Nm) and never back the nut off to align the pin.
• ¾ and 1 ton trucks: 90 ft. lbs. (122 Nm), plus additional torque necessary to align the cotter pin. Do not exceed 130 ft. lbs. (176 Nm) and never back off the nut to align the pin.
9. On C-series vehicles, tighten the ball joint nuts as follows:
• 1988–90 models, tighten the nuts to 17 ft. lbs. (23 Nm) for the 15 and 25 Series and 52 ft. lbs. (70 Nm) for 35 the Series.
• 1991–98 models, tighten the nuts to 18 ft. lbs. (24 Nm).
10. On C-series vehicles, tighten the ball stud nut to 90 ft. lbs. (120 Nm) on 1988–90 models, 84 ft. lbs. (115 Nm) on 1991–95 models and 74 ft. lbs. (100 Nm) on 1996–98 models.
11. Install a new lube fitting and lubricate the new joint.

Lower Ball Joint

INSPECTION

▶ See Figure 19

1. Support the weight of the control arm at the wheel hub.
2. Measure the distance between the tip of the ball joint stud and the grease fitting below the ball joint.
3. Move the support to the control arm and allow the hub to hang free. Measure the distance again. If the variation between the two measurements exceeds ³⁄₃₂ in. (2.4mm) the ball joint should be replaced.

REMOVAL & INSTALLATION

▶ See Figures 20, 21 and 22

1. Raise and support the front end on jackstands.
2. Support the lower control arm with a floor jack.
3. Remove the wheel.
4. Remove the lower stud cotter pin and loosen, but do not remove, the stud nut.
5. Loosen the ball joint with a forcing-type ball joint tool. It may be necessary to remove the brake caliper and wire it to the frame to gain enough clearance.
6. When the stud is loose, remove the tool and ball stud nut.
7. Install a spring compressor on the coil spring for safety.
8. Pull the brake disc and knuckle assembly up and off the ball stud and support the upper arm with a block of wood.
9. Remove the ball joint from the control arm with a ball joint fork or another suitable tool.

To install:

Installation is the reverse of removal but please note the following important steps.

10. On R-series vehicles, start the new ball joint into the control arm. Position the bleed vent in the rubber boot facing inward.
11. On C-series vehicles, force the ball joint into position using a screw-type forcing tool. The ball joint will bottom in the control arm. The grease seal should face inboard.
12. On R-series vehicles, turn the screw until the ball joint is seated in the control arm.
13. Lower the upper arm and match the steering knuckle to the lower ball stud.
14. On C-series vehicles, start ball stud into the knuckle. Install the nut and tighten it to 90 ft. lbs. (122 Nm) on 1988–90 models; 84 ft. lbs. (115 Nm) on 1991–94 models and 94 ft. lbs. (128 Nm) on 1995–98 models. Advance the nut to align the cotter pin hole and insert the new cotter pin. NEVER back off the nut to align the cotter pin hole; always advance it!

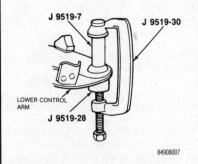

Fig. 20 Remove the lower ball joint using a suitable tool—R-Series shown, C-series similar

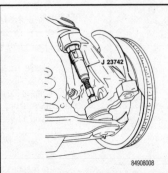

Fig. 21 Use an appropriate tool to separate the lower ball joint from the steering knuckle—R and C-Series

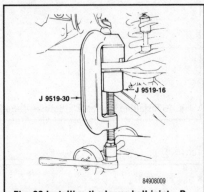

Fig. 22 Installing the lower ball joint—R and C-Series

15. On R-series vehicles, tighten the ball stud nut to 80–100 ft. lbs. (108–135 Nm), plus the additional torque necessary to align the cotter pin hole. Do not exceed 130 ft. lbs. (176 Nm) or back the nut off to align the holes with the pin.

16. Install a new lube fitting and lubricate the new joint.

Stabilizer Bar

REMOVAL & INSTALLATION

R-Series

♦ See Figure 23

1. Raise and support the front end on jackstands.
2. Remove the wheels.
3. Remove the stabilizer bar-to-frame clamps.
4. Remove the stabilizer bar-to-lower control arm clamps.
5. Remove the stabilizer bar and bushings.
6. Check the bushings for wear or splitting. Replace any damaged bushings.
7. When installing, note that the split in the bushing faces forward. Coat the bushings with silicone grease prior to installation. Install all fasteners finger-tight. When all the fasteners are in place, tighten all of them to 24 ft. lbs. (32 Nm).

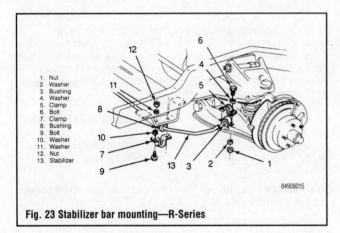

Fig. 23 Stabilizer bar mounting—R-Series

C-Series

♦ See Figure 24

➡On C-series vehicles, the end link bushings, bolts and spacers are not interchangeable from left to right, so keep them separate.

1. Raise and support the front end on jackstands.
2. Remove the nuts from the end link bolts.
3. Remove the bolts, bushings and spacers.
4. Remove the bracket bolts and remove the stabilizer bar.
5. Inspect the bushings for wear or damage. Replace them as necessary.
To install:
6. Install the bar, coating the bushings with silicone grease prior to assembly. The slit in the bushings faces the front of the truck.
7. Tighten the frame bracket bolts to 24 ft. lbs. (33 Nm) and the end link nuts to 13 ft. lbs. (18 Nm).

Upper Control Arm—R-Series

REMOVAL & INSTALLATION

♦ See Figure 25

1. Raise and support the truck on jackstands.
2. Support the lower control arm with a floor jack.
3. Remove the wheel.

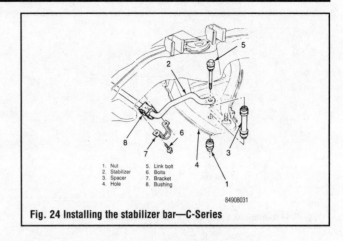

Fig. 24 Installing the stabilizer bar—C-Series

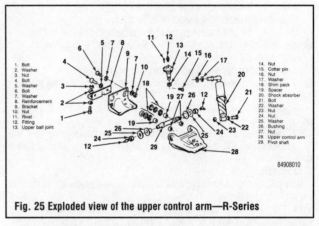

Fig. 25 Exploded view of the upper control arm—R-Series

4. Remove the cotter pin from the upper control arm ball stud and loosen the stud nut until the bottom surface of the nut is slightly below the end of the stud.
5. Install a spring compressor on the coil spring for safety.
6. Loosen the upper control arm ball stud in the steering knuckle using a ball joint stud removal tool. Remove the nut from the ball stud and raise the upper arm to clear the steering knuckle. It may be necessary to remove the brake caliper and wire it to the frame to gain clearance. Do not allow the caliper to hang by the brake hose.
7. Remove the nuts securing the control arm shaft studs to the crossmember bracket and remove the control arm.
8. Tape the shims and spacers together and tag for proper reassembly.
To install:
Installation is the reverse of removal but please note the following important steps.
9. Place the control arm in position and install the nuts. Before tightening the nuts, insert the caster and camber shims in the same order as when installed.
10. Tighten the nuts securing the control arm shaft studs-to-crossmember bracket to 70 ft. lbs. (95 Nm) for 10/1500 and 20/2500 series; 105 ft. lbs. (142 Nm) for 30/3500 series.
11. Tighten the ball stud nut to 90 ft. lbs. (122 Nm) for 10/1500 series and 20/2500 series; 130 ft. lbs. (176 Nm) for 30/3500 series. Install the cotter pin. Never back off the nut to install the cotter pin. Always advance it.

Upper Control Arm and Bushings–C-Series

REMOVAL & INSTALLATION

♦ See Figure 26

1. Raise and support the truck on jackstands.
2. Support the lower control arm with a floor jack.
3. Remove the wheel.

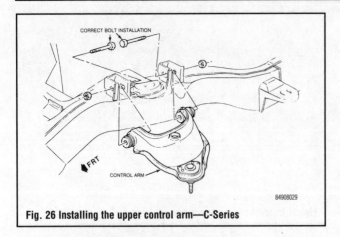

Fig. 26 Installing the upper control arm—C-Series

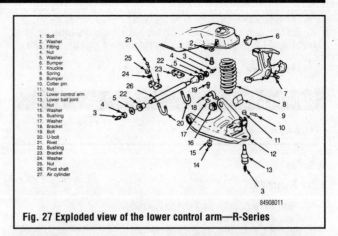

Fig. 27 Exploded view of the lower control arm—R-Series

4. Remove the air cleaner extension (if necessary).
5. Unbolt the brake hose bracket from the control arm.
6. Remove the cotter pin from the upper control arm ball stud and loosen the stud nut until the bottom surface of the nut is slightly below the end of the stud.
7. Install a spring compressor on the coil spring for safety.
8. Using a screw-type forcing tool, break loose the ball joint from the knuckle.
9. Remove the nuts and bolts securing the control arm to the frame brackets.
10. Tape the shims and spacers together and tag for proper reassembly. The 35 Series bushings are replaceable. The 15/25 Series bushings are welded in place.

To install:
Installation is the reverse of removal but please note the following important steps.
11. Place the control arm in position and install the shims, bolts and new nuts. Both bolt heads **must** be inboard of the control arm brackets. Tighten the nuts finger tighten for now.

➡**Do not tighten the bolts yet. The bolts must be torqued with the truck at its proper ride height.**

12. Install the ball stud nut. Tighten the nut to specification.
13. Lower the truck. Once the weight of the truck is on the wheels perform the **Z** height adjustment procedure outlined in this section.
   a. If the figure is correct, tighten the control arm pivot nuts to 88 ft. lbs. (120 Nm) on 1988–90 models; 140 ft. lbs. (190 Nm) on 1991–98 models.
   b. If the figure is not correct, tighten the pivot bolts to specification and have the front end alignment corrected.

Lower Control Arm—R-Series

REMOVAL & INSTALLATION

▶ **See Figure 27**

1. Raise and support the truck on jackstands.
2. Remove the spring.
3. Support the inboard end of the control arm after spring removal.
4. Remove the cotter pin from the lower ball stud and loosen the nut.
5. Loosen the lower ball stud in the steering knuckle using a ball joint stud removal tool. When the stud is loose, remove the nut from the stud. It may be necessary to remove the brake caliper and wire it to the frame to gain clearance.
6. Remove the lower control arm.

To install:
Installation is the reverse of removal. Tighten the U-bolts to 85 ft. lbs. (115 Nm).

Lower Control Arm and Bushing—C-Series

REMOVAL & INSTALLATION

▶ **See Figure 28**

1. Raise and support the truck on jackstands.
2. Remove the coil spring.
3. Support the inboard end of the control arm after spring removal.
4. Remove the cotter pin from the lower ball stud and loosen the nut.
5. Loosen the lower ball stud in the steering knuckle using a ball joint stud removal tool. When the stud is loose, remove the nut from the stud. It may be necessary to remove the brake caliper and wire it to the frame to gain clearance.
6. Remove the lower control arm.

To install:
7. Slowly raise the jack and lower the control arm. Guide the control arm into place with a prybar.
8. Install the pivot shaft bolts, front one first. The bolts **must** be installed with the heads towards the front of the truck! Remove the safety chain or spring compressors.

➡**Do not tighten the bolts yet. The bolts must be torqued with the truck at its proper ride height.**

9. Remove the jack.
10. Connect the stabilizer bar to the lower control arm.
11. Install the shock absorber.
12. Install the wheel.
13. Lower the truck. Once the weight of the truck is on the wheels perform the **Z** height adjustment procedure outlined in this section.
   a. If the figure is correct, tighten the control arm pivot nuts to 96 ft. lbs. (130 Nm) on 1988–90 models; 121 ft. lbs. (165 Nm) on 1991–94 models; 137 ft. lbs. (101 Nm) on 1995–98 models.
   b. If the figure is not correct, tighten the pivot bolts to specification and have the front end alignment corrected.

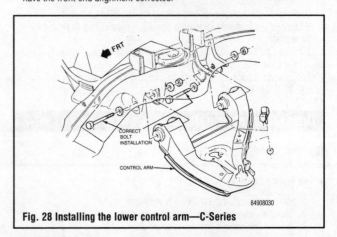

Fig. 28 Installing the lower control arm—C-Series

Upper Control Arm Pivot Shaft and Bushings—R-Series

REMOVAL & INSTALLATION

10/1500 Series

♦ See Figure 29

➡The following special tools, or their equivalents, are necessary for this procedure: J–24435–1, J–24435–3, J–24435–4, J–24435–5 and J–24435–7.

1. Remove the upper control arm as explained earlier in this Section.
2. Remove the pivot shaft nuts and washers.
3. Assemble tool J–24435–1. J–24435–3, and J–24435–7 on the control arm. Tighten the tool until the front bushing is forced out.
4. Remove the pivot shaft.
5. Use the forcing procedure to remove the rear bushing.

To install:

6. Position the new front bushing in the arm and assemble tools J–24435–4, J–24435–5 and J–24435–7. Force the bushing into place until it is fully seated.
7. Install the pivot shaft.
8. Repeat the forcing procedure to install the rear bushing.
9. Install the lower control arm.
10. Install the nuts and washers. Tighten the nuts to 115 ft. lbs. (156 Nm).
11. Install the control arm.

20/2500 and 30/3500 Series

1. Raise and support the front end on jackstands.
2. Take up the weight of the suspension with a floor jack positioned under the lower control arm as near to the ball joint as possible.
3. Loosen, but do not remove, the pivot shaft-to-frame nuts.
4. Tape together and matchmark each shim pack's position for exact installation.
5. Install a chain over the control arm, inboard of the stabilizer bar and outboard of the shock absorber to hold the control arm close to the crossmember.
6. Remove the pivot shaft nuts, bolts and spacers.
7. Remove the grease fittings and unscrew the bushings from the control arm.
8. Remove the pivot shaft. Discard the seals.

To install:

9. Install new seals on the pivot shaft.
10. Slide the shaft into the arm.
11. Start the bushings into the arm and center the shaft in the bushings. Hand tighten the bushings to make sure the shaft doesn't bind.
12. Tighten the bushings to 190 ft. lbs. (257 Nm).
13. Check the pivot shaft for free rotation.
14. Install the grease fittings and lubricate the bushings.
15. Position the control arm on the frame and install the shim packs, spac-

ers, nuts and bolts. Tighten the nuts to 105 ft. lbs. (142 Nm). Have the alignment checked.

Lower Control Arm Pivot Shaft and Bushings—R-Series

REMOVAL & INSTALLATION

10/1500 Series

♦ See Figures 30 and 31

➡The following special tools, or their equivalents, are necessary for this procedure: J–22717, J–24435–7, J–24435–3, J–24435–2, J–24435–6, J–24435–4.

1. Remove the lower control arm as explained earlier in this Section.
2. Remove the pivot shaft nuts and washers.
3. Place the control arm in a press and press on the front end of the pivot shaft to remove the rear bushing.
4. Remove the pivot shaft.
5. Remove the front bushing stakes with tool J–22717, or equivalent.
6. Assemble tool J–24435–7. J–24435–3, J–24435–2 and J–24435–6 on the control arm. Tighten the tool until the bushing is forced out.

To install:

7. Position the new front bushing in the arm and assemble tools J–24435–6, J–24435–4 and J–24435–7. Force the bushing into place until it is fully seated. The outer tube hole must be lined up so that it faces the front, towards the staked bushing.
8. Stake the bushing in at least 2 places.
9. Install the pivot shaft.
10. Install the rear bushing.
11. Install the washers and pivot shaft nuts. Tighten the nuts to 70 ft. lbs. (94 Nm).
12. Install the lower control arm.

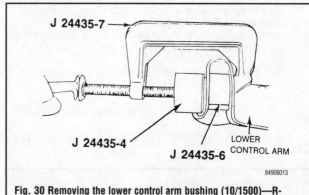

Fig. 30 Removing the lower control arm bushing (10/1500)—R-Series

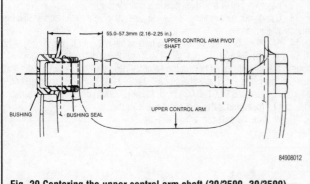

Fig. 29 Centering the upper control arm shaft (20/2500, 30/3500)—R-Series

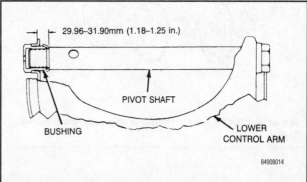

Fig. 31 Centering the lower control arm shaft (20/2500, 30/3500)—R-Series

20/2500 and 30/3500 Series

1. Remove the lower control arm.
2. Remove the grease fittings and unscrew the bushings.
3. Slide out the pivot shaft.
4. Discard the old seals.

To install:

5. Install new seals on the pivot shaft.
6. Slide the shaft into the arm.
7. Start the bushings into the arm and center the shaft in the bushings. Hand tighten the bushings to make sure the shaft doesn't bind.
8. Tighten the bushings to 280 ft. lbs. (380 Nm).
9. Check the pivot shaft for free rotation.
10. Install the grease fittings and lubricate the bushings.
11. Install the lower arm.

Steering Knuckle

REMOVAL & INSTALLATION

♦ **See Figures 32 and 33**

1. Raise and support the front end on jackstands.
2. Remove the wheels.
3. Dismount the caliper and suspend it out of the way without disconnecting the brake lines.
4. Remove the hub/rotor assembly.
5. Unbolt the splash shield and discard the old gasket.
6. Using a ball joint separator, disconnect the tie rod end from the knuckle.
7. Position a floor jack under the lower control arm, near the spring seat. Raise the jack until it **just** takes up the weight of the suspension, compressing the spring. Safety-chain the coil spring to the lower arm.
8. Remove the upper and lower ball joint nut.
9. Using tool J-23742, or equivalent, break loose the upper ball joint from the knuckle.
10. Raise the upper control arm just enough to disconnect the ball joint.
11. Using the afore-mentioned tool, break loose the lower ball joint.
12. Lift the knuckle off of the lower ball joint.
13. Inspect and clean the ball stud bores in the knuckle. Make sure that there are no cracks or burrs. If the knuckle is damaged in any way, replace it.
14. Check the spindle for wear, heat discoloration or damage. If at all damaged, replace it.

To install:

Installation is the reverse of removal but please note the following important steps.

15. Maneuver the knuckle onto both ball joints and tighten the nuts to specifications.

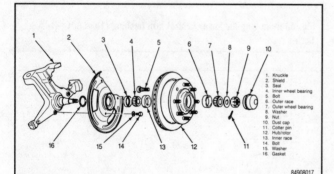

1. Knuckle
2. Shield
3. Seal
4. Inner wheel bearing
5. Bolt
6. Outer race
7. Outer wheel bearing
8. Washer
9. Nut
10. Dust cap
11. Cotter pin
12. Hub/rotor
13. Inner race
14. Bolt
15. Washer
16. Gasket

84908017

Fig. 32 Exploded view of the steering knuckle and components—R-Series

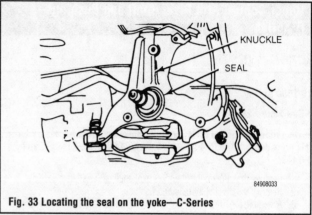

84908033

Fig. 33 Locating the seal on the yoke—C-Series

16. Install a new splash shield gasket and tighten the shield bolts to 10 ft. lbs. (14 Nm) on R-series vehicles. On C-series vehicles, tighten the bolts to 12 ft. lbs. (16 Nm) on 1988–90 models; 19 ft. lbs. (26 Nm) on 1991–98 models.

Front Hub, Rotor and Bearings

REMOVAL & INSTALLATION

♦ **See Figures 34 thru 49**

1. Raise and support the front end on jackstands.
2. Remove the wheel.
3. Dismount the caliper and wire it out of the way.
4. Pry out the grease cap, remove the cotter pin, spindle nut, and washer.
5. Remove the hub. Do not drop the wheel bearings.
6. Remove the outer roller bearing assembly from the hub. The inner bearing assembly will remain in the hub and may be removed after prying out the inner seal. Discard the seal.
7. Using a hammer and drift, remove the bearing races from the hub. They are driven out from the inside out.

To install:

8. Clean all parts in a non-flammable solvent and let them air dry. Never spin-dry a bearing with compressed air! Check for excessive wear and damage.
9. When installing new races, make sure that they are not cocked and that they are fully seated against the hub shoulder.
10. Pack both wheel bearings using high melting point wheel bearing grease for disc brakes. Ordinary grease will melt and ooze out ruining the pads. Bearings should be packed using a cone-type wheel bearing greaser tool. If one is not available they may be packed by hand. Place a healthy glob of grease in the palm of one hand and force the edge of the bearing into it so that the grease fills the bearing. Do this until the whole bearing is packed.
11. Place the inner bearing in the hub and install a new inner seal, making sure that the seal flange faces the bearing race.
12. Carefully install the wheel hub over the spindle.
13. Using your hands, firmly press the outer bearing into the hub. Install the spindle washer and nut.
14. Spin the wheel hub by hand and tighten the nut until it is just snug—12 ft. lbs. (16 Nm). Back off the nut until it is loose, then tighten it finger tight. Loosen the nut until either hole in the spindle lines up with a slot in the nut and insert a new cotter pin. There should be 0.0012–0.005 in. (0.03–0.13mm) end-play on R-series and 0.001–0.008 in. (0.025–0.200mm) end-play on C-series. This can be measured with a dial indicator, if you wish.
15. Replace the dust cap, wheel and tire.

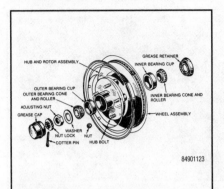

Fig. 34 Front hub and bearing components—2WD

Fig. 35 Pry the dust cap from the hub, taking care not to distort or damage its flange

Fig. 36 Once the bent ends are cut, grasp the cotter pin and pull or pry it free of the spindle

Fig. 37 If difficulty is encountered, gently tap on the pliers with a hammer to help free the cotter pin

Fig. 38 Loosen and remove the castellated nut from the spindle

Fig. 39 Remove the washer from the spindle

Fig. 40 With the nut and washer out of the way, the outer bearing may be removed from the hub

Fig. 41 Pull the hub and inner bearing assembly from the spindle

Fig. 42 Use a small prytool to remove the old inner bearing seal

Fig. 43 With the seal removed, the inner bearing may be withdrawn from the hub

Fig. 44 Thoroughly pack the bearing with fresh, high temperature wheel bearing grease before installation

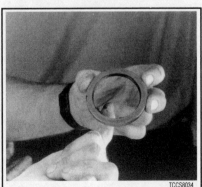

Fig. 45 Apply a thin coat of fresh grease to the new inner bearing seal lip

Fig. 46 Use a suitably sized driver to install the inner bearing seal to the hub

Fig. 48 After the bearings are adjusted, install the dust cap by gently tapping on the flange

Fig. 47 Tighten the nut to specifications while gently spinning the wheel, then adjust the bearing

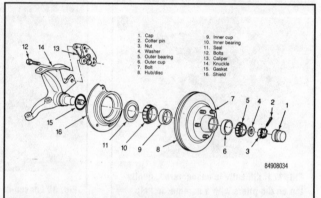

1. Cap	9. Inner cup
2. Cotter pin	10. Inner bearing
3. Nut	11. Seal
4. Washer	12. Bolts
5. Outer bearing	13. Caliper
6. Outer cup	14. Knuckle
7. Bolt	15. Gasket
8. Hub/disc	16. Shield

Fig. 49 Exploded view of the hub, knuckle and bearings—C-Series

V-SERIES 4WD FRONT SUSPENSION

Leaf Spring

REMOVAL & INSTALLATION

♦ See Figure 50

1. Raise and support the vehicle so that all tension is taken off of the front suspension.
2. Remove the shackle retaining bolts, nuts and spacers.
3. Remove the front spring-to-frame bracket bolt, washer and nut.
4. On the 10/1500 and 20/2500 both sides and the 30/3500 left side: remove the U-bolt nuts, washers, U-bolts, plate and spacers.
5. On the 30/3500 right side: remove the inboard spring plate bolts, U-bolt nuts, washers, U-bolt, plate and spacers.

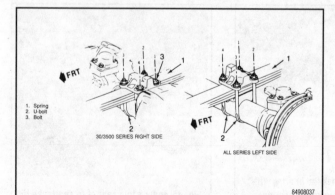

1. Spring
2. U-bolt
3. Bolt

30/3500 SERIES RIGHT SIDE

ALL SERIES LEFT SIDE

Fig. 50 U-bolt tightening sequence—V-Series

6. To replace the bushing, place the spring in a press or vise and press out the bushing.

To install:

7. Press in the new bushing. The new bushing should protrude evenly on both sides of the spring.
8. Install the spring. Coat all bushings with silicone grease prior to installation.
9. Install all bolts and nuts finger-tight.
10. When all fasteners are installed, torque the bolts. Tighten the U-bolt nuts, including the inboard right side 30/3500 series bolts, in the crisscross pattern shown, to 150 ft. lbs. (203 Nm). Tighten the shackle nuts to 50 ft. lbs. (67 Nm). Tighten the front eye bolt nut to 90 ft. lbs. (122 Nm).

Shock Absorbers

REMOVAL & INSTALLATION

Dual or Quad Shocks

♦ See Figure 51

1. Raise and support the front end on jackstands.
2. Remove the nuts and eye bolts securing the upper and lower shock absorber eyes. Quad shocks have a spacer between the lower end bushings.
3. Remove the shock absorber(s) and inspect the rubber eye bushings. If these are defective, replace the shock absorber assembly.
4. Make sure that the spacer is installed at the bottom end on quad shocks. Tighten the upper end nut to 65 ft. lbs. (88 Nm). On dual shocks, tighten the lower end to 65 ft. lbs. (88 Nm). On quad shocks, tighten the lower end to 89 ft. lbs. (120 Nm).

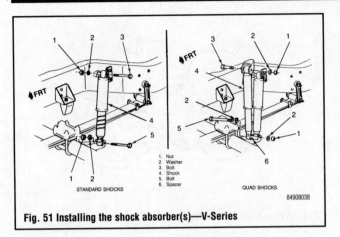

Fig. 51 Installing the shock absorber(s)—V-Series

84908038

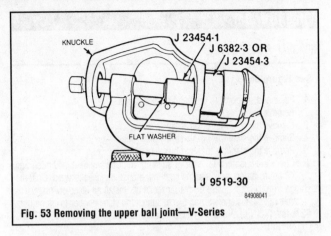

Fig. 53 Removing the upper ball joint—V-Series

84908041

TESTING

Refer to the shock absorber testing procedure in the C/R-series front suspension portion of the section.

Ball Joints

CHECKING TURNING EFFORT

1. Raise and support the front end on jackstands.
2. Remove the wheels.
3. Disconnect the connecting rod and tie rod at each knuckle.
4. Position the knuckle in the straight-ahead position and attach a spring scale to the tie rod hole of the knuckle. Pull at a right (90) angle and determine the amount of pull necessary to keep the knuckle moving after the initial breakaway. The pull should not exceed 25 lbs. (111.2 N) in either direction for each knuckle. If pull is excessive, the ball joint can be adjusted. See the procedure in this section. If no adjustment is required, connect the connecting rod and tie rod.

REMOVAL & INSTALLATION

♦ **See Figures 52 and 53**

➡**The following special tools, or their equivalents, are necessary for this procedure: J–9519–30, J–23454–1, J–23454–4, J–23454–3, J–23454–2, J–23447.**

1. Raise and support the front end on jackstands.
2. Remove the wheels.
3. Remove the locking hubs.
4. Remove the spindle.
5. Disconnect the tie rod end from the knuckle.

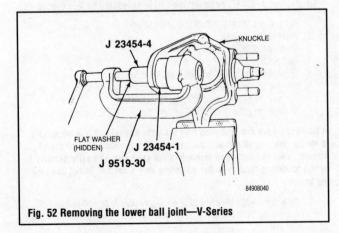

Fig. 52 Removing the lower ball joint—V-Series

84908040

6. Remove the knuckle-to-steering arm nuts and adapters.
7. Remove the steering arm from the knuckle.
8. Remove the cotter pins and nuts from the upper and lower ball joints.

➡**Do not remove the adjusting ring from the knuckle. If it is necessary to loosen the ring to remove the knuckle, don't loosen it more than 2 threads. The non-hardened threads in the yoke can be easily damaged by the hardened threads in the adjusting ring if caution is not used during knuckle removal!**

9. Insert the wedge-shaped end of the heavy prybar, or wedge-type ball joint tool, between the lower ball joint and the yoke. Drive the prybar in to break the knuckle free.
10. Repeat the procedure at the upper ball joint.
11. Lift off the knuckle.
12. Secure the knuckle in a vise.
13. Remove the snapring from the lower ball joint. Using tools J–9519–30, J–23454–1 and J–23454–4, or their equivalent screw-type forcing tool, force the lower ball joint from the knuckle.
14. Using tools J–9519–30, J–23454–3 and J–23454–4, or their equivalent screw-type forcing tool, force the upper ball joint from the knuckle.

To install:
Installation is the reverse of removal but please note the following important steps.

15. Install the lower ball joint first, (the one without the cotter pin hole) squarely in the knuckle. Using tools J–9519–30, J–23454–2 and J–23454–3, or their equivalent screw-type forcing tool, force the lower ball joint into the knuckle until it is fully seated.
16. Install the snapring.
17. Perform the same procedure for the upper ball joint (the one with the cotter pin hole).
18. Start the ball joints into their sockets. Place the nuts onto the ball studs. The nut with the cotter pin slot is the upper nut. Tighten the lower nut to 30 ft. lbs. (40 Nm), for now.
19. Using tool J–23447, tighten the adjusting ring to 50 ft. lbs. (70 Nm).
20. Tighten the upper nut to 100 ft. lbs. (135 Nm). Install a new cotter pin. NEVER loosen the nut to align the cotter pin hole; always tighten it. Tighten the lower nut to 70 ft. lbs. (95 Nm).
21. Attach the steering arm to the knuckle using adapters and NEW nuts. Tighten the nuts to 90 ft. lbs. (122 Nm).
22. Have the front end alignment checked and adjusted as necessary.

ADJUSTMENT

➡**Tool J–23447, or its equivalent, is necessary for this procedure.**

1. Raise and support the front end on jackstands.
2. Remove the wheels.
3. Remove the cotter pin and nut from the upper ball joint.
4. Using tool J–23447, back off the adjusting ring no more than 2 threads, then, tighten the adjusting ring to 50 ft. lbs.
5. Install the upper nut. Tighten the upper nut to 100 ft. lbs. Install a new cotter pin. NEVER loosen the nut to align the cotter pin hole; always tighten it.
6. Install the wheel.

Stabilizer Bar

REMOVAL & INSTALLATION

▶ **See Figure 54**

1. Raise and support the front end on jackstands.
2. Remove the wheels.
3. Remove the stabilizer bar-to-frame clamps.
4. Remove the stabilizer bar-to-spring plate bolts.
5. Remove the stabilizer bar and bushings.
6. Check the bushings for wear or splitting. Replace any damaged bushings.
7. When installing, note that the split in the bushing faces forward. Coat the bushings with silicone grease prior to installation. Install all fasteners finger-tight. When all the fasteners are in place, tighten the stabilizer bar-to-frame nuts to 52 ft. lbs. (70 Nm). Tighten the stabilizer bar-to-spring plate bolts to 133 ft. lbs. (180 Nm).

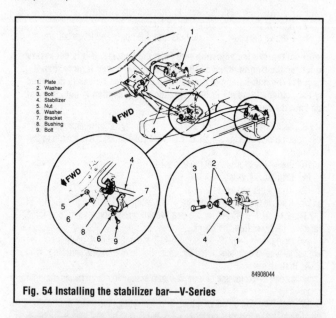

Fig. 54 Installing the stabilizer bar—V-Series

Spindle

REMOVAL & INSTALLATION

▶ **See Figures 55 and 56**

➡ **Special tools J–23445–A/J–8092, and J–21465–17, or their equivalents, are necessary for this procedure.**

1. Raise and support the front end on jackstands.
2. Remove the wheel.
3. Remove the locking hub.
4. Remove the hub and bearing assembly.
5. Remove the nuts and remove the caliper mounting bracket and splash shield.
6. Tap the end of the spindle with a plastic mallet to break it loose from the knuckle. If tapping won't break it loose, you'll have to do the following:
   a. Thread the bearing locknut part way onto the spindle.
   b. Position a 2 or 3-jawed puller with the jaws grabbing the locknut and the screw bearing in the end of the axle shaft.
   c. Tighten the puller until the spindle breaks free. It will be very helpful to spray Liquid Wrench®, WD-40® or similar solvent around the spindle mating area and around the bolt holes. As the puller is tightened, tap the spindle with the plastic mallet. This often helps break the spindle loose.
7. Drive out the bearing and seal.

To install:
Installation is the reverse of removal but please note the following important steps.

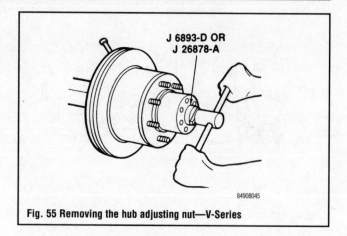

Fig. 55 Removing the hub adjusting nut—V-Series

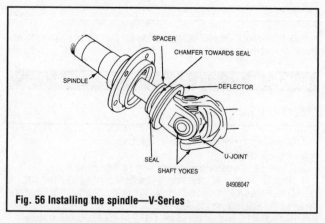

Fig. 56 Installing the spindle—V-Series

8. Drive in a new bearing using bearing installer J–23445–A/J–8092 for 10/1500 and 20/2500 Series or J–21465–17 for 30/3500 Series.
9. Pack the spindle bearing with wheel bearing grease.
10. When you place the spindle on the knuckle. Be sure the seal and oil deflector are in place.
11. Using new washers (30/3500 Series), install new nuts and tighten them to 65 ft. lbs. (88 Nm).

Steering Knuckle

REMOVAL & INSTALLATION

10/1500 and 20/2500 Series

▶ **See Figures 57 and 58**

➡ **Special tool J–23447, or its equivalent, is necessary for this procedure.**

1. Raise and support the front end on jackstands.
2. Remove the wheels.
3. Remove the locking hubs.
4. Remove the spindle.
5. Disconnect the tie rod end from the knuckle.
6. Remove the knuckle-to-steering arm nuts and adapters.
7. Remove the steering arm from the knuckle.
8. Remove the cotter pins and nuts from the upper and lower ball joints.

➡ **Do not remove the adjusting ring from the knuckle. If it is necessary to loosen the ring to remove the knuckle, don't loosen it more than 2 threads. The non-hardened threads in the yoke can be easily damaged by the hardened threads in the adjusting ring if caution is not used during knuckle removal.**

9. Insert the wedge-shaped end of the heavy prybar, or wedge-type ball joint tool, between the lower ball joint and the yoke. Drive the prybar in to break the knuckle free.

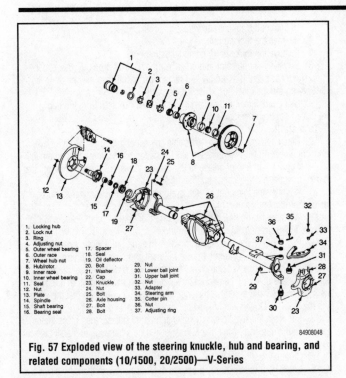

Fig. 57 Exploded view of the steering knuckle, hub and bearing, and related components (10/1500, 20/2500)—V-Series

1. Locking hub
2. Lock nut
3. Ring
4. Adjusting nut
5. Outer wheel bearing
6. Outer race
7. Wheel hub nut
8. Hub/rotor
9. Inner race
10. Inner wheel bearing
11. Seal
12. Nut
13. Plate
14. Spindle
15. Shaft bearing
16. Bearing seal
17. Spacer
18. Seal
19. Oil deflector
20. Bolt
21. Washer
22. Cap
23. Knuckle
24. Nut
25. Bolt
26. Axle housing
27. Bolt
28. Bolt
29. Nut
30. Lower ball joint
31. Upper ball joint
32. Nut
33. Adapter
34. Steering arm
35. Cotter pin
36. Nut
37. Adjusting ring

84908048

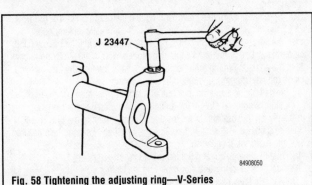

Fig. 58 Tightening the adjusting ring—V-Series

84908050

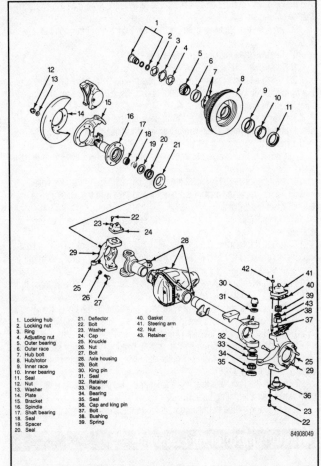

Fig. 59 Exploded view of the steering knuckle, hub and bearing, and related components (30/3500)—V-Series

1. Locking hub
2. Locking nut
3. Ring
4. Adjusting nut
5. Outer bearing
6. Outer race
7. Hub bolt
8. Hub/rotor
9. Inner race
10. Inner bearing
11. Seal
12. Nut
13. Washer
14. Plate
15. Bracket
16. Spindle
17. Shaft bearing
18. Seal
19. Spacer
20. Seal
21. Deflector
22. Bolt
23. Washer
24. Cap
25. Knuckle
26. Nut
27. Bolt
28. Axle housing
29. Bolt
30. King pin
31. Seal
32. Retainer
33. Race
34. Bearing
35. Seal
36. Cap and king pin
37. Bolt
38. Bushing
39. Spring
40. Gasket
41. Steering arm
42. Nut
43. Retainer

84908049

10. Repeat the procedure at the upper ball joint.
11. Lift off the knuckle.

To install:

Installation is the reverse of removal but please note the following important steps.

12. Position the knuckle on the yoke.
13. Install the ball joints into their sockets. And tighten the nuts as outlined in the ball joint removal and installation procedure in this section.
14. Install the hub/rotor assembly and wheel bearings. Adjust the bearings.

30/3500 Series

♦ **See Figures 59, 60 and 61**

➡The following special tools, or their equivalents, are necessary for this procedure: J–26871, J–7817, and J–22301.

1. Raise and support the front end on jackstands.
2. Remove the wheel.
3. Remove the hub/rotor/bearings assembly.
4. Remove the locking hubs.
5. Remove the spindle.
6. Remove the upper cap from the right side knuckle and/or steering arm from the left side knuckle, by loosening the bolts (right side) and/or nuts (left side) a little at a time in an alternating pattern. This will safely relieve spring pressure under the cap and/or arm. Once spring pressure is relieved, remove the bolts and/or nuts, washers and cap and/or steering arm.
7. Remove the gasket and compression spring.

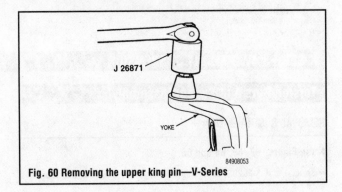

Fig. 60 Removing the upper king pin—V-Series

84908053

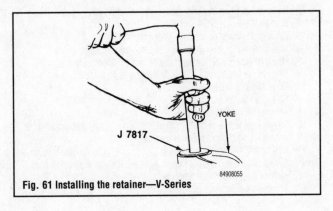

Fig. 61 Installing the retainer—V-Series

84908055

8. Remove the bolts and washers and remove the lower bearing cap and the lower kingpin.

9. Remove the upper kingpin bushing by pulling it out through the knuckle.

10. Remove the knuckle from the axle yoke.

11. Remove the retainer from the knuckle.

12. Using a large breaker bar and adapter J–26871, remove the upper kingpin from the axle yoke by applying 500–600 ft. lbs. (677–813 Nm) of torque to the kingpin to break it free.

13. Using a hammer and blunt drift, drive out the retainer, race bearing and seal from the axle yoke. These are driven out all at once.

To install:

Installation is the reverse of removal but please note the following important steps.

14. Using tool J–7817, install a new retainer and race in the axle yoke.

15. Fill the recessed area in the retainer and race with the same grease used on the wheel bearings.

16. Completely pack the upper yoke roller bearing with wheel bearing grease.

17. Install the bearing and a new seal in the upper axle yoke, using a bearing driver such as J–22301. DON'T distort the seal. It should protrude slightly above the yoke when fully seated.

18. Using adapter tool J–28871, install the upper kingpin. The kingpin must be tightened to 550 ft. lbs. (745 Nm).

19. Position the knuckle in the yoke. Working through the knuckle, install a new felt seal over the kingpin and position the knuckle on the kingpin.

20. Install the bushing over the kingpin.

21. Install the compression spring, gasket, bearing cap and/or steering arm and bolts and/or nut and washer. Tighten the bolts and/or nuts, in an alternating pattern, to 80 ft. lbs. (108).

22. Install the lower bearing cap and kingpin. Tighten the bolts to 80 ft. lbs. (108 Nm) in an alternating pattern.

23. Thoroughly lube both kingpins through the grease fittings.

Wheel Hub/Rotor and Bearing

REMOVAL & INSTALLATION

▶ **See Figure 55**

1. Raise and support the front end on jackstands.
2. Remove the wheel.

K-SERIES 4WD FRONT SUSPENSION

Torsion Bars and Support Assembly

REMOVAL & INSTALLATION

▶ **See Figures 62, 63, 64 and 65**

➡Special tool J–36202, or its equivalent, is necessary for this procedure.

1. Raise and support the front end on jackstands.
2. Remove the wheels.
3. Support the lower control arm with a floor jack.
4. Matchmark both torsion bar adjustment bolt positions.
5. Using tool J–36202, increase the tension on the adjusting arm.
6. Remove the adjustment bolt and retaining plate.
7. Move the tool aside.
8. Slide the torsion bars forward.
9. Remove the adjusting arms.
10. Remove the nuts and bolts from the torsion bar support crossmember and slide the support crossmember rearwards.
11. Matchmark the position of the torsion bars and note the markings on the front end of each bar. They are not interchangeable. Remove the torsion bars.
12. Remove the support crossmember.
13. Remove the retainer, spacer and bushing from the support crossmember.

3. Dismount the caliper and wire it out of the way.
4. Remove the locking hub.
5. Remove the lock nut, ring and adjusting nut.
6. Remove the hub/rotor and outer bearing. Do not drop the wheel bearings. The inner bearing assembly will remain in the hub and may be removed after prying out the inner seal. Discard the seal.
7. Using a hammer and drift, remove the bearing races from the hub. They are driven out from the inside out.

To install:

8. Clean all parts in a non-flammable solvent and let them air dry. Never spin-dry a bearing with compressed air! Check for excessive wear and damage.

9. Apply a thin film of grease to the spindle at the outer wheel bearing seat and at the inner bearing seat, shoulder and seal seat.

10. Apply a small amount of grease inboard of each wheel bearing cup, inside the rotor/ hub assembly.

11. When installing new races, make sure that they are not cocked and that they are fully seated against the hub shoulder.

12. Pack both wheel bearings using high melting point wheel bearing grease for disc brakes. Ordinary grease will melt and ooze out ruining the pads. Bearings should be packed using a cone-type wheel bearing greaser tool. If one is not available they may be packed by hand. Place a healthy glob of grease in the palm of one hand and force the edge of the bearing into it so that the grease fills the bearing. Do this until the whole bearing is packed.

13. Lubricate the seal lip with a small amount of grease, then place the inner bearing in the hub and install a new inner seal. Use a flat plate to install the seal so it is flush with the hub/rotor flange.

14. Carefully install the wheel hub/rotor assembly.

15. Using your hands, firmly press the outer bearing into the hub. Install the adjusting nut.

16. Spin the wheel hub by hand and tighten the nut to 50 ft. lbs. (68 Nm). Back off the nut until it is loose. On models with automatic locking hubs, tighten the adjusting nut to 35 ft. lbs. (47 Nm) while rotating the hub by hand, back off the adjusting nut ⅜ of a turn. On models with manual locking hubs, tighten the adjusting nut to 50 ft. lbs. (68 Nm) while rotating the hub by hand, back off the adjusting nut enough to free the bearing.

17. Install the ring and the lock nut. The tang on the inside diameter of the ring must pass onto the slot on the spindle. Also the hole in the ring must align with the pin on the lock nut. Move the adjusting nut to align the pin. There should be 0.001–0.010 in. (0.025–0.254mm) end-play. This can be measured with a dial indicator, if you wish.

18. Install the lock nut and tighten to 160 ft. lbs. (217 Nm).

19. Install the locking hub assembly and the caliper.

20. Replace the wheel and tire and lower the vehicle.

To install:

14. Installation is the reverse of removal, but please note the following important steps.

15. Position the support assembly on the frame, out of the way.

16. Align the matchmarks and install the torsion bars, sliding them forward until they are supported.

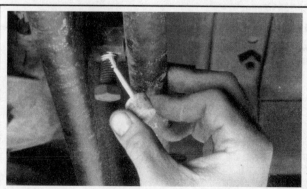

Fig. 62 Matchmark both torsion bar adjustment bolt positions

87988P01

Fig. 63 Increase the tension on the adjusting arm

87988P02

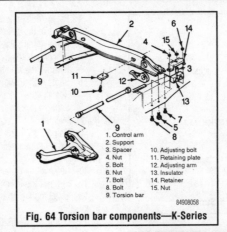

Fig. 64 Torsion bar components—K-Series

1. Control arm
2. Support
3. Spacer
4. Nut
5. Bolt
6. Nut
7. Bolt
8. Bolt
9. Torsion bar
10. Adjusting bolt
11. Retaining plate
12. Adjusting arm
13. Insulator
14. Retainer
15. Nut

84908058

Fig. 65 Torsion bar adjuster height—K-Series

1. Frame
2. Support
3. Adjusting bolt
4. Nut
5. Adjusting arm

34mm

84908059

16. Bolt the support crossmember into position. Tighten the center nut to 18 ft. lbs. (24 Nm); the edge nuts to 46 ft. lbs. (62 Nm).

17. Install the adjuster retaining plate and bolt on each torsion bar.

18. Using tool J–36202, increase tension on both torsion bars.

19. Set the adjustment bolt to the marked position.

20. Release the tension on the torsion bar until the load is taken up by the adjustment bolt.

Shock Absorbers

REMOVAL & INSTALLATION

♦ See Figures 66 and 67

1. Raise and support the front end on jackstands.
2. Remove the upper end bolt, nut and washer.
3. Remove the lower end bolt, nut and washer.
4. Remove the shock absorber and inspect the rubber bushings. If these are defective, replace the shock absorber assembly.

To install:

5. Install the shock and tighten both nuts to 48 ft. lbs. (65 Nm) on 1988–90 models; 66 ft. lbs. (90 Nm) on 1991–98 models. Make sure that the bolts are inserted in the proper direction. The bolt head on the upper end should be forward; the bottom end bolt head is rearward.

TESTING

Refer to the shock absorber testing procedure in the R/C series front suspension portion of the section.

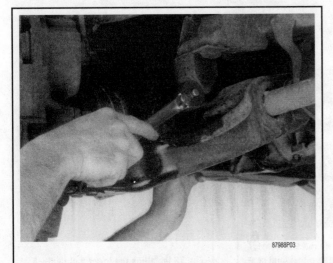

Fig. 66 Remove the shock absorber lower end bolt, nut and washer

87988P03

Fig. 67 Remove the shock absorber and inspect the rubber bushings

87988P04

Upper Ball Joint

REMOVAL & INSTALLATION

♦ See Figures 68 and 69

1. Raise and support the front end on jackstands.
2. Remove the wheel.
3. Unbolt the brake hose bracket from the control arm.
4. Using a ⅛ in. (3.175mm) drill bit, drill a pilot hole through each ball joint rivet.
5. Drill out the rivets with a ½ in. (12.7mm) drill bit. Punch out any remaining rivet material.
6. Remove the cotter pin and nut from the ball stud.
7. Support the lower control arm with a floor jack.
8. Using a screw-type forcing tool, separate the ball joint from the knuckle.

To install:

9. Installation is the reverse of removal but please note the following important steps.

➥Service replacement ball joints come with nuts and bolts to replace the rivets.

10. Install the bolts and nuts. Tighten the nuts to 18 ft. lbs. (24 Nm) for 15 and 25 Series (K1 or K2); 52 ft. lbs. (70 Nm) for 35 Series (K3).

➥The bolts are inserted from the bottom.

11. Start the ball stud into the knuckle. Make sure it is squarely seated. Install the ball stud nut and pull the ball stud into the knuckle with the nut. Do not tighten the nut just yet.

12. Install the wheel.

13. Lower the truck. Once the weight of the truck is on the wheels perform the **Z** height adjustment procedure in this section.

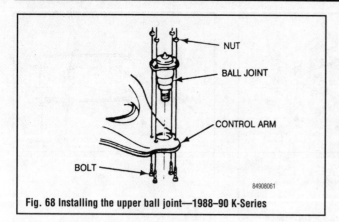

Fig. 68 Installing the upper ball joint—1988–90 K-Series

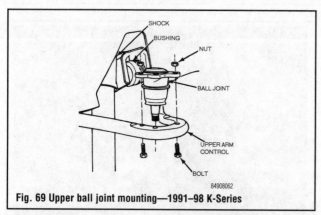

Fig. 69 Upper ball joint mounting—1991–98 K-Series

14. Tighten the ball stud nut to 84 ft. lbs. (115 Nm) on 1988–95 models and 74 ft. lbs. (100 Nm) on 1996–98 models and have the front end alignment corrected.

15. When the adjustment is correct, tighten the control arm pivot nuts to 88 ft. lbs. (120 Nm) on 1988–90 models; 140 ft. lbs. (190 Nm) on 1991–98 models. If the adjustment is not correct, tighten the pivot bolts to specification and have the alignment checked.

Lower Ball Joint

REMOVAL & INSTALLATION

Rivet/Bolted Type

▶ See Figures 70, 71 and 72

➡Special tool J–36202, or its equivalent, is necessary for this procedure.

1. Raise and support the front end on jackstands.
2. Remove the wheel.
3. Remove the splash shield from the knuckle.
4. Disconnect the tie rod end from the knuckle using a ball joint separator.
5. Remove the axle shaft.
6. Remove the caliper assembly and wire it out of the way.
7. Remove the cotter pin and the nut from the lower control arm ball joint.
8. Seperate the lower control arm from the knuckle and remove the knuckle from the vehicle.
9. Using a 1/8 in. drill bit, drill a pilot hole through each ball joint rivet.
10. Drill out the rivets with a 1/2 in. drill bit. Punch out any remaining rivet material.
11. Remove the cotter pin and nut from the ball stud.
12. Support the lower control arm with a floor jack.
13. Matchmark both torsion bar adjustment bolt positions. This will aid in installation.
14. Using tool J–36202, increase the tension on the adjusting arm.
15. Remove the adjustment bolt and retaining plate.
16. Move the tool aside.
17. Slide the torsion bars forward.
18. Using a screw-type forcing tool, separate the ball joint from the knuckle.
To install:
19. Installation is the reverse of removal, but please note the following important steps.

➡**Service replacement ball joints come with nuts and bolts to replace the rivets.**

20. Install the bolts and nuts. Tighten the nuts to 45 ft. lbs. (61 Nm).

➡**The bolts are inserted from the bottom.**

21. Start the ball stud into the knuckle. Make sure it is squarely seated. Install the ball stud nut and pull the ball stud into the knuckle with the nut. Don't final-torque the nut yet.
22. Using tool J–36202, increase tension on both torsion bars.
23. Install the adjustment retainer plate and bolt on both torsion bars.
24. Set the adjustment bolt to the marked position.
25. Release the tension on the torsion bar until the load is taken up by the adjustment bolt and remove the tool.
26. Connect the tie rod end to the steering. Tighten the nut to 40 ft. lbs. (54 Nm).
27. Install the wheel.
28. Lower the truck. Once the weight of the truck is on the wheels perform the **Z** height adjustment procedure in this section.
29. Tighten the ball stud nut to 94 ft. lbs. (128 Nm).

Pressed-in Type

▶ See Figures 73 and 74

1. Raise and support the front end on jackstands.
2. Remove the wheel assembly.
3. Support the control arm with a floor jack.
4. Remove the halfshaft (drive axle).

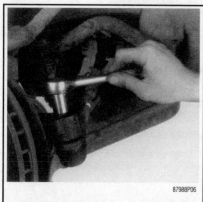

Fig. 70 Remove the tie rod end nut

Fig. 71 Disconnect the tie rod end from the steering knuckle using a ball joint separator

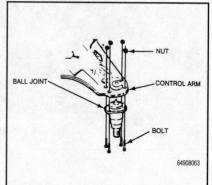

Fig. 72 Installing the lower ball joint—K-Series

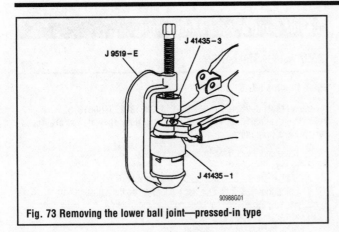

Fig. 73 Removing the lower ball joint—pressed-in type

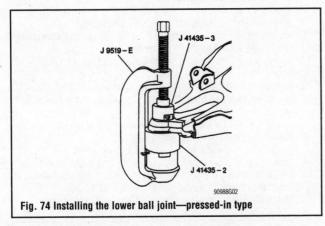

Fig. 74 Installing the lower ball joint—pressed-in type

5. Remove the caliper assembly and wire it out of the way.
6. Remove the cotter pin and the nut from the lower control arm ball joint.
7. Use a suitable tool to separate the ball joint from the knuckle.
8. Seperate the lower control arm from the knuckle and remove the knuckle from the vehicle.
9. Using the tools (or their equivalents) shown in the accompanying illustration, remove the ball joint.

To install:

10. Installation is the reverse of removal, but please note the following important steps.
11. Apply a ¼ inch (6mm) bead of Loctite® 680 evenly to the serration's on the ball joint prior to installation.
12. When installing the ball joint, make sure the grease fitting is facing forward and press the ball joint into the control arm using the tools (or their equivalents) shown in the accompanying illustration.
13. Tighten the ball joint stud nut to 84 ft. lbs. (115 Nm) on 1995 models and 94 ft. lbs. (128 Nm) on 1996–98 models. Install a new cotter pin.

Stabilizer Bar

REMOVAL & INSTALLATION

▶ See Figures 75, 76, 77 and 78

Special tool J–36202, or its equivalent, is necessary for this procedure.

1. Raise and support the front end on jackstands.
2. Remove the wheels.
3. Remove the stabilizer bar-to-frame clamps.
4. Remove the stabilizer bar-to-lower control arm bolts, nut/grommet assemblies and spacers.

➡The bolts, spacers and nuts are not interchangeable from side-to-side. Keep them separated.

5. Remove the stabilizer bar and bushings.
6. Check the bushings for wear or splitting. Replace any damaged bushings.

To install:

7. Installation is the reverse of removal, but please note the following important steps.
8. Matchmark the both torsion bar adjustment bolt positions.
9. Using tool J–36202, increase the tension on the adjusting arm.
10. Remove the adjustment bolt and retaining plate.
11. Move the tool aside.
12. Slide the torsion bars forward.
13. Coat the stabilizer bar bushings with silicone grease and install them on the stabilizer bar. Note, the split in the bushing faces forward.
14. When all fasteners are installed, tighten the frame clamp bolts to 24 ft. lbs. (33 Nm); the end link bolts to 13 ft. lbs. (18 Nm).
15. Using tool J–36202, increase tension on both torsion bars.
16. Install the adjustment retainer plate and bolt on both torsion bars.
17. Set the adjustment bolt to the marked position.
18. Release the tension on the torsion bar until the load is taken up by the adjustment bolt.

Upper Control Arm and Bushings

REMOVAL & INSTALLATION

▶ See Figure 79

1. Raise and support the truck on jackstands.
2. Support the lower control arm with a floor jack.
3. Remove the wheel.
4. Unbolt the brake hose bracket from the control arm.
5. Remove the air cleaner extension (if necessary).
6. Unfasten the brake hose bracket retainer and wire the hose aside.

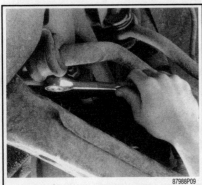

Fig. 75 Remove the stabilizer bar-to-frame clamps

Fig. 76 Remove the stabilizer bar-to-lower control arm bolts, nut/grommet assemblies and spacers

Fig. 77 Remove the stabilizer bar and bushings

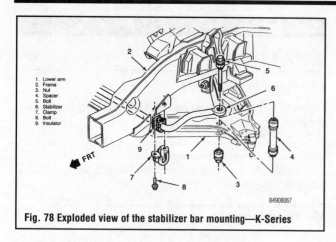

1. Lower arm
2. Frame
3. Nut
4. Spacer
5. Bolt
6. Stabilizer
7. Clamp
8. Bolt
9. Insulator

Fig. 78 Exploded view of the stabilizer bar mounting—K-Series

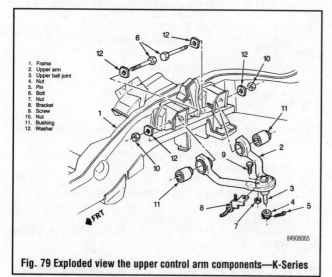

1. Frame
2. Upper arm
3. Upper ball joint
4. Nut
5. Pin
6. Bolt
7. Nut
8. Bracket
9. Screw
10. Nut
11. Bushing
12. Washer

Fig. 79 Exploded view the upper control arm components—K-Series

7. Remove the cotter pin from the upper control arm ball stud and loosen the stud nut until the bottom surface of the nut is slightly below the end of the stud.

8. Using a screw-type forcing tool, break loose the ball joint from the knuckle.

9. Remove the nuts and bolts securing the control arm to the frame brackets.

10. Tape the shims and spacers together and tag for proper reassembly.

To install:

11. Installation is the reverse of removal but please note the following important steps.

12. Place the control arm in position and install the shims, bolts and new nuts. Both bolt heads **must** be inboard of the control arm brackets. Tighten the nuts finger tight for now.

➡**Do not tighten the bolts yet. The bolts must be torqued with the truck at its proper ride height.**

13. Install the ball stud nut. Tighten the nut to 94 ft. lbs. (128 Nm) on 1988–90 models and 1995–98 models and 84 ft. lbs. (115 Nm) on 1991–94 models. Install the cotter pin. Never back off the nut to install the cotter pin. Always advance it. Never advance it more than 1⁄6 turn.

14. Lower the truck. Once the weight of the truck is on the wheels perform the **Z** height adjustment procedure in this section.

15. When the adjustment is correct, tighten the control arm pivot nuts to 88 ft. lbs. (120 Nm) on 1988–90 models; 140 ft. lbs. (190 Nm) on 1991–98 models. If the adjustment is not correct, tighten the pivot bolts to specification and have the alignment checked.

Lower Control Arm and Bushing

REMOVAL & INSTALLATION

◆ **See Figures 80, 81 and 82**

➡**Special tools J–36202, J–36618–1, J–36618–2, J–36618–3, J–36618–4, J–36618–5, and J–9519–23, or their equivalents, are necessary for this procedure.**

1. Raise and support the truck on jackstands.
2. Remove the wheel.
3. Matchmark the both torsion bar adjustment bolt positions.
4. Using tool J–36202, increase the tension on the adjusting arm.
5. Remove the adjustment bolt and retaining plate.
6. Move the tool aside.
7. Slide the torsion bars forward.
8. Remove the adjusting arm.
9. If equipped, remove the splash shield from the knuckle.
10. Remove the hub nut and washer. Insert a long drift or dowel through the vanes in the brake rotor to hold the rotor in place.
11. Using a puller, force the outer end of the axle shaft out of the hub. Remove the shaft.
12. Remove the brake caliper and wire it out of the way. Remove the rotor.
13. Disconnect the shock absorber from control arm and compress the shock absorber.
14. Disconnect the inner tie rod from the relay rod (center link).
15. Support the lower control arm with a floor jack.
16. If necessary, disconnect the stabilizer bar from the control arm.
17. Remove the cotter pin from the lower ball stud and loosen the nut.
18. Loosen the lower ball stud in the steering knuckle using a ball joint stud removal tool. When the stud is loose, remove the nut from the stud.
19. Remove the control arm-to-frame bracket bolts, nuts and washers.

Fig. 80 Disconnect the tie rod end from the steering knuckle

Fig. 81 Matchmark the torsion bar adjustment bolt positions

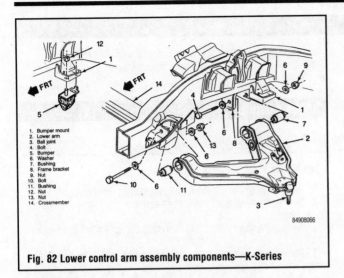

Fig. 82 Lower control arm assembly components—K-Series

1. Bumper mount
2. Lower arm
3. Ball joint
4. Bolt
5. Bumper
6. Washer
7. Nut
8. Frame bracket
9. Nut
10. Bolt
11. Bushing
12. Nut
13. Nut
14. Crossmember

84908066

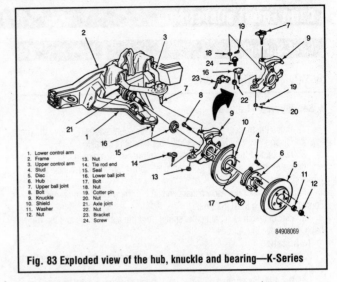

Fig. 83 Exploded view of the hub, knuckle and bearing—K-Series

1. Lower control arm
2. Frame
3. Upper control arm
4. Stud
5. Disc
6. Hub
7. Upper ball joint
8. Bolt
9. Knuckle
10. Shield
11. Washer
12. Nut
13. Nut
14. Tie rod end
15. Seal
16. Lower ball joint
17. Bolt
18. Nut
19. Cotter pin
20. Nut
21. Axle joint
22. Nut
23. Bracket
24. Screw

84908069

20. Remove the lower control arm and knuckle as a unit.

21. Separate the control arm and torsion bar.

22. On 15 and 25 Series, the bushings are not replaceable. If they are damaged, the control arm will have to be replaced. On 35 Series, proceed as follows:

    a. FRONT BUSHING: Unbend the crimps with a punch. Force out the bushings with tools J–36618–2, J–9519–23, J–36618–4 and 36618–1.

    b. REAR BUSHING: Force out the bushings with tools J–36618–5, J–9519–23, J–36618–3 and J–36618–2. There are no crimps.

To install:

23. Installation is the reverse of removal, but please note the following important steps.

24. On 35 Series, install a new front bushings, then a new rear bushing using the removal tools.

25. Raise the control arm assembly into position. Insert the front leg of the control arm into the crossmember first, then the rear leg into the frame bracket.

26. Install the bolts, front one first. The bolts **must** be installed with the front bolt head heads towards the front of the truck and the rear bolt head towards the rear of the truck!

➡**Do not tighten the bolts yet. The bolts must be torqued with the truck at its proper ride height.**

27. Start the ball joint into the knuckle and tighten the nut to specification.

28. Install the adjuster arm.

29. Using tool J–36202, increase tension on both torsion bars.

30. Install the adjustment retainer plate and bolt on both torsion bars.

31. Set the adjustment bolt to the marked position.

32. Release the tension on the torsion bar until the load is taken up by the adjustment bolt.

33. Install the wheel.

34. Lower the truck. Once the weight of the truck is on the wheels perform the **Z** height adjustment procedure in this section.

35. When the adjustment is correct, tighten the control arm pivot nuts to 135 ft. lbs. (185 Nm) on 1988–90 models; 140 ft. lbs. (190 Nm) on 1991–95 models and 121 ft. lbs. (165 Nm) on 1996–98 models. If the adjustment is not correct, tighten the pivot bolts to specification and have the alignment checked.

Hub, Knuckle and Bearing

REMOVAL & INSTALLATION

♦ **See Figure 83**

1. Raise and support the front end on jackstands.
2. Remove the wheel.
3. Remove the caliper and suspend it out of the way.
4. Remove the brake disc.

5. If necessary, remove the left stabilizer bar clamp.

6. If necessary, remove the left stabilizer bar bolt, spacer and bushings at the lower control arm.

7. Disconnect the tie rod end from the knuckle.

8. Remove the hub nut and washer.

9. Using a puller, force the outer end of the drive axle out of the hub. Remove the hub/bearing assembly. Remove the drive axle.

10. Support the lower control arm with a floor jack.

11. Unbolt and remove the splash shield.

12. Remove the upper and lower ball joint nuts and cotter pins. Using a screw-type forcing tool, separate the upper, then the lower, ball joint from the knuckle. Remove the knuckle and old seal.

To install:

Installation is the reverse of removal but please note the following important steps.

13. Drive a new seal into the knuckle using installer tool J–36605 or its equivalent.

14. Attach the ball joints to the knuckle and tighten to specifications.

15. Tighten the splash shield bolts to 12 ft. lbs. (16 Nm) on 1988–90 models; 19 ft. lbs. (26 Nm) on 1991–98 models.

16. Position the axle shaft and install the flange bolts. Tighten them to 59 ft. lbs. (79 Nm).

ADJUSTMENT

Z Height

1. Lower the truck. Once the weight of the truck is on the wheels perform the following height adjustment procedure.

2. Lift the front bumper about 38mm and let it drop.

3. Repeat this procedure 2 or 3 more times.

4. Draw a line on the side of the lower control arm from the centerline of the control arm pivot shaft, dead level to the outer end of the control arm.

5. Measure the distance between the lowest corner of the steering knuckle and the line on the control arm. Record the figure.

6. Push down about 38mm on the front bumper and let it return. Repeat the procedure 2 or 3 more times.

7. Re-measure the distance at the control arm.

8. Determine the average of the 2 measurements. The average distance should be:
- C-series: 89–101mm
- K15/25 without F60 option: 151–163mm
- K15/25 with F60 option: 177–190mm
- K35 without F60 option: 139–151mm
- K35 with F60 option: 167–179mm

9. When the adjustment is correct, tighten the control arm pivot nuts to specification. If the adjustment is not correct, tighten the pivot bolts to specification and have the alignment checked.

C3HD FRONT SUSPENSION

Leaf Spring

REMOVAL & INSTALLATION

▶ **See Figures 84 and 85**

1. Raise the truck and support the axle with safety stands. Remove the tire.
2. Disconnect the lower shock absorber mount at the axle.
3. Disconnect the stabilizer bar link from the bar. Remove the nut, washer and insulator and pull the link from the axle—don't lose the other insulator and retainer.
4. Remove the nuts and washers and lift out the U-bolts and spacer. Disconnect the spring from the axle.
5. Disconnect and separate the spring from the rear shackle and the front hanger. Remove the spring.

To install:

Installation is the reverse of removal but please note the following important steps.

6. Position the spring so it lines up with the shackle and the hanger. The double wrap end should face forward.
7. Tighten the hanger and shackle bolts to 92 ft. lbs. (125 Nm) on 1988–95 models and 136 ft. lbs. (185 Nm) on 1996–98 models.
8. Position the spring spacer so that the aligning pin contacts the edge of the spring and tighten the U-bolt nuts, diagonally to 18 ft. lbs. (25 Nm). Retighten the nuts to 80 ft. lbs. (109 Nm) on 1988–95 models and 92 ft. lbs. (125 Nm) on 1996–98 models.
9. Attach the retainer and insulator and then insert the stabilizer link into the proper hole in the axle. Tighten the nut until the distance between each retainer is 38mm (1½ in.).

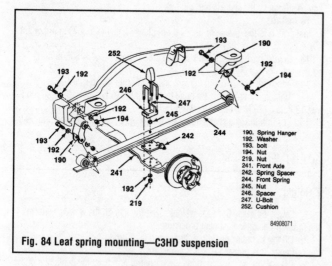

190. Spring Hanger
192. Washer
193. bolt
194. Nut
219. Nut
241. Front Axle
242. Spring Spacer
244. Front Spring
245. Nut
246. Spacer
247. U-Bolt
252. Cushion

84908071

Fig. 84 Leaf spring mounting—C3HD suspension

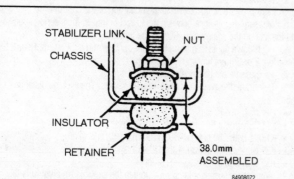

STABILIZER LINK
NUT
CHASSIS
INSULATOR
RETAINER
38.0mm ASSEMBLED

84908072

Fig. 85 Tighten the stabilizer link to this dimension—C3HD suspension

10. Tighten the stabilizer link-to-bar nut to 50 ft. lbs. (68 Nm).
11. Install the shock to the axle and tighten the lower mounting nut to 37 ft. lbs. (50 Nm).

Shock Absorber

REMOVAL & INSTALLATION

▶ **See Figure 86**

1. Raise the truck and support it with safety stands. Remove the wheels.
2. Remove the lower mounting nut and washer and disconnect the shock from the axle.
3. Remove the upper mount nut and washer, pull out the bolt and remove the shock.
4. Install the shock and tighten the upper mount to 136 ft. lbs. (185 Nm) and the lower nut to 37 ft. lbs. (50 Nm).

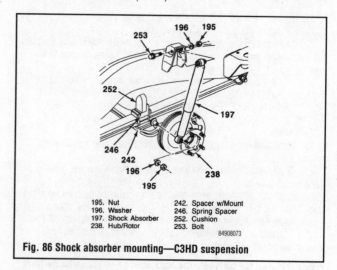

195. Nut
196. Washer
197. Shock Absorber
238. Hub/Rotor
242. Spacer w/Mount
246. Spring Spacer
252. Cushion
253. Bolt

84908073

Fig. 86 Shock absorber mounting—C3HD suspension

TESTING

Refer to the shock absorber testing procedure in the R/C series front suspension portion of the section.

Stabilizer Bar

REMOVAL & INSTALLATION

▶ **See Figure 87**

1. Raise the truck and support the axle with safety stands. Remove the tire.
2. Disconnect the stabilizer bar link from the bar.
3. Remove the clamp bolts and disconnect the bar from the axle.
4. Remove the insulator from the bar.
5. Remove the nut, retainer and insulator and then pull the link from the frame bracket. An additional insulator and retainer will come off with it.

To install:

6. Slide a retainer and insulator onto the link and insert it into the proper hole in the frame bracket.
7. Install the other insulator and retainer and then tighten the nut until the distance between each retainer is 1½ in. (38mm).
8. Connect the bar to the front axle.
9. Slide the insulators onto the bar, install the clamps and bolts and tighten them to 21 ft. lbs. (28 Nm).
10. Connect the bar to the link and tighten the nut to 50 ft. lbs. (68 Nm). Install the wheel and lower the truck.

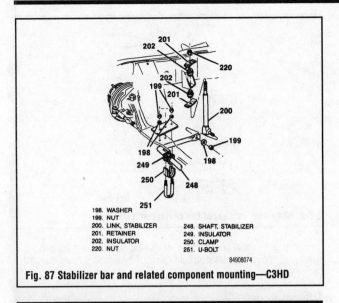

198. WASHER
199. NUT
200. LINK, STABILIZER
201. RETAINER
202. INSULATOR
220. NUT

248. SHAFT, STABILIZER
249. INSULATOR
250. CLAMP
251. U-BOLT

84908074

Fig. 87 Stabilizer bar and related component mounting—C3HD

Steering Arm, Knuckle and Spindle

REMOVAL & INSTALLATION

♦ See Figure 88

1. Raise the front of the truck and support it with safety stands. Remove the wheels.

2. Remove the brake caliper and hub/rotor assembly.

3. Loosen the mounting bolts and remove the anchor plate and splash shield. Press out the steering rod and let it hang by the rods. Unfasten the bolts attaching the anchor plate to the splash shield and separate the steering arm from the tie rod and Pitman arm.

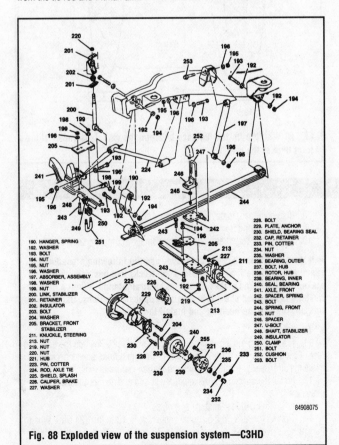

190. HANGER, SPRING
192. WASHER
193. BOLT
194. NUT
196. WASHER
197. ABSORBER, ASSEMBLY
198. WASHER
199. NUT
201. RETAINER
202. INSULATOR
203. BOLT
204. WASHER
205. BRACKET, FRONT STABILIZER
211. KNUCKLE, STEERING
213. NUT
219. NUT
220. NUT
221. HUB
223. PIN, COTTER
224. ROD, AXLE TIE
225. SHIELD, SPLASH
226. CALIPER, BRAKE
227. WASHER

228. BOLT
229. PLATE, ANCHOR
232. CAP, RETAINER
233. PIN, COTTER
234. NUT
235. WASHER
236. BEARING, OUTER
237. BOLT, HUB
238. ROTOR, HUB
239. BEARING, INNER
240. SEAL, BEARING
241. AXLE, FRONT
242. SPACER, SPRING
243. BOLT
244. SPRING, FRONT
245. NUT
246. SPACER
247. U-BOLT
248. SHAFT, STABILIZER
249. INSULATOR
251. BOLT
252. CUSHION
253. BOLT

84908075

Fig. 88 Exploded view of the suspension system—C3HD

4. Remove the brake hose bracket.

5. Remove the gaskets. Remove the caps from the knuckle.

6. Remove the nut, washer and lock pin and then drive the king pin out of the knuckle with a drift. Collect the spacers and bushings.

7. Disconnect the knuckle from the axle.

8. Remove the dust seal, shim and thrust bearing.

To install:

9. Install new bushings and ream them to 1.1804–1.1820 in. (29.982–30.022mm).

10. Install the knuckle to the axle and install the thrust bearing, shim and dust seal. Lubricate the king pin and install it with the spacers in the order in which they came out. Install the washer, nut and lock pin. Tighten the nut to 29 ft. lbs. (40 Nm).

11. Install the gaskets, caps and brake line bracket. Tighten the mounting bolts to 60 inch. lbs. (7 Nm).

12. Connect the steering arm and install the splash shield and anchor plate. Tighten the bolts to 12 ft. lbs. (16 Nm) and the nuts to 230 ft. lbs. (312 Nm).

13. Install the hub assembly and adjust the wheel bearings. Install the caliper and wheels and then lower the truck. Check the alignment.

Wheel Hub/Rotor and Bearing

REMOVAL & INSTALLATION

1. Raise and support the front end on jackstands. Remove the wheel.

2. Dismount the caliper and wire it out of the way.

3. Remove the dust cap, cotter pin, nut and washer.

4. Remove the hub/rotor and outer bearing. Do not drop the wheel bearings. The inner bearing assembly will remain in the hub and may be removed after prying out the inner seal. Discard the seal.

5. Using a hammer and drift, remove the bearing races from the hub. They are driven out from the inside out.

To install:

6. Clean all parts in a non-flammable solvent and let them air dry. Never spin-dry a bearing with compressed air! Check for excessive wear and damage.

7. Apply a thin film of grease to the spindle at the outer wheel bearing seat and at the inner bearing seat, shoulder and seal seat.

8. Apply a small amount of grease inboard of each wheel bearing cup, inside the rotor/ hub assembly.

9. When installing new races, make sure that they are not cocked and that they are fully seated against the hub shoulder. Use a press and a 3 inch (76mm) diameter bar to install the inner race and outer race into position. If the bar diameter is bigger than 3 inch (76mm), it may damage the seal seat.

10. Pack both wheel bearings using high melting point wheel bearing grease for disc brakes. Ordinary grease will melt and ooze out ruining the pads. Bearings should be packed using a cone-type wheel bearing greaser tool. If one is not available they may be packed by hand. Place a healthy glob of grease in the palm of one hand and force the edge of the bearing into it so that the grease fills the bearing. Do this until the whole bearing is packed.

11. Lubricate the seal lip with a small amount of grease, then place the inner bearing in the hub and install a new inner seal. Use a flat plate to install the seal so it is flush with the hub/rotor flange.

12. Carefully install the wheel hub/rotor assembly.

13. Using your hands, firmly press the outer bearing into the hub. Install the adjusting nut.

14. Spin the wheel hub by hand and tighten the nut until it is just snug—12 ft. lbs. (16 Nm). Back off the nut one full flat. If the hole in the spindle lines up with the slot in the nut, insert the cotter pin. If they do not line up, back off the nut until they do, but not more than one additional flat and install the cotter pin. There should be 0.0005–0.008 in. (0.013–0.20mm) end-play. This can be measured with a dial indicator, if you wish.

15. Replace the dust cap, caliper, wheel and tire.

Wheel Alignment

If the tires are worn unevenly, if the vehicle is not stable on the highway or if the handling seems uneven in spirited driving, the wheel alignment should be checked. If an alignment problem is suspected, first check for improper tire inflation and other possible causes. These can be worn suspension or steering components, accident damage or even unmatched tires. If any worn or damaged components are found, they must be replaced before the wheels can be properly aligned. Wheel alignment requires very expensive equipment and involves minute adjustments which must be accurate; it should only be performed by a trained technician. Take your vehicle to a properly equipped shop.

Following is a description of the alignment angles which are adjustable on most vehicles and how they affect vehicle handling. Although these angles can apply to both the front and rear wheels, usually only the front suspension is adjustable.

CASTER

♦ See Figure 89

Looking at a vehicle from the side, caster angle describes the steering axis rather than a wheel angle. The steering knuckle is attached to a control arm or strut at the top and a control arm at the bottom. The wheel pivots around the line between these points to steer the vehicle. When the upper point is tilted back, this is described as positive caster. Having a positive caster tends to make the wheels self-centering, increasing directional stability. Excessive positive caster makes the wheels hard to steer, while an uneven caster will cause a pull to one side. Overloading the vehicle or sagging rear springs will affect caster, as will raising the rear of the vehicle. If the rear of the vehicle is lower than normal, the caster becomes more positive.

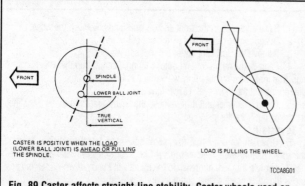

Fig. 89 Caster affects straight-line stability. Caster wheels used on shopping carts, for example, employ positive caster

CAMBER

♦ See Figure 90

Looking from the front of the vehicle, camber is the inward or outward tilt of the top of wheels. When the tops of the wheels are tilted in, this is negative camber; if they are tilted out, it is positive. In a turn, a slight amount of negative

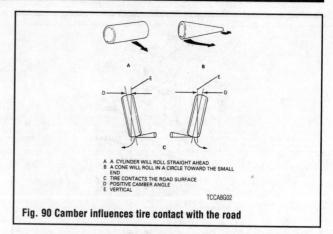

Fig. 90 Camber influences tire contact with the road

camber helps maximize contact of the tire with the road. However, too much negative camber compromises straight-line stability, increases bump steer and torque steer.

TOE

♦ See Figure 91

Looking down at the wheels from above the vehicle, toe angle is the distance between the front of the wheels, relative to the distance between the back of the wheels. If the wheels are closer at the front, they are said to be toed-in or to have negative toe. A small amount of negative toe enhances directional stability and provides a smoother ride on the highway.

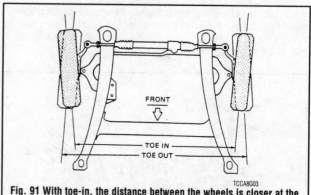

Fig. 91 With toe-in, the distance between the wheels is closer at the front than at the rear

REAR SUSPENSION

Leaf Spring

REMOVAL & INSTALLATION

R/V Series

♦ See Figures 92 and 93

1. Raise the vehicle and support it so that there is no tension on the leaf spring assembly.
2. Remove the stabilizer bar.
3. Loosen the spring-to-shackle retaining bolts. (Do not remove these bolts).
4. Remove the bolts which attach the shackle to the spring hanger.
5. Remove the nut and bolt which attach the spring to the front hanger.
6. Remove the U-bolt nuts.
7. Remove the stabilizer bar anchor plate, spacers, and shims. Take note of their positions.

8. If so equipped, remove the auxiliary spring.
9. Pull the spring from the vehicle.
10. Inspect the spring and replace any damaged components.

➡️If the spring bushings are defective, use the following procedures for removal & installation. ¾ ton and 1 ton trucks use bushings that are staked in place. The stakes must first be straightened. When a new bushing is installed stake it in 3 equally spaced locations. Using a press or vise, remove the bushing and install the new one.

To install:

11. Place the spring assembly onto the axle housing. Position the front and rear of the spring at the hangers. Raise the axle with a floor jack as necessary to make the alignments. Install the front and rear hanger bolts loosely.
12. Install the spacers, shims, auxiliary spring and anchor plate or spring plate.
13. Install the U-bolts, washers and nuts.
14. Tighten the nuts, in a diagonal sequence, to 18 ft. lbs. (24 Nm). When the spring is evenly seated, Tighten the 10/15 and 20/25 Series nuts to 125 ft.

TYPICAL REAR SUSPENSION COMPONENT LOCATIONS

1. Leaf spring   2. U-bolt   3. U-bolt nut   4. Shock absorber

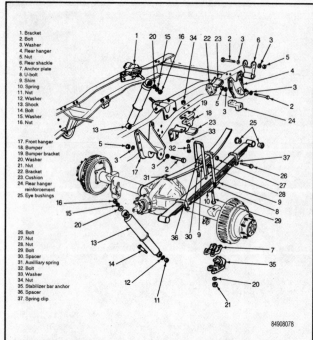

1. Bracket
2. Bolt
3. Washer
4. Rear hanger
5. Nut
6. Rear shackle
7. Anchor plate
8. U-bolt
9. Shim
10. Spring
11. Nut
12. Washer
13. Shock
14. Bolt
15. Washer
16. Nut

17. Front hanger
18. Bumper
19. Bumper bracket
20. Washer
21. Nut
22. Bracket
23. Cushion
24. Rear hanger reinforcement
25. Eye bushings

26. Bolt
27. Nut
28. Nut
29. Bolt
30. Spacer
31. Auxiliary spring
32. Bolt
33. Washer
34. Nut
35. Stabilizer bar anchor
36. Spacer
37. Spring clip

84908078

Fig. 92 Exploded view of a typical rear suspension system—R/V Series 30/3500 shown, others similar

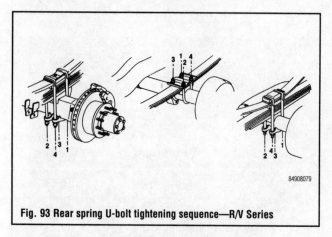

84908079

Fig. 93 Rear spring U-bolt tightening sequence—R/V Series

lbs. (169 Nm). Tighten the 30/35 Series nuts to 147 ft. lbs. (200 Nm). Use the same diagonal sequence.

15. Make sure that the hanger and shackle bolts are properly installed. The front hanger bolt head is outboard as is the rear spring-to-shackle bolt head. The shackle-to-hanger bolt head faces inboard. When all the bolts, washers and nuts are installed, tighten them to 92 ft. lbs. (124 Nm) if you are torquing on the nut; 110 ft. lbs. (149 Nm) if your are torquing on the bolt head.

16. Install the stabilizer bar.

C/K Series

♦ See Figures 94, 95, 96, 97 and 98

1. Raise the vehicle and support it so that there is no tension on the leaf spring assembly.

2. Remove the U-bolt nuts, plates, and spacer(s).

3. Remove the anchor plate.

4. Loosen the spring-to-shackle retaining bolts. (Do not remove these bolts).

5. Remove the bolts which attach the shackle to the rear bracket.

6. Remove the bolt which attaches the spring to the front bracket.

7. Pull the spring from the vehicle.

8. Inspect the spring and replace any damaged components.

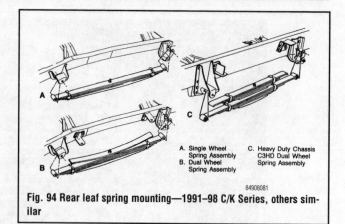

A. Single Wheel Spring Assembly
B. Dual Wheel Spring Assembly
C. Heavy Duty Chassis C3HD Dual Wheel Spring Assembly

84908081

Fig. 94 Rear leaf spring mounting—1991–98 C/K Series, others similar

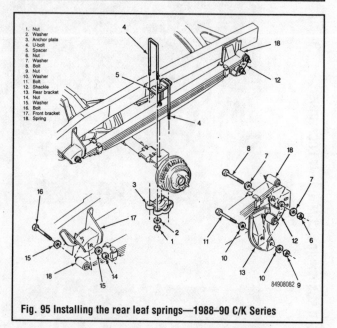

1. Nut
2. Washer
3. Anchor plate
4. U-bolt
5. Spacer
6. Nut
7. Washer
8. Bolt
9. Nut
10. Washer
11. Bolt
12. Shackle
13. Rear bracket
14. Nut
15. Washer
16. Bolt
17. Front bracket
18. Spring

84908082

Fig. 95 Installing the rear leaf springs—1988–90 C/K Series

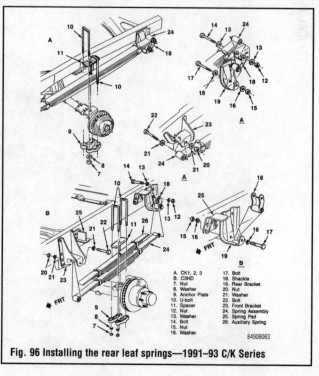

A. CK1, 2, 3
B. C3HD
7. Nut
8. Washer
9. Anchor Plate
10. U-bolt
11. Spacer
12. Nut
13. Washer
14. Bolt
15. Nut
16. Washer
17. Bolt
18. Shackle
19. Rear Bracket
20. Nut
21. Washer
22. Bolt
23. Front bracket
24. Spring Assembly
25. Spring Pad
26. Auxiliary Spring

84908083

Fig. 96 Installing the rear leaf springs—1991–93 C/K Series

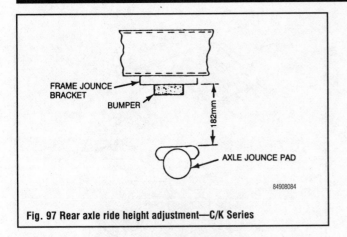

FRAME JOUNCE BRACKET

BUMPER

182mm

AXLE JOUNCE PAD

84908084

Fig. 97 Rear axle ride height adjustment—C/K Series

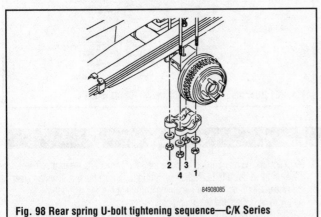

2 3 1
4

84908085

Fig. 98 Rear spring U-bolt tightening sequence—C/K Series

To install:

→If the spring bushings are defective, use the following procedures for replacement. On bushings that are staked in place, the stakes must first be straightened. Using a press or vise, remove the bushing and install the new one. When a new, previously staked bushing is installed, stake it in 3 equally spaced locations.

9. Place the spring assembly onto the axle housing. Position the front and rear of the spring at the brackets. Raise the axle with a floor jack as necessary to make the alignments. Install the front and rear brackets bolts loosely.

10. Install the spacers and spring plate.

11. Install the **NEW** U-bolts, washers and nuts. Install the anchor plate.

12. Tighten the U-bolt nuts, in a diagonal sequence, to 17 ft. lbs. (23 Nm). When the spring is evenly seated, tighten the nuts to the specifications outlined in the specifications chart at the end of this section.

13. Make sure that the hanger and shackle bolts are properly installed. All bolt heads should be inboard. Don't tighten them yet.

14. Using the floor jack, raise the axle until the distance between the bottom of the rebound bumper and its contact point on the axle is 182mm plus or minus 6mm.

15. When the spring is properly positioned, tighten all the hanger and shackle nuts to the specifications outlined in this specifications chart at the end of this section.

Shock Absorbers

REMOVAL & INSTALLATION

♦ **See Figure 99**

1. Raise and support the rear end on jackstands.
2. Support the rear axle with a floor jack.
3. If the truck is equipped with air lift shocks, bleed the air from the lines and disconnect the line from the shock absorber.

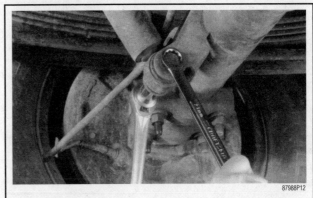

87988P12

Fig. 99 Remove the nut, washers and bolt from the bottom mount

4. Disconnect the shock absorber at the top by removing the retainers and washers.

5. Remove the nut, washers and bolt from the bottom mount. Remove the shock from the truck.

To install:

6. Install the shocks onto the vehicle.

7. Install the retainers until they are finger tight, then tighten the retainers to the specifications outlined in the torque specification chart at the end of this section.

TESTING

Refer to the shock absorber testing procedure in the R/C series front suspension portion of the section.

Stabilizer Bar

REMOVAL & INSTALLATION

R/V Series

♦ **See Figure 100**

1. Raise and support the rear end on jackstands.
2. Remove the stabilizer bar end link nuts, bolts, washers, grommets and spacers. Take note of their respective positions for installation.

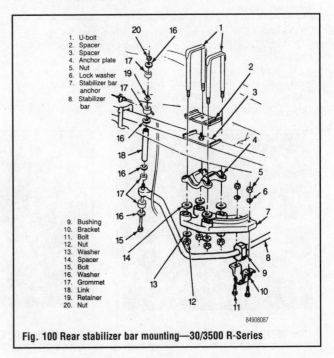

1. U-bolt
2. Spacer
3. Spacer
4. Anchor plate
5. Nut
6. Lock washer
7. Stabilizer bar anchor
8. Stabilizer bar
9. Bushing
10. Bracket
11. Bolt
12. Nut
13. Washer
14. Spacer
15. Bolt
16. Washer
17. Grommet
18. Link
19. Retainer
20. Nut

84908087

Fig. 100 Rear stabilizer bar mounting—30/3500 R-Series

3. Unfasten the clamps securing the stabilizer bar to the anchor arms. Remove the bar.

4. Remove the bushings from the clamps and check them for wear or damage. Replace them as necessary.

To install:

5. Install the bar onto the vehicle, coating the bushings and all rubber parts with silicone grease.

6. Tighten the end link nuts just until they reach the unthreaded part of the bolt.

7. Tighten the clamp-to-anchor bolts to 24 ft. lbs. (32 Nm).

✳✳ CAUTION

Make sure that the parking brake cable is routed over the stabilizer bar!

C3HD Series

▶ See Figure 101

1. Raise and support the vehicle on safety stands. Remove the wheels.

2. Remove the upper nut and insulator. Remove the bolts from the spacer and the bar.

3. Remove the U-bolt nuts, the U-bolts, clamps and lower insulators and lift out the bar.

4. Install the bar and tighten the U-bolt nuts to 22 ft. lbs. (30 Nm). Tighten the upper insulator nuts to 17 ft. lbs. (23 Nm).

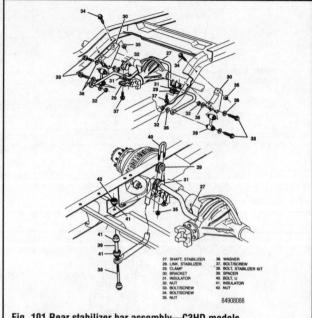

27. SHAFT, STABILIZER	36. WASHER
28. LINK, STABILIZER	37. BOLT/SCREW
29. CLAMP	38. BOLT, STABILIZER KIT
30. BRACKET	39. SPACER
31. INSULATOR	40. BOLT, U
32. NUT	41. INSULATOR
33. BOLT/SCREW	42. NUT
34. BOLT/SCREW	
35. NUT	

84908088

Fig. 101 Rear stabilizer bar assembly—C3HD models

STEERING

Steering Wheel

REMOVAL & INSTALLATION

All Series

▶ See Figures 102 thru 107

✳✳ CAUTION

When performing service around the SIR system components or wiring, the SIR system MUST be disabled. Failure to do so could result in possible air bag deployment, personal injury or unneeded SIR system repairs.

1. Disconnect the battery ground cable.

2. On models equipped with a drivers side air bag, perform the following procedure:

a. Disable the Supplemental Restraint System (if equipped).

b. On all but 1996–98 models equipped with a air bag, unfasten the screws at the rear of the steering wheel.

c. On 1996–98 models equipped with a air bag, turn the steering wheel 90 to access the rear shroud holes to the inflator module. Insert a screwdriver in the holes and push the leaf spring to release the pin. Turn the steering wheel 180 to access the remaining shroud holes and using the screwdriver, release the remaining pins.

d. Tilt the inflator module rearward from the top to access the wiring. Tag and unplug the lead wire from the clip on the module, the lead wire from the clip on the steering wheel and the Connector Position Assurance (CPA) and retainer from the module.

3. If not equipped with a drivers side air bag, remove the horn pad or button cap and disconnect the horn wires.

4. Mark the steering wheel-to-steering shaft relationship.

5. If equipped, remove the snapring from the steering shaft.

6. Remove the nut from the steering shaft.

✳✳ WARNING

Don't hammer on the steering shaft!

7. Remove the steering wheel with a puller.

To install:

8. Install the wheel aligning the marks made earlier. The turn signal control assembly must be in the Neutral position to prevent damaging the canceling cam and control assembly. Tighten the nut to 30 ft. lbs. (40 Nm).

87988P13

Fig. 102 Remove the horn button cap

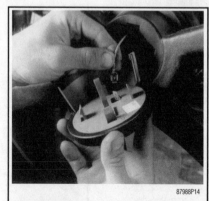

87988P14

Fig. 103 Disengage the horn wiring

87988P15

Fig. 104 If equipped, remove the snapring from the steering shaft

Fig. 105 Remove the nut and washer from the steering shaft

Fig. 106 Use a puller to separate the steering wheel

Fig. 107 Remove the steering wheel

9. Install the horn pad and horn contact (if equipped).

10. If equipped with a drivers side air bag, install the inflator module as follows:

   a. Attach the lead wire to the clip on the module, the lead wire to the clip on the steering wheel and the Connector Position Assurance (CPA) and retainer to the module.

   b. On 1996–98 models, install the inflator module by pressing it firmly into the steering wheel so that all four notched pins in the leaf spring are fully engaged. Be very careful that you do not pinch any wires.

   c. On all but 1996–98 models equipped with a air bag, install the inflator module and tighten the screws to 27 inch lbs. (3 Nm).

11. Connect the battery ground cable and enable the SIR system (if equipped).

Turn Signal (Combination) Switch

REMOVAL & INSTALLATION

1988–94 Models

♦ See Figures 108, 109 and 110

✳✳ CAUTION

When performing service around the SIR system components or wiring, the SIR system MUST be disabled. Failure to do so could result in possible air bag deployment, personal injury or unneeded SIR system repairs.

1. Make sure the switch is in the off position.
2. Remove the steering wheel as outlined in this section.
3. Remove the instrument panel trim cover.
4. Insert a screwdriver into the lockplate cover slot and pry out the cover.

Remove the lockplate. A special tool is available to do this. The tool is an inverted U-shape, with a hole for the shaft. The shaft nut is used to force it down. Pry the wire snapring out of the shaft groove. Discard the snapring.

5. Remove the tool and lift the lockplate off the shaft.
6. Remove the turn signal lever screw and lever.
7. Press the hazard button inward and unscrew it.
8. Remove the switch retaining screws. Pull the switch connector out of the mast jacket and feed the switch connector through the column support bracket.
9. Position the turn signal lever and shifter housing in the downward, or "low" position and pull downward on the lower end of the column using a pliers on the tab provided. Remove the wire protector.
10. Remove the switch mounting screws. Remove the switch by pulling it straight up while guiding the wiring harness cover through the column.

To install:

11. Install the replacement switch by working the connector and cover down through the housing and under the bracket.
12. Install the switch mounting screws and the connector on the mast jacket bracket. Install the column-to-dash trim plate.
13. Install the flasher knob and the turn signal lever.
14. With the turn signal lever in neutral and the flasher knob out, slide the thrust washer, upper bearing preload spring, and canceling cam into the shaft.
15. Position the lockplate on the shaft and press it down until a new snapring can be inserted in the shaft groove.
16. Install the cover and the steering wheel.

1995–98 Models

♦ See Figure 111

✳✳ CAUTION

When performing service around the SIR system components or wiring, the SIR system MUST be disabled. Failure to do so could result in possible air bag deployment, personal injury or unneeded SIR system repairs.

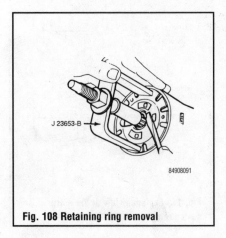

Fig. 108 Retaining ring removal

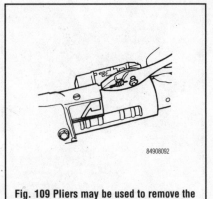

Fig. 109 Pliers may be used to remove the turn signal wire protector

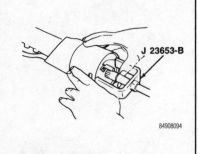

Fig. 110 Install the lockplate and the retaining ring using the tool illustrated (or its equivalent)

1. Make sure the switch is in the off position.
2. Remove the steering wheel as outlined in this section.
3. Disconnect the tilt wheel lever by pulling it out.
4. Remove the knee bolster and the Torx head screws from the lower column cover.
5. Lower the cover by tilting it down and then sliding it back to disengage the locking tabs.
6. Remove the Torx® head screws from the upper column cover.
7. Remove the steering column lock set and the upper cover.
8. Disconnect the wiring harness straps from the steering column wiring harness.
9. Remove the retainer from Connector Position Assurance (CPA) if equipped.
10. Disengage the connector from the Brake Transmission Shift Interlock (BTSI) if equipped.
11. Unplug the gray and black connectors from the bulkhead connector.
12. Unfasten the Torx® head screws from the switch and remove the switch.

To install:

Installation is the reverse of removal but please note the following important steps.

13. Install the switch. Use a small blade screwdriver to compress the electrical contact and move the switch into position. The electrical contact must rest on the canceling cam assembly.
14. Fasten the Torx® head screws on the switch. Tighten the screws to 53 inch. lbs. (6 Nm).
15. Install the upper column cover and fasten the column bracket nuts. Tighten the nuts to 22 ft. lbs. (30 Nm).
16. Install the knee bolster and the steering column cylinder lock. Tighten the column cover Torx® screws to 12 inch. lbs. (1.4 Nm).
17. Install the lower column cover and tighten the Torx screws 53 inch. lbs. (6 Nm).
18. Make sure the switch is in the off position and install the steering wheel. Refer to this section for this procedure.
19. Enable the SIR system (if equipped).

Ignition Switch

REMOVAL & INSTALLATION

1988–91 Models

1. Remove the column shroud halves.
2. Remove the column-to-dash attaching bolts and slowly lower the steering column, making sure that it is supported.
3. Make sure that the switch is in the Lock position. If the lock cylinder is out, pull the switch rod up to the stop, then go down one detent.
4. Disconnect the actuating rod from the switch.
5. Remove the two screws and the switch.

To install:

6. Before installation, make sure the switch is in the Lock position.
7. Installation is the reverse of removal.

1992–94 Models

1. Disconnect the negative battery cable.
2. Lower the steering column.
3. Remove the washer head screw and the hexagon nut.
4. Disconnect the dimmer switch assembly from the rod.
5. Unfasten the dimmer and ignition switch mounting stud.
6. Seperate the ignition switch from the actuator rod.
7. Unplug the ignition switch electrical connection and remove the switch.

To install:

➡ The new ignition switch will come in the OFF-LOCK position. Once the switch is assembled on the column, remove the plastic pin from the switch. If you are installing the old switch, make sure it is in the OFF-LOCK position.

8. Attach the switch to the actuator rod.
9. Move the switch slider to the extreme left position, then move the slider one detent right to the **OFF-LOCK** position. Install the dimmer switch mounting stud and tighten to 35 inch lbs. (4 Nm).
10. Attach the dimmer switch to the rod, then install the washer head screw and hexagon nut. Do not fully tighten at this time.
11. Place a $\frac{3}{32}$ inch drill bit in the hole on the dimmer switch. Position the switch on the column and push against the rod to eliminate all lash.
12. Install the switch and tighten the screw and nut to 35 inch lbs. (4 Nm).
13. Attach the switch electrical connection.
14. Raise and attach the steering column.
15. Connect the negative battery cable and check for proper switch operation.

1995–98 Models

▶ **See Figures 112 and 113**

1. Remove the column shroud halves.
2. Remove the column-to-dash attaching bolts and slowly lower the steering column, making sure that it is supported.
3. Remove the multi function switch if necessary.
4. Remove the key alarm switch, if equipped by gently prying the alarm switch retaining clip with a small screwdriver. Rotate the alarm switch ¼ in. turn and remove.

❊❊ WARNING

Extreme care is necessary to prevent damage to the collapsible column.

5. Make sure that the switch is in the Lock position. If the lock cylinder is out, pull the switch rod up to the stop, then go down one detent.
6. Disconnect the actuating rod from the switch.
7. Remove the two screws and the switch.

To install:

8. Before installation, make sure the switch is in the Lock position.
9. Attach the actuating rod to the switch.
10. Install the switch using the original screws. Tighten the screws to 12 inch. lbs. (1.4 Nm).

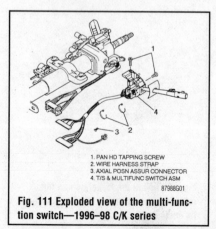

1. PAN HD TAPPING SCREW
2. WIRE HARNESS STRAP
3. AXIAL POSN ASSUR CONNECTOR
4. T/S & MULTIFUNC SWITCH ASM

87988G01

Fig. 111 Exploded view of the multi-function switch—1996–98 C/K series

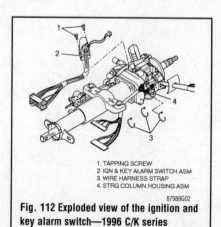

1. TAPPING SCREW
2. IGN & KEY ALARM SWITCH ASM
3. WIRE HARNESS STRAP
4. STRG COLUMN HOUSING ASM

87988G02

Fig. 112 Exploded view of the ignition and key alarm switch—1996 C/K series

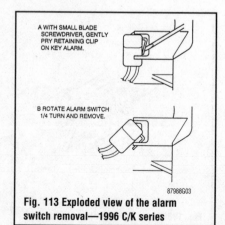

A WITH SMALL BLADE SCREWDRIVER, GENTLY PRY RETAINING CLIP ON KEY ALARM.

B ROTATE ALARM SWITCH 1/4 TURN AND REMOVE.

87988G03

Fig. 113 Exploded view of the alarm switch removal—1996 C/K series

11. Install the key alarm switch, if equipped . Make sure the retaining clip is parallel to the lock cylinder. Rotate the alarm switch ¼ in. turn until locked in place.

12. Install the multi function switch if removed.

❊❊ CAUTION

Use of screws that are too long could prevent the column from collapsing on impact.

13. Replace the column. Tighten the nuts to 22 ft. lbs. (29 Nm); the bolts to 20 ft. lbs. (27 Nm).

14. Install the column shroud halves.

Lock Cylinder

REMOVAL & INSTALLATION

1988–94 Models

▶ See Figures 114 and 115

1. Remove the steering wheel.
2. Remove the turn signal switch. It is not necessary to completely remove the switch from the column. Pull the switch rearward far enough to slip it over the end of the shaft, but do not pull the harness out of the column.
3. Turn the lock to Run.
4. If necessary, remove the ignition key.
5. If equipped, remove the buzzer switch assembly.
6. Remove the lock retaining screw and remove the lock cylinder.

❊❊ WARNING

If the retaining screw is dropped on removal, it may fall into the column, requiring complete disassembly of the column to retrieve the screw.

To install:

7. Rotate the key to the stop while holding onto the cylinder.
8. Push the lock all the way in.
9. Install the screw. Tighten the screw to 40 inch lbs. (5 Nm) for regular columns, 22 inch lbs. (2.5 Nm) for tilt columns.
10. Install the turn signal switch and the steering wheel.

1995–98 Models

▶ See Figures 116, 117 and 118

❊❊ CAUTION

When performing service around the SIR system components or wiring, the SIR system MUST be disabled. Failure to do so could result in possible air bag deployment, personal injury or unneeded SIR system repairs.

When carrying a live inflator module, make sure that the bag and trim cover are pointed away from you. Never carry the inflator module by the wires or connector on the underside of the module. In case of accidental deployment, the bag will then deploy with minimal chance of injury.

When placing a live inflator module on a bench or other surface, always face the bag and trim cover up, away from the surface.

1. Disconnect the negative battery cable and disable the SIR system.
2. Remove the upper and lower shroud, air bag module and the steering column.
3. Remove the retaining ring, SIR coil assembly, wave washer.
4. Remove the shaft lock retaining ring using tool J 23653-SIR or its equivalent to push down the shaft lock shield assembly. Discard the ring.
5. Remove the shaft lock shield and turn signal cancel cam assembly.
6. Remove the park lock cable assembly from the lock module assembly.
7. Remove the key alarm switch, if equipped by gently prying the alarm switch retaining clip with a small prytool. Rotate the alarm switch ¼ in. turn and remove.
8. Remove the two tapping screws and the ignition key and alarm assembly. Let the switch hang freely.

❊❊ CAUTION

The lock assembly is under slight spring tension. Hold the lock bolt in place while removing the lock module assembly.

9. Remove the three pan head tapping screws and the lock module assembly.
10. Remove the backing plate from the module.

➡**Mark the two sector gears at the OFF-LOCK position to ensure proper reassembly.**

11. Remove the sector gears.
12. Remove the positioning tab on the end of the lock cylinder using an ⅛ in. burring tool. Remove all burrs from the lock module and cylinder assembly.
13. Push on the locking tab of the lock cylinder from inside the lock module assembly and remove the lock cylinder.

To install:

14. Align the marks on the sector gears and install the gears and the backing plate to the lock module assembly.
15. Install the lock cylinder set and ensure that the lock module assembly is in the **OFF-LOCK** position.
16. Install the key in the lock cylinder and ensure that it is in the **OFF-LOCK** position.
17. Line up the locking tab with the slots in the lock module assembly and push the cylinder into position.
18. Rotate the lock cylinder to the **ACC** position. The alignment arrows on the sector gears should be pointing towards each other.
19. Rotate the lock cylinder to the **LOCK** position. Push the lock bolt in until it is flush and align the lock module assembly with the head assembly and install the lock module assembly.
20. Install the three pan head screws and tighten to 53 inch. lbs. (6 Nm).
21. Install the ignition and key alarm switch assembly and the fasteners. Tighten the fasteners to 12 inch. lbs. (1 Nm).

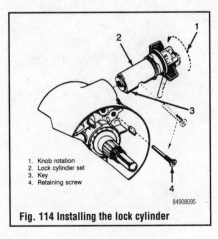

1. Knob rotation
2. Lock cylinder set
3. Key
4. Retaining screw

84908095

Fig. 114 Installing the lock cylinder

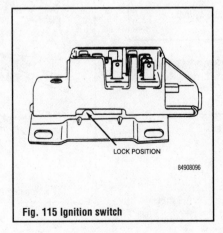

LOCK POSITION

84908096

Fig. 115 Ignition switch

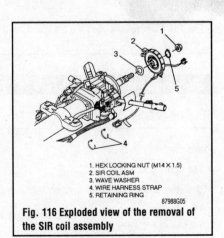

1. HEX LOCKING NUT (M14 X 1.5)
2. SIR COIL ASM
3. WAVE WASHER
4. WIRE HARNESS STRAP
5. RETAINING RING

87988G05

Fig. 116 Exploded view of the removal of the SIR coil assembly

22. Install the key alarm switch. Make sure the retaining clip is parallel to the lock cylinder. Rotate the alarm switch ¼ in. turn until locked in place.

23. Lubricate the lower brass surface of the turn signal cancel cam assembly with synthetic grease and install the assembly.

24. Align the inner block tooth of the lock plate to block tooth of race and upper shaft assembly and install the assembly.

25. Install a new shaft lock ring using tool J 23653-SIR and ensure the ring is firmly seated in the groove on the shaft.

26. Install the center race and upper shaft assembly.

27. Place the ignition switch to the lock assembly and ensure the coil is centered.

28. Install the wave washer and the SIR coil assembly.

29. Install the retaining ring and route the coil wire along the steering column.

30. Install the wire harness straps to the steering column harness.

31. Install the park lock cable assembly with the transmission in Park and the ignition switch in the **OFF-LOCK** position.

32. Install the upper and lower covers, lock cylinder set and tilt lever (if equipped).

33. Install the steering column and enable the SIR system. Connect the negative battery cable.

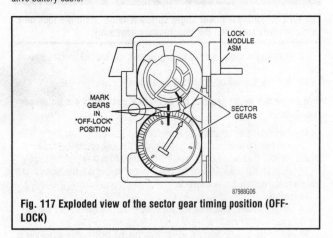

Fig. 117 Exploded view of the sector gear timing position (OFF-LOCK)

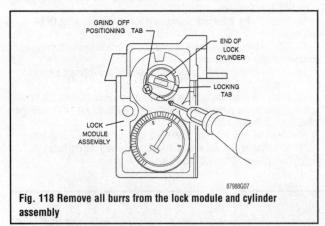

Fig. 118 Remove all burrs from the lock module and cylinder assembly

Steering Linkage

REMOVAL & INSTALLATION

Pitman Arm

♦ See Figures 119 thru 123

1. Raise and support the front end on jackstands.
2. Remove nut from Pitman arm ball stud.
3. On R/V series, remove the Pitman arm or relay rod from ball stud by tapping on side of rod or arm (in which the stud mounts) with a hammer while

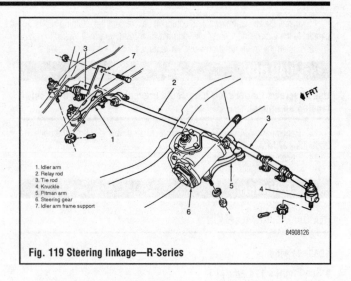

1. Idler arm
2. Relay rod
3. Tie rod
4. Knuckle
5. Pitman arm
6. Steering gear
7. Idler arm frame support

Fig. 119 Steering linkage—R-Series

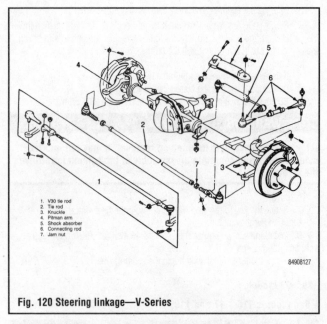

1. V30 tie rod
2. Tie rod
3. Knuckle
4. Pitman arm
5. Shock absorber
6. Connecting rod
7. Jam nut

Fig. 120 Steering linkage—V-Series

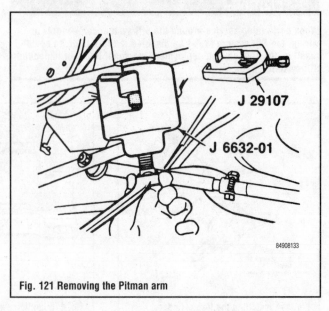

J 29107

J 6632-01

Fig. 121 Removing the Pitman arm

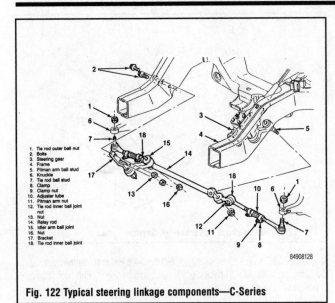

Fig. 122 Typical steering linkage components—C-Series

1. Tie rod outer ball nut
2. Bolts
3. Steering gear
4. Frame
5. Pitman arm ball stud
6. Knuckle
7. Tie rod ball stud
8. Clamp
9. Clamp nut
10. Adjuster tube
11. Pitman arm nut
12. Tie rod inner ball joint nut
13. Nut
14. Relay rod
15. Idler arm ball joint
16. Nut
17. Bracket
18. Tie rod inner ball joint

84908128

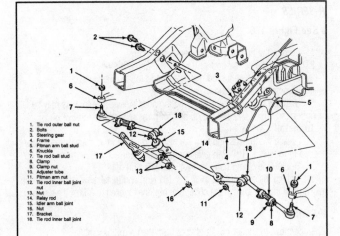

Fig. 123 Steering linkage—1988–91 K-Series

1. Tie rod outer ball nut
2. Bolts
3. Steering gear
4. Frame
5. Pitman arm ball stud
6. Knuckle
7. Tie rod ball stud
8. Clamp
9. Clamp nut
10. Adjuster tube
11. Pitman arm nut
12. Tie rod inner ball joint nut
13. Nut
14. Relay rod
15. Idler arm ball joint
16. Nut
17. Bracket
18. Tie rod inner ball joint

84908130

using a heavy hammer or similar tool as a backing. Pull on the linkage to remove from the stud.

4. On C/K series, break loose the Pitman ball stud from the relay rod using a screw-type ball stud tool. Pull on the linkage to remove the stud.

5. If necessary, unbolt the steering gear from the frame.

6. Remove the Pitman arm nut from the Pitman shaft or the clamp bolt from the Pitman arm, and mark the relation of the arm position to the shaft.

7. Remove Pitman arm, using a large puller.

To install:

8. Install the Pitman arm on the Pitman shaft, lining up the marks made upon removal.

➡ **If a clamp type Pitman arm is used, spread the Pitman arm just enough, with a wedge, to slip arm onto the Pitman shaft. Do not spread the Pitman arm more than required to slip over the Pitman shaft with hand pressure. Do not hammer or damage to the steering gear may result. Be sure to install the hardened steel washer before installing the nut.**

9. Make sure that the threads on the ball studs and in the ball stud nuts are clean and smooth. If threads are not clean and smooth, ball studs may turn in there sockets when attempting to tighten the nut. Check the condition of the ball stud seals; replace if necessary.

10. Install the Pitman shaft nut or Pitman arm clamp bolt and tighten to 184 ft. lbs. (249 Nm) on R and C/K-Series; 125 ft. lbs. (169 Nm) on V-Series.

11. If removed, bolt the steering gear to the frame.

12. Position the ball stud onto the Pitman arm or relay rod.

13. On R/V series, tighten the Pitman arm-to-relay rod nut to 66 ft. lbs. (89 Nm). On C/K series, tighten the Pitman arm-to-relay rod nut to 40 ft. lbs. (54 Nm) on 1988–91 models; 46 ft. lbs. (62 Nm) on 1992–98 models. Always advance the nut to align the cotter pin hole. NEVER back it off!

14. Lubricate ball studs.

15. Lower the vehicle to the floor.

C3HD Series

1. Raise and support the front end on jackstands.

2. Disconnect the drag link from the Pitman arm ball stud.

3. Matchmark the Pitman arm to the Pitman shaft, remove the nut from the steering gear shaft and discard it.

4. Remove the Pitman arm with the proper tool (ball joint puller).

5. Install the arm so the marks line up with those on the shaft. Tighten the nut to 184 ft. lbs. (250 Nm). Tighten the ball stud nut to 48 ft. lbs. (62 Nm).

Idler Arm

◆ **See Figures 119 thru 123**

1. Raise and support the front end on jackstands.

2. Remove the idler arm ball stud nut. Discard the nut.

3. Using a screw-type ball joint tool, separate the idler arm from the relay rod.

To install:

4. Make sure that the threads on the ball stud and in the ball stud nut are clean and smooth. If threads are not clean and smooth, ball stud may turn in the socket when attempting to tighten nut. Check condition of ball stud seal; replace if necessary.

5. Position the idler arm on the frame and install the mounting bolts. On R/V series, tighten the bolts to 30 ft. lbs. (40 Nm). On C/K series, tighten the frame-to-bracket bolts to 78 ft. lbs. (105 Nm) on 1988–92 models, 59 ft. lbs. (80 Nm) on 1993–95 models and 71 ft. lbs. (96 Nm) on 1996–98 models.

6. Install the idler arm ball stud in the relay rod, making certain the seal is positioned properly. On R/V series, tighten the nut to 66 ft. lbs. (89 Nm). On C/K series, tighten the new ball stud nut to 40 ft. lbs. (54 Nm) on 1988–92 and 1996 models, 52 ft. lbs. (70 Nm) on 1993–95 models and 46 ft. lbs. (62 Nm) on 1997–98 models. Always advance the nut to align the cotter pin hole. NEVER back it off! Lower the vehicle to the floor.

Relay Rod (Center Link)

R/V SERIES

◆ **See Figures 119, 120 and 121**

1. Raise and support the vehicle with jackstands.

2. Remove the inner ends of the tie rods from the relay rod.

3. Remove the nuts from the Pitman and idler arm ball studs at the relay rod.

4. Using a screw-type ball joint tool, separate the relay rod from the Pitman and idler arms.

5. Remove the relay rod from the vehicle.

To install:

6. Installation is the reverse of removal, but please note the following important steps.

7. Make sure that threads on the ball studs and in the ball stud nuts are clean and smooth. If the threads are not clean and smooth, ball studs may turn in sockets when attempting to tighten nut. Check condition of ball stud seals; replace if necessary.

8. Connect the relay rod to the idler arm and Pitman arm ball studs, making certain the seals are in place. Tighten the nuts to 66 ft. lbs. (89 Nm). Always advance the nut to align the cotter pin hole. NEVER back it off!

C/K SERIES

◆ **See Figures 121, 122 and 123**

1. Raise and support the vehicle with jackstands.

2. Disconnect the steering shock absorber from the relay rod.

3. Remove the nut and disconnect the inner tie rod ball joint from the relay rod using a screw-type ball joint tool. Discard the nut.

4. Remove the nuts from the Pitman and idler arm ball studs at the relay rod. Discard the nuts.

5. Using a screw-type ball joint tool, disconnect the relay rod from the Pitman and idler arm.

6. Remove the relay rod from the vehicle.

To install:

Installation is the reverse of removal but please note the following important steps.

7. Make sure that threads on the ball studs and in the ball stud nuts are clean and smooth. If the threads are not clean and smooth, ball studs may turn in sockets when attempting to tighten nut. Check condition of ball stud seals; replace if necessary.

8. Connect the relay rod to the idler arm and Pitman arm ball studs, making certain the seals are in place. Tighten the new ball stud nut to 40 ft. lbs. (54 Nm) on 1988–92 and 1996 models, 52 ft. lbs. (70 Nm) on 1993–95 models and 46 ft. lbs. (62 Nm) on 1997–98 models. Always advance the nut to align the cotter pin hole. NEVER back it off!

9. Install the tie rod to the center link. Tighten the new nut to 40 ft. lbs. (54 Nm).

10. Install the shock absorber. Tighten the frame end nut to 30 ft. lbs. (40 Nm); the relay rod end nut to 46 ft. lbs. (62 Nm). Always advance the nut to align the cotter pin hole. NEVER back it off!

Drag Link

C3HD SERIES ONLY

1. Raise the front of the truck and support it on safety stands.
2. Remove the nuts from the Pitman arm and drag link ball studs.
3. Press the link off the arm and the tie rod.
4. Install the link. Tighten the Pitman arm ball stud to 46 ft. lbs. (62 Nm) to seat the tapers. Tighten both ball stud nuts to 40 ft. lbs. (54 Nm).

Steering Linkage Shock Absorber

V SERIES

▶ **See Figure 120**

1. Remove the cotter pins and nuts and remove the unit.
2. Installation is the reverse of removal. Tighten the tie rod end nut to 46 ft. lbs. (62 Nm); the frame end nut to 81 ft. lbs. (109 Nm). Always advance the nut to align the cotter pin hole. NEVER back it off!

C/K SERIES

▶ **See Figures 124 and 125**

1. Raise and support the front end on jackstands.
2. Remove the frame end nut and bolt.
3. Remove the cotter pin and nut from the relay rod end. It may be necessary to separate the shock from the relay rod with a screw-type ball joint tool.
4. Install the shock and tighten the frame end nut and bolt to 33 ft. lbs. (45

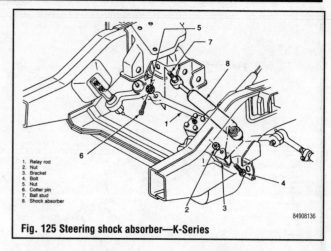

1. Relay rod
2. Nut
3. Bracket
4. Bolt
5. Nut
6. Cotter pin
7. Ball stud
8. Shock absorber

84908136

Fig. 125 Steering shock absorber—K-Series

Nm); the relay rod end nut to 46 ft. lbs. (62 Nm). Always advance the nut to align the cotter pin hole. NEVER back it off! A maximum torque of 59 ft. lbs. (80 Nm) is permissible to align the hole.

Tie Rod Ends

R-SERIES

▶ **See Figure 126**

1. Loosen the tie rod adjuster sleeve clamp nuts.
2. Remove the tie rod end stud cotter pin and nut.
3. Use a screw-type tie rod removal tool to loosen the stud.
4. Remove the inner stud in the same way.
5. Unscrew the tie rod end from the threaded sleeve. The threads may be left or right hand threads. Count the number of turns required to remove it.

To install:

6. Grease the threads and turn the new tie rod end in as many turns as were needed to remove it. This will give approximately correct toe-in.
7. Tighten the clamp bolts to 14 ft. lbs. (18 Nm).
8. Tighten the stud nuts to 45 ft. lbs. (61 Nm) and install new cotter pins. You may tighten the nut to align the cotter pin, but don't loosen it. Adjust the toe-in.

V-SERIES

1. Remove the cotter pins and nuts from the tie rod assembly.
2. Disconnect the steering shock absorber from the tie rod.
3. Use a screw-type tie rod removal tool to loosen the ball studs from the knuckles.
4. Count the number of exposed threads on each tie rod end and record it.
5. Loosen the tie rod end lock nuts and unscrew the tie rod ends.
6. When installing the tie rod ends, turn them in until the same number of threads previously visible are achieved. Tighten the locknuts.
7. Install the tie rod assembly in the knuckles and tighten the castellated nuts to 40 ft. lbs. (54 Nm). Always advance the nut to align the cotter pin hole. NEVER back it off!
8. Tighten the tie rod end locknuts to 175 ft. lbs. (237 Nm).

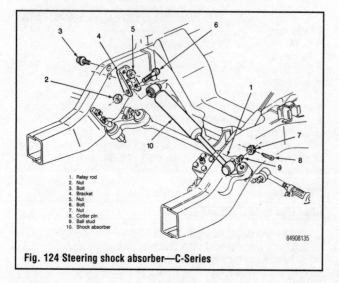

1. Relay rod
2. Nut
3. Bolt
4. Bracket
5. Nut
6. Bolt
7. Nut
8. Cotter pin
9. Ball stud
10. Shock absorber

84908135

Fig. 124 Steering shock absorber—C-Series

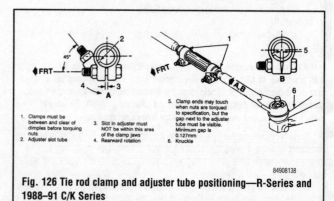

1. Clamps must be between and clear of dimples before torquing nuts
2. Adjuster slot tube
3. Slot in adjuster must NOT be within this area of the clamp jaws
4. Rearward rotation
5. Clamp ends may touch when nuts are torqued to specification, but the gap next to the adjuster tube must be visible. Minimum gap is 0.127mm
6. Knuckle

84908138

Fig. 126 Tie rod clamp and adjuster tube positioning—R-Series and 1988–91 C/K Series

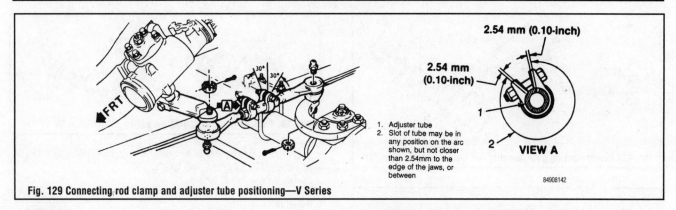

Fig. 129 Connecting rod clamp and adjuster tube positioning—V Series

C/K SERIES

▶ See Figures 70, 71, 80, 126, 127 and 128

1. Raise and support the front end on jackstands.
2. Remove the nut from the knuckle end ball stud. Discard the nut.
3. Using a screw-type ball joint tool, separate the tie rod ball stud from the knuckle.
4. On all except C3HD models, remove the nut from the inner tie rod ball stud.
5. Using a screw-type ball joint tool, separate the tie rod ball stud from the relay rod.
6. Clean the threaded parts of the tie rod ends thoroughly and count the exact number of threads exposed on each tie rod end. Measure the overall length of the tie rod assembly.
7. Loosen the clamp nuts, spread the clamps and unscrew each tie rod end.

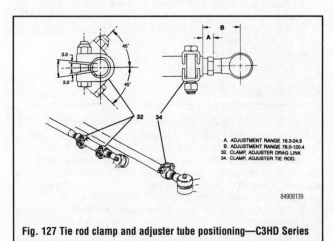

A. ADJUSTMENT RANGE 16.3-24.9
B. ADJUSTMENT RANGE 79.0-120.4
32. CLAMP, ADJUSTER DRAG LINK
34. CLAMP, ADJUSTER TIE ROD.

Fig. 127 Tie rod clamp and adjuster tube positioning—C3HD Series

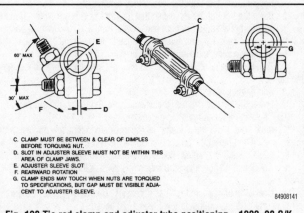

C. CLAMP MUST BE BETWEEN & CLEAR OF DIMPLES BEFORE TORQUING NUT.
D. SLOT IN ADJUSTER SLEEVE MUST NOT BE WITHIN THIS AREA OF CLAMP JAWS.
E. ADJUSTER SLEEVE SLOT
F. REARWARD ROTATION
G. CLAMP ENDS MAY TOUCH WHEN NUTS ARE TORQUED TO SPECIFICATIONS, BUT GAP MUST BE VISIBLE ADJACENT TO ADJUSTER SLEEVE.

Fig. 128 Tie rod clamp and adjuster tube positioning—1992–98 C/K Series

To install:

8. Coat the threaded parts of the new tie rod ends with chassis grease. Screw the tie rod ends into the sleeve until the exact number of threads is exposed on each tie rod end. Check the overall length of the new assembly. Adjust as necessary. Don't tighten the clamp nuts yet.
9. On all except C3HD models, position the tie rod assembly in the relay rod and install a new nut on the ball stud. Tighten the nut to 40 ft. lbs. (54 Nm).
10. Position the other tie rod end in the knuckle. Install the new nut and tighten it to 40 ft. lbs. (54 Nm) on 1988–96 models (except C3HD) and 46 ft. lbs. (62 Nm) on 1997–98 models (except C3HD). On 1988–94 C3HD models, tighten the nut to 40 ft. lbs. (54 Nm) and 65 ft. lbs. (88 Nm) on 1995–98 models.
11. Before tightening the clamp nuts, position the clamp as shown in the accompanying illustrations.
12. Tighten the clamp nuts to 14 ft. lbs. (19 Nm) on 1988–96 models (except C3HD) and 18 ft. lbs. (25 Nm) on 1997–98 models (except C3HD). On C3HD models, tighten the clamp nuts to 50 ft. lbs. (68 Nm) on 1988–95 models and 65 ft. lbs. (88 Nm) on 1996–98 models.

Connecting Rod

V-SERIES

▶ See Figure 129

1. Remove the cotter pins and nuts from each end of the connecting rod.
2. Using a screw type remover tool, break loose the connecting rod from the Pitman arm and steering knuckle.
3. If the connecting rod ends are being replaced, note the length of the complete assembly and record it. Also note the respective directions of the ends when installed.
4. Loosen the clamp bolts and unscrew the ends. If the bolts are rusted, replace them.
5. Install the rod and tighten the clamp bolts to 40 ft. lbs. (54 Nm); the ball stud nuts to 89 ft. lbs. (120 Nm). Always advance the nut to align the cotter pin hole. NEVER back it off!

Power Steering Gear

REMOVAL & INSTALLATION

▶ See Figures 130 and 131

1. Raise and support the front end on jackstands.
2. Set the front wheels in the straight ahead position and disconnect the battery ground cable.
3. Place a drain pan under the gear and disconnect the fluid lines. Cap the openings.
4. On C/K series, remove the adapter and shield from the gear and flexible coupling.
5. On C/K series, matchmark the flexible coupling clamp and wormshaft.
6. Remove the flexible coupling pinch bolt.
7. Mark the relationship of the Pitman arm to the Pitman shaft.
8. Remove the Pitman shaft nut and then remove the Pitman arm from the Pitman shaft, using a puller.
9. Remove the steering gear to frame bolts and remove the gear assembly.

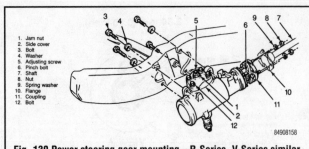

1. Jam nut
2. Side cover
3. Bolt
4. Washer
5. Adjusting screw
6. Pinch bolt
7. Shaft
8. Nut
9. Spring washer
10. Flange
11. Coupling
12. Bolt

84908158

Fig. 130 Power steering gear mounting—R-Series, V-Series similar

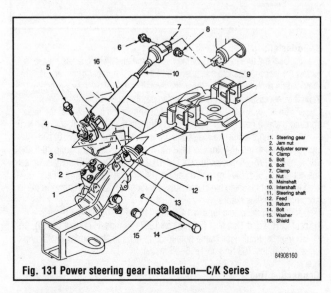

1. Steering gear
2. Jam nut
3. Adjuster screw
4. Clamp
5. Bolt
6. Bolt
7. Clamp
8. Nut
9. Mainshaft
10. Intershaft
11. Steering shaft
12. Feed
13. Return
14. Bolt
15. Washer
16. Shield

84908160

Fig. 131 Power steering gear installation—C/K Series

To install:

10. Place the steering gear in position, guiding the wormshaft into flexible coupling. Align the flat in the coupling with the flat on the wormshaft.

11. Install the steering gear to frame bolts and tighten to 66 ft. lbs. (89 Nm) on R-series. On C/K series tighten to 30 ft. lbs. (41 Nm) on 1988–90 models; 22 ft. lbs. (30 Nm) on 1991–98 models.

12. Install the flexible coupling pinch bolt. Tighten the pinch bolt to 30 ft. lbs. (40 Nm) on R-series and 1988–90 C/K series. On 1991–98 C/K series, tighten to 100 ft. lbs. (135 Nm). Check that the relationship of the flexible coupling to the flange is ¼–¾ in. (6–19mm) of flat.

13. Install the Pitman arm onto the Pitman shaft, lining up the marks made at removal. Install the Pitman shaft nut and tighten to specification.

14. Connect the fluid lines and refill the reservoir. Bleed the system.

Power Steering Pump

REMOVAL & INSTALLATION

R/V Series

▶ See Figure 132

1. Disconnect the hoses at the pump. When the hoses are disconnected, secure the ends in a raised position to prevent leakage. Cap the ends of the hoses to prevent the entrance of dirt.

2. Cap the pump fittings.

3. Loosen the bracket-to-pump mounting nuts.

4. Remove the pump drive belt.

5. Remove the bracket-to-pump bolts and remove the pump from the truck.

To install:

6. If a new pump is being installed, remove the pulley with a pulley puller such as J–25034–B. Install the pulley on the new pump with a forcing screw and washer.

7. Install the pump and tighten all bolts and nuts securely.

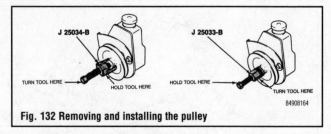

J 25034–B   J 25033–B

TURN TOOL HERE HOLD TOOL HERE   HOLD TOOL HERE TURN TOOL HERE

84908164

Fig. 132 Removing and installing the pulley

8. Fill the reservoir and bleed the pump by turning the pulley counterclockwise (as viewed from the front) until bubbles stop forming.

9. Bleed the system as outlined.

C/K Series

▶ See Figure 132

1. Disconnect the hoses at the pump. When the hoses are disconnected, secure the ends in a raised position to prevent leakage. Cap the ends of the hoses to prevent the entrance of dirt.

2. Cap the pump fittings.

3. Loosen the belt tensioner.

4. Remove the pump drive belt.

5. Remove the pulley with a pulley puller such as J–29785–A.

6. Remove the following fasteners:
- 6–4.3L, 8–5.0L, 8–5.7L engines: front mounting bolts
- 8–7.4L engine: rear brace
- 8–6.2L/6.5L diesel: front brace and rear mounting nuts

7. Lift out the pump.

To install:

8. Installation is the reverse of removal but please note the following important steps.

9. Tighten all mounting bolts and brace nuts and bolts to the specifications shown in the torque chart at the end of this section.

10. Install the pulley with J–25033–B.

11. Fill and bleed the system.

BLEEDING THE HYDRAULIC SYSTEM

The procedures for maintaining, adjusting, and repairing the power steering systems and components discussed in this chapter are to be done only after determining that the steering linkages and front suspension systems are correctly aligned and in good condition. All worn or damaged parts should be replaced before attempting to service the power steering system. After correcting any condition that could affect the power steering, do the preliminary tests of the steering system components.

1. Fill the reservoir to the proper level and let the fluid remain undisturbed for at least 2 minutes.

2. Start the engine and run it for only about 2 seconds.

3. Add fluid as necessary.

4. Repeat Steps 1–3 until the level remains constant.

5. Raise the front of the vehicle so that the front wheels are off the ground. Set the parking brake and block both rear wheels front and rear. Manual transmissions should be in Neutral; automatic transmissions should be in Park.

6. Start the engine and run it at approximately 1500 rpm.

7. Turn the wheels (off the ground) to the right and left, lightly contacting the stops.

8. Add fluid as necessary.

9. Lower the vehicle and turn the wheels right and left on the ground.

10. Check the level and refill as necessary.

11. If the fluid is extremely foamy, let the truck stand for a few minutes with the engine off and repeat the procedure. Check the belt tension and check for a bent or loose pulley. The pulley should not wobble with the engine running.

12. Check that no hoses are contacting any parts of the truck, particularly sheet metal.

13. Check the oil level and refill as necessary. This step and the next are very important. When willing, follow Steps 1–10 above

14. Check for air in the fluid. Aerated fluid appears milky. If air is present, repeat the above operation. If it is obvious that the pump will not respond to bleeding after several attempts, a pressure test may be required.

TORQUE SPECIFICATIONS

Components	Ft. Lbs.	Nm
Wheels		
Lug nuts		
Trucks with single front and rear wheels		
R10/1500 w/5 studs and steel or aluminum wheels	100	140
V10/1500 w/6 studs and steel wheels	88	120
V10/1500 w/6 studs and aluminum wheels	100	140
C/K series		
1988-90 models	90	123
1991-95 models	120	160
1996-98 models	140	190
RV series with 8 studs	120	160
Trucks with single front and dual rear wheels		
RV series with 8 studs	140	190
RV series with 10 studs	175	240
C/K series		
1988-90 models	125	170
1991-98 models with 8 studs	140	190
1991-98 models with 10 studs	175	240
Front Suspension		
C and R series 2 wheel drive models		
Coil spring		
R series	85	115
Cross-shaft-to-crossmember U-bolts	24	32
Stabilizer bar-to-lower control arm nuts		
C series		
Control arm pivot nuts		
1988-90 models	96	130
1991-95 models	121	165
1996-98 models	101	137
Pivot bolts	96	130
Shock absorbers		
R series		
Upper nut	140	190
Lower bolt	59	80
C series		
Upper nut	100 inch lbs.	11
Lower bolts	20	27
Upper ball joint		
R series	18	24
Ball joint nuts		
Ball stud nut		
1/2 ton trucks	50	68
3/4 and 1 ton trucks	90	122
C series vehicles		
Ball joint nuts		
1988-90 models	17	23
15 and 25 series	52	70
35 series	18	24
1991-98 models		
Ball stud nut		
1988-90 models	90	120
1991-95 models	84	115
1996-98 models	74	100

91028C01

TORQUE SPECIFICATIONS

Components	Ft. Lbs.	Nm
Front Suspension (cont.)		
C and R series 2 wheel drive models (cont.)		
Lower ball joint		
C series		
1988-90 models	90	120
1991-94 models	84	115
1995-98 models	94	128
R series		
Ball stud nut	80-100	108-135
Stabilizer bar		
R series		
All fasteners	24	32
C series		
Frame bracket bolts	24	33
End link nuts	13	18
Upper control arm		
R series		
Control arm shaft studs-to-crossmember bracket nuts		
10/1500 and 20/2500 series	70	95
30/3500 series	105	142
Ball stud nut		
10/1500 and 20/2500 series	90	122
30/3500 series	130	176
C series		
Control arm pivot nuts		
1988-90 models	88	120
1991-98 models	140	190
Lower Control Arm		
R series		
U-bolts	85	115
C series		
Stabilizer bar-to-lower control arm nuts	13	17
Control arm pivot nuts		
1988-90 models	96	130
1991-95 models	121	165
1996-98 models	101	137
Upper control arm pivot shaft		
R series		
10/1500 series	115	156
20/2500 and 30/3500 series	190	257
Pivot shaft nuts	105	142
Lower control arm pivot shaft		
R series		
10/1500 series	70	94
Pivot shaft nuts		
20/2500 and 30/3500 series		
Bushings	280	380

91028C02

TORQUE SPECIFICATIONS

Components	Ft. Lbs.	Nm
Front Suspension (cont.)		
C and R series 2 wheel drive models (cont.)		
Steering knuckle		
Splash shield bolts		
R series	10	14
C series	12	16
1988-90 models	19	26
V series 4 wheel drive models		
Leaf spring		
U-bolt nuts	150	203
Shackle nuts	50	67
Front eye bolt nut	90	122
Shock absorbers		
Quad shocks		
Upper end nut	65	88
Lower end	89	120
Dual shocks	65	88
Upper and lower end nut		
Ball Joints	50	70
Adjusting ring		
Ball studs nuts		
Upper nut	100	135
Lower nut	70	95
Steering arm-to-knuckle nuts	90	122
Stabilizer bar	52	70
Stabilizer bar-to-frame nuts		
Stabilizer bar-to-spring plate bolts	133	180
K series 4 wheel drive models		
Torsion bars and support assembly		
Support crossmember		
Center nut	18	24
Edge nuts	46	62
Shock absorbers		
1988-90 models	48	65
1991-98 models	66	90
Upper ball joint		
Nuts		
15 and 25 series (K1 or K2)	18	24
35 series (K3)	52	70
Ball stud nut		
1988-95 models	84	115
1996-98 models	74	100
Control arm pivot nuts		
Upper arm		
1988-90 models	88	120
1991-98 models	140	190
Lower arm		
1988-90 models	135	185
1991-98 models	121	165
Lower ball joint		
Rivet/bolted type		
Nuts	45	61

91028C03

TORQUE SPECIFICATIONS

Components	Ft. Lbs.	Nm
Front Suspension (cont.)		
K series 4 wheel drive models		
Stabilizer bar		
Frame clamp bolts	24	33
End link bolts	13	18
Steering knuckle and seal		
Splash shield bolts		
1988-90 models	12	16
1991-98 models	19	26
C3HD models		
Leaf spring		
Hanger and shackle bolts		
1988-95 models	92	125
1996-98 models	136	185
U-bolt nuts	①	①
Shock absorber		
Upper retainer	136	185
Lower retainer	37	50
Stabilizer bar		
Clamp bolts	21	28
Bar-to-link nut	50	68
Steering arm, knuckle and spindle		
Nut	29	40
Brake line bracket bolts	60 inch lbs.	7
Anchor plate and steering arm-to-knuckle		
Bolts	12	16
Nuts	230	312
Rear suspension		
Leaf spring		
R/V series		
U-bolt nuts	②	②
Shackle-to-hanger bolt		
If you are torquing on the nut	92	124
If you are torquing on the bolt head	110	149
C/K series		
U-bolt nuts	③	③
Hanger and shackle nuts		
Spring-to-bracket nuts		
1988-92 15/25/35 series	89	120
1993-95 15/25/35 series	92	125
1996-98 15/25/35 series	70	95
1988-95 C3HD series	320	435
1996-98 C3HD series	306	415
Leaf spring-to-shackle nuts		
1988-92 15/25/35 series	89	120
1993-95 15/25/35 series	81	110
1996-98 15/25/35 series	70	95
1988-95 C3HD series	136	185
1996-98 C3HD series	157	213

91028C04

TORQUE SPECIFICATIONS

Components	Ft. Lbs.	Nm
Rear suspension (cont.)		
Leaf spring (cont.)		
Shackle-to-bracket nuts		
1988-92 15/25/35 series	89	120
1993-95 15/25/35 series	81	110
1996-98 15/25/35 series	70	95
1988-95 models	136	185
1996-98 models	157	213
Shock absorbers		
R/V series		
Upper mount	140	190
10/15 and 20/25 series	52	70
30/35 series	115	160
Lower mount bolt (all series)		
C/K series except C3HD models		
Upper mounting nuts		
1988-95 models	17-20	25-27
1996-98 models	13	17
Lower mounting nuts		
1988-91 models	52	70
1992-95 models	81	110
1996-98 models	74	100
C3HD models		
Lower mounting nuts		
1988-91 models	52	70
1992-95 models	81	110
1996-98 models	52	70
Upper mounting nuts		
1988-91 models	17	25
1992-95 models	17-20	25-27
1996-98 models	11	15
Stabilizer bar		
R/V series		
Clamp-to-anchor bolts	24	32
C3HD series		
U-bolt nuts	22	30
Upper insulator nuts	17	23
Steering		
Steering wheel		
Steering wheel nut	30	40
Dimmer switch mounting stud	35 inch lbs.	4
Switch screw		
1988-94 models	35 inch lbs.	4
1995-98 models	12 inch lbs.	1.4
Column		
Nuts	22	29
Bolts	20	27

91028C05

TORQUE SPECIFICATIONS

Components	Ft. Lbs.	Nm
Steering (cont.)		
Lock cylinder		
1988-94 models		
Lock screw		
Regular columns	40 inch lbs.	5
Tilt columns	22 inch lbs.	2.5
1995-98 models		
Three pan head screws	53 inch lbs.	6
Ignition and key alarm switch assembly fasteners	12 inch lbs.	1
Steering Linkage		
Pitman arm		
Pitman shaft nut or pitman arm clamp bolt		
R and C/K series	184	249
V series	125	169
Pitman arm-to-relay rod nut		
R/V series	66	89
C/K series		
1988-91 models	40	54
1992-98 models	46	62
C3HD series		
Pitman arm-to-shaft nut	184	250
Idler arm		
Idler arm-to-frame bolts		
R/V series	30	40
C/K series		
Frame-to-bracket bolts		
1988-92 models	78	105
1993-95 models	59	80
1996-98 models	71	96
Idler arm ball stud-to-relay rod nut		
R/V series	66	89
C/K series		
1988-92 models	40	54
1993-95 models	52	70
1997-98 models	46	62
Relay rod (center link)		
R/V series		
Relay rod-to-idler arm and pitman arm ball stud nuts	66	89
C/K series		
1988-92 models	40	54
1993-95 models	52	70
1997-98 models	46	62
Steering linkage shock absorber		
R/V series		
Tie rod end nut	46	62
Frame end nut	81	109
Steering linkage shock absorber (cont.)		
C/K series		
Frame end nut and bolt	33	45
Relay rod end nut	46	62

91028C06

TORQUE SPECIFICATIONS

Components	Ft. Lbs.	Nm
Steering Linkage (cont.)		
Tie rod ends		
R series		
Clamp bolts	14	18
Stud nuts	45	61
V series		
Tie rod-to-knuckle castellated nuts	40	54
Tie rod end locknuts	175	237
C/K series		
Except C3HD models		
Tie rod assembly-to-relay rod nut	40	54
Tie rod end-to-knuckle		
1988-96 models	40	54
1997-98 models	46	62
Clamp nuts		
1988-96 models	14	19
1997-98 models	18	25
C3HD models		
Tie rod end-to-knuckle		
1988-94 models	40	54
1995-98 models	65	88
Clamp nuts		
1988-95 models	50	68
1996-98 models	77	104
Connecting rod		
V series		
Clamp bolts	40	54
Ball stud nuts	89	120
Manual steering gear		
Steering gear-to-frame bolts 100 ft. lbs. (135 Nm).	100	135
Flexible coupling pinch bolt	22	30
Adapter-to-gear box nut	5 inch lbs.	0.5
Pitman shaft nut		
Power steering gear		
R/V series		
Steering gear-to-frame bolts	66	89
Flexible coupling pinch bolt	30	40
Pitman shaft nut	185	250
C/K series		
Steering gear-to-frame bolts		
1988-90 models	69	93
1991-98 models	100	135
Flexible coupling pinch bolt		
1988-90 models	30	41
1991-98 models	22	30

91028C07

TORQUE SPECIFICATIONS

Components	Ft. Lbs.	Nm
Power steering pump		
C/K series		
4.3L, 5.0L, and 5.7L engines		
Front mounting bolts	37	50
7.4L engine		
Rear brace nut	61	82
Rear brace bolt	24	32
Mounting bolts	37	50
6.2L and 6.5L engines		
Front brace retainer	30	40
Rear mounting nuts	17	23

① Step1:Tighten diagonally to 18 ft. lbs. (25 Nm)
Step 2: 1988-95 models retighten to 80 ft. lbs. (109 Nm)
1996-98 models retighten to 92 ft. lbs. (125 Nm)
② Step 2: Tighten diagonally to 18 ft. lbs. (25 Nm)
Step 2: Make sure the spring is evenly seated
Step 3: 10/15 and 20/25 series retighten to 125 ft. lbs. (169 Nm)
30/35 series retighten to 147 ft. lbs. (200 Nm)

③ Step1:Tighten diagonally to 17 ft. lbs. (23 Nm)
Step 2: Make sure the spring is evenly seated
Step 3: 15/25 series: 81 ft. lbs. (110 Nm)
35 series without dual wheels or 6-7.4L engine: 81 ft. lbs. (110 Nm)
35 series with dual wheels: 110 ft. lbs. (148 Nm)
35 series with 6-7.4L engine, without dual wheels: 110 ft. lbs. (148 Nm)
C3HD models
1988-95 C3HD series: 207 ft. lbs. (280 Nm)
1996-98 C3HD series: 187 ft. lbs. (253 Nm)

91028C08

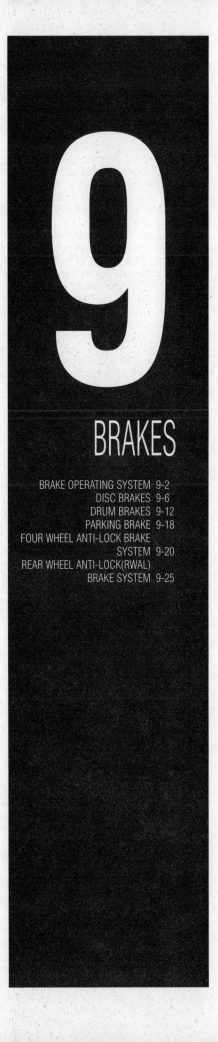

9

BRAKES

BRAKE OPERATING SYSTEM

Basic Operating Principles

Hydraulic systems are used to actuate the brakes of all modern automobiles. The system transports the power required to force the frictional surfaces of the braking system together from the pedal to the individual brake units at each wheel. A hydraulic system is used for two reasons.

First, fluid under pressure can be carried to all parts of an automobile by small pipes and flexible hoses without taking up a significant amount of room or posing routing problems.

Second, a great mechanical advantage can be given to the brake pedal end of the system, and the foot pressure required to actuate the brakes can be reduced by making the surface area of the master cylinder pistons smaller than that of any of the pistons in the wheel cylinders or calipers.

The master cylinder consists of a fluid reservoir along with a double cylinder and piston assembly. Double type master cylinders are designed to separate the front and rear braking systems hydraulically in case of a leak. The master cylinder coverts mechanical motion from the pedal into hydraulic pressure within the lines. This pressure is translated back into mechanical motion at the wheels by either the wheel cylinder (drum brakes) or the caliper (disc brakes).

Steel lines carry the brake fluid to a point on the vehicle's frame near each of the vehicle's wheels. The fluid is then carried to the calipers and wheel cylinders by flexible tubes in order to allow for suspension and steering movements.

In drum brake systems, each wheel cylinder contains two pistons, one at either end, which push outward in opposite directions and force the brake shoe into contact with the drum.

In disc brake systems, the cylinders are part of the calipers. At least one cylinder in each caliper is used to force the brake pads against the disc.

All pistons employ some type of seal, usually made of rubber, to minimize fluid leakage. A rubber dust boot seals the outer end of the cylinder against dust and dirt. The boot fits around the outer end of the piston on disc brake calipers, and around the brake actuating rod on wheel cylinders.

The hydraulic system operates as follows: When at rest, the entire system, from the piston(s) in the master cylinder to those in the wheel cylinders or calipers, is full of brake fluid. Upon application of the brake pedal, fluid trapped in front of the master cylinder piston(s) is forced through the lines to the wheel cylinders. Here, it forces the pistons outward, in the case of drum brakes, and inward toward the disc, in the case of disc brakes. The motion of the pistons is opposed by return springs mounted outside the cylinders in drum brakes, and by spring seals, in disc brakes.

Upon release of the brake pedal, a spring located inside the master cylinder immediately returns the master cylinder pistons to the normal position. The pistons contain check valves and the master cylinder has compensating ports drilled in it. These are uncovered as the pistons reach their normal position. The piston check valves allow fluid to flow toward the wheel cylinders or calipers as the pistons withdraw. Then, as the return springs force the brake pads or shoes into the released position, the excess fluid reservoir through the compensating ports. It is during the time the pedal is in the released position that any fluid that has leaked out of the system will be replaced through the compensating ports.

Dual circuit master cylinders employ two pistons, located one behind the other, in the same cylinder. The primary piston is actuated directly by mechanical linkage from the brake pedal through the power booster. The secondary piston is actuated by fluid trapped between the two pistons. If a leak develops in front of the secondary piston, it moves forward until it bottoms against the front of the master cylinder, and the fluid trapped between the pistons will operate the rear brakes. If the rear brakes develop a leak, the primary piston will move forward until direct contact with the secondary piston takes place, and it will force the secondary piston to actuate the front brakes. In either case, the brake pedal moves farther when the brakes are applied, and less braking power is available.

All dual circuit systems use a switch to warn the driver when only half of the brake system is operational. This switch is usually located in a valve body which is mounted on the firewall or the frame below the master cylinder. A hydraulic piston receives pressure from both circuits, each circuit's pressure being applied to one end of the piston. When the pressures are in balance, the piston remains stationary. When one circuit has a leak, however, the greater pressure in that circuit during application of the brakes will push the piston to one side, closing the switch and activating the brake warning light.

In disc brake systems, this valve body also contains a metering valve and, in some cases, a proportioning valve. The metering valve keeps pressure from

traveling to the disc brakes on the front wheels until the brake shoes on the rear wheels have contacted the drums, ensuring that the front brakes will never be used alone. The proportioning valve controls the pressure to the rear brakes to lessen the chance of rear wheel lock-up during very hard braking.

Warning lights may be tested by depressing the brake pedal and holding it while opening one of the wheel cylinder bleeder screws. If this does not cause the light to go on, substitute a new lamp, make continuity checks, and, finally, replace the switch as necessary.

The hydraulic system may be checked for leaks by applying pressure to the pedal gradually and steadily. If the pedal sinks very slowly to the floor, the system has a leak. This is not to be confused with a springy or spongy feel due to the compression of air within the lines. If the system leaks, there will be a gradual change in the position of the pedal with a constant pressure.

Check for leaks along all lines and at wheel cylinders. If no external leaks are apparent, the problem is inside the master cylinder.

DISC BRAKES

Instead of the traditional expanding brakes that press outward against a circular drum, disc brake systems utilize a disc (rotor) with brake pads positioned on either side of it. An easily-seen analogy is the hand brake arrangement on a bicycle. The pads squeeze onto the rim of the bike wheel, slowing its motion. Automobile disc brakes use the identical principle but apply the braking effort to a separate disc instead of the wheel.

The disc (rotor) is a casting, usually equipped with cooling fins between the two braking surfaces. This enables air to circulate between the braking surfaces making them less sensitive to heat buildup and more resistant to fade. Dirt and water do not drastically affect braking action since contaminants are thrown off by the centrifugal action of the rotor or scraped off the by the pads. Also, the equal clamping action of the two brake pads tends to ensure uniform, straight line stops. Disc brakes are inherently self-adjusting. There are three general types of disc brake:

1. A fixed caliper.
2. A floating caliper.
3. A sliding caliper.

The fixed caliper design uses two pistons mounted on either side of the rotor (in each side of the caliper). The caliper is mounted rigidly and does not move.

The sliding and floating designs are quite similar. In fact, these two types are often lumped together. In both designs, the pad on the inside of the rotor is moved into contact with the rotor by hydraulic force. The caliper, which is not held in a fixed position, moves slightly, bringing the outside pad into contact with the rotor. There are various methods of attaching floating calipers. Some pivot at the bottom or top, and some slide on mounting bolts. In any event, the end result is the same.

DRUM BRAKES

Drum brakes employ two brake shoes mounted on a stationary backing plate. These shoes are positioned inside a circular drum which rotates with the wheel assembly. The shoes are held in place by springs. This allows them to slide toward the drums (when they are applied) while keeping the linings and drums in alignment. The shoes are actuated by a wheel cylinder which is mounted at the top of the backing plate. When the brakes are applied, hydraulic pressure forces the wheel cylinder's actuating links outward. Since these links bear directly against the top of the brake shoes, the tops of the shoes are then forced against the inner side of the drum. This action forces the bottoms of the two shoes to contact the brake drum by rotating the entire assembly slightly (known as servo action). When pressure within the wheel cylinder is relaxed, return springs pull the shoes back away from the drum.

Most modern drum brakes are designed to self-adjust themselves during application when the vehicle is moving in reverse. This motion causes both shoes to rotate very slightly with the drum, rocking an adjusting lever, thereby causing rotation of the adjusting screw. Some drum brake systems are designed to self-adjust during application whenever the brakes are applied. This on-board adjustment system reduces the need for maintenance adjustments and keeps both the brake function and pedal feel satisfactory.

Brake Light Switch

REMOVAL & INSTALLATION

1. Disconnect the negative battery cable.
2. Disable the SIR system (if equipped).
3. Remove the clip (R/V Series) or unclip the switch (C/K Series) and unplug the electrical connector from the brake light switch.
4. Remove the switch.
5. Installation is the reverse of removal.

Master Cylinder

REMOVAL & INSTALLATION

▶ See Figures 1 and 2

✳✳ WARNING

Clean any master cylinder parts in alcohol or brake fluid. Never use mineral based cleaning solvents such as gasoline, kerosene, carbon tetrachloride, acetone, or paint thinner as these will destroy

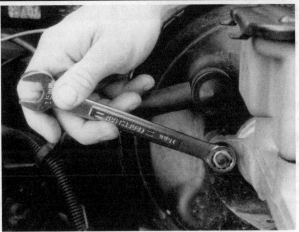

87989P03

Fig. 2 Unfasten the master cylinder attaching bolts and remove the master cylinder

rubber parts. Do not allow brake fluid to spill on the vehicle's finish, it will remove the paint. Flush the area with water.

1. Using a clean cloth, wipe the master cylinder and its lines to remove excess dirt and then place cloths under the unit to absorb any spilled fluid.
2. Remove the hydraulic lines from the master cylinder using a flare nut wrench and plug the outlets to prevent the entrance of foreign material. On trucks with ABS, disconnect the lines at the isolation/dump valve.
3. Remove the master cylinder attaching bolts or, on trucks with ABS, the attaching bolts from the isolation/dump valve, and remove the master cylinder from the brake booster, or, on trucks with manual brakes, the firewall.

✳✳ CAUTION

On trucks with ABS, never let brake fluid or your skin touch the ECU electrical connections! Also, never let the isolation/dump valve hang by its wiring!

To install:

4. Position the master cylinder or, on trucks with ABS the master cylinder and isolation/dump valve, on the booster or firewall. Tighten the nuts to 20 ft. lbs. (27 Nm).
5. Connect the brake lines and tighten them to 13 ft. lbs. (17 Nm) on R/V series and 18 ft. lbs. (24 Nm) on C/K models. Fill the master cylinder reservoirs to the proper levels.
6. Bleed the brake system.

Vacuum Booster

REMOVAL & INSTALLATION

1. Disconnect the negative battery cable.
2. Apply the parking brake.
3. Unplug all necessary electrical connections.
4. Remove the master cylinder from the booster and pull it off the studs, CAREFULLY! It is not necessary to disconnect the brake lines.
5. Disconnect the vacuum hose from the check valve.
6. If necessary, remove the brake light switch.
7. Disconnect the booster pushrod at the brake pedal.
8. Remove the booster mounting nuts, located on the inside of the firewall.
9. Lift off the booster and remove the gasket.

To install:

10. Install the booster with a new gasket.
11. Tighten the booster mounting nuts to 21 ft. lbs. (29 Nm) on all except 1996–98 models. On 1996–98 models, tighten the nuts to 26 ft. lbs. (36 Nm).
12. Install all remaining components.

87989P02

Fig. 1 Remove the hydraulic lines from the master cylinder using a line wrench

Hydro-Boost

Diesel engine trucks and some 30/3500 series trucks and motor home chassis are equipped with the Bendix Hydro-boost system. This power brake booster obtains hydraulic pressure from the power steering pump, rather than vacuum pressure from the intake manifold as in most gasoline engine brake booster systems.

REMOVAL & INSTALLATION

✷✷ CAUTION

Power steering fluid and brake fluid cannot be mixed. If brake seals contact the steering fluid or steering seals contact the brake fluid, damage will result!

1. Turn the engine off and pump the brake pedal 4 or 5 times to deplete the accumulator inside the unit.
2. Tag and disconnect the hoses from the booster.
3. Unfasten the master cylinder retainers, and remove the cylinder keeping the brake lines attached. Secure the master cylinder out of the way.
4. Unplug all necessary electrical connections.
5. Unfasten the pushrod retainer and disconnect the pushrod from the brake pedal, in some cases it will be easier to remove the brake light switch to access the pushrod retainer.
6. Remove the booster unit from the firewall.
7. Remove the gasket.

To install:
Installation is the reverse of removal, but please note the following important steps.
8. Always install a new gasket.
9. Tighten the booster mounting nuts to 22 ft. lbs. (30 Nm) on all except 1996–98 models and 26 ft lbs. (36 Nm) on 1996–98 models.
10. After installation is complete, bleed the Hydro-Boost system.

Combination Valve

This valve is used on all models with disc brakes. The valve itself is a combination of:
1. The metering valve, which will not allow the front disc brakes to engage until the rear brakes contact the drum.
2. The failure warning switch, which notifies the driver if one of the systems has a leak.
3. The proportioner which limits rear brake pressure and delays rear wheel skid.

REMOVAL & INSTALLATION

R/V Series

▶ **See Figure 3**

1. Disconnect the hydraulic lines and plug them to prevent dirt from entering the system.
2. Disconnect the warning switch harness.
3. Unfasten the retaining bolts and remove the valve.
4. Install the valve and tighten the retainers to 150 inch lbs. (17 Nm).
5. Bleed the brake system.

C/K Series

MANUAL BRAKES

▶ **See Figure 4**

1. Disconnect the brake lines at the valve. Plug or cap the lines and ports.
2. Unplug the switch wiring connector.
3. Remove the valve-to-bracket bolts.
To install:
4. Install the valve. Tighten the bolts to 20 ft. lbs. (27 Nm).
5. Bleed the system.

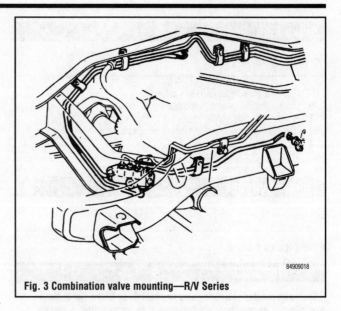

Fig. 3 Combination valve mounting—R/V Series

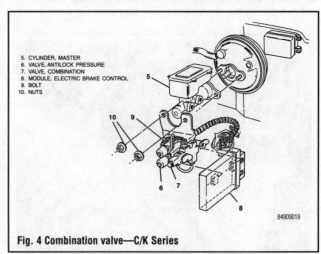

5. CYLINDER, MASTER
6. VALVE, ANTILOCK PRESSURE
7. VALVE, COMBINATION
8. MODULE, ELECTRIC BRAKE CONTROL
9. BOLT
10. NUTS

Fig. 4 Combination valve—C/K Series

POWER BRAKES

▶ **See Figure 4**

1. Disconnect the brake lines at the switch. Plug or cap the lines and ports.
2. Unplug the warning switch wiring connector.
3. Remove the anti-lock brake system control module from the bracket. See the procedure later in this section.
4. Remove the bolts attaching the ABS isolation/dump valve to the bracket. See the procedure later in this section.
5. Remove the nuts that attach the master cylinder and bracket to the booster.
6. Remove the bracket and combination valve assembly.
To install:
7. Position the bracket/valve assembly and install the master cylinder-to-booster nuts. Tighten the nuts to 20 ft. lbs. (27 Nm).
8. Install the ABS isolation/dump valve nuts. Tighten them to 21 ft. lbs. (24 Nm).
9. Install the remaining components in the reverse order of removal.

SWITCH CENTERING

Whenever work on the brake system is done it is possible that the brake warning light will come on and refuse to go off when the work is finished. In this event, the switch must be centered.
1. Raise and support the truck.
2. Attach a bleeder hose to the rear brake bleed screw and immerse the other end of the hose in a jar of clean brake fluid.

3. Be sure that the master cylinder is full.

4. When bleeding the brakes, the pin in the end of the metering portion of the combination valve must be held in the open position (with the tool described in the brake bleeding section installed under the pin mounting bolt). Be sure to tighten the bolt after removing the tool.

5. Turn the ignition key ON. Open the bleed screw while an assistant applies heavy pressure on the brake pedal. The warning lamp should light. Close the bleed screw before the helper releases the pedal.

6. To reset the switch, apply heavy pressure to the pedal. This will apply hydraulic pressure to the switch which will re-center it.

7. Repeat Step 5 for the front bleed screw.

8. Turn the ignition OFF and lower the truck.

➡ **If the warning lamp does not light during Step 5, the switch is defective and must be replaced.**

Height Sensing Proportioning Valve

This valve distributes braking pressure evenly from front-to-rear depending on either a light or heavy load condition. Not all models utilize this valve.

⁕⁘ CAUTION

Adjustment of the valve is determined by the distance between the axle and frame. The addition of such aftermarket items as air shocks, lift kits and addition spring leaves will render the valve inoperable, resulting in unsatisfactory brake performance, accident and injury!

REMOVAL & INSTALLATION

♦ **See Figures 5 and 6**

➡ **Special gauging tools are required for this job.**

1. Raise and support the rear end on jackstands under the frame, allowing the axle to hang freely.

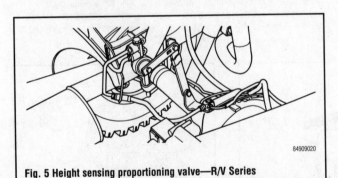

Fig. 5 Height sensing proportioning valve—R/V Series

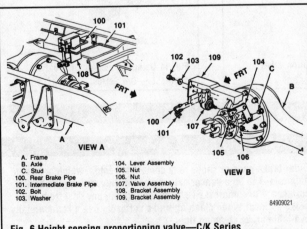

A. Frame
B. Axle
C. Stud
100. Rear Brake Pipe
101. Intermediate Brake Pipe
102. Bolt
103. Washer
104. Lever Assembly
105. Nut
106. Nut
107. Valve Assembly
108. Bracket Assembly
109. Bracket Assembly

Fig. 6 Height sensing proportioning valve—C/K Series

2. Clean the exterior of the valve.

3. Disconnect the brake lines at the valve. Cap the lines.

4. Remove the valve shaft-to-lever nut.

5. Remove the valve-to-bracket bolts.

To install:

6. Position the valve on the bracket and tighten the bolts to 20 ft. lbs. (27 Nm).

7. Adjust the valve as described below.

8. Connect the lever to the valve shaft and tighten the nut to 89 inch lbs. (7 Nm).

9. Connect the brake lines and tighten them to 18 ft. lbs. (24 Nm).

10. Bleed the brakes.

ADJUSTMENT

♦ **See Figures 7 and 8**

If front wheels lock-up at moderate brake pressure is experienced with the vehicle at or near maximum GVWR, or, whenever the valve is replaced, the valve must be adjusted.

➡ **Special gauging tools are required for this job.**

1. Raise and support the rear end on jackstands under the frame, allowing the axle to hang freely.

2. Remove the shaft-to-lever nut and disconnect the lever from the shaft.

3. Obtain the proper gauge:

• R and V with Extra Capacity Rear Spring option: part number 14061394; color green; code A

• R Series without Extra Capacity Rear Spring option, and with either the 6–4.3L or 8–5.7L engine: part number 14061395; color black; code B.

• V Series without Extra Capacity Rear Spring option and with the diesel engine or the 8–5.7L engine: part number 14061396; color blue; code C.

• R and V Series with VD1 tire option: part number 15592484; color red; code D.

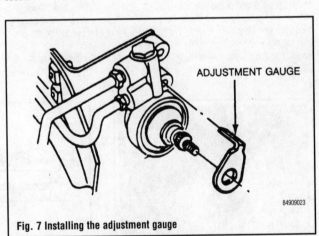

Fig. 7 Installing the adjustment gauge

Fig. 8 After installation, sever the adjustment tang

- V Series, except above: part number 15548904; color yellow; code E.
- C/K Series: part number 15592484.

4. Rotate the valve shaft to permit installation of the gauge. The center hole of the gauge must seat on the D-shape of the valve shaft. The gauge tang must seat in the valve mounting hole.

5. Install the lever on the shaft with a C-clamp to seat the nylon bushings on the serrated valve shaft. Don't force it into position.

6. Install the nut on the shaft and tighten it to 89 inch lbs. (7 Nm) on the R/V series; 8 ft. lbs. (9 Nm) on the C/K Series

7. Break off or cut the tang on the gauge.

8. Road test the truck. The gauge will stay in place.

Bleeding the Brakes

EXCEPT HYDRO-BOOST OR ABS

▶ **See Figures 9, 10 and 11**

To bleed the brakes on a vehicle equipped with ABS, please refer to the ABS bleeding procedure in this section.

The brake system must be bled when any brake line is disconnected or there is air in the system.

➡**Never bleed a wheel cylinder when a drum is removed.**

1. Clean the master cylinder of excess dirt and remove the cylinder cover and the diaphragm.

2. Fill the master cylinder to the proper level. Check the fluid level periodically during the bleeding process and replenish it as necessary. Do not allow the master cylinder to run dry, or you will have to start over.

3. Before opening any of the bleeder screws, you may want to give each one a shot of penetrating solvent. This reduces the possibility of breakage when they are unscrewed.

4. Attach a length of vinyl hose to the bleeder screw of the brake to be bled. Insert the other end of the hose into a clear jar half full of clean brake fluid, so that the end of the hose is beneath the level of fluid. The correct sequence for bleeding is to work from the brake farthest from the master cylinder to the one closest; right rear, left rear, right front, left front.

5. The combination valve must be held open during the bleeding process. A clip, tape, or other similar tool (or an assistant) will hold the metering pin in.

6. Depress and release the brake pedal three or four times to exhaust any residual vacuum.

7. Have an assistant push down on the brake pedal and hold it down. Open the bleeder valve slightly. As the pedal reaches the end of its travel, close the bleeder screw and release the brake pedal. Repeat this process until no air bubbles are visible in the expelled fluid.

➡**Make sure your assistant presses the brake pedal to the floor slowly. Pressing too fast will cause air bubbles to form in the fluid.**

8. Repeat this procedure at each of the brakes. Remember to check the master cylinder level occasionally. Use only fresh fluid to refill the master cylinder, not the stuff bled from the system.

9. When the bleeding process is complete, refill the master cylinder, install its cover and diaphragm, and discard the fluid bled from the brake system.

HYDRO-BOOST

The system should be bled whenever the booster is removed and installed.

1. Fill the power steering pump until the fluid level is at the base of the pump reservoir neck. Disconnect the battery lead from the distributor.

➡**Remove the electrical lead to the fuel solenoid terminal on the injection pump before cranking the engine.**

2. Jack up the front of the car, turn the wheels all the way to the left, and crank the engine for a few seconds.

3. Check steering pump fluid level. If necessary, add fluid to the "ADD" mark on the dipstick.

4. Lower the car, connect the battery lead, and start the engine. Check fluid level and add fluid to the "ADD" mark, as necessary. With the engine running, turn the wheels from side to side to bleed air from the system. Make sure that the fluid level stays above the internal pump casting.

5. The Hydro-Boost system should now be fully bled. If the fluid is foaming after bleeding, stop the engine, let the system set for one hour, then repeat the second part of Step 4.

The preceding procedures should be effective in removing the excess air from the system, however sometimes air may still remain trapped. When this happens the booster may make a gulping noise when the brake is applied. Lightly pumping the brake pedal with the engine running should cause this noise to disappear. After the noise stops, check the pump fluid level and add as necessary.

Fig. 9 Connect one end of a clear plastic tube to the bleeder screw and submerge the other end in clean brake fluid

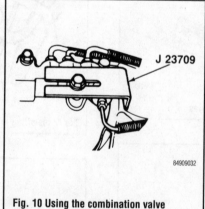

Fig. 10 Using the combination valve depressor—R/V Series

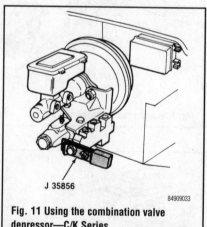

Fig. 11 Using the combination valve depressor—C/K Series

DISC BRAKES

The front brake system uses either a Delco or Bendix system. Refer to the illustration of the brake components to determine which brake system is used on your vehicle. A Bendix system is the only type used on all rear brake applications.

✳✳ CAUTION

Older brake pads or shoes may contain asbestos, which has been determined to be a cancer causing agent. Never clean the brake surfaces with compressed air! Avoid inhaling any dust from any brake surface! When cleaning brake surfaces, use a commercially available brake cleaning fluid.

Brake Pads

REMOVAL & INSTALLATION

Delco System

▶ **See Figures 12 thru 22**

1. Remove the cover on the master cylinder and siphon out ⅔ of the fluid. This step prevents spilling fluid when the piston is pushed back.
2. Raise and support the front end on jackstands.
3. Remove the wheels.
4. Push the brake piston back into its bore using a C-clamp to pull the caliper outward.
5. Remove the two bolts which hold the caliper and then lift the caliper off the disc.

✳✳ CAUTION

Do not let the caliper assembly hang by the brake hose.

6. Remove the inboard and outboard shoe. Use a small prybar to disengage the buttons on the outboard shoe from the holes in the caliper housing.

➡ **If the pads are to be reinstalled, mark them inside and outside.**

7. Remove the pad support spring from the piston.
   To install:
8. Position the support spring and the inner pad into the center cavity of the piston, snap the retaining spring into the piston. The outboard pad has ears which are bent over to keep the pad in position while the inboard pad has ears on the top end which fit over the caliper retaining bolts. A spring which is inside the brake piston holds the bottom edge of the inboard pad.

9. Push down on the inner pad until it lays flat against the caliper. It is important to push the piston all the way into the caliper if new linings are installed or the caliper will not fit over the rotor.
10. Position the outboard pad with the ears of the pad over the caliper ears and the tab at the bottom engaged in the caliper cutout.
11. With the two pads in position, place the caliper over the brake disc and align the holes in the caliper with those of the mounting bracket.

✳✳ CAUTION

Make certain that the brake hose is not twisted or kinked.

12. Install the mounting bracket bolts through the sleeves in the inboard caliper ears and through the mounting bracket, making sure that the ends of the bolts pass under the retaining ears on the inboard pad.

➡ **For best results, always use new bushings, bolt sleeves and bolt boot.**

13. Tighten the mounting bolts to 35 ft. lbs. (47 Nm) for R/V Series; 28 ft. lbs. (38 Nm) for 1988-92 C/K Series and 38 ft. lbs. (51 Nm) for 1993-98 C/K Series. Pump the brake pedal to seat the pad against the rotor. Don't do this unless both calipers are in place. Use a pair of channel lock pliers to bend over the upper ears of the outer pad so it isn't loose.

➡ **After tightening the mounting bolts, there must be clearance between the caliper and knuckle at both the upper and lower edge. On R/V Series, the clearance must be 0.010–0.024 in. (0.26–0.60mm); on C/K Series, it must be 0.005–0.012 in. (0.13–0.30mm) for 1988–91 models, and 0.010–0.024 in. (0.26–0.60mm) on 1992–98 models. If not, loosen the bolts and reposition the caliper.**

14. Install the wheel and lower the truck.
15. Add fluid to the master cylinder reservoirs so that they are ¼ in. (6mm) from the top.
16. Test the brake pedal by pumping it to obtain a hard pedal. Check the fluid level again and add fluid as necessary. Do not move the vehicle until a hard pedal is obtained.

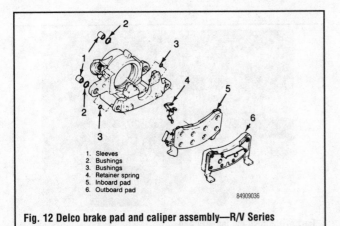

1. Sleeves
2. Bushings
3. Bushings
4. Retainer spring
5. Inboard pad
6. Outboard pad

84909036

Fig. 12 Delco brake pad and caliper assembly—R/V Series

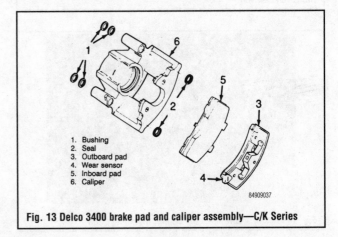

1. Bushing
2. Seal
3. Outboard pad
4. Wear sensor
5. Inboard pad
6. Caliper

84909037

Fig. 13 Delco 3400 brake pad and caliper assembly—C/K Series

3. BUSHINGS
5. SHOE AND LINING, OUTBOARD
6. SENSOR, WEAR
7. SHOE AND LINING, INBOARD
11. VALVE, BLEEDER
12. HOUSING, CALIPER

84909038

Fig. 14 Delco 3486 brake pad and caliper assembly—C/K Series

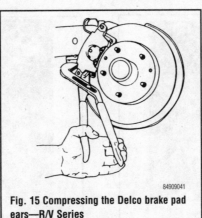

84909041

Fig. 15 Compressing the Delco brake pad ears—R/V Series

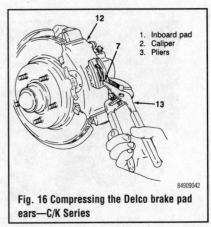

1. Inboard pad
2. Caliper
3. Pliers

84909042

Fig. 16 Compressing the Delco brake pad ears—C/K Series

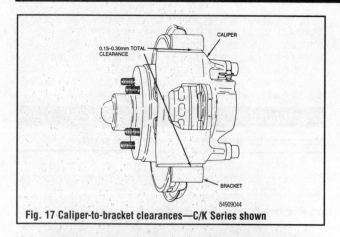

Fig. 17 Caliper-to-bracket clearances—C/K Series shown

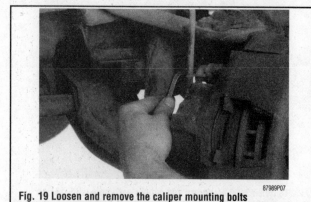

Fig. 18 Push the piston back into its bore using a C-clamp to pull the caliper outward

Fig. 19 Loosen and remove the caliper mounting bolts

Fig. 20 Grasp the caliper assembly and pull it off the rotor

Bendix System

♦ **See Figures 23, 24 and 25**

The Bendix system is used on some front brake applications and all rear brake applications.

1. Remove approximately ⅔ of the brake fluid from the master cylinder. Discard the used brake fluid.
2. Jack up your vehicle and support it with jackstands.
3. Push the piston back into its bore. This can be done by using a C-clamp.
4. Remove the bolt at the caliper support key. Use a brass drift pin to remove the key and spring.
5. Rotate the caliper up and forward from the bottom and lift it off the caliper support.
6. Tie the caliper out of the way with a piece of wire. Be careful not to damage the brake line.
7. Remove the inner pad from the caliper support. Some rear disc brake shoe assemblies have a anti-rattle spring at the inner pad, after removing the inner pad, look for the anti-rattle spring and remove as necessary.
8. Remove the outer pad from the caliper.

To install:

9. Lubricate the caliper support and support spring, with silicone.
10. If equipped on the rear disc brake assembly, install the anti-rattle spring in place before installing the inner pad.
11. Install the lower end of the inboard shoe into the groove provided in the support. Slide the upper end of the shoe into position. Be sure the clip remains in position.
12. Position the outboard shoe in the caliper with the ears at the top of the shoe over the caliper ears and the tab at the bottom of the shoe engaged in the caliper cutout. If assembly is difficult, a C-clamp may be used. Be careful not to mar the lining.
13. Position the caliper over the brake disc, top edge first. Rotate the caliper downward onto the support.
14. Place the spring over the caliper support key, install the assembly between the support and lower caliper groove. Tap into place until the key retaining screw can be installed.

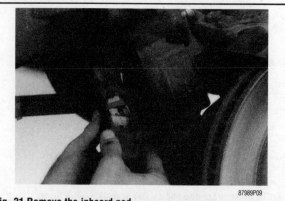

Fig. 21 Remove the inboard pad

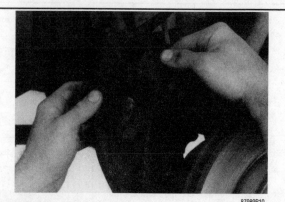

Fig. 22 Remove the outboard pad

15. Install the screw and tighten to 15 ft. lbs. (20 Nm). The boss must fit fully into the circular cutout in the key.

16. Install the wheel and add brake fluid as necessary.

INSPECTION

♦ See Figures 26 and 27

Support the truck on jackstands and remove the wheels. Look in at the ends of the caliper to check the lining thickness of the outer pad. Look through the inspection hole in the top of the caliper to check the thickness of the inner pad. Refer to the brake specifications chart at the end of this section for the brake pad minimum thickness.

➡These manufacturer's specifications may not agree with your state inspection law.

Original equipment pads and GM replacement pads have an integral wear sensor. This is a spring steel tab on the rear edge of the inner pad which produces a squeal by rubbing against the rotor to warn that the pads have reached their wear limit. They do not squeal when the brakes are applied.

The squeal will eventually stop if worn pads aren't replaced. Should this happen, replace the pads immediately to prevent expensive rotor (disc) damage.

Brake Caliper

REMOVAL & INSTALLATION

Delco System

♦ See Figures 12 thru 22

1. Remove the cover on the master cylinder and siphon enough fluid out of the reservoirs to bring the level to ⅔ full. This step prevents spilling fluid when the piston is pushed back.

2. Raise and support the vehicle. Remove the front wheels and tires.

3. Push the brake piston back into its bore using a C-clamp to pull the caliper outward.

4. Unfasten the brake hose fitting from the caliper using a flare nut wrench, cap the fitting to prevent foreign material from entering the or the hose.

5. Remove the two bolts which hold the caliper and then lift the caliper off the disc.

⁂ CAUTION

Do not let the caliper assembly hang by the brake hose.

6. Remove the inboard and outboard shoe.

➡If the pads are to be reinstalled, mark them inside and outside.

7. Remove the pad support spring from the piston.

8. Remove the two sleeves from the inside ears of the caliper and the 4 rubber bushings from the grooves in the caliper ears.

9. Remove the caliper.

10. Check the inside of the caliper for fluid leakage; if so, the caliper should be overhauled.

⁂ CAUTION

Do not use compressed air to clean the inside of the caliper as this may unseat the dust boot.

To install:

11. Lubricate the sleeves, rubber bushings, bushing grooves, and the end of the mounting bolts using silicone lubricant.

12. Install new bushing in the caliper ears along with new sleeves. The sleeve should be replaced so that the end toward the shoe is flush with the machined surface of the ear.

13. Install the brake pads.

14. With the two pads in position, place the caliper over the brake disc and align the holes in the caliper with those of the mounting bracket.

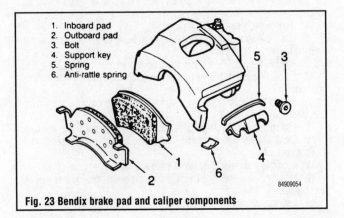

Fig. 23 Bendix brake pad and caliper components

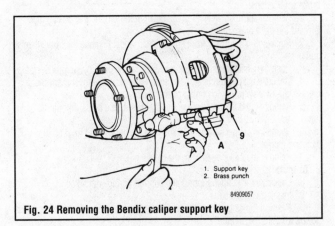
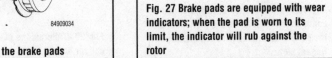

Fig. 24 Removing the Bendix caliper support key

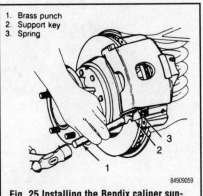
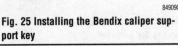

Fig. 25 Installing the Bendix caliper support key

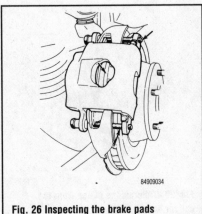

Fig. 26 Inspecting the brake pads

Fig. 27 Brake pads are equipped with wear indicators; when the pad is worn to its limit, the indicator will rub against the rotor

⁕⁕ CAUTION

Make certain that the brake hose is not twisted or kinked.

15. Fill the cavity between the bolt bushings with silicone grease. Install the mounting bracket bolts through the sleeves in the inboard caliper ears and through the mounting bracket, making sure that the ends of the bolts pass under the retaining ears on the inboard pad.

➡ **For best results, always use new bushings, sleeves and bolt boots.**

16. Tighten the mounting bolts to 35 ft. lbs. (47 Nm) for R/V Series; 28 ft. lbs. (38 Nm) for 1988-92 C/K Series and 38 ft. lbs. (51 Nm) for 1993-98 C/K Series.

17. Connect the brake hose to the caliper and tighten the fitting until the are snug.

18. Pump the brake pedal to seat the pad against the rotor. Don't do this unless both calipers are in place. Use a pair of channel lock pliers to bend over the upper ears of the outer pad so it isn't loose.

➡ **After tightening the mounting bolts, there must be clearance between the caliper and knuckle at both the upper and lower edge. On R/V Series, the clearance must be 0.010-0.024 in. (0.26-0.60mm); on C/K Series, it must be 0.005-0.012 in. (0.13-0.30mm) for 1988-91, and 0.010-0.028 in. (0.26-0.71mm) on 1992-98 models. If not, loosen the bolts and reposition the caliper.**

19. Install the front wheel and lower the truck.

20. Add fluid to the master cylinder reservoirs so that they are ¼ in. (6mm) from the top.

21. Bleed the brake system.

22. Check the fluid level again and add fluid as necessary. Do not move the vehicle until a hard pedal is obtained.

Bendix System

♦ **See Figures 23, 24 and 25**

The Bendix system is used on some front brake applications and all rear brake applications.

1. Remove approximately ⅔ of the brake fluid from the master cylinder. Discard the used brake fluid.

2. Raise and support the front end on jackstands. Remove the front wheels and tires.

3. Push the piston back into its bore. This can be done by suing a C-clamp.

4. Unscrew the brake line at the caliper. Plug the opening. Discard the copper washer. Be careful not to damage the brake line.

5. Remove the bolt at the caliper support key. Use a brass drift pin to remove the key and spring.

6. Rotate the caliper up and forward from the bottom and lift it off the caliper support.

7. Remove the brake pads from the caliper.

To install:

8. Lubricate the caliper support and support spring with silicone.

9. Install the brake pads.

10. Position the caliper over the brake disc, top edge first. Rotate the caliper downward onto the support.

11. Place the spring over the caliper support key, install the assembly between the support and lower caliper groove. Tap into place until the key retaining screw can be installed.

12. Use a brass drift pin to remove the key and spring.

13. Install the screw and tighten to 15 ft. lbs. (20 Nm). The boss must fit fully into the circular cutout in the key.

14. Using a new copper washer, connect the brake line at the caliper. Tighten the connector to 33 ft. lbs. (45 Nm).

15. Bleed the brake system.

16. Install the wheel.

OVERHAUL

♦ **See Figures 28 thru 35**

➡ **Some vehicles may be equipped dual piston calipers. The procedure to overhaul the caliper is essentially the same with the exception of multiple pistons, O-rings and dust boots.**

1. Remove the caliper from the vehicle and place on a clean workbench.

⁕⁕ CAUTION

NEVER place your fingers in front of the pistons in an attempt to catch or protect the pistons when applying compressed air. This could result in personal injury!

➡ **Depending upon the vehicle, there are two different ways to remove the piston from the caliper. Refer to the brake pad replacement procedure to make sure you have the correct procedure for your vehicle.**

2. The first method is as follows:
 a. Stuff a shop towel or a block of wood into the caliper to catch the piston.
 b. Remove the caliper piston using compressed air applied into the caliper inlet hole. Inspect the piston for scoring, nicks, corrosion and/or worn or damaged chrome plating. The piston must be replaced if any of these conditions are found.

3. For the second method, you must rotate the piston to retract it from the caliper.

4. If equipped, remove the anti-rattle clip.

5. Use a prytool to remove the caliper boot, being careful not to scratch the housing bore.

6. Remove the piston seals from the groove in the caliper bore.

7. Carefully loosen the brake bleeder valve cap and valve from the caliper housing.

8. Inspect the caliper bores, pistons and mounting threads for scoring or excessive wear.

9. Use crocus cloth to polish out light corrosion from the piston and bore.

10. Clean all parts with denatured alcohol and dry with compressed air.

To assemble:

11. Lubricate and install the bleeder valve and cap.

12. Install the new seals into the caliper bore grooves, making sure they are not twisted.

13. Lubricate the piston bore.

TCCA9P01

Fig. 28 For some types of calipers, use compressed air to drive the piston out of the caliper, but make sure to keep your fingers clear

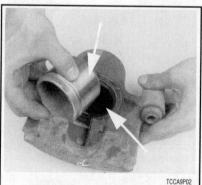

TCCA9P02

Fig. 29 Withdraw the piston from the caliper bore

TCCA9P03

Fig. 30 On some vehicles, you must remove the anti-rattle clip

14. Install the pistons and boots into the bores of the calipers and push to the bottom of the bores.
15. Use a suitable driving tool to seat the boots in the housing.
16. Install the caliper in the vehicle.
17. Install the wheel and tire assembly, then carefully lower the vehicle.
18. Properly bleed the brake system.

Brake Disc (Rotor)

REMOVAL & INSTALLATION

Front

R AND C-SERIES

▶ **See Figure 36**

1. Remove the brake caliper as previously outlined.
2. Remove the outer wheel bearing.
3. Remove the rotor from the spindle.
4. Reverse procedure to install. Adjust the bearings.

V-SERIES

➡**Before starting, you'll need a special wheel bearing nut socket for your ½ inch drive ratchet. These sockets are available through auto parts stores and catalogs. You can't do this job properly without it.**

1. Raise and support the front end on jackstands.
2. Remove the wheels.
3. Remove the hubs.
4. Wipe the inside of the hub to remove as much grease as possible.
5. Using your bearing nut socket, remove the locknut from the spindle.
6. With the locknut off you'll be able to see the locking ring on the adjusting nut. Remove the locking ring. A tool such as a dental pick will make this easier.

7. Using the special socket, remove the bearing adjusting nut.

➡**You'll notice that the adjusting nut and the locknut are almost identical. The difference is, the adjusting nut has a small pin on one side which indexes with a hole in the locking ring. DO NOT CONFUSE THE TWO NUTS!**

8. Dismount the brake caliper and suspend it out of the way, without disconnecting the brake line.
9. Pull the hub off of the spindle. The outer bearing will tend to fall out as soon as it clears the spindle, so have a hand ready to catch it.

➡**Some discs have an anti-squeal groove. This should not be mistaken for scoring.**

To install:
10. Carefully place the hub assembly on the spindle. Take care to avoid damaging the seal on the spindle threads. Make sure the hub is all the way on the spindle.
11. Refer to the V-series wheel hub, rotor and bearing procedure in Section 8 of this manual. Starting at step 15 of the procedure, install and adjust the wheel bearings.
12. After bearing installation and adjustment, install the remaining components.

K1 AND 2-SERIES

1. Raise and support the front end on jackstands.
2. Remove the wheel.
3. Remove the caliper. Do not disconnect the brake hose from the caliper. Use a piece of wire to support the caliper, do not let it hang on the hose.
4. Remove the rotor.
5. Installation is the reverse of removal.

K3-SERIES

1. Raise and support the front end on jackstands.
2. Remove the wheel.
3. Remove the hub nut and washer. Insert a long drift or dowel through the vanes in the brake rotor to hold the rotor while loosening the nut.

Fig. 31 Use a prytool to carefully pry around the edge of the boot . . .

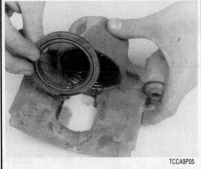

Fig. 32 . . . then remove the boot from the caliper housing, taking care not to score or damage the bore

Fig. 33 Use extreme caution when removing the piston seal; DO NOT scratch the caliper bore

Fig. 34 Use the proper size driving tool and a mallet to properly seal the boots in the caliper housing

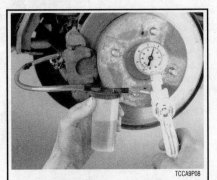

Fig. 35 There are tools, such as this Mighty-Vac, available to assist in proper brake system bleeding

Fig. 36 Remove the wheel and outer wheel bearing so that the rotor can be removed from the vehicle

4. Using a puller, force the outer end of the axle shaft out of the hub. Remove the hub/rotor.

To install:

5. Position the shaft in the hub and install the washer and hub nut. Leave the drift in the rotor vanes and tighten the hub nut to 173 ft. lbs. (235 Nm).

6. Remove the drift.

7. Install the wheel and lower the vehicle.

Rear

1. Raise and support the rear end on jackstands.
2. Remove the wheel.
3. Remove the axle shaft. Refer to Section 7 for this procedure.
4. Using wheel bearing nut wrench, remove the outer lock nut. If equipped, remove the retaining ring.
5. Remove the lock or key washer.
6. Remove the bearing adjusting nut and washer.
7. Remove the hub and rotor assembly.

To install:

8. Install the hub and rotor assembly making sure the bearings and the oil seal are positioned properly.

9. Apply alight coating of high melting point wheel bearing lubricant to the contact surfaces outside diameter of the axle housing tube.

10. Install the washer making sure the tang is engaged in the keyway.

11. Install the bearing adjusting nut and tighten as follows:

a. Tighten the nut to 50 ft. lbs. (68 Nm) while turning the hub.

b. Back off the nut and retighten to 30–40 ft. lbs. (40–54 Nm) while rotating the hub.

c. Back the nut off 135–150°.

12. Install the lockwasher and the locknut. Bend one ear of the lockwasher over the inner nut a minimum of 30° and one ear of the lockwasher over the outer nut a minimum of 60°.

13. Tighten the nut to 65 ft. lbs. (88 Nm).

14. Install the axle shaft, the tire and wheel assembly and lower the vehicle.

INSPECTION

1. Using a brake rotor micrometer measure the rotor thickness in several places around the rotor.

2. If the disc brake rotor minimum thickness varies more than 0.0005 inch (0.013mm) from point-to-point, refinish or replace the rotor

3. Mount a magnetic base dial indicator to the strut member and zero the indicator stylus on the face of the rotor. Rotate the rotor 360 degrees by hand and record the run-out.

➡**If the wheel has to be removed to check run-out, install the wheel lugs and tighten them to specification to hold the rotor in place.**

4. Refer to the brake specifications chart at the end of this section for the rotor run-out specification. If the run-out exceeds specification, it should be replaced.

DRUM BRAKES

✳✦✳ CAUTION

Older brake pads or shoes may contain asbestos, which has been determined to be a cancer causing agent. Never clean the brake surfaces with compressed air! Avoid inhaling any dust from any brake surface! When cleaning brake surfaces, use a commercially available brake cleaning fluid.

Brake Drums

REMOVAL & INSTALLATION

Semi-Floating Axles

▶ **See Figure 37**

1. Raise and support the rear end on jackstands.
2. Remove the wheel.
3. Pull the drum from the brake assembly. If the brake drums have been scored from worn linings, the brake adjuster must be backed off so that the brake shoes will retract from the drum. The adjuster can be backed off by inserting a brake adjusting tool through the access hole provided. In some cases the access hole is provided in the brake drum. A metal cover plate is over the hole. This may be removed by using a hammer and chisel.
4. To install, reverse the removal procedure.

Full Floating Axles

To remove the drums from full floating rear axles, use the axle shaft removal & installation procedure in Section 7. Full floating rear axles can readily be identified by the bearing housing protruding through the center of the wheel.

➡**Make sure all metal particles are removed from the brake drum before reassembly.**

INSPECTION

When the drum is removed, it should be inspected for cracks, scores, or other imperfections. These must be corrected before the drum is replaced.

✳✦✳ CAUTION

If the drum is found to be cracked, replace it. Do not attempt to service a cracked drum.

Minor drum score marks can be removed with fine emery cloth. Heavy score marks must be removed by turning the drum. This is removing metal from the entire inner surface of the drum on a lathe in order to level the surface. Automotive machine shops and some large parts stores are equipped to perform this operation.

If the drum is not scored, it should be polished with fine emery cloth before replacement. If the drum has to be resurfaced, it should not be enlarged more than the maximum wear limit. Refer to the brake specifications chart in this section for the brake drum original inside diameter and maximum wear limit specifications for your vehicle.

It is advisable, while the drums are off, to check them for out-of-round. An inside micrometer is necessary for an exact measurement, therefore unless this tool is available, the drums should be taken to a machine shop to be checked. Any drum which is more than 0.006 in. (0.1524mm) out-of-round will result in an inaccurate brake adjustment and other problems, and should be refinished or replaced.

➡**Make all measurements at right angles to each other and at the open and closed edges of the drum machined surface.**

87989P16

Fig. 37 You may have to back off the automatic adjuster before you can pull the drum from the brake assembly

Brake Shoes

INSPECTION

1. Raise and support the rear end on jackstands.
2. Remove the wheel.
3. Remove the drum from the brake assembly.
4. Use a ruler or a suitable measuring device to measure the lining thickness at the middle and both ends of the shoes.
5. Check the brake linings for peeling, cracks or extremely uneven wear.
6. Compare your readings to the minimum thickness specifications shown in the brake specifications chart in this section. If the lining thickness is less than specified, replace the brake shoes.
7. If their is evidence of the lining being contaminated by brake fluid or oil, replace the shoes.
8. Always replace the brake shoe assemblies on both sides.

REMOVAL & INSTALLATION

Duo-Servo

▶ See Figures 38 thru 46

1. Raise and securely support the vehicle using jackstands.
2. Loosen the parking brake equalizer enough to remove all tension on the brake cable.
3. Remove the brake drums.

✳✳ WARNING

The brake pedal must not be depressed while the drums are removed!

4. Using a brake tool, remove the shoe return springs. You can do this with ordinary tools, but it isn't easy.
5. Remove the shoe guide.
6. Remove the hold-down pins. These are the brackets which run though the backing plate. They can be removed with a pair of pliers. Reach around the rear of the backing plate and hold the back of the pin. Turn the top of the pin retainer 45° with the pliers. This will align the elongated tang with the slot in the retainer. Be careful, as the pin is spring loaded and may fly off when released. Use the same procedure for the other pin assembly.
7. Remove the adjuster actuator assembly.
8. Remove the actuator lever adjuster spring and link.
9. Remove the parking brake strut and the strut spring.

10. Remove the shoes from the backing plate. Make sure that you have a secure grip on the assembly as the bottom spring will still exert pressure on the shoes. Slowly let the tops of the shoes come together and the tension will decrease and the adjuster and spring may be removed.

➡ **If the linings are to be reused, mark them for identification.**

11. Remove the rear parking brake lever from the secondary shoe. Using a pair of pliers, pull back on the spring which surrounds the cable. At the same time, remove the cable from the notch in the shoe bracket. Make sure that the spring does not snap back or injury may result.

To install:

12. Use a brake cleaning fluid to remove dirt from the brake drum. Check the drums for scoring and cracks. Have the drums checked for out-of-round and service the drums as necessary.
13. Check the wheel cylinders by carefully pulling the lower edges of the wheel cylinder boots away from the cylinders. If there is excessive leakage, the inside of the cylinder will be moist with fluid. If there is any leakage at all, a cylinder overhaul is in order. DO NOT delay, as a brake failure could result.

➡ **A small amount of fluid will be present to act as a lubricant for the wheel cylinder pistons.**

14. Check the flange plate, which is located around the axle, for leakage of differential lubricant. This condition cannot be overlooked as the lubricant will be absorbed into the brake linings and brake failure will result. Replace the seals as necessary.

➡ **If new linings are being installed, check them against the old units for length and type.**

15. Check the new linings for imperfections.

✳✳ CAUTION

It is important to keep your hands free of dirt and grease when handling the brake shoes. Foreign matter will be absorbed into the linings and result in unpredictable braking.

16. Lightly lubricate the parking brake and cable and the end of the parking brake lever where it enters the shoe. Use high temperature, waterproof, grease or special brake lube.
17. Install the parking brake lever into the secondary shoe with the attaching bolt, spring washer, lockwasher, and nut. It is important that the lever move freely before the shoe is attached. Move the assembly and check for proper action.
18. Lubricate the adjusting screw and make sure that it works freely. Sometimes the adjusting screw will not move due to lack of lubricant or dirt contamination and the brakes will not adjust. In this case, the adjuster should be disassembled, thoroughly cleaned, and lubricated before installation.

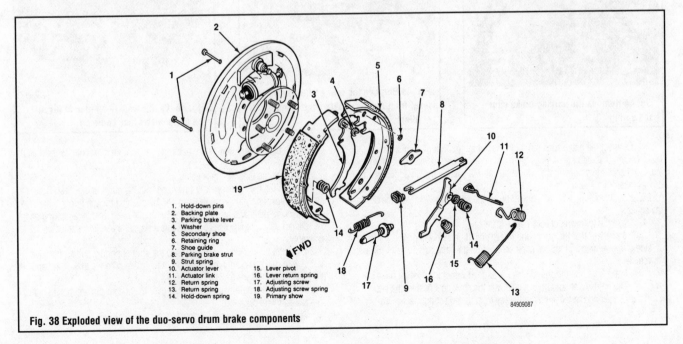

1. Hold-down pins
2. Backing plate
3. Parking brake lever
4. Washer
5. Secondary shoe
6. Retaining ring
7. Shoe guide
8. Parking brake strut
9. Strut spring
10. Actuator lever
11. Actuator link
12. Return spring
13. Return spring
14. Hold-down spring
15. Lever pivot
16. Lever return spring
17. Adjusting screw
18. Adjusting screw spring
19. Primary show

84909087

Fig. 38 Exploded view of the duo-servo drum brake components

Fig. 39 Using a brake tool, remove the shoe return springs

Fig. 40 Remove the self-adjuster actuator spring

Fig. 41 Remove the link from the secondary shoe by pulling it from the anchor pin

Fig. 42 Remove the hold-down pins

Fig. 43 Remove the shoes from the backing plate

Fig. 44 Remove the parking brake strut and spring

Fig. 45 Remove the rear parking brake lever from the secondary shoe using a pair of pliers

Fig. 46 It's always a good idea to lay all the parts out as they come off

19. Connect the brake shoe spring to the bottom portion of both shoes. Make certain that the brake linings are installed in the correct manner, the primary and secondary shoe in the correct position. If you are not sure remove the other brake drum and check it.

20. Install the adjusting mechanism below the spring and separate the top of the shoes.

21. Make the following checks before installation:

 a. Be certain that the right hand thread adjusting screw is on the left hand side of the vehicle and the left hand screw is on the right hand side of the vehicle.

 b. Make sure that the star adjuster is aligned with the adjusting hole.

 c. The adjuster should be installed with the starwheel nearest the secondary shoe and the tension spring away from the adjusting mechanism;

 d. If the original linings are being reused, put them back in their original locations.

22. Install the parking brake cable.

23. Position the primary shoe (the shoe with the short lining) first. Secure it with the hold-down pin and with its spring by pushing the pin through the back of the backing plate and, while holding it with one hand, install the spring and the retainer using a pair of needlenose pliers. Install the adjuster actuator assembly.

24. Install the parking brake strut and the strut spring by pulling back the spring with pliers and engaging the end of the cable onto the brake strut and then releasing the spring.

25. Place the small metal guide plate over the anchor pin and position the self-adjuster wire cable eye.

❋❋ CAUTION

The wire should not be positioned with the conventional brake installation tool or damage will result. It should be positioned on the actuator assembly first and then placed over the anchor pin stud by hand with the adjuster assembly in full downward position.

26. Install the actuator return spring. DO NOT pry the actuator lever to install the return spring. Position it using the end of a screwdriver or another suitable tool.

➡ If the return springs are bent or in any way distorted, they should be replaced.

27. Using the brake installation tool, place the brake return springs in position. Install the primary spring first over the anchor pin and then place the spring from the secondary show over the wire link end.

28. Pull the brake shoes away from the backing plate and apply a thin coat of high temperature, waterproof, grease or special brake lube in the brake shoe contact points.

❋❋ CAUTION

Only a small amount is necessary. Keep the lubricant away from the brake linings.

29. Once the complete assembly has been installed, check the operation of the self-adjusting mechanism by moving the actuating lever by hand.

30. Turn the star adjuster until the drum slides over the brakes shoes with only a slight drag. Remove the drum.

31. Turn the adjuster back 1¼ turns.

32. Install the drum and wheel.

33. Adjust the brakes.

34. If necessary, adjust the parking brake.

Leading/Trailing

▶ See Figures 47, 48 and 49

1. Jack up and securely support the vehicle using jackstands.

2. Loosen the parking brake equalizer enough to remove all tension on the brake cable.

3. Remove the brake drums. If difficulty is till encountered, remove the access hole plug in the backing plate and insert a metal rod to push the parking brake lever off its stop.

❋❋ WARNING

The brake pedal must not be depressed while the drums are removed!

4. Raise the lever arm of the actuator until the upper end is clear of the slot in the adjuster screw. Slide the actuator off the adjuster pin.

5. Disconnect the actuator from the brake shoe.

6. Remove the hold-down pins. These are the brackets which run though the backing plate. They can be removed with a pair of pliers. Reach around the rear of the backing plate and hold the back of the pin. Turn the top of the pin retainer 45° with the pliers. This will align the elongated tang with the slot in the retainer. Be careful, as the pin is spring loaded and may fly off when released. Use the same procedure for the other pin assembly.

7. Pull the lower ends of the shoes apart and lift the lower return spring over the anchor plate. Remove the spring from the shoes.

8. Lift the shoes and upper return spring along with the adjusting screw, from the backing plate. Some spreading of the shoes is necessary to clear the wheel cylinder and axle flange. Remove the upper spring.

9. Remove the retaining ring, pin, spring washer and parking brake lever.

➡ If the linings are to be reused, mark them for identification.

To install:

10. Use a brake cleaning fluid to remove dirt from the brake drum. Check the drums for scoring and cracks. Have the drums checked for out-of-round and service the drums as necessary.

11. Check the wheel cylinders by carefully pulling the lower edges of the wheel cylinder boots away from the cylinders. If there is excessive leakage, the inside of the cylinder will be moist with fluid. If there is any leakage at all, a cylinder overhaul is in order. DO NOT delay, as a brake failure could result.

➡ A small amount of fluid will be present to act as a lubricant for the wheel cylinder pistons.

12. Check the flange plate, which is located around the axle, for leakage of differential lubricant. This condition cannot be overlooked as the lubricant will be absorbed into the brake linings and brake failure will result. Replace the seals as necessary.

➡ If new linings are being installed, check them against the old units for length and type.

13. Check the new linings for imperfections.

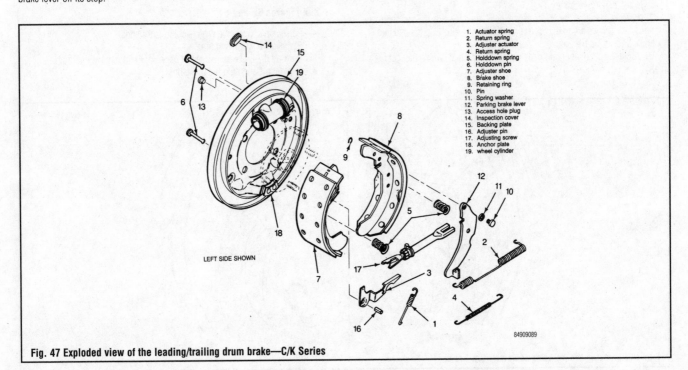

1. Actuator spring
2. Return spring
3. Adjuster actuator
4. Return spring
5. Holddown spring
6. Holddown pin
7. Adjuster shoe
8. Brake shoe
9. Retaining ring
10. Pin
11. Spring washer
12. Parking brake lever
13. Access hole plug
14. Inspection cover
15. Backing plate
16. Adjuster pin
17. Adjusting screw
18. Anchor plate
19. wheel cylinder

LEFT SIDE SHOWN

84909089

Fig. 47 Exploded view of the leading/trailing drum brake—C/K Series

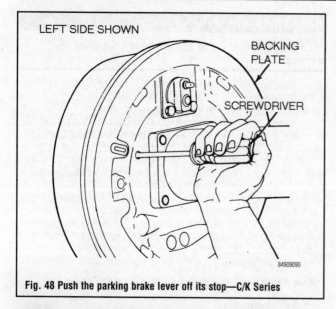

LEFT SIDE SHOWN

BACKING PLATE

SCREWDRIVER

84909090

Fig. 48 Push the parking brake lever off its stop—C/K Series

✳✳ CAUTION

It is important to keep your hands free of dirt and grease when handling the brake shoes. Foreign matter will be absorbed into the linings and result in unpredictable braking.

14. Install the parking brake lever assembly The concave side of the washer should be against the shoe.

15. Install the adjuster pin in the shoe so that the pin projects 0.268–0.276 in. (6.8–7.0mm) from the side of the shoe where the actuator is installed.

16. Apply an approved brake lubricant grease to the threads of the adjuster screw, socket and socket face.

17. Make certain that the brake linings are positioned correctly and connect the upper spring. If you are not sure of which shoe goes where, remove the other brake drum and check it. Don't over-stretch the spring; you'll ruin it. The spring can't be stretched, safely, more than 8.04 in. (204mm).

18. Install the adjusting mechanism between the shoes. Make the following checks before installation:

   a. Be certain that the adjusting screw assembly engages the adjuster shoe and parking brake lever.

   b. Make sure that the spring clip is positioned towards the backing plate.

   c. The linings are in the correct positions. The shoe with the parking brake lever is the rear shoe.

19. Coat the shoe mounting pads on the backing plate with a thin coat of lithium grease.

20. Position the assembly on the backing plate, engaging the upper shoe ends with the wheel cylinder pushrods.

21. Hook the lower return spring into the shoe ends and spread the shoes, guiding the lower spring over the anchor plate. Don't over-stretch the spring; you'll ruin it. The spring can't be stretched, safely, more than 4¼ in. (108mm).

22. Install the hold-down spring assemblies.

23. Place the adjuster actuator over the end of the adjusting pin so its top leg engages the notch in the adjuster screw.

24. Install the actuator spring. Make sure that the free end of the actuator engage the notch of the adjuster nut. Don't over-stretch the spring. Its maximum stretch is 3¼ in. (83mm).

25. Connect the parking brake cable to the lever.

26. Turn the star adjuster until the drum slides over the brakes shoes with only a slight drag. Remove the drum.

27. Turn the adjuster back 1¼ turns.

28. Install the drums and wheels.

29. Adjust the brakes.

30. Adjust the parking brake as necessary.

ADJUSTMENT

1. Raise the vehicle and support it with jackstands.

2. Remove the adjusting hole cover from the rear of the backing plate.

3. Insert a brake adjustment tool into the adjusting hole and turn the star-wheel on the adjusting screw while turning the wheel by hand. Keep turning the starwheel until the wheel can just be turned by hand.

4. On vehicles equipped with duo-servo drum brakes, back off the adjusting screw 33 times.

5. On vehicles equipped with leading/trailing drum brakes, back off the adjusting screw 20 times.

6. Perform this procedure at both wheels.

7. Install the adjusting hole cover and check the parking brake adjustment.

8. Lower the vehicle.

9. Make the final adjustment by driving the vehicle very slowly in reverse and pumping the brakes until the self-adjusting mechanisms adjust to the proper level and the brake pedal reaches satisfactory height.

10. Road test the vehicle.

Wheel Cylinders

REMOVAL & INSTALLATION

♦ **See Figures 50 and 51**

1. Raise and support the vehicle using jackstands.

2. Remove the wheel and tire.

3. Back off the brake adjustment if necessary and remove the drum.

4. Disconnect and plug the brake line.

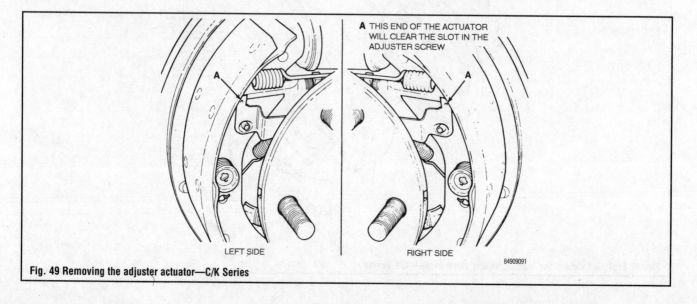

A THIS END OF THE ACTUATOR WILL CLEAR THE SLOT IN THE ADJUSTER SCREW

A

A

LEFT SIDE

RIGHT SIDE

84909091

Fig. 49 Removing the adjuster actuator—C/K Series

5. Remove the brake shoes as described above.
6. Remove the bolts securing the wheel cylinder to the backing plate.
7. Install the wheel cylinder. Tighten the mounting bolts to 15 ft. lbs. (20 Nm). Tighten the brake pipes to 13 ft. lbs. (17 Nm). Bleed the system.

OVERHAUL

♦ **See Figures 52 thru 61**

Wheel cylinder overhaul kits may be available, but often at little or no savings over a reconditioned wheel cylinder. It often makes sense with these components to substitute a new or reconditioned part instead of attempting an overhaul.

If no replacement is available, or you would prefer to overhaul your wheel cylinders, the following procedure may be used. When rebuilding and installing wheel cylinders, avoid getting any contaminants into the system. Always use clean, new, high quality brake fluid. If dirty or improper fluid has been used, it will be necessary to drain the entire system, flush the system with proper brake fluid, replace all rubber components, then refill and bleed the system.

1. Remove the wheel cylinder from the vehicle and place on a clean workbench.
2. First remove and discard the old rubber boots, then withdraw the pistons. Piston cylinders are equipped with seals and a spring assembly, all located behind the pistons in the cylinder bore.
3. Remove the remaining inner components, seals and spring assembly. Compressed air may be useful in removing these components. If no compressed air is available, be VERY careful not to score the wheel cylinder bore when removing parts from it. Discard all components for which replacements were supplied in the rebuild kit.
4. Wash the cylinder and metal parts in denatured alcohol or clean brake fluid.

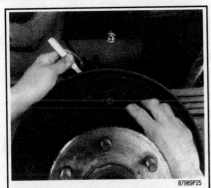

Fig. 50 Remove the bolts securing the wheel cylinder to the backing plate
87989P25

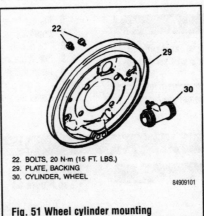

22. BOLTS, 20 N·m (15 FT. LBS.)
29. PLATE, BACKING
30. CYLINDER, WHEEL
84909101

Fig. 51 Wheel cylinder mounting

Fig. 52 Remove the outer boots from the wheel cylinder
TCCA9P13

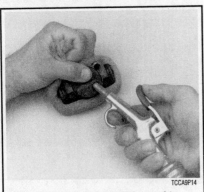

Fig. 53 Compressed air can be used to remove the pistons and seals
TCCA9P14

Fig. 54 Remove the pistons, cup seals and spring from the cylinder
TCCA9P15

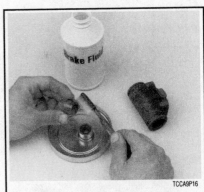

Fig. 55 Use brake fluid and a soft brush to clean the pistons . . .
TCCA9P16

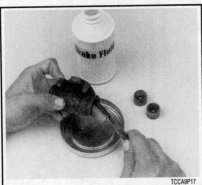

Fig. 56 . . . and the bore of the wheel cylinder
TCCA9P17

Fig. 57 Once cleaned and inspected, the wheel cylinder is ready for assembly
TCCA9P18

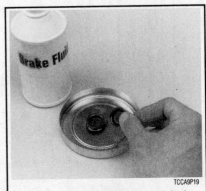

Fig. 58 Lubricate the cup seals with brake fluid
TCCA9P19

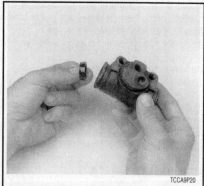

Fig. 59 Install the spring, then the cup seals in the bore

TCCA9P20

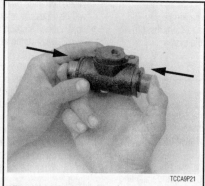

Fig. 60 Lightly lubricate the pistons, then install them

TCCA9P21

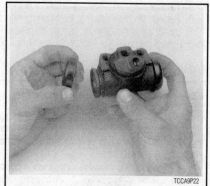

Fig. 61 The boots can now be installed over the wheel cylinder ends

TCCA9P22

✳✳ WARNING

Never use a mineral-based solvent such as gasoline, kerosene or paint thinner for cleaning purposes. These solvents will swell rubber components and quickly deteriorate them.

5. Allow the parts to air dry or use compressed air. Do not use rags for cleaning, since lint will remain in the cylinder bore.

PARKING BRAKE

Cables

REMOVAL & INSTALLATION

Front Cable

DRUM BRAKES

▶ See Figure 62

1. Raise vehicle and support it with safety stands.
2. Remove adjusting nut from equalizer.
3. Remove retainer clip from rear portion of front cable at frame and from lever arm.
4. Disconnect front brake cable from parking brake pedal or lever assemblies. Remove front brake cable. On some models, it may assist installation of new cable if a heavy cord is tied to other end of cable in order to guide new cable through proper routing.

To install:
5. Install cable by reversing removal procedure.
6. Adjust parking brake.

6. Inspect the piston and replace it if it shows scratches.
7. Lubricate the cylinder bore and seals using clean brake fluid.
8. Position the spring assembly.
9. Install the inner seals, then the pistons.
10. Insert the new boots into the counterbores by hand. Do not lubricate the boots.
11. Install the wheel cylinder.

DISC BRAKES

▶ See Figure 63

1. Release the parking brake.
2. Raise the truck and support it with safety stands.
3. Remove the cotter pin and the clevis pin from the brake lever and disconnect the clevis and lock nut from the end of the cable.
4. Pull the cable and grommet out of the lower bracket. Unscrew the bracket bolt on the frame rail.
5. Disconnect the end of the cable at the pedal lever, release the retaining fingers and remove the cable.
6. Install the cable and check the parking brake adjustment.

Center Cable

1. Raise the vehicle on hoist.
2. Remove the adjusting nut from the equalizer.
3. Unhook the connector at each end and disengage the hooks and guides.
4. Install the new cable by reversing the removal procedure.
5. Adjust the parking brake.
6. Apply the parking brake 3 times with heavy pressure and repeat adjustment.

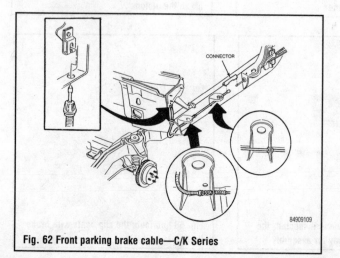

Fig. 62 Front parking brake cable—C/K Series

84909109

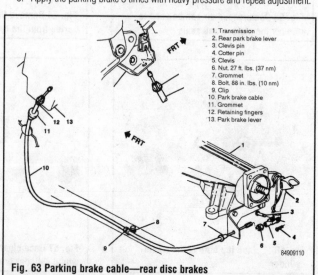

1. Transmission
2. Rear park brake lever
3. Clevis pin
4. Cotter pin
5. Clevis
6. Nut, 27 ft. lbs. (37 nm)
7. Grommet
8. Bolt, 88 in. lbs. (10 nm)
9. Clip
10. Park brake cable
11. Grommet
12. Retaining fingers
13. Park brake lever

Fig. 63 Parking brake cable—rear disc brakes

84909110

Rear Cable

▸ See Figure 64

1. Raise the vehicle and support it on safety stands.
2. Remove the rear wheel and brake drum.
3. Loosen the adjusting nut at the equalizer.
4. Disengage the rear cable at the connector.
5. Bend the retainer fingers at the backing plate.
6. Disengage the cable at the brake shoe operating lever.
7. Install the new cable.
8. Adjust the parking brake.

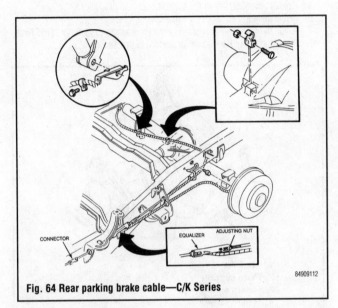

Fig. 64 Rear parking brake cable—C/K Series

84909112

ADJUSTMENT

Duo-Servo Drum Brakes

The rear brakes serve a dual purpose. They are used as service brakes and as parking brakes. To obtain proper adjustment of the parking brake, the service brakes must first be properly adjusted as outlined earlier.

1. Apply the parking brake 4 clicks from the fully released position.
2. Raise and support the vehicle.
3. Loosen the locknut at the equalizer.
4. Tighten or loosen the adjusting nut until a moderate drag is felt when the rear wheels are rotated forward.
5. Tighten the locknut.
6. Release the parking brake and rotate the rear wheels. No drag should be felt. If even a light drag is felt, readjust the parking brake.
7. Lower the vehicle.

➡If a new parking brake cable is being installed, pre-stretch it by applying the parking brake hard about three times before making adjustments.

Leading/Trailing Drum Brakes

1. Raise the rear of the truck and support it with safety stands. Remove the wheels and brake drum.
2. Measure the brake drum inside diameter.
3. Turn the adjuster nut until the brake shoe maximum diameter is 0.01–0.02 in. (0.25–50mm) less than the brake drum diameter.
4. Make sure that the stops on the parking brake levers are against the edge of the brake shoe web. If the cable is holding the stops off the edge, loosen the adjustment.
5. Tighten the cable at the adjuster nut until the lever stops begin to move off the shoe webs.
6. Loosen the adjustment nut until the lever stops are **just** touching the

shoe webs. There should be no more than 0.019 inch (0.5mm) clearance between the stops and the webs.

7. Install the drums and wheels.
8. Pump the brake pedal 30–35 times with normal force. Pause about 1 second between each stroke.
9. Depress the parking brake pedal 6 clicks. The wheels should be locked.
10. Release the parking brake. The wheels should rotate freely.

Disc Brakes

▸ See Figure 65

1. Locate the parking brake drum assembly. Its at the back of the transmission extension housing. Remove the clevis pin from the parking brake lever.
2. Set the parking brake pedal to 4 clicks.
3. Connect a tension gauge to the frame of the truck with a small length of cable and a turn buckle.
4. Connect the tension gauge to the bottom of the parking brake lever and tighten it to 50 lbs. (222N).
5. Loosen the clevis lock nut and turn the clevis until the pin slides freely in the lever. There should be no slack in the cable.
6. Install the clevis pin and a new cotter pin. Tighten the lock nut to 27 ft. lbs. (37 Nm).
7. Remove the gauge and release the parking brake.

Parking Brake Drum

REMOVAL & INSTALLATION

▸ See Figures 66 and 67

➡This applies to rear disc brakes only.

1. Release the parking brake. Raise the vehicle and support it on jackstands.
2. Disconnect the driveshaft at the brake drum.
3. Remove the nut or bolt and pull off the drum/yoke assembly.
4. Remove the bolts and pull the drum off the yoke.

To install:

5. Position the drum on the yoke and tighten the bolts to 27 ft. lbs. (37 Nm).
6. Slide the drum/yoke assembly on and tighten the bolt to 65 ft. lbs. (88 Nm), or the nut to 180 ft. lbs. (255 Nm) on all but 1996–98 models. On 1996–98 models tighten the bolt to 90 ft. lbs. (122 Nm), or the nut to 350 ft. lbs. (475 Nm)
7. Install the driveshaft and lower the truck.

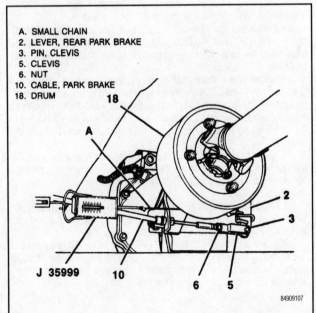

A. SMALL CHAIN
2. LEVER, REAR PARK BRAKE
3. PIN, CLEVIS
5. CLEVIS
6. NUT
10. CABLE, PARK BRAKE
18. DRUM

J 35999

84909107

Fig. 65 Adjusting the parking brake on models with rear discs

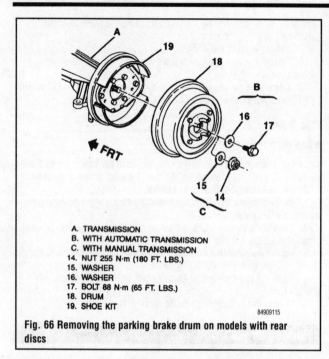

A. TRANSMISSION
B. WITH AUTOMATIC TRANSMISSION
C. WITH MANUAL TRANSMISSION
14. NUT 255 N·m (180 FT. LBS.)
15. WASHER
16. WASHER
17. BOLT 88 N·m (65 FT. LBS.)
18. DRUM
19. SHOE KIT

84909115

Fig. 66 Removing the parking brake drum on models with rear discs

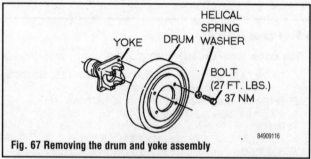

Fig. 67 Removing the drum and yoke assembly

84909116

Brake Shoes

REMOVAL & INSTALLATION

▶ **See Figure 68**

1. Remove the drum. Refer to the procedure in this section.
2. Remove the bolts and washers.
3. Disconnect the support plate and shoe kits.
4. Remove the springs and shoe kits.

To install:

5. Connect the shoe kits to the support plate.
6. Install the springs, support plate and shoe kits.
7. Install the bolts and washers. Tighten the washers to 77 ft. lbs. (105 Nm).
8. Install the drum. Refer to the procedure in this section.

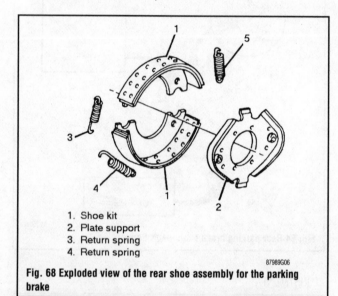

1. Shoe kit
2. Plate support
3. Return spring
4. Return spring

87989G06

Fig. 68 Exploded view of the rear shoe assembly for the parking brake

FOUR WHEEL ANTI-LOCK BRAKE SYSTEM

General Information

The Kelsey Hayes four wheel anti-lock brake system is used on the 1992–98 Suburban, Jimmy, Yukon and Blazer and C/K Series trucks.

The 4 wheel anti-lock system is designed to reduce brake lock-up during severe brake application. The Electro-Hydraulic Control Unit (EHCU) valve—located near the master cylinder—controls the hydraulic pressure within the brake lines.

The control valve is made up of 2 types of valves. Each front wheel and the combined rear wheel circuit are served by a dedicated isolation valve and a dump valve. The isolation valves maintain pressure within their respective circuits; the dump valves release pressure within each circuit as commanded by the EHCU. The valves are controlled by a micro-computer within the EHCU valve.

In a severe brake application, the EHCU valve will either allow pressure to increase within the system or maintain (isolate) the pressure within the system or release existing pressure through the dump valves into the accumulators.

The EHCU valve operates by receiving signals from the speed sensors, located at each wheel, and from the brake lamp switch. The speed sensors connect directly to the EHCU valve through a multi-pin connector.

The system is connected to the ANTI-LOCK warning lamp on the dashboard. The warning lamp will illuminate for about 2 seconds every time the vehicle is started. The warning lamp will illuminate it the computer detects a problem within the anti-lock system during vehicle operation.

System Components

EHCU VALVE

▶ **See Figure 69**

The EHCU valve is mounted near or under the master cylinder and combination valve. The valve is not serviceable and must be replaced if malfunctioning.

FRONT WHEEL SPEED SENSORS

With one exception, on both 2WD and 4WD vehicles, the front wheel speed sensors are permanently mounted to the brake rotor splash shield. With the exception of the 1992–98 Suburban, if the sensor fails the rotor and splash shield must be removed. On 4WD vehicles, the hub and bearing assembly must also be removed for access.

The front wheel speed sensors on 1992–98 4WD Suburban vehicles are removable without disassembly of the hub or brakes.

REAR WHEEL SPEED SENSORS

Except for 1992–93 Suburban, the rear wheel speed sensors are held by 2 bolts at each rear wheel. The brake drum and primary brake shoe must be removed for access.

The 1992–93 Suburban receives the rear wheel speed signal from the Vehicle Speed Sensor (VSS) buffer. The VSS is located at the left rear of the transmission. The buffer, a unit for interpreting the electrical signal from the sensor, is located

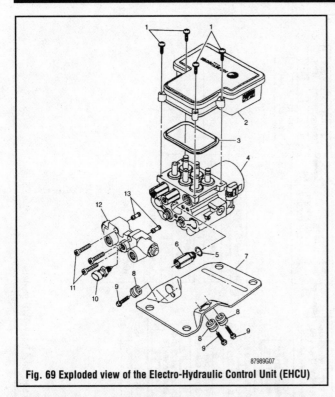

Fig. 69 Exploded view of the Electro-Hydraulic Control Unit (EHCU)

behind the instrument cluster. The buffer, formerly known as the digital ratio adapter controller (DRAC), is matched to the final drive and tire size of each vehicle. If the final drive or tire size is changed, the buffer unit must be replaced to maintain accurate speedometer/odometer readings and proper ABS function.

System Diagnosis

▶ See Figures 70 and 71

PRELIMINARY DIAGNOSIS

System diagnosis begins with the diagnostic circuit check as given in the chart. If the chart is used correctly, it will aid in elimination of simple, non-system problems such as blown fuses of failed bulbs. The chart will prompt the reading of codes at the proper point in the diagnosis.

➡Some of the diagnostic or repair procedures refer to the performance of a Function Test. This test is performed with the scan tool; it operates all components of the EHCU valve and checks their function. The test cannot be performed without the scan tool.

READING CODES

Stored trouble codes are transmitted through the flashing of the amber ANTI-LOCK dash warning lamp. The system may be put into diagnostic mode with a jumper wire, however, the use of the TECH-1 scan tool or its equivalent is highly recommended. The scan tool will allow performance of the specific system tests called for by the trouble tree for each code.

On all models except 1996–98, the codes can be read without the use of a hand scanner. To read the codes, use a jumper wire to connect terminal H on the ALDL to either body ground or to terminal A. The terminals must be connected for a few seconds before the code(s) will transmit. Observe the ANTI-LOCK light on the dash and count the flashes in groups: a group of 4 flashes, a pause and a group of 3 flashes indicates Code 43. Codes 12 and 14 are not trouble codes, but may appear with them to indicate normal operation. Not all vehicles use Code 12 or 14.

After the trouble codes have been read, refer to the correct trouble tree for each code. After repairs, repeat the initial diagnostic circuit check to confirm normal operation of the system.

CLEARING CODES

Stored codes may be erased with the hand scanner if available. If not using a hand scanner, codes may be cleared as follows:
1. Turn the ignition switch **ON** but do not start the engine.
2. Use a jumper wire to ground ALDL terminal H to terminal A for 2 seconds.
3. Remove the jumper wire for 2 seconds.
4. Repeat the grounding and un-grounding two more times. Each connection and opening of the circuit should last 2 seconds.
5. Connect the jumper to terminals H and A for a longer time; no trouble codes should be displayed. If codes are displayed, the system was not properly erased.
6. If no trouble codes appear, the memory has been cleared. Turn the ignition switch **OFF**.

Trouble codes

The following is a list of the OBD-I trouble codes for the four wheel anti-lock brake system.
- Code 21: right front speed sensor or circuit open
- Code 22: missing right front speed signal
- Code 23: erratic right front speed signal
- Code 25: left front speed sensor or circuit open
- Code 26: missing left front speed signal
- Code 27: erratic left front speed signal
- Code 29: simultaneous drop-out of front speed sensors
- Code 35: vehicle speed sensor or open circuit
- Code 36: missing vehicle speed sensor signal
- Code 37: erratic vehicle speed sensor signal
- Code 38: wheel speed error
- Codes 41 through 54: control valves
- Codes 61 through 63: reset switches
- Code 65 and 66: open or shorted pump motor relay
- Code 67: open motor circuit or shorted BPMV output
- Code 68: locked motor or shorted motor circuit
- Codes 71 through 74: memory errors
- Code 81: brake switch circuit shorted or open
- Code 86: shorted anti-lock indicator lamp
- Code 87: shorted brake warning lamp

The following is a list of the OBD-II trouble codes for the four wheel anti-lock brake system.
- Code C0021: right front wheel speed sensor circuit open or shorted to battery
- Code C0022: right front wheel speed sensor signal missing
- Code C0023: right front wheel speed sensor signal erratic
- Code C0025: left front wheel speed sensor circuit open or shorted to battery
- Code C0026: left front wheel speed sensor signal missing
- Code C0027: left front wheel speed sensor signal erratic
- Code C0029: simultaneous drop-out of front wheel speed signals
- Code C0035: rear speed sensor circuit open or shorted to battery
- Code C0036: rear speed signal missing
- Code C0037: rear speed signal erratic
- Code C0038: wheel speed signal malfunction
- Code C0041: right front isolation solenoid circuit open
- Code C0042: right front dump solenoid circuit open
- Code C0043: right front isolation solenoid circuit shorted
- Code C0044: right front dump solenoid circuit shorted
- Code C0045: left front isolation solenoid circuit open
- Code C0046: left front dump solenoid circuit open
- Code C0047: left front isolation solenoid circuit shorted
- Code C0048: left front dump solenoid circuit shorted
- Code C0051: rear isolation solenoid circuit open
- Code C0052: rear dump solenoid circuit open
- Code C0053: rear isolation solenoid circuit shorted
- Code C0054: rear dump solenoid circuit shorted
- Code C0065: pump motor relay circuit open
- Code C0066: pump motor relay circuit shorted
- Code C0067: pump motor circuit open
- Code C0068: pump motor locked or pump motor circuit shorted
- Codes C0071 through C0074: EBCM internal fault
- Code C0081: stoplamp switch circuit always closed or shorted
- Code C0086: anti-lock indicator lamp circuit shorted to battery
- Code Co0087: brake warning lamp circuit shorted to battery

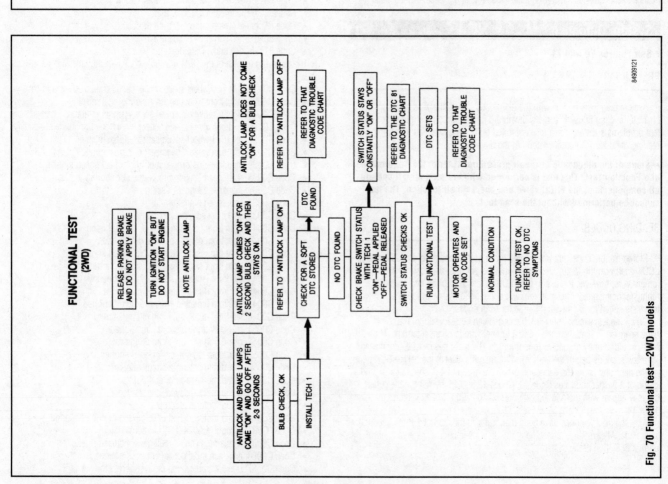

Fig. 71 Functional test—4WD models

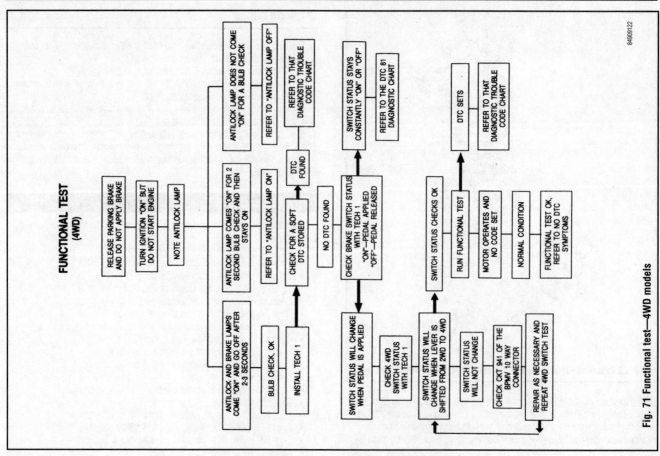

Fig. 70 Functional test—2WD models

Component Replacement

♦ See Figures 72 and 73

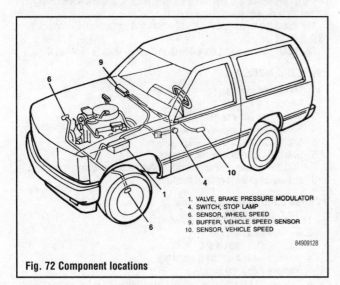

1. VALVE, BRAKE PRESSURE MODULATOR
4. SWITCH, STOP LAMP
6. SENSOR, WHEEL SPEED
9. BUFFER, VEHICLE SPEED SENSOR
10. SENSOR, VEHICLE SPEED

84909128

Fig. 72 Component locations

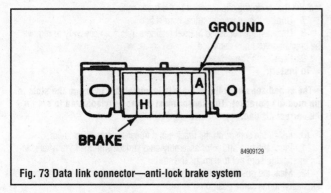

84909129

Fig. 73 Data link connector—anti-lock brake system

REMOVAL & INSTALLATION

Electro-Hydraulic Control Unit (EHCU) Valve

The EHCU valve is not serviceable and must never be disassembled or repaired. If tests indicate the unit is faulty, the EHCU must be replaced.

1. Label and unplug the electrical connectors from the EHCU.
2. Label and disconnect the brake lines from the EHCU.
3. Remove the bolts holding the EHCU bracket to the vehicle. Remove the bracket and hydraulic unit as an assembly.
4. Once removed from the vehicle, separate the bracket from the EHCU.

To install:

5. Assemble the EHCU to its bracket and install the bolts. Tighten the bolts to 5 ft. lbs. (7 Nm). Overtightening these bolts can cause excessive noise during system operation.
6. Install the assembly into the vehicle. Tighten the mounting bolts to 33 ft. lbs. (45 Nm).
7. Connect the brake lines in their original locations. Tighten the fittings to 16 ft. lbs. (25 Nm).
8. Connect the electrical connectors. Make certain each is squarely seated and secure.
9. Bleed the EHCU valve, then bleed the entire brake system.

Bleeding the EHCU

➡Bleeding the EHCU requires the use of the TECH-1 scanner or its equivalent and the appropriate cartridge. Additionally, 3 tools, J–39177 or equivalent, are required. Bleeding cannot be performed without this equipment.

The EHCU must be bled after replacement or if air is trapped within the unit. It must be bled after bleeding the master cylinder and before bleeding the individual wheel circuits.

The Internal Bleed Valves on either side of the unit must be opened ¼–½ turn before bleeding begins. These valves open internal passages within the unit. Actual bleeding is performed at the two bleeders on the front of the EHCU module. The bleeders must not be opened when the system is not pressurized. The ignition switch must be **OFF** or false trouble codes may be set.

1. Open the internal bleed valve ¼–½ turn each.
2. Install one tool J–39177 on the left bleed stem of the EHCU. Install one tool on the right bleed stem and install the third tool on the combination valve.
3. Inspect the fluid level in the master cylinder, filling if needed.
4. Slowly depress the brake pedal and hold it down.
5. Open the left bleeder on the front of the unit. Allow fluid to flow until no air is seen or until the brake pedal bottoms.
6. Close the left bleeder, then slowly release the pedal. Wait 15 seconds.
7. Repeat Steps 4, 5 and 6, including the 15 second wait, until no air is seen in the fluid.
8. Tighten the left internal bleed valve to 5 ft. lbs. (7 Nm).
9. Repeat Steps 3–7 at the right bleeder on the front of the unit.
10. When bleeding of the right port is complete, tighten the right internal bleed valve to 5 ft. lbs. (7 Nm).
11. Remove the 3 special tools.
12. Check the master cylinder fluid level, refilling as necessary.
13. Bleed the individual brake circuits at each wheel.
14. Switch the ignition **ON**. Use the hand scanner to perform 3 function tests on the system.
15. Carefully test drive the vehicle at moderate speeds; check for proper pedal feel and brake operation. If any problem is noted in feel or function, repeat the entire bleeding procedure.

Front Wheel Speed Sensors

TWO-WHEEL DRIVE MODELS (EXCEPT 1995–98)

♦ See Figure 74

1. Elevate and safely support the vehicle.
2. Remove the wheel.
3. Remove the brake caliper.
4. Remove the hub and rotor assembly.
5. Unplug the sensor wire connector.
6. Disconnect the sensor wire from the clip(s) on the upper control arm.
7. Remove the bolts holding the splash shield.
8. Remove the splash shield and sensor assembly.
9. Remove the gasket.

To install:

10. Install a new gasket.
11. Mount the sensor and splash shield to the knuckle. Install the retaining bolts and tighten them to 89 inch lbs. (10 Nm).
12. Connect the wiring to the clips on the upper control arm. Check the wiring for correct routing.
13. Connect the wiring connector.
14. Install the hub and rotor assembly.
15. Install the brake caliper.
16. Install the wheel. Lower the vehicle to the ground.

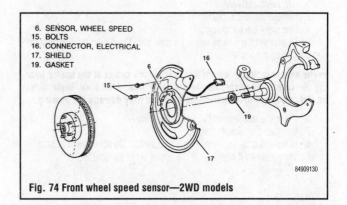

6. SENSOR, WHEEL SPEED
15. BOLTS
16. CONNECTOR, ELECTRICAL
17. SHIELD
19. GASKET

84909130

Fig. 74 Front wheel speed sensor—2WD models

FOUR-WHEEL DRIVE MODELS (EXCEPT 1995–98)

▶ **See Figure 75**

1. Elevate and safely support the vehicle.
2. Remove the wheel.
3. Disconnect the sensor electrical connector.
4. Release the sensor wire from the clip(s) on the upper control arm.
5. Remove the bolts holding the sensor; remove the sensor from its mount.
6. Reassemble in reverse order. Tighten the sensor mounting bolts to 11 ft. lbs. (15 Nm).

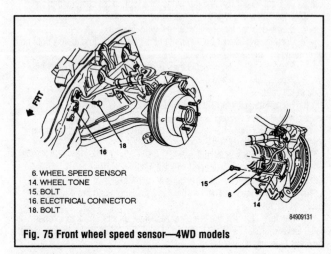

6. WHEEL SPEED SENSOR
14. WHEEL TONE
15. BOLT
16. ELECTRICAL CONNECTOR
18. BOLT

84909131

Fig. 75 Front wheel speed sensor—4WD models

TWO-WHEEL DRIVE 1995–98 MODELS (EXCEPT C3HD)

1. Elevate and safely support the vehicle.
2. Remove the wheel.
3. Remove the brake caliper.
4. Remove the hub and rotor assembly.
5. Unplug the sensor wire connector.
6. Use a ³⁄₁₆ inch drill to remove the sensor harness clip rivets.
7. Disconnect the clips from the sensor wire. Save the clips for the new sensor.
8. Remove the sensor assembly bolts and nut.
9. Remove the bolts holding the splash shield.
10. Remove the splash shield and sensor.
11. Remove the gasket.
To install:
12. Install a new gasket.
13. Mount the sensor and splash shield to the knuckle. Install the retaining bolts and tighten the splash shield mounting bolts to 12 ft. lbs. (16 Nm). Tighten the sensor retainers to 19 ft. lbs. (26 Nm).
14. Install the harness clips in their original position and attach them using ³⁄₁₆ inch rivets.
15. Install the remaining components in the reverse order of removal.

FOUR-WHEEL DRIVE 1995–98 MODELS (EXCEPT C3HD)

1. Elevate and safely support the vehicle.
2. Remove the wheel.
3. Remove the brake caliper.
4. Remove the rotor assembly.
5. Disconnect the sensor wiring harness from the clip on the control arm and the clip on the frame.

➡ **The sensor mount in a bore that leads to the center of the sealed bearing. Be careful when cleaning and working around the bore. Make sure no dirt or contaminates enters the bore or it may damage the bearing.**

6. Clean the area around the sensor thoroughly.
7. Unfasten the sensor retainer.
8. Remove the sensor by pulling it straight out. Do not use a prytool to remove the sensor as it could break the sensor off in the bore.

9. Make sure to remove the sensor O-ring and discard it.
To install:
10. Lubricate the new sensor O-ring with wheel bearing grease, install the O-ring on the sensor and lubricate the area just above and below the O-ring on the sensor body with wheel bearing grease.
11. Install the sensor assembly in the bore and tighten its retaining bolt to 13 ft. lbs. (18 Nm).
12. Install the remaining components in the reverse order of removal.

1995 C3HD MODELS

1. Elevate and safely support the vehicle.
2. Remove the wheel.
3. Remove the brake caliper.
4. Remove the hub and rotor assembly.
5. Unplug the sensor electrical connection.
6. Unfasten the sensor bracket retainers.
7. Unfasten the sensor retainers and remove the sensor from the knuckle.
8. Installation is the reverse of removal.

1996–98 C3HD MODELS

1. Elevate and safely support the vehicle.
2. Remove the wheel.
3. Remove the brake caliper.
4. Remove the hub and rotor assembly.
5. Remove the splash shield.
6. Disconnect the sensor wire mounting clip attached to the upper king pin cap and the mounting clip attached to the frame rail.
7. Unplug the sensor electrical connection.
8. Unfasten the sensor to bracket retainers. It is not necessary to remove the bracket unless it is damaged.
9. Remove the speed sensor.
To install:

➡ **The speed sensor on these models is adjustable by using the slots in the mounting bracket. The sensor must be properly adjusted to obtain the correct air gap.**

10. Install the sensor on the bracket and finger-tighten its retainers.
11. Place the hub and rotor assembly on a surface with the tone wheel facing up making sure not to damage the studs.
12. Mark the position of the rotor relative to the hub so the rotor can be reinstalled in the same position.
13. Unfasthe the bolts attaching the rotor to the hub and separate the rotor from the hub.
14. Install the hub and tone wheel assembly onto the spindle.
15. Install the outer bearing, washer and spindle nut. Tighten the spindle nut to 12 ft. lbs. (16 Nm) while rotating the hub in either direction. Do not back off the nut.
16. Insert a flexible shim stock or equivalent between the tone wheel and the sensor. The shim stock must be 0.050 inch (1.25mm) thick and the length and width of the shim stock must be enough to cover the face of the sensor. If shim stock is nit available, regular notebook or writing paper can be used as long as the specification for thickness, length and width are strictly adhered to.
17. Press the sensor firmly against the shim stock and tone wheel.
18. Tighten the retainers as follows:
   a. Left-hand lower attaching nut: 10 ft. lbs. (14 Nm).
   b. Left-hand upper attaching nut: 10 ft. lbs. (14 Nm).
   c. Right-hand upper attaching nut: 10 ft. lbs. (14 Nm).
   d. Right-hand lower attaching nut: 10 ft. lbs. (14 Nm).
19. Remove the shim stock and make sure the sensor does not contact the tone while when rotated.
20. Install the splash shield making sure to route wire through the opening in the shield. Tighten the splash shield bolts to 13 ft. lbs. (17 Nm).
21. Route the wiring harness to its original location and attach the mounting clips.
22. Install the rotor making sure to line up the reference marks made previously. Tighten the bolts to 175 ft. lbs. (237 Nm).
23. Install the caliper and the wheel. Lower the vehicle.

Rear Wheel Speed Sensor

EXCEPT SUBURBAN

1. Elevate and safely support the vehicle.
2. Remove the wheel.
3. Remove the brake drum.
4. Remove the primary brake shoe.
5. Disconnect the sensor wiring at the connector.
6. Remove the sensor wire from the rear axle clips.
7. Remove the 2 bolts holding the sensor.
8. Remove the sensor by tracking the wire through the hole in the backing plate.

To install:

9. Route the wire through the hole in the backing plate and fit the sensor into position.
10. Install the 2 bolts; tighten them to 26 ft. lbs. (35 Nm).
11. Install the remaining components in the reverse order of removal.

SUBURBAN WITH 4L60E

➥**Speed sensor removal/installation tool J–38417 or its equivalent is required for this procedure.**

1. Elevate and safely support the vehicle. The speed sensor is located on the left side of the transmission.
2. Disconnect the sensor wiring connector.
3. Remove the retaining bolt holding the sensor.
4. Using the removal tool, remove the sensor from the transmission case. Have a pan available to catch fluid spillage.

To install:

5. Coat the O-ring on the sensor with a thin coat of transmission fluid.
6. Using the installation tool, install the sensor into the case. Tighten the mounting bolt to 8 ft. lbs. (11 Nm).
7. Install the remaining components in the reverse order of removal.

SUBURBAN WITH 4L80E AND MANUAL TRANSMISSION

1. Elevate and safely support the vehicle. The speed sensor is located on the left side of the transmission.
2. Disconnect the sensor wiring connector.
3. Remove the retaining bolt holding the sensor.
4. Remove the sensor from the transmission case. Have a pan available to catch fluid spillage.

To install:

5. Coat the O-ring on the sensor with a thin coat of transmission fluid.
6. Install the sensor into the case. Tighten the mounting bolt to 5 ft. lbs. (7 Nm).
7. Install the remaining components in the reverse order of removal.

2WD WHEEL SPEED SENSOR TEMPERATURE VS. SENSOR RESISTANCE (APPROXIMATE)			4WD WHEEL SPEED SENSOR TEMPERATURE VS. SENSOR RESISTANCE (APPROXIMATE)		
TEMP. (°C)	TEMP. (°F)	RESISTANCE (OHMS)	TEMP. (°C)	TEMP. (°F)	RESISTANCE (OHMS)
-40 TO 4	-40 TO 40	1575 TO 2420	-40 TO 4	-40 TO 40	1900 TO 2950
5 TO 43	41 TO 110	1980 TO 2800	5 TO 43	41 TO 110	2420 TO 3450
44 TO 93	111 TO 200	2250 TO 3280	44 TO 93	111 TO 200	2810 TO 4100
94 TO 150	201 TO 302	2750 TO 3850	94 TO 150	201 TO 302	3320 TO 4760

91029G01

Fig. 76 Wheel speed sensor temperature versus resistance chart

VEHICLE SPEED SENSOR

Refer to Section 4 of this manual for VSS testing.

WHEEL SPEED SENSOR

♦ **See Figure 76**

1. Elevate and safely support the vehicle.
2. Unplug the sensor electrical connection.
3. Check the condition of the sensor terminals and the wiring harness terminals. Repair as necessary.
4. Check the sensor wiring harness for an open or short circuit. Repair as necessary.
5. Using a Digital Volt OhmMeter (DVOM) set to read resistance, probe the sensor terminals.
6. If the resistance is not as specified in the accompanying charts, the sensor may be defective.
7. Turn the DVOM to the A/C voltage scale and spin the wheel, there should be a voltage reading. As the wheel speed increases, the voltage should increase. If there is no voltage present, or the voltage does not increase with wheel speed, check the tone wheel for defects. If the tone wheel is found to be in good condition, replace the sensor.

PUMP MOTOR CIRCUIT

1. Check the condition of the fuse in the relay center and replace as necessary.
2. Unplug the pump motor electrical connection.
3. Check the condition of the terminals and the wiring harness terminals. Repair as necessary.
4. Attach the electrical connection.
5. Using a Digital Volt OhmMeter (DVOM) set to read voltage, backprobe between the black (ground) wire and red (power) wire terminals of the harness. The voltage should be between 9–14 volts.
6. If the voltage is less than 9 volts, set the DVOM on the lowest resistance scale, disconnect the harness and the positive and negative battery terminals. Connect one probe to the positive battery cable and the other probe to red wire terminal. Note the reading. Connect one probe to the negative battery cable and the other probe to black wire terminal. Note the reading.
7. If the resistance is less than one ohm the wiring is fine and the control unit should be replaced.
8. If the resistance is more than one ohm, clean and tighten the terminals or repair the wiring as needed.
9. Attach all unplugged wires and recheck the voltage.
10. Clear the trouble codes and road test the vehicle. If the trouble code returns, check the motor supply voltage again.
11. If the voltage is now between 9–14 volts and the pump is still not functioning properly, replace the assembly.
12. If the voltage is still lower than 9 volts, there may be a problem with the EBCM.

REAR WHEEL ANTI-LOCK (RWAL) BRAKE SYSTEM

General Description

♦ **See Figures 77 and 78**

The Kelsey Hayes RWAL system is found on Chevrolet and GMC products including Suburban and C/K Series pick-ups. The system is particularly useful because of the wide variations of loading the vehicle may experience. Preventing rear wheel lock-up often makes the difference in controlling the vehicle during hard or sudden stops.

Found on both 2WD and 4WD vehicles, the RWAL system is designed to regulate rear hydraulic brake line pressure, preventing wheel lock-up at the rear. Pressure regulation is managed by the control valve, located under the master cylinder. The control valve is capable of holding, increasing or decreasing brake line pressure based on electrical commands from the RWAL Electronic Control Unit (ECU) or Electronic Brake Control Module (EBCM).

The RWAL ECU is a separate and dedicated microcomputer mounted next to the master cylinder; it is not to be confused with the engine management ECU. The RWAL ECU receives signals from the speed sensor. The speed sensor sends its signals to the Vehicle Speed Sensor buffer (previously known as the Digital Ratio Adapter Controller or DRAC) within the instrument cluster. The buffer translates the sensor signal into a form usable by the ECU. The RWAL ECU reads this signal and commands the control valve to function. If commanded to release pressure, the dump valve releases pressurized fluid into the accumulator where it is held under pressure. If a pressure increase is called for,

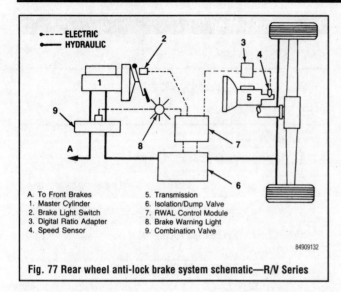

A. To Front Brakes
1. Master Cylinder
2. Brake Light Switch
3. Digital Ratio Adapter
4. Speed Sensor
5. Transmission
6. Isolation/Dump Valve
7. RWAL Control Module
8. Brake Warning Light
9. Combination Valve

84909132

Fig. 77 Rear wheel anti-lock brake system schematic—R/V Series

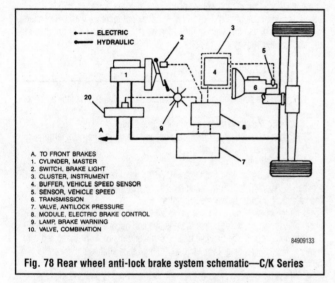

A. TO FRONT BRAKES
1. CYLINDER, MASTER
2. SWITCH, BRAKE LIGHT
3. CLUSTER, INSTRUMENT
4. BUFFER, VEHICLE SPEED SENSOR
5. SENSOR, VEHICLE SPEED
6. TRANSMISSION
7. VALVE, ANTILOCK PRESSURE
8. MODULE, ELECTRIC BRAKE CONTROL
9. LAMP, BRAKE WARNING
10. VALVE, COMBINATION

84909133

Fig. 78 Rear wheel anti-lock brake system schematic—C/K Series

the isolator valve within the control valve pulses, releasing pressurized fluid into the system.

The RWAL system is connected to the BRAKE warning lamp on the instrument cluster. A RWAL self–check and a bulb test are performed every time the ignition switch is turned to ON. The BRAKE warning lamp should illuminate for about 2 seconds and then go off. Problems within the RWAL system will be indicated by the BRAKE warning lamp staying illuminated.

If a fault is detected within the system, the RWAL ECU will assign a fault code and store the code in memory. The code may be read to aid in diagnosis.

System Diagnosis and Testing

▶ **See Figures 79 thru 85**

SYSTEM PRECAUTIONS

• If the vehicle is equipped with air bag (SIR) system, always properly disable the system before commencing work on the ABS system.
• Certain components within the RWAL system are not intended to be serviced or repaired. Only those components with removal & Installation procedures should be serviced.
• Do not use rubber hoses or other parts not specifically specified for the RWAL system. When using repair kits, replace all parts included in the kit. Partial or incorrect repair may lead to functional problems.
• Lubricate rubber parts with clean, fresh brake fluid to ease assembly. Do not use lubricated shop air to clean parts; damage to rubber components may result.

• Use only brake fluid from an unopened container. Use of suspect or contaminated brake fluid can reduce system performance and/or durability.
• A clean repair area is essential. Perform repairs after components have been thoroughly cleaned; use only denatured alcohol to clean components. Do not allow components to come into contact with any substance containing mineral oil; this includes used shop rags.
• The RWAL ECU is a microprocessor similar to other computer units in the vehicle. Insure that the ignition switch is OFF before removing or installing controller harnesses. Avoid static electricity discharge at or near the controller.
• Never disconnect any electrical connection with the ignition switch ON unless instructed to do so in a test.
• Always wear a grounded wrist strap when servicing any control module or component labeled with a Electrostatic Discharge (ESD) symbol.
• Avoid touching module connector pins.
• Leave new components and modules in the shipping package until ready to install them.
• To avoid static discharge, always touch a vehicle ground after sliding across a vehicle seat or walking across carpeted or vinyl floors.
• Never allow welding cables to lie on, near or across any vehicle electrical wiring.
• Do not allow extension cords for power tools or droplights to lie on, near or across any vehicle electrical wiring.

PRELIMINARY DIAGNOSIS

Before reading trouble codes, perform the Diagnostic Circuit Check according to the chart. This test will aid in separating RWAL system problems from common problems in the hydraulic brake system. The diagnostic circuit check will direct the reading of trouble codes as necessary.

READING CODES

▶ **See Figure 73**

The RWAL ECU will assign a code to the first fault found in the system. If there is more than 1 fault, only the first recognized code will the stored and transmitted.

Trouble codes may be read either though the use of TECH-1 or equivalent scan tool or by connecting a jumper wire from pin H on the ALDL to pin A. If the jumper method is used, the fault code will be displayed through the flashing of the BRAKE warning lamp on the dash. The terminals must be connected for about 20 seconds before the display begins. The display will begin with 1 long flash followed by shorter ones—count the long flash as part of the display.

➡**Sometimes the first display sequence will be inaccurate or short; subsequent displays will be accurate.**

If using a hand scanner, note that if a soft code is stored, only the last recognized code will be retained and displayed on the scanner. Soft fault codes 6, 9 and 10 can only be read with a scan tool. Codes 1, 11 and 12 will not read on the scan tool; they must be read using the jumper wire method.

➡**Never ground terminal H of the ALDL to terminal A if the BRAKE warning lamp is not lit. Doing so will set a false code 9 and illuminate the BRAKE warning lamp. With the brake lamp on, the RWAL system will be disabled.**

CLEARING CODES

Stored trouble codes must be cleared with the ignition switch OFF. Remove the STOP/HAZARD fuse for at least 5 seconds, then reinstall the fuse.

Trouble Codes

The following is a list of the trouble codes for the Rear Wheel Anti-Lock (RWAL) brake system.
• Code 2: open isolation solenoid or EBCM malfunction
• Code 3: open dump solenoid or EBCM malfunction
• Code 4: grounded anti-lock pressure valve rest switch
• Code 5: excessive dump valve actuation's during anti-lock stop

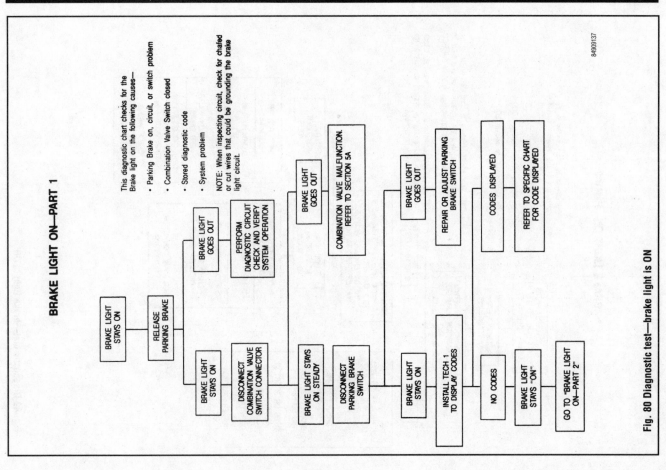

BRAKE LIGHT ON—PART 1

This diagnostic chart checks for the Brake light on the following causes—

- Parking Brake on, circuit, or switch problem
- Combination Valve Switch closed
- Stored diagnostic code
- System problem

NOTE: When inspecting circuit, check for chafed or cut wires that could be grounding the brake light circuit.

Fig. 80 Diagnostic test—brake light is ON

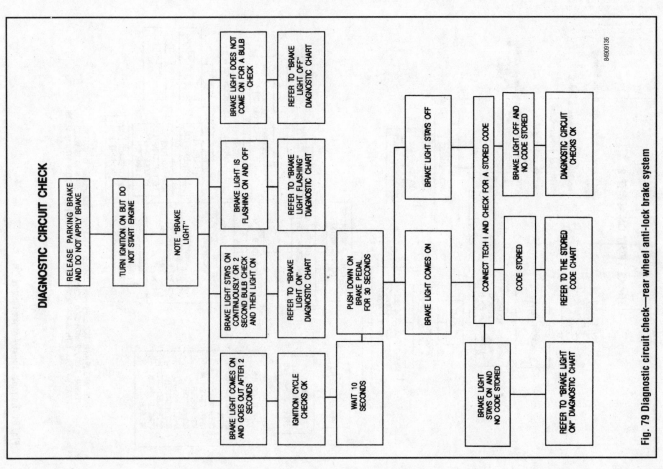

DIAGNOSTIC CIRCUIT CHECK

Fig. 79 Diagnostic circuit check—rear wheel anti-lock brake system

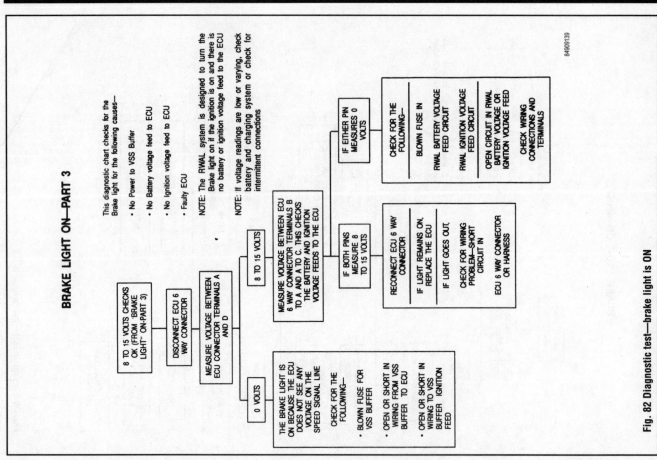

BRAKE LIGHT ON—PART 3

This diagnostic chart checks for the
Brake light for the following causes—

• No Power to VSS Buffer
• No Battery voltage feed to ECU
• No Ignition voltage feed to ECU
• Faulty ECU

NOTE: The RWAL system is designed to turn the
Brake light on if the ignition is on and there is
no battery or ignition voltage feed to the ECU

NOTE: If voltage readings are low or varying, check
battery and charging system or check for
intermittent connections

Fig. 82 Diagnostic test—brake light is ON

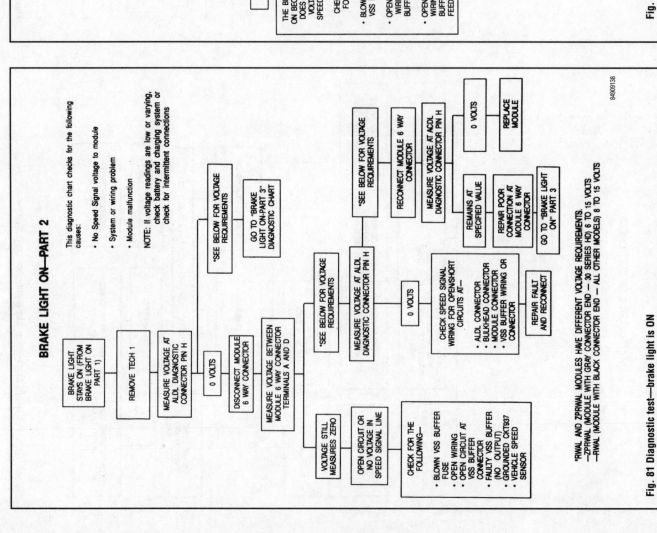

BRAKE LIGHT ON—PART 2

This diagnostic chart checks for the following
causes:

• No Speed Signal voltage to module
• System or wiring problem
• Module malfunction

NOTE: If voltage readings are low or varying,
check battery and charging system or
check for intermittent connections

*RWAL AND ZRWAL MODULES HAVE DIFFERENT VOLTAGE REQUIREMENTS.
—ZPRWAL (MODULE WITH GRAY CONNECTOR END — 30 SERIES HD) 6 TO 15 VOLTS
—RWAL (MODULE WITH BLACK CONNECTOR END — ALL OTHER MODELS) 8 TO 15 VOLTS

Fig. 81 Diagnostic test—brake light is ON

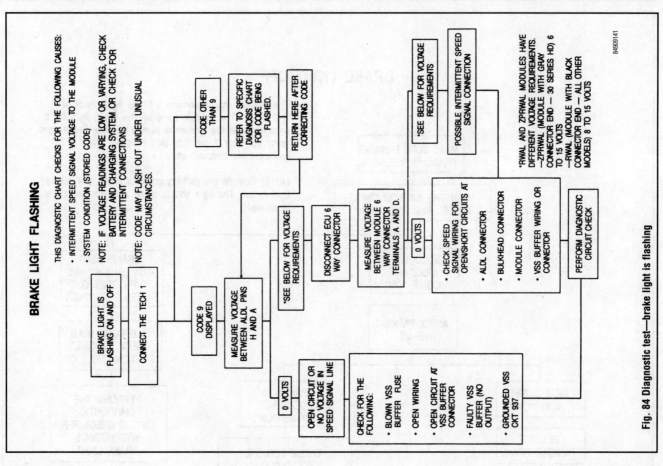

BRAKE LIGHT FLASHING

THIS DIAGNOSTIC CHART CHECKS FOR THE FOLLOWING CAUSES:
- INTERMITTENT SPEED SIGNAL VOLTAGE TO THE MODULE
- SYSTEM CONDITION (STORED CODE)

NOTE: IF VOLTAGE READINGS ARE LOW OR VARYING, CHECK BATTERY AND CHARGING SYSTEM OR CHECK FOR INTERMITTENT CONNECTIONS

NOTE: CODE MAY FLASH OUT UNDER UNUSUAL CIRCUMSTANCES.

Fig. 84 Diagnostic test—brake light is flashing

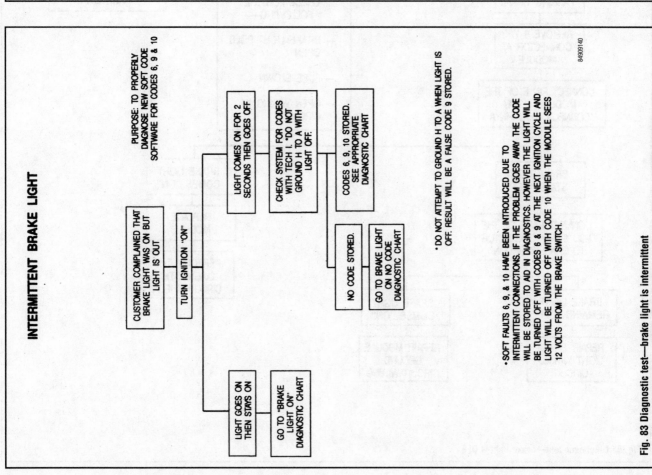

INTERMITTENT BRAKE LIGHT

Fig. 83 Diagnostic test—brake light is intermittent

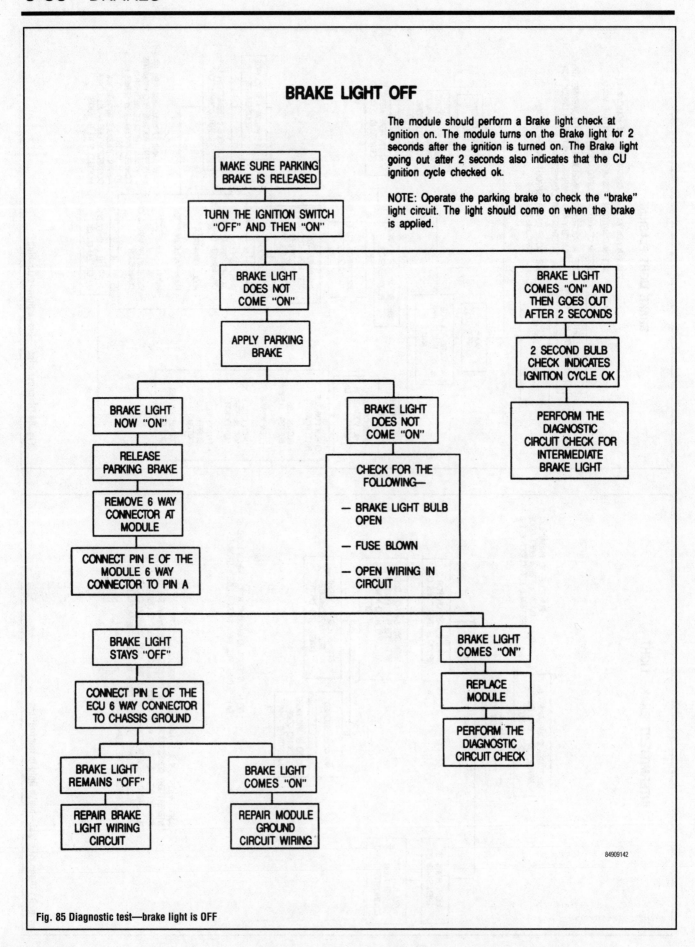

BRAKE LIGHT OFF

The module should perform a Brake light check at ignition on. The module turns on the Brake light for 2 seconds after the ignition is turned on. The Brake light going out after 2 seconds also indicates that the CU ignition cycle checked ok.

NOTE: Operate the parking brake to check the "brake" light circuit. The light should come on when the brake is applied.

MAKE SURE PARKING BRAKE IS RELEASED

TURN THE IGNITION SWITCH "OFF" AND THEN "ON"

BRAKE LIGHT DOES NOT COME "ON"

APPLY PARKING BRAKE

BRAKE LIGHT NOW "ON"

RELEASE PARKING BRAKE

REMOVE 6 WAY CONNECTOR AT MODULE

CONNECT PIN E OF THE MODULE 6 WAY CONNECTOR TO PIN A

BRAKE LIGHT DOES NOT COME "ON"

CHECK FOR THE FOLLOWING—

— BRAKE LIGHT BULB OPEN

— FUSE BLOWN

— OPEN WIRING IN CIRCUIT

BRAKE LIGHT COMES "ON" AND THEN GOES OUT AFTER 2 SECONDS

2 SECOND BULB CHECK INDICATES IGNITION CYCLE OK

PERFORM THE DIAGNOSTIC CIRCUIT CHECK FOR INTERMEDIATE BRAKE LIGHT

BRAKE LIGHT STAYS "OFF"

CONNECT PIN E OF THE ECU 6 WAY CONNECTOR TO CHASSIS GROUND

BRAKE LIGHT REMAINS "OFF"

REPAIR BRAKE LIGHT WIRING CIRCUIT

BRAKE LIGHT COMES "ON"

REPAIR MODULE GROUND CIRCUIT WIRING

BRAKE LIGHT COMES "ON"

REPLACE MODULE

PERFORM THE DIAGNOSTIC CIRCUIT CHECK

84909142

Fig. 85 Diagnostic test—brake light is OFF

- Code 6: erratic speed signal
- Code 7: shorted isolation solenoid or EBCM malfunction
- Code 8: shorted dump solenoid or EBCM malfunction
- Code 9: open or grounded speed signal circuit
- Code 10: stop lamp switch circuit
- Codes 1, 11 and 12: invalid diagnostic trouble codes
- Codes 13, 14 and 15: electric brake control module malfunction

Component Replacement

REMOVAL & INSTALLATION

RWAL Electronic Control Unit (ECU)

▶ See Figure 86

The RWAL ECU is a non–serviceable unit. It must be replaced when diagnosis indicates a malfunction.
1. Turn the ignition switch **OFF**.
2. Disconnect the wiring harness to the RWAL ECU.
3. Gently pry the tab at the rear of the ECU; remove the control unit toward the front of the vehicle.

➡**Do not touch the electrical connectors or pins; do not allow them to contact brake fluid. If contaminated with brake fluid, clean them with water followed by isopropyl alcohol.**

4. Install the RWAL ECU by sliding it into the bracket until the tab locks into the hole.

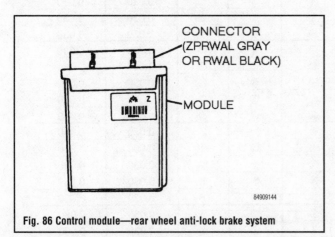

Fig. 86 Control module—rear wheel anti-lock brake system

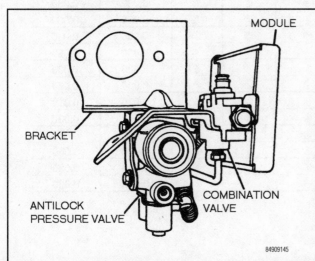

Fig. 87 Anti-lock pressure valve and module assembly—rear wheel anti-lock brake system

5. Connect the wiring harness to the ECU.

Isolation/Dump Valve (Control Valve)

▶ See Figure 87

1. Disconnect the brake line fittings at the valve. Protect surrounding paintwork from spillage.
2. Disconnect the electrical connectors from both the ECU and the isolation valve.
3. Remove the bolts holding the valve to the bracket.
4. Carefully remove the isolation/dump valve from the vehicle.

➡**Do not touch the electrical connectors or pins; do not allow them to contact brake fluid. If contaminated with brake fluid, clean them with water followed by isopropyl alcohol.**

To install:
5. Place the valve in position and install the retaining bolts. Tighten the bolts to 21 ft. lbs. (29 Nm).
6. Connect the electrical connector to the RWAL ECU.
7. Install the brake lines; tighten the fittings to 20 ft. lbs. (27 Nm)
8. Bleed the brake system at all 4 wheels.

Speed Sensor

The speed sensor is not serviceable and must replaced if malfunctioning. The sensor is located in the left rear of the transmission case on 2WD vehicles and on the transfer case of 4WD vehicles.
The speed sensor may be tested with an OhmMeter; the correct resistance is 900–2000 ohms. To remove the speed sensor:
1. Disconnect the electrical connector from the speed sensor.
2. Remove the sensor retaining bolt if one is used.
3. Remove the speed sensor; have a container handy to catch transmission fluid when the sensor is removed.
4. Recover the O-ring used to seal the sensor; inspect it for damage or deterioration.
To install:
5. When installing, coat the new O-ring with a thin film of transmission fluid.
6. Install the O-ring and speed sensor.
7. If a retaining bolt is used, tighten the bolt to 8 ft. lbs. (11 Nm) in automatic transmissions or 9 ft. lbs. (12 Nm) for all other transmissions.
8. If the sensor is a screw-in unit, tighten it to 32 ft. lbs. (43 Nm).
9. Connect the wire harness to the sensor.

Bleeding the ABS System

▶ See Figures 9, 10 and 11

The brake system must be bled when any brake line is disconnected or there is air in the system.

➡**Never bleed a wheel cylinder when a drum is removed.**

1. Clean the master cylinder of excess dirt and remove the cylinder cover and the diaphragm.
2. Fill the master cylinder to the proper level. Check the fluid level periodically during the bleeding process, and replenish it as necessary. Do not allow the master cylinder to run dry, or you will have to start over.
3. Before opening any of the bleeder screws, you may want to give each one a shot of penetrating solvent. This reduces the possibility of breakage when they are unscrewed.
4. Attach a length of vinyl hose to the bleeder screw of the brake to be bled. Insert the other end of the hose into a clear jar half full of clean brake fluid, so that the end of the hose is beneath the level of fluid. The correct sequence for bleeding is to work from the brake farthest from the master cylinder to the one closest; right rear, left rear, right front, left front.
5. The combination valve must be held open during the bleeding process. A clip, tape, or other similar tool (or an assistant) will hold the metering pin in.
6. Depress and release the brake pedal three or four times to exhaust any residual vacuum.
7. Have an assistant push down on the brake pedal and hold it down. Open the bleeder valve slightly. As the pedal reaches the end of its travel, close the

bleeder screw and release the brake pedal. Repeat this process until no air bubbles are visible in the expelled fluid.

➡**Make sure your assistant presses the brake pedal to the floor slowly. Pressing too fast will cause air bubbles to form in the fluid.**

8. Repeat this procedure at each of the brakes. Remember to check the master cylinder level occasionally. Use only fresh fluid to refill the master cylinder, not the stuff bled from the system.

9. When the bleeding process is complete, refill the master cylinder, install its cover and diaphragm, and discard the fluid bled from the brake system.

10. Perform 3 function tests with the TECH 1 scan tool. The brake pedal **must** be firmly applied.

11. On models with rear wheel ABS:

a. Refill the jar with clean brake fluid and attach the bleed hose to the bleed valve on the Isolation/Dump valve.

b. Have your assistant slowly depress the brake pedal and hold it. Loosen the bleed valve and expel the air. Tighten the valve and slowly release the pedal.

c. Wait 15 seconds and repeat this procedure. Repeat bleeding the Isolation/Dump valve until all the air is expelled.

12. On models with 4 wheel ABS, repeat Steps 1–9.

BRAKE SPECIFICATIONS
All specifications given in inches unless otherwise indicated

Year	Model	Brake Disc			Brake Drum Diameter			Minimum Lining Thickness	
		Original Thickness	Minimum Thickness	Maximum Runout	Original Inside Diameter	Max. Wear Limit	Maximum Machine Diameter	Front	Rear
1988	R/V 10, 15	①	③	0.004	④	⑤	⑥	0.030	0.030
	R/V 20, 25	①	③	0.004	④	⑤	⑥	0.030	0.030
	R/V 30, 35	①	③	0.004	④	⑤	⑥	0.030	0.030
	C/K 15, 25	①	③	0.004	④	⑤	⑥	0.030	0.030
	C/K 35	①	③	0.004	④	⑤	⑥	0.030	0.030
1989	R/V 10, 15	①	③	0.004	④	⑤	⑥	0.030	0.030
	R/V 20, 25	①	③	0.004	④	⑤	⑥	0.030	0.030
	R/V 30, 35	①	③	0.004	④	⑤	⑥	0.030	0.030
	C/K 15, 25	①	③	0.004	④	⑤	⑥	0.030	0.030
	C/K 35	①	③	0.004	④	⑤	⑥	0.030	0.030
1990	R/V 10, 15	①	③	0.004	④	⑤	⑥	0.030	0.030
	R/V 20, 25	①	③	0.004	④	⑤	⑥	0.030	0.030
	R/V 30, 35	①	③	0.004	④	⑤	⑥	0.030	0.030
	C/K 15, 25	①	③	0.004	④	⑤	⑥	0.030	0.030
	C/K 35	①	③	0.004	④	⑤	⑥	0.030	0.030
1991	R/V 10, 15	①	③	0.004	④	⑤	⑥	0.030	0.030
	R/V 20, 25	①	③	0.004	④	⑤	⑥	0.030	0.030
	R/V 30, 35	①	③	0.004	④	⑤	⑥	0.030	0.030
	C/K 15, 25	①	③	0.004	④	⑤	⑥	0.030	0.030
	C/K 35	①	③	0.004	④	⑤	⑥	0.030	0.030
1992	C/K 15, 25	①	③	0.004	④	⑤	⑥	0.030	0.030
	C/K 35	①	③	0.004	④	⑤	⑥	0.030	0.030
1993	C/K 15, 25	①	③	0.004	④	⑤	⑥	0.030	0.030
	C/K 35	①	③	0.004	④	⑤	⑥	0.030	0.030
1994	C/K 15, 25	①	③	0.004	④	⑤	⑥	0.030	0.030
	C/K 35	①	③	0.004	④	⑤	⑥	0.030	0.030
1995	C/K 15, 25	①	③	0.004	④	⑤	⑥	0.030	0.030
	C/K 35	①	③	0.004	④	⑤	⑥	0.030	0.030
1996	C/K 15, 25	②	③	0.004	④	⑤	⑥	0.030	0.030
	C/K 35	②	③	0.004	④	⑤	⑥	0.030	0.030
1997	C/K 15, 25	②	③	0.004	④	⑤	⑥	0.030	0.030
	C/K 35	②	③	0.004	④	⑤	⑥	0.030	0.030
1998	C/K 15, 25	②	③	0.004	④	⑤	⑥	0.030	0.030
	C/K 35	②	③	0.004	④	⑤	⑥	0.030	0.030

① Available with 11.57 inch, 12. 5 inch and 14.25 inch rotors

② Available with 11.57 inch, 12. 5 inch and 13.86 inch rotors

③ 11.57 inch and 12.5 X 1.26 inch rotors: 1.215 inch
   12.5 X 1.50 inch and 14.25 inch rotors: 1.46 inch
   13.86 inch rotor: 1.366 inch

④ Available with 10 inch, 11.15 inch and 13 inch drums

⑤ 10 inch drum: 10.09 inch
   11.15 inch drum: 11.24 inch
   13 inch drum: 13.09 inch

⑥ 10 inch drum: 10.05 inch
   11.15 inch drum: 11.21 inch
   13 inch drum: 13.06 inch

91029C01

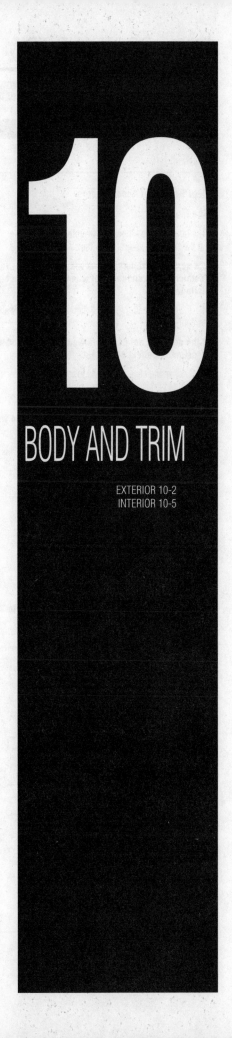

10

BODY AND TRIM

EXTERIOR

Doors

ADJUSTMENT

Except Rear Seat Access Doors

▶ **See Figure 1**

The holes for the hinges are oversized to provide for latitude in alignment. Align the door hinges first, then the striker.

➡**C/K series utilize hinges that are welded to the door and frame. No adjustment is possible except when replacement hinges have been installed.**

1. If a door is being installed, first mount the door and tighten the hinge bolts lightly.

➡**If the door has not been removed, determine which hinge bolts must be loosened to effect alignment.**

2. Loosen the necessary bolts just enough to allow the door to be moved with a padded prybar.
3. Move the door in small movements and check the fit after each movement.

➡**Be sure that there is no binding or interference with adjacent panels.**

4. Repeat this procedure until the door is properly aligned.
R/V Series:
- Door edge-to-rocker panel: 6mm
- Door edge-to-roof panel: 5mm
- Door edge-to-rear pillar: 5mm
- Door edge-to-front pillar: 2mm
C/K Series:
- Door edge-to-rocker panel: 6mm
- Door edge-to-roof panel: 6mm
- Door edge-to-rear pillar: 4mm
- Door edge-to-front pillar: 7mm
- Door front edge-to-fender: 5mm
5. Tighten all the bolts to 26 ft. lbs. (35 Nm).

➡**Shims may be either fabricated or purchased to install behind the hinges as an aid in alignment.**

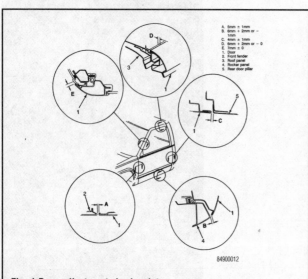

84900012

Fig. 1 Door adjustment check points

Rear Seat Access Door

▶ **See Figure 2**

➡**The holes for the hinges are oversized to provide for latitude in alignment. Align the door hinges first, then the striker.**

1. If a door is being installed, first mount the door and tighten the hinge bolts lightly.

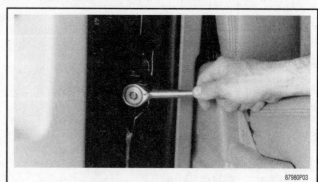

87980P03

Fig. 2 If a door is being installed, first mount the door and tighten the hinge bolts lightly

➡**If the door has not been removed, determine which hinge bolts must be loosened to effect alignment.**

2. Loosen the necessary bolts just enough to allow the door to be moved with a padded prybar.
3. Move the door in small movements and check the fit after each movement.

➡**Be sure that there is no binding or interference with adjacent panels.**

4. Keep repeating this procedure until the door is properly aligned.
- Door panel lower edge-to-platform panel: 5–7mm
- Door outer panel-to-platform panel (closed): 12.5–15.5mm
- Door edge-to-roof panel: 3–7mm
- Door edge-to-pillar: 3–7mm
- Door edge-to-door edge (closed): 3–7mm
5. Tighten all the bolts to 26 ft. lbs. (35 Nm).

➡**Shims may be either fabricated or purchased to install behind the hinges as an aid in alignment.**

Hood

REMOVAL & INSTALLATION

➡**You are going to need an assistant for this job.**

R/V Series

▶ **See Figure 3**

1. Open the hood and trace the outline of the hinges on the hood.
2. While an assistant holds the hood, remove the hinge-to-hood bolts and lift the hood off.
3. Install the hood and tighten the bolts to 18 ft. lbs. (24 Nm).
4. Adjust hood alignment, if necessary.

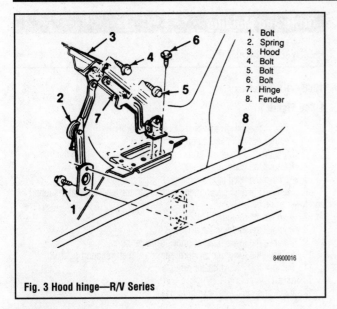

1. Bolt
2. Spring
3. Hood
4. Bolt
5. Bolt
6. Bolt
7. Hinge
8. Fender

84900016

Fig. 3 Hood hinge—R/V Series

C/K Series

▶ See Figure 4

1. Open the hood and trace the outline of the hinges on the hood.
2. Remove the hood seals from the hinges.
3. While an assistant holds the hood, remove the hinge-to-link bolts and lower the hood.
4. Remove the outboard section of the cowl vent grille.
5. Remove the hinge-to-fender bracket bolts.
6. Lift off the hood.
7. Install the hood and tighten the bolts to 18 ft. lbs. (24 Nm).
8. Adjust hood alignment, if necessary.

ALIGNMENT

1. Hood alignment can be adjusted front-to-rear or side-to-side by loosening the hood-to-hinge or hinge-to-body bolts.
2. The front edge of the hood can be adjusted for closing height by adding or deleting shims under the hinges.
3. The rear edge of the hood can be adjusted for closing height by raising or lowering the hood bumpers.

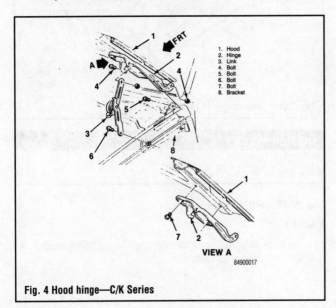

1. Hood
2. Hinge
3. Link
4. Bolt
5. Bolt
6. Bolt
7. Bolt
8. Bracket

VIEW A

84900017

Fig. 4 Hood hinge—C/K Series

REMOVAL & INSTALLATION

Pick-Ups

1988–91 MODELS

1. Open the tailgate and support it with something like sawhorses.
2. Pull up on the side links at the joints.
3. Unfasten the attaching bolts and remove the link and striker plate from each end of the tailgate.
4. Remove the hinge-to-tailgate bolts.
5. Remove the tailgate.
6. Installation of the tailgate is the reverse of the removal procedure.

1992–98 MODELS

▶ See Figure 5

1. Lower the tailgate to the horizontal position.
2. Move the tailgate to the 45⁻ position and support it while disconnecting the cable from each side at the striker bolts.
3. Disconnect the tailgate from the right and then the left side hinge and then remove the gate.
4. To install, position the tailgate into the hinges at 45⁻ angle and then connect the cable.

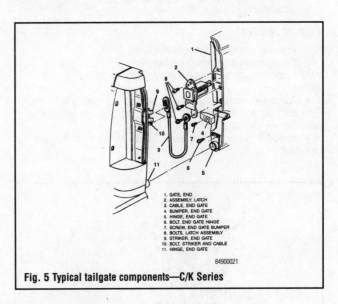

1. GATE, END
2. ASSEMBLY, LATCH
3. CABLE, END GATE
4. BUMPER, END GATE
5. HINGE, END GATE
6. BOLT, END GATE HINGE
7. SCREW, END GATE BUMPER
8. BOLTS, LATCH ASSEMBLY
9. STRIKER, END GATE
10. BOLT, STRIKER AND CABLE
11. HINGE, END GATE

84900021

Fig. 5 Typical tailgate components—C/K Series

Blazer/Jimmy/Yukon

1988–91 MODELS

1. Place the tailgate in the closed position and lower the window.
2. Remove the torque rod-to-frame stud and nut and allow the torque rod to swing down.
3. Open the tailgate and support it with something like a picnic table, so there is no tension on the support cables.
4. Remove the attaching screws and remove the tailgate inner cover.
5. Disconnect the wiring harness connectors in the tailgate.
6. Remove the support cables-to-pillar attaching bolts, spacers and washers.
7. Remove the torque rod brackets.
8. Remove the hinge-to-floor panel bolts.
9. Lift the tailgate off, guiding the torque rods over the gravel deflectors.
10. Installation is the reverse of removal.

1992–98 MODELS

1. Open the tailgate and remove the torque rod.
2. Disconnect the window electrical harness.
3. Support the gate and remove the cable support bolts and washers.
4. Spread the hinge pin clip enough to get it above the recess in the pin. Remove the pins and lift out the gate. Be careful, the pin will fall off as the pin comes out.
5. Install the gate and the hinge pins. Connect the cables and install the torque rod.

Suburban

1988–91 MODELS

▶ **See Figure 6**

1. Open the tailgate and support it with something like a picnic table, so there is no tension on the support cables.
2. Unbolt the torque rod bracket.
3. Remove the attaching screws and remove the tailgate inner cover.
4. Disconnect the wiring harness connectors in the tailgate.
5. Remove the hinge access cover and seal.
6. Lift the tailgate to the almost-closed position, hold it there, and remove the hinge-to-tailgate bolts.
7. Lower the tailgate and support it so there is no tension on the cables and remove the support cables-to-pillars attaching bolts and washers.
8. Lift the tailgate off, along with the torque rod.
9. Installation is the reverse of removal.

1992–98 MODELS

1. Open the tailgate and remove the torque rod.
2. Disconnect the window electrical harness.
3. Support the gate and remove the cable support bolts and washers.
4. Spread the hinge pin clip enough to get it above the recess in the pin. Remove the pins and lift out the gate. Be careful, the pin will fall off as the pin comes out.
5. Install the gate and the hinge pins. Connect the cables and install the torque rod.

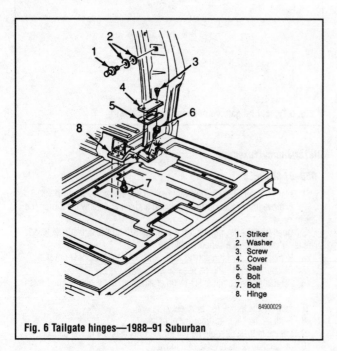

1.	Striker
2.	Washer
3.	Screw
4.	Cover
5.	Seal
6.	Bolt
7.	Bolt
8.	Hinge

84900029

Fig. 6 Tailgate hinges—1988–91 Suburban

Grille and Molding

REMOVAL & INSTALLATION

1988–91 R/V Series

▶ **See Figure 7**

1. Remove the lower radiator grille-to-grille bolts.
2. Remove the radiator support-to-grille bolts.
3. Slide the bottom of the grille out and lower the grille from the truck.
4. Remove the headlight bezels.
5. Remove the headlights.
6. Remove the nuts securing the molding to the fender, radiator support and lower grille panel.
7. Remove the molding.
8. Remove the molding clips.
9. Remove the lower radiator grille-to-fender bolts.
10. Remove the lower radiator grille-to-sheet metal support bolts.
11. Remove the lower radiator grille.
To install:
12. Installation is the reverse of removal.

Except 1988–91 R/V Series

▶ **See Figure 8**

1. Remove the parking lamps and side marker lamps.
2. Remove the grille-to-latch support bolts.
3. Remove the grille bracket-to-latch support bolt.
4. Remove the grille-to-radiator support bolts.
5. Lift the grille and filler panels from the truck.
6. Installation is the reverse of removal.

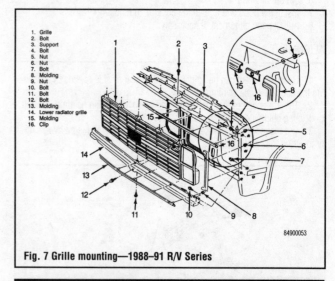

1.	Grille
2.	Bolt
3.	Support
4.	Bolt
5.	Nut
6.	Nut
7.	Bolt
8.	Molding
9.	Nut
10.	Bolt
11.	Bolt
12.	Bolt
13.	Molding
14.	Lower radiator grille
15.	Molding
16.	Clip

84900053

Fig. 7 Grille mounting—1988–91 R/V Series

Outside Mirrors

REMOVAL & INSTALLATION

Standard Type–R/V Series

▶ **See Figure 9**

1. If you are replacing an electrically operated mirror it may be necessary to remove the trim panel upper extension.

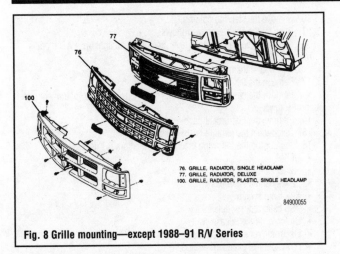

Fig. 8 Grille mounting—except 1988–91 R/V Series

2. Unfasten the mirror to bracket screw and remove the mirror from the door.
3. Unfasten the bracket to door bolts and remove the bracket and gasket from the vehicle.
4. Disengage the electrical connector.
5. Installation is the reverse of removal.

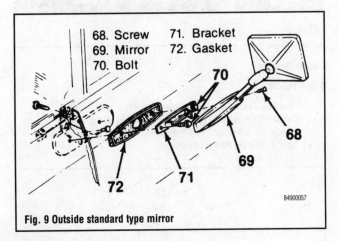

Fig. 9 Outside standard type mirror

Standard Type–C/K Series

1. Remove the interior trim panel or trim panel upper extension.
2. Unfasten the nuts attaching the mirror to the door.
3. If equipped, unplug the mirror electrical connection and remove the mirror.
4. Installation is the reverse of removal.

Below Eyeline Type

▶ **See Figure 10**

1. Remove the mirror cover screw and lift the cover and pivot the mirror towards the window.

INTERIOR

Instrument Panel and Pad

REMOVAL & INSTALLATION

⚹ CAUTION

When replacing cluster components on the C/K Series trucks there are several steps which should be taken to avoid damage to Electrostatic Discharge Sensitive (ESD) parts. They are:

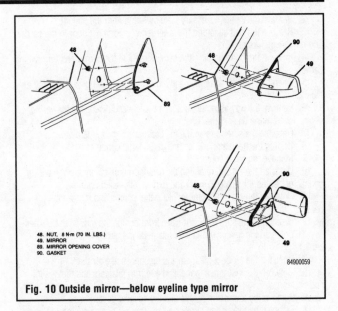

Fig. 10 Outside mirror—below eyeline type mirror

2. Unfasten the mirror to door bolts and remove the mirror and seal from the door.
3. To install, position the mirror and seal to the door and install the retaining bolts.
4. Pivot the mirror away from the window, and lower the mirror cover.
5. Installation is the reverse of removal.

Antenna

REMOVAL & INSTALLATION

Fender Mounted Type

1. Remove the antenna mast.
2. Remove the nut and the bezel.
3. Disconnect the antenna cable from the extension cable.
4. Remove the screws from the body and cable assembly.
5. If equipped, remove the insulator.
6. Installation is the reverse of removal.

Windshield Type

On these models the antenna is part of the windshield. Replace the cable as follows:

1. Disconnect the battery ground cable.
2. Unsnap the antenna cable from the windshield.
3. Remove the bracket to dash panel screws.
4. Disconnect the cable at the rear of the radio receiver and remove the cable assembly.

• Do not open the package until it is time to install the part
• Avoid touching the electrical terminals on the part
• Before removing the part from the package, ground the package to a known good ground on the truck
• Always touch a known good ground before handling the part. You should ground yourself occasionally while installing the part, especially after sliding across the seat, sitting down or walking a short distance

1988–94 Models

1. Disconnect the negative battery cable.

2. Remove the center accessory plate by lifting from the bottom.

3. Remove the bolt attaching the lower left compartment door to the carrier and remove the door.

4. Remove the bolts holding the compartment to the carrier and remove the carrier.

5. Open the ash tray assembly and remove the screws holding the tray to the carrier.

6. Remove the tray assembly from the vehicle and disengage the wiring connector from the back of the assembly.

7. Unfasten the screws retaining the bezel and remove the bezel.

8. Unplug the headlamp switch and cargo lamp connector.

9. Remove the radio control.

10. Unfasten the screws retaining the heater control, disengage the wiring connector behind the heater control and remove the heater control.

11. Unfasten the steering column filler panel screws and remove the filler panel.

12. Disengage the shift indicator cable from behind the instrument cluster.

13. Unfasten the instrument cluster retainers and remove the instrument cluster.

14. Unfasten the air duct retainers and disconnect the air duct.

15. Unfasten the instrument panel pod and trim retainers and remove the pod and trim.

16. Remove the lower trim panels and the speaker covers.

17. Remove the five upper carrier screws. There is one screw located under each speaker cover three located in the defroster vent grille.

18. Disconnect the parking brake handle and cable from the ratchet assembly.

19. Unfasten the hood release handle retainers and remove the hood release handle.

20. Unfasten the ALDL retaining screws and disengage the ALDL.

21. Unplug the door jam switch and remove the fuse box cover.

22. Remove the fasteners holding the carrier to the instrument panel support.

23. Unfasten the nut from both sides of the steering column, lift the steering column up from the support studs and lower it.

24. Remove the left and right kick pads by prying them off.

25. Remove the snap clips and bolts from the left and right bracket mounted studs supporting the carrier.

26. Remove the carrier and disengage the wiring harness from the back of the carrier.

27. Unplug the connector to the instrument panel compartment lamp.

28. Unfasten the bolts holding the A/C duct to the carrier and disconnect the A/C duct.

29. Tag and disengage all electrical connections to the back of the carrier and remove the carrier from the vehicle.

To install:

30. Installation is the reverse of removal but please note the following important step.

31. Install the carrier brackets to the body studs and the bolts through the body and carrier brackets. Tighten the bolts to 15 ft. lbs. (20 Nm).

1995–98 Models

1. Disconnect the negative battery cable and disable the SIR system if equipped.

2. Remove the three relay center bolts from inside the wheel opening and set aside.

3. Unplug the cruise control harness, forward lamp harness, rear lamp harness, SIR system harness, relay center and unfasten the two screws retaining the convenience center to the cowl.

4. Unplug the antenna lead-in and unfasten the steering shaft bolt.

5. Remove the left and right hinge pillar trim panels and disconnect the brake release handle from the cable.

6. Remove the lower bolster fasteners as follows:

  a. Unsnap the bolster.

  b. Twist the brake release cable to disengage.

  c. Disengage the lap cooler hose.

7. Disconnect the reaction plate assembly and the tie bar.

8. Unplug the 8-way column connector and the 48-way connector to gain access to the lower column nuts.

9. Disconnect the shift cable (automatic transmission).

10. Remove the steering column.

11. Remove the shift levers as follows:

  a. Remove the transfer case lever by pulling straight up. 4WD models must be in 4-LO range.

  b. Manual transmission lever (if equipped).

12. Remove the left and right instrument panel bolts.

13. Remove the center support screws and the three upper instrument panel support screws.

14. Remove the instrument panel from the cowl.

15. Disconnect the parking brake release cable.

16. Tag unplug the following electrical connectors (as necessary):

- DERM
- HVAC
- 22-way engine harness
- Stoplamp switch
- VSS calibrator module
- Clutch or brake release switches
- Electronic accelerator (diesel)
- HVAC control cables (if equipped)

17. Remove the instrument panel from the vehicle.

To install:

18. Install the instrument panel in the vehicle and rest it on the lower pivot studs.

19. Install the remaining components in the reverse order of removal.

Console

REMOVAL & INSTALLATION

Center Console

▶ **See Figure 11**

1. Remove the floor tray from the compartment.
2. Remove the storage bin and the plugs covering the screws.
3. Remove the screws and the storage compartment.
4. Installation is the reverse of removal.

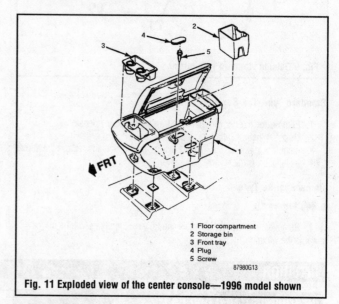

1 Floor compartment
2 Storage bin
3 Front tray
4 Plug
5 Screw

87980G13

Fig. 11 Exploded view of the center console—1996 model shown

Overhead Console

▶ **See Figure 12**

1. Remove the console retaining screws.
2. Unplug the console electrical connectors.
3. Remove the console.
4. Installation is the reverse of removal.

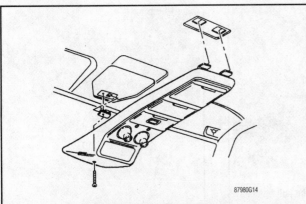

Fig. 12 Exploded view of the overhead console—1996 model shown

Door Panels

REMOVAL & INSTALLATION

R/V Series

▶ **See Figures 13 thru 24**

1. If equipped, remove the window handle by depressing the door panel and removing the retaining clip.
2. Remove the door lock knob.
3. Remove the arm rest-to-bracket screws.
4. Snap off the trim covers and remove the screws retaining the assist strap, if so equipped.

5. Remove the screws securing the lower edge of trim panel.
6. Remove the screws at the door handle cover plate and remove the plate.
7. If necessary, remove the screw located under the arm rest pad.
8. Remove the trim panel from the door by carefully prying out at the trim retainers located around the perimeter of the panel.
9. If equipped, with electric windows, unfasten the window electrical connection retainer and unplug the connection, then remove the panel.

To install:

➡️**Before installing the door trim assembly, check that all trim retainers are securely installed to the assembly and are not damaged.**

10. Pull the door inside handle inward, then position the trim assembly to the inner panel, inserting the door handle through the handle hole in panel.
11. Position the rim assembly to the door inner panel so the trim retainers are aligned with the attaching holes in the panel and tap the retainers into the holes with a clean rubber mallet.
12. Install previously removed items.

C/K Series

1988–94 MODELS

1. Remove the window handle by depressing the door panel and removing the retaining clip.
2. Remove the door lock knob.
3. Remove the arm rest.
4. Snap off the trim covers and remove the screws retaining the assist strap, if so equipped.
5. Remove the electrical switch panel, if so equipped.
6. Remove the trim panel by carefully prying out at the trim retainers located around the perimeter of the panel.

To install:

➡️**Before installing the door trim assembly, check that all trim retainers are securely installed to the assembly and are not damaged.**

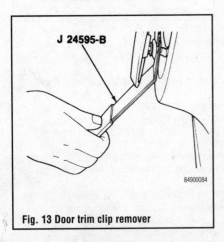

Fig. 13 Door trim clip remover

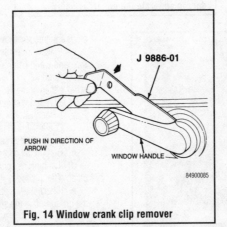

Fig. 14 Window crank clip remover

Fig. 15 Unfasten the screws retaining the door handle trim plate . . .

Fig. 16 . . . hold the handle out and remove the trim plate

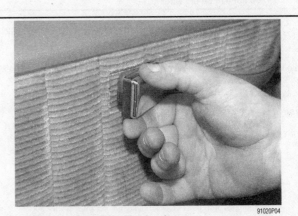

Fig. 17 Remove the pull handle trim pieces

Fig. 18 Use a Torx® head bit to remove the pull handle retainers . . .

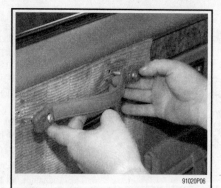

Fig. 19 . . . then remove the pull handle from the door panel

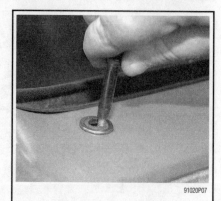

Fig. 20 Unscrew the door lock pull knob

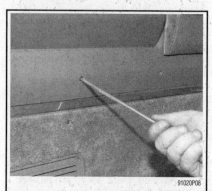

Fig. 21 Unscrew the door panel Phillips head screws

Fig. 22 Lift the door panel up and off the door to separate the panel fasteners

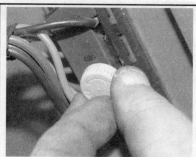

Fig. 23 If the door is equipped with electric windows, unscrew the electrical connection retainers . . .

Fig. 24 . . . and pull gently on the connector to separate it from the switch. Do not pull on the wires

7. Pull the door inside handle inward, then position trim assembly to inner panel, inserting door handle through handle hole in panel.

8. Position rim assembly to the door inner panel so the trim retainers ar aligned with the attaching holes in the panel and tap the retainers into the holes with a clean rubber mallet.

9. Install previously removed items.

1995–98 MODELS

▶ See Figures 26, 27 and 28

1. Remove the door handle bezel as follows:
   a. Insert a flat bladed prytool between the door bezel and the handle assembly.
   b. Bend the retaining tabs outward carefully, then pull out the bezel.
   c. If equipped with power locks, unplug the electrical connection.

2. If equipped, remove the window regulator handle as follows:
   a. Place window handle regulator tool J 9886–01 or equivalent, between the handle and bearing plate.
   b. Align the tool and push to unfasten the handle retaining clip, then remove the handle.

3. If equipped with power accessories, remove the switch as follows:
   a. Disconnect the negative battery cable.
   b. Use a flat bladed prytool to carefully pry the door accessory mounting panel from the door panel.
   c. Unplug the connectors from the switches and if applicable, the speaker.
   d. If applicable, pry the switches from the accessory mounting panel using a flat bladed prytool.
   e. If necessary, spread the speaker grille mounting retainers and remove the grille. Rotate the speaker counterclockwise to remove it from the panel.

4. Remove the trim panel upper extension using a trim panel removal tool and pulling gently upwards on the extension.

5. Using a flat bladed prytool, carefully pry off the armrest screw cover and unfasten the armrest screws.

6. Using a trim panel removal tool, carefully pry the door panel from the door.

7. Unplug all necessary electrical connections.

8. If equipped, remove the courtesy lamp lens and remove the panel.

To install:

➡Before installing the door trim assembly, check that all trim retainers are securely installed to the assembly and are not damaged.

9. Install previously removed items.

Rear Seat Access Door (Extended Cab)

▶ See Figures 29 and 30

1. Remove the armrest screws and the seatbelt retractor cover and "D" ring.

2. Remove the trim panel by carefully prying out at the trim retainers located around the perimeter of the panel.

Fig. 25 Remove the armrest

Fig. 26 Remove the electrical switch panel, if so equipped

Fig. 27 Remove the trim panel by carefully prying out at the trim retainer locations

To install:

3. Install the trim panel on the door and engage the trim retainers.
4. Install the seatbelt "D" ring and retractor cover.
5. Fasten the armrest screws.

Door Lock Assembly

REMOVAL & INSTALLATION

R/V Series

FRONT AND REAR DOORS

♦ See Figures 30 and 31

1. Raise the window completely.

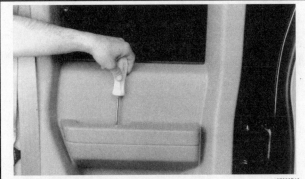

Fig. 28 Remove the armrest screws

Fig. 29 Remove the seat belt retractor cover

2. Remove the door trim panel.
3. Using a suitable flat bladed tool, push on the top of the door lock rod clips and pivot the clip away from the rod.
4. Disconnect the door handle to lock rod from the lock.
5. Disconnect the outside door handle to lock rod clip, using the same procedure as in Step 3.
6. Remove the inside door lock knob.
7. Remove the door to lock assembly screws, then tilt the lock assembly away from the outside lock cylinder. Pull the lock assembly downward to make clearance for the inside lock rod and remove the lock assembly from the door.

To install:

8. Align the lock rod to the hole in the door panel. Tilt the lock assembly onto the outside lock cylinder.
9. Installation of the remaining components is the reverse of removal.

C/K Series

FRONT AND REAR DOORS—1988–94 MODELS

♦ See Figures 32 and 30

1. Remove the door trim panel.
2. Peel off the water deflector.
3. Remove the door module attaching screws and tilt the module out at the top.
4. Disconnect the outside handle lock rod from the lock mechanism.
5. Using a screwdriver, reach between the glass and door and press down on the top of the lock cylinder assembly to disengage the lock cylinder rod from the cylinder.

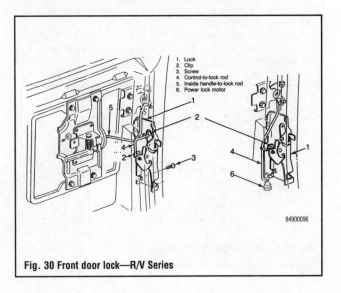

Fig. 30 Front door lock—R/V Series

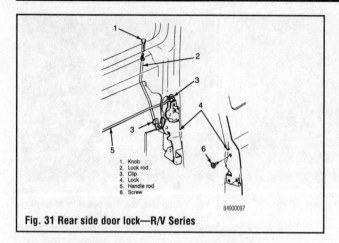

1. Knob
2. Lock rod
3. Clip
4. Lock
5. Handle rod
6. Screw

84900097

Fig. 31 Rear side door lock—R/V Series

6. Remove the lock mechanism attaching screws and remove the mechanism.

7. Install the assembly and tighten the lock screws to 5 ft. lbs. (7 Nm).

FRONT DOORS—1995–98 MODELS

1. Remove the door trim panel and peel back the watershield

2. Remove the inner mounting panel as follows:

a. If equipped, remove the speaker by carefully prying out the retaining clips.

b. Unfasten the inner panel bolts.

c. Disconnect the lock rods from the lock handle, lever and lock rod guides.

d. Unplug the wiring harness.

e. Slide the inner mounting panel rearward to release the regulator roller from the window sash and remove the panel.

3. Disconnect the inside door handle and lock control rods.

4. Unfasten the lock assembly bolts, then disconnect the door handle and lock control rods. Discard the plastic retainers and use new retainers for installation.

To install:

5. Pull the outside handle out of the door opening and slide the latch outside door connector onto the outside handle rod. Twist the latch into the door assembly and install the retaining screws.

6. Connect the inside handle (top) rod and inside lock (bottom) rod to the latch.

7. Insert the key in the lock and adjust the rod up and down by turning the key through the opening.

8. Connect the lock rod to the latch through the opening in the door below the latch.

9. Install the inner mounting panel as follows:

a. Install the inner panel and slide it forward to release the regulator roller from the window sash.

b. Attach the wiring harness.

c. Attach the lock rods to the lock handle, lever and lock rod guides. Install the inner panel bolts.

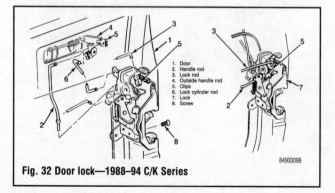

1. Door
2. Handle rod
3. Lock rod
4. Outside handle rod
5. Clips
6. Lock cylinder rod
7. Lock
8. Screw

84900098

Fig. 32 Door lock—1988–94 C/K Series

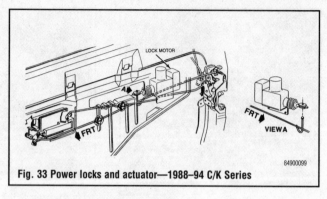

84900099

Fig. 33 Power locks and actuator—1988–94 C/K Series

d. If equipped install the speaker.

10. Attach the water shield and install the door trim panel.

REAR DOORS—1995–98 MODELS

1. Remove the door trim panel and peel back the water shield.

2. Disconnect the inside door handle and lock control rods.

3. Remove the outside door handle.

4. Disconnect the lock control rods or power door lock connector (whichever is applicable).

5. Unfasten the lock assembly bolts and remove the lock.

6. Installation is the reverse of removal.

Front Door Lock Cylinder

REMOVAL & INSTALLATION

R/V Series

1. Raise the window.
2. Remove the door trim panel.
3. Slide the lock cylinder retaining clip off of the cylinder.
4. Remove the lock cylinder and gasket from the door.
5. Installation is the reverse of removal.

C/K Series

1. Remove the door trim panel and peel back the watershield

2. On models equipped, remove the inner mounting panel as follows:

a. If equipped, remove the speaker by carefully prying out the retaining clips.

b. Unfasten the inner panel bolts.

c. Disconnect the lock rods from the lock handle, lever and lock rod guides.

d. Unplug the wiring harness.

e. Slide the inner mounting panel rearward to release the regulator roller from the window sash and remove the panel.

3. Disconnect the outside door handle rod from the rod clip.

4. Disconnect the lock cylinder rod from the rod clip.

5. Unfasten the outsized handle mounting screws.

6. Remove the lock cylinder from the handle housing.

To install:

7. Installation is the reverse of removal, but please note the following important step.

8. Tighten the outside handle mounting bolts to 35 inch lbs. (4 Nm).

Rear Door Lock Cylinder, Rod and Handle

REMOVAL & INSTALLATION

▶ **See Figures 34 and 35**

1. Disconnect the negative battery cable.

2. Remove the door panel, watershield, module and window.

3. If equipped, remove the access hole cover.
4. Disconnect the outside door handle rod from the clip.
5. Disconnect the lock cylinder rod from the clip.
6. Remove the handle mounting screws and pull the cylinder out of the handle housing. Remove the handle.

To install:

7. Installation is the reverse of removal. Tighten the handle screws to 35 inch lbs. (4 Nm).

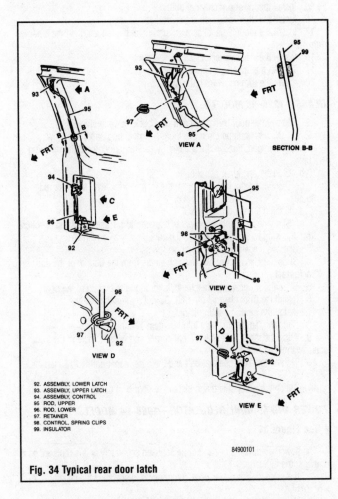

92. ASSEMBLY, LOWER LATCH
93. ASSEMBLY, UPPER LATCH
94. ASSEMBLY, CONTROL
95. ROD, UPPER
96. ROD, LOWER
97. RETAINER
98. CONTROL, SPRING CLIPS
99. INSULATOR

84900101

Fig. 34 Typical rear door latch

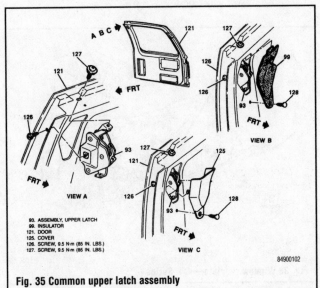

93. ASSEMBLY, UPPER LATCH
99. INSULATOR
121. DOOR
125. COVER
126. SCREW, 9.5 N·m (85 IN. LBS.)
127. SCREW, 9.5 N·m (85 IN. LBS.)

84900102

Fig. 35 Common upper latch assembly

Door Glass and Regulator

REMOVAL & INSTALLATION

R/V Series

GLASS

▶ **See Figure 36**

1. Lower the door glass completely.
2. Remove the trim panel from the door.
3. Remove the vent window assembly as follows:
   a. Pull the run channel molding out of the vent assembly only.
   b. Unfasten the door panel-to-run channel bolt.
   c. Unfasten the door-to-ventilator screws and remove the spacer.
   d. Remove the door vent/window run channel assembly from the vehicle by pulling the top of the vent backwards away from the door frame, then lift and rotate the assembly from the door.
4. Slide the glass forward until the front roller is in line with the notch in the sash channel. Disengage the roller from the channel.
5. Push the window forward and tilt the front portion of window up until the rear roller is disengaged.
6. Put the window assembly in a normal position (level) and raise straight up and out.

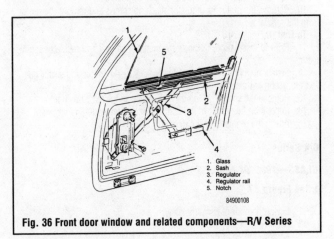

1. Glass
2. Sash
3. Regulator
4. Regulator rail
5. Notch

84900108

Fig. 36 Front door window and related components—R/V Series

To install:

7. Lower the glass into the door frame, push the window forward, then tilt it up and slide the rear roller into the sash channel.
8. Slide the glass backwards until the front roller is in line with the notch in the same channel, then engage the roller to the sash.. Slide the glass rearward into the run channel.
9. Install the door vent/window run channel as follows:
   a. Rotate the assembly into the door and fit the assembly into the door frame.
   b. Install the door-to-ventilator screws and spacers. Start with the screw at the top of the door and work downwards.
   c. Install the door panel-to-run channel bolts.
   d. Install the run channel molding by seating the clip into the vent, then push the remainder of the molding into the run channel.
10. Install the door trim panel.

MANUAL REGULATOR

1. Place the window in the full up position and hold it there with heavy tape.
2. Remove the door trim panel.
3. Remove the door panel-to-regulator attaching bolts.
4. Slide the regulator rearward to disengage the rear roller from the sash channel.
5. Disengage the lower roller from the regulator rail.
6. Disengage the forward roller from the sash channel at the notch.
7. Fold the regulator down and remove it.
8. Installation is the reverse of removal.

POWER REGULATOR AND MOTOR

1. Raise the glass to the full up position and tape it to the door frame with fabric tape.
2. Disconnect the negative battery cable.
3. Remove the door trim panel.
4. Remove the window control bolts and lay the control aside for access.
5. Remove the regulator-to-door panel attaching bolts.
6. Disconnect the harness from the regulator.
7. Slide the regulator assembly rearward, disengaging the rollers from the sash panel.

➡ **A notch is provided in the sash panel to allow disengagement of the forward roller on the window regulator.**

8. Remove the regulator assembly through the access hole in the door.

❊❊ CAUTION

The next step must be performed when the regulator is removed from the door. The regulator lift arms are under tension from the counterbalance spring and can cause serious injury if the motor is removed without locking the sector gear in position.

9. Drill a hole through the regulator sector gear and back plate. DO NOT drill a hole closer than ½ inch (13mm) to the edge of the sector gear or back plate. Install a pan head sheet metal tapping screw at least 3/4 inch (19mm) long in the drilled hole to lock the sector gear in position.
10. Remove the motor-to-regulator attaching screws and remove the motor from the regulator.

To install:

11. Prior to installation, lubricate the motor drive gear and regulator sector teeth.
12. Install the motor to the regulator. Make sure the motor and sector gear teeth mesh properly before installing the retaining screws.
13. Remove the screw locking the sector gear in the fixed position.
14. Reposition the motor in the door and install the wiring connector.
15. Attach the regulator to the door.

C/K Series

GLASS—1988–94 MODELS

▸ **See Figure 37**

1. Lower the door glass completely.
2. Remove the trim panel from the door.
3. Remove the water deflector by peeling it back.
4. Remove the module panel screws.
5. Remove the door lock rods from the module and tape them to the door.
6. Remove the lower run channel bolt.
7. Loosen the upper run channel bolt.
8. Move the run channel away from the glass.
9. Pull the wiring harness towards the door to reach the connector. Remove the boot from the wiring and disconnect the harness at the door hinge pillar.

10. Remove the module and window assembly from the door frame by tilting it and lowering it from the door.
11. Fold back the tab on the channel and slide the glass out.

To install:

12. Slide the glass into the channel and fold over the tab.
13. Fit the glass into the rear channel in the door, then, while pulling the channel towards the glass, fit the glass into the front run channel.
14. Install the boot from the wiring and connect the harness at the door hinge pillar.
15. Install the lower run channel bolt.
16. Install the door lock rods at the module.
17. Install the module panel screws, starting at the top left, then the top right.
18. Install the water deflector.
19. Tighten the upper run channel bolt.
20. Install the trim panel from the door.

GLASS—1995–98 MODELS

1. Remove the door trim panel and peel back the watershield.
2. On models equipped, remove the inner mounting panel as follows:
   a. If equipped, remove the speaker by carefully prying out the retaining clips.
   b. Unfasten the inner panel bolts.
   c. Disconnect the lock rods from the lock handle, lever and lock rod guides.
   d. Unplug the wiring harness.
   e. Slide the inner mounting panel rearward to release the regulator roller from the window sash and remove the panel.
3. Remove the window front channel top screw.
4. Slide the glass out of the glass channels from the bottom of the door.

To install:

5. Slide the window into the channels through the bottom of the door.
6. Install the front channel top bolt. Do not tighten the bolt yet.
7. Install the inner mounting panel.
8. Slide the regulator rollers into the glass channel.
9. Align the inner panel lower front corner bolt with the hole in the front glass channel assembly.
10. Tighten the front channel bolt and the inner panel bolts to 18 inch lbs. (2 Nm).
11. Attach the water shield and install the door trim panel.

POWER AND MANUAL REGULATOR—1988–94 MODELS

▸ **See Figure 38**

The power window motor can not be serviced separately and is replaced as a unit with the regulator.

1. If equipped with power door components, disconnect the negative battery cable.
2. Remove the door trim panel.

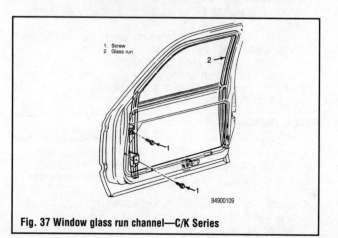

1. Screw
2. Glass run

84900109

Fig. 37 Window glass run channel—C/K Series

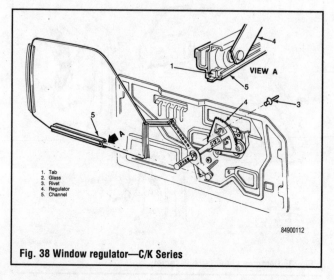

1. Tab
2. Glass
3. Rivet
4. Regulator
5. Channel

VIEW A

84900112

Fig. 38 Window regulator—C/K Series

3. Remove the water deflector by peeling it back.
4. Disconnect the door lock linkage.
5. If equipped, remove the door module.
6. Remove the glass.
7. Drill out the regulator assembly rivets.
8. Remove the regulator.

To install:

9. Install the regulator. Use bolts and nuts to replace the rivets.
10. Install the water deflector by peeling it back.
11. Install the glass.
12. If equipped, install the door module.
13. Install the door lock linkage.
14. Install the door trim panel.
15. If necessary, connect the negative battery cable.

POWER AND MANUAL REGULATOR—1995–98 MODELS

The power window motor can not be serviced separately and is replaced as a unit with the regulator.

1. Remove the door trim panel and peel back the watershield.
2. On models equipped, remove the inner mounting panel as follows:
   a. If equipped, remove the speaker by carefully prying out the retaining clips.
   b. Unfasten the inner panel bolts.
   c. Disconnect the lock rods from the lock handle, lever and lock rod guides.
   d. Unplug the wiring harness.
   e. Slide the inner mounting panel rearward to release the regulator roller from the window sash and remove the panel.
3. Remove the glass.
4. Drill out the front and rear rivets that attach the regulator to the door inner panel.

To install:

5. Place the regulator into position and attach it to the inner door panel using rivets.
6. Install the glass.
7. Install the inner mounting panel.
8. Attach the water shield and install the door trim panel.

Tailgate Glass and Regulator

REMOVAL & INSTALLATION

Glass

▶ See Figures 39 and 40

1. Remove the window run channel caps.
2. Lower the window and pry out the inner and outer glass seals. They clip in place.
3. Remove the tailgate cover plate.
4. Raise the window so that the window sash channel bolts are accessible.
5. Remove the sash-to-channel bolts.
6. Pull the glass/sash assembly from the tailgate. Disconnect the sash rails from the regulator.
7. Installation is the reverse of removal.

Manual Regulator

1. Remove the tailgate cover plate.
2. Disconnect the tailgate handle control rod from the handle.
3. Remove the handle.
4. Disconnect the right and left latch rods from the control assembly.
5. Remove the attaching bolts and lift the control assembly from the tailgate.
6. Remove the window glass as described above.
7. Remove the attaching bolts and lift the regulator from the tailgate.
8. Installation is the reverse of removal.

Power Regulator

▶ See Figure 41

1. Remove the tailgate cover plate.
2. Disconnect the tailgate handle control rod from the handle.

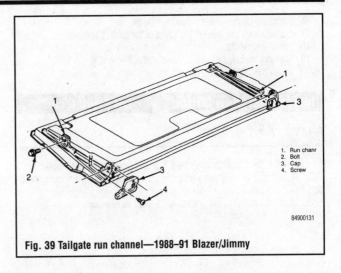

1. Run chanr
2. Bolt
3. Cap
4. Screw

84900131

Fig. 39 Tailgate run channel—1988–91 Blazer/Jimmy

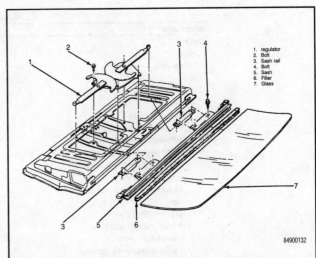

1. regulator
2. Bolt
3. Sash rail
4. Bolt
5. Sash
6. Filler
7. Glass

84900132

Fig. 40 Tailgate window and related components—1988–91 Blazer/Jimmy

3. Remove the handle.
4. Disconnect the right and left latch rods from the control assembly.
5. Remove the attaching bolts and lift the control assembly from the tailgate.
6. Remove the window glass as described above.

⁂ CAUTION

The next step must be performed before if the gearbox is removed or disengaged from the regulator arms. The regulator lift arms are under tension from the counterbalance spring and can cause serious injury if the gearbox is removed without locking the sector gear in position.

7. Drill a ⅛ inch hole through the regulator sector gear and back plate. Install a pan head sheet metal tapping screw in the drilled hole to lock the sector gear in position.
8. Disconnect the drive cable at the regulator.
9. Remove the attaching bolts and lift the regulator from the tailgate.
10. Unbolt the gear assembly from the regulator.

To install:

11. Assemble the gearbox and regulator.
12. Install the regulator in the tailgate.
13. Connect the drive cable at the regulator.
14. Remove the head sheet metal tapping screw used to lock the sector gear in position.
15. Install the window glass as described above.

16. Install the control assembly in the tailgate.
17. Connect the right and left latch rods at the control assembly.
18. Install the handle.
19. Connect the tailgate handle control rod at the handle.
20. Install the tailgate cover plate.

Inside Rear View Mirror

REMOVAL & INSTALLATION

1. Remove the screw retaining the mirror to its glass mounted bracket.
2. If the mirror is equipped with a compass disengage the electrical connection.
3. Install the mirror to the bracket and tighten as necessary.

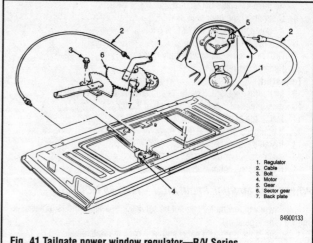

1. Regulator
2. Cable
3. Bolt
4. Motor
5. Gear
6. Sector gear
7. Back plate

84900133

Fig. 41 Tailgate power window regulator—R/V Series

TORQUE SPECIFICATIONS

Components	Ft. Lbs.	Nm
Exterior		
Doors		
Hinge bolts	26	35
Hood		
Hood bolts	18	24
Front fenders		
1988-91 R/V series		
Fender-to-radiator support bolts	13	17
Wheelwell panel-to-fender bolts	13	17
Lower door pillar-to-fender bolt	31	42
Wheelwell panel-to-splash shield bolts	13	17
Fender-to-cowl bolt	31	42
Upper fender-to-door pillar bolt	31	43
Hood spring assembly bolts	20	27
Except 1988-91 R/V series		
Fender-to-door hinges bolts	18	24
Lower fender-to-cab bolt	18	24
Fender-to-radiator support bolts	18	24
Fender-to-wheelwell bolts	18	24
Step side rear fenders		
Fender retainers	13	17
Dual wheel fenders		
Fender retainers	18	25
Cab mount bushings		
Bolt(s)	55	75
Nuts	35	47
Dead weight tow hitch		
R/V series		
Bracket-to-frame bolts	52	70
Bar-to-bracket bolt	70	100
Bar-to-support nuts	52	70
Support-to-bumper nuts	24	32
Front bumpers		
R/V series	66	89
C/K series	74	100
Interior		
Instrument panel and pad		
1988-94 models		
Carrier bracket bolts	15	20
Door lock cylinder		
C/K Series		
Outside handle mounting bolts	35 inch lbs.	4
Seats		
Front seats	41	55
Center seats	41	55
Rear seats		
C/K series extended cab	12	17
All others	41	55

91020C01

GLOSSARY

AIR/FUEL RATIO: The ratio of air-to-gasoline by weight in the fuel mixture drawn into the engine.

AIR INJECTION: One method of reducing harmful exhaust emissions by injecting air into each of the exhaust ports of an engine. The fresh air entering the hot exhaust manifold causes any remaining fuel to be burned before it can exit the tailpipe.

ALTERNATOR: A device used for converting mechanical energy into electrical energy.

AMMETER: An instrument, calibrated in amperes, used to measure the flow of an electrical current in a circuit. Ammeters are always connected in series with the circuit being tested.

AMPERE: The rate of flow of electrical current present when one volt of electrical pressure is applied against one ohm of electrical resistance.

ANALOG COMPUTER: Any microprocessor that uses similar (analogous) electrical signals to make its calculations.

ARMATURE: A laminated, soft iron core wrapped by a wire that converts electrical energy to mechanical energy as in a motor or relay. When rotated in a magnetic field, it changes mechanical energy into electrical energy as in a generator.

ATMOSPHERIC PRESSURE: The pressure on the Earth's surface caused by the weight of the air in the atmosphere. At sea level, this pressure is 14.7 psi at 32°F (101 kPa at 0°C).

ATOMIZATION: The breaking down of a liquid into a fine mist that can be suspended in air.

AXIAL PLAY: Movement parallel to a shaft or bearing bore.

BACKFIRE: The sudden combustion of gases in the intake or exhaust system that results in a loud explosion.

BACKLASH: The clearance or play between two parts, such as meshed gears.

BACKPRESSURE: Restrictions in the exhaust system that slow the exit of exhaust gases from the combustion chamber.

BAKELITE: A heat resistant, plastic insulator material commonly used in printed circuit boards and transistorized components.

BALL BEARING: A bearing made up of hardened inner and outer races between which hardened steel balls roll.

BALLAST RESISTOR: A resistor in the primary ignition circuit that lowers voltage after the engine is started to reduce wear on ignition components.

BEARING: A friction reducing, supportive device usually located between a stationary part and a moving part.

BIMETAL TEMPERATURE SENSOR: Any sensor or switch made of two dissimilar types of metal that bend when heated or cooled due to the different expansion rates of the alloys. These types of sensors usually function as an on/off switch.

BLOWBY: Combustion gases, composed of water vapor and unburned fuel, that leak past the piston rings into the crankcase during normal engine operation. These gases are removed by the PCV system to prevent the buildup of harmful acids in the crankcase.

BRAKE PAD: A brake shoe and lining assembly used with disc brakes.

BRAKE SHOE: The backing for the brake lining. The term is, however, usually applied to the assembly of the brake backing and lining.

BUSHING: A liner, usually removable, for a bearing; an anti-friction liner used in place of a bearing.

CALIPER: A hydraulically activated device in a disc brake system, which is mounted straddling the brake rotor (disc). The caliper contains at least one piston and two brake pads. Hydraulic pressure on the piston(s) forces the pads against the rotor.

CAMSHAFT: A shaft in the engine on which are the lobes (cams) which operate the valves. The camshaft is driven by the crankshaft, via a belt, chain or gears, at one half the crankshaft speed.

CAPACITOR: A device which stores an electrical charge.

CARBON MONOXIDE (CO): A colorless, odorless gas given off as a normal byproduct of combustion. It is poisonous and extremely dangerous in confined areas, building up slowly to toxic levels without warning if adequate ventilation is not available.

CARBURETOR: A device, usually mounted on the intake manifold of an engine, which mixes the air and fuel in the proper proportion to allow even combustion.

CATALYTIC CONVERTER: A device installed in the exhaust system, like a muffler, that converts harmful byproducts of combustion into carbon dioxide and water vapor by means of a heat-producing chemical reaction.

CENTRIFUGAL ADVANCE: A mechanical method of advancing the spark timing by using flyweights in the distributor that react to centrifugal force generated by the distributor shaft rotation.

CHECK VALVE: Any one-way valve installed to permit the flow of air, fuel or vacuum in one direction only.

CHOKE: A device, usually a moveable valve, placed in the intake path of a carburetor to restrict the flow of air.

CIRCUIT: Any unbroken path through which an electrical current can flow. Also used to describe fuel flow in some instances.

CIRCUIT BREAKER: A switch which protects an electrical circuit from overload by opening the circuit when the current flow exceeds a predetermined level. Some circuit breakers must be reset manually, while most reset automatically.

COIL (IGNITION): A transformer in the ignition circuit which steps up the voltage provided to the spark plugs.

COMBINATION MANIFOLD: An assembly which includes both the intake and exhaust manifolds in one casting.

COMBINATION VALVE: A device used in some fuel systems that routes fuel vapors to a charcoal storage canister instead of venting them into the atmosphere. The valve relieves fuel tank pressure and allows fresh air into the tank as the fuel level drops to prevent a vapor lock situation.

COMPRESSION RATIO: The comparison of the total volume of the cylinder and combustion chamber with the piston at BDC and the piston at TDC.

CONDENSER: 1. An electrical device which acts to store an electrical charge, preventing voltage surges. 2. A radiator-like device in the air conditioning system in which refrigerant gas condenses into a liquid, giving off heat.

CONDUCTOR: Any material through which an electrical current can be transmitted easily.

CONTINUITY: Continuous or complete circuit. Can be checked with an ohmmeter.

COUNTERSHAFT: An intermediate shaft which is rotated by a mainshaft and transmits, in turn, that rotation to a working part.

CRANKCASE: The lower part of an engine in which the crankshaft and related parts operate.

CRANKSHAFT: The main driving shaft of an engine which receives reciprocating motion from the pistons and converts it to rotary motion.

CYLINDER: In an engine, the round hole in the engine block in which the piston(s) ride.

CYLINDER BLOCK: The main structural member of an engine in which is found the cylinders, crankshaft and other principal parts.

CYLINDER HEAD: The detachable portion of the engine, usually fastened to the top of the cylinder block and containing all or most of the combustion chambers. On overhead valve engines, it contains the valves and their operating parts. On overhead cam engines, it contains the camshaft as well.

DEAD CENTER: The extreme top or bottom of the piston stroke.

DETONATION: An unwanted explosion of the air/fuel mixture in the combustion chamber caused by excess heat and compression, advanced timing, or an overly lean mixture. Also referred to as "ping".

DIAPHRAGM: A thin, flexible wall separating two cavities, such as in a vacuum advance unit.

DIESELING: A condition in which hot spots in the combustion chamber cause the engine to run on after the key is turned off.

DIFFERENTIAL: A geared assembly which allows the transmission of motion between drive axles, giving one axle the ability to turn faster than the other.

DIODE: An electrical device that will allow current to flow in one direction only.

DISC BRAKE: A hydraulic braking assembly consisting of a brake disc, or rotor, mounted on an axle, and a caliper assembly containing, usually two brake pads which are activated by hydraulic pressure. The pads are forced against the sides of the disc, creating friction which slows the vehicle.

DISTRIBUTOR: A mechanically driven device on an engine which is responsible for electrically firing the spark plug at a predetermined point of the piston stroke.

DOWEL PIN: A pin, inserted in mating holes in two different parts allowing those parts to maintain a fixed relationship.

DRUM BRAKE: A braking system which consists of two brake shoes and one or two wheel cylinders, mounted on a fixed backing plate, and a brake drum, mounted on an axle, which revolves around the assembly.

DWELL: The rate, measured in degrees of shaft rotation, at which an electrical circuit cycles on and off.

ELECTRONIC CONTROL UNIT (ECU): Ignition module, module, amplifier or igniter. See Module for definition.

ELECTRONIC IGNITION: A system in which the timing and firing of the spark plugs is controlled by an electronic control unit, usually called a module. These systems have no points or condenser.

END-PLAY: The measured amount of axial movement in a shaft.

ENGINE: A device that converts heat into mechanical energy.

EXHAUST MANIFOLD: A set of cast passages or pipes which conduct exhaust gases from the engine.

FEELER GAUGE: A blade, usually metal, or precisely predetermined thickness, used to measure the clearance between two parts.

FIRING ORDER: The order in which combustion occurs in the cylinders of an engine. Also the order in which spark is distributed to the plugs by the distributor.

FLOODING: The presence of too much fuel in the intake manifold and combustion chamber which prevents the air/fuel mixture from firing, thereby causing a no-start situation.

FLYWHEEL: A disc shaped part bolted to the rear end of the crankshaft. Around the outer perimeter is affixed the ring gear. The starter drive engages the ring gear, turning the flywheel, which rotates the crankshaft, imparting the initial starting motion to the engine.

FOOT POUND (ft. lbs. or sometimes, ft.lb.): The amount of energy or work needed to raise an item weighing one pound, a distance of one foot.

FUSE: A protective device in a circuit which prevents circuit overload by breaking the circuit when a specific amperage is present. The device is constructed around a strip or wire of a lower amperage rating than the circuit it is designed to protect. When an amperage higher than that stamped on the fuse is present in the circuit, the strip or wire melts, opening the circuit.

GEAR RATIO: The ratio between the number of teeth on meshing gears.

GENERATOR: A device which converts mechanical energy into electrical energy.

HEAT RANGE: The measure of a spark plug's ability to dissipate heat from its firing end. The higher the heat range, the hotter the plug fires.

HUB: The center part of a wheel or gear.

HYDROCARBON (HC): Any chemical compound made up of hydrogen and carbon. A major pollutant formed by the engine as a byproduct of combustion.

HYDROMETER: An instrument used to measure the specific gravity of a solution.

INCH POUND (inch lbs.; sometimes in.lb. or in. lbs.): One twelfth of a foot pound.

INDUCTION: A means of transferring electrical energy in the form of a magnetic field. Principle used in the ignition coil to increase voltage.

INJECTOR: A device which receives metered fuel under relatively low pressure and is activated to inject the fuel into the engine under relatively high pressure at a predetermined time.

INPUT SHAFT: The shaft to which torque is applied, usually carrying the driving gear or gears.

INTAKE MANIFOLD: A casting of passages or pipes used to conduct air or a fuel/air mixture to the cylinders.

JOURNAL: The bearing surface within which a shaft operates.

KEY: A small block usually fitted in a notch between a shaft and a hub to prevent slippage of the two parts.

MANIFOLD: A casting of passages or set of pipes which connect the cylinders to an inlet or outlet source.

MANIFOLD VACUUM: Low pressure in an engine intake manifold formed just below the throttle plates. Manifold vacuum is highest at idle and drops under acceleration.

MASTER CYLINDER: The primary fluid pressurizing device in a hydraulic system. In automotive use, it is found in brake and hydraulic clutch systems and is pedal activated, either directly or, in a power brake system, through the power booster.

MODULE: Electronic control unit, amplifier or igniter of solid state or integrated design which controls the current flow in the ignition primary circuit based on input from the pick-up coil. When the module opens the primary circuit, high secondary voltage is induced in the coil.

NEEDLE BEARING: A bearing which consists of a number (usually a large number) of long, thin rollers.

OHM: (Ω) The unit used to measure the resistance of conductor-to-electrical flow. One ohm is the amount of resistance that limits current flow to one ampere in a circuit with one volt of pressure.

OHMMETER: An instrument used for measuring the resistance, in ohms, in an electrical circuit.

OUTPUT SHAFT: The shaft which transmits torque from a device, such as a transmission.

OVERDRIVE: A gear assembly which produces more shaft revolutions than that transmitted to it.

OVERHEAD CAMSHAFT (OHC): An engine configuration in which the camshaft is mounted on top of the cylinder head and operates the valve either directly or by means of rocker arms.

OVERHEAD VALVE (OHV): An engine configuration in which all of the valves are located in the cylinder head and the camshaft is located in the cylinder block. The camshaft operates the valves via lifters and pushrods.

OXIDES OF NITROGEN (NOx): Chemical compounds of nitrogen produced as a byproduct of combustion. They combine with hydrocarbons to produce smog.

OXYGEN SENSOR: Use with the feedback system to sense the presence of oxygen in the exhaust gas and signal the computer which can reference the voltage signal to an air/fuel ratio.

PINION: The smaller of two meshing gears.

PISTON RING: An open-ended ring with fits into a groove on the outer diameter of the piston. Its chief function is to form a seal between the piston and cylinder wall. Most automotive pistons have three rings: two for compression sealing; one for oil sealing.

PRELOAD: A predetermined load placed on a bearing during assembly or by adjustment.

PRIMARY CIRCUIT: the low voltage side of the ignition system which consists of the ignition switch, ballast resistor or resistance wire, bypass, coil, electronic control unit and pick-up coil as well as the connecting wires and harnesses.

PRESS FIT: The mating of two parts under pressure, due to the inner diameter of one being smaller than the outer diameter of the other, or vice versa; an interference fit.

RACE: The surface on the inner or outer ring of a bearing on which the balls, needles or rollers move.

REGULATOR: A device which maintains the amperage and/or voltage levels of a circuit at predetermined values.

RELAY: A switch which automatically opens and/or closes a circuit.

RESISTANCE: The opposition to the flow of current through a circuit or electrical device, and is measured in ohms. Resistance is equal to the voltage divided by the amperage.

RESISTOR: A device, usually made of wire, which offers a preset amount of resistance in an electrical circuit.

RING GEAR: The name given to a ring-shaped gear attached to a differential case, or affixed to a flywheel or as part of a planetary gear set.

ROLLER BEARING: A bearing made up of hardened inner and outer races between which hardened steel rollers move.

ROTOR: 1. The disc-shaped part of a disc brake assembly, upon which the brake pads bear; also called, brake disc. 2. The device mounted atop the distributor shaft, which passes current to the distributor cap tower contacts.

SECONDARY CIRCUIT: The high voltage side of the ignition system, usually above 20,000 volts. The secondary includes the ignition coil, coil wire, distributor cap and rotor, spark plug wires and spark plugs.

SENDING UNIT: A mechanical, electrical, hydraulic or electro-magnetic device which transmits information to a gauge.

SENSOR: Any device designed to measure engine operating conditions or ambient pressures and temperatures. Usually electronic in nature and designed to send a voltage signal to an on-board computer, some sensors may operate as a simple on/off switch or they may provide a variable voltage signal (like a potentiometer) as conditions or measured parameters change.

SHIM: Spacers of precise, predetermined thickness used between parts to establish a proper working relationship.

SLAVE CYLINDER: In automotive use, a device in the hydraulic clutch system which is activated by hydraulic force, disengaging the clutch.

SOLENOID: A coil used to produce a magnetic field, the effect of which is to produce work.

SPARK PLUG: A device screwed into the combustion chamber of a spark ignition engine. The basic construction is a conductive core inside of a ceramic insulator, mounted in an outer conductive base. An electrical charge from the spark plug wire travels along the conductive core and jumps a preset air gap to a grounding point or points at the end of the conductive base. The resultant spark ignites the fuel/air mixture in the combustion chamber.

SPLINES: Ridges machined or cast onto the outer diameter of a shaft or inner diameter of a bore to enable parts to mate without rotation.

TACHOMETER: A device used to measure the rotary speed of an engine, shaft, gear, etc., usually in rotations per minute.

THERMOSTAT: A valve, located in the cooling system of an engine, which is closed when cold and opens gradually in response to engine heating, controlling the temperature of the coolant and rate of coolant flow.

TOP DEAD CENTER (TDC): The point at which the piston reaches the top of its travel on the compression stroke.

TORQUE: The twisting force applied to an object.

TORQUE CONVERTER: A turbine used to transmit power from a driving member to a driven member via hydraulic action, providing changes in drive ratio and torque. In automotive use, it links the driveplate at the rear of the engine to the automatic transmission.

TRANSDUCER: A device used to change a force into an electrical signal.

TRANSISTOR: A semi-conductor component which can be actuated by a small voltage to perform an electrical switching function.

TUNE-UP: A regular maintenance function, usually associated with the replacement and adjustment of parts and components in the electrical and fuel systems of a vehicle for the purpose of attaining optimum performance.

TURBOCHARGER: An exhaust driven pump which compresses intake air and forces it into the combustion chambers at higher than atmospheric pressures. The increased air pressure allows more fuel to be burned and results in increased horsepower being produced.

VACUUM ADVANCE: A device which advances the ignition timing in response to increased engine vacuum.

VACUUM GAUGE: An instrument used to measure the presence of vacuum in a chamber.

VALVE: A device which control the pressure, direction of flow or rate of flow of a liquid or gas.

VALVE CLEARANCE: The measured gap between the end of the valve stem and the rocker arm, cam lobe or follower that activates the valve.

VISCOSITY: The rating of a liquid's internal resistance to flow.

VOLTMETER: An instrument used for measuring electrical force in units called volts. Voltmeters are always connected parallel with the circuit being tested.

WHEEL CYLINDER: Found in the automotive drum brake assembly, it is a device, actuated by hydraulic pressure, which, through internal pistons, pushes the brake shoes outward against the drums.

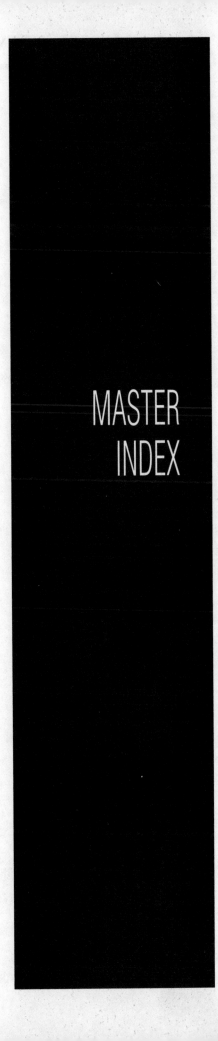

MASTER

INDEX

Total Car Care, continued

Sentra/Pulsar/NX 1982-96
PART NO. 8263/52700
Stanza/200SX/240SX 1982-92
PART NO. 8262/52750
240SX/Altima 1993-98
PART NO. 52752
Datsun/Nissan Z and ZX 1970-88
PART NO. 8846/52800

RENAULT
Coupes/Sedans/Wagons 1975-85
PART NO. 58300

SATURN
Coupes/Sedans/Wagons 1991-98
PART NO. 8419/62300

SUBARU
Coupes/Sedan/Wagons 1970-84
PART NO. 8790/64300
Coupes/Sedans/Wagons 1985-96
PART NO. 8259/64302

SUZUKI
Samurai/Sidekick/Tracker 1986-98
PART NO. 66500

TOYOTA
Camry 1983-96
PART NO. 8265/68200
Celica/Supra 1971-85
PART NO. 68250
Celica 1986-93
PART NO. 8413/68252

Celica 1994-98
PART NO. 68254
Corolla 1970-87
PART NO. 8586/68300
Corolla 1988-97
PART NO. 8414/68302
Cressida/Corona/Crown/MkII 1970-82
PART NO. 68350
Cressida/Van 1983-90
PART NO. 68352
Pick-ups/Land Cruiser/4Runner 1970-88
PART NO. 8578/68600
Pick-ups/Land Cruiser/4Runner 1989-96
PART NO. 8163/68602
Previa 1991-97
PART NO. 68640

Tercel 1984-94
PART NO. 8595/68700

VOLKSWAGEN
Air-Cooled 1949-69
PART NO. 70200
Air-Cooled 1970-81
PART NO. 70202
Front Wheel Drive 1974-89
PART NO. 8663/70400
Golf/Jetta/Cabriolet 1990-93
PART NO. 8429/70402

VOLVO
Coupes/Sedans/Wagons 1970-89
PART NO. 8786/72300
Coupes/Sedans/Wagons 1990-98
PART NO. 8428/72302

SELOC MARINE MANUALS

OUTBOARDS
Chrysler Outboards, All Engines 1962-84
PART NO. 018-7(1000)
Force Outboards, All Engines 1984-96
PART NO. 024-1(1100)
Honda Outboards, All Engines 1988-98
PART NO. 1200
Johnson/Evinrude Outboards, 1.5-40HP, 2-Stroke 1956-70
PART NO. 007-1(1300)
Johnson/Evinrude Outboards, 1.25-60HP, 2-Stroke 1971-89
PART NO. 008-X(1302)
Johnson/Evinrude Outboards, 1-50 HP, 2-Stroke 1990-95
PART NO. 026-8(1304)
Johnson/Evinrude Outboards, 50-125 HP, 2-Stroke 1958-72
PART NO. 009-8(1306)
Johnson/Evinrude Outboards, 60-235 HP, 2-Stroke 1973-91
PART NO. 010-1(1308)
Johnson/Evinrude Outboards, 80-300 HP, 2-Stroke 1992-96
PART NO. 040-3(1310)
Mariner Outboards, 2-60 HP, 2-Stroke 1977-89
PART NO. 015-2(1400)

Mariner Outboards, 45-220 HP, 2 Stroke 1977-89
PART NO. 016-0(1402)
Mercury Outboards, 2-40 HP, 2-Stroke 1965-91
PART NO. 012-8(1404)
Mercury Outboards, 40-115 HP, 2-Stroke 1965-92
PART NO. 013-6(1406)
Mercury Outboards, 90-300 HP, 2-Stroke 1965-91
PART NO. 014-4(1408)
Mercury/Mariner Outboards, 2.5-25 HP, 2-Stroke 1990-94
PART NO. 035-7(1410)
Mercury/Mariner Outboards, 40-125 HP, 2-Stroke 1990-94
PART NO. 036-5(1412)
Mercury/Mariner Outboards, 135-275 HP, 2-Stroke 1990-94
PART NO. 037-3(1414)
Mercury/Mariner Outboards, All Engines 1995-99
PART NO. 1416
Suzuki Outboards, All Engines 1985-99
PART NO. 1600

Yamaha Outboards, 2-25 HP, 2-Stroke and 9.9 HP, 4-Stroke 1984-91
PART NO. 021-7(1700)
Yamaha Outboards, 30-90 HP, 2-Stroke 1984-91
PART NO. 022-5(1702)
Yamaha Outboards, 115-225 HP, 2-Stroke 1984-91
PART NO. 023-3(1704)
Yamaha Outboards, All Engines 1992-98
PART NO. 1706

STERN DRIVES
Marine Jet Drive 1961-96
PART NO. 029-2(3000)
Mercruiser Stern Drive Type 1, Alpha, Bravo I, II, 1964-92
PART NO. 005-5(3200)
Mercruiser Stern Drive Alpha 1 Generation II 1992-96
PART NO. 039-X(3202)
Mercruiser Stern Drive Bravo I, II, III 1992-96
PART NO. 046-2(3204)
OMC Stern Drive 1964-86
PART NO. 004-7(3400)
OMC Cobra Stern Drive 1985-95
PART NO. 025-X(3402)

Volvo/Penta Stern Drives 1968-91
PART NO. 011-X(3600)
Volvo/Penta Stern Drives 1992-93
PART NO. 038-1(3602)
Volvo/Penta Stern Drives 1992-95
PART NO. 041-1(3604)

INBOARDS
Yanmar Inboard Diesels 1988-91
PART NO. 7400

PERSONAL WATERCRAFT
Kawasaki 1973-91
PART NO. 032-2(9200)
Kawasaki 1992-97
PART NO. 042-X(9202)
Polaris 1992-97
PART NO. 045-4(9400)
Sea Doo/Bombardier 1988-91
PART NO. 033-0(9000)
Sea Doo/Bombardier 1992-97
PART NO. 043-8(9002)
Yamaha 1987-91
PART NO. 034-9(9600)
Yamaha 1992-97
PART NO. 044-6(9602)

"...and even more from CHILTON"

General Interest / Recreational Books

ATV Handbook
PART NO. 9123
Auto Detailing
PART NO. 8394
Auto Body Repair
PART NO. 7898
Briggs & Stratton Vertical Crankshaft Engine
PART NO. 61-1-2
Briggs & Stratton Horizontal Crankshaft Engine
PART NO. 61-0-4
Briggs & Stratton Overhead Valve (OHV) Engine
PART NO. 61-2-0
Easy Car Care
PART NO. 8042

Motorcycle Handbook
PART NO. 9099
Snowmobile Handbook
PART NO. 9124
Small Engine Repair (Up to 20 Hp)
PART NO. 8325

Total Service Series

Automatic Transmissions/Transaxles Diagnosis and Repair
PART NO. 8944
Brake System Diagnosis and Repair
PART NO. 8945
Chevrolet Engine Overhaul Manual
PART NO. 8794
Engine Code Manual
PART NO. 8851
Ford Engine Overhaul Manual
PART NO. 8793
Fuel Injection Diagnosis and Repair
PART NO. 8946

COLLECTOR'S SERIES HARD-COVER MANUALS
Chilton's Collector's Editions are perfect for enthusiasts of vintage or rare cars. These hard-cover manuals contain repair and maintenance information for all major systems that might not be available elsewhere. Included are repair and overhaul procedures using thousands of illustrations. These manuals offer a range of coverage from as far back as 1940 and as recent as 1997, so you don't need an antique car or truck to be a collector.

MULTI-VEHICLE SPANISH LANGUAGE MANUALS
Chilton's Spanish language manuals offer some of our most popular titles in Spanish. Each is as complete and easy to use as the English-language counterpart and offers the same maintenance, repair and overhaul information along with specifications charts and tons of illustrations.

TOTAL SERVICE SERIES / SYSTEM SPECIFIC MANUALS
These innovative books offer repair, maintenance and service procedures for automotive related systems. They cover today's complex vehicles in a user-friendly format, which places even the most difficult automotive topic well within the reach of every Do-It-Yourselfer. Each title covers a specific subject from Brakes and Engine Rebuilding to Fuel Injection Systems, Automatic Transmissions and even Engine Trouble Codes.

For the titles listed, visit your local Chilton® Retailer
For a Catalog, for information, or to order call toll-free: 877-4CHILTON.

NP/CHILTON'S® 1020 Andrew Drive, Suite 200 • West Chester, PA 19380-4291
www.chiltononline.com

2P2VerB